THE CUMMERBUND

Waist Sash

AN INDIAN POEM
by
Edward Lear

I

SHE sate upon her *Dobie*,[1]
 To watch the Evening Star
And all the *Punkahs*[2] as they passed
 Cried, "My! how fair you are!"
Around her bower, with quivering leaves,
 The tall *Kamsamahs*[3] grew,
And *Kitmutgars*[4] in wild festoons
 Hung down from *Tchokis*[5] blue.

[1]*Washerman*

[2]*Fan*

[3] *Butler*

[4] *Waiter at table*

[5] *Police or post station*

II

Below her home the river rolled
 With soft meloobious sound,
Where golden finned *Chuprassies*[6] swam,
 In myriads circling round.
Above, on tallest trees remote,
 Green *Ayahs*[7] perched alone,
And all night long the *Mussak*[8] moan'd
 Its melancholy tone.

[6]*Office messenger*

[7]*Ladies maids*

[8]*Water-skin*

III

And where the purple *Nullahs*[1] threw
 Their branches far and wide, —
And silvery *Goreewallahs*[2] flew
 In silence, side by side, —
The little *Bheesties'*[3] twittering cry
 Rose on the flagrant air,
And oft the angry *Jampan*[4] howled
 Deep in his hateful lair.

[1] *Watercourse*

[2] *Groom*

[3]*Water-carrier*

[4] *Sedan chair*

IV

She sate upon her *Dobie*, —
    She heard the *Nimmak*[5] hum, —   [5]*Salt*
When all at once u cry arose:
    "The *Cummerbund*[6] is come!"   [6]*Waist sash*
In vain she fled; — with open jaws
    The angry monster followed,
And so, (before assistance came,)
    That Lady Fair was swollowed.

V

They sought in vain for even a bone
    Respectfully to bury, —
They said, "Hers was a dreadful fate!"
    (And Echo answered "Very.")
They nailed her *Dobie* to the wall,
    Where last her form was seen,
And underneath they wrote these words,
    In yellow, blue, and green:—

Beware, ye Fair! Ye Fair, beware!
    Nor sit out late at night, —
Lest horrid *Cummerbunds* should come,
    And swollow you outright.

NOTE. – First published in *Times of India*, Bombay, July 1874.

SAHIBS, NABOBS AND BOXWALLAHS
A Dictionary of the Words
of Anglo-India

SAHIBS, NABOBS
AND
BOXWALLAHS

A Dictionary of the Words
of Anglo-India

IVOR LEWIS

DELHI
OXFORD UNIVERSITY PRESS
CALCUTTA   CHENNAI   MUMBAI
1997

Oxford University Press, Great Clarendon Street, Oxford OX2 6DP

Oxford New York
Athens Auckland Bangkok Calcutta
Cape Town Chennai Dar es Salaam Delhi
Florence Hong Kong Istanbul Karachi
Kuala Lumpur Madrid Melbourne Mexico City
Mumbai Nairobi Paris Singapore
Taipei Tokyo Toronto

and associates in

Berlin Ibadan

First published 1991
Reprinted 1992
Oxford India Paperbacks 1997

ISBN 0 19 564223 6

Printed at Pauls Press, New Delhi 110 020
and published by Manzar Khan, Oxford University Press
YMCA Library Building, Jai Singh Road, New Delhi 110 001

PREFACE

Broadly speaking, it can be said that the British came to India for one or more of three reasons: to amass enormous and quick wealth (these were the *Nabobs*); to conquer and rule as if by God-given right (these were the *Sahibs*); and lower down the social ladder, as tradesmen (these were the *Boxwallahs*). The mixture of these three varied at different times according to the changing winds of Indo-British history, and one man in his time could play two or even three parts. But whatever the mixture, Indian words found to be necessary by *Nabobs, Sahibs* or *Boxwallahs* in their separate pursuits made their way into the daily speech, the written records of trade and government, and the literature of Anglo-India. To explore anew these three areas of colonial and imperial life and history in the words of India which have attached themselves (some only for the time-being) to English, in and out of India, is the object of this present work.

This is not the first time this has been attempted. About a century ago two English scholar–administrators who had served the government of India from about the middle of the nineteenth century, Col. Henry Yule and Dr A. C. Burnell, collaborated to produce a scholarly master-work, *Hobson-Jobson,* aptly described by Yule in his preface as a 'portly double-columned edifice'. It is unique and has held the field ever since 1886 for its extensive exposition of the history of Indian words, and words of Indian provenance, in English; and more widely, the history of Anglo-India in Indian words. This must be said with some reservation, which will be mentioned later. The present work will attempt to fill in some measure certain *lacunae* in *Hobson-Jobson* in order to achieve a better balance between the words of the common sort and those in the learned registers of theology, indology, philosophy and the like.

These acquired words are to be found in the literature of Anglo-India, and scattered in the pages of dictionaries, especially those compiled on historical principles, notably *The New English Dictionary* which, under the aegis of the Philological Society at Oxford, began publication at about the same time as that of *Hobson-Jobson* and continued to its final part in 1928. Afterwards, its successor, *The Oxford English Dictonary,* has continued the good work up to the present day in seventeen massive volumes. My debt to these lexico-graphical titans is beyond computation, and it would be fair to say that without the solid foundations laid in *Hobson-Jobson* and *The Oxford English Dictionary* this present work would not have been possible.

I am also particularly indebted to G. C. Whitworth's *Anglo-Indian Dictionary* (1885), Horace Hayman Wilson's *Glossary* (1885), G. Subba Rao's *Indian Words in English* (1954), and R. E. Hawkins' *Common Indian Words in English* (1984). All the four authors ploughed the same field to produce in their various ways their Anglo-Indian lexical harvests, though unfortunately, except for Subba Rao, without the historical background that animates the Anglo-Indian presence in India from the reign of Elizabeth I to that of George VI : that is, from 1600 to 1947.

Isle of Wight   Ivor Lewis
September 1990

NOTES

1. The terms 'Anglo-Indian' and 'Anglo-India' are used in this work to refer to the English in India and to the India of the English, their original meanings. No other significance should be attached to them.

2. We have not ventured to speculate on the changing phonetics of Anglo-Indian words from the seventeenth to the twentieth century as there were at least as many pronunciations of the same word as there were variant spellings, as well as varying pronunciations of the same spelling.

Sometimes the pronunciation needs no phonetic gloss as it is obvious from the spelling, for example *soojee. bangle, bungalow, calico,* and where it is not so obvious it is hazardous to use the original Indian word as a model for Anglo-Indian pronunciation. Consequently the Anglo-Indian orthography has been left to speak for itself, as far as it is able to do so.

CONTENTS

CONTENTS

PRINCIPAL ABBREVIATIONS

adj.	adjective
A-I.	Anglo-Indian
Ar.	Arabic
As. R.	Asiatick Researches (Journal of)
Ass.	Assamese
attrib.	attributively
Beng.	Bengali
C.	Century
Ch.	Chinese
coll.	colloquial
CIWIE	(R.E. Hawkins) *Common Indian Words in English*
Corr.	Corruption
Dim.	Diminutive (of)
Du.	Dutch
ed.	edition/edited by
E.I.C.	East India Company
Eng.	English
err.	erroneously
esp.	especially
E. tr.	English translation
Etym.	Etymology
fig.	figurative
fr.	from
Fr.	French
GCW.	George Clifford Whitworth, *Anglo-Indian Dictionary*
Ger.	German
Gr.	Greek
Guj.	Gujarati
HHW.	Horace Hayman Wilson, *Glossary*
H.	Hindi/Urdu/Hindustani
interjec.	interjection
J.	Japanese
Kan.	Kannada
Kash.	Kashmiri
L.	Latin
lit.	literally
M.	Malayalam
Mal.	Malay
Mar.	Marathi

OED	Oxford English Dictionary
occas.	occasionally
OE.	Old English
orig.	originally
ODEE	Oxford Dictionary of English Etymology
Pakht.	Pakhtun
Pal.	Pali
Par.	Parsi
Part.	Partridge, Dictionary of Slang and unconventional English
P.	Persian
perh.	perhaps
Pg.	Portuguese
phr.	phrase
pl.	plural
poss.	possibly
Prak.	Prakrit
Pusht/ Pasht.	Pushto/Pashto
S.	Sanskrit
sb,	substantive
Sin.	Sinhala/Sinhalese
Sp.	Spanish
SR.	Subba Rao, Indian Words in English
Stan.	The Stanford Dictionary of Anglicised Words
Suppl.	Supplement
Tam.	Tamil
Tel.	Telugu
Tibet.	Tibetan
tr.	translation/translated by
transf.	transferable
vb.	verb
vb. trans.	verb transitive
Web.	Webster's New International Dictionary
YB.	Yule and Burnell, Hobson-Jobson

NOTE

Following Platts Dictionary of Urdu, Classical Hindi and English, we have not separated words of Urdu and Hindi stock, preferring to regard them (as they were so regarded by Anglo-Indians) as 'Hindustani' words, indicated by 'H.' in this work.

HISTORICAL INTRODUCTION

A maker of a dictionary on historical principles is a registrar, and very occasionally a registrar-general, of the births, marriages and deaths of words. These are dated and recorded in their accepted order and form, while for historical and sometimes sentimental reasons the old spellings which have lost their way in the corridors of time are occasionally allowed elbow-room.

Such historical variants particularly attach themselves to words journeying from one language to another, 'for', in the words of a former Boden Professor of Sanskrit, 'the human ear is far from accurate, particularly the English ear, which is unaccustomed to a definite system of pronunciation in its own alphabet, especially as regards vowel sounds. The consequences are an entire misrepresentation of the original spelling, and a total want of consistency, the very same word being written in every possible variety of orthography.'[1]

The Great Grey Crane of India (*Grus grus lilfordi*), in Hindi *kulang*, has been variously transcribed since the seventeenth century as *colum, kolong, kullum, coolen* and *coolung*, while the ubiquitous Indian unleavened bread, *chapāti*, emerged in the nineteenth century as *chowpatty* in Anglo-Indian folk etymology, perhaps from a phonetic resemblance to the English 'patty' or even, from its shape, the lowly 'cow-pat'!

Again, when we consider the nature of the Indian plant *kawanch* (*Mucuna pruriens*), with its irritating hairs, we need not be unduly surprised that in the process of striving after meaning it was transformed into 'cowitch' by Dr Fryer in the seventeenth century. And what Anglo-Indian wit contrived the racy 'cock-up' for that succulent East Indian fish the *kakap* (*Lates calcarifer*)?

The prize example in this jungle of verbal exuberance is *Hobson-Jobson* itself. This is a far cry from its origins in the frenzied and impassioned wailings of 'Ya Hassan! Ya Husain!', in the Muslim sections of Indian towns and cities in annual memory of the martyrdom of the grandsons of the Prophet Muhammad. Before its now final Anglo-Indian form it underwent the strangest metamorphoses from Dr Fryer's *Hossen-Gosseen* and *Hossy-Gossy* in the seventeenth century, to *Saucem-Saucem* among the Portuguese in the eighteenth, to *Jaksom-Baksom* among the Dutch in the same century, coming to rest as a respectable term in linguistics in the twentieth, meaning the

1

assimilation of a foreign expression to conform to the *Sprachgefühl* of the recipient language.

A casual excursion into the hinterland of Anglo-India will reveal such gems as 'Corporal Forbes' from *cholera morbus,* a British soldier's grim jest for a British soldier's grim killer, and on a lighter note there is the 'brass knocker', the Anglo-Indian *réchauffé,* of the memsahib's kitchen, meaning yesterday's dinner reheated, from the Hindi *bāsī-khāna,* 'stale food'. Again, the common vegetable the brinjal, alias the egg-plant alias the aubergine *(Solanum melongena),* ended up in West Indies' kitchens as 'brown jolly', with a fine array of Anglo-Indian variants derived from its original Portuguese *beringella,* such as *pallingenie* in *Purchas* (1613), *berenjaws* in Dr Fryer (1681), *bedin-janas* in Shaw's *Travels* (1738) and *badenjana* in *Hajji Baba in England* (1828). These and many more of the same ilk in the ever-growing Anglo-Indian idiom added zest and humour to the workaday wordy mass: yeast to the verbal dough.

It is no wonder then that De Quincey complained that the spelling of Indian words in English was at 'sixes and sevens, so that most Hindoo words are in masquerade',[2] despite the scholarly and persuasive efforts of Sir William Jones, in his *Dissertation on the Orthography of Asiatick Words in Roman Letters* (1784), to standardize the spelling. If the masquerade is less fantastic since then it is largely due to this brilliant Welshman. The days are now gone in India when Lord Anantha's town in old Malabar, Tiruvananthapuram, the 'Sacred Vishnu Town', could be transmuted by means of some Anglo-Indian verbal prestidigitation into present-day Trivandrum, or when Allahabad via Illahabaz could be twisted into 'Isle o' Bats' by British soldiers in the service of the East India Company. Nevertheless, as long as a quick native wit and a feeling for the comedy always lurking below the surface of words are with us we will not lack a supply of 'Hobson-Jobsons' for our verbal 'brass knockers'.

These and the more numerous conventional Anglo-Indianisms illuminate the changing human and bureaucratic, civil and military relationships between the Indian people of all castes and conditions and the British of all classes and occupations from the founding of the East India Company in 1600 to the end of British rule in 1947. The acquisitions from Indian languages, or of Indian provenance, by British soldiers and civilians, merchants and missionaries, teachers, scholars and writers of many kinds, illustrate the varied Anglo-Indian interests, official, social and personal, until the final separation of the rulers from the ruled, the outsiders from the indigenes. Anglo-Indian words which still have common currency in English speech are now often spoken and written in ignorance of their Indian origins and are examples of genuine cultural penetration illustrative of Indo-British relationships at one time or another. For example *bangle, Blighty, bungalow, cheroot, loot, thug, pundit, calico, chintz, cot, cash, dungarees.*

Some of the social history of Anglo-India can be perceived in the different sorts of words acquired at different times and for different reasons, for example the trade words of the seventeenth and eighteenth centuries in contrast to the learned and politically loaded words of the nineteenth and twentieth centuries. Many of these words are obsolete, or exhausted of their novelty or contemporary relevance, or imprisoned in old, half-forgotten letters, ledgers and memoirs, or buried in vast, expanding and uncharted lexical graveyards. Should they be dis-interred and put on parade here? I am content to leave it to that old dictionary-maker and apostle of common-sense, Samuel Johnson: 'Obsolete words are admitted when they are found in authors not obsolete, or when they have force or beauty that may deserve revival.'[3]

Guided by this dictum, we have included obsolete words in company with those that still have breath in them, because a language, like a country, includes the dead and the living. Tombstones and public monuments to ancient and often forgotten heroes are part of the total history of a country, while dead words are undoubtedly part of the totality of a language as well as of the history and literature of those who have written and spoken in that language down the ages. Nowhere is this more true than in the historical array of the acquired words and phrases of foreign origin which a language adopts, befriends and cultivates to enrich and enlarge itself in its material and con-ceptual areas of written and oral expression. But there is no way in which a lexicographer can arrive at a 'total' dictionary. Old, dead words are pushed out through the back door, while new, living ones come swaggering in through the front, for a dictionary is both a graveyard and a nursery of a language. All is in flux, making selection inevitable, difficult, even hazardous. As Henry Sweet, no mean practi-tioner of the craft, says in the preface to his *Anglo-Saxon Diction-ary*: 'A dictionary which is good from a practical point of view – that which is finished in reasonable time, and is kept within reasonable limits of space – must necessarily fall short of total requirements.'[4] We have brought together in generous measure a representative and 'dated' selection of words from many sources to illustrate and exemplify the world of Anglo-India. Nevertheless, the percipient reader will still find pointers to lead him, if he is so inclined, to discover for himself a more bountiful harvest of Anglo-Indian expressions in many fields of cultural and historical interest, such as, for example, indology, archaeology, anthropology, philosophy, theology, music and dance. These will, we hope, correct the opinion of Burnell in the introductory remarks to *Hobson-Jobson*, 'that considering the long intercourse with India, it is noteworthy that the additions which have thus accrued to the English language are, from the intellectual point of view, of no intrinsic value'.[5] From one who made such a significant contribution to the subject this is an astonishing statement, which can only be attributed to his somewhat narrow and limited interpretation of the parameters of Anglo-Indian English. *Hobson-Jobson*, otherwise a master-work of mellow, witty and leisurely scholarship, is sadly lacking, for example, in references to the words arising from interest in the main religions of India: Hinduism, Jainism, Sikhism, Buddhism, Islam and Zoroastrianism, which have provided English with a useful word-bank of widely accepted conceptual and descriptive terms in the linguistic confluence or *doab* of Anglo-India. A small selection of such words, from a large number which Yule and Burnell could with advantage have included, are: *atman* (1785), the supreme principle of life; *karma* (1828) and *kismet* (1849), destiny or fate; *mahatma* (1855), 'great-souled', a superior spiritual being; *rishi* (1766), a sage or saint, and *Vedanta* (1788), one of the six systems of orthodox Hindu philosophy.[6]

II

At this point we should ask ourselves: 'Are these esoteric expressions now considered to be adequately acclimatized or familiarized to be acceptable English? *Quot homines, tot sententiae!* Scholars and others now using them as necessities not oddities in their English texts regard them as familiar and unavoidable technical terms. On the other hand, to British soldiers, for example, serving in India (or afterwards in *Blighty*), they were either completely unknown or outlandish gibberish. Between these two extremes there appears to be a reasonably acceptable and extensive usage. A random selection might well include: *Brahmin*, a member of the top 'twice-born' caste among Hindus; *pariah*, a social outcaste; *pundit*, a learned Brahmin (or nowadays any learned person); *thug*, a one-time professional murderer and thief in India (or today any brutal lout); *suttee*, 'the faithful Hindu wife' who was immolated with her dead husband, or such immolation; *yoga*, the union with the Supreme Spirit and associated practices; *nirvana*, the extinction of individual existence according to the teachings of the Buddha (or, more generally the achievement of eternal bliss); *zenana*, the woman's part of a Hindu family house; *harem*, the same in a Muslim family house, and *swastika*, a Hindu symbol of good fortune, twisted to become the Nazi 'Aryan' emblem in Germany under Hitler.

Yet as soon as these words and others like them are written down the doubts come creeping in, for there is no final, objective test to determine beyond a shadow of a doubt whether they are 'family' or not, or whether they still retain something (or a lot) of their original foreign style, however well-dressed in the English fashion they may appear to be or however long they have been on parade or on active service in English uniforms. 'The final approval', avers Eric Partridge, 'lies with the general feeling of the people as a whole. Yet sometimes there is no vote, no decision: a word or a phrase may gain a place in standard English as if by stealth: by being consonant with and appropriate to the genius of the language. It just drops into place.'[7]

We have perhaps been too hospitable to numerous esoteric or obsolete Anglo-Indian expressions. On the other hand, English is surely the most hospitable and companionable of languages, and just as a man should be known by the company he has kept during his entire life, and not only in his present state, so should a language. Throughout its history a language gathers companionable words from foreign sources, befriends them, adapts them to its grammar, spelling and familiar speech sounds, sometimes changing their appearance and original meanings beyond recognition. For example, *catamaran* (1620) no longer means or sounds in English what it meant or sounded like in its Tamil form, *kattu-marram*, 'tied-wood', and meanwhile it has bred not only the British yachtsman's abbreviated slang variation 'cat', but also the hybrid 'trimaran', whose fibre-glass elegance and ocean-going size do not remotely resemble the tiny, primitive, tied-wood raft described by Dr Fryer in 1672, and still to be seen unchanged on the Coromandel coast today.[8] While for Thackeray a 'catamaran' was simply a spiteful woman; another kind of 'cat'. Similarly, *punch*, the Anglo-Indian quintuplicate tipple,[9] mentioned by Evelyn in his *Diary* on 16 January 1662, has now been transformed into a totally different article of refreshment from that imbibed by the *sahibs, nabobs* and *boxwallahs* of John Company's days, for whom its five ingredients were generally *arrack*, lime-juice (*nimbu-pānī*), spice (*masāla*), sugar (*chīnī*) and water (*pānī*),[1] and Robert Burns' 'toddy (H. *tārī*) in *The Holy Fair*, composed of whisky, sugar and hot water was a world away from the fermented sap of the *tār*-palm, the *palmyra*, of South India, mentioned in Arrian's *Indica*, *c*. 320 BC, and on numerous Anglo-Indian occasions since then.[11] In the same way, *bandicoot* (Tel. *pandi-kooka*, lit. 'pig-dog') underwent a sea-change from a giant Indian rat (*Mus giganteus* or *Indica*) to a genus of small Australian marsupials, the *paramelidae*.[12]

But English is not unselectively friendly. It has cultivated different kinds of foreign companions at different periods of its history according to its changing tastes, needs and discretion, sometimes discarding, forgetting or neglecting some of them from time to time, or associating with them in full-dress or formal functions only: fancy words for fancy occasions. Witness the opulence and fancy dress of some of the words selected by Roget to illustrate the word 'master'. They include: *maharaja, mandarin, nabob, subahdar, sahib, sirdar, sheik, sultan, caliph, pasha, imaum, shah, mogul, khan, rajah, emir, Nizam, nawab, padishah, lama, seyyid,* and, for good measure, *sultana,* and *maharani,* suggesting, perhaps, that mistresses are sometimes masters!

The historical process of accumulating and discarding is notably complex in English, enriched as it is by many ancient and modern languages from many parts of the world. In this ever-changing socio-linguistic spectrum, Indian languages have played a significant role, from the beginning of the seventeenth century, or well before if we count a handful of Sanskrit or Pali words, some of which landed on the shores of England 300 years before the first Englishman, Father Thomas Stevens, set foot on Indian soil as a Jesuit priest in the service of Portugal. Arriving by favour of Greek and Latin, these words have now esconced themselves in the core of English. All of them were carried to the West as verbal freight along the old trade routes from the East: witness their Arabic, Persian, Portuguese, Dutch, Spanish or French forms acquired in transit. An early example by way of Arabic, Greek and some European languages is the titular character of the old story of Josaphat, who renounced the world after the fashion of the Indian *sannyāsīs.* 'It is now evident that Josaphat is the Bodhisat or Bodhisatva, and the story is nothing less than the great renunciation of Gautama Buddha, as narrated in *Lalita Vistara.'*[13] Among the earliest of these old 'Anglo-Indian' words, with their Greek, Latin and Sanskrit forms, and with the centuries in which they arrived in English are the following :

11 C. pepper. Gr. peperi; L. piper; S. *pippalī.*
13 C. beryl. Gr. berullos; L. beryllus; perh. S. *vaidūrya.*
13 C. ginger. Gr. ziggiberis; L. zingiber(i); S. *srngaveram.*
13 C. panther. Gr. panther; L. panthera; perh S. *pandarīkas* (tiger).
13 C. sugar. Gr. sakharon; med. L. succarum; S. *sarkara.*
14 C. musk. Late Gr. mosk(h)os; med. L. mos(c)hus; perh. S. *mushka.*
14 C. sandal. Gr. sandalion; L. sandaium; S. *chandana.*
15 C. camphor. Med. Gr. kaphoura; med. L. camphora; S. *karpūram.*
16 C. opal. Late Gr. opallios; L. opalus; S. *upalas.*

(A fascinating short list of the earliest trade-words redolent of the spices and perfumes of the 'gorgeous' East and foreshadowing so much Anglo-Indian history of succeeding centuries.)

But traffic in words, and in the commodities they denoted, was by no means a one-way East-West affair between India and Europe: far from it as we will see. In the sixteenth century the Portuguese carried to Goa and other parts of their *Estado da India* (which was established by the middle of the sixteenth century), a considerable and powerful cargo of words from Portugal which, with substantial additions from local Indian languages, developed into the Indo-Portuguese patois. This ubiquitious creole Portuguese established itself as the lingua franca for trade and other purposes in India throughout the trading areas, between the Portuguese and other Europeans (mostly English), as well as between Europeans and Indians, often at first with the aid of the 'men of two languages', the *dubashes* or *topasses*. Chaplains or in the Indo-Portuguese patois, *padres*, of the East India Company were required to learn and discourse in Portuguese or in the Indo-Portuguese patois throughout the eighteenth century and Charles Lockyer (1711) declared: 'Thus the Portuguese may justly claim that they have established a kind of lingua franca in all sea-ports of India of great use to other Europeans who would find it difficult in many places to be well understood without it.'[14] The East India Company actually had the liturgy of the Church of England and the psalms of David translated into Portuguese and printed at Oxford in folio, 'so the Gospel and the protestant religion may be made known to those ignorant natives in their own language [!] to the honour of God and the glory of our church'.[15] Even the greatest Englishman of his time in India, Robert Clive, was never able to give an order in any Indian language, it was said, yet he spoke Portuguese with fluency!

This patois endured throughout the seventeenth and eighteenth centuries and remnants of it beyond. But inevitably, with the passage of time, as the strength of the East India Company increased and the Portuguese power waned, much of its vocabulary passed into the lexicon of Anglo-India. Among such inherited words were: *maistry* (Pg. mestre), an artisan; *mosquito* (dim. Pg. mosca), a fly; *castees* (Pg. castico), India-born Portuguese of 'pure', unmixed descent; *mustees* (Pg. mestiço), a person of 'mixed' Indo-Portuguese parentage; *muster* (Pg. mostra), a sample or pattern; *caste* (Pg. casta), pure, unmixed; *padre* (Pg. padre), a Catholic Father or Protestant chaplain; *ayah* (Pg. aia), a nurse or housemaid; *cobra* (Pg. cobra), a snake of the genus *Naja* and related genera, and *kittysol* (Pg. quita-sol), an umbrella. Two interesting relics of the Portuguese possession of Bombay are: foras-lands (Pg. foro, quit-rent), referring to the assiduous reclamation of land from the sea, and *vellard* (Pg. vellado, an embankment or causeway), associated with such reclamation. Hence 'Hornby's Vellard', built about 1752, curiously enough about twenty years before Hornby's time as Governor of Bombay!

Among the verbal relics of the Indo-Portuguese lingua franca many are immediately recognizable by their nasalized endings: *palanquin* (Pg. palanquim, from S. *palyanka*), a covered litter; *mandarin* (Pg. mandarin, from Mal. *mĕntĕri*, from H. *mantrī*), a high civil servant, or,

7

nowadays, an intellectual of the ruling caste; *mangelin* (Indo-Pg., from Tel. *manjali*, Tam. *manjadi*, the seed of the *Adenanthera pavonina*), a small weight for weighing jewels.

The Portuguese also left a legacy of such everyday things as rooms *(cameras)*, boats *(botellos)*, shirts *(cameezes)*, buckets *(baltees)*, keys *(chabees)* and hammers *(martols)*.

And we should not overlook the lowly, obligatory and one-time ubiquitous spittoon, the *cuspidor*, or, more properly, the *cuspidore* (Pg. cuspadeira), as Yule and others have been at some pains to emphasize.

III

It has been possible from the beginning of the seventeenth to the middle of the twentieth century to associate, with varying degrees of certainty, the dates of acquiring Indian expressions broadly with the prevailing social, official, political, commercial and personal relationships existing between the Indians and the British. This is social history documented by dated lexical items appropriate to the various linguistic registers and contexts of Anglo-Indian usage. These extend from the colloquial, slang and unconventional English of the British soldier in India, such as : 'To *bolo* the *bat* a *tora*', 'to speak the lingo a bit'; '*Banged* up to the eyeballs', 'totally "stoned" on *bhang*'; 'The *amen-wallah*', 'the army chaplain or padre'; *Tory peechy*', 'delayed repatriation' (fr. H. *tora pīchchī*, a little later), to the middle ground of the middlemen, the *box-wallahs* or tradesmen who dealt in *chintz, calico, dungarees,* and *seersucker* in *godowns* and *bazaars* and measured their *nafa* (profit) in *crores* and *lakhs* of *sicca* rupees, *goldmohurs* and *pagodas,* having set their minds on 'shaking the Pagoda-Tree', and returning whence they came, if not as ostentatiously wealthy *nabobs,* at least as respectably rich burgesses.[15] From this linguistic middle ground to the upper regions of scholarship, law and government was a gigantic step. In these elevated linguistic spheres Anglo-Indians combined their workaday interests with research into the history, languages, archaeology, religion and the arts of India, acquiring and using strange and powerful expressions from Indian languages, particularly Sanskrit, evocative of ancient *mantras* and *sutras,* the *Vedas,* the *Ramayana,* the *Mahabharata,* the *Upanishads,* the Laws of Manu and a host of other Sanskrit writings from the earliest years of Hindu civilization. Some of the most outstanding of these scholar-administrators and soldier-scholars will be mentioned later. A few lines from Sir Edwin Arnold's *The Light of Asia* (1879) will provide a rich, perhaps a too rich taste of what I mean:

Then 'ten chief sins came – Mara's mighty ones.
Attavada first, the Sin of Self.
Then came wan Doubt – False *Visikitcha.*
Then came she who gave dark creeds their power,
Sillabat – paramasa, sorceress.
Next, *Kama,* the king of passions.
Next came fiercer sins, *Patigha* – Hate –
and *Ruparga* – Lust of Days.
And next him, *Aruparaga* – Lust of Fame,
And haughty *Mano* came, the Fiend of Pride,
And smooth Selfrighteousness – *Udachacha,*
And Ignorance, *Avidya,* hideous hag.

In the spheres of Indian music and dance, Anglo-Indians for the most part were unreceptive to the Indian words associated with these aspects of Indian culture, finding these art forms (when they were aware of them at all) hideous and completely alien to their British and European traditions. For most Anglo-Indians the only Indian dance-form presented for their entertainment was the *Nautch,* often dubbed the *'Poggly'* or frenzied *Nautch,* or the *'Pootly',* the wooden-puppet *Nautch* in description of the movements and the nature of these dances. The infinitely more subtle and refined dance-forms, *Yaksha-gana, Manipuri, Kathak, Bharatanatyam, Kathakali, Kuchipudi,* and *Odissi,*[17] seemed to have remained out of sight of Europeans until comparatively recently in the religious seclusion of Hindu temples where they were traditionally and ritually cultivated by *devadasis,* 'the slave-girls of the gods', for the delectation of the temple *pujārīs* (priests) and other high caste Brahmins. Similarly, the Indian instrumental and vocal music was almost *terra incognita,* largely unexplored by Anglo-Indians, or considered by them to be too outrageously discordant to be thought of as music at all, though at least one nineteenth century Anglo-Indian writer was curious enough to investigate the nature of the *rāga.* 'The Hindoos', he said, 'have a gamut (the *rāga*) consisting of seven notes like our own; which being repeated in three several *ast'hanas* or octaves form, in all, a scale of twenty-one natural notes.'[18] A more usual attitude was that of the Hon. Emily Eden, sister of Lord Auckland, Governor-General of India, 1835-42, when she exclaimed: He '[Col. James Skinner ('Sikander Sahib')] had all the best singers and dancers in Delhi, and they acted passages out of Vishnu's and Brahma's lives and sang Persian songs which I thought made a very ugly noise.'[19] And from the same source: 'People may abuse nautching, but it amuses me extremely. The girls hardly move about at all, but their attitudes are so graceful, I like to see them. Their singing is dreadful and very noisy.'[20] But the inquisitive and fearless *mem-sahib* traveller, Fanny Parks, who was vastly and insatiably curious about everything Indian that came her way, or that she went out of her way to discover, acquired a *sitār*, the classical North Indian stringed instrument, of which she said:

I have received a present that pleases me so greatly, a *sitar*, a musical instrument, in general use all over India; it was made at Lucknow [*sic*!] from a hollow gourd, and is very beautifully put together. It has four strings; the first is of steel wire and the two next are of brass wire, the fourth and smallest of steel. It is played with the first finger of the right hand alone, on which is placed a little steel wire frame, called a *misrab*, with which the strings are struck; the left hand stops the notes on the frets, but you only stop the notes on the first string; the other three strings produce a sort of pedal sound as the *misrab* passes over them, from the manner in which they are tuned. The instrument is most elegantly formed.

She then goes on to describe the *ektara*, a one-stringed instrument, as its name implies, used by wandering minstrels, 'veritable Paganinis of the East' in the critical estimation of the enthusiastic Fanny Parks.[21] One other nineteenth century English traveller was exceptionally enthusiastic about Indian music. Capt. Godfrey Charles Mundy informs us: 'Before the musicians left us I had become quite a fanatico for Indian minstrelsy and gave my "wah! wah!" of applause to a favourite *gazzul* of Hafiz, or sprightly *kuhirwa* air, with at least as much judgment and discernment as is displayed by one half of the pit-frequenting cognoscenti in their distribution of "bravos!" to the production of Rossini or Paesiello.'[22]

As India was never a *colonie de peuplement* for Anglo-Indians as it was for some of its earlier invaders, many of the acquired Indian expressions wear a 'reach-me-down' or 'for-the-time-being' look, underlining the temporary nature of the sojourn in India of the Army, 'civilians', *boxwallahs*, *Feringies* and *Blighty-wallahs*. As Bishop Heber said: 'So few Europeans, however, who can help it reside in India, that it seems strange that any man should prefer it as a residence, without some stronger motive than a fondness for Sanscrit literature.'[23] Or as Sir George Trevelyan asks: 'Who would consent to exchange the common-room in *esse*, and Downing Street in *posse*, for the bungalow and the cutcherry?'[24]

The Anglo-Indian expressions which may well have been absolutely *pukka* for *sahib* and *mem-sahib* in Calcutta or in the *mofussil*, 'up the country', could hardly have been of much use in their retirement in Bath, Cheltenham or Chalfont St. Giles. Who would know there that breakfast was *chota-hazri*; a *badmash*, a scoundrel; a *derzi*, a tailor; a *bundook*, a musket; an *ayah*, a nursemaid; a *bearer*, a manservant; a *panchayat*, a local council; a *burra peg*, a double whisky, and that to *gubbrow*, *lugow*, *foozilow*, *dumbcow*, *puckerow* and *bunow* meant to

bully, to moor a boat, to flatter, to scold, to lay hold of, and to fabricate? They could not have been much used except (with fading relevance) among a declining number of retired Anglo-Indians in the
evening of their lives spent in their salubrious English *compounds*
and *cantonments*. They brought with them into retirement their old
imperial India colonized in their old imperial hearts, with a small but,
to them, vivid vocabulary of Anglo-Indian words, such as I have quoted
above, which set them apart from their stay-at- home neighbours. 'For
he that hath long cultivated another language will find its words and
combinations croud upon his memory, and haste or affectation will
obtrude borrowed terms and exotic expressions.'[25]

The use of Indian words in their Anglo-Indian fancy-dress was a
habit born of long familiarity, sometimes turning to affectation and
jocularity. 'How charmingly and effectively', wrote Aldous Huxley,
'these foreign tags assist one in the great task of calling a spade by
some other name.'[26] The popular notion that foreign words are
acquired to fill gaps in one's own native language is too simplistic and
patently wide of the mark, though they often seem to do so at the time
in situ. The *cutcherry* was felt to be more than the office or the court-
house: it was the core and power-house of British justice and administration. The Indo-Portuguese *peon*, at one time a footslogging *sepoy*,
stood for more than an office-boy or stamp-licker: he was the connect-
ing link not only between one official and another in the *cutcherry*
itself, but also between the *cutcherry* and the outside world. A
tamasha, always a grandiloquent word on the lips of Anglo-Indian
sahibs and *mem-sahibs*, promised more excitement than a mere
entertainment or show, and *bandobast* carried overtones of organization beyond a simple arrangement or 'set-up'. *Koi Hai?* (Is there
anyone there?) summoned the genie and the bottle with more
panache and urgency than lacklustre 'Waiter!' or 'Steward!',[27] while
'*Brandy-shrub* and *Blighty-pani lao!*' was a world away from 'Bring
me a brandy-soda!' *Decko!, Jildi!* and *Chello!* were more immediately
imperative than 'Look!, get a move on!, and 'Let's go!' A *pukka sahib*
was the genuine article, a gentleman of gentlemen, *sans peur et sans
reproche*, and 'a man who is the thorough master of the word 'pucka'
may hold his own in any society in India', proclaimed Sir George
Trevelyan.[28]

This special, often mildly contemptuous use, and frequent misuse,
of the common words of the Indian vernaculars by all classes of Anglo-
Indians gave substance to the notion that Anglo-Indian English never
got beyond being a 'frontier language'. 'Anglo-Indians', said Sir G.O.
Trevelyan, 'are naturally enough wont to interlard their conversation
with native words.... The habit is so universal that a Governor-

General fresh from home complained in a published order that he could not understand the reports of his own officials.[29]

Flora Annie Steel gives a taste, or rather a parody, of this when she makes one of her characters, not a *pukka sahib* it must be admitted, say:

Decko, you want this *admi abhi,* but you ain't goin' to get 'im. *Tumhara nahin.* He's mine, *mehra admi, sumja*? If you want to *lurro,* come on. You shall have a bellyful, and there'll be plenty on you to *phansi.* But wot I say is don't be *pargul soors.* I don't do your temples 'arm. It's *durm shester ram-ram* an' *hurry ganga,* so far's I care. But this man's my guv'nor. You don't touch 'im *kubbi nahin.* I'm a *nek admi, burra ussel,* when I'm took the right way, contrariwise I'm *zulm* an' *ficker* an' *burra burra affut*?[30]

Or another example from another source: You *dekkoed* me *giro* in the *peenika pani* and you *cooch-biwanied.* You *soonoed* me *bolo. Iswasti* I'll *gurrum* your *peechi.*[31]

Though there were many Anglo-Indians who were sustained by high ideals of public service, the notion of impermanance of tenure gradually but inevitably established itself in the minds of Anglo-Indians, undermining the concept of imperial immortality symbolized in Disraeli's 'brightest jewel in the English crown', proclaimed in *durbar* and parliament, though with faltering, sometimes strident tones towards the end. The Mutiny of 1857, the Jallianwalla Bagh massacre of 1919, and two World Wars, among other happenings, eroded beyond repair the British will to rule India imperially.[32] The establishment of telegraphic communication in 1865 and the opening of the Suez canal in 1869 contributed to this by making India more accessible, leading ultimately to the transference of real power from the Anglo-Indians on the spot to the men in Whitehall and Westminster.[33] The Indian Empire had run its course by 1947, ninety years after Queen Victoria had proclaimed it and 347 years after Queen Elizabeth I had granted the first charter of the East India Company. With the death of empire the spring of Anglo-Indian words of the common kind almost dried up, though a trickle of scholarly and political expressions continued to flow into the three and a half centuries-old reservoir of the Anglo Indian glossary. Some of these are the topical slogans of the 'Quit India' movement such as: *Jai Hind*!, 'Victory to India!'; *Mahatma Gandhi zindabad*!, Long live Mahatma Gandhi!'; *Vande Mataram,* 'I bow to thee my Motherland'; *Swaraj,* Self-Rule, Independence; *swadeshi,* 'of one's own country', applied to the patriotic wearing of India-made clothing *(khaddar)*; *Harijan,* 'Man of God', the exalted title Gandhi conferred on the 'Untouchables', the *pariahs,* of Indian society;[34] *Satyagraha,* so-called 'passive resistance', literally 'insistence on truth', the method used by Gandhi and his followers to achieve national independence. To these should be added *shantih,* T.S. Eliot's 'the peace that passeth understanding';[35] *Manvantura*, 'the period or age of a Manu held equal to 4,320,000 human years' in James Joyce's *Ulysses;* and *Pralaya*, the overwhelming destruction of the universe after a *Kalpa* (1000 *Yugas*), or a 'day of *Brahma*', in the same work.[36] Lower down on the scale we become acquainted with *goondas,* hooligans; *jathas,* armed bands, and, finally, the British soldier's euphonious invention, *Doolallytap,* his valedictory gift from India, the mocking appellation for the long-service, sun-induced muddle-headedness and sometimes insanity, treated, not always effectively, at the military sanatorium at Deolali, a *cantonment* town near Bombay.

V

In attempting to 'date' early Anglo-Indian words we cannot be certain of their first use among British travellers and traders, nor can we be sure of how they were pronounced, as spelling was utterly idiosyncratic in an individual writer as well as between one writer and another. In this context it would be wise to take heed once again of the words of Samuel Johnson:

As Language was at its beginning merely oral, all words of necessary or common use were spoken before they were written, and while they were unfixed by any visible signs, must have been spoken with great diversity, as we now observe those who cannot read to catch the words imperfectly, and utter them negligently.... The powers of the letters, when they were applied to a new language, must have been vague and unsettled, and therefore different hands would exhibit the same sound by different combinations.[37]

As an early and apt example of this, in his *Discoveries of the Sect of the Banians* (1630), Henry Lord, for whom every Brahmin 'was an hypocrite and evil-doer, and every mouth speaketh folly', writes *Brammon, Cuttery, Shuddery* and *Wise* (the errant pen following the errant ear) for the four main Hindu castes, *Brahmin, Kshatriya, Sudra* and *Vaisya;* and *Bremaw, Vistney* and *Ruddery* for *Brahma, Vishnu* and *Rudra*.[38] The English translation of Bernier's *Travels in the Mogul Empire 1658-64,* informs us of *Beths, Beschen* and *Mahadeu,* and in *Purchas: His Filgrimage, Nirvana* is written in its Pali form, *Niba*.[39]

Although we may know the first written use of a word, we can only surmise from the circumstances of the author how long before he wrote it he first spoke it. However, with regard to the earliest travellers to India, the approximate first date of the spoken word is not too difficult to surmise in most cases as their individual stay in the country was for a few years only. There is little or no evidence that they knew, before they set sail on their six-month voyage to India, the Indian words they used in their writings though they may have picked up some of them on their way out. To indicate the latitude to be allowed I have shown the length of residence in India of each of these early travellers.

Of the four Englishmen, Ralph Fitch, John Newberry, James Story and William Leedes, brought to Goa as prisoners of the Portuguese on 4 April 1583 after sailing from London to Aleppo on the 'Tyger', and generally reckoned to be the first English arrivals in India after the English Jesuit Priest, Father Thomas Stevens in 1579, Ralph Fitch (1583-91) is the most important for our immediate purpose.[40] He may be said to have laid the foundation, or at least the foundation-stone, of Anglo-Indian writing by introducing into his letters a score of everyday Indian words (dressed in his personal spellings), which were after-wards printed by Hakluyt in *The Principal Navigations* (1599). He tells us of *areca*, the so-called *betel-nut*, and *chunam* the astringent lime that goes with it to form, with other ingredients, the popular Indian masticatory called *pān*, which received so much attention in Anglo-Indian writing thereafter. A score of words is not much to write home about, but a useful start to the 3700 words in this present work.

Eight years after the departure of Fitch, John Mildenhall (or Midnall) arrived in India, stayed for seven years (1599-1606), and posed as the ambassador of Elizabeth I to the court of Akbar. Among other words that he added to the score already contributed by Fitch, two were of some interest. He considered that the Persian word *arz* (a petition or request) was a plural form (natural enough in an English-man), a mistake that was to continue with the spelling *ars* in the writings of others who followed him. He also introduced into the Anglo-Indian vocabulary the Arabic word *tarjuman*, an interpreter, in the form of *drugman*, though the word had been living in English since the fourteenth century and is now standardized as 'dragoman'. We have seen that an interpreter was a necessity for travellers and traders, the Indo-Portuguese patois being the link language commonly used, with the words *topass* and *dubash*, both meaning 'a man of two languages', existing side by side with 'dragoman. (Plural *dragomans*, not *dragomen* as sometimes occurs). Mildenhall was followed by William Hawkins (1608-11), who was all at sea over the spelling of this word, giving us a choice of *trouch-man*, *treuch-man* and *truchman*. He may also have been the first Anglo-Indian to folk-etymologize Rajputs in the guise of *Rashpoots* to fit the well-known bellicosity of the owners of this Rajputana *Kshatriya* caste title.

Another pioneer user of Anglo-Indian words was William Finch, who landed in Surat with William Hawkins on 24 August 1608 and remained in India for three years, leaving to posterity his journal (fortunately preserved by Purchas), a work of considerable literary merit and historical interest. He was the earliest practitioner of what we may call 'Anglo-Indian prose', which freely uses Indian words to enliven and authenticate Indian themes and situations. Many of the expressions he chooses to use of Dravidian, Indo-European or of Portuguese origin are of objects, plants and people possessing no English, or no exact English, equivalents. But Finch uses them, without pedantry or ostentation in the service of exactitude, vividness and local colour, and with his own orthographic representations. The high-ranking Mughal officer, head of the police and in charge of criminal jurisdiction is given his proper title of *phousdar* (H. *foujdar*), as is the religious mendicant, the *gosain, gossyne* (H. *gosain*), who had subdued his passions and renounced the world. On a more secular level, Finch tells us of the *massalgee,* his spelling of the Hindi *mas'alchī,* the link-boy or torch-bearer who runs beside his master's *palankin* at night. The water-chestnut, one of the crops on which revenue was collected is credited with its proper name, the *sringara* (H. *sringhara*), as is the valuable indigo plant, *neel* or *anile,* a name borrowed from the Arabic by way of the Portuguese. India was a 'goodly country' said Finch, 'and fertile... abounding with Date Trees whence they draw a liquor, called *Tarree (toddy)* and *Sure (sura),* both of which are fermented juices of palms, which figure quite often in the literature and the life of Anglo-India in succeeding centuries.

Finch was followed by four Englishmen who were in India at about the same time: Nicholas Withington (1662-16), Thomas Coryat(e), (1616-17), Edward Terry (1616-18), and Sir Thomas Roe (1615-18). Being the first royally appointed English ambassador to the Mughal court of Jehangir, Roe was in many ways – including his self-esti-mate – the most important of these. He was in an eminently favour-able position to observe and comment on the life-styles of the ruling classes in Hindustan and on the relationships between Indian officials and Englishmen who were endeavouring to establish 'factories' (trading posts) in Jehangir's empire. The first of these had already been set up by Hawkins, somewhat shakily, at Surat, about seven years before Sir Thomas Roe landed there. He brought with him a handful of oriental words which he may have picked up on the way or at home as they were by this time gaining some currency in England. These were: *areca, betel, calico* (from Calicut on the Malabar coast); *cuscus,* (Ar. *Kouskous),* millet; *junks* (Pg. *junco;* Mal. *jong*), the sailing vessels of the China seas; and coconuts, perhaps from the Spanish and Portuguese *coco* (monkey-face), with its three holes in the base of the shell. Although Roe was a man of strict protocol – aristocratic, ceremonious, somewhat aloof – he was, at the same time observant, shrewd and worldly-wise. Above all he was determined to maintain his own sovereign's dignity at all cost in the face of the attempts by Jehangir's court, as well as by the attendant Portuguese Jesuits, to abort his aim of establishing by imperial *firman* (patent, licence) the right of the East India Company to trade in Mughal territory. Oaten said of him: 'he should have sometimes removed his gaze from the dazzling splendour of princes' and have given 'more pertinent observations relative to the state of the country and the people'.[41] This is somewhat unfair criticism, for though a score from about seventy of his Indian words smack of the court, the palace, the mosque and the temple, such as *Hawa Gemal*, the Pleasure Garden; *sizeda* and *tessalim*, ceremonial obeisances, and '*larruco*, the publicke sitting of the King to see the games and hear complaints', the rest exhibit his interest in and knowledge of ordinary everyday things, and of the people of India. He tells of 'High *cannates*' (H./Ar. *kanat*), tent walls of a coarse stuff 'made like arras'; of the Prince's *haddy* troops (H./Ar. *ahadi*, single) in the Mughal service who offered their services singly, and were directly responsible to the emperor or prince; of the *alfandica* (Pg. *alfandega*), the custom-house and meeting-place of foreign merchants, and of '*Surat* stuffe', goods of traditionally inferior quality, made in Surat. These and many more are given house-room in the pages of Sir Thomas Roe's account, grandly entitled: *Embassy to the Court of the great Mogoar, King of the Oriental Indyes, of Condahey, of Chismer and of Corason* (1615-19). His keen eye for the details of the life around him is seen in the following extract, in which he says of the Governor of Maladia:

He sent for coconuts to give the Company himself chewing *Bittle*, and the lime of burnt Oyster-shells with a kernel of a nut called *Arraca* like an akorne, it bites the mouth, avoids the rheume, cools the head, strengthens the teeth, and is all their Phisick: it makes one unused to it giddie, and makes a man's spittle red, and in time it colours the teeth, which is esteemed as beautie: this is used by men hourly.

But Withington, Coryat and Terry were not without their interest and importance either, both in their contribution to the growing Anglo-Indian vocabulary and to our knowledge of the Indian people they met on their travels. We learn of bathrooms, *goozul-khanas* (H./Ar. *ghūsl-khāna*) used as rooms of private audience by some of the Great Mughals and their officials, and of the *mansabdars (mancipdares* in Roe), those quasi-feudal noblemen who served the Mughal emperors, in return being given military rank and responsibility for providing a certain number of men and horses, to be put at the service of the emperor when called for. Coryat, who boasted of his great accomplishments as a linguist, used *Musselman* (Muslim) quite correctly as the singular form and *Musselmen* quite incorrectly as the plural, a mistake repeated by Dr Fryer sixty years later and by Queen Victoria, 180 years later still, in a letter to Lady Canning in

September 1857. Another interesting word which seems to have been established in seventeenth century Anglo-Indian usage is to be found in Edward Terry's *A Voyage to East India* (1655). This is the word *Adam*, Terry's rendering of the Hindi word *ādmi*, a man. 'The Indians call a man Adam from our first father Adam, whose wife tempted him with forbidden fruit, took as they say and ate it down, but as her husband swallowed it the Hand of God stopped it in his throat, when a man hath a bunch there, which women have not, called by them Adam's Apple.'[42] As Terry was the East India Company's chaplain to Sir Thomas Roe's embassy (1616-18), this may account for the professional tone of this morsel of ecclesiastical folk-etymology, matched equally by his incredible reason for the Brahmin's *sikha* (top-knot): 'They usually shave off all their haire from their heads,' he wrote, 'reserving only a locke on the crowne for Mahomet [!] to pull them into heaven.'[43]

Religion added its quota of expressions in Anglo-Indian writing of the seventeenth century (e.g. *yogi, hadji, Holi, Juggernaut, khutba, moolvi, mullah, purana, Ramadan, Vishnu*), to be multiplied and analysed by succeeding generations of travellers and others of an enquiring cast of mind. Among these must certainly be included Henry Lord, appointed chaplain by the East India Company to the English 'factory' at Surat for five years in 1624, who gives us an interesting, albeit inaccurate, account of Hinduism and Parseeism (Zoroastrianism) in his *Displaye of two Forraigne Sects in the East Indies: A Discoverie of the Sect of the Banians, and the Religion of the Persees* (1630). In this fascinating and pioneering work, extolled by Sir William Jones[44] (though somewhat beyond its merits), Lord claimed, after the manner of the times, that these two sects were guilty of 'violating the divine law of the dread Majesty of Heaven, and notable forgery coyning Religion according to the Mint of their own Tradition'. He refers to the *shasters*, the Hindu sacred books, and to *Porous (Purusha)* and *Parcoutie (Prakriti)*, the first man and woman in the Hindu universe, who begot four sons (referred to above), *Brammon, Cuttery, Shuddery and Wyse*. In the second book, dedicated like the first to the Archbishop of Canterbury, Lord castigates the idolatrous worship of fire by the Parsis just as he did the false religion of the *Banians* (Hindus). Nevertheless it is to Lord that the West owes one of the first useful introductions to the teachings of the *Zundavasthan (Zend-Avesta)*, the holy scriptures of the Parsis, and to the ritual functions of the priests of the *agiaries* (fire-temples) and the *dokhmas* ('Towers of Silence').[45] We learn of the *dasturs*, the chief priests of the Parsis, of the *mobeds* next below them in the hierarchy, and the *herbuds*, the lowest of them all.[46]

Fate or *kismet* as an aspect of Hinduism does not go unmentioned by one seventeenth-century Anglo-Indian commentator, John Marshall, who, in his *Notes and Observations on the East Indies* (1668-72), observes:

Seranaut the Bamin [Brahmin] Doctor at Pottama saith 'tis writ in their books that Man hath no Freewill, and saith that Man's heart may be compared to God as a Spider webb is to a Spider, for which way soever the Spider draws the webb follows.

He draws our attention, too to his understanding of the contemporary system of Hindu medicine. 'The Hindoos', he says, 'reckon upon 3 humors in man's body, viz. *By, Pitt, Cuff....* The *By* rules the body from 2 *Gurries* before sunrise and rules until 1 *Purr.* The *Pitt* rules till night; then *Cuff,* till *By* begins again.'[47]

Curiosity also tempted some early travellers to observe the exotic plant life of their new surroundings. One of the earliest of these was Peter Mundy, who reached India as a cabin-boy in 1628. His work, *Travels in Europe and Asia* (1634-6), contains striking descriptions of the trees and fruits of Goa, including the *jambu,* a species of *Eugenia,* of which he writes: 'I think few trees More beautiful to the Eye, the flower of a good bigness, fine form and of an excellent vermilion Dye, very thicke sett growing on the stalkes and biggest bowes, not at the end of the sprigges as trees Doe bear with us.' Similar detailed and perceptive descriptions are given by Mundy of *Cajoories* (cashews), *Jackes* (jack-fruit trees), and *cocotrees* (coconut trees), the last- named 'affording Meat, Drink and lodging, Oyle, Wyne, Milk, Sugar, etts., and good cordage [*coir*] Made of the outward rinde of the Nutte, which in Clusters grow outt at the toppe on a sprigge, as Doe alsoe the *Papaes* [papayas].'

At the end of the seventeenth century there appeared on the Anglo-Indian scene one of the most important literary productions, Dr John Fryer's *A New Account of East India and Persia,* begun in 1672, finished in 1681 and printed in 1698. Of this Col. Henry Yule, in his preface to *Hobson-Jobson,* proclaimed: 'No work has been more serviceable in the completion of this Glossary'. 'It is', in the words of Subba Rao, 'a mine of historical and philological information.'[48] Early in the *Account* new and old oriental words come trippingly from Dr Fryer's pen, including several Malay words that established themselves in the Anglo-Indian lexicon. We are introduced to 'Cockatoes and Newries from Bantam', the first being from Malay *kakak tua,* 'old sister', and of the second Linschoten (1598) said: 'There cometh out of the Island of Molucas beyond Malacca a kind of birdes called *Noyras;* they are like Parattes.'[49] The Malay word *kajang,* 'palm-leaves dressed for thatching or matting',[50] is aptly used to describe the way the

Malays use *kajang* branches for 'both Sides and Coverings to their Cottages'. *Rattan*, the English word from Malay *rotan*, a species of *Calamus*, is properly used by Fryer in describing one of its many uses, the making of lattices for native houses. Similarly, he introduces us to *buncos* (Malay, *bungkus*), a bundle, a wrapping, used to describe the *cheroots* (Malay *churuttu*, Tamil *shuruttu*), wrapped in Malacca and Trichinopoly, and to *bank-solls*, later Anglo-Indian *bankshalls*, from Malay *bangsal*, a warehouse or, in Bengal, the office of the Harbour Master. *Proe* (Malay *prahu*, English 'prow'), 'a general name for any vessel, but generally for small craft', is inducted by Dr Fryer into the increasing Anglo-Indian seafaring vocabulary.[51] On the sea, *catamarans* and *mussoolas*, the surf-boats of the Coromandel coast, attract Dr Fryer's attention. 'I went ashore', he tells us 'in a *Mussoola*, a boat wherein ten men paddle... calked with *Dammar*' (resin), another Malay word. On land he sights 'a fair *Pagod* or Temple of the *Gentoos*, the Portugal idiom for Gentiles ... the aboriginees , and soon learns something of the Hindu caste system from the lowly *Holencores (Halalcores)* to the mighty *Brachmin* or *Bramine* and the Warrior *Rashpoots*, whom we have already met. 'At the head were the Brahmines', Fryer writes, 'the Ancient Gymnosophists; out of whom branched their priests, Physicians and their learned men. Next in esteem were the *Rashwars, Rashpoots*, or Souldiers.' His keen eye notes the details of the passing throng of natives and foreigners as *palenkeens* pass by him on the road, as do the pedestrians with their *arundells*, 'which are broad umbrellas held over their heads', on which sit 'small *turbats*'.

As a doctor, Fryer was professionally interested in the drugs and poisons used in India. He mentions '*Bung* [H. *bhang*], the juice of the intoxicating sort of hemp' and *Dutty* (H. *dhatura*), *Datura stramonium*, the thorn apple, 'the deadliest sort of *Solarium* [*solanum*] or Nightshade', earlier mentioned in Mandelslo's *Travels*.[51] He notes that '*Jaugies* [*yogis*] use a factitious stone (which we call snake-stone) and it is Counter-poyson to all deadly bites; if it sticks it attracts the poyson, and put it in Milk it recovers itself again'. There are, he says the *chints* or *chinces* (bugs), mentioned also by Terry, 'raising blisters on us [which] if squeezed leave a most Poysonous Stench'. On a pleasanter note he proceeds: 'On the other hand there were delicious fruits: *Jamboes* and *Guiavas* a kind of pear, *Jawks*, a coat of armour over it, like Hedge-hog, guards its weighty fruit and *Mangoes*, the Delight of India.' Dr Fryer, in company with numerous of his fellow Anglo-Indians before him and since, does not fail to impress upon us the importance in the lives of the natives of 'the only Indian entertainment, called *Pawn* [H. *pān*]', the Indian masticatory with *Arack (areca)* and *Chunam* 'the lime of calcined Oyster Shells'. By day Fryer

19

moved among *palenkeen* boys and *coolies,* at night with *duties* (H. *diutī*), torch-bearers with their 'Mussals [H. *mash'al*] in their hands: 'they are pots filled with Oyl in an Iron hoop, like our beacons, and set on fire by stinking rags'. We learn of men of various callings and castes, whose descriptions by Dr Fryer reveal a more than usually sharp eye for the varied, colourful and ever-changing panorama of life in seventeenth century India. I have given only a taste of the richness of the Anglo-Indian vocabulary used with great effect and authenticity by Dr Fryer. The dictionary and the original work must reveal the rest.

VI

With the passing of the seventeenth century, already richly abundant in its harvest of Anglo-Indian words of the common sort, and to a lesser degree of those belonging to more exalted spheres, the first half of the eighteenth century was marked by a sharp decline in the number of acquired Anglo-Indian expressions. Anglo-Indian English had almost reached a temporary saturation point of the more immediately useful acquisitions. The quota of words of commercial or domestic use that remained to be adopted was relatively small, while time and circumstance were not yet ripe to entertain words of the less common sort. The advance in European interest in the philosophy, religions, literature and languages of India had to wait for the recruitment of men of the intellectual stature of James Forbes, Sir Charles Wilkins, Sir G.A. Grierson, Nathaniel Brassey Halhed, H.T. Colebrooke, Sir William Jones, Joshua Marshman, and Warren Hastings, among others. Nevertheless, the carefree distortions and vulgarizations of words of Indian provenance, often with a racy, robust humour, would continue to be created until the last British soldier had left the barracks, *bazaars* and *cantonments* of India.

The second half of the eighteenth century and the whole of the nineteenth saw a considerable addition of scholarly words (one of the results initially of the encouragement and patronage of Warren Hastings), contributed by outstanding British and European linguists, lexicographers, historians and translators.[52] Sir Charles Wilkins (1769-1836), the first Englishman to master Sanskrit, translated the *Bhagavadgita* (1785), the *Hitopadesa* (1787) and *Sakuntala* (1793), and also compiled grammatical and lexical works, including an important glossary of Anglo-Indian words prepared for *The Fifth Report from the Select Committee of the House of Commons on the Affairs of the East India Company* (1812). Sir William Jones (1746-94) said of him (perhaps over-modestly): 'But for him I never would have learned Sanskrit.'[53] Of this brilliant group of scholar-administrators in the service of the East India Company, Jones was perhaps the most illustrious. His original discovery of the relationship between Sanskrit on the one hand and Greek and Latin on the other was mentioned in a private letter in 1787. This may be said to have marked the beginning of comparative philology, a field of study greatly enlarged and refined since then by European as well as British scholars. Jones died, at the age of forty-eight, after only ten years of residence in India, but not before he had founded the Asiatic Society of Bengal (1784), and published numerous translations from classical Sanskrit and other works including the *Sakuntala* of Kalidas(a) and a massive *Digest of Hindu and Muslim Laws*. His *Dissertation on the Orthography of Asiatick Words in Roman Letters* (1784) was a most valuable guide to writers and lexicographers using the Roman alphabet, through the maze of wildly inaccurate spellings of Anglo-Indian words already mentioned.

One of Jones's friends at Oxford was another orientalist, Nathaniel Brassey Halhed (1751-1830), who was said to have been the first to have called 'public attention' to the affinity between Sanskrit, Persian, Arabic, Latin and Greek.[54] Halhed's other main contribution was his compilation of the *Gentoo Code* at the instigation of Warren Hastings. This was, however, found to be inadequate and was later revised by another extraordinary orientalist, Henry Thomas Colebrooke (1765-1837), sometimes described as 'the first great Sanskrit scholar of Europe'.[55] Of his various works, his *Sanskrit Grammar* (1805) should be mentioned because in it he, too, foreshadowed the new field of comparative philology. His essay on the *Vedas* is also of special interest as perhaps the first authentic account of the Hindu scriptures by a European author. The scholarly expressions contributed to the word-bank of Anglo-India by these and other writers are too numerous and require explanations too lengthy to be mentioned here, but as a foretaste the reader should consult the dictionary for the significance of, for example, *mukti* (1785), *mimamsa* (1788), *bhakti* (1829), *gayatri* (1843), *samsara* (1845), *sandhi* (1874).

The end of the eighteenth century, which saw the birth of the Asiatic Society of Bengal (1784), saw also the founding of the École Nationale de Langues Orientales Vivantes (1795), followed in the next century by the Société Asiatique (1822), the Royal Asiatic Society of Great Britain and Ireland (1823), and the Deutsche Morgenlandische Gesellschaft (1845), affirming the deep and increasing intellectual interest of Europe in the culture, history and languages of India which had been fostered and encouraged by these early Anglo-Indian scholars, and brilliantly developed by that most erudite of Sanskrit scholars Max Mueller.

But of course it was not all culture and scholarship among Anglo-Indians in the eighteenth and nineteenth centuries. In the eighteenth century particularly we see commerce and conquest going hand in hand, the one depending on and harnessed to the other. The victories of Clive at Arcot (1751) and Plassey (1757) demonstrated for the first time in the history of the East India Company how war could be used not only to protect general commercial ends but also to amass colossal private fortunes for specially favoured or unscrupulous individuals. Clive, it was said, received over £ 200,000 from Mir Jafar for services rendered. This atmosphere of greed and its attendant corruption engendered arrogance and a spurious assumption of superiority, both in the military and civilian cadres. In the seventeenth century and even in the days of Clive and Hastings, Englishmen had mixed in free social intercourse with the local population, learnt their languages and appreciated indigenous culture.[56] We learn, also, from Subedar Sita Ram, an Indian officer of the Bengal Army, that even in the early nineteenth century 'the Sahibs could speak our language much better than they do now and they mixed more with us.... The only language they learn now is that of the lower orders which they pick up from servants, and which is unsuitable to be used in polite conversation.'[57] Cornwallis and Wellesley put an end to the easy-going fraternization: militant evangelicalism added extra muscle to bigotry. Yet, despite everything, the second half of the eighteenth century saw an increase in Anglo-Indian vocabulary – none of which, however, is likely to have been contributed by the lower ranks of the British soldiery in India or by the *boxwallahs* of that time. It included: *avatar* (1784) (S. *avatāra*), descent of the deity in bodily form; *dhurna* (1793) (H. *dharna*), the extraction of payment by sitting at the debtor's door; *khalsa* (1776) (H./Ar. *khālsa*), 'pure' in the creed of Sikhism; *musnud* (1763) (H./Ar. *masnad*), in India the cushioned throne of native Muslim princes; and *Prakrit* (1786) (S. *prākrita*), a vernacular dialect developed from Sanskrit.

To these should be added the names of the animals and plants of India, many of which had their Anglo-Indian baptism at this time and later in the works of a growing number of observers who became keen and competent students of Indian natural history. For instance, Edward Ives writes of the *argala* (1754) or Adjutant-bird (H. *hargīlā*): 'In the evening excursions we had often observed an extraordinary species of birds, called by the natives Argill or Hargill, a native of Bengal. They would majestically stalk before us, and at first we took them for Indians naked.'[58] Then follows a description of the 'exact marks and dimensions' of the bird. Sir William Jones comments on the *champak* (1770) *(Michelia champac)*, observing that 'the strong aromatick smell of the gold-coloured champac is thought to be offensive to the bees, who are never seen on its blossoms'.[59] A large number of plants and animals, too numerous to be itemized here, came into the literature of eighteenth and nineteenth century Anglo-India through the publications, *inter alia,* of Edward Ives, Sir William Jones, Nathaniel Brassey Halhed, Thomas Claverhill Jerdon, Warren Hastings and Sir Thomas Munro.

But for historical reasons it was on the battlefield and in the barracks that many Anglo-Indian expressions were minted in the second half of the eighteenth century. The spread of these may be largely attributable to the influence of Robert Orme's *magnum opus, A History of the Military Transactions of the British Nation in Indostan from the year 1745,* a work held in high esteem by Sir William Jones, Macaulay, Thackeray, Scott and Stevenson. In Orme's pages we are introduced to a colourful and true-to-life parade of Indian characters and types, some of whom we have met before and all of whom we meet again in the later literature of Anglo-India.[60] There are *Rajputs, Afghans, Pathans, Morattoes, nabobs, caffres, topasses, subahdars, jemautdars, phousdars, killadars,* and *munsubdars,* all conveying some of the special flavour of Orme's comprehensive and authoritative work, aptly described by Oaten as 'the prose epic of the early achievements of the British in India'. But Orme was not always on parade in the *durbars* of his *Rajputs* or in the impregnable fort-resses of his *killadars.*[61] Born in India, where he lived for most of his life, he introduces us to real life *coolies, cadis, mullahs, lascars* and *peons,* and he is as much at home in the *patnams,* the small town-ships, as in the *killa-kotes,* the fortresses, and in their suburbs, the *pettahs,* the whole varied scene bearing the stamp of authenticity bred of familiarity with the ordinary and everyday events of which he was so much a part by virtue of his birth and long residence.

VII

But above all others, it is to Burke that we must look as the chief exponent and publicist, in parliament and out, of the Anglo-Indian terms in constant use (and sometimes misuse) among the clerks ('writers'), *burra sahibs* and *dorays* of the Bengal and Madras esta-blishments of his days.[62] Burke's vocabulary of Anglo-Indian words of bureaucratic political nature was cunningly chosen and expertly used to contribute pungency as well as verisimilitude to his imposing and, often, savage rhetoric. Nevertheless, his own rich vocabulary of Anglo-Indian terms did not prevent him from complaining bitterly that such terms flowed so freely and obscurely from the pens of the 'writers' of the East India Company as to create feelings of bewilderment and even disgust in the minds of parliamentarians and others whose business it was to make sense out of the never-ending flow of reports, letters and accounts from India. The difference between Burke and these anonymous East India Company officials was that he defined exactly every term he used whereas they (either carelessly or deliberately) did not. Revenue administrators for him were *amins;* petitions were *arzees;* commission was *aumeeny;* contracts were *cabooleats;* poll-taxes were *jusseras;* payment of revenue by instalments was *kistbandi,* to mention a very short-list of Burke's comprehensive corpus of Anglo-Indian bureaucratic expressions.[62] Despite his proclaimed abhorrence of that style of Anglo-Indian English, which was saturated to the point of nausea with Indian words often barbarously misspelt, he prophesied in his impeachment of Warren Hastings that 'the Indian vocabulary will by degrees become familiar to your lordships [on the Select Committee of the House of Commons] as we develop the modes and customs of the country'.[63] How right he was – and not only in regard to their lordships. A list of those eminent persons in politics and literature in the eighteenth century who never set foot on Indian soil but who followed the fashion of incorporating Indian expressions in their writings would certainly include Horace Walpole, Burns, Sheridan, Defoe, Addison, Steele, Gay, Pope, Smollett, Gibbon and Sterne,[64] on whose pages we meet many of the customary ornamental and local-colour words we have met before – *nabobs, pagodas, Brahmans, Moguls, punch* and *arrack* – which were all words generally acceptable to the British reading public without explanatory notes, and which were certainly old favourites of the Anglo-Indian residents in Calcutta, Bombay, Lahore, Madras and in the *mofussil.*

VIII

The English novelists and poets of the nineteenth century employed a great store of Indian words between them for the delight as well as information of their readers, though almost all of them had been the stock-in-trade of Anglo-Indian writers of the preceding generations. Such words on the pages of Scott, Thackeray, Kipling, Southey and Byron, for instance, have an intended exotic appeal, artistically and deliberately used to create interest in the reader by their appearance of authentic foreignness. In this, these authors were often strikingly successful, especially as contemporary British readers were more at ease with such Indianisms than they are now that India has ceased to be the Jewel in the Crown of the erstwhile British empire.

Sir Walter Scott, for example, in *The Surgeon's Daughter* (1827), a novel set in the middle of the eighteenth century, was remarkably at home with Indian terms for one who never set foot in India: a circumstance he much regretted.[65] 'For that is the true place for a Scot to thrive in', he tells us. 'To India!' he makes one of his characters,

Richard Middlemas exclaim, 'Happy dog! To India! Oh, Delhi! Oh, Golconda!... India where gold is won by steel ... where men are making *lacs* of *rupees* ... in the land of *cowries* ... I shall be relieving some *nabob* or *rajahpoot* of his plethora of wealth.' Scott tells, through the medium of another character, Tom Hillary, of 'the good things that were going at the storming of a *Pettah*, or the plundering of a *Pagoda*', of 'the luxuries of a *nautch* ... and of changing sheep-head broth and haggis for *mulagatawny* and *curry*'. We learn of 'gold *mohrs*', and of the 'glittering drapery of gold and silver *muslins* mingled with *shawls*, while the *Begum* of Montreville is revealed to us in her ornate *turban* with a black slave standing behind her 'with a *chowry* or cow's tail, having a silver handle, to keep off the flies'. Thus detail is piled upon detail to form a rich oriental pattern of sights, sounds and words: *zenana, dubash* and *bakshee,* the *looties, vakeels* and *sowars.* The bed of an Indian stream is correctly a *nullah,* a foot-soldier is accurately a *sipahee, Telinga* or *peon,* and the small 'country' horse is rightly a *tatoo,* while the *Cuttyawar* breed of horses is appropriately 'high-crested with broad hindquarters'. All these and many more add a glossy varnish of Indian local colour to a melodramatic tale of skulduggery and romance, with the attendant Indian vocabulary suitable to Scott's theme and treatment, with princes, *nawaubs, nizams* and an almost total absence of the rest of the Indian population.[65]

His use of Anglo-Indian words, almost all of them of Hindustani origin, has been rightly described as masterly.[66] Certainly he benefited from the advice and help of the factual Colonel Ferguson (fictional Colonel Mackenzie), and put the colonel's knowledge of India and of Indian expressions to good effect.

In *Guy Mannering* (1815) the references to India are few and superficial, but such as there are include: *dubash, fakir, hookah, lootie, mango, pariah,* and two unusual ones: *banka,* a bully, and *motakul,* a meeting.

William Makepeace Thackeray (1811-63) (without need of any prompting by a factual or fictional colonel), handled his store of Anglo-Indian words like a conjuror with a pack of cards, with dexterity and wit, often producing a joker which he had kept up his sleeve for surprise occasions. In *Vanity Fair* (1848), *Pendennis* (1849-50), *Henry Esmond* (1852), *The Newcomes* (1854-5), *Major Gahagan* (1838-9) and *The Book of Snobs* (1848), he puts on parade his battalion of Anglo-Indian words, sometimes in odd and comic uniforms. To taste the full flavour, for instance, of the characters of Bobbachy Bahawder, Loll Jewab and Bucksheesh Bay we must understand the original literal meanings of their component parts. The first is a combination of *bawarchi,* a cook and *bahadur,* a champion, a delicious and mischievous juxtaposition of the lowly menial and the high-ranking hero, the mixture of the two producing a self-important and pretentious Colonel Blimp, whom we are delighted to meet on the pages of *The Newcomes* and *Major Gahagan*. The second, Loll Jewab, an Indian servant from *The Newcomes* (1854-5), is a subtle cocktail of the affectionate sobriquet *Lal*, 'sonny' and *jawab*, 'a reply or a duplicate'. The whole name may mean 'young answerer-back', or 'the answer to his master's whims', or 'a double-sided, impertinent young shaver'. Take your choice! Bucksheesh Bay, a combination of the Hindustani *backshīsh*, a tip or gratuity, and Bay (Beg), a Turkish governor, obviously appended for the alliteration, is another example of Thackeray's felicitous juxtaposition of the incongruous to produce a sense of comic delight in the minds of his readers. But even without being an Anglo-Indian cognoscente one can still appreciate much of the wit and humour of Thackeray's inventions and even the best-informed reader cannot be certain that he has extracted the full flavour of these subtle collocations. But one does not need to be an Anglo-Indian to appreciate General Sir Rice Curry, KCB, in *A Shabby Genteel Story*; Mr Mulligatawny (literally Mr Pepper-Water), a magistrate at Budgebudge in *Vanity Fair*, *Major Gahagan* and *The Book of Snobs*, and Mr Chutney the *burra-burra sahib* of Madras 'civilians' in *The Virginians*. Then there are Miss Mac Toddy in *Pendennis*; Mr Mango in *Vanity Fair*, Lady Betty Bulbul in *Our Street*; Baron Bandanna in *Vanity Fair*; Captain and Major Bangles in *Sketches and Travels*; Colonel Goldmore (*gol mohur*) in *The Book of Snobs*, and Miss Goldmore in *The Memoirs of Barry Lyndon*, the former a rich *nabob*, the latter an equally rich *nabobess*.

His particular use of about a hundred ordinary Anglo-Indian words reveals the consummate ease with which he could handle them, perhaps from his family's long residence in and connection with India. He introduces us to '*Brahminical* cousins' and 'City nobs' who eat '*kabobs* with wealthy *nabobs*' in *The Newcomes*, and in the same novel he completely transmogrifies *catamaran*, the tied-wood raft, into a termagant, a shrew, a female catamount, in the person of Mrs Mackenzie.

An examination – even a casual one – of the list of Thackeray's Anglo-Indian words will reveal, as with Scott, a picture of India as the land of *nabobs* and *pagodas*, of *curries* and *pilaus*, of *tatties* and *punkahs*, of *suttee* and the *juggernaut*. The India that Sir William Jones and some of his contemporaries had discovered and opened to the western world had left both novelists unmoved.

Thackeray's penchant for reshaping Indian terms into strange, comic and satiric forms was not his alone. There were other Anglo-Indian scribes before and after him devoted to the same pursuit of extracting as much fun as possible from caricaturing the stereotypes of the Anglo-Indians of their day. William Knighton, for instance, in his *Tropical Sketches, or Reminiscences of an Indian Journalist* (1885) introduces us to Major Subjunta, 'a meretricious know all'; Colonel Bunder, a 'monkey' of a man; Paugal, a pompous half-wit of the Indian Civil Service; Mrs Nutkut, a roguish mischief-maker; Mr Kabob, a glutton for Indian delicacies, and Mr Layjow (Mr Take-away) who elopes with Miss Ducklet. Not very subtle perhaps, but typical of much topical writing of the time.[67]

But above all others of this literary genre we must look for a complete dramatis personae of a typical Anglo-Indian 'station' to George Franklin Atkinson, who with great gusto as well as intimate knowledge, gives us a whole community of oddly and aptly christened Anglo-Indian characters in his *Curry and Rice* (1859) which, dedicated naturally to Thackeray, followed 'as a tiny vessel in the wake of [Thackeray's] big men of war'. These characters inhabit a 'station', rejoicing in the meaty appellation of *Kabob*, situated in the plains of *Deckchy* (stew-pan) where we become acquainted with Mrs Chutney, Mrs Ghee, Mr Chabook, and Messrs Dalbhat and Cheenee, a pair of eligible bachelors; the Nuwab, the oriental potentate; General Bamboo; the *syce*, who is the coachman and Pysa Doss (Penny Slave), the gardener.[68]

This work is an Anglo-Indian classic and, published as it is with delightful and penetrating illustrations done by the author himself, has earned a permanent place in the library of Anglo-India.

IX

Rudyard Kipling (1865-1936), more than anyone else among English men of letters, is the outstanding modern interpreter of Anglo-India in English literature, though it must be added he was sometimes in his life and writings out of tune or at odds with those of his countrymen whom he considered had fallen below or deviated from his strict imperial and class standards and values. In the posthumous autobiographical fragment, *Something of Myself* (1937), we read that at his club in India he 'met none but picked men at their definite task'. It is not difficult to detect here and elsewhere a strong element of caste-pride. He spoke for empire as no English writer had done as whole-heartedly and as brilliantly before him, and because of this he was accused in 1899 by Robert Buchanan of 'hooligan imperialism'. The truth of the matter was that in 1890 at the age of twenty-five he was acclaimed as a new phenomenon in English literature, identical in outlook and character with England's new-found imperial vocation which was to shoulder 'the white man's burden', and to plant the torch of enlightenment in the darkest continents. This is clearly mirrored in his early work, *Departmental Ditties* (1886), *Plain Tales from the Hills* (1888) and *Barrack Room Ballads* (1892). He was proud as well as condescending to acclaim the bravery of Gunga Din, a character based on the real-life water-carrier *(bhīstī)* of the Guides at the siege of Delhi in 1857. He based his *Drums of the Fore and Aft* on a true incident in Orme's *History*, and identified John Chinn in *The Tomb of his Ancestors* with Sir James Outram (1803-63), the friend of Sir Henry Lawrence (1806-1857) and of his brother Lord John Lawrence (1811-79), the English heroes of the Punjab, and of Kipling himself.

Kipling's sometimes sternly critical attitude to Anglo-Indian faults or weaknesses and his social ostracism by the Simla Anglo-Indian Society, however, did not dim his brilliant use of a very large vocabulary of Anglo-Indian words which emerged from his extensive knowledge of Hindustan and Hindustani, picked up in the streets and bazaars of Bombay and Lahore and fortified by his peripatetic journalistic experience in North India as a young man. He was an acknowledged adept at 'slinging the *bat* ', the Anglo-Indian expression for 'speaking the lingo'. The 'lingo' was, of course, Hindustani in his case: he knew little of, and cared less for, the Dravidian south, nor could he understand why anyone in his right mind would want to live with the 'Mulls' (from *mulligatawny*), in 'benighted' Madras, a name discourteously and outrageously deemed to be a corruption of *Manda-rajya*, 'Realm of the stupid'.[69] Even the surrounding Madras countryside was out of bounds for him because of the barbarously named places, 'all *ungas, or rungas or pillays or polliums*', and where the north Indian water-carrier, with his 'heavenly' sobriquet 'bhīstī, became an earthy 'tunny-cutch' (Tam. *tannir-kasatti*, 'water-carrier woman'). In contrast were 'the large open names' of the north, '*Umballa, Ludianah, Phillour, Jullundur*'.[70] India for Kipling and for most of his countrymen was Hindustan, the land of the tall fair-skinned Aryans whose languages Sir William Jones had shown to be cousins of English. The little people of the soft Dravidian south were birds of another kind and of darker plumage. Hence we may search in vain throughout Kipling's works for more than a few southern Anglo-Indian words: *mango, cheroot, tope*, and the already mentioned *tunny-cutch*, the first three from the seventeenth and the last from the eighteenth century.

But when we turn our attention to Kipling's use of Hindustani, his unerring and meticulous use of the right word in the right place, and to his gift for turning the commonplace into high drama or a fascinating fairy-tale, his genius is fully revealed. For instance, when he makes the blunt-nosed *mugger* (H. *magar*) crocodile of the Ganges say: 'I am no fish-hunting *gavial* [H. ghariyal] I, at Kasi [Banaras] today and Prayag [Allahabad] tomorrow.'[71] This is an instance of Kipling's delight in portraying the animals of India in fabled or fairy-tale guise. His *Jungle Books* (1894 and 1895) are worthy descendants of the ancient Indian animal fables in the *Panchatantra*. An inimitable wonderland is opened up for us by Kipling, crowded with animal characters endowed with human virtues and vices in a jungle society ruled by its own self-conceived laws. We meet *Tabaqui,* the jackal, the Dish-licker, and his people the *Gidur-Log* who keep their distance from the great *Shere Khan,* the tiger. On guard, in the book as in nature, is *Sambhur* the barking-deer, and nearby are *Akela,* the great, grey, lone wolf; *Baloo,* the brown bear; *Bagheera,* the black panther; *Ikki,* the porcupine; *Mao,* the peacock; *Kaa,* the rock-snake, and the *Bandar-Log,* the monkey people, 'who boast and chatter and pretend they are great people about to do great affairs in the Jungle, but the falling of a nut turns their mind to laughter and all is forgotten'. Above the jungle soars *Chil,* the kite, and on the ground slithers *Nag,* the cobra, who boasts 'I am *Nag.* The great God *Brahm,* put his mark upon all our people when the first cobra spread his hood to keep the sun off *Brahm* while he slept'. *Karait,* another of his kind, and one of the most venomous of snakes in the Indian jungle, meets his match in the *mongoose,* 'who is the hardest thing in the world to frighten, because he is eaten up with curiosity'. In the river reside the sharp-nosed *gavial* and the blunt-nosed *mugger* of *Mugger Ghaut,* the latter older than any man in the village, a murderer, man-eater and local fetish in one. These and others receive Kipling's lavish attention; the whole jungle is alive with plots and counter-plots, with never a dull moment and with the law of the jungle rightly triumphant in the end.

Lavish though he was in his attention to the beasts, birds and reptiles of India, following in this his father's footsteps,[72] and using their correct names in Anglo-Indian spellings, he turns his observant gaze on occasion to the rich and strange plant life of the Indian countryside. *The Jungle Books* refer to the *dhak*-tree, alias 'The Flame of the Forest' *(Butea frondosa);* the *tulsi* plant, the holy basil of Hindus *(Ocimum sanctum);* the *sal (Shorea robusta), peepul (Ficus religiosa), kikar (Acacia arabica)* and *Mohwa (Madhuca indica)* trees, and *karela,* the bitter gourd (*Momordica charantia*). One fine nature description must suffice here to show Kipling's keen eye for detail and atmosphere:

That spring the *Mohwa* tree never flowered. The greeny, cream-coloured waxy blossoms were heat-killed before they were born.... Then inch by inch, the untempered heat crept into the heart of the Jungle, turning it yellow, brown, and at last black.... The juicy-stemmed creepers fell away from the trees they clung to and died at their feet; the bamboos withered, clanking when the hot winds blew, and the moss peeled off the rocks, till they were as bare and as hot as the quivering blue boulders in the bed of the stream.[73]

Kipling, unlike Thackeray who never returned to India, came back as a young man to do his writing, or much of it, in the land of his birth and infancy. Thackeray employed the seriousness, absurdity and the irony of the human comedy to create his literary effects, whereas Kipling's pathos, humour and cruelty often spill over into tragedy. Henry James spoke of 'his talent enormous but the brutality even deeper-seated'.[74] These qualities are as evident in *The Jungle Books* among the birds and the beasts as they are in *Kim* and the short stories set among the varied populace 'up the country', along the byways and in the hills and the *mofussil* of Kipling's British India. Each of these authors used his stock of Anglo-Indian words in his own way to create his own desired effects, and put the stamp of their distinct personalities on their remarkable creations.

In all, Kipling's work exhibits more than 300 Anglo-Indian words, shaped mainly according to the sound and spelling conventions of his day. Their power, local-colour effect and plain realism could only have come from someone who had lived, moved and had his being among *boxwallahs*, *goondas* and *badmashes*, as well as among *pukka sahibs*, *babus* and *Qui Hyes*. His Anglo-Indian words were as ready to hand when required as were his native English words, to which they added oriental spice, piquancy and aroma but were never paraded extravagantly or for mere show. The words matched the characters and the occasions on which they were used.

For the most part, Kipling's Anglo-Indian expressions were not newly-minted for special occasions but inherited from the verbal treasuries of generations of Anglo-Indians stretching as far back as to the seventeenth century and occasionally earlier. In *Kim*, for instance, we find *Brahmin* from the fifteenth century, *Bunnya*, *bhang* and *lac* from the sixteenth and a host of others from the seventeenth, all of them of street-level usage in the Anglo-India of Kipling's days, after two centuries or more of common Anglo-Indian currency. But there were others which, though they may have played their part in contemporary parlance, had not earned unchallengeable places in the Anglo-Indian lexicon. These Kipling used as casually and naturally as if they had. Here are some from Kim: *arplan*, a medicine for making old men young; *bilaur* (E. *bery*), crystal for spectacles; *chabuk-sawai*, 'a smart chap', and *hawa-dilli*, 'heart-lifter', a sweetheart.

In another special sphere, that of British other ranks in India, Kipling's knowledge, and understanding of what went on in their minds and daily lives guided him unerringly to make dramatic and accurate use of their Anglo-Indian slang and unconventional colloquialisms, omitting the grosser side of barrack-room obscenity, unsanctioned in the literature of the less permissive times in which he wrote. Typical are the oft-quoted lines about Gunga Din, the Indian regimental *bhīstī* mentioned above :

> You limping lump of brick-dust,
> Gunga Din,
> Hi! slippy *hitherao!*
> Water, get it! *Panee lao!*
> You squidgy-nosed old idol, Gunga Din.
> You 'eathen, where the mischief 'ave you been?
> You put some *juldee* in it
> Or I'll *marrow* you this minute
> If you don't fill up my helmet, Gunga Din.[73]

Here is simplicity of purpose and with it 'goes a consummate gift of word, phrase and rhythm'.[76]

The unconventional colloquialisms which Kipling acquired from his contemporaries and bequeathed to succeeding generations were greatly multiplied and diversified before, during and after the two World Wars by the never-failing, superb, impish and often lewd inventiveness of British soldiers serving in India. Delightful as well as outrageous examples are enshrined in Eric Partridge's *Dictionary of Slang and Unconventional English* (1979) and need no repetition here. In any case, samples will be found in the dictionary following this Introduction, though one final nugget from this rich vein must legitimately claim a place here from 'The Three Musketeers' in *Plain Tales from the Hills*:

I purshued a ekka, an' I sez to the dhriver divil, I sez, 'Ye black limb, there's a *Sahib* comin' for this *ekka*. He wants to *go jildi* to the *Padsahi jhil'* ... *'twas* about tu moiles away ... to shoot snipe ... *chirria*. You dhrive *Jehannum Ke marfik, mallum* ... like Hell! 'Tis no manner av use *bukkin'* to the Sahib, bekase he doesn't *samjao* your talk. Av he *bolos* anything, just you *choop* and *chel. Decker?* Go *arsty* for the first *arder* mile from *cantonmints*. Thin *chel, Shaitan ke marfik*, an' the *chooper* you *choops* an' the *jildier* you *chells* the better *kooshy* will that *Sahib* be; an' here's a *rupee* for ye!

The *ekka*-man grinned an' sez, 'Bote *achee*! I goin' damn fast'.[77]

X

Rudyard Kipling (1865-1936) and Edward Morgan Forster (1879-1970) overlapped in their lives but had little else in common, except that they were both successful writers of great stature and chose to write about Anglo-India. This term, however, meant something different for each of them. *Kim* (1921) and *A Passage to India* (1924) could hardly be more different, the one showing a deep and wide knowledge of many aspects of Anglo-Indian and Indian life, the other a specialized knowledge of a small Anglo-Indian community in a fictional location aptly called Chandrapore ('Moon-Town'). Apart from imperial issues given an airing by Forster, he chose certain Anglo-Indian words to add a local flavour to his narrative. These serve a mainly decorative purpose and are inserted into the text like jewels in a crown, generally without explanation or translation, the author perhaps considering them to be as well-known to his readers as they were to himself.

Anglo-Indian expressions, in all about 100 words in 300 pages, are judiciously scattered here and there in the text, doing just enough to preserve the authentic Anglo-Indian flavour in our minds as we follow the drama through mosque, cave and court-house. We find ourselves among the *toddy*-palms, *neem*-trees, *mango-topes* and the 'green-blossomed' *Champak*-trees which provide some of the necessary exotic local-colour for Forster's background to the events in Chandrapore, where Hindu *sadhus* 'stride stark naked' through the streets, and Muslims carry their *tazias*, in memory of the martydrom of Hasan and Hussain, in the Muharram processions along the traditional routes.

In the letters of Forster in *The Hill of Devi* (1953) only a few Anglo-Indian words ornament the easy informal style, but they are enough to convey a sense of history and place. Naturally, etiquette, protocol and courtly customs play a large part in the life and circumstances described in these letters, with the appropriate Anglo-Indian expressions appearing sporadically. The *sirdars* or headmen always accompany the guests of the *Maharaja* in their carriages; the *nuzzers* or gifts of homage are always graciously accepted (and expected) by the *Maharaja* who then remits them to his servants for safe-keeping; the ceremonial of *attar* (H. *itr*) and *pan* is a *sine qua non* of all courtly receptions and *durbars*, the palace levees. We are told of the supreme importance to the *Maharaja* of his investiture (with the sacred thread) as a *Kshatriya* of the Hindu 'warrior' caste, and of *sadhus* coming 'to bless the palace' and demanding rewards of a hundred *rupees* each. The eight-day festival in honour of Lord Krishna's birthday, *Gokul Ashtami*, is given a detailed description, while an aside is spared by Forster to mention the *gaddi*, the 'sacred feather-bed', which is the *Maharaja's* throne. Outside the palace the *swarajists*, 'self-rule' agitators in their 'white Gandhi caps', represent the wind of change which will ultimately blow away the exotic and decadent life of princely India in which Forster had become temporarily involved as the Maharaja's private secretary.

As the Maharaja's life and Forster's account of it draw to a close we are appropriately transported many hundreds of miles south to the *Saivite* temple at Rameswaram, 'one of the holiest places in India', near Kanya Kumari, the Cape Comorin of Anglo-India, at the extreme tip of the Indian peninsula, with its sacred *lingam* 'washed daily with Ganges water'.

XI

Because India is too big, too varied and too populous for one man, native or foreign, to see it whole, it is not to be wondered at that Anglo-Indian writers present only a partial and individual India, reflecting their personal attitudes (with selected Anglo-Indian words) to the social, cultural and political situations in which they set their writings. Unavoidably the more serious writers of the nineteenth and early twentieth centuries foreshadow the increasing racial and political tensions which marked the ending of empire and which ultimately destroyed the older, more comfortable Anglo-Indian relationships. We have seen signs of this in *A Passage to India*, and we see them even more obviously in other Anglo-Indian writers, for example, Edward Thompson (1886-1946) and Edmund Candler (1874-1926), both once held in high esteem, now neglected and underrated.[78]

Thompson, in *An Indian Day* (1927) and *A Farewell to India* (1930), readily uses such terms as *zillah*, the administrative district; *panchayat*, the village council, originally of five (H. *panch*) members; the *Raj*, British rule in India; *Mahatma*, the 'great-souled' one, applied particularly to Gandhi in recent times, and *hartal*, a day of mourning or social protest, when all shops are shut. As religion is never far away from politics in India it is not surprising to find Thompson using deeply emotive religious expressions (all of which have been used before in Anglo-Indian writings), such as: *bhakti*, Hindu religious devotion as a means of salvation; *karma*, fate, the sum of a person's actions in one of his existences; and *suddhi*, 'purification'. These are planted among well-known current Anglo-Indian terms like the names of Indian trees, *banyan*, *palas*, *bel*, *simul* and *mahua*, as well as old friends, such as *pukka*, *babu*, *griffin*, *budgerow*, *bungalow*, and many others.

Another writer, Edmund Candler, in his *Siri Ram Revolutionist* (1912), involves his readers in an intensely melodramatic incursion into the politico-religious arena during the years just before the First World War, when sections of the Indian populace – students and the intelligentsia in particular – were awakening to an awareness of their latent political power: an awareness generated in no small measure by the growth and spread of English education. The words of Abbé Dubois might be considered a prophetic text (in 1816) of the sermon Candler preached (in 1912) in the guise of fiction in *Siri Ram*: 'The European Power which is now established in India is, properly speaking, supported neither by physical force nor by moral influence. It is a piece of a huge complicated machinery, moved by springs arbitrarily adapted to it.'[79] *Siri Ram* is an important Anglo-Indian work in that it captures the burgeoning spirit of the incipient, underground social revolt of the times: a revolt conspiratorial, half-baked, unplanned, deep-seated, dangerous, and powerfully attractive to an increasing number of Indians, particularly students, and feared by an increasing number of Anglo-Indians. This 'transcript from life' projects these signs of revolution closely bound up with religion, by means of a considerable vocabulary of appropriate Anglo-Indian words used by Candler to give force and colour to the language of revolt. 'To sacrifice a goat to *Kali*'[80] has a sharper political cutting edge than 'to assassinate an Englishman on the altar of Independence', which is what it means. Sarcasm, scorn and hatred are encapsulated in the normally harmless phrase, 'Empire-Day-*Wallah*', and there is obvious racial bitterness in 'the meddling *Sahib-log*' and 'the pestilent *Feringhies*' who wear the despised *Wilayiti* shirts imported from England, which should be patriotically discarded for *swadeshi khaddar*, the home-spun cloth advocated by patriotic nationalists. Racial pride and whole-hearted love of country are symbolized in the highly-charged emotional term *Bharat Mata* (Mother India), while the arrogant foreigners are 'accursed *mlechas*' (intruders) and 'hateful *Asuras*' (demons) who ravage *Bharat Mata*. But Candler's Anglo-Indian vocabulary is not all of this highly-charged or bad-tempered kind. He has a veritable treasure-house of Anglo-Indian words, all of which have been used over and over again, many of them since the seventeenth century.

Although the novel *Siri Ram* is now almost forgotten it aroused considerable interest and discussion in India and England when it was published, and 'it marks the emergence of Indian nationalists as major characters in English fiction'.[81]

An extraordinary work deserving of mention in passing, in which Anglo-Indian words of moral and political significance feature, is one ironically entitled *Mother India*, by an American author Katherine Mayo (1868-1946). This book raised the hackles of Indian nationalists and the eyebrows of the English reading public in 1927. It is not a book about which one can be neutral. Critically acclaimed on the one hand as fearless and as an accurate description and analysis of Indian depravity and superstition, it was on the other hand dismissed (by Mahatma Gandhi, among others) as a gross travesty of Indian society, a deliberate (even criminal) insult to the Indian people and to Hinduism itself by a sensation-mongering American pro-British imperialist. *Volume Two* (1931) was Miss Mayo's defence of her indictment. Whatever the truth, the author thoroughly absorbed the necessary Anglo-Indian vocabulary to illustrate her opinion on child-marriage and its attendant physical and mental decadence; on the evils of the caste system; on *purdah*; on the *Padmapurana* which, she maintains, 'incontrovertibly asserts, with the authority of *Puranic* writ', that 'there is no other god on earth for a woman than her husband'; on the plight of child-widows, and indeed of all Hindu widows, despite the official abolition of *suttee;* on the daily torture of a cow by the practice of *phuka,* 'in order that the worth of a few more pennies may be wrung from the pain'. Cow-protection societies which maintain *gaushalas,* 'cow asylums', and similar agencies which provide *pinjrapoles* for all sick animals, receive her caustic criticism. What good there is, is laid at the door of the British, for example, the abolition of the professional Hindu strangler tribes, the *Thugs,* of *suttee* and of the burying alive of lepers.[82]

In the *mofussil,* we learn, the general conditions of life are intolerable, and the ignorant *ryot,* the peasantry, is cloddishly indifferent to the village school, and only interested in the five substances of the cow *(panchagavia)*: milk, *ghee* (clarified butter), curd, dung and urine, 'which mixed together and swallowed surpass in potency all other means of purifying soul and body'. The illiterate class, the *gvalas,* who breed cattle are a hopeless lot, we are told, 'who lack enterprise, capital and intelligence to carry on the work'. Miss Mayo's India is of almost unrelieved backwardness, dirt and depravity and it is not to our purpose to enlarge on this here. Our main interest is in the Anglo-Indian words she uses to add vivid realism to the presentation of her theme. Apart from those already mentioned we meet *dacoits* (bandits), *Swarajists* (Self-rulers), *Moplahs* (Malabar Muslims), *Ulemas* (Muslim divines), *begums* (princesses), *devadasis* (temple prostitutes), *sahibs* and *sahibas* (gentlemen and ladies), *dhais* (wet-nurses), and *banyas* (merchants and money-lenders), and we learn of the backwardness, in her opinion, of *Ayurvedic* and *Unani* systems of medicine, while we are treated to a chorus of other well-worn Anglo-Indian words learnt by Miss Mayo during her investigations and used in a journalistic way to suit her propaganda purposes.

Katherine Mayo's *Slaves of the Gods* followed in 1929: it contains more of the same, though in fictional form.

XII

In contrast, Somerset Maugham's *The Razor's Edge* (1944) avoids the political drama of disaffection and revolt to make fleeting reference to the mythical India of the *Upanishads,* the *Bhagavadgita,* and of the imaginary India of holy *sadhus* and *sanyasis.* These are seen through rose-tinted glasses by a footloose and fancy-free Westerner, Larry, who is unable to tolerate the sordid materialistic and money-grubbing preoccupations of his own country. He, and others of his kind in the modern world, yearn for the magical uplift of hypnotic *mantras* that convey mysterious Sanskrit sounds with no intruding meaningful commonsense. These modern unscholarly seekers after the elusive truths of *Vedantism* and the esoteric enigmas and eroticism of *Tantric* rituals and the Hindu belief in *Punarjanma,* 'rebirth', are of a different breed from the scholarly William Jones, Wilkins, Colebrooke, Elphinstone, James Tod and the rest. The only equipment of the latter-day drop-outs is emotional and sentimental yearning. They wither as the days pass in heat and squalor, and are afflicted by diseases and discomforts unknown in their aseptic homelands. They are, in the end, disappointed and often feel insulted by their Indian hosts whose early affection turns to indifference and sometimes hostility as they increasingly intrude on and pollute native customs and ways of life through ignorance or thoughtlessness.

Maugham does not take us quite as far as this in depicting the character of Larry who, a misfit in the West, derives a kind of spurious spiritual consolation temporarily in his understanding of Hindu philosophy, in *ashrams* and temples, until in the end he finds it is not, after all, for him, and he takes himself off, back to New York to become a taxi-driver.

Before this happens Maugham throws in a few local-colour Anglo-Indianisms as if quoting from a guide-book. We meet *Ramakrishna-swamis,* a *Brahman,* a *guru, Vedantists, Sufis,* and *Aryans,* and are told of *Brahma* the Creator, *Vishnu* the Preserver, and *Siva* the Destroyer; of *Karma,* fate; *samadhi,* the highest state of meditation; *Shri Ganesha,* the elephant-god; and we are taken on a tour of Elephanta and the Ganges, all in twenty pages, as if Maugham wanted to get this India-business off his chest or out of his system as quickly as possible. It is difficult to take him (or Larry) seriously, but he is interesting in so far as he chooses to use some Anglo-Indian words he thinks his readers know, or ought to know, as part of the legacy of generations of Anglo-Indians to the English language.

XIII

Unlike Maugham, who knew little of India and less about its languages, or their influence on English, numerous and prolific women writers, *mem-sahibs* of the nineteenth and twentieth centuries, took their well-known Anglo-India by the scruff of the neck and shook it. Various, copious and of unequal merit was the literary fall-out: novels, short-stories, memoirs, letters, verse, cook-books and traveller's tales.[83] Some were able 'to *bolo* the *bat*' with more than mere domestic fluency, though others, on the other hand, described Anglo-Indian life as if there were no Indians except servants in India and no language but English and a few words of kitchen Hindustani spoken. Like flocks of variously plumaged migrant birds they had their seasons and departed from the literary scene, and are hardly read now except by the curious. Some, though, deserve a better fate, and among these are the novelists Flora Annie Steel (1847-1927); Maud Diver (1867-1945); Alice Perrin (1867-1934); Christine Weston (1904-19??), whose *Indigo* has been compared to Forster's *A Passage to India* 'for its authenticity and understanding of the complexity of the Indian problem',[84] and finally, that fascinating and indomitable traveller Fanny Parks whose *Wanderings of a Pilgrim in Search of the Picturesque, with Revelations of Life in the Zenana* (1850) deserves to be placed beside the brilliant works of the seventeenth century French travellers in India, Bernier and Tavernier.[85] Her Anglo-Indian vocabulary is rich, varied and extensive, amounting in all to about 750 words, and 147 Indian proverbs for good measure, garnered from her travels and contacts with all kinds and conditions of Indians, and used with great gusto and effect to add a special flavour to this remarkable book. To mention a few examples, we learn of *atashbazi* (fireworks), of the *chhach hundar* (musk-rat), of *dulhan* and *dulha* (bride and bride-groom), of *jadu-gari* (magic) and *pagal-i-nach* (fancy-dress ball) and *ras-dhari* (the dancing-boy).

One of the features of the novels of Flora Annie Steel is not only a large vocabulary of Anglo-Indian words but also of phrases and sentences of Hindustani appropriate to the contexts in which she uses them, especially in her novels portraying the lives of the first four Mughal emperors.[86] Although Englishmen are conspicuous by their absence in these novels (Leeds, the seventeenth century jeweller, has a walking-on part only), her Hindustani words are part of the historical Anglo-Indian word-bank for the most part, with some unusual ones of Pushtu, Persian and Turkish origin, such as: *kizzilbashes* (Mughal Persian troops, the Red-Heads); *chaugan* (the original game of polo, 'hockey on horseback'); *badshah* (king);

ghazals (love-lyrics sung to musical accompaniments); *sijden* and *tasleem* (ceremonial prostrations);[87] *jharoka* (balcony-window); *shikast* (a Persian script); *rubai* (poetry); *fatwah* (a Muslim legal decision); *kanjari* (harlot); *ishkh* and *ashkh* (love and tears). A few nursery words are added for good measure: *nani* (grandmother); *amma-jan* ('mummy'); *mata-jee* (mother), and *missi-baba* (girl-child).

Afghanistan and the North-West Frontier Province feature also in two novels by Maud Diver (1867-1945), *The Hero of Herat* (1912) and *The Judgement of the Sword* (1913). She, too, has used an appropriate selection of Afghan and Frontier expressions (well-known to Anglo-Indians serving there), to give an authentic air to the events of The First Afghan War (1838-42), and the defence of Herat by Eldred Pottinger. A few of these are: *badzat* (a bad hat); *top-khana* (arsenal); *ikbal* (prestige); *elchi* (ambassador); *Pae-i-Takht* ('The Foot of the Throne', a public place of justice), and *poshteen* (an Afghan sheepskin coat).

Lady Sale in her memoirs of the First Afghan War contributed not only her trenchant criticism of the conduct of the operations but also a number of expressions with an Afghan flavour, such as: *bosh* (nonsense); *choga* (a cloak); *golundaz* ('ball-thrower', an artilleryman); *khootba* (Friday sermon in the mosque); *shahzada* (a prince); *zubberdust* (overbearing), and *malik* (leader of an Afghan tribe).

XIV

But the most significant verbal contributions from the Pushtu and Pakhtun areas of Afghanistan are revealed in a classic work on the Pathans by Sir Olaf Caroe, especially in the expressions relating to the fundamental, age-old way of life among these northern tribes such as: *Pakhtunwali*, the 'Way of the Pathans', the Pathan Code, which prescribes the vengeance *(badal)* of the sufferer from any wrong, great or small, inflicted on him, the most frequent causes demanding *badal* being one or more of the trinity, *zar, zan, zamin*, gold, woman, land. *Nanawati*, the cessation, by assassination or other appeasement, of the feud. *Melmastia*, the obligatory protection of a guest invited or otherwise, from attack, and the provision of free board and lodging. Sometimes the clan guest-house or *hujra* is used for the protection of the guest from all harassment. *Jirga*, the assembly or council of a sub-group of Pathans in which all matters of common or individual interest are judiciously considered according to established traditions and customs.[88]

Words also came into the Anglo-Indian vocabulary from Tibet and some of them, such as : *Yak*, the Tibetan ox *(Poephagus grunniens)*; *thanka*, a holy Tibetan painting; *chang*, barley beer; *chorten*, a solid square structure containing relics of the dead, and *lama*. a Tibetan Buddhist monk, have become currently well-known because of the increased interest in Tibet in recent years. Others, not so well-known but still to be found in English texts, for instance, in the *Narrative of the Mission of George Bogle to Tibet* (1757) and in the *Journey of Thomas Manning to Lhasa* (1811) by Clements Markham (1876) are: *chupa*, the long, folded Tibetan gown worn by women; *dzong*, a fortress; *penlops*, regional governors, and *kiyang*, the Asiatic wild ass, *(Equus hemionus)*.

The few acquisitions from the Sino-Tibetan source do not by any means disturb the conclusion that the vast majority of Anglo-Indian words are of Indo-Aryan stock. For the British as for Kipling, India was mainly Hindustan, the north-land of the tall fair-skinned Aryans speaking languages that were cousins to English and breeding the robust martial races, *Sikhs* and *Rajputs*, admired and respected by British soldiers and 'civilians' of the East India Company and, later, of the *Raj*. This preference, after the initial influx of South Indian words, is clearly shown in the *Dictionary* by the preponderance of *Hindi, Urdu, Bengali, Marathi* and *Punjabi* words, and the relatively poor showing of words of Dravidian stock: *Tamil, Malayalam, Kannada* and *Telugu.*

From the life of the unsettled mountain regions of Afghanistan and the North-West Frontier Province we descend finally to the calmer domestic atmosphere of the Anglo-Indian households on the plains in the heartland of British India.

This Introduction would lack an essential ingredient if one of the most fruitful sources of Anglo-Indian expressions, namely the internal discipline and management of the Anglo-Indian household organized by Anglo-Indian *mem-sahibs*, was missing. The range of their domestic interests was wide: from the culinary arts to the care of horses, from the careful grading of the hierarchy of the many servants to the equally careful treatment and prevention of the common Indian diseases of children, adults and domestic animals, and from the book-keeping of the household expenses to the endless planning of menus for all occasions, great and small. All this is animated and expressed by a well-tested corpus of Anglo-Indian words suitable for every domestic occasion.

We need refer to one work only, compiled by that *mem-sahib* of many parts and long experience, Flora Annie Steel, in collaboration with a certain Mrs Grace Gardiner. Of unequalled comprehensiveness and authority, *The Complete Indian Housekeeper and Cook, giving the duties of Mistress and Servants, the General Management of the House and Practical Recipes for Cooking in all its Branches* was first published in 1888 and rapidly ran into many editions by 1913. There is no space here for more than a flavour of the verbal contributions of this Anglo-Indian 'Mrs Beeton'.

We learn that the best rice for curry is called *barsi muttee* (*basmati*), that 'country' raisins are *munukha;* dried apricots, *koorbanee;* plums, *aloo-bokhara;* figs, *unjeer;* sultanas, *kishmish;* almonds, *badam;* cauliflower, *phoolgobi;* claret, *lal-sherab;* and so on through the whole gamut of Indian comestibles in the quaint and uncertain Anglo-Indian spellings of the time. We are informed that the language of the servants must be thoroughly understood and kept in mind at all times, from that of the lowest menial, the *matey,* to that of 'the head of House', the *bearer,* who, unless his mistress has ordered him to say 'Durwaza bund' (the door is closed), the somewhat abrupt equivalent of 'Not at home', 'should at once usher the visitors into the drawing-room and present their cards to the mistress wherever she may be. He must not do this with his fingers, and a small tray for receiving the cards should always be on the verandah or hall table.' (O tempora! O mores!) Moving from the drawing-room to the kitchen we discover a veritable armoury of burnished brass, copper, tin and cast-iron utensils, among which are *degchies,* stew-pans or dixies; *momlet-*pans, omelette-pans; *kittlis,* large kettles; *unda-poach-*pans, egg poachers; *imamdustas,* mortars and pestles; *gridamis,* gridirons; *kebab-dans,* roasters; *turkari-ke-chulais,* colanders; *aloo-mulne-ke-lukkris,* potato-mashers, and a host of others. Virtually nothing is omitted and the appropriate Anglo-Indian expressions are insisted on. Many of these originated with the servants in their *Butler-English* attempts to imitate the *sahib-log,* who with condescension and some-times mockery absorbed them into their own Anglo-Indian vocabulary. Champagne became *simkin,* a scrambled-egg was appropriately *rumble-tumble,* while a spiced egg dish became *ackoori,* originally in the Parsi kitchens of Bombay, clearly a corruption of 'egg-curry'. Finally, everyone knew that *Sudden-Death* was only a spatchcock, killed, dressed, cooked and eaten in the shortest possible time.

This account has many omissions, the nature and the extent of which a casual examination of the bibliography and the dictionary will reveal. In addition to the pre-Independence omissions for reasons of space and partiality, there is no mention either of post-Independence 'Indian' writing by British authors who have contributed their own harvest of Indian words to English. They were considered and re-luctantly rejected as being outside the scope of this work, as were the brilliant nineteenth century Bengali writers in English, Torulata Dutt, Romesh Chunder Dutt, Henry Derozio, Rabindranath Tagore and others, in company with Indian writers writing in English from other Indian States, such as Sarojini Naidu, Cornelia Sorabji, Ahmed Ali, Raja Rao, R.K. Narayan, Mulk Raj Anand and a host of others who have suffered 'exclusion for the reason that they are birds of different plumage and sport the colours of Indo-Anglia, not of Anglo-India.'[89]

If, despite faults of commission and omission, we succeed in stimulating some readers, for one reason or another, to browse where they will in the *Dictionary*, one word leading to another, a process for which this Introduction serves only as a starter, we may legitimately consider our efforts will not have been in vain.

REFERENCES

The place of publication of the following works is London, unless otherwise stated.

1. Horace Hayman Wilson, *Glossary of Judicial and Revenue Terms and of useful words occurring in Official Documents relating to the Administration of India* (1855), Preface. (Wilson was Boden Professor of Sanskrit at Oxford, 1835-6).
2. Quoted by Mildred Archer in *Early Views of India* (1984).
3. Samuel Johnson, *A Dictionary of the English Language* (1755), Preface.
4. Henry Sweet, *The Student's Dictionary of Anglo-Saxon* (1896), Preface.
5. Yule and Burnell, *Hobson-Jobson* (1886), (Introductory Remarks), p. xxl.
6. However, a large number of learned words appeared on the Anglo-Indian scene later than the publication of *Hobson-Jobson* in 1886, though the second and third editions of 1902 and 1986 also failed to mention them. All of those quoted appear in the *OED*.
7. Eric Partridge, *Dictionary of Slang and Unconventional English* (1970), Introduction.
8. Dr John Fryer, *A New Account of East India and Persia*, 1672-81 (1698), p. 24
9. Ibid., p. 157.
10. The relation of English 'punch' to Hindi *panch*, 'five', is sometimes questioned. See *ODEE*, p. 723. But there is little doubt about the Anglo-Indian provenance and popularity of the mixture. See YB, pp. 738-9.
11. Also by Robert Burns in *The Holy fair*, 1789, p.xx.
    'The lads and lassies blythely bent
    To mind baith saul an' body
    Sit round the table, weel content
    An' steer about the toddy.'

12. Not from Tel. *pandi-kokku*, wrongly translated as 'pig-rat' by *OED, ODEE*, YB, Skeat, *et al.*, even by Subba Rao whose mother tongue was Telugu! The Telugu word for 'rat' is *eluka*. *Pandi-kooka*, 'pig-dog', is the Telugu expression for the *Mus malabaricus* or *giganteus*, the *bandicoot* of Anglo-India. The etymological inexactitude may well have its origin in Fryer in his *New Account* (1698) where he says: 'For vermin, the strongest huge rats as big as our pigs ... are bold to venture on poultry.'
13. G.T. Garratt, *The Legacy of India* (Oxford, 1937), p.26.
14. Charles Lockyer, *An Account of the Trade in India* etc. (1711), p. 286
15. From *Notes on the Study of Indian Languages by Franciscans* by Fr. Achilles Meersman (QFM, Bangalore), Reprint from *Neue Zeitschrift fur Missionswissenschaft* (1960), p. 60.

16. Botanically the Pagoda Tree is the *Plumeria acutifloria, the Sophora japonica* and the *Ficus Indica;* metaphorically, a tree bearing gold Pagoda-coins which were current in India from Portuguese times to the nineteenth century. (Mentioned by Wellington in his *Despatches* (1837), ii, p. 375. This idea may be traced back to the Malay *pokok emas* (gold tree) customarily sent as tribute to old Siam by certain north Malayan States.
17. *See* Kay Ambrose and Ram Gopal, *Classical Dances and Costumes of India* (1937).
18. James Forbes, *Oriental Memoirs* (1813). Mentioned earlier by Sir William Jones in *Asiatick Researches* (1788), I. 264. More recently we hear of 'raga-rock', rock music improvisation.
19. The Hon. Emily Eden, *Up the Country, letters written to her sister from the upper Provinces of India* (1866), p. 143.
20. Ibid, p. 176.
21. Fanny Parks, *Wanderings of a Pilgrim in Search of the Picturesque* (1850), vol. 1, pp. 250-51.
22. Capt. G.C. Mundy, *Pen and Pencil Sketches, Being the Journal of A Tour of India.* (1832), vol. 1. p. 349.
23. Bishop Reginald Heber, *Narrative of a Journey through the Upper Provinces of India etc. 1824-25* (London, 1866), vol. 1. p. 143.
24. Sir George Otto Trevelyan, *Letters of a Competition Wallah* (1864), p.16.
25. Samuel Johnson, op. cit.
26. Aldous Huxley, *Antic Hay* (1923).
27. Beng. '*Koi hai ?*', 'Is anyone there?' This, without the question mark, was the ironic nickname for a Bengal Anglo-Indian club-man, and, with it, the formula for summoning the Indian cup-bearer.
28. Trevelyan, op. cit., p. 22.
29. Ibid. p.22.
30. Flora Annie Steel, *Voices in the Night* (1900).
    'Look 'ere. You want this man now, but you ain't goin' to get 'im. He's not yours. He's mine, my man, understand? If you want a fight come on! You shall have a bellyful, an' there'll be plenty on you to hang. But what I say is don't be stupid pigs. I don't do your bally temples 'arm. It's the true faith and Lord Ganga, so far's I care. But this man's my guv'nor. You don't touch 'im, never. I'm a virtuous man, very gentle w'en I'm took the right way; contrariwise I'm a tyrant and troublemaker and a very great misfortune.'
31. Charles Allen, *Plain Tales from the Raj* (1975), p.273. 'You saw me fall into the drinking water and you did nothing. You heard me speak. For this I'll warm your backside.'
32. *See* Michael Edwardes, *The Last Years of British India* (1963).
33. On 5 March 1881, in the House of Commons, Disraeli was able to proclaim with the utmost certainty 'the key of India is in London'.
34. It is an old Indian custom to reward the basest menials with the noblest titles, sometimes ironically, sometimes compassionately. A domestic 'sweeper' was called a 'mehtar', a prince, and his wife a 'mehtrani', a princess. Someone addressed as 'Caleefa' (Ar. *Khalifa,* the Caliph) could be the cook, the tailor, the barber or farrier. (*See* YB, p.146).
35. *The Waste Land* (1922), *Poems 1909-22* (1925), p. 85.
36. *Ulysses* (Paris, 1922), p.290.
37. Samuel Johnson, op. cit.
38. Lord is reputed to have acquired a knowledge of Hindustani and Persian, yet he makes the *Sudras* 'merchants' and the *Vaisyas* 'mechanics' (in the Shakespearean sense), instead of vice versa as they should be.
39. This is from the Pali form *nibbana.*

40. See *Macbeth* 1.iii.8. (1606).
'Her husband's to Aleppo gone, master of the Tyger.' And Hakluyt, ii., p. 250. 'I did ship myself in a ship of London called the Tyger, whereon we went to Tripolis in Syria and from thence took the way for Aleppo.'

41. E.F. Oaten, *European Travellers in India* (1909), p. 140.

42. Sir William Foster, ed., *Early Travels in India, 1583-1619* (1921), pp. 288-332.

43. Ibid. p. 308.

44. Sir William Jones, *Works*, ed. John Shore, Baron Teignmouth (1807), lv., pp. 110 seq.

45. But *see* Martin Haug, *Essays on the Sacred Writings and Religion of the Parsees* (1878), p.16, in which he claimed that Thomas Hyde was the first writer to have given an accurate account of Zoroastrianism.

46. Henry Lord, *The Religion of the Persees* (1630), p.29.

47. *By* (H. *bai*, air); *Pitt* (H. *pit*, bile); *Cuff* (H.*kaf*, phlegm); *Gurry* (H. *ghari*, an hour).

48. G. Subba Rao, *Indian Words in English* (Oxford, 1954), p.70.

49. Jan Huygen van Linschoten, *Discours of Voyages into Ye Easte and Weste Indies, 1598.* (Hak. Soc., 1807), i. 307.

50. Fryer, op. cit., p. 17.

51. Ibid., p. 32. See also *The Travels of John Albert de Mandelslo into the East Indies* (1638; E. tr. 1669).

52. 'The effect on European writers was immense. Schlegel, Schopenhauer and Goethe were deeply influenced by translations from the Sanskrit'. Michael Edwardes, *A History of India* (1961), p.266.

53. S.N. Mukherjee, *Sir William Jones, A Study in Eighteenth Century Attitudes to India*, 2nd edn. (Bombay, 1987), p. 88.

54. *Dictionary of National Biography*, vol.iii (1917), p. 925.

55. Ibid, iv, p. 738.

56. J.H. Plumb, *England in the Eighteenth Century* (1963), p. 177.

57. *From Sepoy to Subedar, being the Life and Adventures of Subedar Sita Ram*. Translated and first published by Lt. Col. Norgate, Bengal Staff Corps at Lahore (1873); ed. James Lunt, (Delhi, 1970). (Believed to have been written in Awadhi i.e. (western Hindi)).

58. Edwards Ives, *A Voyage from England to India in the Year 1754* (edn. 1773).

59. Sir William Jones, *Botanical Observations (Works)* (1807).

60. E.F. Oaten, 'Anglo-Indian Literature', *Cambridge History of English Literature* (Cambridge, 1932), vol. xiv (1932).

61. One of the best studies of Anglo-Indian military affairs is Philip Mason's *A Matter of Honour* (1974).

62. Edmund Burke, *Works* (Bohn's Standard Library, 1901-1906). See, *On Fox's East India Bill* (1783); *On the Nabob of Arcot's Debts* (1785); *Report on the Affairs of India* (1783); *Articles of Charge against Warren Hastings* (1783).

63. Ibid. vol., vii, p. 780.

64. Subba Rao, *Indian Words in English* (Oxford, 1954), pp. 77-90.

65. Scott's accuracy in his use of Indian words and in his descriptions of Indian scenes stemmed from the advice and information he received from a Scottish Anglo-Indian, Colonel Ferguson of Hartly Burn. Scott's debt to Orme must also be mentioned.

66. Subba Rao, op. cit., p.81.

67. The Hindi origins and meanings of the titles in the order given in the text are: (1) *Sub-janta*, all knowledge, know-all; (2) *bandar*, monkey; (3) *pagal*, confused; (4) *nat khat*, rascal; (5) *kabab*, skewered roast meat; (6) *le jao*, take away.

68. The Hindi originals and meanings in the order of the text are : (1) *chatni*, an Indian relish, in English 'chutney'); (2) *ghi*, clarified butter; (3) *chabuk*, a whip; (4) *dhal bhat*, pulse and rice, 'daily bread'; (5) *chini*, sugar; (6) *sais*, groom; (7) *paisa das*, 'penny slave'.

69. *Hobson-Jobson*, p. 532.
70. *The Day's Work*, 1898 (Oxford, 1987), p. 163.
71. 'The Undertakers', *Second Jungle Book*, 1895 (Oxford, 1987), p. 69. An ironic reference to the peripatetic pilgrims and mendicants who flock to the Hindu holy places such as ancient Prayag and Kasi, modern Allahabad and Banaras.
72. John Lockwood, Kipling, *Beast and Man in India, a Popular Sketch of Indian Animals in their Relation with the People* (1892).
73. 'How Fear Came', *Second Jungle Book*, 1895 (Oxford, 1987), p. 2.
74. *Oxford History of English Literature: Eight Modern Writers* (Oxford, 1963), p. 226.
75. The italicized words mean: (1) Come here! (2) Bring water! (3) Get a move on! (4) I'll thrash you.
76. T.S. Eliot, *A Choice of Kipling's Verse* (1941), p.11.
77. The Anglo-Indian words and their meanings are : *ekka*, a one-horse trap or buggy; *jildi*, quickly; *bukkin'*, talking; *jhil*, a lake; *Jehannum ke marfik!*, like Hell!; *mallum*, understand; *samjao*, understand; *bolos*, he speaks; *choop*, be silent; *chel*, go on, proceed; *dekker?*, Do you see?; *arsty*, slowly; *arder*-mile, half a mile; *shaitan ke marfik*, like the devil; *the chooper* you *choop*, the less you say; the *jildier* you *chels*, the quicker you go; *kooshy*, satisfied, happy; *bote-achee!*, very good!
78. Edward Thompson is unrecognized in the *Oxford Companion to English Literature* (1985), ed. Margaret Drabble, but his son, the historian, finds a place!
79. Abbé J.A. Dubois, *Hindu Manners, Customs and Ceremonies*. First English translation from MS 1816. Rpt. in H.K. Beauchamp's trans. 1897, p. 4.
80. *See* Cecil Leslie, *Goat to Kali* (1948), which makes use of the contemporary political terms Congress-*Wallah*; *zulm*, tyranny; *ahimsa*, non-violence; *satya-graha*, passive resistance, etc.
81. Saros Cowasjee, *Stories from the Raj* (1985), p.267.
82. *See* Sir William Sleeman, *Ramaseeana; or a vocabulary of the Peculiar Language used by the Thugs* (1836).
83. A select list of Anglo-Indian women writers of journals, memoirs, letters and novels would include: Lady Mary Nugent, *Journal* (1811-15); Maria Graham, *Journal of Residence in India*, Edinburgh (1812); Mary Martha Sherwood, *Little Henry and His Bearer* Wellington, Salop. (1822); Eliza Fay, *Original Letters from India 1779–1819* (1925); Anne Katherine Elwood, *Narrative of a Journey Overland from England* (1830); Lady Sale, *The First Afghan War* (1841-2, ed. 1969); Lady Charlotte Canning, *Letters* (1855-61, ed. 1986); Fanny Parks, *Wanderings of a Pilgrim in Search of the Picturesque* (1850); Catherine Weston, *Indigo* (1941); Maud Diver, *The Hero of Herat* (1912), *The Judgement of the Sword* (1913).
   (The novels of Flora Annie Steel are mentioned below.)
84. Saros Cowasjee, op. cit., p. 260.
85. Francois Bernier, *Travels in the Mogul Empire* (1658-64; E. tr. Constable, 1891); Jean Baptiste Tavernier, *Travels in India* (1638-68; E.tr. Ball, 1889).
86. *King Errant* (1912), about Babur; *A Prince of Dreamers* (1908), about Akbar; *Mistress of Men* (1917), about Jehangir; *The Builder* (1928), about Shahjahan.
87. Both of these expressions, *sijdah* and *tasleem*, were well known to English travellers in the seventeenth century as terms in their courtly and diplomatic vocabulary.
88. *See* Sir Olaf Caroe, *The Pathans* (Oxford, 1958). A former British Governor of the North-West Frontier Province, Caroe is the most eminent British commentator on the Pathans. The earlier work of Mountstuart Elphinstone, *Account of the Kingdom of Caboul* (1815), is also a work of considerable historical importance.
89. *See* K.R. Srinivasa Iyengar, *Indian Writing in English* (New Delhi, 1985).

A

Aal [19C. H./Beng. *aal.*] A red dye used to colour cotton fabrics, extracted from the roots of the *Morinda* plant allied to the **Muddar** (*madar*). [*OED. See also* **Ak** and **Ogg**. Tod, *Anns and Antiqs of Rajasthan* (1820).]

Abad [19C. H./P. *abad.*] A populated or cultivated place that paid revenue or gave supplies to the military. Often suffixed to a proper name to denote a city, e.g. *Allahabad.* [Whitworth, *Anglo–Indian Dictionary* (1885).]

Abada, badak [16C. = Pg. *abada*, Mal. badak.] The (female) *Rhinoceros sondaicus. Cf. Ar. abadat*, a wild animal. An early name for the rhinoceros in India. [*OED* & YB; Barker in *Hakluyt II* (1599; ed. 1812).]

Abdar [19C. H./P. *ab* = water + *dar* agent.] A waiter, servant or bearer whose function was to prepare water for drinking and other domestic uses. Cf. **Beastie (Bhisti)**. *Also* Anglo-Indian slang for a teetotaller, c. 1870. [Wilson, *Glossary* (1855); Partridge, *Dict. of Slang* etc. (Suppl. 1976).]

Abhaya [19C. H./S. *a.* without + *bhaya,* fear.] Fearlessness. Immunity (an assurance of). [Wilson, *Glossary* (1855).]

Abhinaya [20C. H./S. *abhinaya.*] Acting, dramatic action, mime; esp. the use of the face and hands in **Kathakali** dance style. [Webster, *Third New International Dictionary* (1976).]

Abhisheka [20C. H./S. *abhi* to + *shecate*, he pours.] Ceremonial bathing of the god (idol); lustration, coronation of a king. [Webster, *Third New International Dictionary* (1976).]

Abihowa [18C. H./P. *ab-o-hawa*, water and air.] The Hindustani expression for 'climate'. [YB; Kirkpatrick, *Select Letters of Tippu Sultan* (1786; ed. 1811).]

Abir, ubeer [19C. H. *abir.*] A perfumed red powder used at the Hindu vernal festival of **Holi**. [Wilson, *Glossary* (1855).]

Abkar [18C. H./P. *abkar.*] A maker of strong waters; a distiller. (*See* next.)

Abkari, abcaree, abkary [18C. H./P. *ab.* water + *kar*, business + *I*, particle.] Distillation, sale and manufacture of spirituous liquors. Also the excise duty levied upon such sale and manufacture. The Abkari System was the practice of farming out of the sale and manufacture to retail shopkeepers. [*OED* & YB; Letter from the Board of Revenue (Bengal) to Government (1790), MS in India Office Library.] *See* **Sayar**.

Accommodation–boat [19C.] Small craft used to carry passengers from ship to shore and shore to ship on the Coromandel coast (1837). [Maud Diver, *Honoria Lawrence* (1936), 63.]

Achar [16C. H./P. *āchār.* (Mal. achar and L. *acetaria*).] Relishes and pickles (now in nearly all the main Indian languages). Also, *achara*, fr. Tag. *atsara*, a pickled article of food in the Philippines. [Linschoten in *Hakluyt*, E.tr. (1598); Danvers, *Letters* (1612), i. 230]

Acharya, achari [19C. S. *āchārya.*] 'One who knows the rules', fr, *āchāra*, custom, rule of conduct. (1) A Brahmin religious teacher; (2) An illustrious or learned person in India, e.g. Shankaracharya. [Wilson, *Glossary* (1855).]

Achcha, atcha [19C. H. *achcha.*] A frequent expression of approval, interrogation, surprise, doubt, wonder, admiration, understanding, etc., etc., throughout N. India, often accompanied by an expressive and appropriate shake of the head. By the 20C. it had become a popular Anglo–Indian colloquialism in civilian and military circles. [YB; Fisher, *Three Years in China* (1863).]

Achkan [20C. H. *achkan.*] A man's long coat, buttoned up the front. *See* **Anga** and **Sherwani**. [*Encycl. Britannica* (1911); R. Godden, *Black Narcissus* (1939), v. 52.]

Ack dum, ek dum [19C. H. *ek dam.*] At once Anglo–Indian coll. = quickly, at the double. Also, '*Ek dum* and *viggery*' (H. and Ar.), the same idea repeated (by the British Army in India and Egypt), 1919. [Partridge, *Dict. Slang.* (1979); Kipling, *The Day's Work* (1898).]

Ackoori, ekoori [20C.Guj. *akūri.*] Spiced scrambled eggs, corr. of 'egg-curry'? A Parsi dish. *See* **Rumble-Tumble**. [Hawkins, *CIWIE* (1984); Premila Lal, *Indian Recipes* (1968); Madhur Jaffrey, *Indian Cookery* (1982), 83.]

Ada(w)lat etc. [18C. H./Ar. *'adālat.'*] Lit. justice, equity, fr. *'adl,' 'doing justice'*. Various kinds and levels of courts of justice in India since the 18C., e.g. (1) *Nizamat Adalat,* the Supreme Court of Criminal Justice; (2) *Diwani Adalat,* the Civil Court of the **Diwan**, or Chief Civil Court of Appeal; (3) *Faujdari Adalat,* the Court of **Faujdar,** or Chief Magistrate's and Police Court of a District; (4) *Sudder Adalat,* Chief Court of Appeal. [YB; Colebrooke, *Life of Elphinstone* (1884), ii. 131; Hockley, *Pandurang Hari* (1826), 271.] *See* **Sudder**.

Adam's Apple [16C.] A.I. version of the Pg. *Pomo*

d'*Adamo*, applied in Goa to the *Mimusops elengi;* to a variety of lime or bergamotte, *Citrus limetta*, and sometimes to varieties of the orange and **Shaddock**. [*OED* & YB; Hakluyt, *Voy.* (1599), ii. 227.]

Adati(s), addatys [17C. Poss. H. *adha*, half, meaning half-width.] Fine Indian muslin orig. exported from Bengal. See **Piece-Goods**. [*OED* & YB; Hedges, *Diary* (1681-8).]

Adharma [19C. S. *a*, without + *dharma*, virtue.] Hinduism: Disharmony with the nature of things; immorality, sin. Jainism: The ontological principle of rest. Also *adharmi*, outcaste [BBC broadcast (1982).] See **Dharma**.

Adi-Dravida [19C. S. *ādi*, original + *Drāvidā*, Dravidian.] Lit. original Dravidian. Outcast, **Untouchable, Harijan**. [Hawkins, CIWIE (1984).]

Adigar, adhikar(i) [17C. Tam. *adhikāri;*] One possessing authority. A rural headman in S. India; Chief Minister (of Kandyan kings in ancient Ceylon). See **Monegar** and **Patel**. [YB; Knox, *An Hist. Rel. of the Island of Ceylon in the East Indies* (1681), 48.]

Adi-Granth,-Grunth [18C. S. *ādi*, original + H. *granth*, book, code, fr. S. *grantha*, 'tying, literary work, text', fr. *granth* 'to tie'.] The Sikh scriptures; the sayings of the first four gurus collected by Arjun, the fifth guru, with additions by later gurus and Sikh saints (*sants*), the whole being metrical, mostly in Hindi with Gurumukhi characters. [*GCW*.] See **Granth, Granth-Sahib, Grantha, Grunthee, Grunthum**. [G. Forster, *Journey from Bengal to England* (1790).]

Adivasi(s), adibasi(s) [19C. S. *ādi*, original + *vāsī*, inhabitant.] Aboriginal tribe(s) or individual(s) in India. [Hawkins, *CIWIE* (1984).]

Adjutant [18C.] A gigantic Indian Stork, *Ciconia Argala*, so-called by Anglo-Indians from its stiff military gait. (The Hindi word for this bird is *hargilā*). See **Argala** [*OED* & YB; Pennant, *View of Hindustan*, II.156 (1798-1800); Ives, *Voy. England to India* (1754).]

Admi, adam [17C. H. *ādmi*.] Man. [Terry, *A Voyage to East India* (ed. 1655).]

Advaita [19C. S. *a*, without + *dvaita*, duality.] Hinduism: Vedantic non-dualism, emphasizing the impersonal oneness of **Brahma**. In advaitic philosophy the apparent dualism between the individual human soul (*jeevatma*) and the god-head (*paramatma*) is explained as a species of **Maya** (illusion). The process of self-realization consists in perceiving that *jeevatma* and *paramatma* are identical : '*Aham*

brahmasmi, tatvam asi'. [Whitworth, *Anglo-Indian Dictionary* (1885).]

Afghan, Afghaun (sb. and adj.) [17C. Pakht/Pasht. *Afghān(i).*] (1) Native of Afghanistan (1609). (2) A knitted woollen blanket made in Afghanistan (1833); (3) A coarse woven rug or carpet made in Afghanistan (1877); (4) A hunting dog resembling a shaggy greyhound (1895). [Finch in *Purchas* (1609), i.521; *OED* & YB.]

Afghani [20C. Pakht/Pasht. *Afghānī*.] (1) Monetary unit of Afghanistan, = 100 *puls*, from 1926. [*OED; Statesman's Yearbook* (1927), 643.] (2) The Afghan language in the time of Babur (16C).

Afim, affion [16C. H. *afim*; Ar *afium*; Gr *opion*.] See **Opium**. [YB; Linschoten, *Discours of Voyages* etc. (tr. 1598).]

Africo [17C.] An Anglo-Indian expression for a Negro slave. See **Hubshee**. [YB; Hedges, *Diary* (1681-8), 27 Feb. 1682.]

Afridi, Afreedi [19C. Pasht. *Afrīdi*.] A **Pathan** people and person from the mountainous region between what is now Pakistan and Afghanistan. [*OED;* Elphinstone, *Kingdom of Caubul* (1815), III. i. 356.]

Agalloch [16C. Ult. S. *aguru*.] See **Agila, Aloe(s), Eaglewood**. [*OED;* Linschoten, *Discours of Voyages* etc. (1598); T. Newton, tr., Lemnie's *Touchstone of Complexions* (1653), 202.] See **Tambac**.

Agam [17C. H./Ar. *agam/'ajam*.] Lit. one who has a speech impediment. In Arabic, a foreigner. An Anglo-Indian usage in the Piece-Goods trade, 'certain cloths dyed in a particular way'. [YB ; Foster's *Letters* (1614; ed. 1896-1900).]

Agar-agar [19C.] A well-known Anglo-Indian term taken from the Malay language. 'Bengal isinglass', made from sea-weed and, esp. in Sri Lanka, from the moss *Gracilaria lichenoides*. Used for soup, the manufacture of a kind of transparent silk, paper and glue, as well as a solidifying agent in culture media in bacteriology. [*OED;* Milburn, *Oriental Commerce* (1818), II. XXIII. 304.]

Agarbatti [19C. H. *agarbatti*.] Incense, joss-stick. Made from powdered **Costus, Sandalwood** and other aromatic materials for use in temples and the home. See **Putchuk**. [*CIWIE*.]

Agda(u)n [19C. H. *āg* fire + *dan*, holder, case.] A small vessel for holding burning charcoal to light cheroots. (Imit. of *pīk-dān, kalam-dān, shama-dān*, spittoon, pen-case, candlestick). See **Pigdaun**. [Whitworth, *Anglo-Indian Dictionary* (1885); YB.]

Agewallah [20C. H. *age*, 'in front' + *wala*, 'agent'.] A fore-runner. A forward caddy in golf. [Hawkins, *CIWIE* (1984); Charles Chevenix Trench, *The Frontier Scouts* (1985), 20.]

Ag-gharry, ag-gari [19C. H. *āg*, 'fire' + *gāri*, carriage.] A railway-train. Cf. the same idiom in Malay, *kreta*, 'carriage' + *api*, 'fire' [YB (1886).]

Agent (Political) [19C.] Title of the chief representative in some of the former Indian states such as Baroda, Rajputana, central India and some smaller states. In Hyderabad and Mysore, for example, he was known as the Resident. [Whitworth, *Anglo–Indian Dict.* (1885).]

Aghan [19C. H./S. *agrahāyana*, fr. *agra*, first + *hayana*, a year.] A month of the Hindu year; at one time the first month, otherwise known as *Margasirsha*. *See* next.

Aghan(i) [19C. H. *aghan* + *ī*. Winter harvest gathered in the month of Aghan (Nov-Dec.). *See* **Kharif**. [Wilson, *Glossary* (1855).]

Aghori,-a [19C. S. *a*, without + *ghora*, 'terrible'. The euphemistic title of a hill tribe in the Kathiawar region, in the forest of Girnar and elsewhere, reputed to have been cannibals. *See* **Parmahansa**. Tod, *Annals and Antiquities of Rajasthan* (1829).]

Aglary, agiari [17C. S. *agni*, 'fire' + *agar*, 'place'.] A Gujarati term for the Parsi fire-temple as an emblem of Hormazd (*Ahura Mazda*). *See* **Dokhma**. [Whitworth, *Anglo-Indian Dictionary* (1885); Lord, *The Religion of the Persees* (1636).]

Agila [16C. Pg. *aguila*.] A resin or resinous wood. *See* **Agalloch, Aloes, Eagle-wood**. [*OED*; Parke, tr., Mendoza's *China* (1588).]

Agni [19C. S. *agni*, 'fire'. Cf. E. 'ignite'.] The Vedic god of fire. *Agnihotra* (hotra = sacrifice), an oblation to Agni. The sacred fire itself. *Agnihotri*, one who prepares or preserves it. Tod, *Annals and Antiquities of Rajasthan* (1829).]

Agra [17C.] The famous city of central India; corr. of *Akbarabad*. A thick pile carpet with heavy knotting, at one time manufactured there. [Webster, *Third New International Dictionary* (1976).]

Agrahara(m) [19C. S. *agra*, 'first' + *hara*, 'taking'.] (1) Land given to Brahmins free or at low cost; (2) Brahmin quarter in S. Indian towns and villages. [GCW; *Abbé* Dubois, *Desc. of the Character, Manners etc. of the People of India* (1817).]

Agrahi, ajaur [19C. Punj. *agrahi*; H. *ajauri*.] The practice in Punjab villages in which traders, mostly Hindus, give out large loans to the Jat/Sikh farmers against their crop, to be returned with interest after the harvest. [Wilson, *Glossary* (1855).]

Agrom [18C. Guj. *agrūn*.] A rough, cracked and ulcerated condition of the tongue, a result of chronic disease of the alimentary canal; at one time frequent in Bombay, Bengal and some other regions of India. [*OED; Chambers Cycl. Supp.* (1753).]

Agun-boat [19C. H. *agan*, 'fire' + 'boat'.] An Anglo–Indian hybrid term for a steam-boat (in Bombay the expression was *ag-bōt*) [*YB*]. *See* **Ag-gharry**. [Arnold, *Oakfield* (1853), i.84.]

Ahadi(s) [19C. H. *ahadī*, 'single, alone'.] Gentlemen troopers in the Mughal service, so-called because they offered their services singly, and did not attach themselves to any chief. *See* **Haddy**. [Tod, *Annals and Antiquities of Rajasthan* (1829).]

Ahata [H. *ahata*.] An enclosure or **Compound**. [Hawkins, *CIWIE* (1984).]

Ahimsa [19C. S. *a*, 'without' + *himsā*, 'injury'.] In Hinduism, the doctrine of non-violence or of refraining from taking human or animal life. 'In its negative form it means not injuring any living being whether by body or mind... In its positive form, *Ahimsa* means the largest love, the greatest charity.' M.K. Gandhi, *Speeches and Writing* (1915) (quoted by G. Subba Rao in *Indian Words in English* (1954). [*OED*; Monier–Williams, *Indian Wisdom* (1875), x.249.] *See* **Satyagraha**.

Ajnas [17C. H./Ar. pl. of *jins*, goods, merchandise, crops, etc.] In *Mughal* times, payment in kind not in cash. [YB; Bernier, *Travels* (tr. 1684).]

Ak, ogg [18C. H. *āk*, the **Muddar** (*madār*). *See* **Aal**. [YB; Ives, *Voy. from England* (1773); Tod, *Annals of Rajasthan* (1829), i.669.]

Akali,-ee [19C. Punj/S. *a*, without + *kāla*, time.] A member of a Sikh politico-religious monistic sect; also called **Nihang**, alone (Pers.); distinguished by blue clothing and steel armlets. 'But now instead of swords they wield automatic rifles, carbines and pistols.' *The Sunday Times*, 4 March 1984. *See* next. [YB; Burnes, *Travels into Bokhara* (1835), ii.10.11.]

Akali Dal [20C.] A *Sikh* political party, the militant wing of the Shiromani Gurdwara Prabhandak Committtee (SGPC); founded to gain control of Sikh temples (*gurdwaras*) from colonial control, and to reform their management. It took an active part in the struggle for Indian independence and the formation of the Indian states on a linguistic basis. [Day & Dagenhardt, *Political Parties of the World* (1980).]

Ahata [H. *ahata*.] An enclosure or **Compound**. [Hawkins, *CIWIE* (1984).]

Akasa, akasha [19C. S. *ākāsa*, 'ether, atmosphere.'] Hindu philosophy : One of the five elements (ether) produced from the five elementary particles; a diffused, etherial, audible fluid occupying space. [*OED;* Colebrooke, *Religion and Philosophy of Hindus* (1858).]

Akela [19C. 'alone'?] The wolf-pack leader in Kipling's *Jungle Book* (1894). Later, a cub-scout pack leader. [Webster, *Third New Intern. Dict.* (1976).]

Akhara, akhada [19C. H. *akhara*.] A place for physical exercises and games; a wrestling arena; gymnasium; a centre for religious mendicants. Also a gambling den. [Whitworth, *Anglo–Indian Dictionary* (1885).]

Akhrot [19C. H. *akhrot;* S. *akshota*.] The walnut (tree), *Junglans regia*. [Webster, *Third New Intern. Dictionary* (1976).]

Akhundzada [19C. H./P. *Ākhūnzāda*, fr. *ākhūn(d)*, 'teacher' + *zada*, 'son'.] In India, the son of a head officer : used as a title. [Wilson, *Glossary* (1855).]

Akund *See* **Muddar**

Ala-Blaze Pan [19C. Poss. corr. of Pg. *brazeiro*, a fire-pan, fr. *braza*, hot coals.] A tinned copper stew-pan carried by European soldiers for the double purpose of cooking and eating out of. (A Bombay term.) [YB.]

Alap(an), (rag) alapana [20C. S. *alap*.] Indian music term; free expressive synthesis of **Raga** as prologue to its formal expression. [Ravi Shankar, *My Music, My Life* (1969).]

Alarippu [20C. Tam. *allarippu*.] A South-Indian dance term; introductory part of a Bharata-Natyam performance. *See* **Bharata-Natyam**. [R. Singha and R. Massey, *Indian Dances* (1967), 39]

Albacore [16C. Pg. *albacor*, fr. Ar *al bukr*, lit. a young camel or heifer.] Transf. A large kind of tunny-fish, *Thynnus albacora*. *See* **Bonito**. [*OED* & YB; Stevens, *Letter from Goa*, in *Hakluyt* (1579).]

Alcatif [16C. Ar. *katīf*, a carpet with a long pile.] A commonly used word in India in the 16C., introduced into Portugal through the Moors. [YB; Linschoten, *Discours of Voyages* etc. (1598).]

Aldea [17C. Pg *aldea*, fr. Ar. *al-dai'a*.] 'A village'; also a villa or farm in Portugal and her colonies,

e.g. Goa, Daman and Diu in India. [*OED* & YB; Danvers, *Letters* (1609).]

Alfandica [17C. Pg. *alfandega*, fr. Ar *alfunduk*, 'the inn'.] A custom-house and resort for foreign merchants in an oriental port. [YB; Sir T. Roe, *Embassy to the Court of the Great Mogul*, Hak. Soc. (1615-19), i. 72.]

Aljofar [17C. Pg. *aljofa*, seed-pearl, poss. fr. Ar *al-jauhar*, jewel.] [YB; Tavernier, *Travels* (tr. 1684; ed. Ball, 1889), ii. 228.]

Alim [17C. Sing. of '**Ulema**', fr. Ar *'ālim*, knowing, learned.] A Muslim doctor or divine, learned in religious matters. [*London Gazette* (1688), No. 23/3/2,.]

Allahabad [17C.] Place-name given in the time of Akbar to the ancient city of Prayag. Hobson-Jobsonized by English soldiers into *Isle o'Bats*. [Bernier, *Travels* (tr. 1684), ed. Constable, 36.]

Alleja, elatches, alacha [17C. H./Turk. *alcha, alajah*.] A kind of substantial silk and cotton stuff; one of the very many kinds of Piece-Goods exported to England until the trade was killed by the prohibitory duties in the nineteenth century. [YB; Danvers, *Letters* (1612; ed. 1896–1900), i. 205.]

Allygole, alighol, allegole [18C. H./P. *'āligol'*, fr. *'ali'*, lofty, excellent, + S. *gola*, a troop.] A nondescript word used for irregular foot in the Maratha service, without discipline or regular arms. According to some they are so named from charging in a dense mass and invoking 'Ali, the son-in-law of Mohammed, being chiefly Mohammedans'.) [YB; Tone, *Letter on the Maratta People* (1796).]

Almadia, almedia, almaydia [17C. H./Pg./Ar. *al-ma' dīyah*, a ferry-boat, fr. *aday*, to cross.] In India this was a boat about 80 ft. in length and of great swiftness, (but della Valle calls it a light vessel). *See* **Dhony**. [*OED* & YB; *Stanford Dictionary of Anglicised Words and Phrases* (1892); Blount, *Glossogr.* (1681).]

Almira, almyra, almari [16C. H. *almārī;* Pg. *almario*.] A commonly used word in Anglo–Indian households for a cupboard, chest of drawers, wardrobe. (See *The Will of Sir Thomas Cumberlege* (1450), which has *almer* and *almar*). Also *almariole* (1807). [*OED* & YB; Ext. *Records Burgh of Glasgow*, (1589); *Life in the Mofussil* by an Ex-Civilian, (1878), 1.34.]

Aloe(s),[1] **alowes** etc. [16C. H. *aghil;* S. *aguru;* Hebr. *akhaloth*, first mentioned in English c. 950 in *Saxon Leechdoms*, 11.174.] The fragrant resin and wood of the **Agalloch**, derived from species of two E. Indian genera, *Aloexylon* and *Aquilaria. See* **Eagle-wood,** and **Calambac.** [Hakluyt, *Voyages,* (1599), 11.229.; *OED* & YB.]

Aloes² [14C.] The drug prepared from the inspissated juice of the *Aloe Socotrina,* of nauseous odour and purgative qualities. Also: *Aloed,* mixed, flavoured, planted or shaded with *aloes* (1625); *Aloedary,* a purge or treatise on the nature of the genus *Aloe* (1753); *Aloetic,* of the nature of aloes; having aloes as an ingredient (1706). Also *aloetical* (1734); *Aloetic Acid* 2C₇H₂N₂O₂ H₂O (1855). [*OED* & YB; Traheron Vigo's *Chirurg* (1543); Travisa, *Barth De Propmetatus Rerum* (tr. 1398); Burke, *Subl. and Beautiful* (1756), Wks.,1.100.]

Aloo-baloo [19C.] The wild sour cherry of N. India, Pakistan and Afghanistan. [Lady Sale, *The First Afghan War* (1841-2; ed. 1969).]

Aloo Bokhara [17C. P. *ālū-bokhāra,* Bokhara Plum.] A kind of prune exported from Afghanistan to India. [YB; Bernier, *Travels* (tr. 1684); ed. Constable 1891).]

Alpana [19C. Beng. *alpana.*] The **Rangoli** of Eastern India. [Hawkins, *Common Indian Words in English* (1984).]

Alpeen [19C. H. *alpīn,* fr. Pg. *alfinete.*] A common pin. [YB; *Punjab Notes and Queries* (1850), ii. 117.]

Alphonso [Pg. *Alfonso.*] The mango *par excellence* of western India. [Hawkins, *Common Indian Words in English* (1984).]

Alu, aloo [H./S. *ālū.*] The potato, *Solanus tuberosum.*] The Sanskrit word is said to mean the esculent root, *Arum campanulatus,* [Whitworth, *Anglo-Indian Dictionary* (1885).]

Ama(h) [19C. Pg. *ama.*] The Anglo-Indian word for a wet-nurse, but current throughout S.E. Asia. [*OED* & YB; Maitland, *Letters from Madras* (1839), 294.]

Amadavat, avadavat [17C. fr.] The city of Ahmedabad. The Indian song-bird, *Estrilda amandava,* the Red Munia or Waxbill. [Fryer, *New Account* etc. (1672-81); Sheridan, *School for Scandal* (1777) V.i. 114]

Amalaka [19C. S. *āmalaka,* 'myrobalan'.] A bulbous ornament on the **Shikaras** of many Hindu temples and shrines. [Webster, *Third New International Dictionary* (1976).]

Amaltas [H. *amaltas*] 'drum-stick'. Indian Laburnum, *Cassia fistula;* also a tanning extract derived from it. [Hawkins, *Common Indian Words in English* (1984); Webster, *Third New International Dictionary* (1976).]

Aman [19C. H./Beng. *āman.*] The winter long-stemmed rice crop, reaped in December. *See* **Amen.** [Wilson, *Glossary* (1855).]

Amavasya amawasi [19C. S. *amā,* together + *was,* to dwell.] The day of the conjunction of the sun and the moon; the day of the new moon; the last day of the *Krishna-paksha;* the dark night preceding the new moon. [Wilson, *Glossary* (1855).]

Ambari,¹ -ee [19C. H. *ambārā, ambārī;*S. *amla-vatika.*] The plant, *Hibiscus cannabinus,* and the brown hemp produced from it, used as a fibre for ropes and coarse cloth. Also called 'Bombay Hemp'. [*OED; Imp. Dict. Suppl.* (1855), ed. J. Ogilvie.]

Ambari,² -ee [17C. H. *ambārī;* P. 'amari.] A canopied **Howdah,** on elephant or camel. [Bernier, *Travels* (tr. 1684), by John Phillips; ed. Constable (1850).]

Ameen, amin [17C. H./Ar. *amin.* Lit. 'A trustworthy person'.] Applied in India to an inspector, an officer, an accountant in a legal investigation, a land-surveyor, etc. Also, *Sudder Ameen,* the chief *ameen,* the second class of native judge; and *Principal Sudder Ameen,* the highest rank of native judge. [YB; Foster, *Letters* (1616; ed. 1896–1900), iv. 351.]

Amen [H. *amen.*] Winter paddy. *See* **Aman, Aus,** and **Summer Paddy.**

Amil, aumil [19C. H./Ar. 'amal, work. P. *amil,* one who performs a task, an agent.'] Revenue collector; manager; a farmer of the revenue invested with the chief authority in his district. Also called *amaldar,* **Amildar.** [*OED;* Wellington, *Wellesley Desp.* (1800), 200.]

Amildar, aumildar [17C. H./Ar. 'amaldar. *See* prec. The official in charge of a **Taluk;** revenue collector, manager, agent. Later (18C.) an Indian factor. (Not to be confused with Ar. 'Amaldar, an opium-eater). [*OED; English Factories in India* (1618–1669).]

Amir, ameer [17C. H./Ar. *amīr,* 'commander', fr. *amara,* 'tell, order or command'.] A Saracen title, *Emir.* An Indian and Afghan ruler or commander. Note, Ar. *Amīr-al-mār* 'sea captain or admiral'. Also *amirship,* the status or rank of an *amir. See* **Omrah.** [*OED* & YB; Selden, *Titles of Honor* (1614), 49; Hedges, *Diary* (8 Oct. 1683).]

Amla [20C. H./Beng. *āmlā;* S. *āmalakā.*] The feathery-foliaged tree *Emblica officinalia,* and its gooseberry-like fruit, called the Indian gooseberry. [Hawkins, *Common Indian Words in English* (1984); Webster, *Third New Intern. Dict.*, (1976).]

Amok, amock, a muck, etc. [17C. Mal. *amok* ('k' = glottal stop).] An expression current throughout India. (Cf. Pg. *amouco, amuco*.) In English, a noun, adjective or adverb. Running madly about in a frenzied and murderous fashion armed with a sword, dagger (Mal. *krīs*), or other weapon, and attacking all and sundry with desperate resolution to commit indiscriminate slaughter, to engender self-justification and satisfaction, to revenge real or imaginary wrongs without regard for the consequences. Yule spells it *A Muck*, and Dryden also considers it to be a noun in *The Hind and the Panther* (1687): 'He scours the streets and runs an Indian Muck at all he meets.' In English it is an adverb in 'to run *amok*', though its Malay equivalent (and source) is a verb, *mĕngamok*. The first European mention of *amok* (*amokos*) seems to be in *The Suma Oriental* of Tome Pires (1512–15). [*OED* & YB; *English Factories in India* (1618–69).]

Amra [18C. S. *amra.*] The **Mango**, tree and fruit. [Sir William Jones, *Letters* (1791).]

Amrita, amreeta [19C. S. *amr(i)ta*, fr. *a.* priv. + *m'rta*, 'dead'. (Gr. *am(b)rotos*) 'immortal'.] Ambrosial nectar, conferring immortality, produced by the mythical churning of the ocean, and with which the gods renewed their powers and drove out the demons, *daityas*, to *Patala*, the lower regions. [*OED*; Southey, *Kehama* (1810), XXIV.] See **Soma**.

Amrud [19C. H./P. *amrūd*. lit. 'pear'.] In India it indicates the **Guava**, *Psidium guayava*. Often called *safarī ām*, 'journey mango'. [YB.]

Amshom [19C. M. *amsham;* S. *amsha*, fr. *ansa*, 'a part'.] The smallest revenue division in Malabar; a part of a *taluk*, 'formerly called *hobili* greater than a *tara*'. [YB; Gundert, *Malayalam and English Dictionary* (1872) Wilson, *Glossary* (1855).]

Anaconda [17C. Sinh. *Anacondaia*, 'The crusher of buffaloes and yoke-beasts'.] Not (now) a Sinhalese word, but Tamil has *anaikkonda*, 'having killed an elephant'. Orig. a large and vicious snake of Ceylon (Sri Lanka), applied by English writers to the *Python reticulatus* or *molurus* (Gray), and by Daudin mistakenly to the large S. American *Boa Murina* or *B. anacondo*. Also, any large prey-crushing snake. [*OED* & YB; John Ray, *Synopsis Methodica*

Animalium Quadrupedum et Serpentini Generis, etc. (1693).]

Ananas [16C. Sinh/Tam. *annāsi;* Pg./Sp. *ananas*, ult.] Guarani *ānanā*, the pine-apple, *Ananassa sativa*, first described by Thevenot in 1555, and which has flourished in India, Malaysia, China, etc. It was habitually served at the table of Akbar, and much appreciated in Indian and Anglo–Indian households thereafter [*OED* & YB; Master John Hawkins in *Hakluyt* (1564), iii.602.]

Ananda [19C. S. *ānanda*, blessedness, bliss.] One of the three attributes which characterize **Brahman**, the other two being *chit*, 'consciousness', and *sat*, 'being' in the Indian philosophy of the *Upanishads*, [Max Mueller, *Theosophy* (1892).]

Anand Marg [20C. S. *anand marg*, lit. 'the path of bliss'.] A sectarian movement of Hindu extremists started in Bihar in 1955. *See* **Margi**. [Hawkins, *CIWIE* (1984).]

Anatta, anatman [20C. S. *anatta, anātmā*, 'no-self'.] The central teaching of Buddhism, affirming the non-existence of the soul or any other entity underlying phenomenal existence. [Keith, *Buddhist Philosophy in India and Ceylon* (1923).]

Andor [18C. Pg. *andor*, 'a litter.'] A kind of slung hammock or palanquin. *See* **Dandy** and **Muncheel**. [YB; Grose, *Voyage to E. Indies* (1757).]

Andrum [17C. M. *āndram.*] A hydrocele, formerly common in S. India. (first described by Kaempfer in his *Decas*, 1694(Leyden). [YB.]

Anga¹ [19C. H/S. *anga*, 'body'.] A poll tax. [Tod, *Annals and Antiquities of Rajasthan* (1829), ii. 111b.]

Anga² [19C. S. *anga*, 'body (or part of it).] Fig. a branch of literature; a supplement of the Vedas etc. [Wilson, *Glossary* (1855).]

Angadia [19C. Guj. *angaddia.*] Carriers who ran a private postal service for businessmen, and others from Gujarat and Poona (Pune). Also runners who conveyed money and jewels concealed on their persons to various places in W. India. [Wilson, *Glossary* (1855).]

Angarkha [19C. H./S. *anga*, 'body' + *rakshana*, 'protecting'.] A long tunic worn both by Hindus and Muslims, tied on the left breast by the former and on the right breast by the latter. *See* **Sherwani, Achkan**, and **Chupkan**. [Wilson, *Glossary* (1855).]

Angavastram [S. *anga* 'body' + *vastram*, 'cloth'.] A folded scarf worn by men in S. India. Coll. a mistress. *See* **Angocha.** [Hawkins, *CIWIE.*]

Angely-wood, angelina, [16C. Tam. *anjalī-maram* (wood).] *Autocarpus hirsuṭa*, an excellent wood for ship- and house-building. In Malabar, known as *Iynee (ayani).* [Linschoten in *Hakluyt* (E. tr. 1598); Logan, *Malabar* (1887-91), i. 39.]

Anglo-Indian [19C. Adj. and sb.] This expression has undergone a sea-change similar to that which affected *creole* in S. America. It first denoted a person of 'pure' British descent resident or born in India, but in 1911 the Government of India decided to substitute this term for 'Eurasian' as the official one for persons of mixed descent. It also refers to anything composed of English and Indian elements, to terms adopted by English from Indian languages, and to literature about India written by British authors in English. *See* **Eurasian, Castees, Mustees, Chi-Chi.** [*OED*; Malcolm, *Polit. Hist. India* (1784 – 1823), 11.xi.248.]

Anglo-Vernacular [19C.] In India, pertaining to, or consisting of English and an Indian language; esp. descriptive of schools in India, Burma, and Ceylon (Sri Lanka), in which both English and a native vernacular language featured during British rule. [*OED*; Caldwell, *Evangel. Work Tinnevelly,* (1877).]

Angocha [H. *angocha.*] Towel customarily worn by Hindus over the shoulders. *See* **Angavastram.** [Hawkins, *CIWIE* (1984).]

Anicut [18C. Tam. *anai,* 'dam' + *kattu,* 'building'.] A dam constructed across a river in Tamil Nadu, to feed a canal for irrigation purposes. *See* **Ayacut,** and **Calingula.** [*OED* & YB; *East India Papers* (1777), i.836.]

Anil(e), (a)neel [16C. H/Pg. *anil;* Ar. *al-nil;* S. *nīlī,* 'indigo' (and plant), fr. *nīlā,* dark-blue.] (1) The indigo shrub; the Indian name of the Indian shrub *Indigofera tinctoria.* Also,- *Neel-wallah,* an indigo-planter, and *Neel-kothee,* his factory. [Pomet, *Hist. Drugs* (E. tr. 1712).] (2) The indigo dye. *See* Lilac. [Act 23, Eliz. ix. 1581; *OED* & YB; Fitch in *Hakluyt* (1583), ii.395.]

Anjuman, anjaman [19C. H/P. *anjaman.*] An assembly, a society, e.g. the *Anjaman-i-Panjab,* a Punjabi society for the revival of oriental learning. Also, a Parsi society to which all questions concerning the customs of the Parsi community are referred. [Whitworth, *Anglo-Indian Dict.* (1885).]

Ankus(h) [19C. H. *ankus;* P. *anguzh;* S. *ankusa.*] In India, an elephant-goad. [Jacob and Hendley, *Jeypore Enamels* (1886), ii; *OED.*]

Anna [17C. H. *ānna,* fr. S. *anus,* small.] Orig. 1/16th of a rupee, or of any kind of property, esp. of coparcenary shares in land, speculation or chattels. On 1 April 1957 India was decimalized and annas gave way to *Naye Paise,* 100 to the rupee. The term was also used colloquially (offensively) in a number of Anglo-Indian expressions, e.g. '4 annas of dark blood', a quadroon; '8 annas in the rupee', a half-caste; 'a 12-anna crop', only 3/4ths successful. And *annewari,* a land-tax expressed in 16ths of a rupee. [*OED* & YB; Foster's *English Factories in India* (1618-69).]

Ant(s), White [17C.] The voraciously destructive and ubiquitous Indian insect, *Termes bellicosus,* of whom it has been said 'It is an insect greatly to be dreaded in every house (in India); and this is not to be wondered at, as the devastation it occasions is almost incredible'. [*OED* & YB; Capt. Innes Munro, *Narratives of Military Operations* etc. (1789); Dampier's *Voyages* (1688).]

Antarjali [19C. H./S. *antar,* 'inside' + *jali* 'river.'] The old practice among Hindus of bringing a dying man to the river-bank and suffocating him to hasten his exit from this world. Sometimes called by missionaries *Ghaut-Murder.* [*The Private Journal of the Marquess of Hastings* (1858), ii.92; G. Smith, *The Life of William Carey* (1887), 256.]

Antiyoday [20C. H./S. *antiyodaya.*] Uplift of the lowest of the low. [Hawkins, *CIWIE* (1984).]

Anushashan [20C. H/S. *ānushāshan,* discipline.] *Anushāshan parva,* 'discipline stage' (of India's development since 1947). Commonly used to describe the Emergency imposed by Indira Gandhi in 1975.

Anuswara [20C. S. *anuswara,* fr. *anu,* according to, + *svara,* voice.] Linguistics : (1) Sanskrit post-vocalic sound or group of sounds recurring in the interior of a morpheme only before, ś, ṣ, s, or h and at the end of a morpheme only before an initial consonant of a following morpheme. (2) A sign; used in written Sanskrit to represent the *anuswara* sound, and in some MSS and editions, certain other postvocalic sounds. [Webster, *Third New Intern. Dict.* (1976).]

Apil [19C. Anglo-Indian term from English *appeal,* used in Indian law-courts. Also *apīlant,* appellant. [YB; Burton, *Sind Revisited* (1872).]

Appam [M. *appam*.] A sweet cake from Malabar (Kerala). [Hawkins, *CIWIE* (1984).]

Apsara(s), upsara [19C. S. *ab*. 'water' + *sri*, 'to go'.] Wives of the **Gandharvas**; (pictures or carvings of) celestial girls or nymphs for the post-mortem delectation of the spirits of Hindu sages. (The word means 'going in the waters' or 'between the waters and the clouds'.) [*OED*; Tod, *Annals and Antiquities of Rajasthan* (1829); Kipling, *Barrack-Room Ballads* (1892), 105.]

Arab[1] [H. *arab*.] 100 **Crores**, 1000 million. [Hawkins, *CIWIE* (1984).]

Arab[2] [17C.] An Arab horse prized for its speed and breed. [*OED*; Evelyn, *Diary*, 25 Oct. 1644).]

Araba, aroba [19C. H/P. *arābah*, a cart or gun-carriage.] Also a kind of arquebus. [*OED*; Irvine, *Army of the Indian Moghuls*; Tod, *Annals and Antiquities of Rajasthan* (1829).]

Aram [H./P. *arām*.] Rest, repose.] [Hawkins, *CIWIE* (1984).]

Arati, arti [19C. H. *ārati*; S. *ārātrika*.] The light waved before an idol at night as part of the evening ceremonial; in S. India the ceremony is performed to honour bridegrooms and guests at marriages and festivals. [Wilson, *Glossary* (1855).]

Arbol Triste [18C. Indo-Pg. *arbol triste*, 'The Tree of Sorrow'. *Nyctanthes arbor tristis* (H. *harsinghar*).]So-called because this common Indian wild shrub sheds its powerful perfumed blossoms in the morning after opening the evening before. Indian folk-lore has the story of a certain king's daughter who, falling in love impetuously with the sun (*Surya*), was all too soon discarded. In despair she killed herself and was cremated. Where her ashes fell there grew this Tree of Sorrow which, unable to bear the sight of the sun, blooms at night and sheds its flowers like perfumed tears in the morning. From the orange tubes of the flowers a rich dye is obtained for dyeing the robes of Buddhist monks. (Cowen.) [YB; Linschoten, *Voyages* (E. tr. 1598; Hak. Soc. ii. 58–62); Moore, *Lalla Rookh* (1817); Fanny Parkes, *Wanderings of a Pilgrim* etc. (1850), i.312.]

Archana [20C. H. *archana*. fr. *archā*, image, icon.] Temple-prayer. [Sir Charles Eliot, *Hinduism Buddhism* (1921), i.ixx.]

Areca [16C. Pg. *areca*; M. *addekka*; Kan. *adike*; Tam. *adaikay*, fr. *adai*, 'close arrangement of the cluster' + *kāy*, 'nut,' 'fruit'.] The palm-tree and nut of the *Areca catechu*. Erroneously called the *betel-nut*, it is chopped up, rolled in **Betel** leaves with lime, tobacco and other astringents together with flavourings such as cloves, cardamoms, tamarind, etc., and chewed as a masticatory, often being offered to the departing guests. *See* **Pan–(Supari)**. [*OED* & YB; Fitch in *Hakluyt* (1586), ii.395.]

Argala, argeela [18C. H. *hargīlā*.] The **Adjutant-Bird**, a gigantic Indian stork, *Ciconia argala*. [*OED*; Ives, *Voy. India* (1754; ed. 1773).]

Argemone Mexicana [19C.] This American weed (N.O. *Papaveraceae*) has established itself throughout India, where it is known as *Firinghī dhatūra, gamboge-thistle*, etc. [YB; Watt, *Dict. Econ. Prod.* (1889–93), i.306.]

Argus-pheasant [18C.] Anglo-Indians applied this expression not to the *Argus giganteus*, to which it properly belongs, but mistakenly to the Himalayan horned pheasant, *Satyr tragopan*, otherwise known as the **Moonaul** (Nep. *monal*). [*OED* & YB; *Gent. Mag.* (1788), XXXVIII, 521. (*See also* Jerdon, *Birds of India* (1862) and Salim Ali, *Birds of India and Pakistan* (1984).]

Arhant [19C. S. *arhant*.] A person in whom all craving is extinct, and who will not be born again. *See* **Arhat**. [Basham, *Cult. Hist. of India* (1975).]

Arhar, rahar [19C. H. *arhar* (perh. from S. *ādhakē*.] Red **dhal**, the pigeon-pea, *Cajanus indicus*. *See* **Moong, Oord, Tur**. [Wilson, *Glossary* (1855).]

Arhat, arahat [19C. S. *arhat*; Pali, *arahat*, deserving, worthy.] A Buddhist saint, who has reached the fourth or highest stage in his progress to **Nirvana**; a **Tirthankar**. Also *arahatship*. [*OED*.] *See* **Arhant, Vira**. [Hardy, *Eastern Monachism* (1850).]

Arjun [19C. H. *arjun*.] The evergreen tree, *Terminalia arjuna*, indigenous to India and Sri Lanka, whose bark is used for dyeing, tanning and medical purposes. Also called *kumbuk*. [Webster, *Third New Intern. Dict.* (1976).]

Arkatia [19C. H. *arkatia*.] A tout who assisted licensed recruiters of slave-labour or indentured labour of Indians for the sugar plantations of the West Indies and elsewhere. [Hugh Tinker, *A New System of Slavery 1830-1920* (ed. 1974).]

Arrack, rack [16C. H./Ar. 'arak', sweet.] (In many Indian languages.) Orig. from the sap drawn from the date palm, *arak al-tamar*;

afterwards any spirituous liquor of native distillation, esp. that of the coconut palm, or from rice and sugar fermented with coconut juice. Also *rack-punch* [Thackeray, *Vanity Fair*]. *See* **Fool's Rack.** [*OED* & YB; E. Scot (1602-5) in *Purchas* (1625); Barbosa, *Travels*, E.tr. Ld. Stanley in *Hakluyt* (1516).]

Arre-Arre! [H. *arre!*] Exclamation of surprise or wonder. *See* **Achcha.**

Arsty [19C. H. *ahisti!*] Slowly! slow down! Take it easy! British Army in India corr. of the Hindustani word. Opp. of **Jildy** and **Ak** (or **Ek**) **Dum.** [Partridge, *Dict. of Slang* etc. (1927).]

Artha [19C. S. *artha.*] The Hindu has traditionally four goals, the *purushastras:* (1) *Artha*, money, material goods, politics, economics; (2) *Kama*, love; (3) *Dharma*, duty, right-behaviour; (4) *Moksha*, the final liberation of the soul. [Wilson, *Glossary* (1855).]

Arthas(h)astra [19C. S. *artha + shāstra*, instruction.] Sanskrit treatise on statecraft. (Attributed sometimes to Kautilya *c.*500 BC.) [T.R. Trautman, *Kautilya and the Artha- shastra*, Leiden (1977).]

Arthi [19C. H. *arthi, arthiya.*] 'A middle man, broker, go-between.' 'A banker who grants and accepts bills on other bankers or correspondents.' [Wilson, *Glossary* (1855).]

Arusha¹ [19C. H. *arus*, perh. fr. S. *atarusha.*] A small Indian shrub, *Adhatoda vasica*, whose flowers yield a yellow dye. [Webster, *Third New Intern. Dict.* (1976).]

Arusha,² aroosha [19C. Perh. S. *arusha*, red.] An Indian shrub, *Callicarpa cana*, yielding a kind of flax. [Webster, *Third New Intern. Dict.* (1976).]

Arya Samaj [19C. S. *ārya* noble, **Aryan** + *samaj*, society.] A religious reform society founded by Dayananda Sarasvati in 1875, influenced by the *Brahmo Samaj*, in attacking polytheism, idolatry and superstition, and in holding the **Vedas** to be incontrovertibly and literally inspired. *See* **Brahmo Samaj.** [Whitworth, *Anglo-Indian Dict.* (1885).] *See* **Sanatan.**

Aryan, Arian [17C. S. *ārya.* (Vedic *aria*), 'noble, of good family'; Zend, *airya*; Old P. *ariya.*] Worshippers of the gods of the **Brahman.** Linguistics ; *Indo-Aryan*, alias Indo-European, Indo-Iranian, Indo-Germanic, and Japhetic; the proto-language and proto-races from which their more modern languages and races have

sprung. The term includes all the races which speak (or have spoken) the languages akin to **Sanskrit.** *Indo-Aryan* (1850) has superseded the older term, *Indo-Germanic*, of the 18th century, used by Schlegel, and includes Sanskrit, Zend, Teutonic, Celtic, Semitic, Slavonic Iranian, Greek, Latin and Romance languages, as well as Hindi, Urdu, Marathi, Punjabi, Bengali, Gujarati, Kashmiri, Sindhi, etc. The original work of Sir William Jones in this philological field at the end of the 18th C. was of prime importance in establishing the links between Sanskrit and Greek, Latin and Hebrew. Also *Aryanism*, 1888; *Aryanization*, 1889 (e.g. of a Jew in Nazi Germany) and *Aryanize* (1935) (to confer Aryan status on a non-Aryan). The term *Aryan* was also applied to non-Jewish people in Germany under Hitler (1932), and the ancient *Aryan* **Swastika** (in reverse) became the symbol of Nazism. The earlier known use of *Aryan* in an ethnic sense is in the inscription on the tomb of Darius, *c.* 486 BC [*OED* & YB; Holland, fr. *Pliny*, (1601), 1.131; Sir William Jones, tr. Ordin, *Menu*, (1794), x.945.]

Aryawarta [19C. S. *ārya*, 'Aryan, noble' + *varta*, 'abode, dwelling'.] The land of the Aryans; North India, between the Himalayas and the Vindhyas, and the Western and Eastern oceans. [Whitworth, *An Anglo Indian Dict.* (1885).]

Arz, urz, urzee, urjee, [17C. H./P. *'arz(i).*] An oral or written petition, or humble representation from an inferior to a superior. Also: *arz-dāsht*. 'memorializing'. [YB; John Mildenhall in *Purchas* (1606), i. (Bk. iii),115.]

Asana(s) [20C. S. *asana*, fr. *aste*, 'he sits', akin to Gr. *hesthai*, 'to sit'.] Posture or manner of sitting, in the practice of **Yoga**, designed to obviate all effort and strain for the full development of the body, nerves, circulation and organs. According to Patanjali, author of the *Yoga Sutras*, written between the third and second centuries BC, the 84 *asanas* are the easiest and best positions for concentration, meditation and contemplation. *See* **Uddiyana** [J. Hewitt, *Yoga* (1960), 11.42; Basham, *Cultural Hist. of India* (1975), 116.]

As(h)oka [19C. S. *ashoka.*] A small, slow-growing, erect and evergreen tree, sacred to Siva, with orange and scarlet clusters of flowers, called *Seraca asoca* or *Jonesia asoka* in honour of Sir William Jones, who wished that the tree should retain its Sanskrit name, honouring the great emperor Ashoka. Sakyamuni, the founder of Buddhism and the doctrine of **Nirvana,** is said to have been born under one of these trees in the 6th C. BC. Hence it is worshipped by all Buddhists, who plant it round their temples, as also do Hindus. Hindus revere it because it is the symbol of love, dedicated to *Kama Deva,* the god of love, who included an *asoka* blossom among the five flowers in his quiver. Sita, when abducted by Ravana was kept in a garden of *asoka* trees, and on *Ashok Shastri* day Bengali women eat the flower-buds, and Hindu women drink the water in which the flowers have lain, believing their children will thus be protected from worry and grief. An Indian belief says that the tree will flower only where a woman's foot has trod, and another that a tree will bloom better from being kicked by a young and beautiful maiden. [Cowen, *Flowering Trees & Shrubs in India* (1950); M. and J. Stutely, *Dict. of Hinduism* (1977).]

Ashrafi, ashrafee, [17C. H./Ar. *ashrafi,* fr. *sharif,* 'noble'.] Various gold coins, for instance the **Gold Mohur** of India. *See* **Xerafine** (1610), a corruption of Ar. *ashrafī,* and applied to a silver coin about 1/10th the value of the gold one. [YB; *Mem. of Humayum* (1550), tr. Maj. C. Stewart (1832).]

Ashram [19C. S. *āsrama,* 'hermitage' (fr. *ā,* 'near to, towards' + *shrama,* 'exertion, earnest endeavour'.)] In India a place of religious retreat, sanctuary or hermitage. Hence *ashramite,* an occupant of an *ashram,* a Rishi, holy man or pilgrim. *Ashrama*: any one of the four stages of Brahmanic life: **Brahmacharya, Grihastha, Vanaprastha, Sannyas.** [W.W. Pearson, *Shantiniketan* (1917), 17; Whitworth, *Anglo-Indian Dict.* (1885).]

Asura [19C. S. *asura* (fr. *a,* 'no' + sura, 'god').] One of a class of celestial spirits of early **Vedic** and **Zoroastrian** mythology, higher than men but lower than gods. *Asuravidya,* the science of the *Asuras,* i.e. magic. Demons or titans in later Hinduism and Buddhism, the enemies of the gods. [Max Mueller, *Theosophy* (1892).] A Hindu name for a Muslim. [Tod, *Annals and Antiquities of Rajasthan* (1829), 1288.]

Asuri [19C. fem. of *asura.*] (1) A demoness, who produced a remedy for leprosy. [W.D. Whitney, tr. *Atharva-Veda Samhita* (1962).] (2) A dialect of the Munda group of languages. *See* **Bhumij.** (3) Also the name of a plant, *Sinapsis ramosa,* of which the Asuri may be

a personification. [M. and J. Stutely, *Dict. of Hinduism* (1977).]

Asvamedhi, Ashwameda [17C. S. *asva,* 'horse' + *medhi,* 'sacrifice'.] Indo-Aryan horse sacrifice, assimilated from an ancient Indian fertility rite in which a bull (probably) was replaced by the Asian horse brought to India by the Aryans; associated with the spring festival, and originally offered to Varuna (Rig Veda, I, 162, 163). [Bernier; *Travels in the Mogul Empire* (1656-68; tr. 1684).]

Atlas [17C. Ar. *atlas.* lit. 'bare or bald'.] Hist : 'A silk stuff wrought with threads of gold and silver ... at one time exported from India. (Otherwise known as Indian Satin.) [*The Draper's Dict.* quoted in YB.] [Fryer, *New Acct. of E. India* etc. (1672–81), 196.]

Atman [18C. S. *ātman.*] The self or soul; the supreme universal principle of life. (O.E. *edm,* 'breath'; Greek *atmos,* 'vapour' and English *ether* and *atmosphere*). [*OED;* Wilkins, tr., *Bhagavadgita* (1785), xiii. 105.]

Atoll [17C. Prob. M. *adal,* 'closing, uniting', and Maldive *atollon.*] A ring-shaped coral reef; a lagoon belt that may vary from less than a mile to 80 miles or more, occupying the place of a submerged island. Also fig. 'to raise up' (1578). [*OED* & YB; Darwin, *Structure of Coral Reefs* etc. (1842); Purchas, *Pilgrimes* (1625), 11.]

Atta, otta, otter [19C. H./Punj. *atta* 'flour'.] Unsorted wheat-meal flour. Poss. connected with S. *ardra* 'soft' [*See* Platts, *Dict. of Urdu* etc.,1884); W.H. Russell, *My Diary in India* (1860), 11.206; *OED* & YB; Chevers, *A Manual of Medical Jurisprudence for India* (1870).]

Attar, otto, otter [18C. H./P. *atar,* perfume, essence. Ar. *otōr,* pl. of *itr,* 'aroma'.] Fragrant essence of flowers, e.g. *attar* of roses (*atar ghul*), a highly perfumed, volatile essential oil from rose-petals. Earlier otto and otta. [*OED;* Pennant, *Hindostan* (1798), 11.238.]

Aumil (dar) *See* **Amildar.**

Aurung [18C. H./P. *aurang.* 'A cloth factory or depot'.] An East India Company cloth 'factory' or cloth market. [YB; Orme, *Hist. Milit. Trans.* etc. (1778), ii.51.]

Aus [Beng/H. *āus.*] short-stemmed Indian rice, grown in the dry season; the **Kharif** crop in West Bengal and Bangladesh. *See* **Aman, Amen.**

Auto-rick(sha) [20C. Anglo-Indian. Hybrid. E. + Jap.] The ubiquitous motorized taxi three-wheeler throughout India, *See* **Jenny Rickshaw.** Also called 'auto'.

Avadavat See **Amadavat.**

Avadoot, abdhut [19C. H/S. *awadhūta*, 'disciple'.] One who has shaken off wordly feeling and obligations; a sect. of religious mendicants. [Sir Charles Eliot, *Hinduism and Buddhism* (1921), 11.243.]

Avantika [19C.] One of the seven sacred cities of Hinduism; modern Ujjain. [Sir Charles Eliot, *Hinduism & Buddhism* (1921), 1.282.]

Avarna Non-caste Hindu, [fr. '*a*', 'without' + *varna*, 'colour, caste'.] See **Varna.**

Avalokiteswara [19C. S. *avalokita*, looking on + *isvara*, 'lord',] One of **Buddha's** most important disciples, widely venerated in N. India from the 3rd to the 7th century. [Sir Charles Eliot, *Hinduism Buddhism* (1921), 111.120]

Avatar[1] [18C. S. *avatāra*, 'descent' fr. *ava*, 'down'+*tar*,'to pass over'.] The descent of an Indian deity to earth, in Hindu mythology;the incarnation of a god on earth. [*OED* & YB; Sir William Jones in *Asiat. Res.* (1784), 1.234]

Avatar[2] [19C.] Any incarnation in human form. [*OED*; Scott (1815), *Paul's Letters* (1839), 325.]

Avatar[3] [19C.] Manifestation or presentation to the world as a ruling power or object of worship. [*OED*; Masson, *Milton* (1859), 1.226.]

Avatar[4] [19C.] Any manifestation; display; phase. [*OED.* (1850); Hunt, *Autobiog.* (1860), ii. 36.]

Avergal [19C. Tam. *avargul.*] Honorific title affixed to a man's name in Tamil Nadu. [Hawkins, *CIWIE* (1984).]

Avesta, Zend-Avesta [17C. P. *Zand(a)vastā*, or *Avesta-va-Zend.*] *Zend* is the name commonly applied to the dialect of an ancient Iranian language in which the **Avesta** or sacred books of Zoroastrianism are written. This is erroneous. The word *Zend* used alone in Farsi means a 'commentary or explanation'. *Zend Avesta* signifies the law and the commentary. Adjs. *Avestan,* **Avestic.** [*OED;* Sir T. Herbert, *Travels,* etc. (1630); Lord, *The Religion of the Persees, Proeme* (1630).]

Avidya [19C. S. *avidyā.* lit. 'ignorance', fr. *ā* 'without' + *vidyā* 'knowledge'.] Nescience, ignorance, together with non-existence. Blindness to ultimate truth. [Max Mueller, *Theosophy* (1892); Radhakrishnan, *Hist. of Philosophy* (1969), 1.280.]

Awadhi, Avadhi [19C. H. *Avadhi.*] A literary dialect of Eastern Hindi, including the translation of the *Ramāyāna* of Tulsidas. [Whitworth, *Anglo-Indian Dict.*(1885).]

Awam [19C. H. *awam.*] People. See next.

Awami [19C. H. *awami.*] People's [Hawkins, *CIWIE* (1984).]

Ayacut [18C. Tam. *vayal,* irrigated field + *kattu,* 'bank'.] The entire extent of land irrigated by a **Tank.** See **Anicut**

Ayah [18C. Pg. *aia.*] An Indian nanny, nursemaid, housemaid, lady's maid, etc. in many Indian languages. [*OED* & YB; *India Gazette,* (12 Oct. 1782); Busteed, *Echoes of Old Calcutta* (1779; ed. 1857), 225.]

Ayurveda (sb) [19C. S. *āyur,* 'life, vital power' + *veda,* 'knowledge'.] The traditional Hindu system of medicine based largely on homeopathy, or the diagnosis of the bodily 'humours' (*dosha*). See **Hakim, Vaid.** [Sleeman, *Rambles and Recollections* (1844), 107; A. Kaviratna, *The Charaka Samhita* (Calcutta, 1899).]

Ayurvedic (adj) [19C.] See prec. Pertaining to the **Ayurveda,** traditionally regarded as ancillary to the *Artharva-veda.* [*OED;* *Antiseptic* (Madras, 1917), XIV. 389; *Blackwood's Magazine* (July 96/2, 1922).]

B

Baba [17C. H. *bābā.*] Title of respect for father, grandfather and child. Also, applied to children by Anglo–Indians as a term of endearment, often in the form *bābā-lōg* (*lōg* = folk). *Bābājī* is a common form of address to a *Fakīr.* [YB; Pringle, *Diary, Fort St. George* (1685), IV.92.]

Babagooree [17C. H. *bābāghūrī,* fr. *bābā* + *Ghori,* 'a traditional prince'.] The white agate of Cambay. 'So called because of the patron saint or martyr of the district containing the mines, under whose protection the miners placed themselves before descending into the shafts.' [YB; Copland, *Trans. Lit. Soc.* (1818), i.294; Tavernier, tr., *Travels* (1684; ed. Ball 1889), i.68.]

Babu, baboo [18C. Beng. *bābū.*] Originally a Hindu (esp. Bengali) gentleman, but used also in a pejorative or comic way for a Bengali with superficial English education; a half-anglicized, often a somewhat effeminate Hindu. Hence: *Babuism, Babu English, Babudom,* all referring to excessively ornate, often unintentionally comic, English usage and offbeat idioms [*OED* & YB; *India Gaz.* (12 Oct. 1782).]

Babul, babool [18C. H./P. *babūl.*] The thorny mimosa, *Acacia nilotica,* common in most parts of India except the Malabar coast. Also called *kikar.* The **Bhils** use the gum as food, and from the bark, with **Jaggery, Arrack** was distilled. [*OED* & YB; Capt. Symson, *A New Voyage to the East Indies* (1702); Hickey's *Bengal Gaz.* (29 April, 1780).]

Baccha [H. a youngster or 'kid'.] *See* **Balbacche**

Backdore [19C. H. *bāg-dor.*] 'bridle-cord', a halter or leading rein. [YB.]

Backsee [19C. H. *bāksī.*] From nautical 'aback'. [YB; Roebuck, *Naval Dict.* (1811).]

Badega, badaga [19C. Tam. *vadagar,* 'Northerners'.] Applied to the **Telugu** people who invaded the Tamil country from the Kingdom of Vijayanagara. [YB; Caldwell, *Grammar Dravidian Langs.* (1856).]

Badega [19C.] A tribal people living in the **Nilgiris,** speaking an old **Kannada** dialect. The name of these people was usually corrupted to **Burghers** by **Anglo–Indians.** [YB; Caldwell, *Grammar Dravidian Langs* (1856).]

Badgeer, badgir [19C. H./P. *bād,* 'wind' + *gīr,* 'catch'.] Contrivance for catching the wind (in Iran and Sind) to bring it down into the house for ventilation and cooling purposes. [YB; Burton, *Sind Revisited* (1877), 254.]

Badian [19C. H/P. *bādyān.*] The Chinese or Star Anise, or Aniseed Tree, *Illicium anisātum,* used as a substitute for anise. [*OED;* Craig, *Badiane* (1847).]

Badmash, budmash [19C. H./P. *bad,* 'evil' + *ma'ash* 'means of livelihood'.] An evil character, rascal, rogue. *See* **Budzat (Badzat).** [*OED* & YB; Skipwith, *Magistr. Guide* (Calcutta, 1843), 17.]

Badshah, bashaw *See* **Padshah.**

Bael, bel [17C. H. *bel,* Mar. *bail,* S. *bilva.*] An Indian tree, *Aegle marmelos,* and its aromatic fruit; the Bengal Quince, *Marmelos de Benguala,* a name given to it by Garcia de Orta, who first described the virtues of its fruit in the treatment of dysentery (1563). The tree is sacred to **Siva** and holy to all Hindus. [*OED* & YB.] *See* **Palas,** which is sacred to **Brahma** and to the moon. [Foster's *Letters* (1618; ed. 1896–1900), iii.41.]

Baft(a)(s) [16C. H./P. *bafta,* 'Woven'.] Orig. a kind of coarse calico; later, a silk fabric. [*OED* & YB; Phillips, tr., *Linschoten's Trav. India* (1598), 18.] *See* **Zerbaft** and **Zari.**

Bagh[1] [19C. H. *bagh.*] Garden, orchard, a pleasure garden. Cf. **Wada (Wadi).** [Whitworth, *Anglo-Indian Dict.* (1885).]

Bagh[2] [19C. H. *bagh.*] Tiger, **Leopard.** *See* **Wagh.** [Hawkins, *CIWIE* (1984).]

Bahadur, bahaudur, bahawder [16C. H./Nep. *bahadur,* 'hero'; champion'.] A brave soldier; a great and distinguished personage; often affixed as a title to an officer's name, e.g. Rao *Bahadur, Khan bahadur. Bahadur* and *Sirdar Bahadur* were also the official titles of members of the 2nd & 1st class respectively of the Order of British India established in 1837 for native officers of the army. The title of *Rae Bahadur* was also conferred on Indian civil officers. Hence, ceremoniously, 'Jones Sahib Bahadur', etc. Occurs in personal names as early as 1583–91 (Fitch). Phr. 'To play the Bahadur', to act big. 'In Anglo-Indian colloquial parlance the word denotes a haughty or pompous person with a strong sense of his own importance.' [YB.] *See* Thackeray, *Memoirs of Major Gahagan,* where we find the Maratta traitor humorously entitled Bobachee (Anglo-Indian, 'a cook') *Bahaudar.* [*OED* & YB; Hanway, *Hist. Acct. of the British*

Trade, etc. (1753); Thackeray, *Major Gahagan*, (1841), IV; *Trial of James Fowke*, etc. (1776).]

Bahar [16C. H./Ar. *bahār;* S. *bhāra*, 'a load'; M. *baharam.*] A weight formerly used in India and China varying from 223 lbs. to 625 lbs. in different places. [*OED* & YB; Frederike in Hakluyt (1569), ii. 358; Eden, *tr., Varthema's Travels* (1576).]

Baheera [20C. H. *bahera.*] The handsome Bellaric Myrobalan tree of India, Burma and Sri Lanka, *Terminalia bellerica*, whose seeds give oil, fruit and a dye, and its bark produces a gum. [D.V. Cowen, *Flowering Trees and Shrubs in India* (Bombay, 1965).]

Baheerwuttee(a), bahirwuttea [19C. fr. *bahār* 'out' + *wat* 'to withdraw'. Guj. *bahirwatu.*] A kind of outlawry or **Dacoity** in Gujarat,Rajputana, etc. *Baheerwuttea* (Guj. *bāhirwatiā*) = **Dacoit**). [YB; Tod, *Annals of Rajasthan* (1829).]

Bahini *See* **Vahini.**

Bahuvrihi [19C. S. *bahu*, 'much' + *vrihi* 'rice'.] Lit. 'having much rice'. Lingusitics : A compound word composed of an adjective plus a noun, to form generally a possessive adjective : e.g. *bahu* + *vrihi* = 'possessing much rice'. Generally a compound word which is a different part of speech from its head member, e.g. high potency vitamins, high-rise buildings, low-cost commodities, many-splendoured thing. [*OED;* Monier-Williams, *Elem. Gram. Sansct.* (1846), ix.157.]

Bai [19C. Mar. *bai.* 'A lady'.] Respectful form of address to a woman. Madame. [Whitworth, *Anglo-Indian Dict.* (1885); Hawkins, *CIWIE.*]

Baikree, bherki [19C. Guj. *bekrī;* Mar. *bhekar.*] The (Bombay and Marathi) name for the Barking Deer, *Muntiacus muntjak* (Malay, *muntjak)* [YB]. *See* **Kakar.** [Jerdon, *Mammals of India.* (1874); Forsyth, *Highlands of Central India* (1872), 470.]

Bail [19C. H. *bail*, a bullock.] *Bail-gharry* = a bullock cart. *See* **Bylee** and **Bandy.** [Whitworth, *Anglo-Indian Dict.* (1885).]

Bairam [16C. H./P. *bairām.*] The name of two Muslim festivals: the *Lesser Bairam*, lasting three days following the Ramadan fasting month and the *Greater Bairam*, seventy days later, lasting four days. [*OED;* Hakluyt, *Voy.* (1599), 11.i.196.]

Bairamee, byramma, byrampaut, beirame [17C. H./P. *bairamī.*] Fine cotton stuff, resembling the fine linen 'Holland cloths' exported from India until the 19th century. [YB; Danvers, *Letters* (1609).]

Bajra, bajri, bajru, [17C. H. *bājrā*, 'millet'.] Types of Indian-grown millet, e.g. *Penicillaria spicata, Panicum vulgare* and *Pennisetum typhoides*. [*OED* & YB; *English Factories in India* (1618– 69).]

Bakir-khani [19C. H./P. *bāqir-khānī.*] 'A kind of cake almost exactly resembling pie-crust, said to owe its name to its inventor *Bākir Khān*.' [YB; Riddell, *Ind. Domest. Econ.* (1871), 386.]

Baksheesh, buksheesh [17C. H./P. *bakshīsh*, 'gratuity'.]A 'tip', 'hand out', sometimes 'a bribe'. *Also* **Buckshee,** slang for 'extras', and **Buxee** *(bakshi)*, a military paymaster. [*OED* & YB.] *See* **Bhagvat.** 'Christmas-boxes' = 'Christmas-baksheesh'. [Purchas, *Pilgrimes* (1625), 11. 1340.]

Balachong, balachaun, blachang [17C. Mal. *belachan.*] 'A pungent condiment of prawns, sardines, and other small fish (e.g. *ikan-bilis*) allowed to ferment in a heap and then mashed up with salt.' [YB.] Other recipes contain pepper, salt, garlic, tamarind juice, etc.[*OED.*] Marsden, *History of Sumatra* (1784); Riddell, *Indian Dom. Econ.* (1871); Dampier's *Voyages* (1688), ii.28.] *See* **Ngapi.**

Balasore [17C.] A town and district of Orissa; the site of one of the earliest English **Factories** in the 'Bay', established in 1642. [YB. *See* Dryden, *Aurungzebe* ii.1. 'When in the vale of **Balaser** I fought, and from Bengal the captive monarch brought' (1676); A. Hamilton, *A New Acct. of the E. Indies* (1727).]

Balass [16C. Corr. of P. *Badakshān*, a district near Samarkand,cf. Ar. *balakhsh.*] A kind of spinel-ruby. Mentioned by many English writers in Hakluyt, Purchas and others from the 16th century. [Linschoten in Hakluyt (1598); Hawkins in *Purchas* (1611); Fryer, *New Accounts* (1673).]

Balbacche [19C. H. *bal;* 'infant' + *bacche*, 'Children'.] Little children, infants *See* **Baccha.** [Thackeray, *Vanity Fair* (1848).]

Bal(1)oon [17C. Poss. Mar. *balyānw.* 'A kind of barge.'] 'A rowing vessel formerly used in various parts of the Indies, the basis of which was a large canoe or dug-out.' [YB & *OED;* Fryer, *A New Acct. of E. India etc.* (1672); Cogan, *Pinto's Voy.* (1633), xi.; (1663), 35.]

Balty [17C. H. *bāltī.* Pg. *baldē.*] A bucket . [YB.]

Baluch(i), Belooch(i), Bilooch(i) [17C. H./P. *Balūchī.*] (1) A native of Baluchistan; (2) The Iranian language of the Baluchis; (3) Adj. referring to the Baluchis or Baluchistan (poss. connected with S. *melechcha*, in the sense of a despised foreigner. [Whittington in Purchas (1613), i.485; Sir. T. Roe, *Let.* (27 Nov. 1616).]

Baluchitherium [20C. *See* prec. + Gr. *therion*, 'the East'.] A giant extinct land-mammal whose remains have been found in the upper Oligocene deposits of the Bugti Hills of Baluchistan. [*OED*; C. Foster-Cooper in *Ann. and Mag. Nat. Hist.* (1913), xiii.544.]

Balwar [18C.] The native servant's form of *barber*, poss. shaped by H. *bālwālā*, 'hair-man', by 'striving after meaning'. [YB; Meninski, *Thesaurus* etc. (1780).]

Bamboo [16C. Orig. doubtful, but Dutch *bamboes*; Pg. *mambu* or *bambu*; Malay, *bambu*; Konkani, *mambu*; Kan. *banbu*.] A genus of giant grasses, *Bambusa*, natives of Asia, Africa and America. 'This word, one of the commonest in Anglo-Indian daily use, and thoroughly naturalized in English, is of exceedingly obscure origin.' [YB] Attrib. *bamboo*-cane, -shoot, -reed, -basket, etc. Slang:*bamboo backsheesh*, a blow recieved for begging for money (1850). Also vb. to *bamboo*, to beat with a bamboo, or 'to furnish with *bamboo*, or with *bamboo-laths*'. [*OED* & YB; Fitch in Hakluyt (1599). ii.391; W. Phillips, tr., *Linschoten's Trav. Ind.* (1598; ed. 1864).]

Banchut, barnshoot, beteechoot [18C. H. *bahin chut*, 'sister raper'.] A vile term of abuse in India. Yule & Burnell say of such terms : 'We should hesitate to print [them] if their odious meaning were not obscure "to the general". If it were known to the Englishmen who some-times use the words, we believe that there are few who would not shrink from such brutality. Somewhat similar in character seems the word which Saul in his rage flings at his son (I. Sam. xx.30).' Orwell in *Down and Out in Paris and London* (1933) states that '*barn-shoot* is a vile and unforgettable insult in India ... but a piece of gentle badinage in England.' Dirom, *Narrative of the Campaign in India*, etc. (1793), 147; Partridge, *Dict. of Slang* (1979).]

Bandobust *See* **Bundobust.**

Bandanna, bandanno [18C. H. *bandhnū*.] 'Tie and dye' material. Mode of dyeing in which the cloth is tied in different places to prevent parts of it from receiving the dye. Orig. a kind of yellow or red spotted silk handkerchief. Now the pattern is produced chemically. In S. India, **Pulicat** handkerchiefs. [*OED* & YB; J. Long, *Bengal* (1752); Thackeray, *Newcomes* (1854).]

Bandar[1] [19C. H. *bandar* S. *vānara*, fr. *vana*

'forest'.] The rhesus monkey, *macacus mulatta*. Also *bandar-log* (log = people), Kipling's nation of monkeys (1894). Fig. a body of irresponsible chatterers (1917). [*OED*; Kipling, *Dept. Ditties* (1885).]

Bandar[2] (a seaport, harbour). *See* **Bunder** and **Shahbandar.**

Bandaree [17C. Mar. *Bhandārī*.] Name of a caste or occupation; applied (in Bombay) to low caste people who look after coconut groves, draw **Toddy** and, at one time, formed a local militia. (It has no connection with *bhandari*, 'a treasurer or storekeeper.) [YB, Fryer, *A New Acct. of E. India*, etc. (1672–81), 68.]

Bande Mataram [20C. Beng. *Bande mātaram*, 'Hail Motherland!'] Opening words of a patriotic song by Bankim Chandra Chatterji, first published in his novel *Ananda Math*. Since 1905 it has evoked a strong national response and is widespread as India's national song. [G. Subba Rao, *Indian Words in English* (1954).]

Bandejah [17C. Pg. *bandeja*.] A salver; a tray to put presents on. *See* **Dolly** (*dāli*). [YB; Cocks's *Diary* (1621), ii.143 (Hak.Soc. (1883).]

Band-ghari [20C. H. *bandh* + *ghari*.] A box carriage. [Forster, *A Passage to India* (1942).]

Bandh,[1] **bund** [19C. H./P. *band*, 'a dam'.] In India 'any artificial embankment, a dam, dyke or causeway'. Hence, *to make bunds*; vb. trans. '*to bund*' (1883); '*contour bunding*' = terracing of paddyfields on hill-sides (1939). *See* **Anicut.** [*OED* & YB; Williamson, *Vade-Mecum* (1810), ii. 279.] *See* **Rasta-roko.**

Bandh,[2] **bund** [20C. H. *bandh*.] Stoppage of work or a strike.] *Bandh* is a general strike, and **Hartal** a more limited one.

Bandhnu *See* **Bandanna.**

Bandhu [S. *bandhu*.] A relation, generally of a different **Gotra.** [Hawkins, *CIWIE.*]

Bandicoot, brandy-cute [17C. Corr. of Tel. *pandi kūkka*, 'pig-dog'.] The mole-rat. *Bandicota bengalensis* (small), or *B. indica* (large). Also known as *Mus malabaricus*, or *giganteus*. According to Friar Jordanus (*c.* 1330) these rats were 'as big as foxes and venemous exceedingly'.Fryer (1673) called them 'the strongest huge Rats as big as our Pigs !' (The earlier etym. fr. *pandi* + *kokku*, 'pig-rat', is erroneous as *kokku* is not a Telugu word for rat.) *Also* a genus of insectivorous Australian marsupials (1831). [*OED* & YB; *English Fact. in India* (1618–69.]

Bandicoy, banda [19C. Tam. *vendai-khāi*, 'the unripe fruit of *vendai* (H. *bhendi*)'.] The coll.

name in S. India for the fruit of the *Hibiscus esculentis. See* **Bendy** [1] .   [YB; Forbes, *Or. Memoirs* (1813), 1.32.]

Bando! [19C. H. *bandhna*, to tie; *bandho*. 'Tie it up! Make fast!] London docks colloquialism, shouted by a man on board to another on the dockside as a rope was thrown to him (c. 1886). [YB; Partridge, *Dict. of Slang* etc.]

Bandobust *See* **Bundobast.**

Bandook *See* **Bundook.**

Bandy [18C. Tel. *bandi;* Tam. *vandi*, 'a cart'.] A bullock-cart, or **Buggy,** used in S. India. *See* **Bail**-*gharry*, and **Bylee.** [*OED* & *YB; Madras Courier* (29 Sept. 1761).]

Bang *See* **Bhang.**

Bangalore-torpedo [20C.] Anglo-Indian. An explosive tube for blowing up wire-entanglements. Invented by a Royal Engineers officer stationed in Bangalore. [*OED*; McClintock in *R.E. Jrnl.* (1913), 135.]

Banghy, bangy [1] [17C. H. *bahangī;* Mar. *bhangī;* S. *vihamgika*.] A shoulder-yoke for carrying loads, often with baskets or boxes slung at each end. Hence a parcel post. *See* next. [*OED. See* **Pitarrah.** *English Factories in India* (1618–69); R. Broome, *Lett. Simpkin the Second* (1789), 21.] *See* **Pitarrah.**

Banghy [2] [19C.] *See* prec. A parcel post orig. carried in this way was called *bangy* or *dawk bangy*, 'even when this primitive mode of transport had long become obsolete'. [YB.] Hence: a *bangy*-parcel, and *bangy-wallah* (1810). [*OED*; Sir G. Arthur in *Ind. Admin. of Lord Ellinborough* (ed. 1874), 221; Williamson, *E. India Vade-Mecum* (1810), 1.325.]

Bangladesh(i) [20C. Beng. *Bangla*, 'Bengal' + *desh*, 'country' + 'belonging to'.] A citizen of *Bangladesh*, an independent country in the Ganga–Brahmaputra delta in the North Eastern part of the sub-continent of India. Until 1971 it was E. Pakistan, and before 1947 a part of British India (East Bengal).

Bangle [18C. H. *bangrī*.] Orig. a circlet of coloured glass worn on the wrist by Indian women. Applied also to any bracelet or anklet in silver or gold or other ornamental metals. Hence *bangled* (1864). [*OED* & *YB; Archaeol.* (1787), viii.256.(D).]

Bangun (Beng. *baingan*). *See* **Brinjal.**

Bangur [19C. H. *bāngar*.] The higher parts of the plain on which the towns stand in N. India, as opposed to khādir *(khādar)*, the lower alluvium near the great Indian rivers. [YB; Medlicot & Blanford, *Man. of the Geology of India* (1879), i.404.]

Bania, bunnia, banyan, etc. [16C. Pg. *banian;* Ar. *banyan;* Guj. *vaniyo* (pl. *vaniyam*); 'man of the trading caste'; S. *vānij*, 'merchant'.] (1) Hindu trader (esp. formerly one settled in an Arabian port) whose caste enjoined a purely vegetarian diet. Hence a *Banian-day*, nautical coll. for a meatless day (1609); a *Banian hospital* (1813), for the care and cure of sick animals. (*See* **Pinjrapole**). A *Banian-fight*, in which the 'assailants' fail to come to blows (1690); a *Banian-party*, a vegetarian picnic ashore for sailors from a British naval vessel; the *Banyan language* = Gujarati (1677). [Hakluyt, *Voy.* (1599), 11.i.310.] (2) Often applied in Western India to persons of the Hindu faith generally. [Sir T. Herbert, *Trav.* (1634), 37.] (3) 'In Calcutta specifically applied to the native brokers attached to houses of business, or to persons in the employment of private persons doing analogous duties. (Now usually called **Sircars.**) [YB.] Also, in Bengal, *bunya* appears in Anglo-Indian usage to indicate a grain-dealer. [A. Lovell, *Thevenot's Trav.* (1687), iii. 1. xxxii.55.] (4) An undershirt, orig. of muslin, now of cotton, wool, or silk worn orig. by Banias and other Hindus, but later by Anglo-Indians in their domestic surroundings. [Sir W. Langhorne's *Standing Order*, in Wheeler (1672; 1878), ii. 426; *Harl. Misc.* (1725), viii. 297.] (5) The application of the word, **Banyan**, was first made by Europeans to a specific tree of the species near Gombroom on the Persian Gulf, under which the *Banian* traders used to consort and had erected a Hindu temple (1634). *See* **Banyan Tree** [*OED* & *YB*.] and **Vaisya.**

Banjar [20C. H. *banjar*.] Waste or fallow land. [Hawkins, *CIWIE*.]

Banjara *See* **Brinjarry.**

Bankshall, bank-soll [17C. Prob. Beng. *bankasālā*, 'hall of trade'. Perh. from S. *bhāndasālā*, 'store house, or magazine'. Cf Mal. *bangsal*, 'warehouse or shed'.] A word once common throughout India and the Far East. In India, it has had a number of meanings : a warehouse, the office of a Harbour Master (**Shahbandar**) or Port Authority, and in Sea Hindustani, in the forms *bansar* and *bangsal* for a store-room. [*OED* & *YB;* Roebuck (1811); *English Fact. in India*, 1618–69.]

Bansri [20C. H. *bānsri*.] 'A reed-flute.' [Hawkins, *CIWIE*.]

Banyan-(tree) [17C.] *See* **Banian.** The Indian fig-tree, *Ficus indica, -religiosa* or *-bengalensis*, whose branches drop aerial roots which, reaching the ground, take root and grow into separate trunks, thus becoming a veritable forest of tees joined to the parent tree and covering much ground. One famous tree was said to have a circumference of 2,000 feet, and to be able to shelter 20,000 people! The Banyan is venerated by Hindus and special prayers are offered to it on *Vat Savitri* day. (Some Indian names are : H. *bargat;* Mar. *war;* Sinh. *nuga*). Frequently mentioned in English literature though not always by name [e.g. Ben Johnson's *Neptune's Triumph* (1642); Milton's *Paradise Lost* (1667); Tickell's *Epistle from a Lady in England to a Lady in Avignon* (1717); Southey's *Curse of Kehama* (1810); Sir T. Herbert, *Trav.* ii. (1634; 1638); *OED* & YB.]

Baobab [17C.] Prob. some dialect of Central Africa. A tree long naturalized in India and Sri Lanka, *Andansonia digitata*, the fibres and bark of which are used for ropes and cloth. Orig. an Ethiopian tree, & considered by Humboldt to be 'the oldest organic monument on our planet'. *See* **Bottle-Tree**. [*OED;* Prosper Alpinus, *Hist. Nat. Aegypti* (1592); Parkinson, *Theatrum botanicum*, etc. (1632).]

Baoli, bowly, bowry [19C. H./Guj. *bāoli*.] A well with steps leading to the water, generally with landings where travellers may rest in the shade, and sometimes with munificent structures above ground. [YB; Forbes, *Or. Memoirs* (1813), ii.102.]

Bap-re! [18C. H. *bap,* 'father'.] Interj. 'O Father!' 'Gosh!' *See* **Bobbery-Bob**. [YB; Joseph Price, *2nd Letter to Burke,* in *Tracts* (1783), vol. ii.]

Barasinha, barasingha [19C. H. *bāra,* 'twelve' + *singā,* 'horn'.] The East Indian deer *Cervus Wallichii,* which has approx. twelve tines. Bengal *shikaris* applied this name also to the **swamp deer**, *Cervus duvauceli* [*OED* & YB; Blanford, *The Fauna of British Indian Mammalia* (1888–91; *Proc. Zool. Soc.,* 1862), ix.136.]

Barat¹ [19C. H. *barat*.] Bridegroom's marriage procession. [Whitworth, *Anglo-Indian Dict.* (1885).]

Barat² [19C. H. *barat*.] A promissory note. [Lady Sale, *The First Afghan War* (1841–2).]

Barat³ [19C. H. *barat.*] The leather rope used for drawing up a bucket from a well. [Whitworth, *Anglo-Indian Dict.* (1885).]

Barber's Bridge [19C.] A word of curious origin. The bridge, in Madras, was built by an engineer called Hamilton. This name was turned into *Ambuton* and, in due course, identified with

Tamil *ambattan,* 'barber'. Thereafter, it became *Barber's Bridge.* [YB; Le Fanu, *Manual of the Salem District* (1883).]

Barbiers [17C.] An obsolete term, though formerly very common in India and the Far East, for **Beri-Beri**. [*OED* & YB; Fryer, *New Account* (1672–81), 68.]

Barfi [20C. H. *barfi.*] A sweetmeat made of milk and sugar. [Hawkins, *CIWIE.*]

Bargany, bragany [16C. H. *barakani,* 'twelve kanis'.] The name of a small silver coin used among the Portuguese in Goa, Daman and Diu. [YB; Barret in Hakluyt (1584), ii.411.]

Bargeer [19C. H./P. *bargīr.*] Lit. 'A load-taker.', or 'a baggage-horse'. 'A trooper of irregular cavalry who was not the owner of his troophorse and arms (as was the normal practice).' [YB.] *See* **Silladar**. [Tod, *Annals of Rajasthan* etc. (1829).]

Barisal [19C. (After a town now in **Bangladesh**.)] 'Barisal-guns are booming-sounds heard in Barisal and certain other regions near water.' [*OED; Nature* (2 Jan. 1896), 197.]

Barking-Deer [19C.] Popular Anglo-Indian name for the Indian *muntjak, muntiacus muntjac,* alias *Ribfaced-Deer.* 'Its common name is from its call, which is a kind of short bark, like that of a fox but louder.' *See* **Baikree** and **Kakar**. [YB & *OED*; Jerdon, *The Mammals of India* (1875); Cooper, *Mishmee Hills* (1873), 177.]

Barnshoot *See* **Banchut**.

Barsat [19C. H. *barsāt.*] 'The Rains.' *See* next.

Barsati,¹ bursat, bursautee [19C. H. *barsati.*] 'Disease to which horses are liable in *The Rains;* pustular eruptions breaking out on head and fore parts of body.' [YB; *Or. Sport Mag.* reprint (1828; 1873), i.125; Mrs Meer Hassan Ali, *Observations on the Mussulmauns of India,* (1832), ii.27.]

Barsati,² barsautee [19C. H. *barsātī.*] (a) A raincoat. *See* **Brandy-Coortee**; (b) Later, a penthouse, or rain-shelter usually at the top of the house. [YB; *Pioneer Mail* (8 July 1880) pub. at Allahabad.]

Barsi *See* **Varsi**.

Basha [20C. Assam. *basha*.] A thatched bamboo hut. [*OED; Blackwood's Mag* (Feb. 1921), 257/1, 'N.Shute', *Chequer Board* (1947).]

Bashaw [16C. Corr. of *Padishah = Pasha;* Turkish, *Bāshā.*] Lord or master. *See* **Badshah**, and **Padishah**. [*OED* & YB; Marlowe, *Tamburlane the Great* (1584), I. iii. 1; Sir Thomas More, *A Dialoge of Comforts against Tribulation* (1583).]

Basil *See* **Tulsi**.

Basin [19C. H. *besan.*] 'Pease-meal; generally made of **Gram**, and used sometimes mixed with ground orange-peel or other aromatic substances to cleanse the hair, or for other *toilette* purposes.' [YB.] *See* **Calavance, Cajan** and **Gram**. [Mrs Meer Hassan Ali, *Observations* (1832), i.328.]

Bassan [19C. H. *bāsan* Pg. *bacia.*] A dinner-plate. [YB; *Punjab Notes and Queries* (1883), ii.117.]

Basti *See* **Busti**.

Bat [19C. H. *bāt*, 'speech'.] Anglo-Indian, coll. 'Foreign speech', or the local vernacular. 'To sling or *bolo* the *bat*' = 'to speak the foreign (local) language. Milit. slang. [*OED*; Partridge, *Dict. of Slang*, etc. (1979); Kipling, 'Three Musketeers' in *Plain Tales* (1887).]

Batai [19C. H. *batai.*] The division of the crop, after harvesting the grain, between government and the owner, cf. **Kancut**. [Tod, *Annals of Rajasthan* (1829).]

Batara, petara [19C. S. *bhattara*, 'lord'.] A term applied to old Javanese deities, and among Philippine Christians = God. *Petara* = a Sea Dyak god. [YB; Skeat, *Malay Magic* (1900), 86 seqq.]

Batel (o), botella [17C. Pg. *batell* (O. Fr. *batel* fr. *baleau*).] A sort of boat used in Western India, Sind and Bengal. *See* **Patello**. (Also in Med. Eng. Brunne, *Chron.* 241. 1330.) [*OED* & YB; Hedges, *Diary* (1681–8).]

Batta¹ [17C. Indo-Pg. *bata*; H. *bhata*; Kan. *bhatta*, 'rice'. (*Also* among Anglo-Indians, *batty*.)] An extra allowance made to military and civil service personnel in the field or on tours of duty; a travelling allowance. It became a *permanent* addition to officers' pay in India; 'and constituted the chief part of the excess of Indian over English military emoluments'. [YB & *OED*; *Eng. Fact. in India.*]

Batta² [17C. H. *batta*: Beng. *bāttā.*] 'Agio' or difference in exchange; discount on coins not current, or of short weight.' [YB & *OED*; *Ft. St. George Consultations* (10 Feb. 1680).]

Battman [17C. H./Turk. *bātmān.*] A Turkish weight used as the equivalent of the Indian **Maund**. In 'The Journals of Captaine Keeling and that of Captaine Hawkins' [Purchas, *Pilgrimes* (1625); Foster, *Early Travels in India* (1921), 102.]

Batty [Kan. *bhatta*; Mar. *bhāt.*] 'Rice in the husk.' (Cf. Malay. *padi*); maintenance allowance. *See* **Paddy** and **Batta**.¹ [Linschoten in Hakluyt (1598), i. 246.] *See* **Nelly**.

Bawarchee, *See* **Bobberjee**.

Bawustye [19C. Anglo-Indian.] Corr. of *bobstay*, in Lascar dialect. [YB; Roebuck, *Naval Dict.* (1811).]

Bay [17C. Anglo-Indian.] 'In the language of the old Company and its servants in the 17th C., the *Bay* meant the Bay of Bengal and their factories in that quarter.' [YB; Hedges, *Diary* 1681–8.]

Baya [18C. H. *baiā.*] The **Weaver-bird**, *Ploceus Philippinus*, that feeds on insects and grain-crops, and builds an intricately woven hanging nest. [YB; *Asiat. Researches* (1790), ii.110.]

Bayadere, balliadera [16C. Fr. *bayadère*; Pg. *bailadeira*, female dancer.] (1) Hindu dancing-girl : 'The Southern Bayadere, who differ considerably from the *nach* girls of Northern India, being all in the service of different temples, for which they are purchased young.' (Bishop Heber, *Narrative of a Journey*, etc. 1844. [*OED* & YB; Phillips, tr., *Linschoten's Trav.* (1598), 74.] *See* **Nautch, Devadasi** and **Dancing-Girl**. (2) Fabric with horizontal stripes. Also attrib., e.g., *Bayadere*-stripes, -skirts, - shoes. [*OED*; *Illustr. London News* (27 Dec. 1856), 653/ii.]

Bayparee, beoparry [19C. H. *bepārī*; S. *vyāpārin.*] A petty trader or dealer. *See* **Mahajun**. [YB; Hoey, *Monograph on Trade*, etc. (1880).]

Bazaar, bazar [II./P. *bazar*, 'market' (cf. Malay, *pasar*).] (1) An oriental market = place; a permanent market-place or a street of stalls and shops where all kinds of merchandise are exhibited for sale, generally in well-defined sections for each kind. [*OED* & YB; Hakluyt, *Voy.* (1599), 11.1.214.] (2) A shopping centre or area in a modern Indian city or town. (3) A fancy fair in England in imitation of the Eastern bazaar. [*OED*; *Soho Bazaar* (1816).] (4) A shop or arcade displaying fancy goods. [Southey, *Lett. from England* (1807), 1.vii.82; *OED.*]

Bear-tree *See* **Ber**.

Bearer¹ [18C. Anglo–Indian.] In India, a headman of a set of a **palanquin** carriers, or often any one of them. [*OED* & YB.] [Grose, *Voy. to the E. Indies*, etc. (1766).]

Bearer² [18C. Anglo–Indian.] A domestic servant, a valet; also a waiter in more recent times. [*OED* & YB.] *See* **Sirdar-Bearer, Boy** and **Kuhar**. [*India Gazette* (2 Sept. 1782).]

Beastie *See* **Bheestie**.

Beebee *See* **Bibi**.

Beckti *See* **Bhikti**.

Beechman, meechilman [19C.] Sea-Hind. for 'midshipman'. [YB; Roebuck, *Naval Dict.* (1811).]

Beegah *See* **Bigha.**

Beejoo [19C. H. *bijū.*] The Indian badger. *Mellivora indica.* 'Often called in N. India the *Grave-Digger (gorkhodo),* from a belief in its bad practices, probably unjust.' [YB; Blanford, *The Fauna of British India: Mammalia* (1888–91).]

Begar, bigarry [17C. H./P. *begār*(i). 'Forced labour(er)', fr. *be,* 'without' + *gār* (for *kār*); 'One who works'.] 'A person pressed to carry a load or do other work really or professed for public service. In some provinces *begār* is the forced labour, and *begāri* the pressed man; whilst in Karnataka *begāri* is the performance of the lowest village offices without money payment but with remuneration in grain or land' [Wilson]. Wellington, declared 'The *bygarry* system is not bearable; it must be abolished entirely'. [YB; *Despatches* (1800); Fryer, *New Acct. of E. India* (1672–81); Kipling, *Kim* (1901).]

Begti¹ [Anglo-Indian, fr. '*bed-tea*'.] In servants' parlance, early-morning tea in bed. *See* **Chota Hazri** and **Butler-English.**

Begti,² beckti *See* **Bhikti** and **Cock-up.**

Begum, beegum, begaum [17C. H./P. *begam;* Turk. *bigim,* 'princess'.] A Muslim Indian queen, lady or mistress of high rank. The honorific title of a married Muslim woman in Pakistan. (Fem. of Turk. *big,* of which the Osmanli form is *beg,* 'prince'.) [*OED* & YB; Foster, *Letters* (1614), ii.282; Sir T. Herbert, *Travels* (1634), 99.]

Behdin [17C. P. *behdin.*] A minor **Parsi** temple official or priest. *See* **Dastur, Mobed** and **Herbed.** [Henry Lord, *The Religion of the Persees* (1630).]

Beiramee *See* **Bairami.**

Benami [18C. H./P. *be-nāmī,* 'anonymous', or 'second name'.] A *benami* transaction is one in which the main party remains anonymous, his place being taken by a substitute; a proxy. Such transactions may be fraudulent or nearly but not necessarily so. Also known as *farzi.* Cf. **Budli.** [YB; Bruce, in *Moore's Reports of Cases on Appeal,* etc. (1854), vi. 72, ref. Justice Hyde's *Notes* (1778).]

Bendara, bintara [16C. Mal. *běndahāra,* 'Lord'; S. *bhāndārin,* 'a steward, treasurer'.] A term used in Malaysia and Indonesia for a high minister of state. [YB; Cogan's *Pinto,* E. tr. by Gent (1653); Litchfield, tr. Castaneda, *Dis-*

coverie Conquest of the E. Indies (1582).]

Bendy,¹ bhindi [19C. H. *bhendī;* Mar. *bhendā.*] The plant and vegetable, *okra,* or Ladies Fingers, *Hibiscus (or Abelmoschus) esculentus.* [*OED.*] *See* **Bandicoy.** [Maria Graham, *Jrnl. Resid. India* (1812), 24.]

Bendy,² bhendi-tree [19C. H. *bhendī.*] A tree bearing yellow flowers that turn purple. *Thespesia populnea,* or *acutiloba,* otherwise known as the *Umbrella Tree, Portia Tree,* and *Indian Tulip Tree.* From the inner bark is obtained a tough fibre for cordage; the bark and wood contain tannin and yield a red dye. From the flowers and fruit a yellow dye is obtained and the fruit juice is good for scabies. Migraines are relieved by applying crushed capsules to the forehead, and a tonic is concocted from the roots. [Cowen, *Flowering Trees and Shrubs in India* (1965); *OED* & YB. *See* **Portia.** [Sir G. Birdwood, in YB,85; Watt, *Econ. Dict.* (1889-93), vi. pt. iv. 45' seq.; Caunter, *Orient. Ann.* (1834), v. 53]

Bengal¹ [16C.] Name of an Indian state, now partly in Bangladesh (and from 1947 until 1972, in East Pakistan). In Marco Polo (1298) as *Bangala;* in Vasco da Gama (1490) as *Bemgala;* in Ovington (1690) as *Bengāla;* in the 11C. it was *Vangalam* in an inscription in the great Tanjore **Pagoda.** [*OED* & YB; Eden, tr.,Varthema, *Travels* (1576).]

Bengal² [17C.] Applied to different kinds of **Piece-goods** exported from and originating in Bengal from the 17C. Also attrib., e.g. (1) *Bengal Light*: a kind of firework producing a steady blue light, used for signals (1818); (2) *Bengal quince*: the fruit of the *Aegle Marmelos,* belonging to the orange family (1866); (3) *Bengal-root*: the root of the yellow **Zedoary** (1866); (4) *Bengal Silk* (1711); (5) *Bengal Stripes;* Striped **Ginghams** orig. fr. Bengal, afterwards from Paisley (1875); (6) *Bengal-tiger*: the tiger proper, *Panthera tigris,* so called from its (former) abundance in lower Bengal; (7) *Bengal-fire, -flash* = Bengal-light (1941) (8) *Bengal-isinglass*: **AgarAgar** (1863); (9) *Bengal-gram*: a kind of pulse or chick-pea used for horse-fodder, *Cicer arietinum* (H. *chanā*) (1776). [*OED* & YB; Pollexfen, *A Discourse of Trade Coyn, and Paper Credit* (1697); Davenant, *An Essay on the E. India Trade* (1696), 31.]

Bengala [18C.] A sort of cane or swagger-stick carried by Portuguese sergeants etc. in India. [*See* Bluteau, *Vocabulario* (1712-21); YB.]

Bengalese (adj. & sb) [18C.] **Bengali.** [Halhed.

Gram. Bengal Lang. (1778); *OED.*]

Bengali (adj. & sb) [17C.] A native of Bengal; the **Aryan** language of Bengal. *See* **Babu**. [YB & *OED*; Purchas, *Pilgr.* (1613), 1.v.v.404.] Anglo-Indians often applied this term to officers from N. Indian provinces other than Bengal. [YB; Hedges, *Diary* (1699).]

Bengaline [19C. Fr. *bengaline.*] A fabric similar to Bengal piece-goods, of silk and worsted. [*OED; Pall Mall Gaz.* (20 Sept. 1884), 4/10.]

Benighted, The [19C.] 'An epithet applied by the denizens of the other Presidencies, in facetious disparagement of Madras.' [YB]. *See* **Mull, Ducks** and **Qui-hi**. (*Note*: under **Mull**, YB applies the word 'Benighted', to Bombay!) [*Fragment of Sir John Maundevile*, ed. Halliwell (1860).]

Ber, bair, bher, bear (tree) [17C. H. *ber;* Mar. *bora;* Mal. *bĕdara*, S. *badara* and *vadara.*] The edible *Chinese Date* or *Indian Jujube, Zizyphus jujuba,* with tiny pale-green flowers and a juicy plum-like fruit. 'One of the most diffused trees in India, and is found wild from the Punjab to Burma, in all of which regions it is probably native.' [YB & *OED*; Danvers, *Letters* (1618-90 ; ed. 1896-1900), i. 30.]

Beriberi, berry-berry [18C. Sinh. *beri,* 'weakness': '*beri-beri*', 'intense weakness'.] An acute nutritional disease, generally with dropsical symptons and paralytic weakness and numbness of the legs; prevalent in India, S.E. Asia and other tropical regions. **Barbiers** (1673) seems to be an earlier spelling. [Fryer, *A New Account of East India and Persia* (1672-81); *OED* & YB; tr. Nieuhoff, *Voy.* (1703). in A. and J. Churchill, *Voy.* (1704).]

Beryl [14C. Poss. S. *vaidūrya;* Mal. *baiduri;* (Gr. *berillos*).] A transparent precious stone of a pale-green colour. 'Beryll is a stone of Ynde lyke in grene colour to Smaragde.' [Trevisa, *Bartholomeus De Proprietatibus Rerum* (1398), xvi. xx.] [*OED* & YB; Holland, *The Historie of the World* etc. (1601); *Land of Cokayne* (c. 1395), 92.]

Beteela, beatelle, etc. [16C. Poss. Pg. *beatilha,* 'a veil'.] A certain kind of muslin or chintz made at Masulipatam in the 17th and 18th centuries, and known as *Organdi*. [*OED* & YB; Phillips, tr., Linschoten's *Trav. Ind.* (1598), 28.]

Betel, beetle, bethel, etc. [16C. Pg. *betel,* M. *vettiila;* Tam. *vetrilei;* cf. S. *viti,* 'betel'.] The leaf of the plant, *Piper betel* or *Chavica betel,* which is wrapped round the parings of Areca-nut, lime, tobacco, cloves etc. etc. and chewed as a masticatory. The whole ensemble is **Pān-**

supāri. In former times the betel-leaf was a monopoly of the East India Company. [*OED* & YB; Stanford *Dict.* (1855; 1892); Eden, *Treat, New Ind.* (1553), 21.; Phillips, tr., Linschoten's *Trav. Ind.* (1598); Lloyd, *Treas. Health* (1585), Niij.] *See* **Tembool**.

Betel-nut [17C.] The nut or fruit of the **Areca** palm, misnamed (by Anglo-Indians) because it is chewed with the betel-leaf. Also called *Betel-nut Palm (Areca catechu),* from which the 'betel-nut' or areca nut is obtained (1861). [*OED*; Fryer, *New Acct. E. Ind.* (1673), 40.]

Bewauris [19C. H./P. *be-wāris.*] Unclaimed, without heir or owner. [YB; Wilson, *Glossary* (1855).]

Bhabar,¹ bhabur, baber [19C. H. *bābar, bhābar.*] Belt of alluvial soil between the **Terai** and the talus of the Himalayas. [*London Morning Paper,* 26 May 1877; YB.]

Bhabar² [H. *bhabar*]. (1) A valuable Indian fibre grass, *Ischaemum augustifolium,* used for making mats, rope and paper; called also *baib*-grass. [Webster, *Third New Intern. Dict.* (1976).] (2) A sedge, *Eriophorum comosum,* found with *bhabar* and used for the same purposes. [Webster, *Third New Intern. Dict.* (1976).]

Bhadra-lok, -log [19C. Beng./S. *bhadra* 'respectable' + *lok,* 'people'.] Prosperous upper caste people; espec. in Bengal; the aristocratic rentier class and well-to-do **Babus**. [Whitworth, *Anglo-Indian Dict.* (1885); Moorhouse, *India Britannica;* J. McGurie, *The Making of a Colonial Mind* (1984); Edward Thompson, *An Indian Day* (1927).]

Bhādon, Bhādrapad [19C. H. *bhādō,* S. *bhādra pada,* fr. *bhādra,* 'fortunate' + *pada,* 'step foot', 'having fortunate steps or feet'.] A month of the Hindu year (Aug-Sept.) [Wilson, *Glossary* (1855).]

Bhagat [19C. H. *bhagat;* S. *bhakta,* 'devoted to'.] A Hindu saint or religious devotee. [Wilson, *Glossary,* 1855.]

Bhagvadgita [18C. S. *Bhagavadgītā.*] 'The Lord's Song', celebrated Sanskrit philosophical poem in the **Mahabharata**. Prob. written in the 1st or 2nd century AD. [Wilkins, *The Bhagvat-Geeta* (tr. 1785).]

Bhagavat [19C. S. *bhaga* + *vat.* lit. 'possessing good fortune'. *S. bhaga* 'good fortune (akin to S. *bhajati* 'he grants'). Cf. **Baksheesh**.] Blessed One; Lord; used chiefly as adj. attached to names of Hindu and Buddhist deities; a name of God commonly used by **Vaishnavas**. [Whitworth, *Anglo-Indian Dict.* (1885).]

Bhagvata [19C. S. *bhāgavata*, 'relating to the Blessed One'.] A devotee of a deity, esp. Vishnu. Also *Bhāgvata-Purāna*, 'ancient stories of the Lord; Hindu sacred literature known as the *Puranas*. See **Bhakta**. [Max Mueller, *The Six Systems of Indian Philosophy* (1919 reprint).]

Bhagvathar [19C. *See* prec. Tam/Kan. *bhāgvathar*. A singer-preacher. Also a S. Indian caste. [Hawkins, *CIWIE*.]

Bhagwan [19C. H. *bhagwan*; S. *bhagavan*, fr. bhaj, 'to adore'.] God. An epithet of Vishnu and Shiva. [Whitworth, *Anglo-Indian Dict.* (1885).]

Bhai [19C. H. *bhāi*; S. *bhratr*, 'brother'.] Now friend as well as brother; commonly used as an expression of national as well as personal friendship, e.g. India-China *bhai-bhai*. [Wilson, *Glossary* (1855).] *Also*, 'the ordinary title of Sikhs who have acquired a name for holiness.' [Whitworth, *Anglo-Indian Dict.* (1885).]

Bhai-band [19C. H. *bhāi* + *band*, 'bond'.] Blood brother, intimate friend. P. *berādarī*; 'brotherhood'; an exogamous unit within the endogamous caste group (*Enc. Brit.*) *See* **Biradari**. [Wilson, *Glossary* (1855).]

Bhajan(a) [20C. S. *bhajjan*.] Hinduism: A devotional hymn. [*OED*; Fox Strangways, *Music of Hindostan* (1914), xi. 286.]

Bhajia [19C. Guj. *bhajia*.] *See* **Pakora** [Hawkins, *CIWIE*.]

Bhakta [19C. S. *bhakta*, 'One who is a religious devotee; a worshipper'.] Lit. 'Belonging to, devoted to'. Cf. **Batta** and **Bhagavata** [*OED*; H. H. Wilson, in *Asiatic Res.* (1828), xvi. 12.]

Bhakti [19C. S. *bhakti*, lit : 'portion or share'. fr. *bhajati*, 'he allots or grants'.] Hinduism: religious devotion. Adj. *bhaktic*. In Bhakti sects the word is used for sexual love [Zaehner, *Hinduism* (1962)].[*OED*; H. H. Wilson, in *Jrnl. Asiatic Soc.* (Bengal) (1832), 220; E.M. Forster, *Hill of Devi* (1953), 117.] *See* **Thumri**.

Bhakti-marga [19C. S. *bhaktimārga*, fr. *bhakti* + *mārga*, 'path'.] Hinduism:The way to salvation by devotion to a deity as contrasted with *karmamarga*, the path of duty, and *jnana marga*, the path of knowledge. [*OED*.] *See* next. [Whitworth, *Anglo-Indian Dict.* (1885); *Times Lit. Suppl.*, 18 Jan. 57/4. (1936); A. Huxley, *Ends & Means* (1937), xii. 234.]

Bhakti-yoga [S. *bhakti* + *yoga*.] Devotional **Yoga**. [Webster, *Third New Intern. Dict.* (1976).]

B(h)alu [19C. H. *bhālū*; S. *bhallūka*, fr. *balla*, 'a bear'.] Spec. the Sloth-bear of India and Sri Lanka, *Melursus labiatus*. [Kipling, *Jungle Books* (1894-6).]

Bhandar [19C. H. *bhandar*; S. bhanda, 'goods'.] Store, shop. Also Guj. *bhandāri*, 'treasurer'. *See* **Bendara**. [Wilson, *Glossary* (1855).]

Bhang, bang [16C. H. *bhāng*; S. *bhangā*, hemp (cf. *bang*, *benj*, and Pg. *bangue*).] Indian hemp *Cannabis sativa* or *indica*, whose dried leaves, seeds and small stalks are smoked, chewed or drunk in an infusion as a narcotic or hallucinogenic drug. Phr. '*Banged* up to the eye-balls'. As a sweetmeat = **Majun**. [*OED* & YB.] *See* **Charas, Ganja, Subji, Hashish**. [Phillips, *Linschoten's Trav. Ind.* (1598), 19.1.]

Bhangy, bungy [19C. *See* prec. + *ī*. Lit:One addicted to **Bhang**.] An Indian menial, sweeper or scavenger; the caste was generally addicted to drink and drugs; an **Untouchable**, *See*: **Harijan, Pariah, Schedule Caste, Outcaste**. [YB; *Trans. Lit. Soc. Bombay* (1823), iii. 374.]

Bhar [19C. Tribal name.] (A member of) a caste of farm labourers of the Kol tribe in Central India. Poss. origin of **Bharata**, the old name of India or native of India. [Wilson, *Glossary* (1855).]

Bharal, burhel, burrell, etc. [19C. H. *bharal*.] The wild, blue sheep of Tibet and the Himalayas, *Pseudois nayaur*. [*OED*; Blanford, *The Fauna of British India: Mammalia* (1888-91); *Proc. Zoo. Soc.* (1838). 79.]

Bharat [20C. S. *bhārate*, India. Also Malay for 'West'. Hence: *bhāratī*, a citizen of India, or relating to India, officially since 1950. *See* **Bhar** and next.

Bharata [19C. S. *bhārata*, 'of or native to India'.] Descending from Bharata, a legendary King of India, whose descendants are the principal characters in the **Mahabharata**. [Wilson, *Glossary* (1855).]

Bharata-natya(m) [20C. S. *bhārata nātya*, lit. 'Bharata's dancing, fr. *Bhārata*, reputed to be the author of the *Natyashāstra*, a manual of dramatic art.] A traditional S. Indian dance performed formerly only by **Devadasis** in Hindu temples. *See* **Kathak, Manipuri, Cuttack** and **Kathakali**. [Singha and Massey, *Indian Dances* (1967), 218.]

Bharati [19C. S. *bhārati*, fem. of **Bhārata** (adj.)] Of or relating to India. *See* **Indian**. [Wilson, *Glossary* (1855).]

Bharat Mata [20C. S. *bharat* + *māia*, 'mother'.] Mother India. [Katherine Mayo, *Mother India* (1927).]

Bharti [19C. H. *bharti.*] Barnyard-grass or Millet, *Echinocloa crysgalli*. A frequent weed in cultivated land in India, occas. used for hay or grazing. [Webster, *Third New Intern. Dict.* (1976).]

Bhat [17C. H. *bhāt*; S. *bhatta.*] A caste of bards, heralds and genealogists who guaranteed the safety against attack and robbery of those travellers they contracted to accompany. [YB; Forbes, *Or. Mem.* (1813), ii.89; Pietro Della Valle, *Voyages.* (E. tr. Havers (1664).] *See* **Traga**.

Bheel [19C. Beng. *bhīl.*] A marsh or lagoon in Bengal. = **Jheel.** [YB; Grant, *Rural Life in Bengal* (1860), 35.]

Bhil, Bheel [19C. H. *Bhīl*; S. *Bhilla.*] (A member of 'a central Indian people, inhabiting the hills and forests of the Vindya, Malwa and of the N. Western Deccan, and believed to have been the aborigines of Rajputana'. [YB & *OED*; Forbes, *Or. Mem.* (1813), iii.]

Bheel(i), Bhil(i) [19C. H. *Bhīlī*, fr. *Bhīl.*] The **Indic** language of the **Bhil** people. [Webster, *Third New Intern. Dict.* (1976).]

Bheestie, beastie, bhis(h)ti, bheesty [17C. H. *bhīstī*; P. *bihishtī*, fr. *bihisht* 'paradise'.] An Indian water-carrier who carried his burden of water in a **Mussuck**. This lowly Indian menial was thus endowed after the Indian fashion with the elevated title of 'Man of Paradise' and (jocularly) by Anglo-Indians Hobson-Jobsonized into 'a beastie'. 'It is one of the fine titles which Indian servants rejoice to bestow on one another, such as **Mehtar** and **Khalifa'** [*OED*]. *See* **Abdar**. [Tr. Bernier, *Travels* (1684); Fergusson, *Dict. of the Hindostan Language* (1773).] *See* **Puckauly, Tomicatchy**.

Bhikku [19C. Pali. *bhikku*, S. *bhikshū.*] A Buddhist monk or religious mendicant; a bonze. [*OED*; *Jrnl. R. Asiatic Soc.* (Ceylon Branch) (1846).]

Bhikshu [19C. S. *bhikshū*; 'a beggar'.] A Hindu or Buddhist mendicant or religious devotee. *See* **Vinaya**. [*OED*; W. Ward, *Acc. Hindoos,* (1811), II. vi. 400.]

Bhikti [19C.] The Bengali name for the fish, *Lates (calcarifer). See* **Begti (Beckti)** and **Cock-up**. [YB.]

Bhil-a-wan nut [18C. Prob. fr. *Bilawan, Bhilwara*, a district in Central India.] The Indian Marking-Nut tree, *Semecarpus anacardium*. The nut yields a blackish resinous juice used for marking cotton cloth. [*OED*; Ellis in *Phil. Trans* (1756), XLIX. 873.]

Bhojpatra [19C. H. *bhoj*; 'birch' + *patra*, 'a leaf'.] Manuscript written on birch leaf or bark. *See*

Kajang² and **Olah**. [Whitworth, *Anglo-Indian Dict.* (1885).]

Bhojpuri [19C. H. *Bhojpurī*, fr. *Bhojpur*, a village in Bihar.] A dialect of *Bihari* spoken in W. Bihar and E. Uttar Pradesh. [Whitworth, *Anglo-Indian Dict.* (1885).]

Bhokra, bekra [19C. Guj. *bhokra.*] The Indian Four Horned Antelope, *Tetracerus quadei cornis* (the buck has two pairs of horns). Also called *dodra*. [Webster, *Third New Intern. Dict.* (1976).]

Bhonsla, Bhonsle, Bhounsla [17C.] An ancient Maratha caste to which Shivaji and his ancestors and descendants belonged. The family name also of the rulers of the Maratha dynasty of Berar State, not of Shivaji's family. [YB; Jadunath Sarkar, *Shivaji and his Times* (1973); Fryer, *New Acct. of E. India etc.* (1672-81), 171.]

Bhoodan [20C. H. *bhu(mi)* 'earth', 'land' + *dan*, 'gift'.] An Indian social movement initiated by Vinoba Bhave in 1951, designed to encourage landowners to donate land to landless labourers. *See* **Gramdan**. [Koestler, *Lotus and Robot* (1960); *OED*; *Times*, 15 April 1953.]

Bhoosa [19C. H. *bhūs(ā).*] Cattle food from husks and straw, 'beaten up into chaff by the feet of oxen on the threshing floor'. [YB & *OED*; Tod, *Annals of Rajasthan* (1829), 1.700.]

Bhora *See* **Bora**.

Bhotan (Bhutan) pine [19C.] A very resinous pine, *Pinus excelsa*, native to the Himalayas, grown for timber and turpentine. [Webster, *Third New Intern. Dict.* (1976).]

Bhotia, Bhutia, etc. [19C. S. *Bhotīya*, 'Tibetan', fr. *Bhota*, 'Tibet'.] (1) A native and languag(s) of Bhutan. *See* **Bhutanese**. [Schroeter, *Dict. Bhotanta Lang.* (1826); *OED*; Heber, *Narr. Journey Upper Provinces of India* (1826).] (2) A breed of Himalaya ponies. Also attrib. *Bhottan*. [*OED*; R. Godden, *Black Narcissus* (1939).]

Bhumi [H./S. *bhūmi.*] Land. *See* next.

Bhumia [19C.] (1) Landlord; (2) Among the Gonds, a priest God of the homestead or the hearth. [Whitworth, *Anglo-Indian Dict.* (1885); Kipling, *Kim* (1901).]

Bhumidar [19C. H. *bhūmidar*, fr. *bhūmi*, 'land' + *dar*, 'holder'.] A landowner with full title to his land. [Wilson, *Glossary* (1855).]

Bhumij [19C. H. *bhūmij*; S. *bhūmija*, lit. 'earthborn'.] A Munda people of Chota Nagpur, India; the Munda language; a member of this people. *See* **Asuri**. [Wilson, *Glossary* (1855).]

Bhut, bhoot [17C. H. *bhut;* S. *bhuta,* 'formed, existent'.] A demon or goblin of many sorts 'by whom the Indian peasantry is so constantly beset.' [YB.] *See* **Butparast**. [OED.] *Bhut khana,* Freemasons Hall. *See* also **Jadoo Ghar**. [Hawkins, tr., *Bhagavat-Geeta*. (1785), ix; Della Valle, *Voyages* (tr. 1664; Hak. Soc. 1891).]

Bhutan cypress A tall Indian cypress, *Cupressus torulosa,* venerated by the people of Bhutan. [Webster, *Third New Intern. Dict.* (1976).]

Bhutanese [19C.] A native and the language of Bhutan. Adj. of or pertaining to the natives and the language of Bhutan. [OED; Stewart, *Hist. Bengal.* (1813), 47.]

Bhutta [19C. H. *bhuttā*.] Indian corn, *Zea mais*. [Whitworth, *Anglo-Indian Dict.* (1885).]

Bhuta-ta-tha-ta [20C. S. *bhutatathata*.] Buddhism: The essence of suchness. [Sir Charles Eliot, *Hinduism & Buddhism* (1921).]

Bhyacharra [19C. H. *bhayāchāra*.] A term applied to settlements made with the village as a community, according to custom and tradition. 'In its perhaps most common form each man's holding is the measure of his interest in the estate, irrespective of the share to which he may be entitled by ancestral right.' [YB; Wilson, *Glossary* (1855).]

Bibi, beebe [17C. H./P. *bībī*. 'A lady; a lawful wife.'] Has undergone a number of changes of meaning, from a Muslim lady, a European lady (later, Mem-Sahib); a (native) mistress, and even a European maid-servant, or other European woman of that rank, and sometimes applied to a prostitute. (The term occurs in personal names as early as the beginning of the 17C.) Also *burree beebee, a 'first* **Chop'** *lady*. [OED & YB; Coryat, *Crudities* (1611).]

Bicnana, bechanah [17C. H. *bichauna*.] Bedding of any kind. *See* **Bistra**. [YB; Ovington, *Voy. to Surat* (1696).]

Bidri, bidree, bidry [18C. H. *bidrī*. fr. *Bidar,* a town formerly in the Nizam's territory.] An alloy of copper, lead, tin and zinc used for inlaying with gold and silver to make the ornamental *bidri*-ware, e.g. hookah-bells, rosewater bottles, etc. [OED & YB; *Europ. Mag.*, 1794, 209.]

Bigha, beega(h) [H. *bīghā*.] At one time the commonest Indian land-measure, from $\frac{1}{2}$ acre to 1 acre. There is also a **Pucka** *bigha* and a **Kutcha** *bigha,* the latter being naturally some-

what less than the former. [OED & YB; Gleig, *Mem. Hastings* (1763), 1. 129.]

Bihar(i), Bearra [17C. From *Bihār,* a State in N. Eastern India.] A native and the Indo-Aryan language of that state. [OED & YB; Sir G. Birdwood, *Report on the Old Records of the India Office* (1676; 1891).]

Bikh, bish [19C. H./S. *visha,* 'poison'.] An Indian poison extracted from the *Aconitum ferox* and other aconites. Also applied (in the Himalayas) to the effect of the rarefied atmosphere at great heights on the body, and to poisonous emanations from the soil or from plants. [OED & YB.] *See* **Biscobra**. [Frazer, *Journal of a Tour* etc. (1820), 442; Lindley, *Introd. Bot.* (1830), 7.]

Bilabundi, bilabundy, bilabundee [19C. H. *bilabandī,* corr. of *behrī bandī*slare arrangements, a share, an allotment'.] An arrangement for securing the payment of revenue from each *mahal* (estate) and of rendering an account of such revenue payments, specifying the name of the farmers and the amount of the rents. [YB; H.H. Wilson, *A Gloss.of Judicial and Revenue Terms* (1855); Sleeman, *A Journey through Oudh in 1849-50* (1858), 1.208.]

Bilayat(i) *See* **Blighty and Vilayati**.

Bildar [19C. H/P. *beldār*.] A ditcher, excavator, or digging labourer (in the P.W.D.). [YB; *Ye Dreme of an Executive Engineer* (1847).]

Bilimbi, blimbee [18C. Tam. *bilimbi,* M. *vilimbī;* H. *belambū;* Mal. *bēlimbing*.] The fruit of the *Averrhoa bilimbi;* two species are cultivated in India. Used to cure skin diseases. *See* **Carambola**. [OED & YB; Cook, *Voy.* (1772-84), 1.247.]

Bilva [19C. S. *bilva*.] Shiva's favourite tree, whose edible fruit is called the Fruit of Fortune (*srī phala*). Its triple leaf symbolizes the three gods of the *trimurti*.[Whitworth, *Anglo-Indian Dict.* (1885).]

Bindi [19C. H. *bindī*.] Dot marked on the forehead of a Hindu wife, or as an ornament. [Hawkins, *CIWIE*.]

Binky-Nabob [18C. Kan. *benkī,* 'fire' + **Nawab**.] A commandant of artillery. A title recorded in documents concerning Hyder and Tippoo. [Gen. Stewart's despatch, 8 March 1799; YB; Wilks, *Mysoor* (Madras, 1810-17; 1869), ii. 346.]

Binturong, benturong [19C. Malay *binturong*.] (*Arctitis binturong*) A prehensile-tailed civet, *Arictis binturong,* an inhabitant of S. & S.E. Asia, from Nepal to Malaysia & Indonesia.

[*OED;* Raffles, *Trans. Linnean Soc.* (1822), XII, 253.]

Biradari [19C. H. *birādari* (cf. S. *bharatr*, 'brother').] Brotherhood. *See* **Bhai-Band.** [Wilson, *Glossary* (1855).]

Biryani [19C. H. *biryāni.*] Dish of rice cooked with meat and vegetables. [Hawkins, *CIWIE.*]

Biscobra [19C. H. *biskhopra.* (Poss. **Bish,** 'Poison' + *khopra*, 'shell, scale').] A name applied to any large and allegedly poisonous lizard. *See* J. L. Kipling, *Beast and Man in India* (1892), who gives the Zoological name as *Varanus-dracaena. See* **Cobra, Ghor-pad** and **Iguana.** [YB; *Tribes on my Frontier* (1883), 205.]

Bismillah [18C. H/Ar. *bi'smillah*] 'In the name of Allah.' A pious expression used by Muslims at the start of any undertaking. The full form is:*Bi-'smi'llahi 'r-rahman' r-rahīm.* 'In the Name of God, the compassionate, the Merciful.' [*OED* & YB; Stanford, *Dict.* (1776; ed. 1892); Byron, *Giaour* (1813).]

Bison [19C.] The popular Anglo-Indian name among Southern Anglo-Indian sportsmen of the great wild ox, *Bos gaurus. See* **Gaur.** [YB; *Saturday Review* (1881), 10 Sept. 335.]

Bistra [H. *bīstra.*] Bedding-roll. *See* **Bichana.** [Hawkins, *CIWIE.*]

Black(s) [17C. Anglo-Indian.] (Adj.) and (sb.) denoting natives of India; used by 'lower class of Europeans and by old officers of the Queen's Army'. [YB; Foster, *Letters* (1896-1900; 1614).] Also *Black Act.* The name given in denigration by Anglo-Indians to the Act of 1836, which placed them on a level with Indians in all civil cases in the East Indian Company's law-courts, including those under Indian judges *Black-doctor* (1787), an Indian dresser or medical orderly. *Black-Hole,* a confinement or punishment cell, esp. the Black Hole of Calcutta (1756). *Black-Jews* (1891), the Jews of S. India (intermarried with Indians). *Black language,* an old expression for Hindustani, used by the military. *Black-Partridge,* the game bird, *Francolinus francolinus,* with a ventriloquial call. *Black-town* (1673), the native section of a city (espec. of Madras). [YB; Trevelyan, *Life of Macaulay* (1876), 1. 398.]

Blackbuck [17C.] The male Indian antelope' *Antilope cervicapra.* [*OED* & YB.] *See* **Sasin.** [Ovington, *Voy. to Suratt* in 1689.]

Black-wood [17C. Chinese ebony used in carving and furniture.] Timber of the **Sissoo.** 'The popular name for what is in England termed "rosewood", produced chiefly by several species of *Dalbergia,* and from which the celebrated

furniture of Bombay is made.' [YB & *OED;* Cocks's Diary (1615; Hak. Soc. 1883), i. 35; Elphinstone, *Hist. Ind.* (1841), 1.9]

Blanks [18C.] Pg. *branco,* 'Whites', or 'Europeans'. [YB; Ziegenbalg and Plutscho, *Propagation of the Gospel in the East* (1718).]

Blatty [17C. Corr. of *wilāyatī,* 'foreign'.] *See* **Blighty.** (1) Two plants in S. India, *Son-neratta acida* and *Hydrolea zeylanica.* [YB; Mad. Admin. Man. Gloss. (1893).] (2) Obs. A kind of cloth. [YB; Danvers' & Foster's *Letters* (1610; 1896-1900).] (3) The land-wind in Arabia. [YB; Owen, *Narrative of Voyages,* etc. (1833).]

Blighty, Blattie [19C. H/Ar. *wīlayat(ī), bilāyat(ī)* 'kingdom', foreign (Indian) army slang, corr. of *bilāyatī.*Kipling, *belait* (1886). Cf. **Deshi.**] (1) England 'Home', sb. adj., attrib. Hence:*Blighty-pani* (pawnee), 'foreign' water, 1885 = soda-water, and *Blighty-baingan* (brinjal) = the tomato. [Kipling, *From Sea to Sea* (1886).] (2) A wound (sometimes self-inflicted), securing return home to Britain (1916). [Partridge, *Dict. of Slang* (1976).]

Blood-sucker [19C. Anglo-Indian.] Harmless Indian lizards, genus *Calotes* which change colour from grey to blood-red when excited. [*OED* & YB; Forbes, *Or. Mem.* (1813); Merton's *Life of Leydon* (1819).]

Blue-sheep *See* **Bharal.**

Bobbachce, bobberjee, etc. [19C. H. *bāwarchī* (Perh. fr. P. *bāwar,* confidence).] A male cook in Anglo-Indian households. [*OED* & YB; Williamson, E. *Ind. Vade Mecum* (1810), 1. 238.]

Bobbachee-connah [19C. H. *bāwarchī-khāna,* 'a cook house'.] The kitchen in Anglo-Indian households, 'detached from the main house with a covered way from one to the other'. [YB; Or. *Sport.Mag.* (1829), i. 118.]

Bobbery [18C. H. *bāpre* 'Oh father!' Exclamation of surprise or grief.] This Anglo-Indian expression indicates any noisy disturbance. In the general dialect of East Anglia in 1830. [*OED.*] Also *Bobbery-bob = Baprebap,* 'Father-O-Father!' (1864) and *Bobbery-pack* (1878), a scratch pack of noisy hounds of different and indifferent breeds, or a scratch match at cricket etc. *See* **Bap-Re!** [*OED* & YB; Joseph Price, *Tracts,* Vol. ii. (1783); 'A. Cheem', *Lays of Ind.* (1873), 2nd Ser., 86.]

Bocha [19C. H. *bochā.*] A chair-palanquin formerly used in Bengal. [YB; Williamson, *Vade Mecum* (1810), i. 322.]

Bodhisattva [19C. S. *bodhi,* 'perfect knowledge + *sattva,* 'reality'.] One destined to become a

Buddha; of infinite compassion, and whose essence is perfect knowledge. [*OED; Asiatic Res.* (1828), xvi. 422.]

Bogie [19C. (Unknown orig).] In India, a railway carriage. [*OED,* specif. J. Wright's Patent No. 10173 (1844).]

Boliah, bauleah [18C. Beng. *bhauliyah.*] A river passenger boat with a cabin, on Bengal rivers. *See* **Paunchway.** [YB; Ives, *Voy. from England to India* (1754 etc.; 1773).]

Bolta [19C. Sea-Hind. Pg. *volta.*] A turn of a rope. [YB; Roebuck, *Naval Dict.* (1811).]

Bombay [17C.] Name of the Indian city, capital of Maharashtra State, derived perh. from *Mumba-Devi (Parvati),* whose shrine was on the Esplanade until about 1650 when it was removed to its present site in the S.E. part of the city. Used attrib, in: (1) *Bombay*-chair (cf. *Bombay-furniture)* (1896). (2) *Bombay*-duck. *See* **Bummalo** (1860). (3) *Bombay*-furniture, combines European forms with Indian ornamentation (1910); (4) *Bombay*-hemp, *Crotolaria juncia,* yields valuable fibre from its inner bark (1866); (5) *Bombay*-shell, the Bull's Mouth shell, *Cassis rufa,* used for cutting shell-cameos (1858); (6) *Bombay*-pearls, from the Persian Gulf, of highest quality, sold in Bombay (1885); (7) *Bombay*-box-work, boxes decorated with veneers of geometrical mosaic (1810); (8) *Bombay*-bowler, the **Sola-Topi** (1836); (9) *Bombay*-Marine, 'A meritorious but somewhat depressed naval service which functioned from about ʰ810 to 1863, in the China War (1841-2), and against the pirates of Western India and the Persian Gulf. Otherwise known as the *Crab* service and the *Bombay Buccaneers. (Crab,*H. *kharab,* 'bad'.) [YB & *OED*; Fryer, *New Acct. of E. India* etc. 1672-81.]

Bombil [19C. Mar. *bombīl(a).*] *See* **Bummalo.** [YB; Molesworth, *Marathi & English Dictionary* (1857).]

Bonito [16C. Pg. and Sp. *bonito,* 'pretty' (cf. Ar. *bainīth).*] The fish, *Sarda orientalis,* the striped tunny growing to the length of three feet, common in Indian and other tropical seas, and living chiefly on the flying-fish. *See* **Albicore.** [*OED* & YB; Hakluyt, *Voy.* (1599) 11. ii. 105.]

Bora(h)[1] [17C. Beng. *bhada.*] A kind of light rowing-boat used for carrying cargo on the rivers of Bengal. [YB; Hedges' *Diary,* 1681-8.]

Bora,[2] **Bohra** [17C. H. and Guj. *Bohra,* poss. fr. S. *vithavahāri,* 'a trader'.] (a) A **Shia** Muslim community of traders and money-lenders,

often called **Box-Wallahs** in Bombay, and once numerous in Surat, Burhanpur and Ujjain. Also attrib. [*OED* & YB; *English Factories in India* (1618-1669; ed. 1906-27); Forbes, *Or. Mem.* (1813). (b) **A Sunni** Muslim community of peasants and traders, once numerous in Gujarat, Baroda and the Northern Konkan, and generally of Hindu descent. *See* **Khoja, Shia** and **Sunni.** [YB; Fryer, *New Acct.* (1672-81).] (c) The village money-lender in Rajasthan (Rajputana). [Tod, *Annals* (1829).]

Bosh, bash [19C. Turki. *bosh.*] Vain, useless, humbug, stuff & nonsense. [*OED* & YB; Morier, *Ayesha* (1834); Lady Sale, *Journal* (1843); Dickens, *Bleak House* (1852).]

Bosman, bochman [19C.] Lascars'. 'boatswain'. [YB; Roebuck, *Naval Dict.* (1811); Small, *A Laskari Dict.* (1882).]

Boson [20C.] Named after Bengali scientist, Dr S.N. Bose. Any particle which has a symmetrical wave-function and which therefore obeys the Bose-Einstein statistics. [*OED;* Dirac. *Prin. Quantum Mech.* (1947), ix. 210.]

Botickeer [18C. Pg. *botiqueiro.*] A shop-or stall-keeper [YB]. *See* **Boutique.** [A Hamilton. *A New Acct. of the E. Indies* (1727), 1.268.]

Bo-tree [18C. Sinh. *bō,* corr. of Pali. *bothi* (S. *bodhi),* 'the bo-tree'; more fully, S. *bothi-taru,* fr. *bodhi,* 'perfect knowledge' + *taru,* 'tree'.] The *Ficus religiosa* or **Pipal**-tree, under which the Buddha attained enlightenment. *See* **Banyan.** [*OED* & YB; Knox, *Hist. Ceylon,* (1681), 18.]

Bottle-tree [19C.] This term seems to have been applied to three different Indian trees : (1) The Baobab, *Andansonia digitata* (H. *gorakamlī,* alias Monkey-Bread tree, with an enormously thick stem; orig. African, now naturalized in Sir Lanka and parts of India. The juice of its fruit is used as an anti-scorbutic and febrifuge medicine, and the fibres of the bark are used for ropes and cloth [YB]. *See* **Baobab.** [*Sir Ali Baba, Twenty-one Days in India,* (1880) by Aberigh Mackay; Parkinson, *Theat. Bot.* (1632).] (2) *The Oreodoxa Regia,* or Bottle Palm-tree; orig. W. Indian; whose young trees have a bottle-shaped swelling towards the top of the trunk. Its leaf-sheaths are used for making sleeping-mats, and the top part of the palm is cooked as a vegetable. [Cowen, *Flowering Trees* etc. (1950).] (3) The Babul-tree (H. *babūl*). *Acacia arabica* or *mimosa,* - suggested becaused the **Baya** bird often builds its bottle-shaped nest in this tree! [YB; Heber, *Narrative* (1824; ed. 1828).]

Bound-Hedge [18C. Anglo-Indian corr. of *boundary hedge*.] Bamboo and prickly pear around Indian forts. [YB; Wilks, *Historical Sketches* (1792), iii. 217.]

Boutique, butica, batteca, [18C. Old Pg. *botica*, and Fr. *boutique*.] A small S. Indian & Sri Lankan shop or stall. 'It would appear that the use of *butica* was peculiar to Portuguese India.' [YB & *OED*; Wheeler, *Madras in the Olden Times* (1799; ed. 1861); J. Long, *Sel. Unpubl. Rec. Govt. (Fort William)* (1767; ed. 1869).]

Bowla [17C. H. *bāolā*, fr. Pg. *baul*, 'a trunk'.] A portmanteau. [YB.]

Box-wal(l)a(h) [19C. Anglo-Indian hybrid, fr. box + *wālā*.] Orig. an Indian itinerant pedlar or packman; later a shop-keeper, retailer or businessman, Indian or European. *See* **Bo(h)ra, Sundook-Wallah.** [*OED* & YB; Mrs Sherwood, *Lady of the Manor* (1847); Kipling, *From Sea to Sea* (1889).]

Boy [17C. Anglo-Indian.] 'In Southern India ... a native personal servant is so termed and is summoned with the vocative 'Boy'. [YB & *OED*; Hawkins in Purchas,*Pilgr.* (1609), 211.]

Boy(i) [17C. Tel. and H/Mar *bhoi*.] The name of a caste of palanquin bearers. (Wilson gives II. & Mar. *bhoi*. [YB.] *See* **Bearer**[1] and **Kuhar.** [Fryer, *New Acct. of E. India*, 1672-81.]

Boya [19C. Sea-Hind.] A buoy. [YB; Roebuck *Naval Dict.* (1811).]

Boyanore, baonor [19C. Corr. of M. *Vāllunavar*, 'ruler'.] A ruler in Malabar. [YB; Logan, *Malabar* (1887), i. 345.]

Brab [17C. Pg. *brava*, 'wild'.] The **Palmyra** palm, *Borassus flabelliformis*. The Portuguese called this *Palmeira brava*, whence the Anglo-Indian corruption *brab*. (H. name, *tāl* or *tār*). [*OED* & YB; Fryer, *New Acct. of E. India*, etc., 1672-81.]

The following words are derived from **Brahm.**

Brahm(a)[1] [18C. S. Brahmā] (a) The supreme god of the Hindu trinity (*trimurti*) of post-vedic Hindu mythology, the second being **Vis(h)nu** and the third **S(h)iva.** [*OED*; Wilkins, tr., *Bhagavat* (1785), viii. 55.] (b) In the later pantheistic systems, the Divine Reality, of which the universe of matter and mind is only a manifestation. Hence:*Brahmahood*, the state of *Brahm(a)*, being the absorbtion into the divine essence. (Various spelling are traceable to the 14C., e.g. *Bragman, Brachman, Bahman,*etc.) [*OED*; Fitzedward Hall, *Refut. Hindu Philos. Syst.* (1862), 194.]

Brahma[2] Shortened form of **Brahmapootra.**

Brahmacharya [20C. S. *brahman*, 'prayer, worship' + *charya*, 'conduct'.] Purity of life, celibacy, sexual restraint. The first stage of Hindu life; studentship under a **Guru.** *See* **Grihasta** and **Sanyas.** Hence:*brahmachari*, one who practises *brahmacharya* (used in modern times particularly in connection with the teachings of Mahtma Gandhi). M.K. Gandhi, *Self-Restraint v. Self-Indulgence* (1920; ed. 1947).]

Brahman [19C. S. *Brahman*, 'prayer'.] Also the infinite in nature. *See* **Brahmin.** [Max Mueller, *Theosophy* (1892).]

Brahmana [19C. S. *Brāhamana*.] One of the scholastic treatises belonging to the **Vedas.** [Max Mueller, *Intro. to the Science of Religion*, (1870).]

Brahmi [19C. S. *Brāhmi*.] One of the oldest Indian alphabets, probably of Semitic origin, which was popularly used in the third century BC throughout India. Among its many descendants are the Devanagri, Bengali, Gujarati and Dravidian scripts. *See* **Kharosthi.** [*OED*; Buhler, *Orig. Indian Brahma Alphabet*, (1895).]

Brahmic [19C. S. *Brahmā*.] Adj. Pertaining to the Indian society **Brahmo Samaj,** or to the older **Brahma Sabha.** [*OED*; *Calcutta Rev.*, (1852), XVII. xvii.]

Brahmin,-an, Bragman etc. [15C. S. *Brāhmana*, 'praise' 'worship'.] A member of the highest, 'twice-born', priestly caste of the Hindus. 'The form **Brahmin,** a corruption of the Indian vernacular pronunciation is still all but universal in popular use. During the present century orientalists have adopted the more correct **Brahman.**' [*OED*.] The older English spelling was **Brachman,** which came from the Greek and Latin authors, Strabo, Megasthenes, Aristobulus, etc. Acosta has **Bragmen.** [Caxton, *The Mirror of the World* (tr. 1481).]

Some learned derivatives found in English indological texts are: *Brahmadarsana,* 'insight into truth'; *Brahmānubhava,* intuition of reality; *Brahmasākshātkara,* 'direct apprehension of reality'; *Brahmasamsparsa,* 'contact with the Supreme'; *Brahmavithāra,* 'living in the Brahman heaven'. The four noble practices in Buddhist philosophy necessary for rebirth in the Brahman heaven: sympathy, compassion, joy, equanimity. [Basham, *A Cultural History of India* (1975).] Attrib. *Brahmin-slayer* [Muir, *Sanskrit* Texts (1858)]; *Brahmin-pope* = Chief Brahmin (obs). [Purchas, *Pilgr. Descr. India* (1613);

Brahmin-beads; the seeds of *Elaeocarpus*, worn as a necklace by Brahmins and others. [*OED*.] *Brahmin-ox* = **Zebu** (1847). Also, Brahminhood, the rank or status of a Brahmin. [H.H. Wilson, *Vishnu Purana* (1840)]; spec. *Boston Brahmin*. An uppercrust Bostonian (USA). [*Homes and Haunts of our Elder Poets* (1881); *OED*.] *See* **Samskara**.

Brahminee (sb)[1] [18C. S. *Brāhmanī*, fem. of **Brahmana**.] A female *Brahmin*. [*OED*; Sir W. Jones, *Inst. of Manu* (1794), x. 66.]

Brahminee (adj.)[2] [19C.] Pert. to the *Brāhmin* caste, on analogy with *Bengali, Punjabi*, etc. [*OED*; Mrs Sherwood, *Henry & Bearer* (1811).]

Brahminee-bull [19C. = Brahmin(ee)-ox (1847).] S(h)iva's sacred bull. More generally the humped Indian *Bos indica*, 'frequenting Hindu bazaars, and fattened by the run of Bunnya's shops'. [YB & *OED*; Rev. Lal Behari Day, *Govinda Samanta* (1874); Lady Brassey, *The Trades* (1885), 99.] *See* **Zebu**.

Brahminee-butter [18C.] **Ghee** [*OED* & YB; India Office M.S.,Acct. Charges Dieting etc., at Fort St. David, 1746-7.]

Brahminee-duck [19C.] The Anglo-Indian term for the *Tadorno ferruginea*, or Ruddy Sheldrake, (H. *chakwa-chakwa*.). [*OED* & YB; Jerdon, *Birds of India* (1862).]

Brahminee-fig-tree [19C.] The **Banyan**, *Ficus indica* or *religiosa*. [*OED*; Mrs Sherwood, *Henry & Bearer* (1811).]

Brahminee-kite, the handsome Indian raptor, *Haliastur Indus*. (H. *Brahminī chīl*.) [*OED* & YB; Fryer, *A New Act. of E. India*, 1673-81.]

Brahminic(al), Brahmanic(al) (adj.) [19C.] Pert. to the *Brahmins*. [*OED*; Wilford, 'Sacred Isles' in *Asiat. Res.* (1809), IX. 71.]

Brahminicide [19C.] (a) One who has killed a *Brahimin*, a **Brahmin-Slayer**. [*OED*.] (b) The act of killing a *Brahmin*. [*OED*; Ward, *Hist. Hindoos* (1817-96).]

Brahminism [19C.] The principles and practices of the *Brahmins*. Hence: Brahminist(ic)(al) (1816) and *Brahminise* (1883). [*OED*; Faber, *Orig. Pagan Idol* (1876), 1.124.]

Brahmism[1] [19C.] The religion of **Brahma** (obs.). [*OED*; *Month Rev.* (1813), 1. XXI. 478.]

Brahmism[2] [19C.] The tenets of the Indian society *Brahma Sabha*, or of the more recently founded **Bramo Samaj**. Also, *Brahmoism* (1857). [*OED*.] *See* **Arya Samaj**. [Balfour, *Cycl. India* (1885), 1. 438.]

Brahmo, Brahmoism, Brahmoist *See* **Brahmo Samaj**.

Brahma(putra) [19C. Indian river; lit. 'Son of **Brahma**'.] A variety of domestic fowl, said to have had its origin in Lakhimpur on the river Brahmaputra. (Anglo-Indian terms, *Burampooter, Baramputrey, Berhumputter*, etc. Usually abbreviated to *Brahma*. [Wright, *Bk. Poultry* (1885), 245.]

Brahmo-Samaj [19C. S. *Brāhma Samaja*, 'Assembly of Brahmists'.] The monotheistic reform of Hindu society begun by Ram Mohun Roy in 1830 and developed by Debendranath Tagore and Keshub Chandra Sen. Advocated widow remarriage, abandonment of **Caste**, abolition of **Purdah** and of child marriage. [*OED* & YB.] *See* **Arya Samaj**. [Dass, *Supreme Being of Brahmo Theol.* (1857); Collet, *Brahmo Year Bk.* (1876), 5.]

Brahui [19C. Tribal name.] (Pert. to) a pastoral people of Baluchistan, and their **Dravidian** language. [*OED*; Pottinger, *Trav. Baluchistan* (1816).]

Brandul [19C. Sea-Hind. Pg. *brandal*.] Backstay. [YB; Roebuck, *An English and Hindoostanee Naval Dictionary* (1811).]

Brandy-coortee, -coatee [18C. H/P. *bārān*, 'rain' + *kurtī, 'jacket'*.] Hobson-Jobsonism: A raincoat. '*Bārānī* is now commonly used to describe those crops which depend on the annual rains not on artificial irrigation.' [YB; Hanway, *Hist. Acct. of British Trade* (1753).]

Brandy-pawnee [19C. A.I. hybrid: *brandy* + H. *panī*, 'water'.] 'A specimen of genuine **Urdu**, i.e. camp jargon, which hardly needs interpretation.' [YB & *OED*.] Williamson, in *The East India Vade Mecum* (1810) has 'brandy-shraubpauny'. *See* **Shrub** and **Sherbet**. [*Thackeray, Newcomes* (1854), ch. 1.]

Brass[1] [19C. A.I. sea-dialect.] A brace. [YB; Roebuck, *An English and Hindostanee Naval Dictionary* (1811).]

Brass[2] [Pg.] 100 cu. ft. (of sand and other material); 100 sq. ft. (of wall surface). [Hawkins, *CIWIE*.]

Brass-knocker [19C. A.I. slang, poss. a corr. of H. *bāsī khāna*, 'stale food'.] Yesterday's dinner re-heated and served for the second time. *See* Winwood Reade's *Liberty Hall*. [YB; *Fifth Series, Notes & Queries*, 34.77.] *See* **Maladoo**.

Bratty [19C. Tam. *varatti* or *virātti*, 'dried dung'.] In S. India, cakes of dried cow-dung used as fuel. (H. *uplā* (**Oopla**) in North India.) [YB; Welsh. *Military Reminiscences* (1830), ii.318. seq.]

Brawl, borrel, burral [17C. Poss. H. *biral*, 'open in texture fine'. Obs.] Blue and white striped cloth once manufactured in India. (*See* **Piece-**

Goods.) [YB; Danvers & Foster, *Letters received by the E.I. Co., from its servants in the East* (1616; 1896-90).]

Brazil-wood [16C. Pg. *brasil.*] Of unknown orign. Perh. corr. of the oriental word for the dye-wood of an Indian tree yielding a red dye; *Caesalpine Sappan.* (The country was named originally Tierra de Brasil, 'red dyewood land', from an allied species of the tree in S. America). See **Sappan-wood** [*OED;* Evelyn's *Diary* (19 Aug. 1641); Richard Eden, *A Treatyse of the Newe India* (tr. 1553).]

Bridgeman, brijman [19C.] Anglo-Sepoy Hind. *brijman,* corr. of 'prisoner'. [Whitworth, *Anglo-Indian Dict.* (1885).]

Bridge-party [20C.] An Anglo-Indian arrangement or **Bundobust** in which Indian and Europeans of both sexes were brought together socially to attempt to bridge the gap that separated the one from the other in their unofficial lives. [Forster, *A Passage to India* (1944).]

Brinjal; Brinjaul, berenjaws, etc. [17C. Pg. *bringella;* S. *vātingana.*] The fruit of the eggplant or aubergine, *Solanum melongena.* (H. and Beng. *baingan.*) See **Bilayati** and **Bangun.** [*OED & YB;* Downton in purchas, *Pilgr.* (1613), 1.298.]

Brinjarry, binjaree, bungaree, etc. [17C. H. *banjārā,* S. *vanij,* 'trade' + *karu,* 'doer'.] A travelling grain and salt-merchant in the Deccan, who often followed the army with goods for sale, or as commissariat carriers. [*OED & YB; Eng. Fact. in India,* 1618-69; J. Briggs, *Acct. Bunjaras (Life of Mohabat Khan)* (c. 1632).]

Buck¹ [20C. Anglo-Indian.] A rupee. Ex. USA. [Hawkins, *CIWIE.*]

Buck,² bukh [19C. H. *bak(na),* 'to talk'.] Anglo-Indian slang; talk, espec. boastful or insolent talk as in 'Don't give me any of that old *buck*'. Hence: impudence or impertinence. *Also,* vb. (1880), 'to chatter', 'to talk with egotistical insistence'. A *buck-stick* (1880) is a chatterer or natterer. [*OED & YB;* Partridge, *Dict. of Slang* etc. (1895; ed. 1979); Aberigh Mackay, *Sir Ali Baba, Twenty One Days in India* (1880); Mrs Croker, *Village Tales* (1895).]

Buckaul [19C. H. *bakkāl.*] A shop-keeper, a **Bannia.** (In Ar., a second-hand dealer). [YB; Wellington, *Despatches* (1800; ed. 1837), i. 196).]

Buckshaw,¹ buckshoe, bubsho, batchwa[17C. H. *bacchuā.*] An edible fish, the Pseudotropius garua or *murius,* which abounds in the Ganges and other N. Indian rivers. [YB; Day, *The Fishes of India* (1876-8); Fryer, *New Acct. of E. India* etc. (1672-81).]

Buckshaw,² boxshah, bouchha [17C. Poss. P. *bukchah,* 'a bundle'.] This word seems to mean some kind of Indian piece-goods as well as its ordinary meaning of a bundle of clothes or other personal belongings. [YB; Foster, *Letters* (1614; ed. 1896-1900), ii. 88.]

Bu(c)kshee, bakshee, bukshi, etc. [17C. H/P. *bakshī.*] (a) *Adj. & Adv.* Free, spare, extra. (b) Sb. something extra, free or to spare; an allowance over and above the usual amount (1916). Also a light wound (1914-18); a *buck-shee*-king,a military paymaster (20C.); a *buck shee* bombardier = an N.C.O. with no additional pay (1940). *Buckshee* lance-jack = a lance corporal (1914-18). [*OED;* Partridge. *Dict. of Slang,*etc. (1979); (c) a senior Mughal military administrative officer (1615), the paymaster general of the army in Indian native states = **Buxee.** [YB; Sir T. Roe in Purchas (1615).] (d) Also a European civil officer. See **Buxee.** [Rev. James Long, *Selections, Records Ft. William* (1753), 43.]

Bucksheesh, Buxees See **Baksheesh.**

Buckyne [19C. H. *bākayan.*] The Indian tree, *Melia semervivens* or *azedarac,* resembling the **Neem**-tree, and, in Bengal, called *mahānīm.* Sometimes erroneously called *Persian Lilac,* the **Bead**-tree, *Pride of India* and *China-berry.* [Cowen, *Flowering Trees and Shrubs in India* (1950); *Penny Cyclopaedia* (1838), 801.]

Buddha [17C. S. *Buddha,* 'enlightened, awakened' (past part of *budh,* 'to awake, know, perceive'.] The title of the founder of **Buddhism,** *Sākyamuni* **Gautama,** or *Siddartha,* who flourished in N. India in the 5C. BC. *Sākyamuni* is regarded as only the latest of a series of *Buddhas* or infallible religious teachers; which is hereafter to be continued indefinitely. Hence *Buddhahood,* the condition of a *Buddha* (1837); and *Buddhi,* 'wisdom'. [Cocks' *Diary,* i. 200 (1615 ; ed. Hak. Soc. (1883); R. Knox, *Hist. Ceylon* (1618), 18.]

Buddhic [19C.] *Buddhist* (adj.). [*OED;* Faber, *Orig. Pagan Idol* (1816).]

Buddhism [19C.] The religious system founded by **Gautama.** [*OED;* Joinville in *Asiatic Res.* (1801), vii. 400.]

Buddhist [19C.] A follower of *Buddha* [*OED;* Joinville in *Asiatic Res.* (1801), vii. 398.]

Buddhist (adj.) [19C.] Relating or pertaining to *Buddhism.* [*OED; Asiat. Jrnl.* (1816), 1.21.]

Buddhistic [19C. *Buddhist*. (adj.).] Also *Buddhistically*, in a *Buddhistic(al)* manner (1920). [*OED;* Anthon, *Classical Dict.* (1841) (*Buddhistic*); Turnour, *Mahāwanso* (1837).]

Buddhite [19C. Obs.] An early synonym of *Buddhist* (sb. and adj.). [*OED;* Percival, *Ceylon* (1803).]

Buddhu A stupid person (cf. Malay *bodoh*, with the same meaning). [Hawkins, *CIWIE*.]

Budg(e)rook, bazaruke, etc. [16C. Pg. *bazarucco*, (H. *bāzār*, 'market' + Kan. *ruka*, 'money').] A coin of low denomination and of various values and metals (copper, tin, lead, **Tutenague**) formerly current in Goa and Western India. [YB; Linschoten in Hakluyt, (1598; ed. 1889).]

Budgerow [17C. H. and Beng. *bajra*.] A lumbering keelless barge employed on the Gangetic rivers. [*OED* & YB; Caesar Fredericke, *Voyage* etc. in Hakluyt (*c.* 1570; ed. 1807), ii. 358.]

Budlee, muddle [19C. H. *badlī*, 'exchange'. (Ar. *badal*, 'he changed').] A person taken in exchange for another; a *locum tenens*; a substitute in public or domestic service; a proxy. Cf. **Benami.** [YB; Julia Charlotte Maitland, *Letters from Madras* (1836-7; ed. 1843).]

Budmas *See* **Badmash.**

Budzat, badzat [19C. H/P. *badzāt*, 'evil race, low-born' fr. *bad*, 'evil + *dat*, 'substance, nature'.] A low fellow, scoundrel, blackguard. Cf. **Badmash.** [YB; G.O. Trevelyan, *The Dawk Bungalow* (1866).]

Buffalo [16C. Pg. *bufalo*, fr. L. *bubalus*.] The name of several species of oxen, esp. *Bos bubalus*, orig. native of India. When domesticated it is commonly known as the *Water-buffalo*, ubiquitous in Indian and S.E. Asia. [*OED* & YB; Fitch in Hakluyt (1585), 389; Parke, tr., *Mendoza* (1588).]

Buggalow [19C. Mar. *bag(a)lā*.] 'A name commonly given on the W. coast of India to Arab vessels of the old native form.' [YB.] (Yule regards this word as corr. of the Pg. *bajel*, or *baixel*, 'vessel' fr. Lat. *vascellum*. [*OED* & YB; Sir G. Arthur in *Ellenborough, Ind. Admin.* (1842), 222.] *See* **Sambook.**

Buggy [18C. Etym. unknown.] Conjecturally connected with **Bogie**, also with 'bug'. There are no grounds for supposing it to be of Anglo-Indian origin, but the word and the vehicle were commonly used in India. A light one- or two-horse gig, for one or two persons; in India, with a hood. [*OED* & YB, *Gentleman's-Magazine* (1773), XL. 111. 297.]

Bulbul [17C. H/P. *bulbul*.] Various species of birds of the genus *Pycnonotus*, of the thrush family, much admired for their song; sometimes called the 'nightingales of the East', and found in many parts of India. Also transf. and attrib. 'A sweet singer.' [Thackeray, *Vanity Fair* (1848).] [*OED* & YB; Sir William Jones, *Memoirs* (1784); Forbes, *Oriental Memoirs* (1813); *Stanford Dict.* (1665; 1892).]

Bulgar, bolgar [P. *bulghār*. 'Russian-leather'.] (Orig. fr. a place on the Volga). The word was in use among Anglo-Indians until the beginning of the 19C. [YB; Danvers, *Letters,* etc. (1614; ed. 1896-1900).]

Bulkut [19C. Tel. *balla*, 'a board'.] A ferry-boat [YB; C.P. Brown, *Zillah Dict.* (1852).]

Bullumteer [19C. Anglo-Sepoy dial. for 'Volunteer'.] Applied to certain regiments of the old Bengal Army, who could be required to serve overseas. [YB.]

Bummalo, bummelo, etc. [17C. Mar. *bombil(a)*.] A small fish, *Harpodon nehereus*, abounding in Indian and other S. Asian waters; used, when dried, as a relish known as **Bombay-Duck**. [*OED* & YB; Fryer, *A New Acct. of E. India* (1672-81); Molesworth, *Mahratti Dict.* (1857).]

Bumba, bomba [19C. H. *bamba* fr. Pg. *bomba*, 'a pump'.] 'Applied in modern times in N. India to canal distributary, and in Ahmedabad to water towers. [YB; Camöens, *Lusiads* (1572); E.T. by Burton 1880), VI. 72.]

Buncus, bunco [18C. Mal. *bungkus*.] 'A wrapper, bundle or contents of bundle.' A **Cheroot.** [YB; Lockyer, *Acct. of the Trade in India,* (1711), 61.]

Bund [19C. H/P. *band*. S. *band*.] 'Any artificial embankment, a dam, a dyke or cause-way.' [YB.] *Also* vb. trans. to *bund*, = to embank (1883). *See* **Anicut.** [*OED* & YB; Williamson, *Vade Mecum* (1813), ii. 279.]

Bunder, bandar [17C. H/P. *bandar*.] 'A landing place or quay, a seaport; a harbour, sometimes a custom-house.' [YB.] Also *Mir-bandar*, Port-Master (in Sind) (*c.* 1565); **Shahbandar,** Harbour-Master. And in S. India *Bunder* is the popular name of Masulipatam = *Machli-bandar* (fish-quay). [*OED* & YB; Foster, *Letters,* (1616), iv. 328; Fryer, *Acct. E. India & Persia,* (1673), 115.]

Bunder-boat [19C.] A boat communicating with ships anchored off Bombay and Madras, and also employed in coastal trade and government business. [*OED;* Bishop Heber, *Narrative,* etc. (1825; ed. 1844), ii. 121.]

Bundobust, bandobust [18C. H/P. *bandobust,* 'tying and binding'.] *See* **Bando.** Organization, arrangement, preparation. A set-up [OED & YB; Verelst, *View of Bengal* (1772).]

Bundook [19C. H. *bandūk;* P. *bandūq.*] 'Filbert-nut'; musket, fire-arm, cannon-ball, match-lock; rifle. Also, *bundookdar,* a musketeer, rifleman, or Master of Artillery. [OED & YB; Burton, *Arabian Nights* (1894), xii. 38; Drew, *Jummoo and Kashmir* (1875), 74.]

Bungalow [17C. H. *bangla,* 'belonging to Bengal'.] Orig. a one-storied thatched house in Bengal and afterwards throughout India. Now any one-storied house anywhere (1886). *See* **Dawk Bungalow** (1855). *Also,* adj. *bungaloid* (1927), having the style of a bungalow; a complex of bungalows, and adj. a bungaloid building development (1968). [OED & YB; Foster, *English Fact. in India* (1618-69; ed. 1906-12).]

Bungarum, -us, bungar, bongar [19C. Beng/S. *bhangura,* 'bent, curled', fr. *bhanj* 'to break, bend'.] Any of the venemous snakes of India of the genus *Bungarus,* esp. the **Krait.** In Bengal it is called *Bangarum Pamah* or *Sackeenee.* [OED; *Encyc. Metrop.* (1835), xxiii. 640/1; Wall's *Snakes of Ceylon* (1921), 435.]

Bungy *See* **Bhangy.**

Bunow [19C. H. *banao,* imp. of *banāna,* 'to make, prepare, fabricate'.] Used in the sense of *banawat,* 'fabrication, invention, sham'. The Anglo-Indian word is applied to anything fictitious or factitious, and as a verb, to pretend, to fabricate. *See* also **Dumcow, Foozillow, Lugow** and **Gubbrow.** [YB; W.D. Arnold, *Oakfield* (1854), ii. 58.]

Bur(r) [19C. H. *bar;* S. *vata.*] The **Pipal** or **Banyan-Tree,** *Ficus indica* or *religiosa.* [OED; Forbes, *Orient. Mem.* (1813), 111. 14).]

Burgher¹ [19C. Du. *burger,* 'citizen'.] In Ceylon (Sri Lanka), a descendant of a Dutch East India Company servant. Now-Eurasian. Cf. **Anglo-Indian, Eurasian** and **Mustees.** [YB; Cordiner, *Desc. of Ceylon* (1807).]

Burgher² [19C.] Anglo-Indian name for tribal people of the Nilgiri Hills in S. India; properly *Badegas* or 'Northerners', speaking an old **Kannada** dialect. *See* **Badega.** [YB; Caldwell. *Comparative Grammar* (1875).]

Burgher³ [19C. H. *bargā.*] A rafter.[YB.]

Burhal *See* **Bharal.**

Burka, boorka [19C. H/Ar. *būrqā.*] A strict **Purdah** gown enveloping the face and form of Muslim women in public in order to screen them from the view of strangers. [OED; J.T. Bealey, tr., *Hedin's Through Asia* (1898), 1.viii.]

Burkundaz, -auze [18C. H/Ar. -P. *barq-andāz,* 'lightning-darter'.] A matchlockman, 'but commonly applied to a native of Hindustan, armed with a sword, who acts as doorkeeper, watchman, guard or escort'. H. H. Wilson, *Gloss. Judicial Terms* (1855). [OED & YB; .Stanford Dict. (1776; 1892); Ann. Reg. (1781), 14/1.]

Burra, barrow [19C. H. *barā,* 'great' (adj.).] Used in conjunction with a large selection of nouns, e.g. *Burra-beebee* (1807) fr. H. *barā-bībī,* 'Grande Dame'. Anglo-Indian colloquial applied to the lady claiming social precedence at a party or *Burra-Khana,* 'a great feast'. [*Lord Minto in India,* (1807-14); ed. 1880.] *Burra-Din* (1880). H. *barā-din,* 'Great Day'. Term applied by Indians (and by Anglo-Indians jokingly) to a great (European) festival or occasion, espec. Christmas (**Kiss-miss**) Day. [V. Ball, *Jungle Life in India* (1880).] *Burra-Khana* (1875); H. *barā-khana,* 'Big dinner', 'a banquet'. 'A vast & solemn entertainment.' [YB; A. Wilson, *The Abode of Snow* (1875).] *Burra-peg,* Hybrid fr. H. *barā* + Anglo-Indian, *peg,* 'a liquid measure'. A big measure for a drink; a double tot. *Burra-Sāhib* (1807), 'The Head Man.' A title of respect denoting the head of a family, the chief in a station, the judge, the general, the head of a department of a business etc. etc. [*Lord Minto in India* (1807-14; ed. 1880).] Also *Burra-memsahib,* a similar title for a wife of the *Burra sahib* (1848). [J. H. Stoqueler, *Oriental Interpreter* (1848).] *Barrow-wallah.* Army colloquial for *Burra-Sahib,* 19C. [Partridge, *Dict. of Slang,* etc.] *Burra sahib log,* the ruling (European) race. *See* **Chota** [OED & YB.]

Bus, bas [H/P. *bas.*] Interj. 'Enough!', 'Stop!'. 'That'll do! Basta! [YB; W. D. Arnold, *Oakfield* (1854), 1. 42.]

Bustee, -i [19C. H. *bastī,* fr. S. *vas,* 'to dwell'.] A village; now generally, a slum in an Indian city; a collection of mean huts; a shanty town, insanitary and lacking ordinary amenities. Cf. **Basha.** [Kipling, *City of Dreadful Night* (1889)], 54. [OED & YB; *Daily Telegraph,* 25 Dec. 1885.]

Butler [17C. Anglo-Indian.] In S. India, the title of the head-servant in an Anglo-Indian house-hold, who did the daily marketing, and superin-tended the table and domestic stores. 'As his profession affords a large scope for feathering his nest at his master's expense, he is generally of good caste.' [YB.] *See* **Khansama.** [OED &

YB; Cocks's *Diary* (1616; Hak. Soc. 1883);
Ovington, *Voyage to Surat* (1689; ed. 1696).]

Butler-English [18-20C. Anglo-Indian.] 'The
broken English spoken by native servants in
the Madras Presidency; which is not much
better than the Pigeon English of China. It is a
singular dialect; the present participle, e.g.,
being used for the future indicative and the
preterite indicative being formed by "done".
Thus I telling = "I will tell"; I *done tell* = "I
have told"; *done come* = "actually arrive".
Peculiar meanings are also attached to words:
thus *family* = "wife".' 'The oddest thing
about this jargon is (or was) that masters
used it in speaking to their servants as well as
servants to their masters.' [YB.] Obs. by about
1900. [YB; *See*, Partridge, *Slang*, etc. (1979).]

Butparast [19C. H. *bhutparast*.] Image worshipper. *Butparasti* = Idolatry. *See* **Bhut**.
[Kipling, *Kim* (1901).]

Buxee [17C. H. bakshi.] A military paymaster.
See **Buksheesh**. [*OED* & YB; Sir T. Roe, in
Purchas, *His Pilgrimes* (1624, Hak. Soc.
1819).]

Buxerry, baksariyah [17C. Etym. uncertain.
Perh. fr. *Buxar*, which upto 1857 was a great
recruiting ground for **Sepoys**.] Now. obs. but
meant a *matchlockman*, used in much the
same sense as **Burkun Dauze**. [Br. Museum
MS. No. 1641. fol. 586. (1690).] [*OED* & YB;
Clive in Grant, *Hist. of India* (1757), 1. ix.
52/2.]

Byde, or Bede Horse [18C.] A predatory tribe of
mercenary cavalry, 'the same as *Pindarehs*,
Looties and *Kuzzacks* (*see* **Pindarry, Looty**
and **Cossack**) who served in Hyder's wars in
Mysore and elsewhere. [YB; Rice, *Gazetter of
Mysore* (1897); Meer Hussein Ali Khan Kirmani,
Hist. of Hyder Ali Naik, tr. Miles (1758;
1842), 20.]

Bylee [19C. H. *bahlī, ballī*, fr. S. *vah*. 'to carry'.]
A small two-wheeled vehicle drawn by two
oxen. [YB.] *See* Lockwood Kipling's *Beast and
Man in India*. (1892). (This word has
apparently no connection with **Bail** 'a
bullock'). *See* **Bail**-gharry and **Bandy**.
[*Society in India, by an Indian Officer*
(1841), 1. 162.]

C

Cabaya, Kabaya [16C. Indo-Pg. *cabaya;* Mal. *kebaya.*] A long Muslim tunic introduced into India by the Portuguese. This word is now obsolete in India, but still current in Malaysia and Indonesia. [*OED* & YB; Fitch in Hakluyt (1585), ii. 386.]

Cabob *See* **Kebab.**

Cabook [19C. Sinh/Pg. *cavouco* 'quarry'.] The Sri Lankan term for **Laterite** (in Tamil Nadu, **Moorum**), a reddish gneissoid building stone, soft when quarried, but hardening on exposure to air. [*OED* & YB; *Ceylon Gazetter* (1834), 33.]

Cachoombar [Guj/ *kachumba.*] Spiced onion salad. [Hawkins, *CIWIE* (1984).]

Caddy [18C. Poss. fr. **Catty** (Mal. *kati*).] A tea-caddy (containing a *catty* or so of tea). [*OED* & YB; *Madras Courier,* 2 Dec. 1792.]

Cadet [18C. Fr. *cadet* (Lat. *caput,* 'head').] In India applied to all young officers appointed to the Indian army before promotion to ensigns and posting to their regiments. A junior in the East India company's service. [*OED* & YB; Court's Letter in Long, *Fort William Records* (1748-67; ed. 1869); Foote, *Nabob* (1772). 1.9.]

Cadi, Kazi, Kaji, Cazee [16C. H/Ar. *qadi,* fr. *qada,* 'judge'.] A Muslim civil judge; exponent of Muslim law; registrar of Muslim marriages. [*OED* & YB; Finch in *Early Travels in India* (1583-1619).]

Cadjan¹ [17C. Mal *kajang.*] Coco–, or *nipah* palm-fronds matted for thatch in S. India and Malaysia. [*OED* & YB; *English Factories in India* (1618-69).]

Cadjan² [18C. *kajang*] A strip of palm leaf of the **Talipot** or of the **Palmyra**, prepared for writing on; a document on such a strip. *See* **Olliah** and **Bhojpatra.** [*OED* & YB; Wheeler, *Madras in the Olden Times* (1707; 1861).]

Cadjowa [P. *kajawah.*] 'A frame or pannier, of which a pair are slung across a camel, sometimes made like litters to carry women or sick persons, sometimes to contain sundries of camp equipage.' [YB; Tavernier, *Six Voyages* (E. tr. 1684)]

Caffa¹ [16C.] A rick silk damask cloth, much used in the 16C. [*OED;* Wardrobe Acc., *Hy., viii.,* 18th May 1531.]

Caffa² [18C.] A kind of painted cotton cloth made in India and occurring in commerce in the 18C. [*OED;* Beawes, *Lex Mercat,* (1750).]

Caffer, Caffe, Cofferee *See* **Kafir.**

Cafila, Kafila [16C. H/Ar. *kafilah,* 'caravan, marching company'.] Hist.: A company or convoy of travellers in Arabia, Persia and India; sometimes a sea-convoy. [*OED* & YB; Linschoten, *Discourse of Voyages* etc (1598.)]

Caimal [Pg/M. *kaimal.*] 'A Nair chief; a word often occurring in the old Portuguese historians.' [YB; *The Three Voyages of Vasco-da-Gama* (1512-61; E. tr. by Lord Stanley, Hak. Soc., 1869).]

Cajan, kachang [17C. H/Mal. *kachang,* 'bean'.] The leguminous plant, *Cajanus cajan,* which gives **Dhal;** called in Jamaica 'Pigeon-peas'. [*OED* & YB.] *See* Calavance, *Gram* and Basin. [*Phil, Trans.* (1693), xvii. 688.]

Cajeput, cajuput [17C. Mal. *kayu.* 'wood' + *puteh,* 'white'.] The Malay name appeared in the vernaculars as *kayaputeh, kayapoote,* etc. (i) One or more species of the *Melaleuca* tree introduced into India from the Far East. (ii) The aromatic oil of these trees, used medicinally as a stimulant, antispasmodic and sudorific. [*OED* & YB; *English Factories in India* (1626).]

Caksen [19C.] *See* Hindi for Coxswain. [YB; Roebuck, *Naval Dict.* (1811).]

Calalux, caluz [17C. Pg/Mal. *ke-lulus,* fr. *lulus,* 'to go straight'(through anything).] 'A kind of swift rowing vessel often mentioned by Portuguese writers from the 16C. as used in the Indian Archipelago.' [YB; Andrade's Letter to Albuquerque of 22 Feb. 1513 (India Office MS); F.M. Pinto, *Voyages and Adventures,* E. tr. by H.C. Gent (1653).]

Calamander [18C. Etym. uncertain, but may be a corruption of Coromandel (cf. D. *Kalamander* (hout)).] A beautiful and extemely hard cabinet wood of Sri Lanka and India, the product of the tree *Diospyros quaesita.* See **Omander.** [*OED* & YB; Thunberg, *Travels* (1770-79; E. tr. 1799).]

Calambac [16C. Mal. *kalambak.*] The finest kind of aloes-wood or **Eagle-wood,** from the tree *Aquilaris agallochia,* akin to ebony. [*OED* & YB.] *See* **Aloes, Eagle-Wood** and **Agallocha.** [Litchfield's tr. of *Castañeda, Historie of the Discoverie and Conquest of the E. Indies* (1582).]

Calash [17C. fr., *caleche* (Russ. *kolaska*)] (1) A light carriage with low wheels and folding hood. 'This seems to have been the earliest precursor of the **Buggy** in Eastern Settlements.' [YB & *OED*.] Hence, to *calash*, to furnish with a *calash*. (2) *Also* a seaman of Far Eastern extraction. [Web; MS *Report in India Office Proceedings* 'Monday, 30th March. 1702; *London Gazette* (1666), 104.]

Calavance, Caravance [17C. Sp. *garbanzo*; Pg. *ervanco* 'chick-pea'.] A name for certain varieties of pulse, as *Dolichos sinensis* etc. [*OED* & YB.] *See* **Cajan** and **Gram**. [Cocks's *Diary* (1620), ii. 311; Hak. Soc. (1883).]

Calay, calin [16C. H *kala'i*; Pg. *calaim*; Ar. *kala'i*, 'tin', and Malay *Něgěri Kalang*, 'tin country' (Perak).] *Also* H. vb. *kala'i karnā*, 'to tin copper vessels'. [YB.] *See* **Tutenag**. [Litchfield, tr. of *Castañeda* (1582).]

Caleefa [19C. Anglo-Indian corr. of the Ar. *Khalifa*, the Caliph or Vicegerent.] Hist.: 'Used in Anglo-Indian households, at least in Upper India, for two classes of domestic servants, the tailor and the cook, and sometimes the barber and farrier. The tailor was always addressed as *Caleefa-jī* by his fellow servants.' [YB.] *See* **Maistry, Bheestie, Mehtar,** and **Matranee** for similar (ironic) honorifics for menial servants. [YB; Broughton, *Letters written in a Mahratta Camp*(ed.1892), 164.]

Caleeoon, calyoon [19C. P. *kaliyūn*.] The Persian form of the **Hubble-Bubble**. [YB.] *See* **Hooka**. [Morier, *Journey through Persia*, etc. (1812), 13.]

Calico [16C. From place-name, Calicut.] A cotton cloth orig. exported from Calicut, often in gay colours. Now applied chiefly to plain white cotton cloth; in the U.S.A. coarser than muslin. Attrib. *Calico*-ball, where the ladies wore cotton dresses. Also Calico-diaper (1969);–*lawn* (1592); –*printer* (1706). [Dunbar, *Worldis Instabilitie*. (c. 1505), 62; Dekker, *The Honest Whore* (1604), Act. ii. Sc. v.]

Calingula [19C. Tam. *kalingal*, 'sluice, water-gate'.] Much used in reports of irrigation works in S. India. [YB.] *See* **Anicut**. [T.V. Row, *Manual of Tanjore District* (1883), 322.]

Calputtee [19C. H. *kālāpattī*; Pg. *calafate*; Ar. *kālāfat*.] A ship's caulker and the process of caulking. [YB; Jal, *Archeologie Navale* (1840).]

Caluat [17C. Ar. *khilwat*, 'privacy'.] A private place or interview. [YB; Bernier, *Voy*. (E. tr. 1684; 1822); Elphinstone in *Life* (1884), 11.144.]

Caluete, caloete [16C. M. *kaluetti*.] The fatal torture of impalement. *See* **Impale**. [YB; Litchfield, E. tr.of *Castañeda* (1582),142- 3.]

Camise, cameeze, kameez [15C. H. *kamis*; Pg. *camisa*; Ar *kamīs*, 'a tunic'. (Cf. S. *kshauma*,

'linen stuff').] This word is used in India for 'shirt', espec. in *shalwar-kameez*, baggy trousers and long shirt (in the Punjab and Pakistan), for men and women. And **Churidar-kameez**, tight-fitting trousers and shirt, a modern fashion for women throughout India and even in Britain. [*OED* & YB; Will of Richard Strode of Newnham, Devon (1464); Byron,'Childe Harold' (1812).]

Camp [19C. Anglo-Indian.] In India a person not at his station or headquarters was (and sometimes still is) addressed as 'in Camp', or 'Camp Agra' (or any other place.) [YB.]

Camphire [16C.] A common Indian shrub of ancient lineage. 'My beloved is unto me as a cluster of camphire in the vineyards of Engedi.' (Song of Solomon 1:14.) (H. *mehndi*, 'henna'.) Now identified with the *Lawsonia inermis*, the henna-plant. Also called Egyptian Privet, Tree Mignonette and Cypress of Egypt (Pliny). [*OED*; Bible; Camphire, *Song of Solomon* (1611); Eden *Treat. New Inde* (1553)]. *See* **Mehndi**.

Camphor [14C. H. *kapur*, Ar. *kāfūr*; Prak. *kappūram*; S. *karpūram*.] (Early forms in English are various, *camphire* prevailing from the 15C. to c. 1800.] A white translucent vegetable oil, $C_1 H_{16}$, distilled from the wood of the tree *Camphora officinarium*, and *Dryobalanops camphora*, purified into a whitish, crystalline, volatile substance, with a bitter, aromatic taste and characteristic smell. Also called in India *Bhimseni*, after the demi-god Bhimsen, second son of Pandu. Also *Camphorate; Camphor-wood (chest); camphor*-balls; -julep; -oil; -pill; -posset, etc. [*OED* & YB; Cocks's *Diary* (1613), ii. 343 (Hak. Soc. (1883); Ward, *Edward II* (1313), Act. 7.]

Campoo, Campo. [19C. H. *kampū*. Corr. of E. *camp*, or Pg. *campo*.] 'Used for a "camp" but formerly was specifically applied to the partially disciplined brigades under European commanders in the Mahratta service.' [YB.] There may be a link between this word and **Kampong** & **Compound.**, in Grant, *Hist. India* (1803), i.ixx, 368/1.]

Canaut, connaught, conaut, khanat [17C. H/Ar. *kanāt*.] The side wall of a tent, or a canvas enclosure. *See* **Surrapardah**. [*OED* & YB; Sir T. Roe, *Embassy to the Court of the Great Mogul* (1615-19), ii. 325; Hak. Soc. (1889).]

Candle-nut oil *See* **Kekune-oil**.

Candy[1] [16C. Tam./Tel./M. *kandi*; Pg. *candil*; fr. S. *khand*, 'to divide; break.'] A weight of about 500 lbs., or 20 **Maunds**; used in S. & W.

India. 'A candy of land is supposed to be as much as will produce a candy of grain, approx. 75 acres.' [OED & YB; Linschoten, *Discours of Voyages* etc. (1598); Purchas, *Pilgr.* (1618), 1.657; *Hak. Soc.* (1885), 1. 245.]

Candy² (Sugar) [15C. S. *khanda* 'sugar in pieces', orig. 'piece, fragment', fr. *khand*, 'break' (cf. P. *kand*, 'sugar').] Sugar-candy; sugar clarified and crystallized after repeated slow boiling. 'Though it came no doubt to Europe fr. the P. and Ar. *kand* [it] is of Indian origin.' [YB & OED; *Liber Cocorum* (c. 1420), 7; Minshell, *Guide into the Tongues* (1627).]

Canongo, canango (e) [18C. P. *kānūn-go*, 'law-utterer'.] A subordinate native revenue officer and, in Bengal, the registrar of a **Tahsil**, or other revenue sub-division, who received reports from the **Patwaris**, or village registrars and kept a record of them. [YB; Long, *Records of Government* etc. (1748-67; ed. 1869), 157.]

Canteroy, canteray [18C. Tam. *Kanthiravā Rāyā*, lit. 'The Lion-voiced', fr. S. *kantha*, 'throat' + *rava*, 'noise'.] A gold coin formerly used in the S.E. part of the Madras territory, worth Rs 3. Properly *kanthiravi hun* (or **Pagoda**) from *Kanthiravā Rāyā*, who ruled in Mysore from 1638 to 1659. [YB; Dalrymple, *Oriental Repertory* (1791-7), i.237.]

Cantonment (pron. cantoonment) [18C. tr. Fr. *cantonnement*, 'quarters'.] 'Constantly used in India, and so little used elsewhere. It was applied to military stations in India, built usually on a plan which was originally that of a standing camp. At first reserved for troops and government officials only, but now often merely a part of a town that was formerly so reserved.' [YB & OED; *Gentl. Mag.* (1756); xxvi. 554. Thackeray, *Vanity Fair* (1848), 11, ch. 8.]

Capass, kapas [18C. H. *kapās; S. karpasa*.] The cotton plant, *Gossypium*, and cotton wool. See **Cotton** and **Kapok**. [YB; Long, *Records of Government*, etc. (1748-67).]

Cape Gooseberry See **Tiparry**.

Capel, kapal [16C. M *kappal*, 'a ship' (cf. Mal. *kāpal*).] 'This word appears to be still in use [1886] on the West Coast of India.' [YB.] It is commonly used throughout Malaysia and Indonesia. [Varthema's *Travels*, tr. by Eden (1576).]

Caracoa, caracolle, karkollen [17C. Mal *kūra-kūra*, 'a tortoise', (or poss. fr. Ar. *kurkur*. pl. *karakīr*, 'a large merchant vessel').] The Malay galley, measuring often 100 ft. long and 10 ft. wide with as many as 90 rowers.

Caracore, 'a sort of vessel used in the Phillipines Isles' (1794). [OED.] Cf. **Carrack**. [*Middleton's Voyage* (1606), 2.]

Carambola, cumrunga [16C. fr. Mar. *karanbal; Pg. carambola; S. karma-ranga*.] The acid fruit, golden-yellow, ellipsoid, 10-ribbed, of a small E. Indian tree, *Averrhoa carambola*. [OED & YB.] See **Blimbi**. [Linschoten, *Discours of Voyages* etc., 96 (E. tr. 1598); *Hak. Soc.* (1885), ii. 33.]

Caravel, carvel [16C. Pg. *caravela*.] A ship variously described, but the Portuguese *caravela* was a small ship with lateen sails, rounded, but not long or sharp like a galley and ordinarily of about 200 tons burden. [OED & YB; R. Thorne, in Hak., *Divers Voy.* (1527); Beaumont & Fletcher, *Wit Without Money* (1615), Act 1, Sc. I.]

Carboy, karboy [18C. P. *karābah*. 'a large flagon'.] A large globular bottle of green or blue glass, covered with basket-work, for holding acids and other corrosives. [OED & YB; Hanway, *Hist. Acc. of the British Trade* etc. (1753), i. 102.]

Carcan, carcoona, karkhana, karkoanna [17C. H/P. *kār–khāna*.] 'A place where business is done.' 'A workshop, a departmental establishment, such as that of the commissariat, or the artillery park, in the field.' [YB.] Fig. any great fuss or bustle (obs). [Bernier, (E. tr. 1684), 83; ed. Ball (1889), 1800; Wellington, *Despatches* (1837), i. 144.]

Carcoon, karkun See prec. [17C. Mar. *kārkūn*, 'clerk'; P. *kārkun*, operator, 'manager'; fr. *kar*, 'action, work, business'.] A clerk. [OED & YB; Foster, *Letters* (1615; ed. 1896-1900).]

Cardamom, cardamum [14C. Gr. *kardamōmon* fr. *kardomon*, 'cress' + *amomōn*, Indian spice.] A spice consisting of the seed, cardamom, *Elletaria cardamomum*, the only kind included in the British pharmacopoeia. Used medicinally as a stomachic and also for flavouring sauces and curries. 'Cardomomum helpyth ayenst wambling and indygnacyon of the stomach.' (Trevisa, *Barth De P. R. XVII, XXIII*, 1398.) [OED; Eden, *Treat, New Ind.* (1553).]

Carnac, cornac [18C. Pg. *cornaca*; perh. Sinh. *kūrawanāyaka* (cf. Du. *cournakeas*) (*Valentijn*).] Used by Fr. writers as equivalent of **Mahout**, elephant driver (fr. S. *kari*, 'elephant'). Supposed to be of Indian origin, but the word apparently is not found in any Indian language. [OED & YB; *Collect Voy. (Churchill)* (1704), iii. 825/2, Hamilton, *New Acct. of the E. Indies* (1727), ii. 110.]

Carnatic *See* **Karnataka** & **Kannada**.

Carpet-snake [19C. Anglo-Indian.] In India applied to any kind of snake found in a dwelling house, other than a Cobra, or a **Dhaman** (rat-snake); most commonly the *Lycodon aulicus*. [Whitworth, *Anglo-Indian Dict.* (1885).]

Carom, carrom [18C. Ar. Shortening of 'carambole', a cannon stroke as in billiards.] A game played on a square enclosed board, with corner pockets into which discs are cannoned (carommed); popular throughout India. [*OED*; C. Jones, *Hoyle's Games Impr.* (1779), 260.]

Carrack, carrick, etc. [14C. Pg. *carraca* (origin uncertain).] *See* **Caracoa**. 'A large ship of burden, also fitted for warfare, such as those ships formerly used by the Portuguese in trading with the East Indies; a galleon.' [*OED*.] In use from the Middle Ages down to the 17C. [Beaumont & Fletcher, *The Coxcomb* (1613), i.3.] The *'Madre de Deus'* captured by the English in 1592, homeward bound from India, was about 1600 tons. [Chaucer, The Prologue of the Somonours Tale (c. 1386; 1615); Terry in *Purchas* (1625-6; ed. 1777), 34.]

Cartmeel [19C. Anglo-Indian.] Mail-cart. 'This was the ordinary form, at least among the Punjabis. Such inversions were not uncommon. Sir David Ochterlony was known as Loniokhtar among his Sepoys.' [YB.]

Cartouce [19C. Anglo-Indian. fr. Fr. *cartouche*; Sepoy-Hindi, *kārtūs*, 'a cartridge'.] *See* **Tostdaun**. [YB; *Society in India*, by an Indian Officer (1841).]

Caryota [18C.] The name of a magnificent palm, *Caryota urens*, growing in S. India, Bangladesh and Sri Lanka, and yielding an abundance of **Toddy** and **Jaggery**. In Sri Lanka it is the *Kitul-palm* and in Bombay the *Hill* – or *Sago-palm*. [YB; Knox, *An Historical Relation of the Island of Ceylon* (1681), 15; Thunberg, *Travels*, 1770-79 (E. tr. 1799).]

Cash, cass [16C. Tam. *kāsu*.] Name of a small coin or of a weight of silver and gold in the E. Indies and China. Also Sinh. *kāsi*, 'coin' and S. *karsha*, 'a weight of silver or gold equal to 1/400 **Tola**. Applied by Europeans to coins of low value in India and elsewhere. The basis of the monetary system of S. India up to 1818. (*See* Dubois.) [Varthema, *Travels* (E. tr. 1576); Linschoten, *Discourse of Voyages*, etc. (E. tr. 1598; 1600); John Davis in *Purchas*, 1625-6, i. 117.]

Cashew, kaju, acajou [16C. Pg. *caju*; Braz *acajoba* var. of *acaju* (whence Fr. *acajou*, 'mahogany'); Fr. Brazilian, *acajoba*.] The tree, *Anacardium occidentale*, and its edible nut. Widely diffused as a wild tree in India before the end of the 17C., and described by Acosta (1598) as an Indian Tree. Also cashew-apple (1813);–nut (1796);–bird (*Tanagra zena*) (1852); kaju-gum. [*OED* & YB; Linschoten, *Discours of Voyages*, etc. (1598), 94; Fryer, *New Account* etc. (1672-81), 182.]

Cashmere [19C. (Place-name **Kashmir**.)] A **Shawl** (properly a *Cashmere*-shawl) made from the fine wool of the Kashmir goat, and of the wild Tibetan goat. Now the name is also applied to woollen fabrics made elsewhere in imitation of the genuine article, e.g. *Cashmerette* (1886), *See* **Kerseymere**. [*OED* & YB; Forbes, *Or. Mem.* (1813), iii. 177; Foster (1615), *Letters* (ed. 1896-1900), iii. 283.]

Cassab, cussab [19C. H/Ar. *kassāb*, 'butcher'.] A seaman of Asian origin employed in the merchant service. [*OED*; *Instr. Census Clerks*, (1881), 35.]

Cassanar, cattanar [19C. M. *kattanār*, 'chief'.] A priest of the Malabar Syrian church. (According to YB formed eventually from S. *kartri*, 'an achiever'). [YB; Logan, *Malabar* (1887-91), i.211.]

Cas(s)umunar [17C. (A corr. of some Eastern name?)] The tuberous root of the E. Indian plant *Curcuma aromatica*: warm, bitter, aromatic, smelling like ginger, and used medically in hysterical, epileptic and paralytic afflictions. *See* **Zedoary** & **Zerumbet**. [*OED*; Pechey, *Observations on the Root called Casmunar* (1693).]

Caste, cast [17C. Anglo-Indian, fr. Pg. *casta*, 'race', 'lineage', 'breed', 'pure or unmixed stock'.] (Cf. E. *chaste*.) The Portuguese applied this term in India about the middle of the 16C. [Garcia, 1563]. Before 1800 it was written 'cast' generally, and 'caste' exceptionally. The S. word is *varna*, 'colour'. A moral and social system, of several hereditary classes, developed and maintained in India over the last 2000 years, categorizing and polarizing the **Hindu** population into hereditary and corporate units defined by descent, marriage and occupation, and differentiated by strict laws of commensality, 'pollution' and other taboos and regulations governing precise and complex interrelationships of the four main castes (**Brahmin, Kshatriya, Vaishya, Sudra**), and of innumerable sub-castes within the total system. In recent times the 'occupation' element differentiating the castes (scholar-priest, warrior, merchant, labourer) has largely fallen into disuse, but recent political attempts to weaken or destroy the caste system have met with only limited success, though inter-caste marriages defying the endogamy principles, and 'inter-dining', disregarding the commensality rules, as well as inter-caste socializing, have become more noticeable, especially among 'westernized' and professional Hindus and particularly among men. Attempts to improve the lot of low-caste and caste-less Hindus have met with some opposition and limited success.

See **Jati, Gotra, Pariah, Harijan, Scheduled Caste** and – **Tribe**, and **Interdine**. In Tamil Nadu castes are, also, Right-hand (*Valakai*) and Left-hand (*Idakai*) (or *Valathu kai* and *Edathu kai*); the agricultural classes on the one hand and the artisans on the other. Faction fights were at one time common between these two. *Transf*: Any hereditary classes resembling those in India, or whose members keep themselves socially distinct or inherit special privileges, e.g. 'Boston Brahmins' of the U.S.A. Hence: To lose *caste; outcast* (sb); *half-caste; caste* feeling; -system; -ridden; -mark; -bound; *caste*-hood; castism; *caste-less, low-caste; high-caste*. (This is also applied to breeds of animals, as in a '*high-caste* Arab horse', and to social distinctions in a community of social insects, such as ants (Darwin, 1859). [Withington in Purchas, *Pilgr.* (1613); i. 485.]

Castees [17C. Indo-Pg. fr. Pg. *castico*, fr. *casta*, 'pure, unmixed, noble'.] Hist.: Long obsolete, this word indicated persons of pure Portuguese descent, alike in the home land, Portugal, and in India, while *mistices* applied to those of 'mixed' parentage whether born in Portugal (generally of Moorish and Portuguese antecedents), or 'country-born' in India (usually of Indian and Portuguese parents). German, French, as well as Portuguese writers emphasized the 'purity' of descent of 'country born' *castees*, at least up to the last decades of the 17th century. [YB.] It seems, however, that the original purport of the word suffered a 'sea-change' and came at last to be confused with *mistices* on some occasions (espec. perhaps, among the British in India) before both expressions sank into an Indian oblivion. This semantic change, and for the same personal and social reasons, resembled that which happened to **Anglo-Indian**, a term which gradually ceased to apply solely (and ultimately not at all) to **Pukka** Britishers, and was taken over by Eurasians in India, who preferred it because of its narrower and less derogatory social implications and overtones. [Linschoten, *Discours of Voyages* etc. (E. tr. 1598; Hak. Soc. 1885; 1887), i. 184; Wheeler, *Census of English on the Coast* (1669; 1878), i. 356.] *See* **Reinol**.

Casuarina [Poss. Mal. *kasuari*, 'the *cassowary* bird'.] A tree, *casuarina equisetifolia*, indigenous to the coast of Chittagong, Burma, Malaysia and the Indonesian archipelago. Now established in Bengal and S. India. The name appears based, as Skeat suggests, on the Malay name of the *cassowary* bird because the needles of the tree resemble the quills of the bird. 'The tree has considerable superficial resemblance to a larch or other finely-feathered conifer.' [YB & *OED; Naval Chron.* (1806), xv. 460; Lewin, *A Fly on the Wheel* (1885). 362.]

Catamaran, cuttmurram [17C. Tam. *kattu*, tie bond' + *maram*, 'wood'.]

I. Orig. a raft of two or more logs tied together; used on the Coromandel coast for transit of goods and passengers to and from ships anchored in the roads. Later, spectacular developments in Britain and the U.S.A. produced twin-hulled sailing vessels built for racing, and called by the yachting fraternity, 'cats' (1957). More recently, a three-hulled variety, inevitably denominated '*Tri*-maran', was invented, capable of trans-oceanic sailing in competition with other large yachts. [*OED* & YB; *English Factories in India* (1618; 1669; ed Foster 1906-27); Fryer, *New Accounts*, etc. (1672-81), 24.]

II. Obs. *Catamaran* also came to mean a kind of fire-ship or instrument of naval warfare (resembling the modern torpedo), invented in 1804 to counter Napoleon's expected cross-channel invasion of England. [Lord Stanhope, *Life of Pitt.* (1861-2), iv. 218; *Chron. in Ann. Reg.* (1804) 419/2.]

III. A cantankerous, quarrelsome female, 'an old hag', by Association with slang use of 'cat'. [*OED* & YB; Marryat, *Peter Simple* (1833); Thackeray, *Newcomes* (1854–5).]

Catechu, cutch [17C. Tam. *kacchu*; Tel. *kaychu*; Kan. *kāshu*; Pg. cacho, Fr. *cachou*.] An astringent substance with much tannin, extracted from the wood of various species of Acacia, e.g. *Acacia catechu; A. suma; A. sundra.* Also known as *Terra Japonica* as it was brought from Japan to Europe in the 17C. Used in medicine, tanning, calico printing and dyeing. Also Catechin (1853) and *catechuic* (1838). It is also a component of *pān,* mixed with **Areca,** lime (**chunam**) tobacco, etc. and wrapped in **Betel** leaves. Also cachou (1703), a sweetmeat for sweetening the breath. [*OED* & YB.] *See* **Cutch & Cauth.** [Foster, *Letters* (1616; ed. 1896-1900), iv. 227.]

Catla [Beng. *kātlā.*] A cyprinoid fresh-water fish, catla-catla of the Bengal rivers. [Webster, *3rd New Intern. Dict.;* Hawkins, *CIWIE.*]

Cat's Eye [16C. E./Pg. *Olhos de gatos.*] A variety of chalcedonic quartz which, cut *en cabochon,* displays a peculiar floating lustre when held up to the light, resembling the contracted pupil of a cat's eye. The finest come from Sri Lanka and Kerala. [*OED* & YB; Hakluyt, *Voy.* (*c.* 1599), II. i; Boyle's *Hindu Medicine* (1837), 103.]

Cattimandoo, callemundoo, etc. [19C. Tel. *kattimandu.*] A resin from the juice of the plant *Euphorbia cattimandu* and other species of *Euphorbia.* Used as a cement and as a medicine for rheumatism. [*OED; Catalogue of the Great Exhibition* (1851), IV. 1. 877/2.]

Catty, katty [16C. Mal. *kati.*] *See* **Caddy.** A weight (*c.* $1\frac{1}{2}$ lbs) used from China to Malaysia, and formerly in Indo-Malaysian and Indo-Chinese trade. [*OED* & YB; Phillips tr. Linschoten (1598), 34; Hak. Soc. (1807), 1. 113.]

Catur [16C. Poss. fr. Indo-Pg. *catur,* or fr. E. 'to cut' (cf E. cutter.)] Hist.: A light boat on the Malabar (Kerala) coast in the early days of the Portuguese in India; sharp at both ends and curving back, with sails and oars. *See* **Cutter** [*OED* & YB; Litchfield, E. tr. of Castañeda's *Historie of the Discoverie and Conquest of the East Indies* (1582).]

Cauth [19C. H. *kath.*] An Anglo-Indian name for **Catechu, Cutch,** occasionally used in commerce. *Also* Mar. *kāt.* [*OED;* Simmonds, *Dict. Trade* (1858).]

Cavally, Cavalloe [17C. Pg. *cavalla,* 'mackerel'.] A tropical fish, also called 'horse-mackerel', *caranx caballus* and *cubium caballa,* described by Pyrard de Laval (*c.* 1610), and by Day (1878). 'Many of the species are extensively salted or sun-dried and eaten by the poor.' [YB & *OED;* Sir T. Herbert, *Trar.*

(1634), 213.]

Cawney, cawny [19C. Tam. *kāni,* 'property, land', fr. *kān,* 'to see', 'what is known and recognised'.] A variable measure of land in Tamil Nadu, but the standard *cawney* is considered to be 1.322 acres. *See* **Ground.** (Buchanan, *Mysore,* etc. (1807), 1.6. [*OED* & YB.]

Cazee, kaji *See* **Kazi.**

Cerame, carame [16C. M. *srāmbi,* 'a gate-house'; Mal. *sĕrambi,* 'a house verandah'.] A gatehouse with a room over the gate and generally fortified. A feature sometimes of temples as well as private dwellings. The word is also applied to a room elevated on four posts. [YB; Litchfield, tr. of *Castañeda* (1582).]

Cha, char, chai [16C. Anglo-Indian.] Various Indian languages. Mandarin *Ch'a* (leaves of) the tea plant, *Thea chinesis,* or *Camilla theifera,* from which the beverage is brewed; the beverage itself. In the 17C. the form *cha* was occasionally used in English middleclass society; in the 19C. it was christened *chai* among soldiers; in the 20C. *char* became popular espec. in the military vernacular. Hence *charwallah,* soldier's *argot* for a teetotaller. [Frank Richards, *Old Soldiers Never Die* (1933).] A *charwallah squadron* was an R.A.F. squadron consisting of Indian personnel. *See* **Tea.** [*OED* & YB; Linschoten, *Discours of Voyages into Ye Easte and Weste Indies,* (1598).]

Chabi, chabee [19C. H. *chāb(h)ī;* Pg. *chave,* 'a key'.] In Bengal it became *ṣabī;* and in Tam. *sāvī.* [YB.]

Chabootra, chabutra, cherbuter [19C. H. *chābutrā.*] A paved or plastered platform or terrace attached to a house, or in a garden (to sit and converse on). [*OED* & YB; Williamson, *Vade Mecum* (1810), ii. 114; Scott, *The Surgeon's Daughter* (1827).] *See* **Pyal.**

Chabouk *See* **Chawbuck.**

Chackram *See* **Chackrum.**

Chackur, chakar [19C. H/P. *chākar.* Obs.] 'The word is hardly ever used in Anglo-Indian households except as a rhyming amplification to *Naukar* [**Nokur**], viz. *Nauker-chākar.* 'The whole following [of servants].' 'But in a past generation there was a distinction made between *naukar,* the superior servant, such as a **munshi, gomashta, chobdar, khansama,** etc. and *chakur,* a menial servant (such as a "sweeper" or *totī*).' [YB; Williamson, *Vade Mecum* (1810), i.187.]

Chadar *See* **Chudder.**

Chagal, chagul, chaghal [20C. H. *chāgal;* S. *chāgala,* 'coming from a goat'.] A leather or canvas water-bottle. [*OED;* Webster (1909); *Blackwood's Mag.,* Oct. 1920.]

Chait, chaitra [19C. H. *chait;* S. *chaitra.*] A month of the Hindu year (March-April); the others being: *Baisakh* (April-May); *Jeth* (May-June); *Asar* (June-July); *Sawan* (July-Aug.); *Bhadon* (Aug-Sept.); *Asin* (Sept-Oct.); *Kartik* (Oct.-Nov.); *Pus* (Dec.-Jan.); *Magh* (Jan.-Feb.); *Phagun* (Feb.-March). [Whitworth, *Anglo-Indian Dict.* (1885).]

Chaitya [19C. S. *chaitiya* fr. *chitā.*] (1) Relating to a funeral pile, mound, monument, sacred trees, etc. (2) A Buddhist place or object of reverence or worship (Tibetan: **Chorten**). (3) A Jain temple. See **Dagoba, Stupa** (1875), **Tope, Chorten, Vihara.** [*OED; Encycl. Brit.* ii. 394; A. Huxley, *Proper Studies* (1927), 181.]

Chajja [19C. H.] Projecting screen above window. [*CIWIE.*]

Chakara, chaakara [18C. H. *chākara.*] Crescent-shaped mud-banks, 10-25 sq. kms., which appear off the Kerala coast during the S.W. monsoon, providing heavy catches of prawns, sardines and mackerel for Kerala fishermen. [A. Hamilton, *A New Account of the East Indies* (1727).]

Chakdar [Punjab. *chakdār,* fr. *chak,* 'tenure'; S. *chakra* + P. *dar,* 'having'.] A native land tenant of India intermediate between the proprietor and cultivator. [Wilson, *Glossary,* (1855).]

Chakra(h) [19C. H/S. *chakra,* 'wheel'.] (1) A sharp-edged circular weapon of the **Sikhs** (1883). [*Encycl. Brit.* (1883), xx. iii/2.] (2) A discus or mystic circle in the hands of pictured Hindu Gods. [Murray's *Handbook, India & Ceylon* (1891), 384/1. (3) Yoga: One of the centres of spiritual power in the human body. [Basu, *Theosophist* (March 1888), 373.] (4) The emblem on the flag of India; the Ashokan wheel.] Constituent Assembly of India, Resolution 22. (1947).] (5) Decorations for valour in the Indian armed services are called *Param Vir Chakra; Maha Vir-, Ashoka-, Kirti-,* and *Shaurya-,* [*CIWIE.* (1984); *OED.*]

Chakravartin [19C. S. *chakravartin,* 'one who turns'.] A universal sovereign; an ideal ruler; one who turns the wheel (of life or government). [Webster; Whitworth, *Anglo-Indian Dict.* (1885).]

Chalak [19C. H. *chālak.*] crafty, cunning. [*CIWIE.*]

Chalan [19C. H. *chalān.*] (1) An invoice, a pass, a voucher, a way-bill; (2) A draft of prisoners; (3) To put on a charge (milit.) [*OED; CIWE;* Simmonds, *Dict. of Trade* (1858).]

Chalu [19C. H. *chalū.*] Ordinary, easy-going, cunning. [CIWIE.]

Chamar,[1] chumar [19C. H. *chamar.*] One of the inferior caste of leather-workers, tanners, shoe-makers found throughout N. India. In S. India the equivalent is **Chuckler.** (The S. is *charman,* 'skin leather' + *kāra,* 'worker'). Also, in N. and Central India an agricultural labourer. [*OED* & YB; Malcolm, *Central India,* 2nd ed. (1824), ii. 179; Kipling, *Kim* (1901), iii. 81.]

Chamar[2] [19C. H. *chanwar, chaunri;* S. *chāmara.*] A fan, made of Yak's tail or peacock's feathers, used as a mark of royalty or in temples. See **Chowry** and **Cow-Tails.** [YB; *Nic. Conti in India in the 15th C.,* ed. Major (Hak. Soc., 1857); Maria Graham, *Journal* (1812).]

Chamcha [20C. H. *chamcha,* 'spoon'.] Slang: A stooge, toady, sycophant, boot-licker, flatterer, toad-eater. Note modern Indo-Anglian usage: 'I watched the pathetic spectacle of my husband, a young man, a professional, *chamchaing* and *maskalagaoing* (buttering up) a callow youth whose voice had not even cracked properly.' See **Toady-Bacha.** Namita Gokhale, *Paro* (1984): 'Indians ate with their fingers, Britishers with knives, forks and spoons. To please their masters, Indians also paraded their cutlery when entertaining them.' [Tariq Ali, *The Nehrus and the Gandhis* (1985).]

Champak, champac, chumpuk, champ, etc. [17C. H/S. *chāmpākā;* M. *chempaka.*] A small tree, a species of magnolia (*magnoliaceae*), *Michelia champaca,* bearing highly fragrant, creamy-white yellow flowers, held in high and religious esteem by Hindus and Buddhists. The tree-blossoms are used for worship (**Puja**) and rubbed on the body at marriages. Hence this is found everywhere in temples and gardens. It is also valuable for its timber, for cabinet-making, while a decoction of the bark makes a good tonic, and the flowers are thought to be a cure for coughs and rheumatism. The scented oil from the flowers is reputed to relieve eye troubles and gout. Also called the Temple Tree. (There is also another tree called the Temple Tree, *Plumeria Rubra,* the Frangipani, alias Jasmine Tree, Dead Man's Flower, Life Tree and Pagoda Tree.) [Pietro Della Valle, *Voyages,* E. tr. by

G. Havers (1664); Sir W. Jones, *Mem. of the Life of* by Lord Teignmouth (1786; ed. 1807), ii.9.]

Champana See **Sampan.**

Chana [19C. H. *chana.*] The chick-pea, *Cicer arietinum.* See **Gram.** [Whitworth, *Anglo-Indian Dict* (1885).]

Chandal, chandaul [19C *chandāl,* 'an outcaste'.] 'A man of the lowest and most depised of mixt tribes, sprung from a **Sudra** father and a **Brahmin** mother.' [YB.] See **Halalcore.** [Maria Graham, *Journal of a Residence in India* (1812), 31.]

Chandu chandoo [19C. H. *chandū.*] Preparation of opium for smoking. [*OED;* John Craig, *Dict. of Eng. Lang.* (1849); Simmonds, *Dict. of Trade* (1858).]

Chang, chong [19C. Tibetan, *chang.*] Tibetan barley-, or rice-beer, or -wine. [*OED;* S. Turner, *Acc. Embassy Court of Teshoo Lama* (1800), I. ii.]

Chank, chunk [17C. H. *chankh.* S. *chankha,* cf. Pg. *chanco, chanquo.*] A large kind of shell (*Turbinella rapa*) used by Hindus for offering temple libations, as a horn to blow at temples, and for fashioning into ornaments. 'The abnormal *chank,* with its spiral opening to the right, is of exceptional value.' [YB.] See **Conch.** [*OED* & YB; *Eng. Fact in India,* (1618-69); ed. Foster (1906-27).]

Chapat(t)i See **Chupatty.**

Chapkan See **Chupkun.**

Chappal [19C. H. *chappal.*] A sandal, usually of leather, but nowadays frequently of rubber or plastic. [*OED.*] Pl. *chappals* and *chapplees.* [E. F. Knight, *Where Three Empires Meet* (1893), 52.]

Chappow, chapao, chupao [19C. Pushtoo. *chapa'o* 'raid; foray inroad'; P. *chapū,* 'plunder'.] A plundering expedition or raid. See **Dour.** [*OED;* Mayne Reid, *Odd People,* (1860), 240; Pottinger, *Travels in Beloochistan* and Sinde (1816), 172.]

Chaprassi See **Chuprassi.**

Char [20C.] Popular spelling of **Cha,** 'tea'. [*OED; Athenaeum,* 25 July (1919), 664/1.]

Char, chaur, churr [19C. H/S. *char,* 'to move'.] New alluvial land formed when a river changes its course, as the floods sink, claims to which were regulated by the Bengal Reg. XI. 1825. [Wilson, *Gloss.* (1855).] [YB; *Life in the Mofussil,* by an Ex-Civilian (1878), ii. 3 seq.]

Charan [19C. H. *chāran.*] A bard, minstrel, genealogist, panegyrist of the gods. [Whitworth, *Anglo-Indian Dict.* (1885).]

Charas, churrus[1] [19C. H. *charas.*] The narcotic resinous exudation of the *Cannabis sativa* or *indica* plant. 'Said to be so-called because the drug is collected by men who walk with leather aprons through the fields.' [YB.] See next. [*OED* & YB.] See **Bhang, Ganja, Subji** & **Hashish.** [Elphinstone, *Caubul* (1839), i. 344.]

Charas, churrus[2] [19C. H. *charas.*] An irrigation apparatus, worked by oxen, for drawing water from a well, by means of pulley ropes and a large leather bag (H. *charsa*), into irrigation channels in the fields. Hence, also, the area irrigated from the well. [YB; Forbes. *Or. Mem.* (1813), i. 153.]

Chark(h)a, churka [19C. H. *charkhah, charkhā,* 'Spinning-wheel', S. *chakrā,* 'wheel'.] (1) A roller cotton gin in frequent use in India. [*OED;* Markham, *Peru* (1880), 122.] (2) A symbol of Gandhian ideology (20C.) See **Takli.**

Charnockite [19C. Pers. name.] (Job) Charnock (d. 1693), founder of Calcutta, whose tombstone- is made of this black Hypersthene-granite. Typically found near Madras. Also *charnockitic* (adj.) [*OED;* T.H. Holland, in *Jrnl. Asiat. Soc. Beng.* (1893), LXII. ii.164.]

Charpoy [19C. H. *chārpāi,* fr. *chahār,* 'four' + *pāi* 'foot'.] Lit. 'four-footed'. A light Indian bedstead with a mattress of string or webbing. See **Cot.** *Charpoy-***bashing,** = R.A.F. slang, 'sleeping', 'sleep'. c. 1920. [*OED* & YB; Stoqueler, *Handbk. Brit. India* (1845); Partridge, *Dict. of Slang* (1979).] See **Teapoy.**

Charsaubis [20C. H. *char* (4), *sau* (100), *bis* (20) = 420.] This refers to Section 420 of the Indian Penal Code, dealing with fraud and cheating. [Hawkins, *CIWIE.*]

Chat [19C. H. *chāt.*] A salad of spiced cut fruit and vegetables. [*CIWIE.*]

Chatta, chatter, chitory [17C. H. *chhata;* S. *chhatra.*] (1) An (Indian) umbrella. Also *chattri,* an umbrella-shaped pavilion. [Fryer *New Acct. of E. India* etc. (1672-81), 160.]

Chatta [19C.] (2) The Umbrella-Tree, *Magnolia tripetula.* [*OED;* Caunter, *Orient Ann.* (1834), V. 58.]

Chatty [18C. Tel. *chatti;* Tam. *shāti;* H. *chātī;* Pali. *chādi.*] A spheroidal earthenware water pot of S. India. [*OED* & YB.] See **Ghurra.** [*Lives of the Lindsays* (1781; ed. 1849), iii. 285.]

Chaudhri, chaudhari, chaudhury See **Chowdry.**

Chauki, choky, chowki, etc. 17C. H./P. *chauki,* 'shed'.] (1) Guard-house, custom house, toll-station, palanquin bearers' station, police station, lock-up, etc. (In English slang this last sense has an association with *choke*. [*OED* & YB.] *See* **Jail-Khana**. [Saris in Purchas, Pilgr. (1608), 1.391.] (2) A chair, almost peculiar to Bengal, poss. connected with *chatur*, *'four'*. [YB; *Gleig, Mem. of Warren Hastings* (1772; ed. 1841), i. 238.]

Chaukidar, chokidar *See* **Chowkidar**.

Chaulmoogra, chalmaugra [19C Beng. *cāul*, 'rice' + *mugrā*, 'a type of plant'.] An E. Indian tree of the family *Flacourtiaceae*, especially *Taraktogenos Kurzii* from whose seeds an oil was formerly obtained for the treatment of leprosy. Also *chaulmoogric acid* (1909). [*OED*.] *See* **Chout**. [Roxburgh, *Flora Indica* (1815), III. 836.]

Chaung [20C. Burm. *chaung*.] A watercourse in Burma (*Further India*). [*OED*; Fergusson, *Beyond Chindwin* (1945), V. 71.]

Chauth *See* **Chout**.

Chaw [17C. Obs.] Tea. *See* **Cha, Char, Chai**. [YB; Cocks' *Diary* (1616), i. 215; Hak. Soc., (1883).]

Chawbuck, chabouk [17C. Obs. H. *chābuk*.] 'horse-whip'. In India, also a flogging with a whip. [Fryer, 1682.] And *chabuckswar* fr. *chābuksuwār*, a 'rough rider'. [Kipling, *Beast and Man in India* (1820)] Note: Malay *chabok*, and Cape Dutch *Sjambok*. [*OED* & YB; *Eng. Fact. in India* (1618-69).]

Chawl [19C. 'a row of rooms let for lodgings'. Mar. *chāl*; S. *shālā*, 'a house'.] An Indian tenement house, especially in Bombay. [*OED*; *Pall Mall* Gaz., 7 Dec. (1891), 7/2.]

Chay(a), choy(a) [16C. Tam. *saya*.] The root of the Indian plant *Oldenlandia umbellata*, sometimes called 'Indian Madder' and 'Dye Root, yielding a deep red dye for Indian cottons. [*OED* & YB; *Early Travels in India* (1583-1619; ed. Foster, 1921); tr. *c*.1598 Frederike (1566) in Hakluyt.]

Chebuli, chebule [16C. Poss. H. *Kābulī*, 'of Kabul'.] One of the numerous kinds of prune-like astringent fruits, **Myrobalans**, exported from India from ancient times. The fruit of the *Terminalis chebula*. Hence *chebulic* (adj) (1727). [*OED* & YB; Eden, *Decades W. Ind.* (1555), III. iv.]

Chee-chee *See* **Chi-chi**.

Cheel [19C. Hindi *chīl*.] The Indian kite, *Milvus migrans govinda* alias 'Pariah Kite'. 'This abundant and successful scavenger can be seen soaring and flapping around villages and towns at all times.' [Woodcock, *Birds of the Indian Sub-continent* (1980); V. Ball, *Jungle Life* (1880). xiv; Kipling, *Jungle Book* (1894).]

Cheeny, chini [19C. H. *chīnī* 'Chinese'.] The whiter kinds of common sugar in India. *See* **Jaggery**. [YB; Williamson, *Vade Mecum* (1810), ii. 134.]

Cheese [19C. poss. H/P. *chīz*, 'thing'.] The right, correct thing; wealth and fame; something first rate, someone important, the 'boss', the 'Big Cheese'. *See* **Subcheese**. The expression used to be common among Anglo-Indians, e.g. 'My new Arab is the real *chīz*.' 'These *cheroots* are the real *chīz*, 'the real thing'. [YB & *OED* (1818); *London Guide* (cited in *Slang Dict.* (1873); Thackeray, *Conningsby* (*c*. 1850), iii.

Cheetah, chittah [18C. H. *chītā*.] 'the *Hunting Leopard, Felis jubata*' (S. *chitraka*, fr. *chitra*. 'spotted, variegated'; orig. 'visible' from *chit*, 'to perceive'. Now extinct in the wild in India, but formerly tamed for hunting deer. [*OED* & YB; *Phil. Trans.* (1781), 1. LXX.]

Chehlum [20C. H. *chehlum*.] The fortieth day of (Muslim) mourning for the dead. [Hawkins, *CIWIE*.]

Chela, cheyla [18C. H. *chēlā*, fr. S. *chētaka*. Lit. 'a servant'.] 'Many changes have been rung upon it in Hindu life, so that it has meant a slave, a family retainer, a household slave, an adopted member of a great family, a dependant relative and a soldier in its secular sense; a follower, a pupil, a disciple and a convert in its ecclesiastical senses.' [Col. Temple, *Indian Ant.* (July 1896).] 'In Anglo-Indian usage it came to mean a special battalion made up of prisoners and converts.' [YB.] 'In esoteric Buddhism, a novice qualifying himself for initiation.' [*OED*; Seton-Karr, *Selections from Calcutta Gazettes* (1784-1823), ii. 311; Sinnet, *Esoteric Buddhism*. (1883), i. 15.]

Chelinga, chelingo [18C. Tam. *chalanku*; perh. fr. S. *jalanga*, 'water-going'; or poss. Ar. *shalandi*.] A large boat of light draught, used on the Coromandel coast at one time for transport of goods, troops and horses. [*OED* & YB; Account charges at Fort St. David (MS in India Office) (1746); *Hist. Europe* in *Ann. Reg.* (1761), 55.]

Chello!¹ Chul(lo)! [19C. H. *chalo*, imp. of *chalna*, 'to go speedily', 'to make off'.] Get on! Let's go! Scram! 'Another common use of the word in Anglo-Indian slang is "It won't *chul*" = "It won't answer, succeed."' [YB.] A variant of **Jildi, Jillo**. Cf. Romany *jido, jidilo*, 'lively'. [Partridge, *Dict. of Slang* (*c*. 1800; ed. 1979).]

Chello,² **chilla, challo** [18C.] Obs. Indian fabric commonly used in the 18C. *See* **Shalee, Shaloo.** [*OED* & YB; *Lond. Gaz.*(1712), No. 5051/3.]

Chena [19C. Sin *hena*.] Forest clearing for temporary cultivation in Sri Lanka. Also, the scrub resulting from such cultivation. [*OED*.; Colebrooke, in *Parl. Papers 1831-2* (1832), XXXII. 104.]

Chenar, chinar, cheenar [17C. H/P. *chīnār*.] The Iranian name of the Oriental Plane Tree, *Platanus orientalis*, which abounds in Kashmir and is found in other parts of N. India. Called the *Arbre Sec* by Marco Polo. [*OED* & YB; Sir. T. Herbert, *Trav.* (1634), 136.]

Cheri [17C. Tam. *chēri*.] 'slum'; town, village, parish quarter, e.g. *Pondicherry (puddu + chēri)* = New Town). [YB; Pringle, *Fort St. George Consultations* etc. (23 May 1681).]

Chernamrit [20C. H/S.] Sanctified drinking water. [*Hawkins, CIWIE.*]

Cheroot, sharoot etc. [17C. Tam. *shuruttu*, 'roll (of tobacco)'.] A cigar, open at both ends, made especially at Trichinopoly (Tiruchirapalli), and in the Godavari delta; known as **Trichies** and **Lungkahs.** *See* **Buncus.** [*OED* & YB; T.B. *Asia*, fol. 46 (1669-79) (cited in *OED*); Long, *Rec Bengal* (1759).]

Cherry fouj [19C. H. *charī-fauj?* (etym. obscure).] Lightly-equipped mobile detachments (in the Maratha armies), used to levy contributions, as well as to plunder the countryside; 'a flying brigade'. [YB; Colebrooke, *Life of Elphinstone* (1803; ed. 1884), 1.59.]

Cherry-merry [19C. H. (etym. obscure). Anglo-Indian.] **Baksheesh.** A present of money. [*OED*; Partridge, *Dict. of Slang* etc. (1979).]

Cherry-merry bamboo [19C. (*see* prec).] Lit. 'a present of bamboo'; Anglo-Indian: A thrashing; a sound drubbing. [Partridge, *Dict. of Slang.* (1979).]

Chetty, chettiar [19C. M. *chetti;* Tam. *shetti;* Tel. *satti;* Sin. *seddi;* S. *Setha*.] Name of S. Indian trading caste; banker; broker; money-lender; merchant. Also attrib., e.g. *Chetty custom* (1908). [*OED* & YB.] *See* **Sowcar, Bania, Seth.** [W. Phillip, tr.,*Linschoten's Voy. E. Indies* (1598), 1. 582.]

Chi [Abbr. of Tam. *chiranjeevi*.] A term of blessing prefixed to the names of male persons. [*Hawkins, CIWIE.*]

Chi-Chi, chee-chee [18C. H. *chhī-chhī.* Lit. 'filth'.] (1) Fie-fie! Pah! Ugh! (2) A term of disparagement applied to Eurasians in India,

and to their alleged mincing manner of speaking English. (In Indonesia, *lip-lap*, in Malaysia, '*stinger*' *(Sa-těngah*, lit. 'half'). [*OED*; Hickey's *Bengal Gazette* (17 March 1781).] *See* **Tarbrush, Mustees**.

Chicane, chaugan, chukan [19C. P. *chaugān*, 'the crooked stick used in Polo'; Poss. fr. Prak. *chaugana*, 'four-fold'.] The ancient game of 'horse-golf' or 'horse-hockey'. Also the stick used in this game. *See* **Polo** & **Chukka.** [*OED* & YB; Vigne, in *J.A.S. Bengal* (1837), vi. 774.]

Chick(s)¹ [17C. H/P. *chik*.] A screen blind made of split bamboos, which can be rolled up or down as needed. [*OED* & YB.] *See* **Jill Mill.** [Sir T. Roe, *Embassy to India*, 1615-19 (Hak. Soc. (1827), ii 321.]

Chick² [17C.] Short for *chicken (chequeen)* worth Rs 4 (cf. Venetian *zecchino*, E. *sequin*).] A gold coin for a long time current in India. A term in frequent Anglo-Indian use at one time, e.g. 'I'll bet you a *chick*'. Also, gambling phrases 'chicken-stakes', and 'chicken hazard'. [*OED* & YB.] *See* **Sicca**, [Coryat, *Crudities* (1611; ed. 1776), ii. 68; Trevelyan, *Dawk Bungalow* (1866).]

Chicken, chikan [19C. H/P. *chikīn*, 'art needle-work'.] (Hand-) embroidery, especially in Lucknow.] Hence *chickenwallah*, itinerant pedlar of embroidered articles. [*OED* & YB; Hoey, *Monograph on Trade* etc. (1880), 88.]

Chickoo [20C. H. *chiku*; Mal. *chiku*.] The edible fruit of the tree *Achras zapota*. The sapodilla (Sp. *zapotilla*). [Hawkins, *CIWIE*.]

Chikara *See* **Chinkara.**

Chikor(e), chukor, chickore, chikhor [19C. H. *chakor*.] Name of various Indian game-birds, especially the red-legged Himalayan partridge, *Alectoris chukor*, and its sub-species, common in the Western Himalayas, N. Punjab and Afghanistan. They are renowned fighting birds. [*OED* & YB; Mrs Sherwood, *Autobiog.* (1815; ed. 1857), 440; Elphinstone, *Acc. Caubul*, (1815), 144.] *See* **Ramchukor**.

Chil *See* **Cheel.**

Chillum [18C. H. *chilam*.] Part of the **Hookah** containing the tobacco & charcoal balls; loosely used for the hookah itself; the 'fill' of tobacco; the act of smoking. [*OED* & YB; *Lives of the Lindsays* (1781; ed. 1849); Thackeray, *Vanity Fair* (1848), ii. xxiii.]

Chillumchee [17C. H. *chilamchī*.] A brass or copper wash basin. *See* **Gindy.** [*OED* & YB; *Diaries of Streynsham Master* (1675-80

1715) in Wheeler, *Madras in the Olden Time*
(ed. 1861).]

Chilly, chilli [17C. Mex. *chilli*.] Popular Anglo-
Indian name for the *Capsicum frutescens*
and *C. annuum fastigiatum*. (H. *mirch*.)
[*OED* & YB; Stubbe, *Indian Nectar* (1662), ii.
10.]

Chimney-glass [19C.] 'Gardeners name on the
Bombay side of India, for the flower and plant,
Allamanda cathartica.' [YB; Sir G. Birdwood,
The Industrial Arts of India (1880).]

China [16C.] A 'foreign' name for the country; of
unknown origin, but found in Sanskrit as
China about the Christian era. [*OED*; Eden,
Decades, W. Ind. (1555), 260.]

China-root [16C.] 'A once famous drug, *Radix
Chinae* and *Tuber Chinae*, being the tuber of
various species of *Smilax*, the same to which
sarsaparilla belongs.' Reputed to be good for
gout. Now obs. in England. [YB; Linschoten,
(1598), 124; Hak. Soc. (1807); ii. 112.]

Chinar *See* **Chenar**.

Chinkara, chikara [19C. H. *chinkārā* fr. S.
chikkāra.] The Indian gazelle, *gazella
bennetti*. [*OED*; *Chambers Encycl.* (1860), i.
287/2.]

Chinny *See* **Cheeny**.

Chints, chinch [Pg. *chinche* (L. *cimex*).] Obs. in
India and England. A bed-bug. [YB; Terry, *A
Voyage to East India* etc. (1616; ed. 1665),
372.]

Chintz, chints [17C. H. *chīnt*; Mar. *chīt*; S.
chitra; 'variegated, speckled'.] Orig. Indian
painted or stained calicoes. Now, a cotton
cloth with flower designs, usually glazed. Some
kinds of chintz are termed **Pintado** (painted).
[*OED* & YB.] Also *chintzy*, cheap, mean, stingy,
petit bourgeois. [*OED*; Cocks, *Diary*. (1616),
i. 171 (Hak. Soc. 1883; 1614); Peyton, *Voy*.
in Purchas, *Pilgrimes* (1625), iv. xv.]

Chip [late 19C.] Anglo-Indian (Milit) slang: A
rupee. Orig.: Regular Army use, now general.
[Partridge, *Dict. of Slang* etc. (late 19C.; ed.
1979.]

Chipe [17C. Tam. *shippi*, 'an oyster'.] The pearl-
oyster from the pearl fisheries of Tuticorin and
Manar. In Indo-Pg. use from 17C. (*See* Couto,
Ribeiro, Sousa, etc.) *See* **Aljofar**. [YB.]

Chipko [20C. H. *chipak*, 'embrace, stick to,
hug'.] The practice of villagers embracing the
trees which the fellers are attempting to cut
down, in order to prevent the felling process.
Also the *Chipko Movement*, an Indian eco-
logical organization for the protection of Indian
forests.

Chir, cheer¹ [19C. H. *chīr*.] The Himalayan
pheasant, *Catreus wallichi*. *See* **College
Pheasant**. [YB; Jerdon's *Birds of India*
(1862).]

Chir, cheer² [19C. H. *chīr*.] The Himalayan pine
tree, *Pinus roxburghii*, akin to Punjabi *chir-
pine*. [*OED*; *Enc. Brit*. (1882), xiv. 155/1.]

Chiragh, chirak [19C. H/P. *chirāgh*, 'lamp–
light'.] A simple earthenware oil-lamp used in
India, and adjacent countries. [*OED*;
Westminster Gaz.(1899), 15 Aug. 1/3.]

Chirayta, chiretta [18C. H. *chirāitā*; Mar.
kirāitā; fr. S. *kīrata-tikta*, the 'bitter plant'.]
The Kiratas, an ancient Indian forest tribe of
N. E. Bengal. The *Ophelia chirayta* plant of N.
India and the bitter febrifuge and tonic
obtained from it. Hence *chiraytin, chiratin,
chiratogenin*. (Chem. bitter principles
obtained from *chirayta*.) (1847). [*OED* & YB
(1754); Ives, *Voy. from England to India*
(1773), 71.]

Chit *See* **Chitty**.

Chital, cheetal [17C. H. *chital*; S. *chitra*.] The
Indian **Spotted Deer**, *Axis axis*. Also *chitra*.
[Fryer, *New Acct. E. India and Persia* (1672-81;
ed. 1698); Gray, *List Mammalia Brit. Mus*.
(1843).] *See* **Para**.

Chitchky [19C. Beng. *chhechkī*.] A curried
vegetable mixture, often eaten with meat
curry. [YB; L.B. Day, *Govinda Samanta* etc.
(1874), i. 59.]

Chit-fund [20C. Anglo-Indian hybrid.] A fund to
which regular contributions are made to be
repaid as a lump sum. [Hawkins. *CIWIE*.]

Chitnis [19C. H. *chit* + a 'letter' + P. *navīs*, ' a
writer'.] In India, the head clerk in the vernacular division of an office. *See* **Sheristadar**
and **Cranny**. [Whitworth, *Anglo-Indian Dict*.
(1885); Wilson, *Glossary* (1855).]

Chittack¹ [19C. Beng. *chhatak*.] (1) An Indian
weight: one ounce, 17 penny–weights, 12
grains troy. [Kipling, *From Sea to Sea*
(1899), ii. 305; Wilson, *Glossary* (1855).]

Chittack² [19C.] (2) A land measure in Bengal.
[*OED*; *Statesman*, 22 Aug. 1905; Wilson,
Glossary (1855).]

Chittagong [19C. Poss. S *Chaturgrāma* or
Saptagrāma ('4 or 7 villages').] A port town
and district in Bangladesh. A variety of
domestic fowl of the Malayan type. [*OED*; 'B.
Moubray', *Poultry*, 2 edn. (1816).]

Chittagong-wood [19C.] The wood of two Indian
trees, *Chukrasia tabularis* & *Toona ciliata*,
family *Meliaceae*. Used for their mahogany-
like qualities in cabinet-making. [Webster,

3rd New Intern. Dict. (1917).]

Chitty [17C. H. *chitthī*, S. *chitra*, 'spot mark'.] 'A letter or note, also a certificate given to a servant or the like; a pass.' [YB.] This word is now rare or obsolete, **Chit** (1608); being more common. Also, the *chit-system* (1845), promissory notes for articles purchased. *See* **Chit-fund.** [*OED* & YB; Finch, *Early Travels in India, 1583-1619* (1608; ed. Foster 1921); *Mem. of Col. Mountain* (1829), 80.]

Cho [20C. Sandy bend of seasonal Himalayan torrent. [Hawkins, *CIWIE.*]

Chobdar [17C. H/P. *chobdar*, 'stick-bearer'.] In India, a staff-bearer or usher attending on a V.I.P., 'who bears as his ensign of office a staff overlaid with silver'. [YB & *OED; Eng. Fact. in India* (1618-69; ed. Foster, 1906-27).]

Choga [19C. Turki. *choghā*.] Long-sleeved garment worn by Afghans. (In Salman Rushdie's *Midnight Children* (1981) a 'chugha coat'.) [*OED* & YB; Watson and Kaye, *People of India* (1869), iv. no. 209.]

Chokidar *See* **Chowkidar, Ramoosy.**

Chokra [19C. H. *chhokrā*. 'a boy, youngster'.] One employed as a servant in a regiment or household. Also, an office boy. *Chuckaroo* was British soldiers' slang for *chokra*. [*OED* & YB; Wilson, *Abode of Snow* (1875), 136; G. Orwell, *Burmese Days* (1934), ii.29.]

Choky, chowky *See* **Chauki.**

Cholera Morbus [17C. The disease.] *See* **Mordeshin, Mort-de-Chien, Corporal Forbes.** [*OED* & YB; Fryer, *New Account of East India and Persia* (1672-81), 113-14; J. Harris, *Lex Techn.* (1704).]

Cholera-horn *See* **Collery-horn.**

Choli [20C. H. *choli*.] A short-sleeved bodice, worn by Indian women, leaving the midriff bare, worn with a sari and *lehenga* (skirt). [*OED; Imp. Gazetteer India* (1908), iii. 199.]

Cholum [19C.] A grass, the Indian Millet, *Sorghum vulgare*. [*OED;* Drury, *Useful Plants of India* (1858), 413.]

Choola(h), chula [19C. H. *chūlhā;* S. *chulli*.] The Indian extemporized fireplace or cooking-place, often made of clay; a stove. [Forbes, *Or. Mem.* (1813), iii. 120; *OED* & YB.]

Choolia *See* **Chulia.**

Choop, chup [19C. H. *chuprao*, 'silence.] 'to keep *choop*' = to stay quiet'. Also, **Chubarrow,** - military colloquial, 'shut up' and *'choops!',* 'be quiet!' [Partridge, *Dict. of Slang* etc. (ed. 1979); Kipling, *Plain Tales from the Hills* (1888).]

Chop [16C. H. *chhāp*, 'stamp, brand, point'.] A seal, stamp, impression, licence, passport (1699); first or other *chop* = first or other rank (1823); a trade-mark, brand of goods; signature. Also: *'no-chop'* (1888) = 'no class', 'no quality'; *chop boat,* 'a licensed lighter for transporting goods'; *chop house* (1882), 'a custom-house', *to chop* (*chhāpnā*), 'to mark goods outward bound' (1698).

The word has become obsolete in India, its country of origin, but still survives in the Pigeon English (Pidgin) of the Chinese ports and other Far East countries. [*OED* & YB; *Castañeda,* tr. Litchfield (1582); Milward in *Purchas Pilgr.* (1614), i. 526.]

Chopper, chupper [17C. H. *chhappar*.] 'thatched roof'. Also *choppered*, 'thatched'. [*OED* & YB.] [*English Factories* (1618-69), ed. Foster (1906-27).] [19C. H. *chhappar-khāt.*] A curtained bedstead or tent-bed. [*OED* & YB; Buchanan, *Eastern India*, (1807; ed. 1839), ii. 92.]

Chor, choor [19C. H. *chòr.*] A thief. [Wilson, *Glossary* (1855); Kipling, *Kim* (1901).]

Chorten [19C. Tibet. *chorten*.] A Tibetan **Stupa** = **Chaitya.** [*OED;* Rockhill, *Land of Lamas* (1891), 63.]

Chota, choota, chutta [19C. H. *chota*, 'small, younger, junior, minor'.] Hence: *chota peg,* 'a small measure of spirits'; *chota hazri,* 'a light breakfast', lit, 'a little get-together; *chutta paise,* 'loose change'; *chota sahib,* 'a junior partner or officer, or the son of the (*burra*) sahib, the 'boss'. [*OED* & YB; Sherwood, *Little Henry and his Bearer* (1815); Arnold. *Oakfield.* (1854) ii. 179.]

Choultry[1] [17C. M. *chāwatī;* Tel. *chāwadi*, S. *chatur*, 'four + *vāta*, 'road, a place where four roads meet'. (YB.) A rest-house; a court-house, hall, shed, inn, caravanserai. [*OED* & YB; *Eng. Fact. in India* (1618-69; ed. Foster, 1906-27).]

Choultry[2] The pillared hall or colonnade of a temple [*OED;* Call, *Signs Zodiac in Phil, Trans*, LXII (1772), 353.]

Chouse, chiause, chiauze [17C. [sb & vb). Turk. *chāush*, 'messenger herald, sergeant'.] This word has come to mean swindle (sb & vb), swindler, dupe (vb), etc. in allusion to a messenger (*chiaush*) sent by Sir Robert Shirley in 1609 to England, who swindled some Turkish and Persian merchants of £4000 and absconded. In its original meaning it has been in Anglo-Indian use since the 17C. [*OED* & YB; B. Jonson

Alchemist (1610), I. ii. 25; Pepys, *Diary* 15 May 1663.]

Chout, chauth, chowt [17C. Mar. *chauth*, a 'fourth part'.] An exaction of one-fourth of the revenue of a province, levied by the Mahrattas from the provincial governors in return for immunity from plunder. Or any similar exaction. [*OED* & YB; Orme (1674), *Historical Fragments,*.etc. (1782), 45.]

Chow-chow [19C. *Chinese Pidgin*.] 'Mixed preserves, or a mixture of any kind.' Used by Viscountess Falkland, whose husband was the Governor of Bombay, as the title of her book on Bombay, published in 1857, in which the expression is given the wider meaning of a mixture of all things, good, bad and indifferent, e.g. the itinerant **Boxwallah's** and **Borah's** bag of mixed oddments brought to the houses of **Memsahibs**. [*OED* & YB; Viscountes Falkland, *Chow Chow* (1857); A. Anderson, *Narr. Brit. Embassy China* (1795).]

Chowdry, chaudhri [18C. H. *chaudharī*, lit. 'a holder of four', but poss. fr. S. *chakradharin*, 'the discus bearer as a sign of authority'.] Headman of a craft in a town; government agent for supplying workmen, materials, etc. for public works; village headman (cf. **Vendumaster**). Also an honorific title given by servants to one of their number, probably the **Mali** (Molly), as **Khalifa** to the cook or tailor, **Jemadar** to the **Bhishti** (**Beastie**)—itself already an honorific for the water-carrier, **Sirdar** to the **Bearer**, **Mehtar** to the sweeper, and **Mehtrani** to his wife. [YB. Verelst, *View* etc. (1772); Long, *Selections*, etc. (1748-67; 1869); ed. 1876).]

Chowk [19C. H. *chauk*. Poss. fr. S. *chatushka*, 'four ways'.] An open space, a main street or open-air market in a city centre. (E.g. *Chāndnī Chowk* in Delhi). Cf. Ar. *sūk*. [*OED* & YB; Capt. T. Skinner, *Excursions in India* (1832), ii. 49.]

Chowkidar, chokidar [17C. H. *chauki*, 'prison, guard-house' + *dar*, 'agent suffix'. A watchman. See **Choky**. [*OED* & YB; *Eng. Fact. in India* (1618-69; ed. Foster, 1906-27).]

Chownee [19C. H *chāonī*. Lit: 'a thatched roof'.] 'The usual native name, at least in the Bengal Presidency, for an Anglo-Indian **Cantonment**. [YB; Tod, *Annals* (1829), ii. 611.]

Chowry, chowrie [17C. H. *chaunrī*, fr. S. *chāmara*.] A fly-whisk, or 'fly flapper', orig. from the bushy-tail of the Tibetan **Yak**. In 17th and 18th centuries called **Cow-tails** by Anglo-Indians. 'One of the insignia of ancient Asiatic royalty.' [YB & *OED*; Stewart, *Thibet in Phil. Trans.* (1777), LXVII. 484; Valentia, *Voyages*, etc. (1802-1806), i. 428.] Also: *Chowry burdar* (H/P *chaunrī-bardar* (1774), the servant who carries the *chowry.*) See **Cow-Tails**. [Markham's *Tibet* (1876); Hodivala (1632), *Notes on Hobson-Jobson,* I.A. (1931), LX; Lord Valentia, *Voyages and Travels* (1802-06; ed. 1809).]

Chowsingha [H. *chousingha.*] The four-horned (Indian) antelope, *Tetracerus quadricornus*. [Hawkins, *CIWIE.*]

Choy(a), chay(a), chey [16C. Tam. *shāyaver*, M. *chāyaver* (*chaya* 'colour' + *ver* 'root').] A root generally known as *chay-root*, *Oldenlandia umbellata*, of the Nat. Ord. *Cinconaceae*, giving a red dye, otherwise called 'India Madder', 'Dye Root' and 'Rameshwaram Root'. [*OED* & YB; tr. Frederike (c. 1566) in *Hakluyt*, ii. 354; *Mem. S. Master*, in *Kistna Man* (1679), 131.]

Chubarrow, chuprow [Mid. 19C. H. *chuprao.*] Be quiet! Shut up! Whisht. See **Choop**. [Partridge *Dict. Slang* (1979).]

Chuckaroo See **Chokra**.

Chucker [17C. H. *chakar*; S. *chakra*, 'wheel, circle'.] (a) A quoit. See **Akali**. [Lewin, *A Fly on the Wheel* (1885), 47.] (b) A sharp discus, an ancient Hindu weapon, carried by Sikh **Akalees**. See **Chakra**. [*OED* & YB; Lord, *Disc. of the Banian Religion* (1630), 12.] (c) To lunge a horse; 'the lunge' fr. H. *chakarnā* and *chakar karnā*. [Shipp, *Memoirs* (1829), i. 53.] (d) In Polo, a period, usually **Chukka**. Also **chukka**-boot, ankle-high polo boot (1948). [W.A. Morgan *et al.*, *House on Sport* (1898), 221.]

Chuckerbutty [19C. Hobson-Jobsonism.] This vulgarized Bengal Brahmin name is a corruption of *Chakravartī*, 'the title assumed by the most exalted ancient Hindu sovereigns; a universal Emperor whose chariot wheels rolled over all (so it is explained by some)'. [YB.] See **Chakravartin**. [Phayre's *Mission to the Court of Ava* (1858), 154.]

Chuckla, –ee [18C. Poss. H. *chaklā*.] Obs. 'a kind of cloth made of silk and cotton. [Platts.] [*OED* & YB; C. King, *Brit. Merchant* (1721), i. 298.]

Chucklah [18C. H. *chaklā*; (S. *chakra*, 'wheel').] A district or territorial sub-division under Muslim rule in India. [YB; Harington, *Analysis of the Laws* etc. (1805-9), vol. i. 5; Warren Hastings, *Explanation of Terms* etc. (1759).]

Chuckler [18C. Tam. & M. *shakkili.*] A S. Indian low-caste person: a tanner, cobbler, leather-worker, shoemaker, like the **Chamars** of N. India. [*OED* & YB; Ives, *Voyage from England to India* (1754; ed. 1773), 26]

Chuckmuck [18C. Corr. of H. *chakmak*, 'flint & steel'.] Title conferred on Hyder Ali = 'Firelock of War'. [YB; *see Hist. Hyder Ali*, tr. Miles (1842), 112.]

Chuckrum [18C. M. *chakram;* Tel. *chakramu,* fr. S. *chakra*, 'wheel'.] An ancient coin once current in S. India of varying value. *See* **Pagoda, Anna, Rupee, Cash.** [YB; Wheeler, *Madras in the Olden Times* (1711; ed. 1861), ii. 165.]

Chudder, chadar [16C. H. *chādar*, 'a sheet'.] A large sheet used as a **Shawl** or mantle in India. It is also applied to the cloths spread over **Muslim** tombs. 'The *Rampore chudder* was a kind of shawl of the Tibetan shawl wool of uniform colour without pattern, made originally in Rampur.' [YB] [*OED* & YB; Peyton, in Purchas (1614), i. 530.]

Chukka *See* **Chucker.**

Chulia, choolia [18C. Mal. and Sinh. *Chūliā;* poss. Sanskrit *chūda;* 'top-knot' worn by Hindus.] A name given in Sri Lanka and in Malabar to a particular class of Shia Muslims though there is much obscurity about the origin and proper application of the term. 'The word is by some derived from Sanskrit *chūda*, the top-knot which every Hindu must wear, and which is cut off on conversion to Islam.' [YB.] The Madras *Glossary* associates the word with the Kingdom of *Chola*, meaning 'a person of S. India'. [Ives, *Voy.* (1754; ed. 1773); Miss Bird, *The Golden Chersonese* (1879), 254.]

Chul(lo)! *See* **Chello!**

Chumar *See* **Chamar.**

Chummery [19C. Anglo-Indian.] In India, a house, or chambers where European bachelor employees of an Indian firm lived together. [*OED;* Besant and Rice, *Son of Vulcan* (1876); Kipling *Plain Tales from the Hills* (1888), 183.]

Chunam [16C. H. *chūnā;* Tam. *chunnam;* S. *chūrna*, 'powder'.] Prepared lime; fine polished plaster, made of shell, sea sand. [*OED* & YB; in Mrs Muter, *Travels in India* etc. (1864), 'a *chunammed* bungalow'. Vb. to *chunam*, 'to set in mortar, or to plaster over with *chunam*' (1687). [Wheeler, *Madras in the Olden Times* (1861), i. 168.] Also, lime used with **Betel**-leaf in preparing **Pan.** [Varthema, *Travels* (tr. 1576); *Early Travels in India* (1583-91; ed. Foster, 1921).]

Chup *See* **Choop.**

Chupatty, chupatti, chapat(t)i, chowpatty [19C. H. *chapatī.*] Small, flat, round or unleavened bread (generally of coarse wheaten meal), 'patted flat with the hand and baked on a. griddle ... the staple food of N. India.' [*OED* & YB.] There is an early reference in Purchas (1615) though not by name. *See* **Hopper.** Also *Chowpatty*, an Anglicization by attraction to an existing English comestible *patty*, a pasty. (Called this by Capt. Thomas Williamson in *The East Indian Vade Mecum*, 1810.) [F.M. Crawford, *Mr. Isaacs* (1883), v. 87.] *See* **Naan.**

Chupkan, chapkan [19C. H. *chapkan*.] The long frock-coat or cassock worn by men (of substance) in N. India. (Poss. of Turki or Mongol provenance.) *See* **Angarkha, Achkan, Sherwani.** [YB; Vambery, *Sketches of Central Asia*, etc. (1868), i. 59; Candler, *Siri Ram.* (1912), 277. C. Weston, *Indigo* (1943).]

Chupras(s)i,-y, chaprasi [19C. H. *chaprāsī.*] 'The bearer of a *chaprās*, a badge-plate inscribed with the name of the office to which the bearer is attached'; an attendant, henchman, messenger. [YB.] Equivalent of **Peon** in S. India, and **Puttywala** (H. *pattīwālā*), 'a man of the belt', in Bombay. A modern usage is to denote a political errand-boy. [*OED* & YB; *Indian Express*, 1 April 1984; Heber (1828), *Indian Jrnls* (1861), II. xxv. 104.]

Chuqzam [19C. Kash. *chuksam.*] A crude suspension bridge, made of birch twigs, common in many parts of Ladakh. [Henry D. Oyley Torrens, *Travels in Ladakh and Kashmir* (1862).]

Churel [19C. H. *churail.*] The ghost of a woman who has died in childbirth, believed to haunt lonely places, to act malevolently and spread disease. [*OED;* Kipling, *Kim* (1901).]

Churidar [20C. H. *churi* + *dar*, 'tight-fitting'.] Esp. of trousers, from the ankles up; worn with a shirt, **Kameez**, by a woman, and with a **Kurta**, a loose fitting tunic, or **Achkan**, a long coat, by men. [Hawkins, *CIWIE*.]

Churr *See* **Char².**

Churruck, charak [19C. Beng. *charak*, fr. P. *charkh*, 'a wheel'.] Cf. S. *chakra*. 'A wheel or any rotating machine; particularly applied to simple machines for cleaning cotton.' [YB.] *See* next.

Churruck-poojah [17C. Beng. *charak* + **Puja.**] 'The Swinging Festival of the Hindus held on the Sun's entrance into Aries. The performer is suspended from a long yard, traversing round on a mast, by hooks passed through the muscle, over the blade bones, and then whirled round so as to fly out centrifugally.... It is the *Shirry* of S. India . [Kan. and Tel. *sidi;* Tam. *shedil,* 'a hook'.] [YB; Purchas, *Pilgrimes* (1614), 1000.]

Chuthachuth [19C. H. *chūth,* 'touchable' + *achūth,* 'untouchable'.] 'Deranging, upsetting,' Writing spoilt by too many corrections, erasures, etc. [Wilson, *Glossary* (1855).]

Chutkarry, chattagar [19C. Tam. *shatti-kar.*] 'One who wears a waistcoat.' In S. India a Eurasian, with reference to imitation of European clothing. [YB.] *See* **Topi wallah.** [C.P. Brown, in YB.]

Chutney, chutny [19C. H. *chatnī.*] A relish made of condiments, fruits, coconut, lime juice, garlic, chillies, etc., the whole concoction ground into a paste. British *chutney* is milder and a sort of pickle, which Indians would call **Achar.** [*OED* & YB; Forbes, *Or. Mem.* (1813), ii. 50. seq.]

Chutt [19C. H. *chhat.* 'A roof', a platform'.] In Anglo-Indian usage this term was applied to the coarse cotton sheeting, stretched on a frame and white-washed, which formed the usual ceiling of rooms in tiled or thatched houses. Properly **Chadar-chhat,** 'sheet-ceiling'. [YB; Wilson *Gloss.* (1855).]

Chuttrum [19C. Tam. *shattiran.* Corr. of Sanskrit *sattra,* 'abode'.] In S. India, a house where pilgrims and travelling members of the higher castes are entertained and fed gratuitously for a day or two. [YB.] *See* **Choultry, Dharmsala.** [Buchanan, *Mysore* (1807), i. 11. 15.]

Cingalese (sb. & adj.) [16C. S. *sinhalam,* Sinh. *sinhalas.*] Ceylon (Sri Lanka), 'Lions' Abode'. A native or the people of Ceylon; its language; adj. pert. to the country and its people. [OED.] *See* **Sinhalese** and **Serendib.** [*OED* & YB; Purchas, Pilgr. (1613), 1. v. xvii. 460; Fitch, *Early Trav. in India.* (1583-1619; ed Foster 1921).]

Cintra oranges *See* **Sungtara.**

Civilian [18C. Anglo-Indian.] A **Covenanted Servant** of the E.I.C; not in military service; classified as **Writers** (First Five years); **Factors** (to the eighth year); from the 9th to 11th as Junior Merchants, and thenceforward as Senior Merchants. These names were abolished in 1842, when the titles were changed to Civil Servants 1st, 2nd and 3rd Class. [*OED* & YB; Malcolm, *Life of Clive* (1766), 54.]

Civil lines [19C. Anglo-Indian.] The area of a town reserved for government officials. [Hawkins, *CIWIE.*]

Civil Service [18C. Anglo-Indian.] The *Civil Service* was a term originally applied to the part of the service of the E.I.C. carried on by *Covenanted Servants* who did not belong to the Army or Navy. [OED.] *See* **Civilian.** [Carracioli, *Life of Clive* (1785), iii. 164.]

Classy, clashy, clashee [18C. H. *khalasi,* fr. Ar. *khalās,* 'tent-pitcher'.] A surveyor's chain-man or staff-man, artillery-man, porter, dock-worker, labourer, native sailor, or **Matross.** *Khalāsī* also means an 'escape channel' of a canal, and *classy (khalāsī)* may have been a person in charge of such a work. [YB & *OED.*] *See* **Khalasi.** [Colebrooke, *Life of Elphinstone* (1801; ed. 1884), i. 27; Tippoo's *Letters* (1785), 171.]

Clearing Nut, Water Filter Nut [19C. Anglo-Indian.] The seed of *Strychnos potutorum;* a tree of S. India (known in N. India as *nirmalā, nirmalī,* 'dirt cleaner'); so-called from its property of clearing muddy water, if well rubbed on the inside of the vessel to be filled. [YB & *OED; Penny Cycl.* (1842), xxiii. 152/2.]

Coast, The [18C. Anglo-Indian.] This term since the 18C. has meant the Madras or Coromandel Coast. and often the Madras Presidency. *Coast* Army = *Madras* Army. [YB & *OED; India Gazette,* 15 Sept. 1781; Hugh Boyd, *The Indian Observer* (1798), 78.]

Cobily mash, goomulmutch etc. [18C. Maldive, *kalu-bill-mās,* 'black bonito fish'.] Hobson-Jobsonism for the dried **Bonito;** staple food of the people of the Maldive Islands. Esteemed also in Malaysian countries, where the fish is called *bilis.* (Sinh. *balaya.*) [YB; A. Hamilton, *New. Acct. of the E. Indies* (1727), i. 347.]

Cobra (de Capello) [17C. Pg. *cobra de capello,* 'hooded cobra'.] The venomous snake *Naja tripudians* of India and Sri Lanka. Called the 'Chapel Snake' in 1700 by Christopher Fryke in *A Relation of Two Several Voyages,* etc. [*OED* & YB; Cogan's tr. of Pinto's *Voyages and Adventures* (1653), 17.]

Cobra lily The flower of the *Arum campanulatum,* 'which stands on its curving stem just like a cobra with a reared head'. [YB.]

Cobra Manilla or Minelle [18C. Mar. *cobra maner,* fr. S. *muni,* 'a jewel'.] A popular name in S. India for venomous snake, 'perhaps a little uncertain in its application, but poss. the Chain-viper, *Daboia elegans.* [YB; Lockyer, *Acct. of the Trade in India* etc. (1711), 276.] *See* **Manilla-man** and **Tic-polonga.**

Cochin-Leg [18C. Anglo-Indian.] An old name for elephantiasis in Malabar. Also called 'St. Thomas Leg'. The Tamil name is *anaikkal*. [YB.] *See* **Panicale**. [Ives, *Voy. from England to India*, (1754; 1773), 193.]

Cock-up [19C. Anglo-Indian. Corr. of Malay *kakap*.] A large fresh-water and estuarine fish of India, *Lates calcarifer*. 'The daily breakfast dish of half the European gentleman [in Calcutta].' [*OED & YB*.] *See* **Begti (Beckti), Bhikti**. [Stocqueller, *Handbk. Brit. India* (1845; 1854), 283]

Coconut-day [Anglo-Indian.] Festival held by Hindus at full moon in the month of *Shravana* (Aug.–Sept.) to mark the end of the rough monsoon seas. [*CIWIE*.]

Coggage, coggidge [Mid. 19C./20C. Anglo-Indian fr. H. *kaghaz*, 'paper'.] Writing paper, a newspaper. (Regular Army colloquial.) [Patridge, *Slang Dict.* (1979).]

Coir, cairo, cayar [16C. M. *kāyar*, 'cord', fr. *kāyāru*, 'to be twisted'.] The fibre of coconut husks for making matting, ropes, etc. Attrib. *coir*-fibre, *coir*-rope, *coir*-yarn, *coir*-cable, etc. [*OED & YB*; Fitch, *Early Travels in India* (1583-91).]

Coja(h) [17C. H/P. *khojah* for *kwājah*.] Respectful title; in India especially applied to eunuchs. [YB.] *See* **Khoja**. [Foster, *Letters* (1615); ed. 1896-1900), iv. 16.]

Collector [18C. Anglo-Indian.] The chief administrative official of an Indian **Zillah** or district, whose special duty is to collect revenue; he also has magisterial powers, except in Bengal. 'The title was originally no doubt a translation of *Tahsīldār*.' [YB.] *Collectorate*, the district under the jurisdiction of a Collector (1825). [*OED & YB*; *Reg. of 14th May* (YB.); Burke, *Warren Hastings*. Wks. (1722; 1788), xi. 484.]

College-Pheasant [19C. H. *kālij*.] Hobson-Jobsonism for *kālij*; the name of a Himalayan bird of the *Lophura leucomelana*, intermediate between pheasants and jungle-fowl. [YB.] *See* **Kaleej** and **Chir**. [Jerdon, *Birds of India* etc. (1862); Ball, *Jungle Life* (1880), 538.]

Collery[1] [18C. Tam. *kallar*, 'thieves', fr. *kallan* (singular) 'thief'.] A S. Indian, non-Aryan race, notorious thieves by reputation. Hence *Cholera-horn* (1832), 'of hideous sound', (corr. of *collery-horn*); *collery-stick* (1801), a boomerang used as a weapon by *colleries*. [*OED & YB*; Orme, *Hist. of the Milit. Trans.* (1763), i. 208.]

Collery[2] [18C. Beng. *khālāri*.] 'salt pan, or place for making salt.' [YB; Verelst, *View of Bengal* (1772), app. 223.]

Comaty [17C. Tel. & Kan. *kōmati*, 'a trader', (poss. fr. S. *go* 'eye' + *mushti*, 'fist', 'from their vigilant habits').] 'A term used chiefly in the north of the Madras Presidency, and corresponding to **Chetty**, which the males assume as an affix.' [YB; Purchas, *Pilgrimes* (1625), 997.]

Comboy [17C. Perh. fr. *Cambay* (place name).] A Sinhalese *sarong* worn by both sexes, usually white cotton, 'but in mourning, black is used'. [YB; Cocks' *Diary* (1615); Hak. Soc. (1883), i. 15.]

Commissioner [18C. Anglo-Indian.] A civil servant (not in Madras) in charge of a Division, embracing several Districts or **Zillahs**, ranked between **Collectors** and Magistrates of these districts on the one side, and the Revenue Board and the Local Government on the other. The officers immediately under him were termed 'Deputy Commissioners'. The *Chief Commissioner* governed a province, subordinate to the *Lieutenant Governor* and directly so to the *Governor–General* in Council. [YB; H. H. Wilson, *Brit. India* (1844), III. 65.]

Community [19C. Anglo-Indian.] A sub-caste or body of co-religionists. Also communal (adj.) (with stress on the second syllable). [Elphinstone, *Acc. Caubul* (1815), 11. 27.]

Company [16C. Anglo-Indian.] In full 'John Company', alias the East India Company. Called by some *Company Jahan* or *Kumpani Jehan*, 'recalling Shah Jehan and Jehangir, and the golden age of the Moguls'. [YB.] Hence *Company Bagh*, 'a public garden'. [*OED & YB*.] *See* **John Company** [Hakluyt, *Voy.* (1553): Note in Hak. *Voy.* (1589), 265; Andreas Spurrman, *Travels* etc. (1784), 9. 347; 1599 Minute Bk. E. Ind. Co. in H. Stevens, *Dawn Brit. Trade* (1886), 10.]

Competition-wallah(s). [19C. Anglo-Indian hybrid of English and Hindustani.] Applied to members of the Civil Service admitted by the competitive system introduced in 1856, and probably known in England through Sir G.O. Trevelyan's *Letters of a Competition Wallah* (1864). They were looked upon with some disfavour by their colleagues who had been recruited straight from Haileybury, the Company's earlier recruiting centre. [*OED & YB*; *All the Year Round* (1863), x. 203.]

Compound [17C. Pg. *campon* (1613) fr. Mal. *kampong*. (A misprint in S.R. attributes the word to Malayalam.)] (1) An enclosed or fenced-in area around a building or a group of buildings. Used in this sense throughout India. [*India Gazette*, 3 March, 1781.] (2) Such an area occupied by a particular nationality or community : e.g. *Kampong China* in Malacca, *Kampong Mëlayu* in many places in Malaysia. [*OED & YB*; 1679 *Notes & Extracts*, Fort St. George (1670-81; ed. 1871).]

Compounder [19C. Anglo-Indian.] A pharmacist attached to Indian army medical corps or government hospitals and clinics. [*OED & YB*; Dr E. Downes in *Rep. Calcutta Missionary Conference* (1883), 414.]

Compradore, compodore [17C. Pg. *comprador*, 'purchaser' fr. *compra* 'to purchase'.] Formerly the chief house-steward or **Butler** who kept accounts and purchased provisions etc. for the houshold employing him. [*OED & YB*; Cocks, *Diary* (1615), i. 19; Hak. Soc. (1883).]

Conbalingua, comolanga. [16C. Tel, Kan, M, *kumbalam, kumbalanu.*] The common pumpkin, *Cucurbita pepo.* [YB; Varthema, *Travels*, E. tr. by Eden (1576).]

Conch [18C. Pg. *concha*.] A spiral mollusc shell used as an instrument of call in Hindu temples. [*OED*.] *See* **Chank**. [J. Grainger, *Sugar Cane* (1764), IV. 163; 1784 Cook's *Voy.* (1790; 1991, IV.).]

Confirmed [19C. Anglo-Indian.] 'Applied to an officer whose hold of appointment is made permanent.' [YB.] In Bengal and elsewhere the popular term was **Pukka**. [YB.] *See* **Cutcha** (1805) in *Life of Colebrooke* (ed. 1873), 223.]

Congee, conjee [17C. Tam. *kanjī*, 'boilings'; H. *ganji*. (of doubtful origin).] (1) Used throughout India for the water in which rice has been boiled; an invalid diet of 'slops'. *See* **Kanji**. [*OED & YB*; Fryer, *Acct. E. Indies* (1673), iv. vi. 200.] (2) Generally used as starch by **Dhobies**. *Congee-cap*, a starched night-cap. *Also* vb. 'to starch with rice-water'. [*OED & YB*; *Eng. Fact. in India.* (1622; ed. 1906-27).] (3) *Congeehouse*, a military lock-up (**Choky**), 'so called from the traditional regimen of the inmates'. [YB & *OED*; Sir C. Napier in Mawson's *Records* (1835).]

Congress (Indian National) [19C.] The Indian National Congress, whose foundation in 1885 is generally credited to a retired **Civilian**, Allan Octavian Hume, as a political 'safety-valve', elected a Bengali leader and lawyer, W.C. Bonnerjee, as its first president. Other leaders of the Congress in the following years

included Surendranath Banerjea, Mahatma Gandhi, Nehru, Patel, Subash Chandra Bose (Netaji), Indira Gandhi, and her son Rajiv Gandhi. Muslims formed only a small percentage of the Congress, which has undergone many changes of policy, composition and direction since its inception. Derivative expressions : *Congress-grass*, a ubiquitous weed, *Parthenium hysterophus*, said to be poisonous to the touch; *Congress-wallah*, a member of the Congress party, a *Congressman*; *Gandhi* cap, a white, homespun cotton-cap worn by *Congress-men*. [*OED*; F. P. Crozier, *Men I Killed* (1937), xii. 269.]

Conicopoly, conucopola etc. [17C. Tam. *kanakkapillai*, 'account person'.] An Indian clerk or accountant (in S. India). *See* **Curnum, Coolcurnie & Cranny**. [*OED & YB*; 1680 *Notes & Extracts*, Fort St. George (1670-81; ed. 1871-73), iii. 34.]

Conner [19C. Military slang fr. H. *khana*, 'food', 'grub', 'nosh'. [*OED*; Brophy and Partridge, *Songs & Slang of the British Soldier* (1914-18; ed. 1931).]

Consumah *See* **Khansama**.

Cooja, kooza [17C. H/P. *kuza*.] Earthenware water-vessel.] (Not long-necked like the *surāhī*). A word used in Bombay chiefly. [*OED & YB*.] *See* **Serai**[2] [Danvers, *Letters* (1611; ed. 1896-1900), i. 128; Riddell *Ind. Domest. Econ.* (7 ed. 1871), 362.]

Cook-room [18C. Anglo-Indian.] Kitchen; in Anglo-Indian establishments always detached from the house, but often joined to it by a covered way. [YB.] [Long, *The Court's Letter* (3 March 1758).]

Coolcurnie, kulkarnee, etc. [18C. Mar. *kulkarnī*, fr. *kula* 'tribe' + *karana* 'writer'.] 'Village accountant and writer in some of the western and central parts of India.' [YB.] (In N. Indian = **Patwari**. *See* **Cranny**. [Gladwin's *Ayeen Akbery* (1783), ii. 57; Hockley, *Pandurang Hari* (1826; ed. 1873), ii. 47.]

Coolie, cooly[1] [16C. Guj. *Kulī, Kolī*.] An aboriginal tribe of Gujarat and the Konkan, formerly robbers, now labourers and cultivators. 'Their savagery, filth, and general degradation attracted much attention in former times.' [YB & *OED*; Linschoten, *Discours of Voyages* (E. tr. 1598), xxvii; Hamilton, *Descr. of Hindostan* (1820), i. 609.]

Coolie, cooly[2] [17C. Of uncertain origin, Poss. H. & Beng. *kūli*.] Perh. to be identified with prec., the name being brought by the Portuguese to S. India. Hired labourer, burden-carrier in India and the Far East. [*OED* & YB; *Eng. Fact. in India* (1618-69; ed. 1906-27).] (The word has entered into English slang in the sense of a 'private soldier' (– 1859; obs. 1900.) [*See* Partridge, *Dict. of Slang* (1979).] (The formal correspondence of Tamil *kūli*, 'hire', is probably coincidental. [*ODEE.*]

Coolie-Christmas [20C.] The Muharram ceremonies observed by Indian immigrants in S. Africa. [*The Graaf Advertiser*, 2 May 1902.]

Coolin [19C. Beng. *kulīnas*, fr. S. *kula*, 'a caste, clan or family'; *kulīna*, 'belonging to a noble family'.] 'A class of Bengali Brahmins who made extraordinary claims to purity of caste and exclusiveness, who were much sought after in marriage for daughters of 'lesser' Brahmins and who often took many brides just for the sake of the dowries they received.' [YB; Risley, *Tribes and Castes of Bengal* (1891), i. 146 *seqq*; W. Ward, *Hist., Lit., & Relig. of the Hindoos* (Serampore, 1811).]

Coolung, coolen, kullum [17C. H. *kulang*; P. *kulank*; Mar. *kallam*.] The great grey crane, *Grus grus lilfordi* or, perhaps mistakenly, the Demoiselle Crane, *Anthropoides virgo*. 'Great companies of these are common in many parts of India, especially on the sands of the less-frequented rivers; and their clanging trumpet-like call is often heard as they pass high overhead at night.' [YB & *OED*; Fryer, *New Acct. of E. India* etc. (1672-81), 117.]

Coomkee,[1] kummeky, kumaki [18C H/P. *kumak*, 'aid'.] Auxiliary troops in the Mughal Army. [YB; c. 1590 Gladwin, *Ayeen Ackbery* (tr. 1783; ed. 1800), i. 188; Sleeman, *Journey Through Oudh* (1849-50; ed. 1858), i. 30.] **Kumaki** [19C. Kan. *kumaki*.] Area in Karnataka from which the proprietor of the village or estate is privileged to supply himself with timber for house-building etc. [YB.] *See* **Coomry**. [Sturrock, *Man. S. Canara*. (1894-5), i. 16. 224. seqq.]

Coomkee,[2] koomki [19C. Beng. *kumki*.] A decoy female elephant employed in capturing a male elephant (in Bengal). [YB; Williamson, *Oriental Field Sports*, folio ed. (1807), 30.]

Coomry [19C. H. *kumrī*; Mar. *kumbari*; Kan. *kumari*.] 'a hill-slope of poor soil'. A system of shifting cultivation in S. India by hill people in which a forest is cut down and burnt and the ground planted with crops for one or two seasons, after which a new site is similarly treated. Also *kumridar :* one who cultivates in this fashion. *See* **Jhoom**. [YB; Sturrock, *Man.*

S. Canara (1894–5), i. 17.] *See* **Taungya**.

Coorsy, kursi [19C. H. Ar. *kursī*. A chair.] In Bengal a more dignified term for **Choky**. *Kursī* is the stand on which Muslims lay the Koran. [YB; Kirmani, *Hist. of Hydur Naik* (tr. 1842), 452.]

Coosumba [19C. H. *kusum(bha)*.] **Safflower**, *Carthamus tinctorius*. The name was applied by the Rajputs and others to tincture of opium and to an infusion of **Bhang**. [YB; Malcolm, *Hist. of Central India* (1823; 2nd ed. 1824), ii. 146.]

Cootie [20C. Mal. *kutu*.] Body-louse. Army slang in India and the Far East. [Partridge, *Dict. of Slang* (1979); *OED*; Empey, *From Fire Step* (1917), 24.]

Cooter goosht [19C. H.] 'dog's meat'. [Frazer & Gibbons, *Soldier & Sailor Words & Phrases* (1925).]

Coppersmith [19C. Anglo-Indian. (Hindi name *chhota basanth*.)] Popular name for the crimson-breasted Barbet, *Megalaima haemacephala*, found in India from about 2500 ft. in the Himalayan south. Also in Bangladesh, Pakistan, Sri Lanka and Burma. [*OED* & YB; Salim Ali, *The Book of Indian Birds* (1979), 60; Jerdon, *Birds of India* (1862; ed. 1877), I. 316; Arnold, *Light of Asia* (1879), 20.]

Copra(h) [16C. Pg. *copra* fr. M. *koppara*, 'coconut'. (H. *khoprā*).] The dried flesh of the coconut from which coconut oil has been expressed. [*OED* & YB; Barret in Hakluyt (1584; ed. 1807), ii. 413.]

Coral-tree [18C. Popular name for the tree *Erythrina Indica* (H. *dapap*).] So-called from the rich scarlet colour of its flowers from which a red dye is obtained. Its leaves are used for **Curry** and cattle fodder. Legend affirms that this tree grew in **Indra's** garden, whence **Krishna** stole the flowers. Then Rukhmini and Satyabhama quarrelled for the possession of these precious blossoms. [*OED* & YB; Mason, *Burmah* (1806), 531; P. Browne, *Jamaica* (1756), 288.]

Corropali [16C. M. *koduka* (the tree) + *puli*, acid.] The tree *garcinia indica*, of the Konkan and Karnataka, belongs to the same genus as the mangosteen, and produces gamboge and an agreeable acid fruit. The seeds give a fatty oil known as *kokan* butter. Also called 'Mate mangosteen' (Cook *mangosteen*' a ship fern. [Varthema *Travels*, Fr. Eden., 1576.]

Corge, coorge [16C. Kan. *korji*; Tel. *khorjam*.] A measure of capacity, about 44 **Maunds** and a cloth measure of 20 pieces. Once used as a mercantile term for 'a score'. [YB, 255; Varthema, *Travels*, tr. Eden (1576).]

Corinda, karvanda [H. *karaundā.*] Thorny shrub, *Corissa carandas*, bearing small black berries. *See* **Curounda.**

Corle [18C. Sinh. *kōrale*, 'a district'.] 'A *Coraal* is an overseer of a *Corle* or District (in Sri Lanka). [YB; Valentijn, *Names of Native Officers in the Villages of Ceylon* (1726), 1.]

Cornac [18C.] *See* **Carnac.**

Coromandel [16C.] The eastern sea-coast of India from point Calimere to the mouth of the River Kistna, fr. *Cholamandalam* 'the kingdom of the Cholas'. [*OED* & YB; Litchfield's *Castañeda* (1582).] (1) *See* **Calamander.** (2) In 1878, used attributively for oriental lacquer transhipped on the Coromandel coast in transit to England. [*OED*; Mrs B. Palliser, tr., Jacqumart's *Hist. Furnit.* (1878), IV. VIII. 454.]

Corporal Forbes [19C.] Regular Army Hobson-Jobsonism for *cholera morbus*, espec. in India. [Shipp, *Memoirs* (1829), ii. 218.]

Corral [19C. Pg. *curral*, 'a cattle pen'.] An enclosure used in Ceylon (Sri Lanka) for the capture of wild elephants). [*OED* & YB.] *See* **Keddah.** [Emerson Tennent, *Acct. Island of Ceylon.* (1859); Darwin, *Voy. Nat.* (1845), viii.]

Corundum [18C. Tam. *kurundam*; Tel. *kuruvindam*; H. *kurand*; S. *kuruvinda*, 'ruby'.] A mineral allied to sapphire and ruby (Al_2O_3), used for polishing and dressing millstones etc. Hence : *Corundum-wheel; Corundum-point; Corundum-tool.* Also called *Adamantine spar.* [*OED* & YB; Woodward, *Catal. For. Fossils* (1728).]

Coss, cos, kos, course [17C. H. *kōs*, S. *krosa.*] A measure of distance, about 2 miles. Originally the distance a particular 'call' would carry. Anglicized to 'course' in Hakluyt and Purchas. (*Pl.* same as *sing.*) [Sir T. Roe, in Purchas. i. 541. (1616; Hak. Soc. I. 105.] [*OED* & YD.]

Cossack, kuzzak, etc. [16C. Turki. *kuzzūk*, 'vagabond, nomad, guerilla adventurer'. In India the word became common in the sense of a predatory horseman and freebooter. [YB.] Also *attrib.* [*OED*, & YB; Hakluyt, *Voy.* (1598), i. 388.] Hence *Cossackee*, 'predatory', used by the Marathas, borrowed from the Mughals. [YB; Malcolm, *Central India* (1823).]

Cossid [17C. Ar. & P. *kāsid.*] A courier or running messenger (Turki *kaz*, 'to wander').

[*OED* & YB; *Eng. Fact. in India* (1618-69; ed. Foster, 1906-27).]

Cossya, kasia [18C. *Khāsi*. Name of Mongoloid-matrilineal, hill-people occupying the mountains immediately north of Sylhet, who erect rough stone monuments of the *menhir* and *dolmen* kind. [*OED*; *Lives of the Lindsays* (1780; ed. 1849), iii. 182.]

Costus [17C. S. *kustha*; Gr. *kostos.*] The Kashmiri plant, *Saussurea lappa*, that yields an essential oil. Once used in charms and rituals, now in the manufacture of perfumes and **Agarbatti (Joss-stick).** [*OED* & YB.] *See* **Putchock,** [Topsell, *Foure-footed Beasts* (1607), 376.]

Cot [17C. H. *khāt*; Pr. *khatta*; S. *khatwā*; Tam. & M. *kattil.*] (1) A light bedstead; hammock; bier; couch; **Charpoy.** [*OED* & YB; *Eng. Fact. in India* (1618-69); Danvers, *Letters* (1613; ed. 1896-1900), i. 227.] (2) A nautical hammock [*OED*; Falconer, *Dict. Marine* (1769).] (3) A child's bed. [*OED*; H. J. Todd, *Dict. of English Lang.* (1818).] Note : *Cot-death*, or *cot-death* syndrome. A largely unexplained fatality of very young infants when lying in their cots. [*OED*; *Guardian*, 11 May 4/5 (1970).]

Cotia, kotyeh [16C. M. *kottiya*; Sinh. *kotyeh.*] A fast, two-masted sailing boat with lateen sails employed on the Malabar coast. [YB; Litchfield, *Castañeda*, (E. tr. 1582).]

Cotta, cottah [18C. H. *katthā.*] A small land-measure (in Bengal and Bihar); the twentieth part of a **Beegha** (*bīgha*) and containing 80 sq. yds. [*OED* & YB; Verelst, *View of Bengal*, (1772), 221.]

Cotton [Ar. *qutn*; Pg. *cotāo.*] As cotton was so important to India, though the word is Arabic and has no Indian derivatives, it has been strongly reinforced in Anglo-Indian English by Indian associations since the 17th century because of the flourishing export trade in cotton **Piece-Goods** to England until 1783, when English import duties killed this trade and boosted the Manchester cotton-goods trade in India. [*OED* & YB.] *See* **Piece-Goods, Capass (Kapas)** and **Kapok.** [Hakluyt, *Voy.* (1598), i. 93.]

Cotton-Tree, Silk. *See* **Simul.**

Cotwal, cutwal *See* **Kotwal.**

Counsillee [19C. Anglo-Indian.] Designation of English barristers by the natives of Calcutta. 'It is the same use as the Irish one of *Counsellor*, and a corruption of that word. [YB.]

Country (adj.) [16C. Anglo-Indian for 'Indian'

(H. *desi*, 'country, State'.)] This word is applied to indigenous (Indian) rather than foreign ('phoren') articles, people etc., with a sub-indication of disparagement: e.g., *country-liquor*, **Arrack**; *country-horses*, not Arabs or **Walers**; *country*-born, of European descent but born in India (e.g. **Castees**); *country-gooseberry*, the *Sicca disticha; country-potato,* the *Batatas edulis,* the sweet-potato; *country craft,* small vessels, used by fishermen and for river traffic (e.g. a **Budgerow**); *country-almond (dēsī-badam),* applied to the nut of the *Terminalia catappa;* etc., etc. This idiom was also used by the Portuguese in India, e.g., '*açafrao da terra*' (**Safflower**), the 'bastard' saffron, sometimes applied to turmeric. [YB.] In contrast is the term 'foreign (*phoren*), an expression of praise in such collocations as *Foreign*-liquor, -educated, -returned, etc., etc., generally with the implication of 'European' or 'British' and not of 'African' or 'Asian'. Also note: 'Up [the] country' 'in the **Mofussil**'. [*OED* & YB.] *See* **Surat, Castees, Lip-lap, Dacey**. [Danvers, *Letters* (1608; ed. 1896-1900), i. 20; Litchfield, Castañeda's *Conqu. India* (1582).]

Country-captain [18C.] A special dry curry served as a breakfast dish. 'We can only conjecture it was a favourite dish at the table of the skippers of '*country ships*', who were themselves called '*country captains*'. [YB; *Madras Courier*, 26 April 1792.]

Courap [18C. Mar. *kharpadī* 'scale, scab'; *kharapne*, 'to scratch'; S. *kshur*, 'to scratch'.] Name given in India to cutaneous eruptions, sometimes called *Scabies indica;* cf. W. Indies vernacular *khurup*, 'herpes'. [*OED*; E. Phillips, *The New World of English Words* (1658; ed. 1706).]

Course [17C. H. *coss*.] A fashionable riding or driving place usually frequented by Europeans at an Indian **Station**. (The *OED* gives this use of the word from Fr. *cours;* It. *corso,* and first English date 1646.) [*OED* & YB.] *See* **Coss**. [Evelyn, *Mem.* (1646); Arnold, *Oakfield,* (1854), ii. 124.]

Covenanted Servants [18C. Anglo-Indian.] Regular members of the Indian Civil Service who entered into a formal covenant with the East India Company, and after 1858 with the Secretary of State for India. [*OED* & YB.] *See* **Civilian**. [Long, *Records, Fort St. William,* (1748-67), 112.]

Covid [17C. Prob. fr. Indo-Pg. *covado,* 'a cubit or Flemish ell'.] A measure of varying lengths in India from 14 to 36 inches. [*OED* & YB; Danvers, *Letters* (1612; ed. 1896-1900), i. 24. 1.]

Covil [18C. Tam. *kō-v-il,* 'God-House'.] A Hindu temple or Malabar palace. In S. India it was used among the French and by some un-enlightened Englishmen for a church. [YB; Logan, *Malabar* (1796; ed. 1889-91), iii. 254.]

Cowage, cow-itch [17C. H. *kewānch;* S. *kapikachchu*.] A climbing plant, *Mucina prurita* with stinging hairs on its pods. Hence the obvious Hobson-Jobsonism striving after meaning, 'cow-itch'. Formerly used as an anthelmintic. [*OED* & YB; Parkinson, *Theat. Bot.* (1556; 1640); R. Hooke, *Microgr.* (1665), 145; Fryer, *New Account* (1672-1681; ed. 1698), 422.]

Cowle, Kaul [17C. Ar. *kaul*.] 'word, promise, bargain, compact, written undertaking, lease'. 'It has become a technical word in the Indian vernaculars, owing to the prevalence of Mohammedan law. [YB.] In India also a safe-conduct pass, or amnesty. [*OED* & YB; Danvers, *Letters* (1611; ed. 1896-1900), i. 236.]

Cowra [19C. Beng. *cowra,* Low caste cook in Bengal.] *See* **Motiya**. [Domestic sketch, *A Letter from an Artist in England* (1849).]

Cowrie, cowry, caurie [16C. H. *kaurī* fr. S. *kapar, kapardika.*] The small white porce-lain-like shell of the gastropod, *Cypraea moneta,* formerly used as currency in India, S. Asia and elsewhere, and found abundantly in the Indian Ocean. (Mentioned in Chinese literature 14 BC.) [*OED* & YB; *The Indian Antiquary* (1610; ed. 1871-1933); Litch-field's *Castañeda* (1582).]

Cowry [19C. Tam. *kāvadi*.] The yoke for carrying burdens in S. India. *See* **Bangy** and **Kavadi**. [YB; Campbell, *Old Forest Ranger* (1853), 178.]

Cow-tails [17C.] 'The name formerly in ordinary use for what we now more euphoniously call **Chowries**.' [YB.] The bushy tail of the Tibetan **Yak**, used as a whisk. [*OED;* Bernier, *Travels in the Mogul Empire* (1658-64; E. tr. Constable (1891), 261.]

Crab-bat [19C. H. *kharāb* 'bad' + *bāt,* 'speech', 'word'.] Anglo-Indian coll. for 'bad language', 'all the swear words in the Hindoostani language, and a few more from the other Indian dialects to help these out.' [Frank Richards, *Old Soldier Sahib* (1936).]

Crab-lanthorn [Late 18C. Anglo-Indian hybrid,

H. *kharab*, 'bad + *lanthorn*.] 'a servant or low fellow', a peevish fellow. [Partridge, *Dict. of Slang* (1970).]

Crab-wallah [19C-20C. H. *kharāb + wala*.] 'An evil man.' Regular Army slang in India. [Partridge, *Dictionary of Slang* (1970).]

Cranchee [19C. Beng. *karānchi*.] A rickety carriage, drawn by wretched ponies, for hire in Calcutta. *See* **Shigram** and **Jutka**. [OED; Bishop Heber, *Narrative of a Journey* (1844).]

Cranny [17C. H. *karānī; S. karan*, 'a doer'.] A **Writer**, accountant or clerk. Orig. a member of a mixed caste (Anglo-Indian slang, 'a half-caste' whose occupation was that of a 'writer' or 'accountant'. (Also Anglo-Malay *kērani*, 'a clerk'.) [YB; Danvers, *Letters* (1611; ed. 1896-1900), i. 117]

Creeper [19C. Anglo-Indian.] A paying pupil to a Ceylon (Sri Lanka) tea planter, from about 1890. [Partridge.] [OED & YB] *See* **Griffin**. [A.L. Mayhew, *Notes and Queries* (1894), v. 124.]

Crore, crow, carror, etc. [17C. H.*kror;* Prak. *krodi;* S. *koti*.] Ten million or 100 lakhs (of **Rupees** etc.) Also *crori* (1675), the possessor of a crore (of money) or the 'collector of revenue to the extent of a crore'. [YB & OED; Hawkins, in Purchas, *Pilgrimes* (1609; ed. 1625–6), i. 216.] *See* **Padma**.

Crow-butterfly A long-winged spotted butterfly, genus *Euploea*. [CIWIE.]

Crow-pheasant [19C.] Anglo-Indian name for an ungainly black bird with chestnut wings and long tail, *Centropus sinesis*, common all over the plains of India, Burma etc. It was held in India to give omens. [YB.] (Hindi names, *majokā, kūkā*.) [P. Robinson, *In My Indian Garden* (1878), 7.]

Cubeb(s) [14C. H. *kabāb (chīnī)* fr. Ar. *kabābah*.] The fruit of the *Piper Cubeba*, or *cubeba officinalis*, first used as a pungent spice in the Middle Ages and, later, as a medicine and in cookery in the 19C. (1874). (Usually in the plural *cubebs*.] In English since 14C. Also attrib. as cubeb-pepper,–tree. [OED & YB; *King Alisaunder (c.* 1300; ed. Weber, 1810); Eden, *Decades* (1555), 238.]

Cuddoo [19C. H. *kaddū*.] 'A generic name for pumpkins, but especially for the musk-melon, *Cucurbita moschata*.' [YB; Riddell, *Ind. Dom. Econ.* (1871), 568.]

Cuddy [18C. (uncertain origin).] 'Public or captain's cabin of an Indiaman or other passenger ship.' [YB & OED; Pepys' *Diary*, 14

May 1660); *Life of Lord Teignmouth* (1769, ed. 1843).]

Culgee [17C. H. *kalghī*.] Rich, silk cloth for turbans and curtains etc. Also, 'A jewelled plume surmounting a *sirpesh* or aigrette upon the **Turban**' (1714). [YB & OED.] *See* **Surpeach**. [*London Gazette*, no. 2312/4, 1688; Wheeler (1715), *Madras in Olden Times* (1861), 11. 246.]

Culmureea, koormureea [19C. Nautical H. *kulmarīya*, fr. Pg. *calmaria*.] A calm at sea. [YB; Roebuck, *Naval Dict.* (1811).]

Culsey [19C. prob. S. *kalasi*, 'a water-jar', and hence a grain-measure.] (The *Madras Gloss.* gives Kan. *kalasi*, a measure of capacity holding 14 seers.) [YB; Forbes, *Or. Mem.* (1813), 1.30]

Cumbly, cumly, cummuel [16C. H. *kamlī;* S. *kambala*.] A blanket; a coarse woollen cloth. [OED & YB; Fitch, *Early Travels in India* (1583-91; ed. Foster (1921).]

Cummerbund [17C. H/P. *kamār-band*, 'lion-band'.] A waist-band or girdle. 'Habitually worn in India by domestic servants, peons and irregular troops; but any waist-belt is so termed.' [YB & OED; Cocks, *Diary* (1616; ed. Hak. Soc., 1883), i. 147.]

Cumra [19C. II. *kamrā*, fr Pg. *camera*, 'a chamber, a cabin'.] 'In upper India the drawing-room was the *gol kamrā* (round chamber) because one end of it was usually semi-circular.' [YB.]

Cunchunee, kanchanee, etc. [17C. H. *kanchanī*, fr. *kanchan*, 'gold'.] A dancing-girl. [YB.] *See* **Dancing-girl, Devadasi, Nautch**. [Bernier, *Travels in the Mogul Empire* (1658-64; ed. Constable, 273 seq.]

Curnum [19C. Tel. *karanamu;* S. *karana*.] A village accountant. [YB.] *See* **Cranny**. It corresponds to the Tamil *kanakan* (*See* **Conicopoly**.) [Arbuthnot, *Mem. of Sir. T. Munro* (1827); ed. 1881, 1. 285.] *See* **Pula**.

Curounda [19C. H. *karaunda*.] A small plum-like fruit of the shrub *Carissa carandas*, which makes good jelly and tarts, and a pickle. [YB.] *See* **Corinda**. [Riddell, *Ind. Dom. Econ.* (1870), 338.]

Currig jema [17C. H. *khārij jama*.] 'Separated or detached from the rental of the State, as lands exempt from rent, or of which the revenue has been assigned to the individuals or institutions.' [YB; Wilson, *Gloss of Judicial & Revenue Terms*, etc. (1855); Yule, Hedges,' *Diary* (1681-8, Hak. Soc.), ii (xiii).]

Curry [16C. Tam. *kari;* Pg. *caril*, 'sauce'.] A dish

of meat, fish, fruit or vegetables cooked with spices and served with rice, **Chapatties** etc. Attrib. *curry*-sauce; -stuff (chillies, onions, turmeric, cardamom, cloves, etc. ground into a paste or powder (1860); –powder; –leaf; –leaf tree (*Bergera konigii*); –paste. *Also vb. to curry* (1739). [*OED* & YB.] *See* **Mussalla** [W. Phillips, *Linschoten* (E. tr. 1598; Hak. Soc., 1885), ii. 11.]

Cusbah, kasbah [18C. H/Ar. *kasba, kasaba*.] In India, the chief place of a **Pergunnah**. [*OED* & YB; *Ayeen Akbery*, tr. Gladwin (1783), ii. 1.]

Cuscus(s) *See* **Khus-khus**.

Cushmawauni, kuchparwani [19C. H. *kūcch + parwa* (care) + *nahin* (no).] Don't care. Never mind! Indian Army Slang (obs.) [J.C. Otter, *The Slang Dict.* (1859).]

Cushy, cushey [20C. Poss. fr. H. *khūsh*, 'pleasure', or Romany *khushto*, 'good'.] Easy, pleasant, comfortable, well-off. Orig. Indian Army slang from the 1st Great War or before [Partridge]. (Erroneously associated with 'cushion', a piece of folk-etymology.) [YB.] Descriptive of slight wound. Also *cushiness*. [Blackwood's *Magazine*, 91/2, Jan. 1916.]

Cuspador(e) cuspidor(e) [16C. Pg. *cuspidor*, 'spitter'.] A spittoon. [*OED* & YB; Litchfield's *Castañeda* [1582]; Wheeler, *Madras in the Olden Time* (1861).]

Custard apple [17C. Anglo-Indian.] The fruit of the *Anona reticulata*, introduced in the 16th C. to India from S. America. It has a rind and a yellowish pulp resembling custard in appearance and flavour. Also called 'Bullock's Heart'. *See* **Sitaphal**. [*OED* & YB; Ovington, *Voy. to Surat* (1689), 303.]

Custom [17C. Anglo-Indian.] 'In India the equivalent of **Dustoor(y)** of which it is a translation. Both words illustrate the origin of *Customs* in the solemn revenue sense.' [YB; Hedges' *Diary* (1681-8).]

Customer [17C. Anglo-Indian.] *See* prec. In India the native official who exacted duties. [YB.] (This word was in common use in England from 1448 to 1748. *See OED*).

[Danvers, *Letters* (1609; ed. 1896-1900), ii. 225.]

Cutch [17C. Kan. *kāchu*.] *See* **Catechu**. [*OED* & YB; Cocks' *Diary* (1617).]

Cutcha, kutcha [19C. H. *kachcha*.] 'raw, crude, unripe, uncooked, imperfect'; unmetalled (of a road); mud-walled (of a house). The opposite of **Pukka**. Also, *Cutcha-pucka*, 'a mixed kind of building in which burnt brick is used but which is cemented with mud instead of lime-mortar.' [YB.] A great variety of metaphorical Anglo-Indian collocations are attached to these two terms. E.g. *Cutcha* – appointment, not permanent, not confirmed; *Cutcha-colour* – one that will fade or 'run'; *Cutcha-scoundrel* – an amateur, slapdash ne'er do well. [*OED* & YB.] *See* **Pucka**. [**A. Prinsep**, *The Baboo and Other Tales* (1834).]

Cutcher(r)y, kuchurry etc. [17C. H. *kachahrī*, 'hall of audience etc.'] (1) A court-house, office (1610). *See* **Dufter (Dafter)**. [*OED* & YB] (2) A brigade of infantry (1799). [Hawkins in Purchas (1610; ed. 1625-6), i. 439; Harris in Owen, *Wellesley's Desp.* (1799), 119.]

Cutchnar [19C. H. *kachnār*, S. *kānchanāra* (*kānchana*, 'gold'). The beautiful flowering tree, *Bauhinea variegata* or Mountain Ebony. [YB; Yule, *Mission to Ava* (1855), 95.]

Cuttlee, cutli [20C.] Domestic Hindi for 'cutlet'. [M. Jaffrey, *Indian Cookery* (1982), 9.

Cuttanee, cottanee, cottony [16C. H/P. *kattāni*; Ar. *kattān*. 'flax or linen cloth'.] Silk, or mixed silk and cotton piece-goods. (*Kattan* is now in India the waste selvage in silk weaving, which is used for stringing ornaments.) [*OED* &YB; Linschoten, *Discours of Voy*. etc. (E. tr. 1598); Cocks, *Diary* (1622).]

Cutter [16C. The *OED* rejects its derivation from Indo-Pg. *catur*.] Ship's rowing or sailing boat; small single-masted sloop-rigged vessel. *See* **Catur**. [*OED;* Varthema, *Travels* (E tr. by Eden, 1576).]

Cuttry *See* **Khuttry**.

Cyrus *See* **Sarus**.

D

D.A. [20C. Anglo-Indian.] Dearness Allowance = Cost of living allowance; addition to earnings to compensate for inflation or other additional expenses. *See* **Batta**. [*OED; Times*, 1 July 1/4 (Advt.) (1955);*National Herald*, New Delhi, 29 July 8/6 1969.]

Daboya, daboia [19C. H. *daboyā*, 'a lurker', from *dabha*, 'to lurk'.] The large viper of the East Indies. [*OED;* W. Aitkin, *Sci. and Pract. Med.* (1863).]

Dacca [17C. H. *dhākā*, 'the wood of the **Dhak** trees'.] The capital city of Bangladesh, famous formerly for its 'Dacca muslins'. '*Dāka* [was] throughout Central Asia applied to all muslins imported through Kabul.' [YB; Sir. T. Roe, *Embassy* etc. (1615-19).]

Dacey [19C. H. *dēsī*.] A native of India, or belonging to India, e.g. *dacey*-cotton, -silk, -manufacture. *See* **Country, Deshi**. [*OED;* L. P. Brockett, *Silk Weaving* (1876).]

Dacoit, dacoo, decoit [19C. H. *dakait;* S. *dashtaka*, 'crowded'.] Indian gang-robber. Hence *dacoity* or armed robbery (1813). 'By law to constitute *dacoity* there must be five or more in the gang committing the crime.' [YB.] Also formerly pirates on the Ganges between Calcutta and Burhampore. [*OED* & YB; Williamson, *VadeMecum*(1810), ii. 396.] *See* **Thug, Pindar**.

Dada [19C. H. *dādā*.] Paternal grandfather; respectful form of address to elders. Also a gangster leader. Cf. Mafia 'Godfather'. [G. C. Whitworth, *Anglo-Indian Dict.* (1885).]

Dadny [17C. H. *dādnī*, fr. P. *dādan*, 'to give'.] 'An advance made to a craftsman, a weaver, or the like, by one who trades in the goods produced.' [YB; Hedges, *Diary* (2 Oct. 1683); Hak. Soc. (1886), i. 21.]

Dadra [20C. H. *dādra*.] A North-Indian melody. [*(CIWIE* (1984).]

Dagbail [19C. H/P. *dāgh-i-bel*, 'spade-mark'.] 'The line dug out to trace on the ground, a camp, or a road or other construction. As the central line of a road, canal, or railway it is the equivalent of English 'lockspit'. [YB.]

Dagoba, dhagope, daghope [19C. Sin. *dāgaba;* Pali. *dhātugabbho;* S. *dhātu-garbha*, 'relic receptacle'.] Any dome-like **Buddhist** shrine containing relics. *See* **Tope, Pagoda, Stupa**. [*OED* & YB; Salt, *Caves of Salsette*, in *Tr. Lit. Soc.* Bo. (1819), i. 47 pub.]

Dah, dha, dao, dhar [19C. Burmese *dah*.] A short, heavy sword or cutting tool; used espec. in Burma. Attrib. *dah*-blade (1888). [*OED;* J. Bell, *Syst. Geogr.* (1832), iv. 588.]

Dahi [19C. H. *dahī*.] Curds. [Mrs Meer Hassan Ali, *Observations on the Mussulmans of India* etc. (1832).] *See* **Tyre**.

Dai, dhai, dhye, daye [18C. H. *dāī;* S. *dātrikā;* P. *dāyah*.] Nurse, wet-nurse, midwife. Also, 'A female commissioner employed to interrogate and swear native women of condition, who could not appear to give evidence in a court.' [Wilson, *Glossary of Judicial & Revenue Terms*. etc. (1855); *OED* & YB; India Gazette, 12 Oct. 1782.]

Daincha *See* **Danchi**.

Daiseye [19C.] Hobson-Jobsonism for **Desai** (1698). *See* **Dessaye**. [YB; Kirkpatrick, *Letters of Tippoo* (1811).]

Dak, dawk, dhak, etc. [17C. H & Mar. *dāk*. (Perh. related to S. *drak*, 'quickly'.)] Postal service; letter delivery, mail. Post or transport by relays of runners, carriages or horses. Hence, '*To lay a dawk*, to cause relays of bearers or horses, to be posted on a road', and 'to travel *dāk'*, to proceed in this way by relays'. Attrib. *Dawk Bunglow*, 'a **rest-house** for the accommodation of travellers . . . maintained by . . . the Government of India' (1853); *Dak-bearer* (1796). *Dak-ghar*, post-office; *Dak-wala*, postman (1828). [*OED* & YB; *Eng. Fact. in India*(1618–69).] *See* **Patamar**.

Dakhma, dokhma [17C. P. *dokhma*.] **Parsi** 'Tower of Silence', where the corpses of Parsis are exposed on an iron grating to be consumed by predatory birds. [*OED;* Chambers, *Encycl.* (1865), vii. 300; Henry Lord *The Religion of the Persees* (1630).]

Dakshina [19C. S. *dakshinā*.] A gift to a Brahmin, 'A good & prolific cow suitable to be given to a Brahmin'. [G. C. Whitworth, *An Anglo-Indian Dict.* (1885).]

Dal, dhal(1), doll. [17C. H. *dāl;* fr. S. *dala* 'split'.] Split pulse, e.g. *Cajanus indicus*. (See **Cajan**), and the porridge and soup made from it. 'It should be noted that in its original sense *dal* is not the name of a particular pea, but the generic name of pulses prepared for use by being broken in a hand-mill.' [YB.] Some varieties are: (1) *arhar dal*, red gram, *cajanus cajan;* (2) *moong dal*, green gram, *Vigna radiata;* (3) *tur dal*, arhar, the red gram *cytisus cajan* or *cajanus indicus;* (4) *urad (oord) dal*, black gram, *Vigna* *mungo. See* **Moong and Oord**. Also, *dal bhat,* 'rice and *dal'; dal roti,* '**Chapati** and *dal',* both the Indian equivalent of 'daily bread'. [*OED* & YB; *Eng. Fact. in India* (1618-69).]

Dal [20C.] Group, political party. Hence, *dal badal,* political defection. Also, *Akali-dal.* (*See* **Akali**.)

Dalal, deloll [17C. H/Ar. *dallāl.*] One who directs (the buyer and seller to their bargain) [YB]. A broker; an auctioneer. *See* **Neelam.** [*Eng. Fact. In India* (1618-69).]

Dalaway [18C. Tamil *talavāy;* Kan. *dhalavāy;* H. *dal,* 'army'; S *dala,* 'army' + *vah,* 'to lead'.] The Commander-in-chief of an army in S. India. [YB; Cambridge, *Acct. of the War in India* (1750-60), App. 29.]

Dalit panth(er) [20C. 'Depressed class'.] Imit. Black Panther. *See* **Panth.**

Daloyet, deloyet [18C. H. *dhalait,* fr. *dhāl,* 'a shield'.] Obs. an armed attendant and messenger; **Peon**. [YB; Gleig, *Mem. of Warren Hastings* (1772; ed. 1841), i. 237.]

Dam, daum, dawm [18C. H. *dām.*] An obsolete Indian copper coin of little value : 1/40th of a rupee. Hence maybe (?), 'I don't care a dam(n)!' or 'a twopenny dam(n)'. [*OED* & YB; Balfour, *Forms of Herkern* (1781), 39.]

Damani A kind of squall. [YB.] *See* **Elephanta.**

Dam(m)ar, dammer [15C. Mal. *damar,* resin.] Botanical genus *Dammara* (N.O. *Coniferae*). A number of species of trees yielding various resins or *dammars,* e.g., *Dammar orientalis,* used for caulking ships and water-proofing roofs, and various resins from India, Malaysia, New Guinea; etc., e.g. White *Dammar* (*Valeria indica*); Black *Dammar* (1880) (*Canarium strictum*). The word is commonly used in Malaysia and sometimes in India for torches which are made by dipping rags in *dammar,* or by filling bamboo sections with the resin and igniting them. [*Secreta secretorum c.* 1400 (Early English Text Society (1898; 165), *Eng. Fact. in India.* (1618–69).] *See* **Sal.**

Dana [17C. Beng. *dana,* 'grain'.] *See* **Dhan.**[2] = **Gram**. [YB; Terry in Purchas (1625–6), ii. 1471.]

Danchi, dhanicha, dhunchee [19C. Beng. *dhanicā.*] A valuable forage or green-manure shrub of India (*Sesbania aculeata*); planted for soil improvement; the bast fibre obtained from it; cultivated in Bengal during the rains. [Roxburgh, *Flora Indica* (1815).]

Dancing-girl [17C. Anglo-Indian.] In India, a **Nautch**-girl = Pg. *bailadeira;* Fr. *bayadère.*

See **Cunchunee** (*kanchanī*), **Bayadere, Nautch, Devadasi, Rum Johnny** (*ramjanī*). 'Alias Dancing Wench among the older Anglo-Indians.' [YB & *OED;* Sir T. Roe, *Emb. to the Court of the Great Mogul* (1615-19).]

Danda [H/S., *'dānda'.*] A short stick or truncheon. *See* next.

Dandy, dandi, dandee[1] [17C. H. *dāndī,* fr. *dānd,* 'staff, oar'.] A boatman of the Ganges. [*OED* & YB; Hedges, *Diary* (6 Jan. 1685).]

Dandy, dandi, dandee[2] [19C. H. *dāndī,* Ar. *dānd,* 'staff, oar'.] A **Saiva** mendicant who carries a wand or staff. [*OED* & YB; Wilson, *Sketch of the Religious Sects of the Hindus* (1832).]

Dandy, dandi, dandee[3] [19C. H. *dāndī,* fr. *dānd,* 'staff, oar'.] 'A kind of vehicle used in Himalayas, consisting of a strong cloth slung like a hammock to a bamboo staff and carried by two or more men (*dandy-wallahs*).' [YB.] Much of the same as the Malabar **Muncheel.** [*OED;* Cumming, *Good Words* (1870).]

Dangur [19C. H. *dhāngar.*] Name of various tribes of *Chūtiā Nāgpūr* who sought work on coffee and tea plantations. [YB; Dalton, *Descriptive Ethnology of Bengal.* (1872), 245; Risley, *Tribes and Castes* (1891), i. 219.]

Darcheenee [17C. P. *dār-chīnī,* 'china stick'.] Cinnamon. [YB: P. Della Valle, *Voyages* (tr. 1664).]

Dargah *See* **Durga.**

Daroga, darogha, droga, etc. [17C. H/P. *dārōgah.* 'governor, overseer'.] Originally a provincial or city governor under the Mughals but later degraded to a chief police-officer, superintendent, manager, controller of customs, etc. [*OED* & YB; *Eng. Fact. in India* (1618-19).]

Darshan [19C. H/S. *darshan,* fr. S. *darshana,* a 'view', *drsh,* 'to see'.] The sight of an august or holy personage, such as a **Mahatma,** and the blessing that proceeds therefrom. [*OED;* Gandhi, in *Young India* (1920). Wilson *Gloss.* (1855).]

Darter, or Snake-bird [19C. E. H. *Pan dubi,* Beng. *goyar.*] An Indian water-bird resembling a cormorant (*Anhinga rufa melaongaster*). [*OED;* Lydekker, *Roy. Nat. Hist.* (1895), IV. 280.]

Darwaza *See* **Durwan.**

Das(a) [19C. S. *dāsa.* a slave.] Hence, *Bhagwandas,* 'the slave of God' and **Devadasi,** a slave-girl of the gods. Often used to form a Hindu name, e.g. Haridas, Tulsidas. Also, Hindus dedicated to a god and seeking favours for themselves or for their first-born. See **Ghulam.** [Whitworth, *Anglo-Indian Dict.* (1885); Wilson, *Gloss.* (1855).]

Das(h)ara *See* **Dussera(h).**

Dastur[1] [17C. H/P. *dastūr*] *See* **Dustoory.**

Dastur,[2] **Destoor** [17C. Guj/P. *dastur*, fr. Pah. *dastobar*, a prime-minister; councillor of State; a high priest; a Parsi bishop. *See* **Herbed, Mobed** and **Behdin.** [*OED* & *YB*; Haug, *Essays on the Sacred Language, Writings and Religion of the Parsis* (1878); Henry Lord, *The Religion of the Parsees* (1630).]

Datchin, dachin [17C. Mal. *daching;* Cant. *t'okch'ing.*] A steelyard or balance. [*Eng. Fact. in India* (1651-4; ed. Foster (1915).]

Datura, dewtry [16C. H. *dhatūra;* Mar. *dhutrā;* S. *dhattūra.*] Also, the early form 'dewtry' [Phillips, tr., *Linschoten* (1598).] (1) The Indian name of *Datura fastuosa* and *Datura metel,* common Indian species used to stupefy and poison. [J. Davis, tr., *Mandelslo's Travels* (1662), 104.] (2) A genus of poisonous plants (N.O. *Solonaceae*) of which *Datura stramonium* or Thorn-Apple is a powerful narcotic. Hence *daturine*= atropine. [R. Christison, *Poisons* (1832).] (3) Also *Yellow datura* or *Yellow Thistle,* a Bombay name for 'the *Argemone mexicana,* the *fico del inferno* of Spaniards, introduced accidentally from America and now an abundant and pestilent weed all over India. [*OED* & *YB*; Linschoten, *Discours of Voyages* etc. (E. tr. 1598); Burton, *Anatomy of Melancholy* (1621).]

Dawa [20C. H. *dāwa,*] Medicine. *Dawa khana,* 'medicine house', pharmacy, dispensary. [*CIWIE.*]

Dawk See **Dak** (post) and **Dak-bungalow.**

Dawk *See* **Dhak** (tree).

Dayal, dhyal *See* **Dial-Bird.**

D.C. Abbr. Deputy Commissioner. *See* **Commissioner** and **Chief Commissioner.**

Deccany [19C. H. *dakhinī;* S. *dakshina,* 'the right hand or the South'.] Coming from the Deccan; an inhabitant of the Deccan. Also, the dialect of Hindustani spoken by the inhabitants of the Deccan. [*YB*; Forbes, *Or. Mem.* (1813).]

Deck, dick [19C. H. *dekh-nā,* 'to look'; Romany, *dick.*] A look, a peep, a glance. *See* **Dekko** [*OED* & *YB*; Or. *Sporting Mag.* (1828-33).]

Deen! Deen! [18C. H. *dīn.*] The excited war-cry of militant Muslims: 'For the Faith.' Espec. in quarrels with those of other beliefs. [*YB*; Orme

Milit. Transactions (1763).]

Deepavali *See* **Diwali, Divali.**

Dekko, dekho [19C. H. *dekho.* Imp. form of *dekhnā,* 'to look'.] Army slang: 'Lets have a dekko'; 'Take a dekko'. *Also* vb. 'to look, to see'. *Dekkoscope* (20C.) a telescope. *See* **Deck.** [*OED; Daily News* (8 Sept. 1804); Partridge, *Dict. of Slang* (1979); Kipling, *Kim* (1901).]

Delhi-boil [19C. Anglo-Indian.] A form of Oriental sore, similar to Biskra Button, Aleppo Evil, Lahore or Multan sore. [*YB; Delhi Gazetteer,* 15 (1886).]

Deling [16C. Etym. obscure. Perh. corr. M. **Manchil.**] A sort of palanquin. [*YB*; Fitch (1587) in Hakluyt (ed. 1807), ii. 391]

Deloll *See* **Dalal.**

Denkli [19C. H. *dhenklī.*] A contrivance for raising water (in N. India) for irrigation purposes. *See* **Picot(t)ah.** [Whitworth, *Anglo Indian Dict.* (1885).]

Deodar [19C. H. *dēodār;* S. *dēva dāru,* 'tree of the Gods' (lit. 'divine wood').] The great cedar tree of the Western Himalayas, *Cedrus deodara,* a variety of the cedar of Lebanon, *Cedrus Libani.* [*OED* & *YB*; Roxburgh, *Flora Indica* (1804).]

Deri [19C. Kash. *deri.*] An inflated buffalo-hide for carrying men and baggage across a river. [Henry D. Oyley Torrens, *Trav. in Ladakh, Tartary and Kashmir* (1862).]

Dervish [17C. P. *darvesh.*] Member of a Muslim religious order.] Among Anglo-Indians the word fell into disuse, and was replaced by **Fakir.** [Terry in *Purchas* (1625-6).]

Desai, dessaye, daiseye [17C. Mar. *desaī.*] In W. & S. India an Indian revenue officer or petty chief, often a hereditary office. *See* **Dissave** & **Deshmukh.** The Hobson-Jobsonism *daiseye* 'repeatedly occurs in Kirkpatrick's *Letters of Tippoo* (1811) for a local chief of some class'. [*YB* & *OED*; **Dessaye.** [Fryer, *Account of E. India* etc. (1698).]

Desh(i) [19C. H. *desh;* S. *desa.* 'country, land', e.g. *Bangladesh,* 'Bengal country'; *Madhya Pra-desh,* Middle (Central) Province.] *Deshi* = made in the country (India). Cf. **Country** & **Dacey.** Derogatively: inferior, in contrast to 'Phoren' (Foreign), made abroad, in Europe or the U.S.A. usually, or to Wilayati (**Blighty**). [Whitworth, *Anglo-Indian Dict.* (1885).]

Deshmukh [19C. H. *dēsmukh,* 'country head', or chief.] Hereditary revenue official; petty chief. [*OED.*] *See* **Desai** and **Dissave.** [Patton, *Asiat. Monarchies* (1801); Elphinstone, *Hist. Ind.*

(1841); ii. 461.] *See* **Saswat, Patel, Vakil**.

Des(h)pande [19C. Mar. *dēspande.*] Hereditary revenue official, superior to the district **Kulkarni**. *See* prec. [Wilson, *Glossary* (1855).] *See* **Saswat**.

Deuti, duty [17C. H. *diutī*; S. *dīpa*, 'a lamp'.] A lamp-stand, also a link-bearer. [YB; *Notes and Exts. (Ft. St. George)* (1671-81), ii. 72.]

Deva, dewa, deo [18C. S. *dēva*, 'a shining one', fr. *divya*, 'to shine'.] One of the good spirits or gods of Hindu mythology. Also *dēvī*, goddess; servant of God, or honorific title. (Fem. form of **Deva**). *See* next. [*OED*; Hope, *Anastasius* etc. (1819); Wilkins (1781), in *Asiat, Res.* (1799), i. 294.]

Devadasi [19C. S. *dēva-dāsī*, 'female-servant, or slave-girl of a god'.] A dancing girl, **Nautch-girl**, or temple prostitute, formerly belonging or dedicated to a Hindu temple, in S. India especially. [*OED* & YB.] *See* **Nautch, Baya-dere, Deva** and **Dancing-girl**. [Dubois, *Manners and Customs of India* (1817).]

Devadaya [Tam. fr. S. *deva*; 'a god' + *dāya*; 'a gift' = **Devaswam**.]

Devanagari [18C. H/S. *dēvanāgarī*, 'town-script of the gods'.] The formal alphabet of the Sanskrit and Hindu languages. [*OED*; Wilkins, *Asiatic Res.* (1781).] *See* **Mahajan(i)**.

Devaswa(m) [19C. Mar. *dēvaswam.*] Temple property or endowment. [Wilson, *Glossary* (1855).] Also, H. **dewasthan**, fr. S. **deva**, 'a god' + *sthana*, 'a place'. A temple and endowment to support a temple. [Whitworth, *Anglo-Indian Dict.* (1885).]

Devata [19C. S. *devāta.*] A divinity, a god, an idol of a god. [Wilson, *Glossary* (1855).]

Devi *See* **Deva**.

Devil [19C. A small whirlwind.] *See* **Pisachee, Shaitan, Typhoon**. [*OED* & YB; Forbes, *Or. Mem.* (1813).]

Devil-bird [17C.] The Brown Owl of Sri Lanka with a wild and wailing cry presaging death and misfortune. [*OED* & YB; Knox, *Ceylon*, (1681), 78; Pridham, *Ceylon* (1849); 737.]

Dewal(é) [17C. H. *dewal;* S. *dēva-ālaya.*] Hindu temple or **Pagoda**. 'This or *dewalgarh* is the phrase commonly used in the Bombay territory for a Christian church. In Ceylon *Dewalé* is a temple dedicated to a Hindu god.' [YB; Knox, *Ceylon* (1681).]

Dewaleea [19C. H. *diwāliyā.*] 'a bankrupt', fr. *diwālā*, 'bankruptcy'. [YB; Drummond, *Illustrations* (1808).]

Dewally [17C.] *See* **Diwali**.

Dewan, diwan, divan, dewaun etc. [17C. H./Ar./P. *dīwān, dīvān.*] Register (of accounts);

Council of State; Hall of State (*dīwān-i-khas* for private audience, and *dīwān-i-am* for general or public audience). The chief meanings in Anglo-Indian usage of this word are : (1) The chief Mughal financial minister of a state or province, 'invested with extensive judicial powers in all civil and financial causes' [Wilson]. 'It was in this sense that the grant of the **Dewauny** to the E.I. Company in 1765 became the foundation of the British Empire in India.' [YB; Holwell, *Hist. Events* (1766), i. 74.] (2) The Prime Minister of a princely State. [Danvers, *Letters,* (1610), i. 51] (3) The chief Indian officer of certain Government establishments, e.g. the Mint or of a **Zemindary**. [Mill, *Brit. India* (1818), v.v.] (4) '[In Bengal] a native servant in confidential charge of the dealings of a house of business with natives, or of the affairs of a large domestic establishment.' [YB.] 'These meanings are perhaps reducible to one conception, of which "Steward" would be an appropriate expression.' [YB.] Hence *dewanship* (1818) = **Dewani**. (5) The word 'divan' was also, and still is, used to denote a sofa, couch, ottoman. [Bruyn, *Voy. Levant* (1702); Tavernier, *Voy.* (E tr. 1684).] (6) Rare: a collection of oriental poems or a brochure (Sismondi, *Lit. Eur.* (1846). [*OED* & YB.] (Cf. *douane, dogana*, etc.)

Dewani, dewauny [16C. H/P. *dīwānī.*] The office of **Dewan**; especially the right to collect the revenue of Bengal, Bihar and Orissa, 'conferred upon the E.I. Company by the Great Mogul Shah Alam in 1765. Also sometimes used for the territory which was the subject of that grant.' [YB. & *OED*; Finch, *Early Travels in India* (1583-1619; ed. 1921); Burke, *Report Affairs India,* Wks. (1783), xi. 141.]

Dewani-Adalat *See* **Adawlut**.

Dewtry *See* **Datura**.

Dh In the Anglo-Indian spelling of Indian words it represents the Indian dental sonant-aspirate, *dha;* also the lingual or cerebral-aspirate, *dha.* In earlier spellings these were simply represented by *d.* Some words are erroneously spelt with *dh* under the notion that an oriental appearance is thus given to a word, e.g. *dhooly, dhow, dholl, dhoney, dhoop dh(o)urra, dhurrie.* [*OED*.]

Dhagope [19C.] *See* **Dagoba**.

Dhak,[1] **dak, dhawk** [18C. H. *dhak.*] An Indian jungle tree *Butea frondosa,* the Flame of the Forest, also called **Palas**, which from January to March becomes a riot of orange and vermilion flowers. The seeds give a clear oil, and from the stem an astringent gum exudes, known as *Bengal Kino*, useful to pharmacists, and to leather workers because of its tannin. From the flowers may be obtained a brilliant yellow or orange dye. Hindus venerate the tree as being sacred to the moon and to Brahma. Hence it is used for a number of religious ceremonies. It is said to have sprung from the feather of a falcon impregnated with **Soma**, the nectar of the Hindu gods. When a Hindu boy becomes a **Sadhu** he is given a *Palas* leaf to eat, the trifoliate formation representing **Vishnu** in the middle, **Brahma** on the left and **Shiva** on the right. During the sacred thread ceremony the boy holds a staff of *Dhak* wood. [*OED* & *YB*.] *See* **Palas**. [Sir T.E. Colebrooke, *Life of Henry Colebrooke* (1799); ed. 1873).] *See* **Teesoo**.

Dhak² (Post) *See* **Dak**.

Dhal(1) *See* **Dal**.

Dhaman¹ [19C. H. *dhāman*.] The **Rat-Snake**, *Ptyas mucosus*. [*OED*; Robinson, *In My Indian Garden* (1878), 92.]

Dhaman² [19C. H. *dhaman*.] The grass, *Cenchrus celiaris*, used for fattening cattle. [*OED*; Coldstream, *Illust. Grasses*, S. *Punjab*. (1889) Pl XI, no. II.]

Dhaman,³ dhamnoo [19C. H. *dhāman*.] An Indian tree, *Grevia tiliaefolia*, with strong flexible wood, used for wheel-axles, spokes and athletic equipment. [*OED*; Royle, *Illustr. Bot. Himal. Mts.* (1839), i. 104.]

Dhamma The **Pali** form of the **Sanskrit Dharma**, meaning 'piety', 'morality', 'the social order'. (The tenets of the Buddhist religion.) [Keith, *Buddhist Phil. in India & Ceylon* (1923); Sir Charles Eliot, *Hinduism & Buddhism* (1921).]

Dhamnoo *See* **Dhaman.³**

Dhan¹ [19C. H. *dhana*; fr. *dadhāte*, 'he puts, places'.] Property or wealth. Spec. the village cattle. [Wilson, *Glossary* (1855).]

Dhan² [19C. II. *dhān*; S. *dhāna*.] Unhusked rice. [*OED*.] *See* **Dana**. [Roxburgh, *Flora Indica* (1832).]

Dhandh [19C. Sind. *dhandh*.] A lake or swamp in Sind. [*OED*; Burton, *Sindh* (1851).]

Dhani, dhunny [20C. H. *dhanī*.] A palm, whose fronds are used for thatching. [*OED*; Chambers, *Journal* (Jan. 1926).]

Dhania [20C. H. *dhania*.] Coriander, *Coriandrum sativum*. [*CIWIE*].

Dhansak [20C. Guj. *dhansak*.] Coriander-

flavoured **Dal** cooked with vegetables or meat. [*CIWIE*.]

Dhanyawad H. *dhanyawad*. Thanks! Thank you! [*CIWIE*.]

Dharana [19C. S. *dhāranā*, 'act of holding'.] Hindu, Buddhist, Jain. Fixed attention; esp. a state of unwavering concentration on an object. [Sir Charles Eliot, *Hinduism & Buddhism* (1921).]

Dharani [19C. S. *dhārani*.] Hinduism and Mahayana Buddhism; a mnemonic formula containing **Mantras**. Popularly *dharanis* are spells protecting against demons, diseases and other malign influences. [Eliot, *Hinduism & Buddhism*]

Dharma, dhurm [18C. S. *dharma*. Lit. 'That which is established', fr. *dharayati*,'he holds'.] (1) Hinduism: (a) social customs regarded as one's duty, e.g. respecting **Brahmins** and abstaining from eating beef. *See* **Dhamma**. (b) Caste customs, espec. the sacrament of spiritual regeneration. (c) Obedience to the civil and criminal law. (d) The corpus of cosmic principles by which all things exist. (e) The essential function inherent in each being, e.g. of the tiger to be fierce. (f) The Natural Law, Moral Law and Justic; all are instruments of *Dharma*. (g) Conduct fitting to one's essential nature, as opposed to **Adharma**. (2) Buddhism: Ideal truth. In *hinayana*, an element of existence. *See* **Dhamma**. (3) Jainism: The uncreated and eternal substance; the necessary movement of souls and matter, the ontological principle of movement. Derivatives; (1) **dharmsāla**, pilgrim's rest-house. [Wellington, *Dispatches* (1805).] (2) *dharma shastra* (1796), Hindu sacred law-book or code of ethics. [Sir W. Jones, tr., *Inst. Hindu Law* (1796).] (3) *dharmasutra*, book of aphorisms on *dharma*. [Max Mueller, Let. 20 July in *Sacred Bks. East* (1849).] (4) *dharmakaya*, the law-body of Buddha. S. Beal, *Buddhism in China*, (1884); *OED*.]

Dharna, dhurna [18C. H. *dharnā*, fr. S. *dhr*, 'to place'.] The act of sitting at the debtor's door without tasting food to force payment of his debt, or compliance with a demand, by shaming him in this way. An offence under the Indian Penal Code. Anglo-Indian phrase 'to sit *dharnā*', and 'to put in *dharnā*', (fr. *dharnā denā* or *baithnā*). Sometimes called *takaza* (Persian), 'dunning' or 'importunity'. [*YB*.] Some different and melodramatic kinds of *dharna* were: (1) *Tasmīwallahs* ('strap riggers'), who twisted a strap around their necks and threatened to choke themselves to death (in the Punjab). (2) *Doriwallahs*, who threatened to hang themselves. (3) *Dandiwallahs*, 'stick rattlers', who rattled until they got what they wanted. (4) *Urimars*, who stood all day and every day before a shop or house until they got alms. (5) *Gurzmars* and *Chharimars*, who suffered self-inflicted wounds with knives and spiked clubs until their beggary was satisfied. [*OED* & YB; Crooke, *Pop. Relig. and Folklore of N. India* (1893), ii. 42, *seq.* See **Traga** & **Gherao**. Shore, in *Asiat. Researches* (1799) (c. 1793), iv. 332.] See **Takaza**.

Dhatura See **Dhatura, Dewtry.**

Dhaura Mardhā vadā See **Dhawa.**

Dhauri [20C. H. *dhārī*.] Indian red-flowered shrub, *Woodfordia floribundia*, yielding a tragacanthic gum. [Web., *3rd New Intern. Dict.* (1976).]

Dhawa, dhava [H. *dhavā*; S. *dhava*.] Indian tree, *Anogeissues latifolia*, used for timber, tanning and its gum. [Web., *3rd New Intern. Dict.*]

Dhobi(e), dhoby, dobee [17C. H. *dhō* fr. S. *dhār*, 'to wash'.] (1) A low caste Hindu employed as a washerman; a laundry-man: Also *dhobin*, a washerwoman. (2) Clothes to be washed and clothes returned from the wash. Attrib. *dhobi*-itch, ring-worm in armpits and crotch communicated by clothes washed by the *dhobi*, vb. to *dhobi* = to launder. [*OED* & YB; *Eng. Fact. in India* (1618-69).]

Dhol, dholuk, dholkee [19C. H/S. *dhola*.] A large cylindrical Indian drum beaten at each end. [*OED*; *Proc. R. Irish Acad.* (1865), ix. i. 116.]

Dhole [19C. Kan *tōla*, 'wolf'?] The wild dog of the Deccan, *Cuon alpinus*. [*OED*; Smith in Griffith, *Cuvier's An. Kingd.* (1827), 11.326.]

Dhoney, doney, dony [16C. Tam. *dōni*; H. *doni* S. *droni*, 'trough, tub'.] A small S. Indian sailing vessel. Also *tony* (M. *toni*), 'a ferry boat' (H.H.W.). See **Almadia.** [*OED* & YB; Litchfield, tr., Castañeda's *Conq. E. Indies* 1582.] See **Telinga.**

Dhooly See **Dooly.**

Dhoon, dhun, doon [19C. H. *dūne*, 'valley'.] Any of the flat valleys at the base of the Himalayas, the Siwaliks; especially the valley of Dehra. [*OED* & YB; Gillespie, *Asiat. Jrnl.*, 29 Oct. 1814.]

Dhoona [19C. H. *dhūna.*] A resin obtained from the *Shorea robusta* tree. See **Dammar.** [*OED*; Lindley, *Veget. Kingd.* (1846).]

Dhoop [19C. H. Beng. *dhūp*, 'incense, resin,

gum'.] An Indian plant, *Vateria indica*, also its pitch. [*OED*; Sleeman, *Ramaseana* (1836).]

Dhoop-ghurry See **Ghurry.**

Dhoti, dhootie, dhuti [17C. H. *dhoti*] 'The loincloth worn by all respectable Hindu castes of upper India, wrapt round the body, the end being then passed between the legs and tucked in at the waist, so that a festoon of calico hang down to either knee.' *Also*, the fabric used for dhotis. [YB & *OED*; Danvers, *Letters*, (1609; ed. 1896-1900), i. 29.]

Dhourra, dhurra, durra [19C. H/Ar. *dhurah*.] Indian millet, *Sorghum vulgare*. Also called Guinea-corn. [*OED*; Malthus, *Population* (1798) ix.]

Dhow, dow [19C. Orig. language unknown, but Ar. and Mar. have *daw*. Webster suggests an 'Indic origin'.] The *dh* in the spelling seems to be an attempt to orientalize the look of the word, which has been applied to various sailing crafts, but 'in the mouths of Englishmen it is applied specially to the old-fashioned vessel of Arab build, with a long **Grab** stem... with one mast and lateen rig.' [YB. & *OED*; *Naval Chron.* (1802), viii. 255.]

Dhrupad [19C. S. *dhraupada*. Lit. 'a kind of dance'.] A classical form of N. Indian vocal music with a prelude and four sections, usually in slow temp developing various parts of the *raga*. [*OED*; Pringle, *Indian Music* (1898), ii, 63.]

Dhurrie, durry [19C. H. *darī*.] An Indian cotton carpet. [*OED*; Eliot James, *Indian Industries*, (1880), iv. 19.]

Dhyal See **Dial-bird.**

Dhyana [19C. S. *dhyāna*.] In Hinduism and Buddhism: profound meditation; the penultimate (7th) stage of **Yoga**; mental concentration. [*OED*; Hardy, *Eastern Monachism* (1850), xxi. 253.]

Dial-bird [18C. H. *dhyal, dahiyāl*.] The magpie-robin, *Copsychus saularis*. A trim black- and-white bird with cocked tail. The Indian Magpie-Robin. Found in the forested areas of India, Bangladesh, Sri Lanka and Burma, up to about 3500 ft. elevation. [*OED*; Salim Ali, *The Book of Indian Birds* (1979); Albin, *Nat. Hist. Birds* (1735), iii. 17.]

Diara [19C. H. *daira*.] Alluvial island formed by recession of a river. See **Char (Churr).** [Wilson, *Glossary* (1855).]

Didwan [17C. H/P. *dīdwān*.] 'A lookout, watchman, messenger, collector of revenue.' [YB; Pringle, *Diary of Fort St. George Cons.* 9 Nov.

(1680),3.38.]

Digambar [19C. S. *digambara*. Lit. 'sky-clad, naked'.] Member of major **Jain** sect formed in 3C. BC., notable (1) for its original abandonment of all worldly goods and possessions, including clothes. (They do not now go naked but wear coloured clothes.) (2) For its denial that women can attain salvation. Also, Svetambara (who wear white clothes). [*OED*; Colebrooke (1805), *Asiat. Res.* (1808) v. 482.]

Diggory, digri, degree [19C.] 'Anglo-Hindustani law-court jargon for 'decree.' [YB; *Confessions of an Orderly* (1866), 138.]

Dikamali, decamalee [19C. Mar. *dikāmāli*.] A fragrant resinous gum exuding from the ends of young shoots of *Gardenia lucida*, a rubiaceous Indian shrub. [*OED*; Simmonds, *Dict. Trade* (1858).]

Dikh, dick, dikk [19C. Ar./P./H. *dik(k)*, 'vexation', 'worry', 'trouble', 'botheration'. So, *dik honā*, 'to be worried'. The noun *dikk-dārī*, worry, has become an adjective in Rudyard Kipling's *In Black and White* (1889). [*OED* & YB; Heeley, *A Lay of Modern Darjeeling* (1873).]

Dilruba, dirub [19C. H. *dilrūba*.] An Indian three or four-stringed long-necked instrument, played with a bow with several sympathetic strings. [*OED*.] See **Sarangi**. [*Hindu Mus. and Gayan Samaj* (1887), iii. 53.]

Dimdam [19C.] Biting black fly of family *Simulidae*, found in the eastern Himalayas. [*CIWIE*.]

Din [10C. E. *din*; S. *dhuni*, 'roaring, a torrent.'] 'A loud noise; particularly a continued confused or resonant sound, which stuns or distresses the ear.' [*OED* (1969), iii. 373.]

Dinar [17C. H/P./Ar. *dīnār*.] Name of various oriental coins once in use in India (corresponding to the **Gold-mohur**), and elsewhere. Latin, *denarius*. [*OED* & YB; Sir T. Herbert, *Travels* (1634).]

Dingar [19C.] A large wild bee of East India, *apis dorsata*. [Sharp in *Camb. Nat. Hist.* (1899), vi. 70; *OED*.]

Dinghy [17C. Beng. *dingī*, H. *dīngi*.] A native Indian rowing boat; (gen.) a small rowing boat or skiff. Dim. of *dēnga, dōnga*, a larger kind of boat, sloop, coastal vessel. [*OED* & YB; *Eng. Fact. in India* (1618-69; ed. Foster,1906-27).]

Dissave, dissava, dissuava [17C.Sinh. *disawa*, S. *desa*, 'a country'.] Governor of Province under the Kandyan government, or a Collector or Government Agent in Ceylon (Sri Lanka). [YB.] See **Desai**, and **Deshmukh**. [Knox, *Hist.*

Rel. of Ceylon etc. (1681), 35.]

Dirzee *See* **Durzee**.

Ditch, ditcher [18C. Anglo-Indian.] Disparaging soubriquet for Calcutta and its European citizens for the rationale of which *see* **Mahratta Ditch**. [*OED* & YB.]

Divan *See* **Dewan**.

Diwali, divali, dewally, deepavali [17C. H. *diwālī*, S. *dīpāvalī*, 'a row of lights'.] Hindu autumn festival of lights in the month of *Asvina* (the dark half) or *Kārtīka* (the new moon), celebrating various divinities, e.g. *Lakshmi, Bhavāni, Krishna's* slaying of the demon Naraka. But there are variations of the timing of the festival in different parts of India. In Bengal it is called *Kālī Pūjā*, the feast of the goddess of destruction, celebrated on the most moonless nights of the month with illuminations and fireworks, with feasting, carousing, gambling and sacrifice of goats, sheep and buffaloes. [YB & *OED*; *Eng. Fact. in India* (1618-69).]

Dixie, dechsie, etc. [19C. H. *degchi, degachī*; Punj. *dekachi, degāchi*; P. *degcha*, dim. of *deg, dīg*, iron pot, cauldron.] A saucepan without a handle for cooking stew, rice, vegetables etc., used by soldiers. [James, *Ind. Househ. Management.*] [*OED* (1879), 40.]

Doab, duab [19C. H/P. *doāb*; lit. 'two waters', i.e. 'Mesopotamia'.] The tract of land between two confluent rivers; espec. that between the Ganges (Ganga) and Jumuna. [*OED* & YB; Wellington, *Desp.* (1803), 1.605.]

Doai! Dwye! [19C. H. *dohāī*! Guj. *dawāhī*! Mal. *adohi!*, alas!] Interjection or exclamation shouted aloud by a petitioner for redress from a prince, Court of Justice, or anyone else deemed able to render justice, e.g. *Dohai Maharaj!* Justice, O King! *Dohai Kompani bahadur!* Justice O Company's Officer! [YB; A. Prinsep, *Baboo* etc. (1834), ii. 242.]

Doar, the Duars [19C. Poss. S. *dvāra*, 'a gate or entrance'.] 'A strip of partially cultivated moist land at the foot of the eastern Himalayas, South of Bhutan, corresponding to the **Terai** further west.' [YB.] A frontier district. [Wilson, *Glossary* (1855).]

Dobund [18C. H. *dōbund*.] 'a new and additional embankment'. [YB; Burke, *Articles Against W. Hastings* (1787), vii. 98.]

Doctor, The [19C. Anglo-Indian.] A refreshing sea-breeze in India peculiar to Bombay, so-called because of its most salubrious properties which 'cause it to be resorted to by invalids from the other presidencies and the interior'.

(Known in the W. Indies since the 18C.). [YB.] Orig. 'Cape Doctor' when the Cape was used by Anglo-Indians as a sanatorium. [Pettman, *Africanderisms* (1913); John B. Seely, *The Wonders of Ellora* (1825).]

Dogra [19C. H. *Daggar*.] The warlike Hindu race of the Duggar district, formerly in N.W. India, now in Pakistan. A well-known Indian Army regiment. *Dogri* = the language of the Dogras. Also adj. [*OED;* Elliot, *Suppl. Gloss. Indian Terms* (1845).]

Dokhma [Guj. *dokhmā*.] *See* **Tower of Silence** [Whitworth, *Anglo-Indian Dict.* (1885).]

Doli, dulha [19C. H. *dulhā*, bridgeroom.] Hindu bridegroom's ceremonial of taking away the bride. *See* **Ghori**. [Whitworth, *Anglo-Indian Dict.*]

Dolly, dhaulie [19C. H. *dālī*. lit. a basket or tray.] (An anglicization attracted to an existing-word in English.) 'A complimentary offering-of fruit, flowers, vegetables, sweet meats and the like, presented usually on one or more trays; also the daily basket of garden produce laid before the owner by the **Malī** or gardener.' ('The Molly with his Dolly.') [YB & *OED;* Mrs Meer Hassan Ali, *Observations,* (1832), i. 333.]

Dom, Dhome, Dombaree [19C. H. *dōm;* S. *dōma; dombas;* Tel. *dommara.*] Member of a menial Dravidian caste; sometimes basket-makers, sometimes professional thieves. 'In many places they perform such offices as carrying dead bodies, removing carrion, etc. They are often musicians and sweepers.' [YB; Abbé Dubois, *Desc. of the Character, Manners of the People of India,* etc. (E. tr. 1817).]

Domba [19C. Sinh. *dombe.*] A large E. Indian & Malaysian tree, *Calophyllum inophyllum,* whose seeds yield a thick, dark green, strong-scented, medicinal and lamp oil. [*OED;* Simmons, *Dict. Trade* (1858).]

Doob [18C. H. *dūb,* S *dūrvā.*] Nutritious Indian dog's tooth grass, *Cynodon dactylon,* used as cattle fodder. [*OED* & YB; *Indian Antiquary* (1795; ed. 1871-1933), vol. xxi.]

Doocaun [19C. H/P. *dukan.* Ar. *dukkan.*] A native shop or a stall. (*dukandar,* a shop-keeper.) [YB; Mrs Meer Hassan Ali *Observations* (1832), ii. 36.]

Doolally [19C. Anglo-Indian.] The spoken form of *Deolali,* a town near Bombay. Orig. Service slang, *Doolali-tap* (fever); an unbalanced mental state requiring treatment at the Army hospital at Deolali, or acquired in the pre-embarkation camp there. [*OED.*] *See* **Puggled**. Also *Doolally-tapped,* 'knocked silly'. [Fraser and Gibbons, *Soldier & Sailor Words and Phrases* (1925).]

Doolie, dooly, dhooly [17C. H. *dōlī,* dim of *dōlā,* 'swing, cradle'; S. *dōlā,* fr. *dūl,* 'to swing'.] 'A covered litter consisting of a cot or frame, suspended by the four corners from a bamboo pole, and carried by four men.' [YB.] A rudimentary palanquin used by Indian lower classes and as an army ambulance. [*OED.*] *See* **Dandy**[3] and **Palanquin.** [Hawkins in *Purchas* (1625), i. 435.]

Doombah, doombur [19C. H/P. *dunba, dumba, dumb,* 'tail'.] The name commonly given in India to the fat-tailed sheep breed. [YB; Parkes, *Wanderings of a Pilgrim,* etc. (1828), i.128.]

Doonga, dunga [20C. H. *dongā.*] A flat-bottomed dug-out, with a square sail; kind of a house-boat in Kashmir. [*OED; Westm. Gaz.,* 3 Jan. 1905.]

Dooputty *See* **Dupatta.**

Doordarshan [20C. H. *dur* (far) + *darshan,* seeing.] Television. [*CIWIE*].

Dopeage [17C. Anglo-Indian, perh. fr. Du. *doop,* 'sauce', fr. *doopen,* 'dip, mix'.] Curry (?) [*The Travels of Peter Mundy in Europe & Asia* (1608-67) (quoted in Woodruffe; *The Men Who Ruled India,* vol. I, 53.]

Dorai, doray, durai [17C. Tam. *turai;* Tel. *dora;* 'master', 'lord'. 'European gentleman.'] S. Indian equivalent of **Sahib.** *Sinnaturai* (Sinnadurai) personal name, 'small gentle-man' = **Chhota Sahib.** Tel. *dorasāni* = 'Lady' or 'Madam'. [YB; *Fort St. George Cons.* (Aug. 5, 1680), in *Notes & Extracts* (1670-81), iii. 31.]

Doria,[1] **doriya** [18C. H. *doriyā;* fr. *dori(ī),* a cord or leash.] A dog-keeper. [*OED*] [*India Gazette,* 17 March 1781.]

Doria,[2] **doorea, doriya, dorea** [17C. H. *doriya* 'striped stuff'.] Orig. striped cotton or muslin, later also silk, silk and cotton, tussore, etc. 'As the characteristic pattern of the *charkhana* is a check, so that of the *doriya* is stripes running along the length of the *than,* i.e. warp threads.' [Yusif Ali, *Mon. on Silk* (1900); *OED* & YB; Hedges, *Diary* (1683); (Hak. Soc. 1886), i. 94.]

Dosa [20C. Tam. *dōsa.*] Fried rice pancake. [*CIWIE.*]

Dosooty [19C. H. *do-sūtī,* 'double thread'.] Coarse cotton – stuff woven with doubled threads. [YB; Davidson, *Diary in Upper India*

(1843), i. 10.]

Double-Grill [19C.] Domestic Hindustani of the kitchen for a 'devil' in the culinary sense: i.e. (highly seasoned) fried or broiled. [YB.]

Double-roti [20C. Domestic Hindustani for leavened bread, as opposed to *roti*, unleavened. *See* **Chapatty**. [*CIWIE*.]

Dour [19C. H. *daur*, 'a run'.] A foray or hasty expedition of any kind. Also *to dour*, 'to run', 'to make such an expedition'. *See* **Chappow**. [YB; Arnold, *Oakfield* (1853), ii. 67.]

Dow [19C. H. *dāo*; S. *dātra*, fr. *dā*, 'to cut'.] A hewing knife of various forms. Cf Burmese **Dha**. [YB; Lewin, *Wild Races of S.E. India* (1870).]

Dragoman, drugman, etc. [17C. H/Ar. *tarjumān*.] An interpreter. *See* **Truchman**. [Mildenhall in Purchas, *Pilgrimes* (1625); Coryat, *Crudities* (1611).]

Dowle [19C.] H. *daul(ā)*.] A ridge of clay serving as the boundary between two rice-fields and retaining the water. (In S. India this is called a **Bund**.) [YB; *Notes and Queries, 1st Series.* (1851), iv. 161.]

Dowra [19C. H. *daurāhā, daura*.] 'a village runner', 'a guide', fr. *daurnā*, 'to run; S. *drava*, 'running'. [YB; Scott, *The Surgeon's Daughter* (1827), ch. xiii.]

Drabby, drabi, draby [19C. Anglo-Indian.] An Indian muleteer, transport driver, or, loosely, a camp-follower. Corr. of the English 'driver'. [*OED* & YB; *Pioneer Mail*, 16 March 1900.]

Dravidian (sb. & adj) [19C. An Anglo-Indian formation fr. S. *Drāvida*, province of S. India, in which Dravidian languages are spoken.] Member(s) and language(s) of a non-Aryan race in S. India & Sri Lanka, e.g. Tamils, Telingas, Malayalis, Kannadigas, Coorgis, etc. Hence *Dravidic* (1888). [*OED* & YB; Caldwell, *Compar. Gramm. Drav. Lang.* (1856), 527.]

Drawers, Long [18C.] An old-fashioned Anglo-Indian term for **Pyjamas**. [YB; Seton-karr, *Selections from Calcutta Gazettes* (1784-1823).]

Dressing-boy, Dress-boy [19C.] Old Madras term for a servant who acted as a valet, corresponding to the **Bearer** of N. India. [YB; Maitland, *Letters from Madras* (1843), 106.]

Drongo [19C. *Malagasy drongo*.] Insectivorous black bird with forked tail, of family *Dicruridae*, also called *Drongo-shrikes*. Some Indian species are : (1) The Black drongo or King crow (*Dicrurus adsimilis*), 'a slim and agile glossy black bird with long, deeply forked tail'. [Salim Ali.] (2) The White-bellied Drongo *(Dicrurus cuerulescens)*. 'Glossy indigo above, with white belly and under-tail coverts.' [Salim Ali.] (3) The Southern Large Racket- tailed Drongo (*Dicrurus paradiseus*). 'Glossy black with prominently tufted forehead and two long wirelike spatula-tipped feathers or streamers in the tail.' [Salim Ali.] [Penny Cycl. (1841), xxi; *OED*; Salim Ali & S.D. Ripley, *Handbook Birds Ind. & Pak.* (1972), vol. 5.]

Drongo cuckoo [19C.] A species of the cuckoo *genus Surniculus* (a bird native of Nepal). [Salim Ali.] [*OED*.]

Droog [19C. Kan. *drug*.] Name given to hill-forts in Karnataka. [Thomas and William Daniell, *Oriental Scenery* (1801).]

Drumstick [19C.] 'The colloquial Anglo-Indian name (in the Madras Presidency) for the long slender pods of the fast-growing *Moringa oleifera*, the **Horse Radish Tree** of Bengal.' [YB; Haafner, *Voyages* (1811).]

Dub (sb. vb) [18C. Tel. *dabba*.] A small copper coin, value 20 **Cash**. Slang: 'to *dub* up', 'to pay on the nail'. [*OED* & YB; *Lives of the Lindsays* (1781; ed. 1849), iii.]

Dubash, dobash [17C. fr. H. *dōbāshī*, 'man of two languages'.] An interpreter. In mercantile houses, the broker transacting business with Indians and corresponding to the Calcutta **Banyan**. In Gujarat reputed to act like Bunyan's Mr Two Tongues. Also *dūbāshī, dōbāshī*. *See* **Topass, Truchman**. [*OED* & YB; *Eng. Fact. in India* (1618-1669).]

Dubba, dubber [18C. H. *dabbah*; Mahr. *dabara*; Guj. *dabaro*.] A bag made of buffalo hide 'used for holding and transporting **Ghee** or oil'. [YB & *OED; Eng. Fact. in India* (1618-1669).]

Dubbawalla [20C. Mar. *dubba-* or *dabara-wala*.] In Bombay and elsewhere one who delivers food in **Tiffin Carriers** from houses to offices. *See* **Khana** & **Coolie**. [*CIWIE*.]

Dubeer, dubbeer 18C. H/P. *dabīr*.] 'a **Writer** or secretary'. 'The King's Dubbeer, or minister, which among the Indians, is equivalent to the Duan (Dewan) of the Mahomedan Princes.' [YB; Orme, *Hist. of the Milit. Trans. of the Brit. Nation in Indostan* (1778), ii. 601.]

Ducks [19C.] Slang: an officer of the Bombay service, 'the correlative of the **Mulls** of Madras and the *Qui-Hi's* of Bengal'. [YB.] Any inhabitant of Bombay. Also *Bombay Ducks*. See **Bummalo**. [Colebrooke, *Life of Elphinstone* (1803; 1884), i. 53.]

Duffadar [19C. H/P. *dafadār*.] A person in

charge of a small body of troops; a cavalry subaltern. A petty officer of native police (*see* **Burkandauze**.) An N.C.O. (corporal **Naik**) in regiments of Irregular Cavalry. [*OED* & YB; Wellington, *Dispatches* (1800; ed. 1844.), ii. 242.]

Dufter, dafter [17C. H/Ar. *daftar*.] 'record, register; bundle of official papers.'] Coll. 'the office' (**Cutcherry**) = *dafter khāna* (records room). 'In S. India *daftar* means a bundle of connected *papers* tied up in a cloth [the *basta* of Upper India.' YB.] Also the *dufteri* (1810), who kept the records in order, repaired pens, bound papers and books and performed other 'office boy' duties. (In S. India a **Moochy**.) [*OED* & YB; *Eng. Fact. in India* (1621; 1618-69).]

Dufterdar, dafterdar [19C. *See* prec.] A record-keeper. 'The head native revenue officer on the Collector's and Sub-Collector's establishment of the Bombay Presidency.' [YB; Wilson, *Glossary* (1855).]

Duggie [19C. Anglo-Burmese. Poss. corr. of Burm. *htāp-gyĭ*, 'big-beam'.] 'Word used in the Pegu teak-trade for a long squared timber.' [YB; Milburn, *Or. Commerce* (1813).]

Dugong [19C. Mal. *dūyong*.] A large cetaceous aquatic herbivorous mammal, *Halicore dugong*, alias the Indian Walrus, native to the Indian seas. [*OED* & YB; Shaw, *General Zool.* (1800).]

Dumbcow(ed) [19C. Prob. H. *dhamkhānā*, 'to chide, scold, threaten, to repress by threats or reproof'.] To browbeat, cow, to put down. Hobson-Jobsonized into a transitive verb (to *dambkcow*), 'both spelling and meaning being affected by English suggestions of sound'. [YB.] 'This is a capital specimen of Anglo-Indian dialect.' [YB.] For similar Anglo-Indian constructions, *see* **Foozilow, Bunnow, Gubrow** & **Lugow**. [YB; Platts, *Dict.* (1884).]

Dumdum [19C.] (Place near Calcutta, headquarters of the old Bengal artillery.) 'The name poss. means 'a mound or elevated battery'. H/P *damdama*' [YB]. Now the name of a soft-core expanding bullet made originally in the arsenal at Dumdum. [*OED* & YB; *Or. Sport. Mag.* (1830); Thackeray, *Vanity Fair* (1848).]

Dumpoke(d) [17C. H/P. *dampukht*, 'air-cooked', i.e. baked.] Baked, broiled, or steamed meat, boned and stuffed with raisins, almonds, ginger, cardamom, butter, etc., especially chicken or duck. (The word is used in all the

English tense forms and attributively.) [*OED* & YB; Fryer, *New Acct.* (1672-81, 93); Ovington, *Voy. Suratt* (1696) 397.]

Dumree [19C. H. *damrī*.] A copper coin of very low value. See **Dam**. [YB; Malcolm, *Central India* (1824).]

Dun *See* **Dhoon**.

Dungaree [17C. H. *dungrī*.] 'A coarse kind of cloth.' A kind of coarse Indian calico 'woven with two or more threads together in the warp and woof.' [YB.] Also, trousers of this material. [Kipling, *City of Dreadful Night* (1891); *OED* & YB; Capt. Saris in Purchas, *Pilgrimes* (1613; ed. 1625-6).]

Dupatta, dooputty, dopatta [17C. H. *dopattah*; fr. *do*, two & *pattah*, a strip.] 'A piece of cloth of two breadths.' 'Formerly these pieces were woven narrow and joined alongside of one another to produce the proper width. Now it is worn either round the head or over the shoulders with ends hanging down, and is used by both Hindu and Muslim women.' [YB; Yusef Ali, *Mon. on Silk* (1900); *Foster's Letters.* (1615; ed. 1896-1900), ii. 156.]

Durbar, darbar [17C. H/P. *dārbār*, fr. *dār*, 'door' + *bar* (suffix of place-names).] (1) A public levée held by a ruler or British governor, viceroy, etc. in India. [Hawkins in Purchas, *Pilgrimes* (1609; ed. 1625-6); (2) The court or hall of audience (of a king or chief). [Sir T. Roe, in Purchas, *Pilgrimes* (1616; ed. 1625-6); (3) The Executive Government of a Native State, as distinguished from the British agent and his officers. [Whitworth; Lord Valentia, *Voy. and Trav. to India* (1809), i. 362.] The word is also found in 'Durbar Sahib', in the Golden Temple of the Sikhs in Amritsar. [*OED* & YB.]

Durga(h)-Pooja [19C. S. *durgā* (the goddess) + *pūjā*, worship.] *Durga*, the Hindu goddess daughter of Himawat and consort of Siva the terrible destroyer. *Durga Pooja*, 'the chief Hindu festival in Bengal, lasting for ten days in Sept./Oct.,commonly termed "the Poojas".' [YB.] *See* **Dusserah**. [Parker, *Bole Pongis* (1851).] *See* **Sakti, Siva, Tantra**.

Durgah, dargah, durgaw [18C. H/P. *dargah*, 'a royal court', gate, door or large bench.] 'But the habitual use in India is for the shrine of a Muslim saint, a place of religious resort and prayer.' [YB & *OED*; Hodges, *Travels in India* (1780-83; ed. 1793).]

Durjun [19C. Domestic. H. *darjan*.] Corr. of English 'dozen'. [YB.]

Durra *See* **Dhourra**. (But **Durra** is the more

acceptable modern spelling.)

Durwan, darwan, door-van [18C. H/P. *darwān*.] A doorkeeper. A porter at the gate of the **Compound**. Also, *darwaza*, a gateway, portal, door. [*OED* & YB; Ives, *Voy. from England to India* (1754; ed. 1773).]

Durwauza-Bund [19C. H. *darwaza-band* (*hai*), the door is closed.] The formula by which an Indian servant in an Anglo-Indian household intimated that his master or mistress could not receive a visitor: 'the door is closed' = Not at home. [YB; Allardyce, *The City of Sunshine* (1877), i. 225.]

Durzee, dirzee, dirgee [19C. H/P. *darzī*, fr. *darz* 'sewing, hem, seam'.] An Indian tailor. [*OED* & YB; Mrs Sherwood, *Autobiog.* (1817); Maria Graham, *Jrnl. Resid. India* (1812).]

Dusserah, Dassehra, etc., [18C. H. *dasahrā; S. dasaharā;* Mar. *dasrā.*] The 'nine nights' (or 'ten days'). Hindu festival in Sept./Oct. celebrated on the tenth day of the Hindu month Jaishtha in honour of **Durga** and **Rama.** The origin of the word is obscure. *See* **Durga Poojah.** [Sir John Malcolm in *Trans. Bomb. Lit. Soc.* (1799), iii. 73.]

Dustak, dastak, dustuck [17C. H/P. *dastak.*] 'a little hand, hand-clapping to attract attention'. (1) a passport, pass or permit, applied espec. to the passports granted by the convenanted servants of the East India Company, in the first half of the 18th Century. (2) 'The modern sense of the word in N. India is a notice of the revenue demand served on a defaulter.' [YB &

OED; Eng. Fact. in India; 1618–69; Orme *Hist. Milit. Trans.* (1778), vol. ii; Burke, *Rep. Indian Affairs,* Wks. (1776), xi. 173.] *See* **Rowannah**.

Dustoor(i), dustoory [17C. H/P. *dastur(ī).*] (1) Custom, usage, fashion. (2) 'Customary commission or percentage on the money passing in any cash transaction which, with or without acknowledgement or permission, sticks to the fingers of the agent of payment.' [YB.] *See* **Dastur.** [*Embassy of Sir Thomas Roe* (1618-19); Trevelyan, *Dawk Bungalow* (1886), 217.] *See* **Tarega**.

Dvanda, dwandwa [19C. S. *dvamdvā.*] The repeated nom. of *dva*, 'pair', 'couple'. Philolophy: A *dvandvā* compound, in which the elements are related to each other, as if joined by a copula, e.g. Prince Consort = Prince and Consort. [*OED;* Monier-Williams, *Elem. Gram. Sanscr.* (1846), ix. 158.]

Dwaita, dvaita [19C. S. *dvaita.*] Hindu philosophy: Dualism. The doctrine affirming that matter and spirit are separate existences. [Whitworth, *Anglo-Indian Dict.* (1885).]

Dwarpal [19C. S. *dwārpāla.*] A door-keeper, especially a painted or sculptured one at a Hindu temple doorway or entrance. [Whitworth, *Anglo-Ind. Dict.*]

Dzo *See* **Zo.**

Dzong, jong [19C. Tib. *rdzon.*] Tibetan, building, castle, fortress, monastery. Also a territorial and administrative division. [*OED; Encycl. Brit.* (1888); Times, 11 May 1904.]

E

Eagle-wood, agal-wood [16C. S. *agaru;* Mal. *kayu,* wood + *gharu.*] The diseased aromatic wood of the Indian tree, *Aquilaria agallocha,* burnt as incense. Also called 'aloes-wood'. *See* **Aloes**[1] and **Calambac.** [*OED* & YB; Linschoten, *Discours,* E. tr. (1598; Hak. Soc., 1807, i. 120. 1. 50); Subba Rao, *Indian Words in English* (1954); Ref. Thomas Bowrey (1669-79), ed. Sir R. C. Temple (Hak. Soc., 1905).]

Earth-oil [18C. Anglo-Indian tr. of the Indian expression *mitti ka tel.* (Also Malay, *minyak tanah).*] Kerosene, petroleum. [*OED* & YB; Dalrymple, *Or. Rep.* (1755), i. 172.]

East India [17C. Obs. except attributively, as in the *East India Company* (1600); *East Indiaman* (1844); *East India Fly* (Blister-Fly, Spanish-fly, *Cantharis vesicatoria* (1816). [Herbert, *Trav.* (1634), 187.]

East Indian [16C.] (1) Pertaining to the East Indies; West Indian of East Indian origin; a large ship in the East India trade; a Catholic community indigenous to Bombay. [*OED;* Eden, *Treat. New. Ind.* (1533).] (2) In Anglo-Indian, parlance = **Eurasian** (sb. and attrib.) [*OED; Asiatic Jrnl,* New Ser. (1831), VI. ii. 106.]

East Indies [16C.] A term used to include Hindustan (now India, Pakistan & Bangladesh), Sri Lanka, the Malay Archipelago and the Indonesian islands. Opposed to *West* Indies. [*OED;* Shakespeare, *Merry Wives* (1598).]

Ecka *See* **Ekka.**

Eid, Eed [H/P.] *See* **Id.**

Eedgah [18C. H/P. *īdgāh,* 'place of *Id'.*] A place of assembly and prayer for Muslim festivals. 'In India usually a platform of white, plastered brickwork enclosed by a low wall on three sides outside of a town or village.' [YB.] Also known as *Namāzgāh,* 'place of prayer'. [Seton-kerr, *Selections* (1792; ed. 1864-9).]

Ekadashi [19C. H. *ekadasi,* eleventh.] The eleventh day of either fortnight in a lunar month on which Hindus fast. [Wilson, *Glossary* (1855).]

Ek-dum *See* **Ack-dum.**

Ekka, ecka [19C. *ekka,* fr. *ek,* 'one'.] A one-horse Indian carriage. *See* **Hackery.** (Described and sketched in J.L. Kipling, *Beast & Man in India,* 1892.) [*OED* & YB; Augustus Prinsep, *Baboo and other Tales* (1834), ii. 4.]

Ekteng [19C. E. *acting.*] Indian pronunciation. Temporary, unconfirmed, not **Pukka.** Indian folk-etymology associated this word with *ek-tang,* 'one leg', 'only one leg in the official stirrup'. [YB.; H. Yule, *Quarterly Review,* April 1883, 297.]

Elaichi [H. *ilāchī.*] 'a cardamom'. *See* next.

Elatches allega, elatcha [17C. H. *ilāchā* (See prec.)] 'A kind of cloth woven of silk and thread so as to present the appearance of cardamoms.' [YB; Platts, *Dict. of Urdu, Hindi & English* (1884); Downton in Purchas (1613), i. 504.]

Elchee [17C. Turk. *īlchī* fr. *īl,* 'a (nomad) tribe'.] An ambassador (a rep. of the *īl*). Kinglake in *Crimea* (1863) described Sir Stratford Canning as the great Eltchi. [*OED* & YB; Hakluyt, *Voyages* (1599; ed. 1807), II. ii. 67.]

Elephant(a) elephanter [17C. Anglo-Indian, fr. Pg. *elephante.*] A name given (originally by the Portuguese) to the stormy weather at the end (or as some say, at the onset) of the monsoon. The Portuguese named it after H. *hathiya,* the sign of *hathi,* the Elephant, the 13th lunar asterism at the end of the rains. [*OED* & YB.] *See* **Damani.** [Danvers, *Letters,* (1611; ed. 1896-1900), i. 126.]

Elephant-apple [19C. Anglo-Indian.] The wood-apple tree of India, *Feronia elephantum.* [Lindley and Moore, *Treas. Bot.* (1866); *OED.*]

Elephant-creeper [19C. Anglo-Indian.] The creeper, *Argyreia speciosa,* N.O. *Convolvulaceae,* the leaves of which are used in Indian medicine as poultices, etc. [YB.]

Elephant-grass [19C. Anglo-Indian.] Various kinds of grass or grass-like plants growing in India, especially *Pennisetum purpureum.* (Elephants are said to be fond of it.) [*OED;* Roxburgh, *Flora Indica* (1832), iii. 566.]

Elk (Indian) [Anglo-Indian.] 'The name given in S. India by sportsmen, with singular impropriety, to the great stag *Cervus unicolor,* the **Sambur** of Upper and W. India.' [YB & *OED;* Forbes, *Or. Mem.* (1813).]

Elu, Helu, Hela [19C. Corr. of Pali *Sinhala.*] An ancient form of **Sinhalese** from which the modern Indo-Aryan vernacular of Sri Lanka is derived. [YB; *Ceylonese Vocabulary* (Colombo, June 1869).]

Emblic *See* **Myrobalans.**

Emir *See* **Amir.**

Esraj [20C. Bengali, *esrāj.*] An Indian musical

instrument with three or four main strings, and extra sympathetic strings, played with a bow and resembling the Sarangi. [*OED*; Popley, *Music of India* (1921), 109.]

Estimauze [17C. A.I. corr. of Ar/P. *iltimās*.] 'a prayer, petition, humble representation.' [YB; Hedges, *Diary* (1681-8; Hak. Soc., 1886), ii. lxx.]

Eurasian [19C.] A person of mixed European and Indian parentage, devised as being more euphemistic than 'half-caste' and more precise than **East Indian.** [YB.] *See* **Anglo-Indian, Chi-Chi, Mustees.** [*OED* & YB; J.M., *Local Sketches* (Calcutta) in *6th Ser. Notes and Queries* (1844), xii. 177.]

Europe (adj.) [17C.] 'Commonly used in India at one time for "European", in contradistinction to **Country,** so designating goods imported from Europe,' e.g. *Europe shop* (1781), selling imported goods; *Europe morning* = lying late in bed, as opposed to the Anglo-Indian's habit of early rising; *Europe engineer* (1673); *Europe ship* (1711). [YB; Fryer, *New Acct. of E. India* etc., 87.]

Eysham, ehsham [18C. H/Ar. *ahshām*, pl. of *hashm*, 'a train or retinue'.] 'Irregular infantry with swords and matchlocks.' [YB; Irvine, *Army of the Indian Moghuls*, in *J.R.A.S.* (July 1896, 528); *Hist. Hyder Naik*, E. tr. by Miles (1842), 398; *Letters of Tippoo Sultan*, E. tr. Kirkpatrick (1811).]

F

Factor [16C. Anglo-Indian. fr. Pg. *feitore*.] A member of the third of four classes of the covenanted civil servants of the East India Company who were divided into Senior Merchants, Junior Merchants, Factors and Writers. These terms disappeared from the E.I.C register in 1842, and thereafter six, and later five, classes took their place. [*OED & YB*; Litchfield, *Castañeda*, tr. (1582), f. 46; Sainsbury, *Calendar of State Papers, East Indies* (1600; ed. 1862-84), i. iii.]

Factory [16C. *See* prec. Pg. *feitoria*.] A trading establishment at a foreign port or other trading centre. More than fifty such Indian factories are listed in Robert Burton's *The English Acquisitions in Guinea and East India* (1728). [*OED & YB*; Litchfield, *Castañeda* (tr. 1582), f 54.] *See* **Presidency**.

Failsoof [19C. H/Ar. *failsūf*, 'philosopher'. (Gr. *philosophos*).] 'But its popular sense is a crafty schemer', 'an artful dodger'. [YB.]

Fakir, fakeer [17C. H/Ar. *fakīr*, 'poor'.] 'Properly an indigent person, but specially 'one poor in the sight of God, applied to a Mahommedan religious mendicant, and then, loosely and inaccurately, to Hindu devotees and naked ascetics.' [YB.] For example, Gandhi, 'That half-naked fakir'. [Churchill.] Barbarie, in Purchas, *Pilgrimes* [*OED & YB*; (1625-6), ii. 857.] *See* **Sannyas** and **Tuckiah**.

Falaun, forlone [19C. H/Ar. *falāna, fulān*; Pg. *fulano*, 'such a one', ' a certain one', 'so and so'.] 'Gradually, by a process of Hobson-Jobson this was turned into Forlone.' [*OED & YB*; Colebrooke, *Life of Elphinstone* (1803; ed. 1884), i. 81.]

Falooda [20C. H. *falūda*.] A farinaceous sweet drink. [*CIWIE*.]

Faltu [20C. H. *faltū*.] Worthless. [*CIWIE*.]

Fanam [16C. Tam. *panam*, 'money'. S. *pana* (fr. *pan*, 'to barter') 'wealth'.] 'Originally a small gold coin long in use in S. India. Latterly of silver or base gold. It bore various local values.' [YB; Varthema, *Travels*, E. tr. by Eden (1576).] *See* **Pun**.

Fan-palm [19C.] Name applied in India and elsewhere to the palm *Borassus flabelliformis* (*see* **Brab, Palmyra**). Sometimes applied to the **Talipot**, and erroneously to the Traveller's Tree, i.e. the Madagascar Ravenala (*Urania speciosa*). [YB; Green, *Universal Herbal* (1820).]

Farash, ferash, frash [17C. H/Ar. *farrash*, fr. *farsh* 'to spread' (a carpet).] A menial servant, carpet-spreader, tent-pitcher, odd-job man. One of the highest hereditary officers of Sindhia's court (was) called *Farāsh-khāna-wālā*. (This is the opposite of the Indian fashion of calling a menial by a princely name, e.g. **Mehtar**, prince = **Sweeper**). [YB; Fryer, *New Acct. E. India and Persia*;Fitzgerald,*Omar Khayyam* (1859), xiv.]

Farsi [P/Ar. *fārsī*.] The Arabic name of the Persian (Iranian) language. *See* **Parsi**.

Fasli [19C. H/Ar. *fasli*, fr. *fasl*, 'to divide'.] Era established by Akbar and observed in the former Hyderabad State ruled by the **Nizam**, in which the *Samvat* year was made to agree with that of the *Hijra* by cutting off 649 years from the former. Also called the harvest year. [Wilson, *Gloss*. (1855).]

Fateha, fatiha [19C. H/Ar. *fataha*, 'to open'.] Prayers for the dead. The opening *Surah* of the Koran. [*OED*; Whitworth, *Anglo-Indian Dict*. (1885); G.F. Lyon, *Narr. Trav. N. Afr.* (1821), ii. 74; J. Morier, *Hajji Baba* (1824), iii. i. 20.]

Fatwa, fetwa, futwa [17C. H/Ar. *fetwa*.] A judicial decision given by a Mufti, or by a man learned in Muslim law on any point of law and morals, usually in writing. [*OED & YB*.] *See* **Adalat, Kazi** and **Law-Officer**. [Purchas, *Pilgrimes* (1608; ed. 1625), II. ix.]

Fedea, fuddea [19C. Mar. *p'hadya*.] Money, formerly current in Bombay and the adjoining coast, of various values, e.g. 4 *fedeas* = 1 **Tanga** and 20 *fedas* = one **Pardoe** according to Nunez (*Livro dos Peso de Ymdia e assy Medidas a Moedas* (1554). [YB.] [Milburn, *Oriental Commerce*, etc. (1813).]

Feni, fenny [20C. Mar. *pheni*.] Alcoholic drink distilled in Goa from cashew or coconut. [*CIWIE*.]

Ferash *See* **Farash**.

Ferazee [19C. H/Ar. *farāizī*, 'the divine ordinances'.] A name applied to a body of Mahommedan Puritans in Bengal, kindred to the Wahabis of Arabia. Founded by Hajji Shariyatullah, killed in 1831. [YB, 350.]

Feringhee, Frangi, Firinghee, Firangi, etc. [17C. H. P. *farangī*.] (1) A term, corr. of 'Frank', applied by Indians to persons of Portuguese descent, and (contemptuously) to other Europeans. [*OED & YB*; *The Indian*

Antiquary, lx, 'Journal of John Jourdain', cited by S. H. Hodivala (1609); Foster, *Letters* (1614; ed. 1896-1900), ii. 299.] (2) 'In the Dravidian languages the word is also used to mean a cannon or a piece of ordnance.' [Dr S.R. Dalgado, *Portuguese Vocables in Asiatic Languages.*] *See* **Parangi** and **Wallandez**.

Fetwa *See* **Fatwa**.

Fire-temple *See* **Agiary**.

Firman, firmaun, phirmaund [16C. H/P. *fermān,* 'an order, patent or passport'. Imperial order. Cf. S. *pramāna,* 'command'. [*OED* & YB.] *See* **Dustuck**. [E. tr. Litchfield, *Castañeda* (1582); Foster, Letters (1614; ed. 1896-1900), ii. 28.]

Firni [20C. H. *firni.*] Sweet dish of milk and ground rice. [*CIWIE.*]

Fiscal [17C. Du. *Fiscaal.*] In Ceylon (Sri Lanka) and in Dutch settlements in Bengal = Sheriff. In Malabar = Dutch Police Superintendent, J.P. & Attorney-General. In British Cochin, the office or title existed until 1860. [Logan, *Malabar* (1887-91), iii. Gloss; *OED* & YB; Hedges, *Diary,* 28 Aug. 1684.]

Fishing fleet [19C.] Unmarried European women visiting India after the opening of the Suez Canal (1869), in the 'cold weather'; popularly said to be bent on matrimony with susceptible European bachelors in India. The unsuccessful ones were cruelly designated 'Returned Empties'. [*CIWIE.*]

Five K's [18C.] The five personal belongings of an orthodox *Sikh* (man): *kesh, kangha, kacha, kara, kirpān;* i.e. long hair, comb, short drawers, iron bangle, sword. *See* **Sikh**. [*Seir Mutaqherin, or a View of Modern Times* etc. (E. tr. 1789).]

Floose, fluce [17C. H/Ar. *fulūs,* pl. of *fals.*] Formerly a small copper coin of India, Arabia and North Africa. [*OED* & YB; Haklyut, *Voy.* (1599), ii. 272.]

Flamboyant *See* **Gulmohr**.

Flame of the Forest *See* **Dhak**.

Florican, florikin, flanderkin [18C. (origin unknown).] Two species of small bustards at home in the tall grass country in India, alias the Lesser Florican, *Sypheotides auritus,* (Hindi name *līkh.*) and the Bengal Florican, *Eupodotis bengalensis bengalensis* (Hindi name *charas.*) [YB; *OED;* Munro, *Narrative* (1780; ed. 1789-99).]

Fly [19C.] In India orig. the roof of a tent (outer or inner) as distinct from the **Kanaut** or wall. (Origin obscure.) [*OED* & YB; Williamson, *Vade Mecum* (1810), ii. 452.]

Flying-fox [19C.] Popular Anglo-Indian name of

the great fruit-eating Indian bat of several species. The *Pteropus giganteus* is the most common. (The *Roursette* of Sri Lanka.) [*OED* & YB; Forbes, *Or. Mem.* (1813; 2nd ed. 1834), iii. 246.]

Folium Indicum [19C.] *See* **Malabathrum**.

Fool's rack [16C. H/Mar. *phūl,* 'flower', + *rack.* (**Arrack**).] This is a combination of anglicization and folk-etymology). The strongest distillation from toddy, or **Sura**, the 'flower' of the spirit, which if taken in large doses is likely to make a 'fool' of anybody. 'It causes those that take it to be fools.' [Fryer, 1673.] [*OED* & YB; Linschoten, *Discours* (E. tr. 1598; Hak. Soc., 1885), ii. 49.] *See* **Pariah-arrack**.

Foozilow, To [19C. H. imp. *p'huslā* of vb. *p'huslānā,* 'to flatter or cajole'.] Used in a common Anglo-Indian fashion as a verbal infinitive. [YB.] Cf. **Bunnow** (1853); **Puckarow** (1866), **Dumbcow** (1884); **Lugow** (1839) **Sumjow** (1826); **Gubbrow** (1886). [YB; Partridge, *Dict. of Slang* (1976).]

Foras Lands [17C.] In Bombay, land reclaimed from the sea. Hence *Forasdars,* holders of Foras Lands. [YB; *Bombay Selections* no. 111 (New Series, 1854).]

Foujdar, faujdar, phousdar [17C. H/P. *fauj-dār,* military force + agent suffix.] A military commander or a military governor of a district. In India under Mughal rule, an officer of government invested with the charge of the police, and with jurisdiction in criminal matters. Also used in Bengal in the 18C. for a criminal judge. Hence *Foujdāri,* a district under a *Foujdār;* the office and jurisdiction of a *Foujdār* (1802). And *Foujdāri Adawlat,* chief criminal court in Madras and Bombay up to 1863 = the *Nizamut Adawlut* of Bengal. [*OED* & YB; Finch, *Early Travels in India* (1608-11; ed. Foster 1921), 122.87.]

Fowra [17C. H. *phāorā.*] In upper India, a mattock or large hoe; the tool generally used in most parts of India. [YB.] *See* **Mamooty** [Streynsham Master, in *Kistna Man* (1679), 147.]

Frank *See* **Feringhi**.

Frazala, farasola, frazil, frail [16C. H/Ar. *fārsala.*] 'A weight formerly much used in trade in the Indian seas. It varied from place to place from about 20 to 30 lb.' [YB.] *See* **Bahar**. [Varthema, *Travels* (E. tr. 1576); Danvers, *Letters* (1611; ed. 1896-1900), i. 123.]

Freguezia [18C. Indo-Pg.] A parish. (A word that appears to have been once common in western

India.) [YB; Grose, *Voy. to the East Indies, etc.* (1757), i 45.]

Fuleeta [19C.] P. *palīta* or *fatīla*, 'a slow match' as of a matchlock, but usually in Anglo-Indian parlance a cotton slow-match in an ornamental tube used to light cigars. [YB.] *See* **Ramasammy.**

Fuleeta-Pup [19C.] A well-known dish in Bengal. Corr. of 'fritter puff'. [YB.]

Fulwa [19C. Beng. *phulwara*.] A solid buttery oil obtained from the *Bassia butyracea.* Also *fulwabutter.* [*OED;* Penny Cycl. (1835), iv. 2.]

Furlough [19C. Dutch *Verlof,* 'leave of absence'.] This word for a soldier's leave has acquired a peculiar citizenship in Anglo-Indian colloquial, from the importance of the matter to those employed in Indian service. [YB.] Also attrib. 'furlough allowance' [Stoqueler, *Hanbk. British India* (1845).] [*OED* & YB; Ben

Jonson, *The Staple of News* (1625), v.i.; Wellington, *Gurw. Desp.* (1804), iii. 41.]

Furnaveese [19C. P. *fard-navīs,* 'statement-writer or secretary'.] A term almost synonymous with that of minister of finance, who receives the accounts of the renters and collectors of revenue. [YB; Malcolm, *Central India* (1823), i. 531.]

Fusly [19C. H/Ar/P. *faslī,* relating to the *fasl,* season or crop.] 'This name is applied to certain solar eras established for use in revenue and other civil transactions under Mohommedan rule in India, to meet the inconvenience of the lunar calendar of the Hijra, in its want of correspondence with the natural seasons.' [YB; *Ain-i-Akbarī,* E. tr. Jarrett (1891-94), ii. 30; H. H. Wilson, *Glossary* (1855).]

G

Gadi, guddy, guddee [19C. Mar. *gādī*, H. ¯*gaddī*, 'cushion'.] (1) 'The Throne', the seat of royalty. 'To be placed on the *guddee (gadī)*' is to succeed to the kingdom. [OED & YB.] (2) The expression is still used to denote any seat of authority or eminence symbolic of authority. [OED & YB.] Also *gadi-nashin* (P. 'who sits'.) One who sits upon the throne; sometimes an heir-apparent. (GCW.) (3) 'The word is also used for the pad placed on an elephant's back.' [YB; Broughton, *Letters from a Mahratta Camp* (1809; ed. 1813), 28.] *See* **Musnud**.

Gaekwar, Gaikwar, Guicowar [19C. Mar. *gāekwād*, lit. 'cow-herd'.] 'The title of the Mahratta kings of Guzerat descended from *Dāmāji* and *Pīlājī* Gaekwar, who rose to distinction among Mahratta warriors in the second quarter of the 18th century.' [YB.] (2) Until the abolition of the Indian princely states, the native ruler of Baroda, and now still the family name of the ex-ruler. [OED & YB; Forbes, *Oriental Mem.* (1813), ii. xviii. 84.]

Gajra [20C.] Flower-bracelet. *See* **Veni**. [CIWIE.]

Galabha [20C. II. *galabha*, 'noise'.] A noisy commotion, disturbance. [CIWIE.]

Gali, galee [19C. H. *gālī*, 'abuse; bad language'.] *See* **Crab Bat**. [YB; Broughton, *Letters from a Mahr. Camp* (1809; ed. 1813).]

Galleece [18C. Domestic Hindustani *gālīs*, 'a pair of braces'.] Orig. from E. *gallows(es)* (obs. in E., and dialect in Scot. & U.S.). [OED & YB; Nathan Bailey, *Dictionarium Britannicum* etc. (1730-36).]

Gallegalle [17C. H. *galgal*.] A mixture of lime and linseed oil forming a waterproof mortar. [YB; Cocks, *Diary* (1621, ii. 190; Hak. Soc., 1883).]

Gallivat, gallevat, galley-watt [17C. Pg. galeota. Obs.] 'A large boat used in Eastern seas, having a triangular sail as well as oars.' [OED.] Like a **Grab** but smaller. *See* **Jalebote** (Jolly-boat). [OED & YB; Downton in Purchas (1618; 1625-6), i. 501.]

Gambier [19C. Mal. *gambir*.] 'An astringent extract prepared from an Eastern plant, *Uncaria gambir*, and largely used for tanning and other purposes.' [OED.] 'The substance in chemical composition and qualities strongly resembles **Cutch**, and the names **Catechu** and Terra Japonica are applied to both.' [YB & OED; De Bry, *Indien Orientalis* (1599-1614); Lindley, *Nat. Syst. Bot.* (1830), 205.]

Ganda [19C. H. *gainda*; S. *ganda*.] 'a rhinoceros.' [YB; D'Albuquerque, *Commentaries* (1557; E. tr. by de Grey Birch, Hak. Soc., 1875-84); Barbosa, *Desc. of the Coasts of E. Africa and Malabar* (1516; E. tr. by Stanley, Hak. Soc., 1866).]

Gandharva, Gandharba,-arwa [19C. S. *gandharva*. (Cf. Gr. *kentauros*).] Hindu myth. A class of genii in the retinue of **Indra**, considered in the epics as celestial musicians. *Ghandharva music* is 'celestial music', also called *marga music* and **Vedic** *music*, said to please the gods. It lost its popularity and was replaced by *deshi music* in the 3rd and 4th centuries AD. [OED.] *Ghandharva* marriage: a love-match; marriage by mutual consent as opposed to an 'arranged' marriage. Cf. **Glendower**. [H. H. Wilson, *Sk. Relig. Sects Hindus* (1846), ii. 17.] *See* **Kinnar**.

Gandhi [20C. Family name fr. H. 'gandhi', a **Banya**.] The name of M.K. Gandhi (1869-1948), otherwise known as **Mahatma** (Great Soul) Gandhi; great Indian political leader and social reformer. Noted for his espousal of non-violence in political protest (**Ahimsa**), adherence to truth (**Satyagraha**), and the dignity of labour. *Gandhi-cap*: a close-fitting **Khadi** cap worn by Gandhi's followers and disciples and by a great many Indian politicians, but not by him. *Gandhian, Gandhism*: The principles and policies advocated by Mahatma Gandhi (1921). [OED.] Also, 'Gandhi's revenge' (slang) 'Matches that, made in India, would, when struck either ignite explosively or lose their heads'. (R.A.F. slang (1935-48). [Partridge, *Dict. of Slang* (Supp.) (1979), E.M. Forster, *Hill of Devi* (1953), 125.]

Ganesh, Ganapati, Ganesa [19C. S. *Ganesa*, fr. *gana*, 'a flock' + *isa*, 'a lord'.] The elephant-headed god of wisdom, son of **Parvati** and **Shiva** (or of Parvati alone). His *Vahan* (vehicle) is the rat. [Whitworth, *Anglo-Indian Dict.* (1885).]

Ganges [H. *Ganga*; S. *ganga*.] The great river of India, most sacred to Hindus. (*See* next.)

Gangetic [17C.] (*See* prec.) Belonging or pertaining to the river Ganges, e.g., the Gangetic plain; –delta; –crocodile (the **gavial**). *Gangetics:* those who live on the banks of the Ganges (obs.) [*OED;* Sir. T. Herbert, *Trav.* (1677), 57.]

Gang-rape [20C.] A self-explanatory expression, of common usage in Indian English-language newspapers. Also vb. 'to gang-rape' and 'to be gang-raped'.

Ganj, gunge, gunj [18C. H/P. *ganj;* a store(house), granary, market.] [*OED* & YB; Vansittart, *Narrative* (1760-64; ed. 1766), 1. 229; *Trial of Nundocumar* (1776), 93/1.]

Ganja, gunja [17C. H. *gānjhā.*] A preparation of Indian hemp (*Cannabis sativa,* variety *indica*), strongly intoxicating and narcotic. *See* **Bhang.** [*OED* & YB; T. Bowrey, *New Acct.* (1669-79; ed. Temple, Hak. Soc., 1905).]

Ganjifa [19C. H/P. *ganjifa.*] The card-game or the pack of cards, with eight suits and twelve cards in each. [Whitworth, *Anglo-Indian Dict.* (1855).]

Gar, gur, gad [17C. H. *garh;* Mar. *gar.*] A hill-fort; a village mud-fort. [Fryer, *New Account* (1672-81; ed. 1698), 340.

Garba [20C. Guj. *garba.*] Folk dance and song of Gujarat. [*CIWIE.*]

Garbha griha [19C. S. *garbha,* 'the womb' + *griha,* 'building'.] The *sanctum sanctorum,* innermost shrine of a Hindu temple. [Whitworth, *Anglo-Indian Dict.* (1885).]

Garce [17C. Tel. *gārisa,* Kan. *garasi,* Tam. *karisai.*] A measure for rice, salt, etc; in use on the Madras coast, as usual varying much in value. In Salem, for example, a *garce* was 400 *markals.* [*OED* & YB.] *See* **Mercall.** [*Notes and Exts. Fort. St. George* (1670-81; ed. 1871-3).]

Gardee [18C. fr. E. guard.] 'A name sometimes given in the 18th C. to native soldiers disciplined in European fashion, i.e., **Sepoys.** Women in the Amazon corps at Hyderabad (Deccan) known as the *Zafar Pultan* or 'Victorious Battalion' were called *gardunee (Gārdanī),* the feminine form of *Gārad* or *Guard.*' [YB; Vansittart, *Narrative* etc. (1760-64), i. 141.]

Garden(s), garden-house [17C.] 'In the 18th C. suburban villas at Calcutta and Madras were so called. 'Garden Reach' below Fort William took its name from these.' [YB; Hedges, *Diary,* 24 July 1682; Hak. Soc., i. 32.]

Garib(i), gharib(i) [20C. H. *gharibi,* 'poverty', fr. *gharib,* 'poor'.] This word combined with *hatao,* (away with!) to form the expression *garibi hatao,* was the **Lok Sabha** election slogan of the Congress(I) party led by Mrs. Indira Gandhi

in 1971. Also, *gharibon ka masiha,* Protector of the poor. [Whitworth, *An Anglo-Indian Dict.* (1885).]

Garuda[1] [19C. S. *garudā,* 'wings of speech', fr. gr, 'to speak'.] Hinduism: The name of a fabulous Hindu mythological creature, half-eagle, half man, ridden by Vishnu, said to represent the occult utterances of the **Vedas,** 'the magic words on whose wings man can be transported from one world into another with the rapidity of light, the strength of lightning.' [Danielou, *Hindu Polytheism,* (1964), 160.] Garuda is also taken as the embodiment of courage and is the great enemy of serpents. [*OED;* M. Lockwood, tr., Lenormant's *Beginning Hist.* (1882), ii. 89.]

Garuda[2] [19C. *Garuda.*] A family priest of the aboriginal tribe, the Dheds, in Gujarat. Also a priest of the **Chamars.** [Whitworth, *Anglo-Indian Dict.* (1885).]

Gaum, gong, gram [19C. H. *gāon,* S. *grāma.*] A village. Also *gāonwār,* a village head in Portuguese India. *See* **Gramdan.** [*Arch. Port. Orient.* (1519; ed. 1857).]

Gaur,[1] **gour, gore** [19C. H. *gaur.*] A large species of wild Indian ox, *Bos gaurus,* alias the **Bison.** [*OED;* Colebrooke, *Life of Elphinstone* (1806; ed. 1884), 1. 156.]

Gaur,[2] **gour** [19C. Kan. *gaur(a).*] The headman (anglice *Gowda*) of a village in **Karnataka,** corresponding to **Patel,** or to the **Zemindar** of Bengal. [YB; F. Buchanan, *Mysore* (1807), i. 268.]

Gaurian [19C. Beng. *Gauda;* Northern Bengal.] A generic name for the Aryan languages of India. [YB; *JRAS N.S.,* vols. xi & xii (Brandreth)].

Gautam, Gotam, etc. [17C. S. *Gotama.*] 'The surname, according to **Buddhist** legend of the Sakya tribe from which Sakya Muni sprang. One of the most common names for Buddha.' [YB; Cogan's *Pinto,* E. tr. by Gent (1653), 222; Hamilton, *New Acct. E. Indies* (1727).]

Gavee [19C. Pg. *gavea,* 'the Top'.] Nautical: Topsail. [YB; Roebuck, *Naval Dict.* (1811).]

Gavial, gharial, etc. [19C. H. *ghariyāl.*] The crocodile of the Ganges and other Indian rivers, *Gavialies gangeticus,* distinguished by its slender elongated muzzle. *See* **Mugger.** [*OED* & YB; Buchanan, *The Fishes of the Ganges* (1822).]

Gayal, gyaul [18C. H. *gayāl;* S. *go,* 'an ox'.] A semi-domesticated kind of ox, *Bibos frontalis,* common in Bengal, Assam and Burma. By some said to be a relative of the **Gaur.** *See*

Mithan. [*OED; Asiatic Res.* (1790), ii. 188.]

Gayatri [19C. S. *gāyatrī*, fr. *gā*, 'to sing'.] (1) An ancient 24-syllable metre. (2) A hymn etc., composed in this metre, especially the verse of the Rig-Veda repeated daily as a prayer by **Brahmins**. [*OED; Penny Cycl.* (1843), xxvi. 177/1.] See **Jagati** and **Tristubh**.

Gazat [19C.] Domestic Hindi for 'dessert'. [YB; *Punj. Notes & Queries*, ii. 184.]

Gecko, gekko, chacco, jackoa, [18C. Mal. *gekok.* The final 'k' is a glottal stop.] A house-lizard found in tropical areas, including India, remarkable for its peculiar cry (of which the word is echoic), and for its wall-climbing abilities. Similar echoic forms, e.g. *chacco* and *ackoa*, were found in Anglo-Indian usage, which have long become obsolete. [*OED & YB;* Lockyer, *Account* etc. (1711), 84.]

Gentoo, Jentoo Sb. & adj. [16C. Pg. *gentio*, 'gentile or heathen'. (Obs.)] Applied:(1) to the Hindus and their language by the Portuguese in contradistinction to the *Moros* (Moors), i.e. Muslims. [*OED & YB;* Litchfield, *Castañeda* (1582), f. 31. (2) To the **Telugu** speaking Hindus and their language. [YB; Fryer, *New Acct.* etc. (1672-81).]

Ghagra [20C. H. *ghāghra*, 'petticoat'.] A long skirt gathered with a drawstring. [Hawkins, *CIWIE.*]

Ghanta, gunte [19C. H. *ghanta*.] A bell or gong used as an instrument in Indian music. [*OED; Proc. R. Irish Acad.* (1865), IX. i. 108.]

Gharana, gharwana [20C. H. *gharānā*.] Indian music: A school of musicians, who practise a particular style of musical interpretation. [*OED;* Gosvami, *Story Indian Music* (1957) XXIV. 260.]

Gharry, garry, g'horry [19C. H. *gārī*: a cart or carriage.] 'The word was used by Anglo-Indians in both senses, at least in Bengal.' [YB & *OED;* Williamson, *Vade Mecum* (181), 1. 329.] Also *palkee-garry* (*palankin* carriage); *sej-garry* (chaise); *rel-garry* (railway carriage); *dawk-garry* (mail-cart), in its original form called the 'Equirotal Carriage'; *ghora-garry* (horse-carriage). [YB; Grant, *Rural Life in Bengal* (1860).]

Ghaslet [20C.] Corr. of 'kerosene'. [*CIWIE* (1984).]

Ghat, ghaut, gate, etc. [17C. H. *ghāt*.] In the form of *gate* the date given is 1603. The order of development of the word is: (1) A path or stairs leading down to the river, hence a quay or place of a ferry. [*Eng. Fact. in India* (1618-69); Rennell, *Mem. Map Hindostan* (1783),

28.] (2) A path down from a mountain, a mountain pass or defile. [Fryer, *Acct. E. India* (1698), 126.] (3) Name given by Anglo-Indians to the mountain ranges parallel to the east and west coasts of India, the Eastern and Western Ghats. [*OED & YB;* K. Johnson, *Kingdom and Commonwealth* (1603), 200.]

Ghat-murder See **Antarjali**.

Ghats, The Burning [19C. See prec.] Cremation platforms or other level areas at the top of a river *ghat* on which Hindus burn their dead on funeral pyres. [*OED; Encycl. Brit.* (1877); vi. 567/1; Kipling, *Life's Handicap* (1885).]

Ghazal, gazel [19C. H/P. *ghazal*.] (1) A kind of (generally erotic) Eastern lyric poetry with a limited number of verses and a recurrent rhyme scheme. [*OED; Asiat. Ann. Reg. Acc. Bks.* (1800), 17/1. (2) A musical piece wih a simple recurring theme. [*OED;* Stainer and Barrett, *Dict. Musical Terms* (1876).]

Ghazi [18C. P. *ghazi*, pr.pple of *ghazā*, 'to fight'.] A Muslim champion or warrior against infidels (**Kafirs**). Also a title of honour. A Muslim fanatic devoted to the destruction of non-Muslims, esp. on the N.W.F.P. against the British. Such *Ghazism* is not unknown in India against Hindus. [*OED;* Hanway (1753), *Trav.* (1762), II. vi. i. 144.]

Ghee, gee, ghi [17C. H. *ghī;* S. *ghrita;* fr. *ghr*, 'to sprinkle'.] Butter boiled and clarified, used in cooking throughout India, as well as an addition to prepared dishes. Also *Ghee-pot*, –bowl, –fed, etc. [*OED & YB;* Sir. T. Herbert, *Trav.* (1665).] See **Nercha, Vanaspati**.

Ghedda wax [20C. Prob. Tel. *gedda*, 'lump'.] Beeswax from Indian bees. [Webster, *Third New Intern. Dict.* (1976).]

Gherao [20C. H. *gherna*, 'to surround, beseige'.] The besieging of industrial employers or managers, within their offices or factories, by their employees and others in sympathy with them, detaining them until they agree to meet the workers demands. [*OED.*] See **Dharna, Traga, Takaza.** [*Statesman* (Calcutta), 7 April 1967.]

Ghetchoo [19C. H. *ghetchu.*] An Indian aquatic root plant, *Aponogetum monostachyon*, whose 'roots are nearly as good as potatoes'. [*OED;* Simmonds, *Dict. Trade* (1858).]

Ghilzai [18C.] One of the most famous tribes of Afghanistan. [*OED & YB;* Hanway, *Hist. Acct.* (1753), iii. 24.]

G(h)oongat [20C. H. *ghūnghat.*] A face-veil. [Hawkins, *CIWIE.*]

Ghori [H. *ghorī.*] Hindu brideroom's ceremonial

ride on horseback to bride's house; a king for the day. *See* **Doli (Dulha).**

Ghorpad [17C. H. *ghorpad.*] 'The monitor lizard. *Varanus bengalensis.*' [Hawkins, *CIWIE.*]

Ghoul [19C. H/Ar. *ghūl;* P. *ghol.*] A goblin or man-devouring demon, especially haunting wildernesses. [*OED* & *YB*; Elphinstone, *Caubool* (ed. 1839), i. 291.]

Ghulam [19C. H/Ar. *ghulām,* 'The son of a slave'.] Often used to form a Muslim name, e.g., Ghulam Mohammed. *See Dās(a).* [Whitworth, *Anglo-Indian Dict.* (1885).]

Ghurra [19C.] A spheroidal clay water-pot, known in S. India as the **Chatty.** [Mundy, *Pen and Pencil Sketches* (1827), 66.]

Ghurry, gurree [17C. H. *gharī,* 'water-clock'.] A clepsydra; a space of time (24 minutes) or in Anglo-Indian parlance 'an hour'; a metal plate on which the hours are struck. Also (1) *Pun-ghurry* (*pānī-ghurry*) water-clock; (2) *Dhoop-ghurry* (*dhūp,* sunshine) sun-dial; (3) *Ret(a)-ghurry,* (*ret(a),* sand), hour-glass. [*OED* & *YB*; Terry, *Early Travels in India* (1583-1619; ed. 1921); Mrs Meer Hasan Ali, *Observations Mussulmauns India* (1832; ed. 1978), 82.]

Ghuslkhana, goozulkhana, gusle-can [17C. H/Ar/P. *ghusl-khāna.*] 'A bathroom. Sometimes used by the great Mughals as a place of private audience.' [*YB*; T. Coryat, *Crudities* (1611); Sir T. Roe, *Embassy to the Court of the Great Mogul* (1615-19).]

Gian, jnani [20C. H. *gian, jnani.*] A knowledgeable person; an expert. [Hawkins, *CIWIE.*]

Gilli-danda [20C. H. *gilli-danda,* 'tip-cat' game with a 'cat', a small piece of wood, tapered at both ends, struck with a stick (*danda*) and knocked to a distance while in the air. [Fisher, *The Life of Mahatma Gandhi* (1951).]

Gindy [16C. Tel. *gindi;* M. *kindi,* 'a basin or pot'.] 'In Anglo-Indian usage [in Bombay] a wash-hand basin of tinned copper, such as is in common use there.' [*YB.*] *See* **Chillumchee.** Also a coffee-pot without the handle, used to drink from. [Litchfield, *Castañeda* (1582), 106.]

Gingal(l), Jinjall [19C. M. *janjāl.* 'A swivel or wall piece.'] A heavy musket fired from a rest; or a light swivel-gun, sometimes on a carriage. Also *gingall*-ball (1834); –battery (1857); –fire (1884). [*OED* & *YB.*] *See* **Jezail.** Colebrooke (1818), *Life of Elphinstone* (ed. 1884), ii. 31.]

Ginger, gyngevere. [11C. Ult. S. *Sringavēram;* Prakrit *singabera.* Poss. fr. *sringgam,* 'horn' + *vera,* 'body'.] So named from its antler-shaped root. [*YB*; considers this to be 'an etymologising', or 'an imaginary etymology' of a Dravidian root.] The rhizome of the tropical plant, *Zingiber officinale,* remarkable or its hot spicy taste. Used in cookery, medicine and as a sweetmeat candied in syrup. Black-ginger = the un- scraped root from India and S.E. Asia. White Ginger = the scraped root from Jamaica. Green ginger = the undried root, used in preserves. Slang: mettle (1843), spirit. A red-haired person (1885). Numerous combinations, e.g. *ginger*-ale, –brandy; –comfit; –cordial; –grass (*Andropogon nardus,* and *Punicum glutinosum*); –nut; –snap; –wine; –beer; –pop, etc. etc. Also: vb. to ginger, to treat with ginger, to ginger up, to put spirit into somebody. [*OED* & *YB*; Haliburton, *Attaché* (1843), I. xv. 261; 'Sax. Leechd.' (c. 1000), Chaucer, *Rom. Rose* (c. 1366), ii. 56.]

Gingham [17C. Poss. ult. fr. Mal. *ginggang,* 'striped', perh. through Dutch *gingang,* or Pg. *guingao.*] A material of the old Indian piece-goods trade, made from cotton dyed before weaving, often in stripes, checks and other patterns. Also, *gingham*-frock (1853), –mill (1860), –waistcoat (1793), –umbrella (1851). [*OED* & *YB*; Cocks, *Diary* (1615; ed. Hak. Soc. 1883), ii. 272.]

Gingili, gingeli, gingelly [16C. H/Mar. *jinjalī.*] The seed and oil of the E. Indian plant *Sesamum indicum,* the trade name of **Til.** 'The Gingili Coast', from the Godavari delta to Puri. [*OED* & *YB*; Litchfield, *Castañeda* (1582); *Eng. Fact. in India* (1618-69; ed. Foster, 1906-27.]

Girijan [20C. H. *giri,* 'hill' + *jan,* 'man'.] A hillman. [Hawkins, *CIWIE.*]

Girja [19C. Pg. *igreja.*] A Christian church, in India (corr. of *ecclesia*). [*YB*; *Punjab Notes & Queries* (1885), ii. 125; Wilson, *Gloss* (1855).]

Gita, The *See* **Bhagvadgita, The.**

Glendower, Glendoveer [19C. S. *gandharva.*] A kind of semi-divine spiritual being. 'One of a race of beautiful sprites in Southey's artificial quasi-Hindu mythology.' [*OED.*] [Southey, *Kehama* (1810), vi. ii.] *See* **Gandharva.**

Goa¹ [16C. The Madras Glossary connects this with S. *go,* 'a cow', in the sense of 'cowherd country'.] City and territory on W. Coast of India, founded by the Portuguese in 1510, now part of the Indian Union since annexation in 1962. Used attrib. in the names of certain articles; e.g. *Goa-bean,* the seed of the *Psophocarpus tetragonolobus* (1882); –plum, the fruit of the *Parinarium excelsum* (19C.);

–potato, *Dioscurea aculeata* (19C.); –powder, a medicament derived from the *Andera araroba*, the active principle of which is Chrysophanic acid, a specific for 'Bombay eczema' (1874); –stone or -ball (1673); a factitious article, once a popular fever medicine, alias 'snake-stone', made up of various drugs compounded into a ball, from which a portion was scraped as required. Also *Goan* (1927), *Goanese* (1851). See **Gomantak**. [*OED* & YB; Varthema, *Travels*, E. tr by Eden (1576); Ovington, *Voy. Suratt* (1696), 262.]

Goa² [19C. Tib. *dgoba*.] A Tibetan antelope, *Procapra picticauda*. [*OED*; Hodgson, *Jrnl. Asiatic Soc. Bengal* (1846), xv. 335.]

Goa³ [19C. (Place name.)] A name of the marsh crocodile, *crocodilus palustris*, alias **Mugger**. [*OED*; Wood, *Nat. Hist.* (1863), iii. 31.]

Gobar (sb. & adj.) [20C. H. *gobar*, 'cow-dung'.] *Gobar*-gas = gas from cow-dung and other organic matter, produced in the Indian countryside in a specially designed system, and used for cooking purposes.

Godown [16C. Of disputed origin but probably Malay *gĕdong*, 'warehouse', store, customs-shed', etc. But cf. Tam. *kidangu*, 'a place where goods lie', fr. *kidu*' to lie; and Pg. *gudao;* Tel. *gidangi;* Sinh. *gudama*.] A warehouse or store for goods in India, Malaysia and other parts of S.E. Asia. (Some early writers state that these stores were underground which may partly account for the form this word has assumed.) [Bluteau, *Vocabulario* etc. (1712-28.); *OED* & YB; Fitch, *Early Travels in India*. (1583-1619); Litchfield, *Castañeda* (1582).]

Goglet, guglet [16C. Pg. *gorgoleta*.] A long-necked, porous earthenware water-pot, 'out of which the water runs and guggles'. [Lacerda, *Pg. Dict.; OED* & YB; Fryer, *Acct. E. Indies and Persia* (1698).] See **Scrai, Surahi**.

Golah [18C. H. *gola*, fr. *go*, 'round'.] A circular storehouse with a conical roof, used for storing grain or salt. 'One of the most famous of these is the gola at Patna, completed in 1786, but never used.' [YB & *OED; Gentl. Mag.* (1771), xli.]

Golconda [16C.] Place-name, old Hyderabad, once famous for its diamonds. A metaphor for 'a mine of wealth'. [*OED*; Fitch, *Early Travels in India* (1583-91; ed. Foster, 1921).]

Gold Mohur (Flower) [19C.] Anglo-Indian for **Gulmohr** (H. *gulmor*). See **Mohur**. [YB; Allardyce, *City of Sunshine* (1877), iii. 207.]

Gole [P/H. *ghol;* S. *kula*, 'an assemblage'.] 'The

main body of an army in array; a clustered body of troops; an irregular squadron of horsemen.' [YB; Skinner, *Mil. Mem.* (1803); ed. Fraser, 1851) i. 298).]

Golmal, goolmaul, goolmool [19th. H. *golmāl*.] 'confusion, jumble, a mess, uproar, disorder, etc.' *Gol-māl karna*, 'to make a mess'. [YB; Allardyce, *City of Sunshine* (1877), ii 106.]

Gomantak A native of **Goa**; a Goan, a Goanese.

Gomashta, gomasta [17C. H/P. *gumāshtah*, 'appointed, delegated'.] A native agent or factor, or, in Madras, a clerk for vernacular correspondence. [*OED* & YB; *Eng. Fact. in India* (1621; 1618-69; ed. Foster, 1906-27).]

Gompa [19C. Tib. *gōnpa, gōmpa*.] 'a solitary place, a hermitage.' Tibetan Buddhist monastery or temple. [*OED;* Schlagintweit, *Buddhism in Tibet* (1863), XIII. 179.]

Gomuti [18C. Malay *gēmuti*.] 'sugar-palm fibre', from a palm tree, *Arenga Pinnata*, native to the East Indies, and cultivated elsewhere, particularly in India. 'A substance resembling horsehair, & forming excellent cordage.... The tree also furnishes *kalams* or reed-pens for writing, and the material for the poisoned arrows used with the blow-tube.' [YB.] See **Sagwire**. [*OED;* Marsden, *Hist. Sumatra* (1783).]

Gond [19C. H/S. *gonda*.] 'fleshy navel.' A person with this physical feature; a Gond. A member of a Dravidian, jungle-dwelling people of Central India. Gondi = the language of the Gonds, and the people (1855). [*OED;* Moxon *in* G. Smith, *S. Hislop* (1810).] See **Muria**.

Gondwana [19C. S. *gondavana* fr. *gond* + *vana* forest.] Sandstone and shale rocks in India. [*OED;* Blanford, *Rud. Phys. Geogr. Indian Sch.* (1873), X. 116.]

Gondwanaland [19C.] An ancient land mass, broken up in the Mezozoic or late Palaeozoic times. [*OED;* Blanford, *Rec. Geol. Survey India* (1873), XXIX. 52.]

Goodry [16C. H. *gudrī*.] A quilt. 'As distinguished from the **Rezai**, it is the bundle of rags on which the **Fakirs** and very poorest people sleep.' [YB; Linschoten, *Voyages* (E. tr. 1598; Tr. Lit. Soc. Bo., 1819), i. 113.]

Googul, gogul. [19C. S. *guggula;* H. *gugal*.] The aromatic gum resin of the *Balsamodendron mukul;* the *mukti* of the Arabs, and generally supposed to be the *bdellium* of the ancients. [YB & *OED;* Milburn, *Or. Commerce* (1813).]

Goojur, Gujar [18C. H. *Gūjar;* S. *Gūrjara*.] The name of a great and populous Hindu clan, formerly thieves. In the Punjab they are

Muslims. Their diffusion over nearly the whole of Northern India is instanced by their having given the name to the State of **Gujarat,** (and *Gujrāt* now a district in Pakistan). [YB; Forbes, *Or. Mem.* (1813), 11.246.]

Goolail [19C. H. *gulel;* Ar. *kaus-el-bandūk.*] A pellet-bow. *See* next. [YB; Chevers, *Ind. Med. Jurisprudence* (1870), 337.]

Gooly [20C. H. *goli.*] A bullet, ball, pill. The testicle(s) (usually plural, *goolies*) in Australian slang; a stone or pebble (1925). [*OED;* Partridge, *Dict. Slang* (1937), 345/1; Baker, *Dict. Austral. Slang* (1941).]

Goonda(h) [20C. H. *gundā,* 'a rascal'.] A hired rowdy, desperado, hooligan. [*Glasgow Herald,* 27 April 1926.]

Goont [17C. H. *gūnth, gūth.*] A strong Himalayan pony; 'a true travelling scale-cliffe beast'. [Finch in Purchas (1625-6), i. 483; YB; *Early Travels in India* (1583-1619; ed. Foster, 1921).]

Goorzeburdar, gooseberdar [17C. H/P. *gurzbardār.*] 'A mace-bearer,' 'whose business it was to preserve order in assemblies, to carry the King's orders & execute his commands with the utmost speed.' [Bernier, *Travels* (E. tr. 1684); YB; Yule's *Hedges Diary* (1717), Hak. Soc., ii. ccclix.]

Gopi [19C. S. *gopi.*] A cowherds wife, of the *Gop* caste. A milkmaid of Brindavan. The *gopis* were devotees, playmates and companions of **Krishna.** [*OED;* Kipling, *A Day's Work* (1893).] *See* **Raslila.**

Gopura(m) [19C. S. *gōpura,* 'City-gate', fr. *gō* 'eye' + *pura,* 'city'.] The great ornamental pyramidal tower over the entrance gate of S. Indian temples. [*OED* & YB; Markham, *Travels,* etc. (1862), 408.] *See* **Vimana, Mantapa.**

Gora [19C. H. *gorā.*] 'fair complexioned'. 'A white man'; a European soldier; any European who is not a *sahib;* was often used in a derogatory sense. [YB.] Plural *gōra-lōg, 'white people',* cf. Tagore's novel, *Gora.* [Cave Browne, *Punjab & Delhi* (1861), i. 243; Kipling, *Kim* (1901).]

Goral, goorul]19C. H. *gūral.*] The *thar* or Himalayan goat-antelope, *Cemas goral. See* **Tahr.** [*OED* & YB; *Penny Cycl.* (1834), ii. 89/2; Lloyd & Gerard, *Narrative etc.* (1840), ii. 112.] *See* **Serow.**

Gorawallah [17C. H. *ghorā,* 'a horse + *wālā,* 'agent'.] A groom, **Syce** or **Horse-keeper.** [YB; *Notes and Extracts, Fort St. George* (1680), ii. 63.]

Gorayt, gorayit, goret [19C. H. *goret, gorait;* poss. connected with S. *ghur,* 'to shout'.] 'A village watchman and messenger, remunerated

by a piece of rent-free land; a villager whose special duty was to watch crops and harvested grain.' [YB.] *See* **Chowkidar.** [Buchanan, *Eastern India* (ed. 1838), ii. 231.]

Gordower, goordore [18C. Anglo-Indian corr. prob. of P. *girdāwa,* 'a patrol' and *girdāwar,* 'all around, a supervisor'.] A kind of paddleboat used in Bengal by officials on their supervisory or inspection tours. [YB; Ives, *Voyage* etc. (1754; ed. 1773), 157.]

Gosain, cossyne [17C. H/Mar. *gosāin;* S. *goswamīn,* 'lord of passions', (lit. 'lord of cows').] A Hindu religious mendicant who is supposed to have subdued his passions and renounced the world. [*OED* & YB; Finch in *Early Travels in India* (1583-1619; ed. Foster, 1921).]

Gosha, goshanashin [19C. H./P. *gosha(nishin),* 'sitting in a corner', cf. **Purdah**-*nashīn.*] 'An Anglo-Indian technicality to indicate that a woman was secluded and cannot appear in public.' [YB.]

Goshala [19C. H. *go,* 'cow', + *shala,* 'shed'.] A cow-shed. *See* **Pinjrapole.** [Hawkins, *CIWIE.*]

Gosht [H. *gosht.*] Cooked meat. [Hawkins, CIWIE.]

Gotra [19C. H/S. *gotra,* lit. 'a cattle-yard', fr. *go,* 'cow' + *tra,* 'protection.'] A group of families, supposedly of the same lineage, derived from one or other of the seven mythical sages, and belonging to one of the three higher **Castes** (Brahmin, Kshatriya & Vaishya). It is forbidden for a man of a particular *gotra* to marry a woman of the same *gotra* as himself, though strictly according to caste laws he is required to marry one of the same caste as himself. (*gotra* = the battalion; *caste* = the regiment). *See* **Caste.** [*OED;* Monier-Williams, *Hinduism.* (1877), xi. 160.]

Gour *See* **Gaur.**

Gourami, goramy [19C. Malay *gorami.*] A large freshwater food fish, *Osphronemus goramy.* [*OED;* Day, *Fishes of India* (1876-8), i. 372.]

Gow, gaou [17C. Dak. H. *gau.*] An ancient measure of distance in S. India and Ceylon (Sri Lanka), of various lengths, from $2\frac{1}{2}$ to 9 miles. [YB. Tavernier, *Voyages* (1684; ed. 1889), E. tr. ii. 30.]

Gowala, goala [19C. H. *gō,* 'cow' + *wala,* 'agent.'] A cowherd; milkman. [Hawkins, *CIWIE.*]

Grab, gurab [17C. Mar/Konkani, *gurāb,* fr. Ar. *ghorab,* 'a galley', (lit: 'a raven.'] 'A kind of vessel which is constantly mentioned in the sea and river-fights of India, from the arrival of the Portuguese down to near the end of the

18th century.' [YB.] A large, coastal two-imasted sailing ship of shallow draught. [*OED*; Fryer, *New Acct.* (1672-81), 153; Morden, *Geog. Rect.* (1680), 405.]

Gram [16C. H/Pg. *grāo* = Latin *granum* 'grain'.] The chick-pea, or Egypt-pea; a kind of vetch, *Cicer arietinum*. Also called 'Bengal gram'; any kind of pulse used as horse-fodder. *See* **Calavance, Basin** and **Chana.** [*OED* & YB; Wheeler, *Madras Official Records* (1702; ed. 1861), ii. 10; Litchfield's *Castañeda* (1582).]

Gram-fed [19C. *See* prec.] 'Properly the distinctive description of mutton and beef fattened upon *gram*, which used to be the pride of Bengal. But applied figuratively to any "pampered-creature".' [YB; Smith, *Life of Lord Lawrence* (ed. 1883), i. 338.]

Grama [19C. S. *grāma*, lit. a 'village'.] A scale in Indian music so called 'because there is in it the assemblage of all the notes'. [*OED*; J.D. Paterson, *Asiatick Researaches*, ix. 446.

Gramdan [20C. H. *grāma*, 'village', + *dan*, 'gift'.] In India, a movement for the free gift of a *village* for the benefit of the community. *See* **Bhoodan** and **Gaum.** [*Economist*, 28 Sept. 1957), 1038/i.]

Gramraj [20C. H. *grāma*, 'village' + *raj*, 'rule'.] Government by the village. Introduced by Vinoba Bhave. Cf. **Swaraj** & **Ramraj.**

Grandon(ic) [17C. fr. **Grantha,** 'a book'.] Refers to books of classical Indian literature in **Sanskrit.** *See* **Grantha(m)** [YB; Sonnerat, *Voyages* (1781), i. 224.]

Granth, grunth [18C. H/Punj. *granth;* S. *grantha.* Lit. 'a knot,' leaves tied together by string.] The Book, *Granth Sahib.* The sacred scriptures of the Sikhs containing the hymns composed or compiled by their leaders from Nanak (1469-1539) onwards. [*OED* & YB; Gholam Hussain Khan, *Seir Mutaqherin* (E. tr. 1789), i. 89. G. Forster, *Journey from Bengal to England.* (1790), i. xi. 255.]

Grantha [19C. S. *grantha* (as prec).] A S. Indian alphabet used by **Tamil** Brahmins in their sacred books, often called **Grandonic** in the 17th and 18th centuries. [*OED*; Burnell, *Elem. S. Indian Palaeogr.* (1874), ii. 34.]

Granthee, grunthee [19C. Punj. *granthī,* fr. **Granth.**] A native 'chaplain; or reader of the Sikh scriptures attached to Sikh regiments. (The name *Granthī* appears among the *Hindi Mendicant Castes of the Punjab* in Maclagan's *Census Report* (1891), 300). [YB; Whitworth, *Anglo-Indian Dict.*]

Grantham, grunthum S. *grantham* = **Grantha.**

Grass (Congress) [20C. Anglo-Indian.] The poisonous white, flowering weed, *Parthenium hysterophorus,* so called (after the Congress Party) because of its ubiquity in India. [?]

Grass-cloth [16C. Anglo-Indian.] A kind of cambric made from grass, e.g. from *Rhea,* or from the *Nilgiri* nettle, *Girardinia heterophylla.* [YB; Fitch, in Hakluyt (1585; ed. 1807), ii. 387.]

Grass-cutter [18C. fr. H. *ghāskātā,* 'the digger, or cutter of grass', fr. S. *ghāsa,* grass.] A servant who collected grass and hay for horses. A **Syce's** assistant. [*OED* & YB; Munro, *Narrative* (1780-84; ed. 1789), 28; Mrs M. E. James, *Ind. Household Management* (1879), 46.]

Grasshopper Falls [19C. *Gersoppa,* fr. Kan. *geru,* '**Marking-nut**' + *soppu,* 'a leaf'.] An Anglo-Indian corruption (Hobson-Jobsonism) of *Gersoppa Falls* (otherwise **Jog Falls**) in Karnataka. *See* Grey's note on P. della Valle (Hak. Soc. 1891), ii. 218. [YB.]

Grassia [19C. H. *grās* (said to mean 'a mouthful'). *See* A.K. Forbes, *Ras Mala, or Hindoo Annals of the Province of Goozerat* (1856) which refers to alienation of lands for religious purposes. But its usual sense is the portion of land given for subsistence to cadets of chieftains' families. Later the term often became one of opprobrium, conveying the idea of 'protection money' by a village paid to a professional robber or blackmailer. [YB.] *See* **Hafta.** [Drummond, *Illustrations* (1808).]

Grass-widow [19C. Anglo-Indian (etym. confused, but hardly likely to be the ironic and punning ref. to 'grace-widow').)] In Anglo-Indian parlance, a married woman living away from her husband. *See* **Widow** (H. *avira*). 'In English it seems to have appeared first as Anglo-Indian.' [*OED* & YB; J. Lang, *Wanderings in India* (1859); *Life in the Mofussil* (1879), ii. 99-100.]

Grave-Digger *See* **Beejoo.**

Green-Pigeon [17C. Anglo-Indian (H. *harial*).] An Indian bird, *Treron phoenicoperta.* It has been said that it can never be tamed or domesticated. (Aslian *De Natura Animalium, c.* 250 AD.) Distribution: practically throughout the Indian Union, Bangladesh, Burma & Sri Lanka. [YB; Fryer, *New Acct.* (1672-81), 176.]

Grey Partridge [19C. Anglo-Indian. H. *safed titar.*] The common Anglo-Indian name of this bird; found in the drier portions of the entire Indian Union (excepting Assam) and upto

1500 ft. in the Himalaya. Also in Sri Lanka and Pakistan. Ornith. name: *Francolina pondicerium pondicerianus*. [YB; Jerdon, *Birds of India* (1862), 11.566; Salim Ali, Ripley, *Handbook*, Vol. 1 (2nd, ed. 1980), 31.]

Griblee [19C. Lascar's language.] A graplin or grapnel. [YB; Roebuck, *Naval Dict.* (1811).]

Griffin, griff, griffish (adj) [18C. Anglo-Indian (etym. unknown).] Any new arrival in India, a green horn, a Johnny-come-lately, ignorant of Indian life and customs. In Sri Lanka such a newcomer was called a **Creeper** (1894) and in Malaya *orang baharu* (a new man). [*OED* & YB; Hugh Boyd, *The Indian Observer* (ed. 1798), 177; Child (1798) in Southey, *Life Bell* (1844), 1. 459.] *See* **Orombarros**.

Grihasta, gr(h)astha [19C. S. *grastha*, fr. *griha*, 'a house' + *stha*, 'to stay'.] A married Brahmin householder, in the 2nd stage (*āsrama*) of life, with social and family obligations. 'The word is now the common word for gentleman.' [*GCW*.] *See* **Brahmacharya, Vanaprastha** and **Sannyasin**. [*OED*; E. Balfour, *Cycl. India* (1857), 11. 409.]

Ground [19C. Anglo-Indian.] A measure of land used in the neighbourhood of Madras. Also called *munny* (Tam. *manai*). [YB.] *See* **Cawney**. [YB; Buchnan, *Mysore*, etc. (1807), i. 6.]

Gruff adj [17C. Anglo-Indian, probably fr. Dutch *grof*, 'coarse'.] A term applied to bulky goods. [YB; Pringle, *Diary, Ft. St. Geo.* (1682-5; ed. 1894-5), 1st ser., vol. ii. 3-4.]

Guar [19C. H. *guar*.] The Indian plant, the cluster bean, *Cyamopsis tetragonoloba*, grown in dry regions as a vegetable, fodder crop and green manure, and as the source of *guar*-gum, used in the food, paper and other industries. [*OED*; Carey, *Roxburgh's Flora Indica* (1832).]

Guaranteed Railway [19C. Anglo-Indian.] A privately constructed and worked railway in India to which government guaranteed a certain rate of interest and gave the land free. [Whitworth. *Anglo-Indian Dict.* (1885).]

Gubber [18C. Perh. fr. P. *dīnar-i-gabr*, 'infidel-money.'] A gold ducat or sequin. 'A Dutch ducat.' [*OED* & YB.] [Milburn, *Oriental Commerce* (1813); Lockyer, *Acct. of Trade in India* (1711), 201.]

Gubbrow [19C. H. *ghabrāo*, imp. of *ghabrānā*.] 'To bully, to dumbfound, to browbeat or perturb a person.' Or to be dumbfounded or perturbed. *See* **Dumbcow, Foozilow, Lugow** & **Bunnow**. [YB; Partridge, *Dict.*

of Slang (1979); YB.]

Gudda, guddha [19C. H. *gadhā*, fr. S. *gardabha*, 'the roarer'.] 'A donkey, literal & metaphorical.' [YB.]

Gudge *See* **Guz.**

Guebre [17C. P. *gabr*.] A Parsi; a **Zoroastrian** fire-worshipper. [*OED*.] *See* **Parsi** [J. Davies, tr., Olearius' *Voy. Ambass.* (1662), vi. 302; attrib. Moore, *Lalla Rookh, Fire-Worshippers* (1817), 191: 'The Gheber belt that round him clung.']

Guicowar *See* **Gaekwar.**

Guinea-cloths, -stuffs [17C. Anglo-Indian. poss. H. *gōnī* (gunny) sack(ing).] Piece-goods bought and manufactured in India to be used in the West African Trade. [YB; Birdwood, *Rept. on Old Recs.* etc. (1675; ed. 1891), 224.]

Guinea deer [18C.] An old name for some species of chevrotain, such as the *Tragulus memminna* or Mouse-Deer. [YB; Ives, *Voy. from England* (1754; ed. 1773), 57; Blanford, *Mammalia* (1888-91), 555.]

Guinea-pig(s) [18C. Anglo-Indian.] 'A nickname given to midshipmen or apprentices on board Indiamen in the 18th century, when the command of such a vessel was a sure fortune, and large fees were paid to the captain with whom the youngsters embarked.' [YB; Carey, *The Good Old Days* etc. (1779; ed. 1882), i. 73.]

Guinea-worm [17C. Anglo-Indian.] A parasitic worm, *Filaria Medinensis*, found in some parts of W. India, Egypt, the Middle East, Guinea and elsewhere, 'inhabiting the subcutaneous cellular tissue of man, frequently in the leg, varying from 6 inches to 12 feet in length'. [YB & *OED*; Purchas, Pilgrimes (1625-6), ii. 963.]

Gujerati, Guzeratee [17C.] Pertaining to the language and natives of the state of Gujarat, taking its name from the Gujar (**Goojur**) tribe. [*OED*; Birdwood, *First Letter Book* etc. (1600-19; ed. 1893), 85.]

Gulab [19C. P. *gul*, 'a rose' + -*ab*, '-water'.] Rose-water. Either that from which the essential oil has been skimmed to make *attar*, or that which retains its cream. Given to a visitor on his departure. [Whitworth, *Anglo-Indian Dict.* (1885).]

Gul-Gul [19C. H. *galgal*.] A kind of cement made of oil and pounded sea-shells used to preserve a ship's bottom from worms. [*OED*; Smyth, *Sailor's Word Book* (1867).]

Gully [19C. Anglo-Indian. H. *galli*.] A lane, an alley. [Whitworth, *Anglo-Indian Dict.* (1885).]

Gulmohr, gold-mohur [19C. H. *gulmor*. Said to mean 'Peacock Flower'. (Properly speaking **Gold Mohur** refers to a gold coin).] An exotic Indian deciduous tree, *Delonix regia* or *Poinciana regia* bearing English names, 'Flamboyant', and 'Flame-tree'. [YB; Allardyce, *City of Sunshine* (1877), iii. 207.]

Gumla(h) [19C. H. *gumlā*.] A large earthenware water jar; flower-pot. [*OED*; H. Caunter, *Oriental Ann.* (1834), ix. 144.]

Guna,[1] goon [19C. S. *guna*.] The middle grade of an ablaut series of vowels in Sanskrit; the process of raising a vowel to the middle grade by prefixing *ā*. Sometimes used in Indo-European comparative grammar for the *ē*–grade of the *o:ē:ū* Series. Also *gunate* and *gunation* (1864). [*OED*; Carey, *Skr. Gram.* (1804), 12.]

Guna[2] [19C.] Any one of the three dominating principles or qualities of nature in the **Sankhya** philosophy, of which all matter consists. The three principles or **Gunas** are: **Tamas** (inertia, heaviness, darkness), **Rajas** (activity, aggression, passion), **Sattva** (harmony, lightness, purity). [*OED*; Vijnana Bhikshu, *Sankhya-Sara* (1862); Sir Charles Eliot, *Hinduism & Buddhism* (1920), 11. 298.]

Gunja *See* **Ganja.**

Gunge [H. *ganj*.] *See* **Ganj.**

Gunny, gunny-bag [17C. H/Mar. *gōnī*; S. *gōni*, 'a sack; sacking'.] Coarse sacking material made from the fibre of jute or sun-hemp; a sack of this material. *See* **Guinea-cloths.** Also *gunny*-bag, –sack(ing) (1764). [*OED* & YB; *Eng. Fact. in India* (1618-69; ed, Foster 1906-27).]

Gunta [19C. H. *ghantā*, 'a bell or gong'.] This is the common term for expressing a European hour in modern Hindustani. *See* **Pandy** for *Gunta Pandy*, the quarter-guard who struck the gong every hour. [YB.]

Gup, gup-gup [17C. H. *gap*.] Idle gossip, silly talk, tittle-tattle, blather. [*OED* & YB; *The Indian Antiquary* (1617; ed. 1871-1933), viii.]

Gupta [19C. S. *gupta*.] 'protected.' From Chandragupta, name of the founder of the Vaishya dynasty that ruled in N. India from the 4th to the 6th century AD. Also, a member of this dynasty. Hence *guptan*. [*OED*; *Encycl. Metropolitana* (1845), xvi. 354/2.]

Guptavidya [19C. S. *gupta* + *vidya*, 'knowledge, science'.] Theosophy: Hidden or secret knowledge. [Blavatsky, *Secret Doctrines* (1888).]

Gupti [19C. H. *gupti*.] A sword-stick. [Hawkins, *CIWIE*.]

Gur, goor [19C. H. *gur*.] Coarse sugar or molasses from sugarcane, made in India. [*OED* & YB; Burnes, *Trav. in Bokhara* (1835).]

Gurdwara [20C. Punj. *gurduārā*, fr. S. *guru*, 'teacher' + *dvāra* 'door', lit. 'The Guru's door'.] The place of worship of the Sikhs. [*OED*; M.A. Macauliffe, *Sikh Religion* (1909), 1. i. 47.]

Gureebpurwur, Gurreebnuwaz [19C. Ar./P. *Gharībparwar*, 'provider of the poor'. *Gharīb-nawāz*, 'Cherisher of the poor'.] [YB.] Respectful greetings used in Hindustani. [Heber, *Narrative* etc. (1844), i. 266.]

Gurjaut (sb. plural) [19C. H. *garh*., 'a fort + P. *jāt*, plural form.] 'The popular and official name of certain forest tracts of Orissa. The manner of denominating such tracts from the isolated occupation by fortified posts seems to be very ancient in that part of India.' [YB; Hamilton, *Desc. of Hindustan*, etc. (1820), ii. 32.]

Gurjun, gurjan [19C. H. *gārjan*.] A tree, *Tripterocarpus alatus* (or *Dipterocarpus*) yielding timber and a balsamic oil, variously known as *gurjun-oil*, wood-oil or *gurjun balsam*; used as a varnish or medicinally, e.g. as a remedy for leprosy. Hence *gurjunic-acid*. $(C_{34} H_{64} O_5 + 3H_2O)$. [YB, 971 & *OED*; Simmonds, *Dict. Trade* (1858).]

Gurkha, goorkha, etc. [19C. H. *Gurkhā*, poss. S. *go*, 'cow' + *raksha* 'keeper'.] A member of the dominant race of Nepal, taking the name from a town so called 53 miles W. of Kathmandu. The Gurkhas are perhaps the most renowned soldiers of modern India, and several regiments- of the Anglo-Indian army were recruited from among them. [*OED* & YB.] *See* next. [Kirkpatrick, *Acct. King. Nepaul* (1811), App. 1.339.]

Gurkhali [18C. H. *Gurkhālī*, sb. + adj.] The Sanskritic language of the Gurkhas and pertaining to them. [*OED* & YB; Long, *Selections* etc. (1748-67; ed. 1860), 526.]

Gurmukhi, gurumukhi [19C. Punj. fr. S. *guru*, 'teacher' + S. *mukha*, 'mouth'.] The language of the Sikh gurus, but applied most commonly to the modification of the **Devanagari** alphabet used by them and used today in writing Punjabi. Also *attrib.* or as *adj.* [*OED*; M.H. Court, *Hist. of Sikhs* (1888), iv 1.]

Gurrah[1] *See* **Ghurra.**

Gurrah[2] [17C. H. *gārha*.] Muslin. [*OED*; *Eng. Fact. in India* (1618-69; ed. Foster 1906-27).]

Gurrawaun [19C. Anglo-Indian.] Corr. of 'coach-man', by Indians. [Partridge, *Dict. of Slang* (1979).]

Gurry [17C. H. *garhī*.] A hill-fort. Also *gurr* fr. H. *garh*, 'a fort'. [*OED* & YB; Fryer, *New Acct.* (1672-81), 165.]

Guru, gooroo [17C.] H. *guru*, 'a teacher', 'priest'; S. *guru*, 'weighty, dignified'.] A Hindu spiritual teacher or head of a religious sect. In a general sense, an influential teacher, a mentor or pundit. Also *guruship*, and *gurukul* (school). One of ten spiritual leaders in Sikhism, beginning with Guru Nanak (1469-1518) and ending with Guru Gobind Singh(d.1708). [*OED* & YB; Purchas, *Pilgrimes* (1613).]

Guz, gudge [17C. H/P. *gaz*.] In India, 'linear measures of very varying lengths from the *hath* or natural cubit, to the English yard'. [YB & *OED; Eng. Fact. in India.* (1618-69; ed. Foster; 1906-21).]

Guzzy [18C. H/P. *gazi* (see prec.).] A very poor kind of cotton cloth, so called perhaps 'from its having been woven from a *gaz* (**Gudge**) in breadth'. [YB; Seton-Karr, *Selections* etc. (1794-1823; 1864-9), i. 4.]

Gyaul, gayal, ghyal [18C. H. *gayāl*, S. *go*, 'an ox'.] A large animal, *Gaveus frontalis* or *Bos frontalis*, of the **Ox** tribe, found wild in various forest tracts in eastern India. In Assam it is called **Mithan**. [*OED* & YB; *Asiatic Res.* (1790), II. 188; Heber, *Narrative*, etc. (1824-5; 1828), i. 34.]

Gyelong [18C. Tib. *dGe-sLong*, 'beggar of virtue'.] A **bhikshu**. Latterly a priest of the highest Buddhist order. [YB; Bogle *in* Markham's *Tibet* (1784; ed. 1876), 25.]

Gymkhana [19C. Anglo-Indian hybrid of *gym*(nastics) + (*gend*) *khana* ball-house.] In India a public resort or club for games. Also a sports meeting. *Sb.* and *attrib.* Apparently first used in Roorkee in 1861. [YB & *OED; Pioneer Mail*, 3 Nov. 1877.]

Gymnosophist [15C. Gr. *gymnosophistēs*.] (One of) a sect of ancient ascetic, mystical, contemplative and naked Hindu philosophers. [*OED; Alliterative Romance of Alexander, c.* 1400-50 (Roxb. cl., 1849); Fryer, *New Account* (1672-81).]

Gynee, giani, ghinee [19C. A.I. H. *gaini*.] A dwarf cow bred in Bengal, not more than 3 ft. high. Mentioned by Aelian, *c.* 250 AD. [*OED* & YB; John Shipp, *Memoirs* (1829), iii. 132.]

H

Habshi, Hubshee [17C. Ar. *Habashī;* P. *Habshī.*] 'An Abyssinian'; an Ethiopian; a negro. Formerly a slave brought from Africa to India. *See* **Sidi.** [YB; Fryer, *A New Acct.* (1672-81), 147.]

Hackery [17C. A.I./H. *chhakrā;* S. *sakata,* 'a waggon'.] Two-wheeled cart. An Indian bullock-cart. 'It is probably one of those numerous words which were long in use, and undergoing corruption by illiterate soldiers and sailors before they appeared in any kind of literature.' [YB.] *See* **Ekka.** [*OED;* Fryer, *A New Acct.* 1672-81), 83.]

Haddy, ahadi(s) [17C. Ar. *ahad,* 'single, alone, one'.] A grade of troops in the Mughal service, who offered their services singly and stood under Akbar's immediate orders. A gentleman trooper. [YB; Sir T. Roe, *Embassy,* etc. (1615-19; Hak. Soc., 1899), 11.383.]

Hadis, hadith [19C. H/Ar. *hadith.*] Traditions relating to the prophet Mohammed which now form the **Sunna,** a supplement to the Koran. [*OED;* Burkhardt, *Trav. Syria and Holy Land* (1817), 326.]

Hafiz, hafeez [17C. H/P/Ar. *hafiz,* 'protector, guard'.] One who knows the Koran by heart. *Khuda hafiz,* Muslim 'goodbye'. [*OED.*] [J. Davies, tr. *Olearius Voy. Ambass.* (1662) 314; T. Hope, *Anastasius* (1819), 1. x. 192.]

Hafta, hapta [19C. H/P. *hafta.*] Periodical payment of money. Slang: protection money. *See* **Grassia.** [Whitworth, *Anglo-Indian Dict.* (1885).]

Hai-hai [H. *hai-hai.*] Alas! [Hawkins, *CIWIE.*]

Hai-toba [H. *hai-tobā.*] Alas! [Hawkins, *CIWIE.*]

Haj, hadj [17C. Ar. *hajj,* 'pilgrimage'.] A pilgrimage to Mecca. [*OED.*] *See* next. [Fryer, *A New Acct.* (1672–81).] *See* **Ziarat.**

Ha(d)ji, Hajji, Hadgee [17C. Ar. *hāji,* 'a pilgrim'.] (1) A Muslim who has performed the Haj (on the 8th to the 10th day of the 12th month) at Mecca. [*OED* & YB; Danvers, *Letters* (1611; ed. 1896-1900), 1.26.] (2) An Oriental Christian who has visited the Holy Sepulchre at Jerusalem. [*OED;* Willis, *Pencillings* (1835), ii. LVII.]

Hajam [H. *hajām.*] A barber. [Hawkins, *CIWIE.*]

Hakim, hakeem¹ [17C. H./Ar. *hākim.*] 'governor, judge, master', in Muslim countries and in India. [*OED* & YB; Danvers, *Letters* (1611; ed. 1896–1900), i. 158.]

Hakim, hakeem, huckeem² [16C. H/Ar. *hākim,* 'wise, learned, philosopher, physician'.] A physician, in India and Muslim countries, of *Unani* medicine. *See* **Vaid.** [*OED* & YB; *Eng. Fact. in India* (1622; ed. 1906-27); T. Washington, tr., *Nicholay's Voy.* (1585), iii. xii. 93.] *See* **Vaid.**

Halal, hallal [17C. H/Ar. *halāl* 'lawful'.] Ritual slaughter of an animal to provide lawful food for Muslims. Also the animal slaughtered in the ritually prescribed manner. Also *attrib.* and as *adj* and *vb.* [*OED* & YB.] *See* next. Cf. **Jhatka.**

Halalcor(e) [17C. H/Ar/P. *halālkhōr,* lit. 'one who eats what is lawful'.] A term euphemistically applied to a person of the lowest class, a sweeper or scavenger, implying 'to whom all is lawful food', that is, 'who eats anything and everything'. Applied ironically for *harāmkhūr,* 'one who eats what is not lawful'. For similar ironic usage *see* **Beastie** and **Mehtar.** [*OED* & YB; *Eng. Fact. in India* (1618-69; 1622; ed. Foster., 1906-27). *See* next.]

Halallcur [19C. H/Ar. *halāl-kar,* 'to make lawful'.] 'Verb used in the imperative for infinitive as is common in the Anglo-Indian use of Hindi verbs, meaning put (an animal) to death in the manner prescribed to Muslims when it is to be used for food.' [YB.] *Halalled* = butchered ritually. [Burton, *Pilgrimage* (1855-6; ed. 1893), i. 255.]

Haldi, huldee [19C. H. *haldi. See* **Turmeric.**] The ceremony of anointing the bride & bridegroom with *turmeric* between betrothal and the actual marriage among Muslims and Hindus. [Wilson, *Gloss. of Judicial & Revenue Terms* (1855).]

Haldu [19C. H. *haldu.*] The tree *Adina cordigolia* and its yellowish hardwood found in India, Burma and Thailand. [*OED;* J. S. Gamble, *Man. Indian Timbers* (1881), 220.]

Half-caste [18C. Anglo-Indian.] A person of mixed European and Indian (or other non-European) blood. *See* **Mustees, Eurasian, Chi-Chi.** [*OED* & YB; Munro, *Narr. of Milit. Operations* (1780-84; ed. 1789), 51.]

Halwa, hulwa, halva [17C. H/Ar. *halwa,* 'sweetmeat'.] In India the ingredients usually are: milk, sugar, almond paste and ghee, flavoured with cardamom. Also *halwāi,* sweetmeat-seller. [*OED* & YB; Fryer, *A New Acct. of E. India & Persia* (1672-81; ed. 1698).]

Hamadryad [19C.] Large venomous hooded

snake of India; the king cobra, *Ophiophagus hannah. See* **King Cobra.** [Wood, *Illustr. Nat. Hist.* (1863), III. 140.]

Ham(m)al, hummaul [18C. H/Ar. *hammal,* 'a porter'.] A porter, messenger, carrier or domestic servant. In Western India a palanquin bearer. Also *hammalage,* 'cooly-hire'. (1711). [*OED* & YB; Grose, *Voy. to E. Indies* (1766), i. 120; Lockyer, *Acct. of the Trade in India* (1711), 243.]

Hammam, hummum, hummaum [17C. H/Ar. *hammām,* 'a bath'.] A bathing establishment; a Turkish bath. [*OED* & YB; Purchas, *Pilgrimage* (1625), II. ix. 1419.]

Hanger [17C. Prob. E. and not fr. H/P. *khanjar.*] A kind of short sword, orig. 'hung' from the belt. [*OED* & YB; Tavernier, *Voyages* (E. tr. 1684); Wheeler, *Early Records* (1717; ed. 1878).]

Hangul, hungal [19C. Kash. *hāngul.*] Kashmiri stag, *Cervus elaphus hanglu,* 'related to and perhaps a race of the red deer'. [*OED;* A. L. Adams in *Proc. Zool Soc.* (1858), xxvi. 329.]

Hansaleri [19C. Anglo-Indian.] Domestic Hindustani for 'horse-radish', apparently influenced by *saleri,* 'celery'. [YB; M.L. Dames in *Punjab N & Q,* ii. 284.]

Hansil [19C. Nautical Hindustani for 'hawser'. [YB; Roebuck, *Naval Dict.* (1811).]

Hanspeek, uspuck, etc. [19C. Nautical Hindustani, *aspak.*] A handspike. [YB; Roebuck, *Naval Dict.* (1811).]

Hanuman, hoonimaun [19C. H. *Hanūmān* S. *hanumant,* fr. *hanumat,* 'large-jawed'.] Name of the monkey-god in the **Ramayana.** Also name of the **Langur,** a slim, long-tailed Indian monkey, *Presbytis entellus,* identified with the monkey-god by Hindus. [*OED.*] *See* **Hoonimaun.** [Southey in J.W. Robberds, *Mem. W. Taylor* (1843), 11. 427.

Haram *See* **Harem** and **Hirrawen.**

Haramzada [19C. H/Ar/P. *harāmzādā.* 'Son of the unlawful'.] Misbegotten, 'Son of a bitch', scoundrel. A common term of abuse. [YB; Smith, *Life of Lord Lawrence* (1883), ii. 251.]

Hare Krishna [20C. H. *hare,* O god! + *Krishna.*] Title of a **Mantra** in praise of **Vishnu.** A foreign 'religious' cult, in Britain, the USA and elsewhere, of a pseudo Hindu nature. Also *attrib.* or *absol.* to designate this cult or its members. [*OED; New Yorker,* 17 Aug. 1968.]

Harem, haram [17C. H/Ar. *haram,* 'prohibited, forbidden'.] Women's apartments in a Muslim household. Also, 'women of the family'. *See*

Purdah, Zenana, Hirrawen. [*OED* & YB; Herbert, *Travels,* etc. (1634), 62.]

Harijan [20C. H. *hari* **Vishnu** + *jana,* 'person'. 'The Elect of God'.] Name bestowed on the untouchables (**Pariahs**) by Mahatma Gandhi. *See* also **Outcaste** and **Scheduled Caste** [*OED;* M.K. Gandhi, *Bleeding Wound* (1931), ix. 40.]

Harry [18C. (obs.) S. *hadda,* 'a bone'. Beng. *hārī,* 'A collector of bones'.] A servant of the lowest class, a sweeper. [YB; Risley, *Tribes of Bengal* (1891), i. 314, seq.; Fort William, MS. in India Office Lib. (Nov. 1706).]

Hartal [20C. H. *hattāl,* 'locking of shops'. S. *hatta,* 'shop' + *talaka,* 'lock, bolt'.] In India, a day (of mourning) when (all) shops are (voluntarily) shut as a form of protest against government legislation or a political situation. [*OED; Blackwood's Mag.,* Apr. 1920, 441/1.]

Hashish, hasheesh [16C. H/Ar. *hashish,* 'dry herb, hay, powdered hemp-leaves'.] An intoxicant made from them. The leaves and tender parts of Indian hemp, *Cannabis indica* or *sativa,* are smoked or chewed for their narcotic effect. *See* **Bhang, Charas, Ganja, Subji, Majun.** [*OED;* W. Phillips, tr., *Linschoten* (1598).]

Hatao [20C. Imp. of H. *hatana.*] Away with! *See* **Garibi.**

Hatha-yoga [20C. S. *hatha,* 'force, violence, forced meditation + **Yoga.**] 'A system of exercises (*āsanas*) and control of breathing forming part of the Hindu philosophy.' So *hatha-yogi(n),* a devotee of *hatha-yoga.* [*OED; Encycl. Brit.* (1911), xxvi. 79/1.]

Hathi, hatty, hotty [19C. H. *hāthī;* S. *hastin.*] The elephant, *Elephas-maximus.* Also attrib. *hathi-tractor,* used in the 1914-18 war. [*OED* & YB; Leyden & Erskine, tr., *Mem. Zehir- Ed-Din.* (1826), 315; Emily Eden, *Up the Country* (1838), i. 269.]

Hattychook [19C. H. *hāthīchak.*] Domestic Hindustani for the globe artichoke. The word 'artichoke' itself is a corruption of the Arabic *alkharshōf.* [YB.]

Haut[1] [17C. H. *hāth,* 'the hand or forearm'.] Hence a 'cubit', from the elbow to the tip of the middle finger; a measure of 18 inches and sometimes more. [YB; Foster, *Letters* (1614; ed. 1896-1900), ii. 112.]

Haut,[2] **hat** [19C. H. *hāt,* fr. S. *hatta.*] A market held on certain days, e.g. a weekly market. [YB; Buchanan, *Mysore* (1807), i. 19.]

Hauz [H. *hauz.*] Reservoir. *See* **Tank.** [Hawkins, *CIWIE* (1984).]

Haveli [19C. H/Ar. *haveli*.] 'a mansion, palace, the big house.' Also 'lands attached to a capital town or administered from headquarters'. [Whitworth, *Anglo-Indian Dict.* (1885).]

Havildar [17C. H. *havildār*. fr. P. *hawāldār*, 'a charge-holder'; 'one holding an office of trust'.] 'A sepoy non-commissioned officer corresponding to a sergeant.' [YB; *Eng. Fact. in India* (1618-69; ed. 1906-27).] *Havildar's Guard*, 'A common way of cooking the fry of freshwater fish as a breakfast dish, by frying them in rows of a dozen or so, spitted on a small skewer. (A whimsical Bombay term.)' [YB & *OED*.]

Hazri [19C. Ar. *hāziri*, 'muster', fr. *hāzir*, 'ready, present'.] Breakfast (in Anglo Indian households in Bengal Presidency). 'It is not clear how it got this meaning.' [YB.] *See* **Chota Hazri.** [Herklots, *Qanoon-i-Islam* (1832; ed. 1863), 183.]

Heavenly-blue *See* **Morning glory.**

Henna, hina [17C. Ar. *hennā*.] (Dye obtained from) Egyptian privet, *Lawsonia inermis*. *See* **Mehndi.** Also made into a cosmetic with **Catechu.** Attrib. and comb., as in *henna-scented, –stained, –coloured*. [*OED*; Purchas, *Pilgrimes* (1613).]

He Ram! Hare Ram! [20C. Hindi.] O God! [Hawkins, *CIWIE* (1984).]

Herbed [17C. P. *hirbad*; Pahl. *aerpat*; Avestan, *aethrapati*. 'A Parsee priest, not specially engaged in priestly duties.' [YB.] *See* **Dastur; Mobed** and **Behdin.** [Lord, *The Religion of the Parsees* (1613).]

Hickmat [19C. H./Ar. *hikmat*.] An ingenious device or contrivance. [YB.] Also *hikmata-mali*, judicious management. [Fanny Parkes, *Wanderings of a Pilgrim* (1850), ii. 240.]

Higher Standard, H.S. [19C.] A government examination in an Indian language (generally **Hindustani**). Failure to pass, denied promotion of military officers to staff appointments. *Sirca baksheesh*, gratuity granted to successful candidates. 'Aliph Cheem' (Water Yeldham), *Lays of Ind.* (1875; ed. 1888), 35.]

Hijra [19C. H. *hijra*.] Eunuch, often dressed as a woman; transvestite. [Hawkins, *CIWIE*.]

Hill-appointment [19C. Anglo-Indian.] An appointment to a government post in a **Hill-Station** in India. [*OED*; *Westm. Gaz.*, 30 Dec. 1896, 3/2.]

Hill-station [19C. Anglo Indian.] Town and surrounding countryside above *c.* 1500 metres to which government officials and European wives and families moved in the **Hot weather,** espec. Simla in N. India and Ooty (Ootacamund) in the South. *See* **Station.** [*OED*; F. Pollock, *Sport Brit. Burmah* (1879), I. 42.]

Hilsa [19C. H. *hilsā* fr. S. *ilisa*.] A rich and savoury sea-fish *Hilsa ilisha*, also found and taken in larger rivers, such as the Jamuna and Irrawaddy. [YB & *OED*; Williamson, *Vade Mecum* (1810), II. 154.] *See* **Sable-Fish.**

Himalaya, Himalya [19C. S. *hima*, 'snow', + *alaya*, 'abode'.] The name of the great range, 'The abode of Snow', the *Himalayas*. Also *Himalayan*, pertaining to the *Himalayas*. Fig. enormous, gigantic, massive, and attrib. *Himalo-Chinese* (1858); *Himalayan* blackbear (*Selenarctos thibetanus* (1858); *Himalayan* rhubarb (*Rheum nobile*) (1866); *Himalayan–pine*, the Neoza Pine (*Pinus gerardiana*), alias the Nepal Nut-pine (1866); the *Himalayan primrose* (*Primula sikkimensis*) (1882) [*OED* & YB; Colebrooke *Life of Elphinstone* (1822; ed. 1884), ii. 139.]

Hinayana [19C. S. *hinayana*. 'The Little Vehicle.' S. *hina*, 'lesser' + *yāna*, 'vehicle'.] The earlier austere form of Buddhism, of S. India and elsewhere. Cf. **Mahayana,** 'The Great Vehicle'. Also *Hinayanism –ist, –ian,* [*OED*; J. Fergusson, *Tree & Serpent Worship* (1868), 65.]

Hindi, Hindee [19C. H. *Hindi*, (sb. & adj.) from P. *Hindwi*, India (whence formerly in English, *Hindevi, Hindawee, Hinduvee*, etc.)] (1) The The dominant Aryan (Indo-European) vernacular of N. India written in the **Devanagri** script, with **Sanskritized** vocabulary. The official language of the Indian Union. The earliest literary work in Hindi is the great poem of Chand Bardai (c. 1200), which records the deeds of Prithviraja, the last Hindu Sovereign of Delhi. [YB & *OED*; *Asiatic Ann. Reg. Acc. Bks.* (1800), 6/1; Grierson, *The Modern Vernacular Literature of Hindustan*, in *J.A.S.B.* (1888), Pt. 1.] (2) Of or belonging to N. India or its language. [*OED*; W. T. Adam, *Stewart's Hist. Anecd.* (1825).] (3) A native of N. India (rare). [*OED*; Elliot, *Hist. Ind.* (1853), III. 539.]

Hindki, Hindeki [19C. H. *hind*, 'India' + *ki*, 'people'.] The name of a people and their language. Hindus converted to Islam, in what is now N. Pakistan and in Afghanistan. They were bankers, and held a large part of the trade in their hands. [YB & *OED*; Elphinstone, *Acct. Kingd. Caubul.* (1815).]

Hindu, Hindoo [17C. H/P. *Hindū*, 'Indian'; S. *Sindhū*, 'river', espec. the Indus, hence the region, *Sindh*.] [*OED*.] (1) Sb. Originally an Aryan of N. India (**Hindustan**) who professed the religion of **Hinduism**. Now any Indian who professes this religion. [*OED;* Davies, tr., *Mandelso* (1662).] (2) Adj: pertaining to Hindus or their religion. [*OED;* Fryer, *Acct. E. Ind. & P.* (1698).] Also in such expressions as *Hindū Mazdoor Sabha*, an important Indian Trade Union. (20C.) *Hindū Kūsh* = Caucasus.

Hinduism [19C.] *See* **Hindu**. The polytheistic religion, or way of life, of the Hindus, a development of Brahmanism. So, *Hinduize*, 'to render Hindu in character, customs or religion'. [*OED; Sat. Review* (1857), iv. 460/1.]

Hindu Raj [20C.] The term used by Jinnah and the Muslim League to denote the state of affairs were India to be undivided after Independence in 1947.

Hindustan, Hindostan [18C. H/P. *Hindū* + *stān*, 'country'.] The country of the Hindus. The northern part of the Indian sub-continent, the languages of whose natives are of the Indo-European family. *See* **Hindustani**. [*OED*.] But used, too, as the equivalent of India proper. [YB; Raynal, *History* etc. (tr. 1776); Wellington, *Despatches* (1837), ii. 209.]

Hindustani, Hindostanee [17C. adj. + sb.] *See* prec. + *ī*, pertaining to Hindustan.] (1) A native of Hindustan. [*OED* & YB.] (2) The language of Hindustan (*Hindūstānī zabān*). A mixture of **Hindi** and **Urdu** (the language of the *Urdu* ('horde' or 'camp') which contains a great many Arabic, Persian and other elements). Hindustani was for a long time a kind of Muslim *lingua franca* all over India. Formerly called *Indostan, Indostans*. 'Old fashioned Anglo-Indians used to call it the **Moors**.' [*OED* & YB.] Also *Hindoostanish* (1811). [Terry, *Voyage*, etc. (1616; ed. 1777).]

Hing, hingh, hinge [16C. H. *hing* S. *hingu*.] *Asafoetida*, a resinous gum yielded by plants of the genus *Ferula*, with a strong smell of garlic, or 'a repulsive smelling gum-resin which forms a favourite Hindu condiment, and is used in Western and Southern India as an ingredient in certain cakes eaten with curry'. [YB.] *See* **Popper Cake** [*OED* & YB; Fitch (1585) in *Early Travels in India* (1583-91; ed. 1921).]

Hirava [16C. M. *Iraya*.] A very low caste in Malabar, one section of the *Cherumar*, of slightly higher social standing than the *Pulayar*. (*See* **Polea**.) 'Their name is derived from the fact that they are allowed to come only as far as the eaves [*ira*] of their employers' houses.' [YB; Varthema, *Travels* etc., E. tr. by Eden (1576); Logan, *Malabar* (1887-91), i. 148.]

Hircarrah, hurcarra(h), hurkaru [17C. H. *harkārā*.] 'A messenger, a courier.' An emissary, a spy. (Whitworth's etymology is: *har*, 'every' + *kār*, 'business'). [*OED* & YB; *Eng. Fact.* (1618-69; ed. Foster, 1906-27).]

Hirrawen [17C. Obs. Corr. of Ar. *ihrām;* 'prohibition, unlawful'.] The Muslim pilgrim dress, so-called as being 'equivalent to our mortification'. [YB.] Purchas, *Pilgrimage* (1614; ed. 1893), ii. 138. *See* **Harem (Haram)**. [*OED* & YB.]

Hitherao [19C. H. imp. *idharao*, 'Come here!' fr. *idharana*, 'to come'.] 'Come here!'. Also *hitherao jildi*, 'come here at the double!' (cf. E. 'come *hither*'.) [Partridge, Dict. of Slang. (1979), vol. ii.]

Hobson-Jobson [17C. Ult. fr. Ar. '*Yā Hasan! Yā Husain!*'.] The excited shouts and the wailing of Muslims (Shias) as they beat their breasts in the **Moharram** processions in memory of the martyrdom of Hasan and Husain, the grandsons of Prophet Mohammed killed while fighting for the faith. *Hobson-Jobson* is an excellent example of the habit of British soldiers and other Anglo-Indians to incorporate native expressions into their own special *argot*, where they undergo strange and often delightful metamorphoses hardly resembling the originals at all. *Hobson-Jobson*, however, was the end not the beginning of the process which chronologically produced *Hosseen Gosseen* (1673), *Hossy Gossy* (1673), *Saucem Saucem* (1710), *Hossein Jossem* (1720), *Jaksom Baksom* (1726) and *Hobson-Jobson* (1829). As this was considered by Yule & Burnell to be the apotheosis of Anglo-Indian folk etymology, they used it as the concise main title for their glossary, and more recently it has entered the professional vocabulary of linguistics to denote the assmilation of a foreign expression to conform to the linguistic predelictions (*Sprachgefühl*) of the target language. Hence *Hobson-Jobsonism* = folk etymology. Also, any **Tamasha** or festal excitement. [YB & *OED;* T. Herbert, *Travels*, (1634), 67; *Oriental Sporting Mag.* (1829; ed. 1873), i. 129; Morris, *Australian English* (1898), 287/2.]

Hodgett [19C. Ar. *hujjat*, 'evidence'.] Perh. Mar *hojat*, 'account current between landlord and tenant'. Or, 'a government acknowledgement or receipt. [YB: Molesworth, *Marathi and English Dict.* (1857), 2nd. ed.]

Hog-bear [18C. Anglo-Indian.] Another name for the Indian sloth-bear, *Melurus labiatus.* [YB; Miller in *Phil. Trans.* (1777), lxviii. 171; Kipling, *The Jungle Book* (1895).]

Hog-deer [18C. Anglo-Indian.] (1) The Anglo-Indian popular name of the *Axis porcinus,* the *pārā* of Hindustan, a smaller relative of the **Chital.** Sometimes used to include the *Axis Maculatus.* [*OED* & YB; Pennant, *Synops. Quadrup.* (1771), 52; Lady Dufferin, *Viceregal Life* (ed. 1890), 146.] (2) The *babiroussa* or Indian hog. [*OED* & YB; Miller in *Phil. Trans. Quadrup.* (1777), lxviii. 171.]

Hog-plum [19C. Anglo-Indian.] The austere fruit of the *amra* (Hind), *Spondius mangifera.* Also called the wild mango; used in curries, pickles and tarts. 'It is native to various parts of India and is cultivated in many tropical countries.' [YB; Mason, *Burmah,* etc. (ed. 1860), 461.]

Holi, Hooli, Hohlee, etc. [17C. H. *holī,* S. *holāka.*] Hinduism: 'The spring festival, held at the approach of the vernal equinox, during the 15 days preceding the full moon of the month *Phālguna* (cf. Persian **Nauroz**). It is a sort of carnival in honour of **Krishna** and the milkmaids (*Gopīs*). Passers-by are chaffed and pelted with red powder, or drenched with yellow liquids from squirts. Songs, mostly obscene, are sung in praise of Krishna and dances performed round fires. [YB.] (*See* Frazer, *Golden Bough* for the saturnalian idea behind this rite.) *Holi* songs: Folk songs sung to the accompaniment of the *pakhawaj* in *dhama tala.* Also called *dolā-yātrā, hutāsani,* and *simgā.* [*OED* & YB; *Eng. Fact.* (1618-69; ed. Foster, 1906-27).]

Holkar [19C. Mar. *Hol.* Name of a village on the Nira + *kar* 'resident of'.] Family name of the one-time rulers of Indore state.

Hom(a) [19C. P. *hōm;* S. *sōma;* Zend *hāoma.*] The sacred plant (acid asclepias?) of the ancient Persians and **Parsis;** an oblation, a sacrifice. Also its juice, orig. the same as the **Soma** of the **Vedas.** *See* **Soma.** [*OED.*] Also *attrib* and *comb.* [Bailey, *Mystic,* (1855), 35.]

Home [19C.] In Anglo-Indian speech this meant England. *See* **Blighty.** '*Home* always means England; nobody calls India *home.*' [*OED* & YB; Maitland, *Letters from Madras* (1836-9; ed. 1843), 92.]

Hooghly-mud [19C. Nautical H.] Butter. [Partridge

Dict. of Slang (1979).]

Hookah, hooka, hooker [17C. H/Ar. *hukkah,* 'casket, vase, cup'.] The Indian narghile or waterpipe for smoking tobacco, with spice, molasses, fruit, etc. *See* **Hubble-Bubble, Caleoon.** [*OED* & YB; Bowrey, *A Geog. Acct.* etc. (1669-79); ed. Temple (Hak. Soc., 1905).]

Hookah-burdar [18C. H/P. *hukka-bardar,* 'hookah-bearer'.] The servant who attended to his master's hookah, 'and who considered that duty sufficient to occupy his time'. [YB; Carey, *Good Old Days* (1779; ed. 1882), i. 71.]

Hookum *See* **Hukum.**

Hoolock, hooluck, hulluck [19C. Poss. fr. Beng. *hūlak* (but obviously imitative).] The black Assamese and Arakanese gibbon, *Hylobates hoolock,* of 'gentle engaging ways and plaintive cries'. [YB & *OED;* Buchanan, *Eastern India* (1809), iii. 563.]

Hoon [19C. H. *hūn.* Perh. Kan. *honnu,* 'gold'. S. *huna.*] A gold coin; the gold **Pagoda** (coin). [*OED* & YB; Buchanan, *Jour. Madras* (1807), II. 310.]

Hoondi, hoondy, hundi [17C. H. *hūndī;* S. *hūndikā.*] A bill of exchange; a banker's draft; a negotiable instrument. [*OED* & YB; *Eng. Fact. in India* [1618-21; ed. Foster, 1906-27).]

Hoonimaun from **Hanuman** The great ape; also called **Langur.**

Hoowa [19C. Sinh. *hūwa.*] 'A peculiar call used by the Singhalese, and thence applied to the distance over which this call can be heard.' [YB.]

Hopper [16C. Tam. *appam,* fr. *apu,* 'hand-clap'.] A cake made of rice-flour in S. India, somewhat resembling the wheaten *chapati* of N. India. (Folk etymology.) [YB; Litchfield, tr. *Castañeda* (1582) f. 38.]

Horse-gram [19C. H. *kulthi.*] Fodder for horses (*dolichos uniflorus*). [Whitworth, *Anglo-Indian Dict.* (1885).]

Horse-keeper [17C.] An old provincial English term, used in the Madras Presidency and in Ceylon, for 'groom'. The usual corresponding words are in N. India **Syce** and in Bombay *ghorāwālā* (**Gorawallah**). [YB & *OED;* Hawkins *in* Purchas (1609; 1625-6). i. 216.]

Horse-radish tree [17C.] The common name in India for the *Moringa pterygosperma,* called in Hind. *sahajnā* (S. *sobhanjana*). 'The name is given because the scraped root is used in place of horse-radish, which it closely resembles in flavour. In S. India it is called the **Drumstick Tree** from the shape of the long slender fruit, which is used as a vegetable, or in curry, or made into a native pickle (**Achar**) 'most nauseous to Europeans'. [YB; Stewart, *Punjab Plants* (1869).] Its pod-like capsules are eaten fresh or pickled; its winged seeds (*ben-nuts*) give oil of ben. [*OED;* Salmon, *Bates Dispensatory* (1694).] *See* **Myrobalan**.

Hosbolhookum [17C. H/Ar. *hasb-ul-hukm,* lit. 'according to order'.] 'The initial formula of a document issued by officers of State on royal authority, and thence applied as the title of such a document.' [YB.] Official order, passport. [Hedges, *Diary* (1681-8, Hak. Soc.), ii. xlvi).] *See* **Purwana**.

Hot-winds [19C.] Anglo-Indian name of one of the seasons of the year in N. India 'when the hot dry westerly winds prevail and such aids to coolness as the **Tatty** and **Thermantidote** are brought into use. May is the typical month of such winds.' [YB; Wellington, *Despatches* (1804; ed. 1837), iii. 180.]

Houri [18C. P. *hūrī,* a nymph of the Muslim paradise.] Hence any voluptuously beautiful woman 'with large dark eyes like close-kept pearls, a recompense for labours past'. (Koran, 56. 10) [*OED;* Johnson, *Irene* (1737), iv. v.]

Howdah, howder, houda [17C. Ar. *haudaj* (P. *haudah*).] Orig. a litter carried by a camel or elephant. 'A great chair or framed seat carried by an elephant.' [YB & *OED;* Bernier, *Travels,* (E. tr. 1684; ed. Ball, 1889), 119; Carraccioli, *Life of Clive* (1775-6), III. 133.]

Hubba [18C. Ar. *habba,* 'a grain'.] A jot, a tittle. [Burke, Art. against Hastings (1786), in *Writings & Correspondence* (ed. 1852), vii. 141.]

Hubble-bubble [17C. Imitative.] A kind of rudimentary **Hookah** in which tobacco-smoke is drawn from a terracotta **Chillum** through water in a coconut shell with a bubbling sound. A rhyming jingle on 'bubble'. *See* **Caleeoon**. [*OED* & YB; Terry, *Voyage,* etc. (1617); ed. 1665), 363.] *See* **Narghile**..

Huck [19C. Ar. *hakk*.] A just right; a lawful claim; a perquisite claimable by established usage. [YB; *Confessions of an Orderly* (1866), 50.]

Huckeem [17C. Ar. *hakīm*.] *See* **Hakīm,²** a physician.

Hukum, hookum [17C. Ar. *hukm*] 'Command, order' (old army colloquial term); regulation, the correct thing. *See* **Hakīm** [YB; Hedges, *Diary* (Hak. Soc., 1681-8), ii. xlvi.]

Huldi, huldee [19C. H. *huldī*.] The plant, *curcuma longa,* the tubers of which yield turmeric; also, the powdered turmeric itself. [*OED;* Herklots, tr., *Customs Moosulmans India* (1832), 97.]

Hullia [19C. Kan. *Holeya,* fr. *hola,* 'land, soil'.] The same as **Polea** (*pulayan*) equivalent to **Pariah**. *Hullias* were agricultural labourers and serfs (bonded labourers) in S. Canara (Karnataka). [YB; Wilks, *Hist. Sketches* (1810-17; ed. 1869), i. 151.]

Huma [19C. H/P. *humā,* 'phoenix'.] The 'Indian Eagle', a fabulous oriental bird, a restless wanderer, fabled to bring luck to those it hovers over. [*OED;* R. C. Wellesley, *Primitiae et Reliquiae* (1841), 104.]

Humhums, humpum [17C. Ar. *hummām,* 'Turkish bath'.] *See* **Hammam**. Coarse cotton cloth of 'thick stout texture and generally worn as a wrapper in the cold season'. ('Apparently so named from its having been originally used at the bath.') [YB; Taylor, *A Descriptive Account of the Cotton Manufacture* etc. (1851).]

Humming-bird(s) [19C. Anglo-Indian.] This word was popularly applied in some parts of India to the sun-birds, e.g. the purple-rumped Sun-bird (*Nectarinia zeylonica*), H. *Shākarkhorā;* the purple Sun-bird (N. *asiatica asiatica*); the Manipur Yellow-backed Sun-bird (*Aethopyja gouldia isolata*). [YB.] [Salim Ali & Ripley, *Handbook of the Birds of India & Pakistan,* Vol. 10 (1974).]

Hump [17C.] '"Calcutta humps" were the salted humps of Indian oxen, *Bos indica.'* [YB & *OED*.] *See* **Buffalo**. [Ovington, *Voy. to Suratt* (1689); 1807 in *Spirit of the Public Journals* (1808), XI. 41.

Hurtaul [18C. H/S. *haritalaka, hartal.*] Yellow arsenic; orpiment. [YB.] [Darymple, *Oriental Repertory* (1791-7; ed. 1808), i. 109.]

Huzoor [18C. H/Ar. *huzūr.* 'The presence' (a title of respect) fr. *hazara,* 'to be present'.] A title of respect for Indian potentates, or sometimes of a master, or any European **Sahib** in the presence of another European. Also, *huzooriahs,* personal attendants of a chief. [*OED* & YB; *The Trial of Joseph Fowke for Conspiracy against W. Hastings* (1776).]

Hydel [20C.] Abridgement of Hydroelectric station. [Hawkins, *CIWIE.*]

I

I.C.S. [18C.] The Indian Civil Service, first organized by Warren Hastings, was succeeded by the I.A.S., The Indian Administrative Service, after 1947. See **Civilian,CompetitionWallah,** and **Convenanted servants.**

Id, Eid, Eed [17C. Ar. *Id.*] A Muslim holy festival, espec. *Bakr-Id* (commemorating Abraham's sacrifice, the victim of which was, according to Muslims, Ishmael), and *Id-ul-fitr* (1734), the feast on breaking the **Ramzan** fast, the Lesser Bairam, on the 1st of *Shawwāl. Id-mubarak* = the *Id*-day greeting. [*OED* & .YB; Hedges, *Diary* (Hak. Soc., 1681-8), ii. cccx.]

Id-gah, Eedgah [18C. Ar. *Idgah*, 'place of *Id*'.] A. place of assembly and prayers on occasion of Muslim festivals. 'In India usually a platform of white plastered brickwork, enclosed by a low wall on three sides, and situated outside of a town or village.... It is also known as *Namazgah*, 'place of prayers'. [YB; Seton-Karr, *Selections* (1784-1823; ed. 1864-9), ii. 89.]

Idli [19C. Tam. *idli.*] Steamed cake of rice and black gram. [Hawkins, *CIWIE.*]

Illom [M. *illom.*] A patriarchal Nambudhri Brahmin family group in Kerala State. See **Nayar.**

Illuk [19C. Sinh. *illuk.*] Coarse *Imperata cylindrica* grass = Malay *lalang.* [*OED*; Thwaites, *Enumeratio Plantarum Zeylaniae* (1864), v. 369.]

Illupi [19C. Tam. *iluppai, iruppai.*] An evergreen tree, *Bassia longifolia*, native to S. India. Also *illupi-oil* obtained from its seeds and *illipi-butter* (1904). [*OED*; Piddington, *Eng. Index Plants India* (1832).]

Imam, imaum, eemawm [17C. Ar. *imām*, fr. *amma*, 'to precede'.] (1) A title technically applied to the Caliph (Khalifa) or 'Vicegerent' or Successor, who is the head of Islam. [*OED* & YB; Fryer, *Acc. E. India* (1698), 220.] (2) The title is also given – in its religious import only – to the heads of the four orthodox Muslim sects, but the title has been perhaps most familiar as that of the Princes of Oman or the 'Imaums of Muscat'. [*OED*; Fryer, *Acc. E. India* (1698), 220.] (3) In a more restricted sense still, to the ordinary functionary of a mosque who leads in the daily prayers of the congregation. [*OED* & YB; Purchas, *Pilgrimage* (1613), 301.]

Imambara, Imaumbara, Eemaumberra [18C.

Hybrid Ar. *Imām* + H. *barā*, 'an enclosure'.] A building maintained by the **Shia** Muslims for the express purpose of celebrating the Muhurrum ceremonies, to which they bring their **Tazias** and **Taboots.** See **Hobson-Jobson.** 'The great Imambara at Lucknow was probably the most magnificent modern oriental structure in India.' [YB & *OED*; Bishop Heber, *Narrative* etc. (1824-5); Miss Eden, *Up the Country* (1866), i. 87; Mrs Mir Hassan Ali, *Observations on the Mussulmans of India*, etc. (1832).]

Imli [H. *imli*; S. *amlikā.*] See **Tamarind.**

Inam, inaum, enaum [17C. H/Ar. *inām*, 'a gift (from a superior), a favour'.] Especially (in India) a gift of rent-free land; also land so held. (*See* Wilson, *Glossary of Indian Terms*, (1855) [YB; *Eng. Fact. in India* (1618-69; ed. Foster 1906–27).] See **Nuzzer.**

India [16C. S. *Sindhu*, 'Great River', espec. the Indus: Gr. *Indos* (the river) and *Indiā* (the country); O.E. *India, Indea;* Ar. *Hēndū;* P. *Hind* (O.P. *Hindu*). The word is in O.E. [(King Aelfred: Oros, Cott. MS. (c. 893) but its present use in English dates from the 16C. and may partly reflect Spanish and Portuguese usage.] (1) Orig. the subcontinent of S. Asia lying east of the Indus and South of the Himalayas. (Also called *Hindustan.*) Extended sometimes to include the region further east (Further India) to the border of China, 'the lande of Prester John'. [*OED*; J. Rustell, *New Interlude Four Elements* (1519).] (2) Since 1947 it has come to represent the South Asian subcontinent excluding Pakistan, Bangladesh and Sri Lanka. (3) Used allusively for a source of immense wealth, where adventurers came 'to shake the **Pagoda-Tree',** and return **Home** to become **Nabobs.** Some of the numerous attributive uses are: *India*-calico (1805), –cotton (1881), –cracker (1799), –docks (1837), –house (1794), –ink (1665), –lake (1658) muslin (1796), –Office (1869), –pale ale (1895), –paper (1750), –red (1732), –rubber (1788), –silk(s) (1758), –Stock (1769), –shawls (1822), –tags (1912), etc. etc. Also, I.M.F.L. (India Made Foreign Liquor) (20C.). [Eden, *Hist. of Travayle*, etc. (1577).] (4) Slang, 'The female pudend is literary rather than coll.' (Donne.) [Partridge, *Dict. of Slang* (1979).] (5) *India husband,* owner of an East India-man, chartered to the

E.I. Co., 18C. (Partridge.)

Indialite [20C.] Hexagonal mineral; dimorph of cordierite, $(Mg.Fe^{-2})_2 Al_4Si_5O_{18}$, found in the Bokaro coalfield. [*OED;* Miyashiro and Iiyama, *Proc. Jap. Acad.* (1954), xxx. 746.]

Indiaman [18C.] A large vessel engaged in trade with India; espec. a ship of large tonnage in the service of the East India Company. [*OED.*] Also *Indianeer* (1845). [Steele, *Tatler* (1709), No. 31. 2.]

Indian (adj. and sb) [14C.] (1) Adj. Belonging or related to India (1566); of Indian manufacture, material, pattern, kind etc. (1635). [*OED &* YB; J. Alday, tr. 'Boaystuau', *Theatrum Mundi.* D.ij. (1566).] (2) Sb. A member of any of the native races of India; after 1947, of the Republic of India. [*OED;* Trevisa's *Barth. de Propriatibus rerum.* (1398), xviii. XLII.] (3) Sb. A European, espec. a Britisher, resident (or ex-resident) in India. Otherwise known as an **Anglo-Indian** (not a **Eurasian**) (1751). Also **Old Indian** and *Returned Indian.*[*OED;* Eliza Heywood, *Hist. Betsy Thoughtless* (1751), III. 254.] (4) Sb. **Mahout** [YB.] (5) Sb. Name of a constellation (*Indus*) between Saggitarius and the N. Pole (1838). [*OED;* Moxon, *Tutor Astron* (1674), 3 edn, i.iii. 10. 19.] (6) Some of the numerous compounds are: *Indian*-almond (*Terminalia catappa*) (1887); –antelope (**Black Buck**) (1888); –ass, the Unicorn (1594); –berry (*Cocculus indicus*) (1765); –blue = **Indigo** (1509); –calico (1702); –cane (bamboo) (1578); –carpet (1896); –chints (chintz) (1718); –club (1857); –cock (the turkey) (1638); –corn (1642); –cotton (1852); –crocus (genus *Caelogyne*) (1888); –cuckoo (koel) (*Eudynamis honorata*) (1826), –elephant (*Elephas maximus*) (1607); –English (1907), *see* **Babu;** –eye (*Dianthus plumarius*) (1573); –fig (pricklypear) (1712); banyan (1594) or banana (1613 obs.); –fire (sulphur, realgar + nitre) (1875); –geranium (Andropogon) (1866); –grass (silkworm gut for anglers (1696); –hay (marijuana) (1939); –heart (*Cardiaspermum corindum*) (1884); –head (cotton stuff) (1911); –hemp (*Cannabis indica*) (1873); –hog (*babiroussa*) (1774); –ink (1665); –leaf (*Cinnamomum malabathrum*) (1884); –light (*Bengal-light*) (1787); –lotus (*Nelumbo speciosum* or *nucifera* (1901); –mouse (*Ichneumon*) (1617); –muslin(s) (1793); –nut (coconut) (1613); –oak (teak) (1866); –ocean (1727); –oil (1626); –rat (= Indian Mouse) (1647); –red (1753); –reed (*Canna indica*) (see -*shot*) (1886); –roller (blue-jay,

Coracias benghalensis) (1809); –shot (*Canna indica*) (see -reed) (1760); –silk (1873); –summer (1784); –tea (1884); –walnut (the Candleberry-tree, *Aleurite triloba*) (1866); –*wood* (**Teak**); –work (= Drawn work) (1865); –yellow (*Euxanthate of Magnesium*) (1866).

Indian (or Oriental) Region: one of the six zoological regions of the world, bounded on the north by the Palaearctic and on the south-west by the Australian, divided into three sub-regions. (1) the *Indo-Chinese* (including the southern slopes of the Himalayas, Assam and the Andamans); (2) the Indo-Malayan (including the Nicobars); and (3) the Indian sub-region, the peninsula south of the Himalayas, from the Indus to the Ganges delta, and southwards to include Sri Lanka. [*OED.*]

Indianesque [19C.] Of an Indian type. [*OED;* Winthrop, *John Brent* (1883; a. 1861), iv. 36.]

Indianist [19C.] One versed in Indian languages, history, philosophy, anthropology, etc. = Indologist. [*OED;* Hall, *Benares Mag.*, 1851, v. 22.]

Indianness [20C.] The quality or state of being Indian or of displaying Indian characteristics. [*OED; Evening Standard,* 20 Sept. 1967.]

Indianite [19C.] (1) A kind of *Anorthite* found in India. It forms the matrix of corundum. [*OED;* Allan, *Min. Nomen.* (2) A solution of India-rubber. [*OED; Eng. Mech.* (1870), 11 March 625/3.]

Indianize [18C.] (1) To act like an Indian; to play the Indian (Obs.) [*OED;* Mather, *Magn. Chr.* (1702), vi. v.; (1852), 400.] (2) To make Indian in character, habit, appearance, etc. [*OED; Bengalee,* 1829, 408.] Also *Indianization* (1918). (a) The process of Indianizing [*OED; Pall Mall Gaz.* (1918), 29 June 5/2]. (b) The replacement of foreigners by Indians in positions of authority. [*OED; Q. Rev.,* July, 1922.]

Indiary [17C.] Obs: Relating to India. [*OED;* Sir T. Browne, *Pseud. Ep.* (1646), I. viii. 30.]

Indic [19C.] Indian (adj.); *Hindu* (adj.); the Indian branch of the Indo-European languages: Sanskrit, Hindi, Marathi, Punjabi, Bengali, Gujarati, etc. [*OED;* Rawlinson, *Orig. Nations* (1877), vi (1883), 24.]

Indicum [14C.] = **Indigo**. [*OED;* Trevisa, Barth. De P. R. (1398), xix. xxxii. (Bodl. MS.).]

Indies [16C.] A name given to India and regions and islands adjacent = East Indies and also to the West Indies. [Eden, *Decades* (1555), 174.]

Indigo, indico [16C. Lat. *indicum,* Gr. *indikon.*] The blue dye. Lit. 'The Indian substance', obtained from the indigo plant, *Indigofera tinctoria*. [*OED* & YB; Haklyut, *Voy.* (1599), II. 218. a.] Also attrib. *indigo*-blue (1712); –vat (1765); –planter (1849), etc.

Indish (adj.) [16C.] Obs. = Indian. [*OED*; Turner, *Names of Herbs* (1548).]

Indo-Anglian (adj. and sb) [20C.] Pertaining to the literature in English written by Indian authors; also a writer of such literature = *Indo-British* (1954). [*OED*; K.R. Srinivasa Iyengar, *Indian Writing in English* (1933).]

Indo-aniline [19C.] A violet dye, $O:C_6H_4:N.C_6H_4$. [*OED*; *Jrnl. Chem. Soc.* (1886), L. 146.]

Indo-Arabic [19C.] A mathematics system with the zero. [*OED*; *Encycl. Brit.* (1884), xvii. 627/1.]

Indo-Aryan adj. and sb. [19C.] Person belonging to, or speaking any of the languages of the Indic group of the Aryans, or the languages themselves. [*OED*; Torrens, *Jrnl. Asiatic Soc. Bengal* (1850), 1.]

Indo-European (adj. and sb.) [19C.] Common to India and Europe; spec. applied to the group of languages spoken over the greater part of Europe and extending into Asia as far as and including Northern India. Also called *Indo-Germanic* (1823) or *Indo-Teutonic* (1850), representing the ethnological and linguistic chain stretching from India to Britain. [Klaproth, *Asia Polyglotta*], or *Indo Celtic* as emphasizing Celtic as the most western member of the group. See **Aryan** (1871). Also *Indo-Europeanist*, a student of the Indo-European family of languages (1927). [*OED*; Dr T. Young (1814) in *Q. Rev.*, x. 255.]

Indo-Gangetic [19C.] Of, or pertaining to, the Ganges and the Indus, esp. to the great Indo-gangetic plain of North India. [*OED*; *Encycl. Brit.* (1880), xii. 735/2.]

Indo-Iranian (adj.) [19C.] Spec. a division of the Indo-European languages, with Indian and Iranian branches. Sb., the Indo-Iranian languages collectively. A member of the Indo-Iranian people. [*OED*; Papillon, *Man. Compar. Philol.* (1876), ii. 10.]

indology [19C.] The study of Indian culture, religion, philosopy, literature, etc. Also *Indologist* (1904), *indological* (1950). [*OED*; Trubner's *Monthly List.* (1888), Oct. 134.]

Indo-Pak(istan)(i) [20C.] Pertaining to India and Pakistan or to their inhabitants; also *Indo-Pak* colloq. abbr. [*Punch* (1965), 27, Jan. 116/1.]

Indra [S. *Indra*.] The celestial ruler, king of the vedic gods, shown riding on an elephant. (See

Ganesh). One of the three main aspects of **Siva:** Might (Indra), the Devourer (Agni) and the Devoured (Soma). [Whitworth, *Anglo-Indian Dict.* (1885).]

Indus See **India.**[5]

Inglees [19C. H. *Inglis*, corr. of 'English'.] 'Invalid soldiers and sipahis [**Sepoys**], to whom allotments of land were assigned as pensions; the lands so granted.' [Wilson, *Gloss. of Judicial & Revenue Terms* etc. (1855).] The word was later used as the equivalent of a *sepoy's* pension with no reference to land. (Poss. corr. of 'invalid'.) [YB; Carnegy, *Kachahri Technicalities* etc. (1877).]

Ingrez [19C. Corr. of 'English'.] An Englishman. *Ingrezi*, adj. 'English', or sb. 'the English language', or 'the English rule or dominion'. [Whitworth, *Anglo-Indian Dict.* (1885).]

Inqilab [19C. H/Ar.] Revolution. See **Kranti.** [Hawkins, *CIWIE* (1984); Platts *Dict.* (1884).]

Inshallah! [19C. H/Ar.] Please God! If Allah wills! [Hawkins, *CIWIE.*]

Inter (adj; sb.) [20C.] A class of railway travel between 2nd and 3rd. (No longer in use.) [Hawkins, *CIWIE.*]

Interdine [20C.] Eat with someone of another Indian community or caste, in this way entailing caste 'pollution' and ostracism. This is becoming less of a 'sin' than formerly. See **Caste** and **Jamat.** [*OED*; Ghurye, *Caste and Race in India* (1932), iv. 73.]

Interloper [16C. E. *inter* + *loper* (leaper); Du. *loopen*, 'to run'.] Trader infringing the East India Company's charter of monopoly. A ship trading without authority in countries allotted to a merchant company. Also *interloperie* (1612-13) and *interloping* (1615). [*OED*; H. Lane in Hakluyt, *Voy.* (1590), I. 375.]

Intermarriage [18C.] In India, marriage between persons of different caste, religion or race. [Colebrooke, *Misc. Ess.* (1798) (ed. 1873), II. 163.] Also, vb. to *intermarry*, and sb. *intermarrying*. [Mickle, *Inq. Bramin Philos.* (1789).]

Iqbal [20C. Ar. *iqbāl*.] Prosperity, good fortune. [Hawkins, *CIWIE* (1984).]

Iron-wood, Iron-Tree [19C.] In India applied to the hard wood tree and timber of the *Mesua forrea*, (H. nagkesar) and in Burma to the *Xylia dolabriformis*. [*OED*; Tennent, *Ceylon* (1859), I. 1. iii. 94.]

Ishwar, Iswara [S. *Īsvara*. Hinduism: 'God', fr. *is*, 'to own'.] The monotheistic concept of god as unity in polytheistic diversity. [Whitworth, *Anglo-Indian Dict.* (1885).]

Iskat [19C. Pg. *escada*.] Ratlines; an Indo-

Portuguese marine term. [YB; T. Roebuck, *An English & Hindoostanee Naval Dict.* (1811).]

Islam [17C. Ar. *Islām;* fr. *aslama,* 'to be or become safe'.] Resignation, surrendering to god; the religion of Muslims; the Muslim world. In India and Pakistan there are approx. 100,000,000 each, mostly of the Sunni sect and in Bangladesh 115,000,000 predominantly of the same sect. Also *Islamism* (18C.) (Fr. *Islamisme,* Voltaire); 18C. (Fr. *Islamite*) [*OED* & YB.] *See* **Moors.** [Foster's *Letters* (1616; ed. 1896-1900), iv. 125; Purchas (1613), *Pilgrimage* (1614), 311.]

Ispaghul, ishabgul [19C. H/P. *asp,* 'a horse' + *gol,* 'ear'.] The plantain *Plantago ovata,* native to India and Persia, the seeds of which are used medicinally to improve digestion. (The name alludes to the shape of the leaves or the seeds.) [*OED;* Fleming in *Asiatick Researches* (1810), xi. 174.]

Istana, astanah [19C. S. *ā-sthāna.*] 'place, assembly'. In Malaysia the Malay ruler's palace. [Newbold, *Pol. & Statist. Acct. Straits of Malacca* (1839).]

Istoop [19C. Corr. fr. Pg. *estopa.*] Oakum; an

Indian marine term. [YB; Roebuck, *An English and Hindoostanee Naval Dict.* (1811).]

Istubbul [19C. H/Ar. *istabl.*] 'stable, manger'. (This is apparently not a corr. of the English word, but is derived from the Arabic.) [YB.]

Ixora [19C. fr. *Iswara,* 'Hindu God' = S. *īsvara,* 'Lord, master'.] A genus, *Rubiaceae,* of so many species and varieties of evergreen flowering shrubs and small trees in India bearing white to brightly-coloured flowers. The commonest is *Ixora coccinea* or *Thesaurus zeylanicus,* known as the Scarlet Ixora or Flame Tree of the Woods; *Bakora* in Marathi, *Vedehi* in Tamil, and *Rat Mal* in Sinhalese. Various parts of the shrubs are used medicinally by the country people, and are held sacred to **Shiva** and **Vishnu,** while the flowers are offered to the god Ixora (*Iswara*). [*OED;* Cowen, *Flowering Trees & Shrubs of India* (1965); *Bot, Reg.* (1816), 11. 154.]

Izzat, izzut [19C. H. *izzat,* Ar. *izzah,* 'glory'.] Honour, reputation, credit, prestige. [*OED;* Letter, 26 Feb. in Edwardes and Merivale, *Life of Sir H. Lawrence* (1857).]

J

Jacaranda [18C. Tupi-guarani, *jacarandā*.] The exotic blue-flowering *Jacaranda acutiflora*, *–ovalifolia*, *–filicifolia*, one of the loveliest flowering trees in India, was introduced from Brazil by the Portuguese and yields a fragrant 'rose-wood' and a drug for catarrh of the bladder. [*OED;* Chambers' *Cyclopedia Suppl.* (1753).]

Jack [19C.] Short for *Jack-***Sepoy.** 'In former days a familiar style for the native soldier; kindly rather than otherwise.' [YB.] Cf. 'Tommy Atkins' (1st World War). [YB; Arnold, *Oakfield* (1854), ii. 66.]

Jack (-fruit), jak [16C. M. *chakka;* Pg. *jaca;* S. *chakra,* 'round'.] The oblong-shaped fruit of a large evergreen tree, *Autocarpus integrifolia* or *heterophyllos,* bears the largest edible fruit in the world. A single fruit perhaps weighing as much as 100 lbs. grows from the trunk or, in a very old tree, from the root. Inside the fruit are many small cavities, each containing one seed surrounded by a soft, yellowish pulp. Sticky white juice from young shoots provides bird-lime; the fruit juice gives a sort of rubber; the leaves are used medicinally for wounds. The heart-wood is good for furniture and building; and produces a yellow dye. Nambudhri Brahmins are said to produce sacred fire from the friction of the branches. [*OED* & YB; Cowen, *Flowering Trees,* etc. (1965); Linschoten, *Discours of Voyages* (E. tr. 1598).]

Jackal [17C. Pg. *chacal;* Turk. *chakāl;* P. *shaghāl;* cogn. with S. *s'rgāla*.] An animal related to the dog, about the size of a fox. The *Canis aureus* 'takes the place of the fox as the object of hunting 'meets' in India; the indigenous fox being too small for sport'. [YB.] (H. *gīdar,* 'the greedy one'.) [*OED;* Sir Edwin Sandys, *Relation of the State of Religion.* (1615), 205.]

Jack-Snipe [19C.] Alias the Fantail Snipe, *Gallinago gallinago gallinago.* Distributed throughout India, Pakistan, Bangladesh, Sri Lanka and Burma. (Hindi name, *Chāhā.*) [*OED* & YB; Jerdon, *Birds of India* (1862-4).]

Jaconet, jaconot,etc. [18C. Corr. of H. *jaganāthī* (*purī*).] the **Juggernaut** town in Orissa. A cotton fabric originally from Jaganathpuri, afterwards from elsewhere in India and England. Now it denotes 'a plain cotton cloth, lighter than shirting and heavier than a mull'.

[*OED; Publ. Advertiser* (1769), 14 Nov. 3/3. 260.]

Jadoo [19C. H/P. *jādū,* 'enchantment'; S. *yātu.*] 'conjuring, magic, hocus-pocus.' Also *jadoo-wallah* (1890), a Hindu conjuror or magician and *jadooghar,* a Masonic Lodge. [*OED* & YB; Hockley, *Pandurang Hari* (1826; ed. 1873), i. 127; Kipling, *Plain Tales from the Hills* (1888), 126.]

Jaffery, jaffry [Poss. corr. of Ar. *zafirat,* 'a braided lock of hair'.] Lattice-work, usually of bamboo. [YB; *Trans. Agri. Hort. Soc. Ind.* (1832), ii. 202.]

Jagati, gagati [19C. S. *gagatī.*] A vedic metre of 12 syllables. [*OED.*] See **Gayatri** and **Trishtup.** [*Penny Cycl.* (1843), xxvi. 177/1.]

Jaggery [16C. Indo-Pg. *jag(a)ra;* Kan. *sharkare,* fr. S. *sarkarā,* 'sugar'.] Coarse, brown, sometimes almost black sugar made from the sap of various palms, e.g. the wild-date tree, the palmyra, the caryota and the coco-palm. See **Sugar.** Also *jaggery-palm, caryota urens* (H. kitul), 1859. [*OED* & YB; Caesar Frederike (*c.* 1567), in Hakl. ii. 344; Hakluyt, *Voy.* (1598), II. i. 252.]

Jaghir, jagheer, jaghire [16C. H/P. *jāgīr* fr. *jā,* 'place' + *gīr,* 'holding or holder'.] A hereditary assignment of land and of its rent as annuity from the king's or government's share of the produce of a district to a person or body empowered to administer it. Also, the district so assigned. [*OED* & YB.] See **Surinjaum** (*Saranjām*). [*Early Travels in India* (1583-1619; ed. 1921).]

Jaghirdar, jagheerdar [17C. H. *jāghīrdār.*] The holder of a **Jaghir.** [*Eng. Fact. in India,* (1618-69; ed. 1906-27); Burke, 'sp. against Warren Hastings', *Wks.* (1794), xv. 385.]

Jai-Hind! [20C. H. *jai,* 'victory(to)' + *Hind,* 'India'.] Long live India! Victory to India! A patriotic salutation at meetings and among individuals during the Indian Freedom Movement and after independence. [*OED;* A. Moorhead, *Rage of Vulture* (1948), v. 76.]

Jail-khana [19C. E. 'jail' + H. *khana,* 'house'.] 'A hybrid word for a gaol, commonly used in the Bengal presidency.' [YB.] See **Choky** (**Chauki**). [YB.]

Jain, Jaina (sb. + adj) [19C. H. S. *jainas,* fr. *jinas,* 'saint, Buddha'; lit. 'over-comer', fr. *ji,* 'overcome'.] A member of a non-Brahminical sect established about the 6C. BC; a follower of

Mahavira (Great Hero), the last **Thirthankar,** 'Founder of the Path'. The Jains are generally merchants, often of enormous wealth. Also Jainism (1858) and Jainist (1816). [*OED* & YB.] *See* **Digambar.** [Colebrooke, in *Asiatic Res.* (1805), v. 483.]

Jaipur [19C.] Former Indian State and capital city. Now capital of Rajasthan. *Jaipuri* = the dialect of this former state. Also *attrib.,* eg. *Jaipur-enamel.* [*OED;* Kipling, *Macm. Mag.* Dec. 1889, 152/1.]

Jajmani system [19C. H. *jajman;* S. *yajamāna,* pres. part of *yajati,* 'he sacrifices'.] A system of village organization under which *jajmans* (landowners, Brahmins, etc.), are served by *jajmani* families (cultivation, barbering, rituals, etc.) in exchange for protection and regular payment, usually in kind. [Hawkins, *CIWIE;* Wilson, *Glossary* (1855).]

Jali [19C. H. *jal;* S. *jāla,* 'a net'.] Pierced marble screen. *See* **Jarokha.** [Whitworth, *Anglo-Indian Dict.* (1885).]

Jalebote, jalibot, jolywat [18C.] A marine corruption of 'jolly-boat'. *See* **Gallevat** [*OED* & YB; Roebuck, *Naval Dict.* (1811).]

Jam¹ [19C. Poss. Sindhi *Jām.*] A title once borne by certain chiefs in Kutch, Kathiawar and on the lower Indus (Sind). *The Jam Sahib,* ruler of Nawanagar. [*OED* & YB; G. Smith, *Life J. Wilson* (1843).]

Jam,² geme [17C. Ar. *zām.*] A nautical measure, 12 nautical miles. Also, a nautical watch. *See* **Puhur.** [YB; Foster, *Letters* (1614; ed. 1896-1900), ii. 177.]

Jama(h), jamma [18C. H/P. *jāmah,* a piece of clothing.] A long cotton gown, tied round the middle with a sash worn by Hindus. *See* **Pyjama.** [*OED* &YB; *Trial Thomas Fowke* (1776), 1.]

Jamadar, jamdar *See* **Jemadar.**

Jaman, jambhool, jamun, jamoon [19C. H. *jāman, jāmun.*] The Java Plum Tree *Eugenia jambolana,* also called the Indian All-spice. A tall, handsome evergreen tree of India, Burma, Sri Lanka and Malaysia, producing an astringent purple-black fruit used in tarts and puddings. 'Sometimes confounded with the Rose-apple or **Jambo,** *Eugenia Jambos.*' [*OED.*] Sacred to **Krishna** and **Ganesh,** hence planted near Hindu temples. Buddhists also venerate this tree. Vinegar is made from the ripe fruit, and the bark is used for tanning, dyeing and dysentery-medicine. [*OED* & YB; Leyden and Erskine, tr., *Mem. Baber* (1826), 325.]

Jamat, jamiat [19C. H. *jamāt.*] Meeting, society, community; a caste of persons who may **Interdine.** [Whitworth, *Anglo-Indian Dict.* (1885).]

Jambhool M. *jambhūl* = **Jaman.**

Jambo, jambos, jambu, jumboo, etc. [16C. H/S. *jambū.*] The Rose-Apple (tree), *Syzigium* or *Eugenia jambos;* its shiny, pinkish fruit containing sweet white pulp, sometimes erroneously applied to the guava (H. *amrūd*). [*OED* & YB.] *Also* **Jamrosade** 1866 = Rose-apple + rose + ade. [Linschoten, *Discours of Voyages* (E. tr. 1598).]

Jamdani [19C. H/P. *jāmahdānī,* lit. 'a box for holding a suit'.] The *jamdānī* was a loom-figured muslin, woven with spots or flowers, 'the most expensive productions of the Dacca looms'. [YB & *OED;* Taylor, *A Descriptive and Historical Account of the Cotton Manufacture of Dacca in Bengal* (1851).]

Jampan, jompon [18C. Beng. *jhāmpān;* H. *jhappān.*] 'A kind of sedan, or portable chair used by the ladies at the Hill Sanitaria of upper India. It is carried by two pairs of men who are called Jomponnies.' Jampan(n)ee (1859). [*OED* & YB; G. Forster, *Journey from Bengal to England* (1808), ii. 3.]

Jamrosade [19C. App. from **Jambu** + rose + ade.] The fruit of the *Eugenia jambos,* the Rose Apple. [*OED; Treas. Bot.* (1866), 635/1.]

Jamwar [17C. H/P. *jāmahwār,* 'sufficient for a dress'.] A kind of **Chintz;** a flowered sheet or shawl. [*OED* & YB; *Eng. Fact. in India* (1618-1635; ed. 1906-27).]

Janai *See* **Juneo.**

Janapa, -um [19C. Tam. *janapa.*] The *Crotolaria juncea,* **Sunn** hemp, cultivated in most parts of India for its fibre. [*OED; Illustr. Catal Gt. Exhib.* (1851), iv. 882/3.]

Jancada [19C. M. *changādam,* Tulu, *jungāla,* 'a raft'.] 'Responsible guides in the **Nair** country who escorted travellers from one inhabited place to another, guaranteeing their security with their lives, like the **Bhats** in Gujarat.' [YB.] Cf. **Jangada** and **Jangar.** [Hak. Soc. (1807), i. 339; Burton, *Goa and the Blue Mountains* (1851), 198.]

Jangada [16C. Pg. *jangada;* M. *changādam;* S. *samghāta,* 'union, joinery, fitting and joining together'.] A log-raft. In Tulu *jangāla,* 'raft'. Junction of two boats; a ferry-boat. Taken by the Portugese to S. America where it was chiefly used. [*OED* & YB; Philips, tr., *Linschoten's Voy.* (1472; 1598).]

Jangar [19C.] *See* **Jangada.** A raft of logs joined

together and furnished with a lateen sail. [*OED* & *YB*; Wellington, *Suppl. Desp.* (1800; ed. 1858), 1. 519.] See **Catamaran**.

Janwar [19C. H/Ar. *jānwar*, 'animal', 'fauna'.] [Edmund Candler, *Siri Ram Revolutionist*, (1912), 180; Wilson, *Gloss.*, 1855.]

Jargon, jargoon, zircon [18C. Pg. *zarcão*, Ar. *zarcūn*, 'zircon'.] ... smoky ... of the mineral Zircon found in Si... (1...

Jarok ... win...

Jarool ... or ... *regim*... addit... Amon... uses:... narcoti... [*OED* & ... 318.]

Jasoos [19... Colebroo... 1884), i. ...

Jat,¹ **jati** [19... Also *jati*, a... (1855).]

Jat,² **Jaut, Ju**... tribe settled ... North-West ... female *Jat*. [... (1622-3).]

Jataka [19C. S. *jātaka*, 'nativity', fr. *jāta*, p. ple. of *jan*, 'to produce'.] A story of one or other of Buddha's previous births, preceding **Gautama**; also the **Pali** collection of these stories. [*OED*; *Asiatic Researches* (1828), xvi. 427.]

Jatha [20C. H/Punj. *jathā*.] An armed (Sikh) band or procession. [*OED*; *Glasgow Herald*, 9 Sept. 1922.] See next.

Jathedar [20C. H/Punj. *jathā*, 'procession of protest' + *dar*, agent.] A Sikh leader who takes out a procession of religious or political protest.

Jati [19C. S. *jati*.] An Indian musical term. One of five sub-divisions of the seven **Talas**. [*OED*; Day, *Mus. and Mus. Instruments S. India* (1891), iii. 36.] See **Rag(a)**.

Jatra [19C. H. *jatra*; S. *yatrā*; fr. *ya*; 'to travel'.] Pilgrimage; fair. Also *jatri*, a pilgrim. [Whitworth, *Anglo-Indian Dict.* (1885).]

Jaun [19C. Beng. *yān*; S. *yāna*, tr. *ya*, 'go'.] (In Calcutta) formerly a small palankin-carriage, commonly used by businessmen in going to

and from their places of business. See **Jampan**. (The *Jaun-bazaar* was a wellknown low quarter in Calcutta. [*YB* & *OED*; Parker, *Bole-Ponjis* (1836), ii. 215.]

Ja... **Plum(tree)** See **Jaman**.

... **Radish** [19C.] A variety of radish, *Rapha- caudatus*, of which the pods are eaten, ... the roots; cultivated in Western India, ... the name of *mogra*. [*YB*; Baden Powell, ... *ab Products* (1872), i. 260.]

...**juwan** [19C. H. *jawān*.] 'young man', ... soldier in the Indian Army. [*OED*.] See ... and **Sainik**. [Taylor, *Confessions of a* ... 1839), I. i. 6.]

...**awab** [19C. H/Ar. *jawāb*, 'reply'.] 'In ... has besides this ordinary meaning, ... dismissal. And in Anglo-Indian collo- ... esp. used for a lady's refusal, of an ... the verb passive 'to be *jawaub'd*'. ... *Sport Mag.* (1830; ed. 1873), i. ... anything planted, erected or placed ... metrical double, e.g. identical wings ... pictures on opposite walls or in ..., etc. [*YB*; Further, *Monumental* ... *W.*, 64; Whitworth, *Anglo-Indian* ... See **Respondentia**.

...*anthi*, 'blue throat'.] The name, ...*cias bengalensis*, given by ... the Nilkanth or 'blue-throat' ... over India. [*YB*; Robinson, *In My Indian Garden* (1878), 3. ed.]

Jeera [H. *jīra*.] Cum(m)in: a plant *Cuminum cyminum* cultivated for its aromatic seed. [G. *Kümmel*.] [Hawkins, *CIWIE* (1984).]

Jeetul [17C. H. *jītal*.] A very old Indian copper coin, now entirely obsolete. [*YB*; Fryer, *New Acct.* (1672-81; ed. 1909).]

Jelabi, jelaubee [19C. H. *jalebī*, corr. of Ar. *zalābiya*.] Ring-shaped, saffron-coloured sweetmeat, made of sugar, ghee and flour, melted and trickled into a pan. [*YB*; Chevers, *Med. Jurisp.* (1870), 178.]

Jelly [19C. Tel. *zalli*, Tam. *shalli*, 'bits & pieces'.] In S. India this was the Anglo-Indian word for vitrified brick refuse used for metalling roads. See **Kunkur** (*kankar*). [*YB*; Nelson, *Man. of Madura.* (1868), v. 53.]

Jemadar, jemautdar, jamadar [17C. H/Ar./P. *jama'dar*, (*jama'*, 'collection (of men)' + *dar*, 'holder'.)] (1) A native officer in a sepoy regiment ranking next below a **Subahdar**. [*OED* & *YB*; Orme, *Hist. of the Military Transactions* etc. (1763).] (2) A junior officer (under the **Dārogha**) of police, customs and other civil departments. [*OED* & *YB*.]

(3) Honorific title of the head servant of a large domestic establishment, or the title often used by other servants for the water-carrier or **Bheestie.** [YB; *The Diaries of Streynsham Master* (1675-80; ed. 1911).] (4) The head of a staff of **Peons.** [YB; Heber, *Narr. Journey through Upper Provinces of India.* (1844), i. 65.]

Jenny-rickshaw, jinrickshaw [19C. Japanese (corr. of *jin-riki-sha,* fr. *jin,* 'man' + *riki,* 'strength' + *sha,* 'vehicle'.)] This conveyance was introduced into India and used at first at Simla and other hill-stations. *See* **Ricksha(w), Trishaw.** [*OED* & YB; Lady Dufferin, *Viceregal Life* (1890), 89.]

Jerrypuranawallah [19C. H. *dzeri,* 'gold (thread)' + *purāna,* 'old' + *wala,* 'agent'.] Dealer in old bottles and newspapers. Originally he bought old saris for their gold thread. *See* **Kabaddiwala.** [Hawkins, *CIWIE.*]

Jezail, juzail [19C. H/P. *jazāil.*] Long, heavy, Afghan musket, generally fired with a forked rest. Hence *jezāilchī,* one armed with a *jezāil,* a matchlockman (1862). [*OED* & YB; Gen. A Abbot, *Jrnl. Afghan War* (1838-42).]

Jezia *See* **Jizya.**

Jhamp, jhaump [19C. H. *jhānp;* Mar. *jhānpa.*] Screen of bamboo matting, used as a shutter or a door. [YB.]

Jharan [19C. H. *jhāran.*] A duster. [Wilson, *Gloss.* (1855).]

Jharu [19C. H. *jhāru.*] A broom. [Wilson, *Gloss.* (1855).]

Jhatka (–meat) [H. *jhatka.*] Sudden death, when the animal is killed with one stroke, in contrast to *halal*-meat of Muslims and Jews. Cf. **Halal.**

Jheel, jeel [18C. H. *jhīl.*] A pool or small stagnant lake left after inundation; a mere, lagoon or swamp. *See also* **Bheel.**[1] [*OED* & YB; Wheeler (1757), *Early Records* (ed. 1878), 250.]

Jhompri [19C. H. *jhōnpri.*] Hut or hovel. [Wilson, *Gloss.* (1855).]

Jhoom, joom [19C. Arak./Beng. *jhūm.*] System of cultivation in hill forests of India under which a tract is cleared by fire, cultivated for one or two years and then abandoned for another tract. *See* **Coomry.** [*OED* & YB; Buchanan,*Mysore*(1807),ii.177.]*See***Taungya.**

Jhoota [19C. H. *jhūtā.*] Uneatable (leavings of food); defiled, polluted. [Wilson, *Gloss.* (1855).]

Jhora [19C. Beng. *jhora.*] Bed of a seasonal torrent; **Nullah.** [Hawkins, *CIWIE.*]

Jhow, jow [19C. H. *jhāū,* fr. S. *jhāwuka.*] Various species of the scrubby tamarisk (e.g. *Tamarix indica*) in Indian rivers and marshes, used for rough basket-making and the like. [*OED* & YB; Buchanan-Hamilton, *Eastern India* (ed. 1809; 1838), iii. 597; D. Johnson, *Ind. Field Sports* (1827), 274.]

Jhuggy [19C.] A slum colony. *Jhuggy-jhonpris;* dwellers in a *jhuggy.* [Hawkins, *CIWIE.*]

Jhula, joola [19C. H. *jhūlā,* 'a swing'.] Himalayan suspension bridge. [*OED* & YB; *Asiat Res.* (1812), xi. 475.]

Ji [19C. H. *–ji;* S. *jaya,* 'conquering'.] Respectful suffix, e.g. *swami-ji; mata-ji; guru-ji; babu-ji; sahib-ji; Nehru-ji,* etc. Also termination of Parsi names, e.g., *Jamsetji, Cawasji.* [Whitworth, *Anglo-Indian Dict.* (1885).]

Ji! [19C.] *See* prec. Yes! Yes Sir! [Wilson, *Gloss.* (1855).]

Jibbah *See* **Jubbah.**

Jihad, jehad, jehaud [19C. H. fr. *jihād,* 'an effort, a striving'.] Holy war of the Muslims against the infidels (**Kafirs**), inculcated as a duty by the Koran and Islamic traditions. [*OED* & YB; M. Wilks, *Sk. S. India* (2nd ed. 1869), ii. xlviii. 381.]

Jildi, jildy, jildo, jillo [19C. H. *jaldī,* 'quickness'.] Get a move on! Quick! Look sharp! At the double! Also as adv. 'on the jildi'. Also 'Get a jildi on'; and 'Do a jildi move' = 'To retreat hastily'. Anglo-Indian military slang. [*OED;* Kipling, *Barrack-Room Ballads* (1892).]

Jillmill [19C. Etym. obscure but poss. fr. H. *jhilmilā,* 'sparkling', acc. to Platts. But it may be an echoic word from the rattle of the shutters.] Venetian blind or shutter. *See* **Chick.** [*OED;* Mrs Meer Hassan Ali, *Observations* etc. (1832), i. 306.]

Jina, Gina [19C. S. *jina.*] Jainism: Title given to Mahavira or to any of the 24 **Tirthankars.** Buddhism: any one of the five Dhyani Buddhas; a sculpture of such a saint. *See* **Jain, Jaina.** [*OED; Asiatick Res.* (1807), ix. 303.]

Jinriksha *See* **Jenny Rickshaw.**

Jirga, jeerga(h) [19C. Pushtu. *jirgah.*] Assembly of Pathan or Baluchi tribal headmen. [*OED;* F. Sale, *Jrnl. Disasters Afghanistan* (1843), xii.]

Jiva [19C. S. *jīva.*] Hinduism & Jainism: 'Life, the vital principle; the soul, the self.' [*OED; Asiatick Res.* (1807), ix. 290.]

Jiwan [20C. S. *jīvana,* 'a son'.] An Indian youth. *See* **Jawan.** [*OED;* Kipling, *New Army* (1914), 29.]

Jizya, jezia [17C. H./Ar. *jizya.*] Poll-tax which Muslim law imposed on non-Muslims; espec.

that imposed by the Mughal emperors in India. [*OED* & *YB*; *The Diaries of Streynsham Master* (1675-80).]

Jnana [19C. S. *jnāna*, fr. *jna*, 'to know'.] Hinduism: Spiritual knowledge, as the way to salvation. [*OED*; *Trans. R. Asiatic Soc.* (1827), i. 576.]

Jnani [19C. S. fr. prec.] A knowledgeable person; an expert; a worshipper of *jnānamārga*, the path to spiritual salvation. *See* **Gian.** [*OED*; Balfour, *Cycl. India*, 3rd ed. (1885), II. 442/2.]

Jodhpur(s) [19C.] Jodhpur: district and city of Rajasthan, formerly the native state of Rajputana. (1) A form of riding-breeches, tight from knee to ankle. [*OED*; G. W. Steevens, *In India* (1899), iv. 28.] (2) –*pyjamas*: Indian trousers cut loosely at the top but close fitting below the knee. Also *jods*, coll. abbr. of *jodhpurs*. *Jodhpuri* = citizen of, or pertaining to *Jodhpur*. [*OED*; E. M. Forster, *Hill of Devi* (1953), (Let. 1 Jan. 1913).] (3) –*jacket*: short close fitting jacket with tight collar buttoned at the neck.

Jogi, jogee *See* **Yogi.**

Johar, jouhar, joar [19C. H. *jauhar*, fr. S. *jatugriha*, 'a house built of combustible materials'.] Ritual mass suicide by immolation of (Rajput) women, at times of military defeat of their men, to avoid being dishonoured by the victors. [*OED*.] *See* **Suttee.** [C. James, *New Milit. Dict.* (1802).]

John Company [18C.] Personification of the East India Company, frequently abridged to 'Company'. Possible connection with (Shah) Jehan in the title *Kumpani Jehan*, to flatter and exalt the E.I.C., 'which in English mouths became 'John Company'. Or fr. Dutch *Jan Kompanie*, the Indian name of the Dutch East Indian Company and Government. *See* **Company.** [Partridge and *OED*; Andreus Sparrmann, *Travels*, etc. (1784), 347; Haklyut, *Voy.* (1553; 1807), (Note) 265.]

Johukum [20C. H. *jo.* 'affirmative + *hukm*, 'the correct thing'.] 'A yes-man'. [Hawkins, *CIWIE*.]

Joint-Family [19C.] Extended Hindu family, including married children. Attrib. 'Joint-family affairs', etc. [*OED*; W.K. Sullivan, *Encycl, Brit.* (1876), V. 779/2.]

Jolar, jolah [19C. H. *jholāh*.] Haversack. Reg. Army usage in India. [Partridge, *Dict. of Slang* etc. (1979).]

Jonga [20C.] Portmanteau-word, *jeep* + *tonga* (two-wheeled-vehicle). A jeep-like motor vehicle. [Hawkins, *CIWIE*.]

Jool, jhool [19C. H. *jhūl*.] 'Body clothing of a

horse, elephant, or other domesticated animal; often a quilt used as such. In colloquial use all over India.' [YB.] (Platts derives it from *jhūlnā*, 'to dangle'). [*OED*; Tod, *Annals*, etc. (1829).]

Joshi [19C. H. fr. S. *jyotisha*, astrologer, astronomer.] A Brahmin who prepares the calendar, casts nativities and announces propitious times for events. Also a painter of idols and pictures of the gods. [Whitworth, *Anglo-Indian Dict.* (1885).]

Jotedar [H. *jōtidar*.] Landlord, a small landowner. [Whitworth, *Anglo-Indian Dict.* (1885).]

Jowar, jowaur, jowari, jawari [17C. H. *jawār(i)*.] The tall, extensively cultivated millet of India, *Sorghum vulgare*. The reedy stems are 8 to 12 feet high. [*OED* & YB; *English Fact. in India* (1618-19; ed. Foster 1906-27).]

Jowaula Mookhee [16C. H. *jwālā-mūkhī*, 'flame-mouthed'.] 'a generic name for quasi volcanic phenomena'. [YB.] Esp. applied to the *Devī* shrine in the Kangra district where the jets of gas are kept constantly burning. [YB; Terry in *Early Travels* (1583-1619).]

Joy [19C. Anglo-Indian, fr. Pg. *joia*.] A jewel or ornament. [*OED*; *Asiatic Ann. Reg. Chron.* (1800), 17/1; Maria Graham, *Jrnl. Resid. India* (1809), 3.]

Jubbah, jibbah [16C. H/Ar. *jubbah*.] A cotton outer garment of Parsis and Muslims, consisting of a long coat, open in front, with long sleeves. [*OED*.] *See* **Kurta.** [Hall, *Chron. Hen.* (1548), viii. 83. a.]

Jubo [20C. Beng. *jūbo*, 'youth'.] [Hawkins, *CIWIE*.]

Jubtee, juptee [19C. Corr. forms of Ar. *zabti*, lit. 'keeping, guarding'. (Mar. *japtū*.)] 'Produce of lands sequestered by the state, an item of revenue' [Wilson.] *See* **Zubt.** 'In Gujarat the title given to the keepers of the **Pargana** revenue records, who have held the office as a hereditary right.' [Wilson.] [YB; Drummond, *Illustrations* etc. (1808).]

Jugal bandhi [20C. H. *jugalbandhi*, 'yoked together'.] Indian music: A duet of musical instruments. [Hawkins, *CIWIE*.]

Jugboolak [19C.] Marine Hindi for *jack-block* [YB; Roebuck, *Naval Dict.* (1811).]

Jugger, –ar, –ur [19C. H. *Jāggār*.] Common Indian falcon, *Falco jugger*, or *biarmicus*, alias the *Laggar Falcon*, found in India from about 2500 ft. in the Himalayas; rare in Assam & S. India. *See* **Laggar.** [*OED*; Jerdon, *Birds of India* (1862).]

Juggernaut, Juggurnaut, Jagganath [17C. Corr. of H. *jagannāth*; fr. S. *jagannātha* fr. *jagat*, 'world' + *nātha*, 'lord', 'protector' = 'Master of the World'.] (1) Hinduism. A title of **Krishna**, the eighth avatar of **Vishnu**; espec. the idol of this deity at *Purī* in Orissa, annually dragged on an enormous chariot or *rath* under whose wheels devotees were said to have thrown themselves, to be crushed to death in an ecstasy of devotional abandonment. The first European account is by Friar Odoric, *c* 1321. [*OED* & YB; Yule, *Cathay and the Way Thither* (1868), 28; Sir. T. Roe, *Embassy*, etc. (1616-19).] (2) Hence, an object or force which relentlessly crushes anything in its path, or 'an institution or organization to which persons blindly devote themselves or are ruthlessely sacrificed'. [*OED*; J. W. Warter, *Last Old Squires* (1854), iv. 32.] (3) A heavy lorry or similar vehicle. [*OED*; Thackeray, *Second Funeral of Napoleon* (1841), iii. 58.]

Jujube (The Indian) See **Ber** (*Zizyphus jujuba*).

Julibdar [17C. H/P. *jilaudār*, (fr. *jilau*.)] 'the string attached to the bridle by which a horse is led; the servant, who leads a horse, also called *janībahdār*.' [YB; Fryer, *New Acct.* etc. (1672-81).]

Juma(h) [19C. H./Ar. *juma*.] Muslim congregational prayers (**Namaz**) in the mosque (**masjid**) on Fridays. [Whitworth, *Anglo-Indian Dict.* (1885); Wilson, *Gloss.* (1855).]

Jumbeea [19C. H/Ar. *janbiya*, prob. fr. *janb*, 'the side'.] A kind of dagger, slightly curved, worn in the girdle, so as to be drawn across the body. [YB; *Ain-i-Akbari*, E. tr. Blochman (1873), i. 110; Egerton, *Handbk. of Indian Arms* (1880).]

Jumdud [19C. H. *jamdad, jamdhar*, perh. fr. S. *yama-dhara*, 'death-bearer'.] 'A kind of dagger, broad at the base and slightly curved; the hilt with a cross grip like that of the *katār*.' See **Kuttaur**. [YB; Forbes, *Or. Mem.* (1813).]

Jumma(h), jama [18C. H. *jama*, fr. Ar. *jama'*, 'total, aggregate, collection, amount, account'.] During British rule, the total land revenue assessment of an estate or division of country. [*OED* & YB; Verelst, *View of Bengal* (1772), 214.]

Jummabundi, –ee [18C. H/Ar. *jama'bundī* (*jama* + *bundī*, 'a tie, band', fr. S *bandh* 'bind').] The settlement of the revenue; the document recording this settlement. [*OED* & YB; Verelst, *View of Bengal* (1772), 214.]

Juneo, janeo, janiwara [19C. S. *yajnopavita* (*yajna*, 'a devotional act' + *upavita*, investiture).] The sacred **Thread** of the Brahmins, Kshatriyas and Vaishyas. See **Jamai**. [Abbé

Dubois, *Desc. of the Character, Manners and Customs of the People of India* (1817).]

Jungle, jungal, jingle [18C. H./Mar. *jangal*, 'desert, waste-land, forest'; S. *jangala*, 'dry, dry ground, desert'.] (1) Orig. waste ground; land overgrown with tangled vegetation. [Halhed, *Gentoo Code* (1776), xiii. 190.] (2) Dwelling place of wild beasts [Burke, sp. India Bill (1783), *Wks*. iv. 24.] (3) Fig. a tangled mass. [Carlyle, *Latter Day Pamphlets* (1850), III.] (4) The tropical rain-forest. Comb: Jungle-bear (*Prochilus labianus*); –cat, *Felis chaus*, the Marsh Lynx (1895); –cock; –fever (1808); –fowl, *Gallus ferrugineus* (1800); –hog (1845); –rice, *Panicum colonum* (1886); –wood (*Terminali cariacea*) (1880); –market, the Stock Exchange (1900), –ox, the *Gayal, Bibos sylhetanus* (1824); –sheep (*Kemas hypocrinus*). Also: *Jungle*-bashing (1963); –fever, (1808); –green (1946); –juice (1945); blackboard–*jungle* (1954); asphalt–*jungle* (1906); concrete–*jungle* (1969). [*OED* & YB.]

Junglo [19C. Guj. *janglo*.] 'This term was used [at the beginning of the 19th century by the less polite, to distinguish Europeans]; 'wild men of the woods', that is, 'who did not understand Guzerati!'. [YB; Drummond, *Illustrations* etc. (1808).]

Jungly, Jungli [19C. adj. & sb. See prec.] Abounding in *jungle*; inhabiting the *jungle* (1860); an inhabitant of the *jungle* (1920); uncouth, unrefined. Also, *Jungled* (1842). [Wellington, *Guru Desp.* (Let. to Lt. Col. Close, 22 May 1800).]

Junkameer, juncaneer [17C. M. *chungakāran*, fr. *chungam*, 'customs'.] 'A collector of customs.' See **Junkeon**. [YB; *Fort St. George Notes and Extracts* (1670-81), iii. 39.]

Junkeon [17C. See prec. fr. M. *chungam*.] Toll or customs duties. [YB; Bruton's 'Narrative' in Hakluyt (1638), v. 53.]

Juribasso [17C. Mal. *juru*, 'master' + *bahāsa*, 'speech' (S. *bhāshā*).] An intrepreter. See **Dubash** and **Topass**. [YB; Capt. Saris in Purchas, *Pilgrimage* (1614), 378; Cocks' *Diary* (1615-22), I. 33.]

Jute [18C. Beng. *jhuto*; S. *jūta*, var. of *jatā*, 'braid of hair'.] Fibre from the bark of Indian trees (genus *Corchorus*) used for canvas, gunny bags, cordage, etc. Also, the tree itself. [*OED* & YB; 22 Sept. 1746, Log of Ship 'Wake', quoted by Col. R.C. Temple in *Indian Antiq.* (1901).]

Jutka [19C. H. *jhatkā*, 'swift'.] 'The native cab of Madras, and of *mofussil* towns in that

Presidency; a conveyance only to be characterised by the epithet *ramshackle*.... It consists of a sort of box with venetian windows on two wheels and drawn by a miserable pony. It is entered by a door at the back.' [YB & *OED*.] *See* **Cranchee, Shigram** and **Tonga**. [YB.]

Jyedad, jaidad [19C. H/P. *jāidād*, fr. *jā*, 'place' + *dād*, 'that gives'.] Territory assigned for the support of troops. [YB; Malcolm, *Central India* (1823), i. 223.]

Jyshe [18C. Ar. *jaish*, 'an army, a legion'.] This term was applied by Tippoo to his regular infantry, the body of which was called the *Jaish Kachari* (*Cutcherry*). **Cutcherry** was used by Tippoo in a special sense for a division or a large brigade. [YB; Hussein Ali Khan Kermani (1864), *Hist. of Tipu Sultan* (1782), 32.]

K

Kabab *See* Kebab; Cabob.

Kabad(d)i [20C. Tam. *kabāddi*.] A vigorous chasing game between two teams of nine, popular in India and Pakistan. [*OED*; Ryburn, *School Organisation* (1935), 278-80.]

Kabaddi-wallah [20C.] Poss. corr. of Kebuli-or Kabuli-wallah. An itinerant (orig. from Kabul?) buyer of old bottles, newspapers, etc. = Jerrypurana-Wallah. [Hawkins, *CIWIE*.]

Kabaragoya [17C. (Etym. unknown).] A water-lizard or monitor of S. Asia and elsewhere, sometimes achieving a length of seven feet, the *Varanus salvator*. [*OED*; R. Knox, *Ceylon* (1681), I. vii. 30.]

Kabay(a), kebaya, cabie [16C. P/Ar. *kabāy*; Pg. *cabaia*, Mal. *kabaya*.] A light, loose tunic commonly worn in the East; now spec. worn by Malay women 'and by Europeans in *dishabille*' [*OED* & *YB*; Fitch in Hakluyt (1585; 1810), II. 386.]

Kabir-Panthi [16C. H. *Kabīrpanthi*, fr. *Kabīr* (1440-1518), Hindu mystic poet, *panthī*, 'follower'.] A member of a reform sect of India with doctrines derived from Kabir's teachings of *Sahaja Yoga*, 'Simple Union' of Hinduism and Islam. [Whitworth, *Anglo-Indian Dict.* (1885).]

Kachnar, cutchnar [19C. H. *kachnār*; S. *kanchanāra* (*kānchana*), 'gold'.] The variegated Mountain Ebony, *Bauhinia variegata*, with magenta, mauve, pink or white flowers. The tree yields an oil, the seeds a gum; the leaves are used for wrapping Bidis, and the bark for tanning. [Cowen] [YB; Yule, *Mission to Ava.* (1855), 95; Cowen, *Flowering Trees & Shrubs in India* (1965).]

Kadamba [20C. Tam./M. *katampu*.] An Indian shade tree, *Anthocephalus cadamba*, having a hard yellowish wood, with clusters of globular flowers. Also the wood of the *kadamba*. [Webster, *3rd New Intern. Dict.* (1976).]

Kadaya-gum [20C. H. *karayal*, 'resin'.] Sterculia gum, similar to tragacanth. [Webster, *3rd New Intern. Dict.*]

Kadir *See* Khadar.

Kafila *See* Cafila.

Kafir, caffer, caffre, coffree [16C. Ar. *kafīr*, 'infidel', unbeliever'.] A giaour. Also applied to the fair, non-Muslim tribes of the Hindu Kush; sometimes specified as the *Siah-posh* or 'black-robed' kafirs. Also a native of Kafiristan, a land between the Oxus and the Indus.

[*OED* & *YB*; Litchfield's *Castañeda* (1582), f. 42. b.] *See* Wahabi.

Kahar, kuhar [17C. H. *kahār*.] One of a Hindu caste whose occupation is that of a carrier, espec. a palanquin carrier. (S. *skandha-kāra*, 'one who carries loads on his shoulders'.) [YB; Fryer, *New Account* (1672-81; ed. 1696), 68.]

Kaisar-i-Hind [19C. P. *Kaisar*, 'Caesar'.] Title of the British monarch in India, 1876-1947. *See* Padishah. [Whitworth, *Anglo-Indian Dict.* (1885); F.A. Steel, *Voices in the Night* (1900); Kipling, *Kim* (1901).]

Kaithi, [20C. H. *kaithī, kāyathī*, fr. *kāyath*, Kayasth. S. *kāyastha*.] An alphabet of Nagari type used for writing in Bihari and Eastern Hindi. [Webster, *3rd New Intern. Dict.* (1976).]

Kaivalya [19C. S. *kevala*, 'exclusively one's own: alone; whole'. (akin to 'celibate').] Absolute bliss, being the final state of Jain and Vedantic salvation; absolute release of one's *jiva* from all entanglement with one's *ajiva*. [Webster, *3rd New Intern. Dict.*]

Kajal [19C. H. *kājal*.] A black cosmetic, used by Indians to beautify the eyes or to avert the evil eye. [Whitworth, *Anglo-Indian Dict.* (1885).]

Kajang [19C. Mal. *kajang*.] Matting made from the leaves of palms, of the *Pandanus* (screwpine). [*OED*; J. Leyden, tr., *Malay Annals* (1821), viii. 261.]

Kajawa, cadjowa, cajava [17C. H/P. *kajāwah*.] A camel litter reserved for women or sick persons; a large pannier or wooden frame, a pair of which are fitted to a camel, one on each side. [*OED* & *YB*; J. Philips, tr., Tavernier, *Travels* (1678; 1684), i, ii, iii, 63; Sir T. Herbert, *Travels* (1634), 151.]

Kaji, kajee *See* Cadi, Cazee. (*kājī*, is also the title of Ministers of State in Nepal and Sikkim.)

Kakar, kakur karkur [19C. H. *kākar*.] The barking deer, *Muntiacus muntjak*. (Malay. *muntjak*). *See* Baikree. [*OED*; A.A.A. Kinloch. *Large Game Shooting* (1876), 11. 26.]

Kakri [19C. H. *kakari*.] The snake cucumber, *Cucumis melo*. [Hawkins, *CIWIE*.]

Kala *See* Kullah.

Kala-azar [19C. Assamese, *kāla*, 'black' + *āzār*, 'disease'.] The black visceral disease *Leishmania, donovani*, or *Dum-Dum Fever*. A virulent, infectious, sand-fly borne malaria, finally conquered by a Bengali doctor, Sir U. N. Brahmchari, with an antimony based treatment. [*OED;* J. J. Clarke in *Ann. Sanitary Rep. Assam* (1883).]

Kaladana [19C. H. *kālā,* 'black' + *dānā,* 'grain seed'.] The convolvulaceous plant *Ipomoea nil,* with cathartic seeds. [*OED; Treas. Bot.* (1866), 643/2.]

Kala-juggah [19C. H. *kālā-jagah.*] A 'dark place', arranged near Anglo-Indian ballrooms for the purpose of flirtation or 'poodle-faking'. *See* **Poodle Faker.** [YB; Lady Dufferin, *Viceregal Life* (1890), 91.]

Kala-pani [19C. H. *kala,* 'black' + *pani,* 'water'; the sea.] Transportation as punishment, and the forbidden, polluting voyage for Brahmins. [YB; Sir J. Malcolm, *Central India* (2nd ed. 1823), i. 446.]

Kaleej, kalij, college [19C. Anglo-Indian corr. of H. *kālij.*] The 'College Pheasant' of the Himalayas, intermediate between the pheasant and the jungle-fowl; genus *Euplocamus* or *Gallophasis.* [*OED.*] An 'absurd' Hobson-Jobsonism. [YB & *OED;* Owen, *Power of God* (1864), 43.]

Kali [19C. S. *kālī,* fem. of *kālā,* 'black', also fem. of *kala,* 'time' (as destroyer).] The dark-complexioned Hindu mother-goddess, Devi, consort of *Siva,* the Destroyer. She is depicted as swarthy, and blood-spattered, wearing a necklace of skulls and a belt of serpents. [*OED;* W. C. Blaquire, tr., in *Asiatick Res.* (1798), v. 369.] *See* **Thug.**

Kali-Yug [18C. S. *kālī* + *jugā,* 'yoke'.] In Hindu cosmology, the present Iron Age or Age of Action. Also called *karma-yug;* the period of 432,000 years at the end of each **Kalpa.** [*OED;* W. Hastings in *Asiatick Res.* (1784).]

Kalla-nimmack [18C. H. *kālā-namak.*] 'black salt', a common mineral drug, muriate of soda, having a mixture of oxide of iron and some impurities, used especially in the treatment of horses. [YB; Royle, *Hindoo Medicine* (1837).]

Kalpa [18C. S. *kalpa.*] A fabulous period of time; 4,320,000,000 years, or a day of **Brahma**; a thousand **yugas.** [*OED;* Sullivan, *View Nat.* (1794), ii. xliv. 287.] *See* **Manvantara.**

Kamala [19C. H. *kamīlā, kamēlā; S. kamala.*] A fine orange-coloured powder from the glandular hairs of the fruit capsules of the tree *Mallotus phillipinensis* or *Rottlera tinctoria* used for dyeing silks yellow, and as a vermifuge. [*OED;* Roxburgh, *Flora Indica* (1820-32).]

Kama Sutra [19C. S. *kāma,* 'love' + *sūtra,*

'rule'.] An ancient Sanskrit treatise on the art of love and sex techniques; also used allusively. [*OED.*] *See* **Sutra** [Burton and Arbuthnot, *Kamasutra of Vatsyayana* (1883).]

Kamaraj, vb. [20C.] Tamil politician's name. To arrange political resignations for the good of the party. [Hawkins, *CIWIE.*]

Kameez *See* **Camise.**

Kamgar [19C.] H. *kām,* 'work' + *gar,* 'agent'.] Workman. [Wilson *Gloss.* (1855).]

Kami(s) [20C.] Workers. *See* prec. [Kuldip Nayar, *The Judgement* (1975); Wilson, *Gloss.* (1855).]

Kampong *See* **Compound.**

Kanat[1] *See* **Canaut.**

Kanat[2] [P/Ar *kanāt* (1855).] *See* **Karez.**

Kangani, canganeme [19C. Tam. *kankāni,* fr. *kan,* 'eye' + *kān,* 'to see'.] An overseer or headman of a gang of labourers in Sri Lanka, S. India and Malaysia. [*OED;* 'Philalethes' *Hist. of Ceylon* (1817), lvi. 324.]

Kangri [20C. H. *kangri;* Kash, *kanguru.*] A small, wicker-covered, clay-lined, pot filled with glowing charcoal, carried (esp. by Kashmiris), next to the skin to warm the air beneath the clothing. [*OED;* Allbut, *Syst. Med.* (2nd ed., 1911), IX. 591.] *See* **Pheran.**

Kanjar [19C.] A generic name for certain small aboriginal gypsy communities which wander about India. [*OED; Encycl. Brit.* (1875), iii. 508/i.]

Kanji *See* **Congee.**

Kanjus [H. kanjus.] Stingy, miserly. [Wilson *Gloss.* (1855).]

Kankar, kunkur, conker [18C. H. Kankar, S. Karkaram, gravel.] Coarse limestone, sometimes burnt to lime, used for road-making in India. [*OED* & YB; Hodges, *Travels,* etc. (1780–83), 110.]

Kannada [19C.] Now the official Dravidian language in **Karnataka** for erstwhile *Kanarese, Canarese* (1598). *See* **Karnataka.** [*OED;* Linschoten, E. tr. (1598); Caldwell, *Compar. Grammar Dravidian* Lang. (1856).]

Kancut [19C. H. *kankut,* fr. kan, 'grain' + *kut,* 'evaluation'.] 'The *kancut* is a conjectural assessment of the standing crop by the united assessment of the government, the **Patel,** the **Patwari,** or registrar, and the owner of the field.' [Tod, *Annals of Rajasthan* (1829), vol. 1. 582.]

Kanoon [19C.] A sort of dulcimer, harp or sackbut, with 50 or 60 strings, played by plucking. [*OED;* Moore, *Lala Rookh* (1817).]

Kaṇṣ [19C. H. *kans,* fr. S. *kasha.*] Coarse grass, *Saccharum spontaneum,* allied to the cane, used for thatching. [*OED*; Atkinson *et al.*, *Statistical Acct. N. W. Provinces India* (1874), i. 89.]

Kanungo *See* **Canongo.**

Kapal [19C. Mal. *kapal*; Tam. *kappal*.] A ship. Applied to any square-rigged vessel with top and top-gallant masts.' [YB; Marsden, *Memoirs of a Malay Family* (1830), 57.]

Kapas *See* **Capass.**

Kapok [18C. Mal. *kapok*.] Fine, silky fibres, resembling cotton wool floss, surrounding the seeds of the White Silk-Cotton Tree, *Eriodendron anfructuosum*, used for pillow and mattress filling. Both the word and the tree are well-established in India where the substance is much used. Also, attrib. *kapok*-tree, –filling. [*OED*] *See* **Capas.** [T. Salmon, *Mod. Hist.* (1735), xxvii. vi. 186.]

Kapur [20C. Mal. *kāpūr*; H. *kapur*, fr. S. *karpūra*, 'camphor'.] A tree, esp. *Dryobalanops aromatica*, from which *Borneo Camphor* is produced. *See* **Camphor.** [*OED*; Burkill, *Dict. Econ. Products Malay Peninsula* (1935).]

Kapurala [19C. Sin. *kapurāla*.] A Buddhist temple priest in Sri Lanka. [Hawkins, *CIWIE*.]

Karana [20C. S. *kārana*. 'doing, posture'.] One of the 108 basic postures in the **Bharata Natya** dance, set out by Bharata Muni in the *Natya Sastra* after instruction from the god **Siva.** [*OED*; B.V.N. Naidu *et al.*, tr. Bharata's *Tandava Lakshanam* (1936), ii. 19.]

Karani, kerani, cranny [17C. H. *karānī*, fr. S. *karan*, 'a doer'.] In India a **'Writer'** or clerk; sometimes of mixed race or caste, e.g. **Sudra** mother and **Vaisya** father, or pure **Kshatriya** mother and 'mixed' **Kshatriya** father. 'The word was probably at one time applied by natives to the junior members of the Covenanted Civil Service – 'Writers' as they were designated'. [YB; Risley, *Tribes & Castes of Bengal* (1891); Danvers, *Letters* (1611: ed. 1896-1900), i. 117.]

Karaya [19C. H. *karāyal*.] Karaya-gum, exuded by the Indian tree *Sterculia urens*. Used as substitute for gum tragacanth. [*OED*; Watt, *Econ. Products of India*, (1893).]

Karbaree [19C.] H. *kārbārī*, 'an agent, a manager'. 'Used chiefly in Bengal Proper.' [YB; Chevers, *Ind. Med. Jurisp.* (1870), 467.]

Karbi [19C. Guj. *karbī*.] Dried stalks of Indian corn (**Jawar**) or other grain. [Wilson, *Gloss.* (1855).]

Karcanna *See* **Carcanna.**

Kardar [19C. H. *kārdār*.] An agent (of the government) in Sindh. [YB; Napier, *Conquest of Scinde* (1851), 149.]

Kareeta, khalita [19C. H/Ar. *kharīta*.] The silk bag enclosing a letter from a native noble. Also, the letter itself. [YB; Fanny Parkes, *Wanderings of a Pilgrim* (1850), ii. 250.]

Karela, kurilla [19C. H. *karēla*, fr. S. *kāravella*.] The bitter gourd, *Momordica charantia*, with edible, rough-skinned, yellow or white, lemon-shaped fruit sometimes about 8 inches long, used in pickles and medicinally. [*OED*; J. W. Masters in *Trans. Agric. & Hort. Soc. India*, (1830), iii. 200.]

Karez [19C. Push/P. *kārez*.] In Afghanistan and Baluchistan, a subterranean irrigation canal. Also **Kanat.** [*OED*; *Encycl. Brit.* (1875), i. 232/i.]

Karma [19C. S. *kārma*, 'action, fate': Hinduism and Buddhism.] The sum of a person's action in one of his existences, regarded as determining his fate in his next existence. Hence inevitable destiny following as effect from cause. [*OED*.] Also, *kārmic*, of the nature of *kārma*. And (1) [*kārmadhārya* (1846), fr. S. *kārma* + *dhāraya*. 'that which holds, maintains'.] Linguistics: A class of compound words typically a noun as second constituent and a descriptive adjective as first (blue-grass, black-berry); or a noun as second constituent and an attributive noun as first (house-boat, street-camp), or an adjective as second constituent and an adverb as first (everlasting, wide-spread). [*OED*; Hodgson, *Trans. Roy. Asiatic Soc.* (1829), II. 250; Monier-Williams, *Elem. Gram. Sanskrit Lang.* (1846), ix. 158.] (2) *karmachari* [H. *karma*, + (a)charya, 'a maker, or doer'.] One who does his duty. An old Indian university expression. (3) *karma-marga* [1817 fr. S. *kārma* + *mārga*, 'path'.] Strict observance of caste rules and rituals as the path to a happier life in one's next incarnation. The way of action, contrasted with **Bhakti-Marga** and **Jnana-Marga.** [*OED*; Monier-Williams, *Hinduism* (1877), i. 11.] (4) *karmayoga* (1896). **Yoga** through disinterested service or the selfless performance of duties. So *kārma-yogī*, a *kārma-yoga* devotee. [*OED*; 'Vivekananda', *Addresses Vedanta Philos.* (1896), i. 19; Koestler, *Lotus and the Robot* (1960), 1. i. 36.]

Karnataka, Karnata, Carnatic [17C. fr. *kar*, 'black', + *nādu*, 'country'.] State name, *Karnātaka*. (Formerly Mysore.) (1) A state of S. India. **Kannada** (Canarese) the language of Karnataka, and *Kannadiga*, a native of Karnataka. [*OED* & YB; Fryer, *New Acct.* etc.

(1673).] (2) The music of S. India, purer in form and older than N. Indian music. [*OED;* Mudaliyar, *Oriental Mus. in European* Notation (1892).]

Karta [19C. H/S. *kartā*, 'a doer, a provider'.] Head of a Hindu (joint) family. (An epithet of Brahma, Vishnu and Siva. [Whitworth, *Anglo-Indian Dict.* (1885).]

Kartik [19C. H. *kārtik*, S. *kārtika* fr. *krittikā*, Pleiades.] The eighth month of the Hindu year when the moon is full in the Pleiades. [Wilson, *Gloss.* (1855).]

Kartikiya [19C.] God of war; Shiva's son, 'fabled to have been reared by the Pleiades, the *nakshatra*, from which the month **Kartik**, the first suitable after the rains for military operations, is named.' [*Anglo-Indian Dict.* (1885).]

Karuna [19C. S. *karuna*.] Loving compassion, as that sought and obtained by a *Bodhisattva*. [*OED;* R. S. Hardy, *Eastern Monachism* (1850), xx. 246.]

Karvanda *See* **Corinda**.

Kashmir [19C.] *See* **Cashmere**.

Kashmiri [19C.] A native or the Dardic language of Kashmir. [*OED; Encycl. Brit.* (1880), XIII. 821/2.]

Karvi [19C. Mar. *karvi*.] Various species of coneheads or strobilanthes, hill-side shrubs whose massed blue and pink flowers appear at intervals of several years. [Hawkins, *CIWIE*.]

Kasturi, kastura [19C. H. *kastūrī*.] Musk-deer, *Moschus moschiferus*, native to the Himalayas. [*OED;* T. Hutton in *Jrnl. Asiatic Soc. Bengal.* (1837), vi. 936.]

Kata [18C (?) Tib. *kata*.] Tibetan prayer-shawl, traditionally given to a **Lama** by those visiting him.

Katel [Afrikaans fr. Pg. *'catel*, 'cot'; fr. Tam/M. *kattil*, 'a hammock.'] In Africa a bed in a waggon. *See* **Cot**. [Webster, *3rd New Intern. Dict.* (1976).]

Kathak [20C. S. *kāthāk*.] (1) Caste name of N. Indian religious troubadours or storytellers; story-telling, religious discourse. [*OED;* Blunt, *Caste System of N. India* (1931), 244; (2) Northern Indian style of classical dancing by men and women. [*OED;* 'La Meri', *Gesture Lang. Hind. Dance.* (1941), 17.]

Kathakali [19C. M. *kathakali*, 'drama'; fr. *kathā*, 'story' + *kali*, 'play'.] Dance-drama of Kerala, all parts being acted and danced by men, with stylized costume and mime. [*OED;* T.K.G. Panikkar, *Malabar and its Folk* (1900),

v. 74.] *See* **Ottam-thullal**.

Kathal [H. *kat-hal* fr. S. *kanthaka*, 'thorn' + *phala*, 'fruit'.] Jackfruit. [Webster, *3rd New Intern. Dict.* (1976).]

Kathiawari [Guj. *Kāthiāwādī*.] (Of *Kathiawar*, on W. coast of India). A breed of small hardy horses of Indian and Arab descent. [Webster, *3rd New Intern. Dict.* (1976).]

Katori, katora [19C. H. *katori*.] A small semi-spherical metal bowl or dish. [Whitworth, *Anglo-Indian Dict.* (1885).]

Katuka [Perh. S. *katuka*, 'sharp, bitter, fierce'. Tam/M. *katu* '(to be) pungent'.] Russell's Viper. [Webster, *3rd New Intern. Dict.* (1976).]

Katyayana-veen = Santoor.

Kaul¹ *See* **Cowle**.

Kaul² [19C. H. *kāl*, 'time'.] 'Period, death, and popularly, the visititation of famine.' [YB; Drummond, *Illustrations* etc. (1808).]

Kaurava *See* **Mahabharata**.

Kavadi [20C. Tam. *kāvati*.] A decorated arch carried like a yoke on the shoulders and hooked into the flesh of penitent devotees of Lord Subramanian, esp. by Hindus in Malaysia. [*OED;* V. Bartlett, *Rep. from Malaya* (1954), ii. 27.]

Kavya [S. *kāvya*, 'poetical'.] Sanskrit and other Indic compositions with decorative elaborations. [Webster, *3rd New Intern. Dict.* (1976).

Kawi, kavi [19C. S. *kāvya*, 'poem'.] The classic or ancient poetic language of Indonesia and Malaysia, containing many Sanskrit words. [*OED;* Raffles, *Java*, (1817), I. 411.]

Kayasth, kayath [19C. S. *kayastha*. Prob. fr. *kāya*, 'body, group' + *stha*, 'standing'.] (1) The writer caste of S & W India, a division of the **Prabhu** caste. (2) In Bengal, a mixed caste (**Kshatriya** father + **Sudra** mother). (3) The **Patwaris** of Bengal. [Whitworth, *AngloIndian Dict.* (1885).]

Kazi [17C.] *See* **Cadi**.

Kebab, kabab, cabob, keebaub, etc. [17C. H/Ar. *kabab*.] In Anglo-Indian households, roast-meat, usually following the name of the dish, e.g. *murghi kebab*, 'roast fowl'. But specifically it is 'Roast Meat on Skewers cut in little round pieces no bigger than a Sixpence, and Ginger and Garlick put between each'. [Fryer, *New Acct. E. India & Persia* (1672-81); *OED* & YB; Forbes, *Orient Mem.* (1813), II. xvi. 12.]

Kebuli(–wallah), Kabuli *See* **Myrobalans** and **Kabaddi-wallah**.

Keddah *See* **Kheddah**.

Kedgeree, kitchery [17C. fr. *khichrī*, S. *k'rsara*, 'dish of rice and sesamum.'] An Indian dish of rice, **Dhal**, onions, etc. An Anglo-Indian variant was a breakfast dish called 'Fish-kedgeree', often with re-cooked fish served with rice and the trimmings. (*See* **Brass-knocker**.) Also *transf.* and *fig.* (1909), meaning any extraordinary mixture of styles, objects, architecture, etc. [OED & YB; Coryat in *Early Travels in India* (1583-1619).]

Kedgeree Pot [19C. *See* Prec.] A round pipkin such as is in common Indian use, both for holding water and for cooking purposes. [YB & OED.] *See* **Chatty, Ghurra**. [Heber, *Jrnl.* (1823), I, 123; Thackeray, *Major Gahagan* (1839).]

Keema [20C. H. *kīma*.] Minced meat. [Hawkins CIWIE.]

Kef, kyfe [19C. H/Ar. *kaif*, 'well-being, enjoyment'.] State of drowsiness or dreamy intoxication; enjoyment of idleness. Also Indian hemp, *Cannabis indica* or *sativa*. [OED & YB; Drummond, *Illustrations* (1808).]

Kekune-oil [Sinh, *kekkŭn*.] **Candlenut-oil,** from the seeds of the *Aleuritis moluccana*. A drying oil for paints, soaps and local candles. [OED; Todd, *Cycl. Anat.* (1835-6), I. 58/1.]

Kendra [H. *kendra*.] Centre. [Hawkins, CIWIE.]

Keora [19C. H. *keorā*.] The Indian plant, *Pandanus adoratissimus*, from the male flowers of which an essential oil, also called *Ketgee-oil*, is obtained. [OED; Simmonds, *Dict. of Trade* (1858).]

Kerala [20C.] Modern Indian state formed in 1956 from ancient **Malabar**, with its capital at Trivandrum. An Ashoka rock inscription, 3rd C. BC, is the first known mention; then known as Keralaputra. [G. Woodcock, *Kerala, a Portrait of the Malabar Coast* (1967).]

Kerseymere, kassimere [18C. Corr. of *cassimere* (cashmere) by association with *kersey* (a kind of coarse cloth made in Kersey, in Suffolk).] Described as a twilled, fine woollen cloth by YB and OED. [Seton-Karr, *Selections* etc. (1784-1823), i. 47; Jane Austen, *Let.* 30 June (1808; 1952), 204.]

Keruna [19C. S. *kerūna*, 'charity', 'compassion'.] The fundamental quality of the Bodhisattva. [OED.] [R.S. Hardy, *Eastern Monachism.* (1850), xx. 246.]

Ketu [19C. S. *ketu*.] A planet; an auspicious time.] 'The dragon's tail, or the point where the moon in its southward course cuts the ecliptic.' [Whitworth, *Dict.* (1885).] *See* **Rahu**.

Key-money [19C. Anglo-Indian.] A premium (**Dasturi**) exacted from prospective tenants in India. This expression originated in England in the 19th C. [*Daily News*, 19 Dec. 1898.]

Kewanch *See* **Cowage (Cow-Itch)**.

Khabber *See* **Khubber**.

Khabbardar *See* **Khubberdaur**.

Khadar, khadir, kadir [19C. H. khadar.] (1) A flood-plain of a river (1832) [OED]; (2) Recently deposited alluvium, bordering a large river (1919). [OED.] Cf. **Bangur**. [G. C. Mundy, *Pen & Pencil, Sk.* (1832), I. v. 269; D. N. Wadia, *Geol. India* (1919), xxii. 251.]

Khaddar, khadi [20C. H. *khādar*.] Indian homespun, hand-woven cotton cloth. *Khadi* = made of *Khaddar*. Associated with the **Swadeshi** (self-government) movement. [OED; *Glasgow Herald*, 27 Dec. 1921.]

Khair, kyar [19C. H. *khair*; S. *khadira*.] A tree *Acacia catechu*, yielding a gum from which **Cutch** is made. [OED & YB; Trelawney, *Advice Younger Son.* (1831), ii. 198.]

Khaki, khakee kharkee (sb. adj.) [19C. H/P. *khākī*, 'dusty', fr. *khāk*, 'dust'.] Dust-coloured; dull, brownish; made of *khaki* cloth (1863); a cloth of this colour used for army uniforms, 'worn by some of the Punjab regiments at the siege of Delhi, and became very popular in the army generally during the campaigns of 1857-8... (introduced) in place of the red uniforms which gave the British soldiers the name of 'Lal Coortee Wallahs'. [YB.] Also: *khaki*-clad; -bound; -coloured; -policy; *khaki*-drill; -serge; -election (1913). 'Cannon and *Khaki*', a round beef-steak pudding and a dump of pease pudding (1909). *Khaki*-patch (1880), a small steak. [OED & YB; H. B. Edwardes in *Lumsden of the Guides* (1857); ed. 1899); Partridge, *Slang Today & Yesterday* (1953).]

Khal [20C. Beng. *khāl*.] A narrow, natural channel of water; a creek. [OED; *Jrnl. Trop. Med.* (1903), vi. 200/2.]

Khalasi *See* **Classy (Clashy)** and **Matross**.

Khalifa, Caliph, Caleefa [18C. H/Ar. *Khalīfa*.] The Caliph or Vicegerent. In Anglo-Indian households this word refers to the Indian tailor (*durzee*), and cook (*bobachee*), and sometimes to the barber and farrier. This was a common honorific practice among Indian domestic servants. *See* **Mehtar** and **Maitrani** ('prince and princess'), **Beastie (Bhishti)**, 'Paradise' man. Also *Caliphate*, the office or rule of the Caliph. [YB; Broughton (1813) *Letters* (ed. 1892), 164.]

Khalistan [20C. 'The Land of the Pure.'] The Punjab; the object of militant Sikhism. *See* next.

Khalsa [18C. H/P. fr. Ar. *khālsa*, 'pure, real, proper'.] (1) The **Sikh** community and religion. *See* **Granth Sahib**. [*OED* & YB; G. Forster, *Journey Bengal to England* (1790), i. 267.] (2) The revenue department or exchequer in Indian states. [*OED; Trial of Joseph Fowke* (1776), B. 14/1.] (3) Militant Sikh theocracy from 17C. founded in *Ānandpur* by Guru Gobind Singh, and continued today as the basis of a politico-religious movement demanding an independent Sikh State, **Khalistan**. Cf. **Nanak Panth**, founded by Guru Nanak (1538) with emphasis on peaceful social tenets. *See* **Namdharis**. [W.H. Mcleod, *Gurū Nānak* and *the Sikh Religion* (1968).]

Khan,[1] **Can, Chan** [17C. H/P. *khān*, 'ruler'.] Persian title of nobility; lord or prince. (1) A **Pathan** title applied at first to various chiefs, now often equivalent to the English 'Esquire' in India for those claiming Pathan descent. [*OED* & YB.] Also *Khanate*, a Khan's rule or district; **Khansama**, butler, steward. [*OED;* Sir Thomas Roe, *Embassy to the Court of the Great Mogul* (1615-19).]

Khan[2] [15C.] (2) A public unfurnished building for the accommodation of travellers; a caravanserai; inn. [The word appears in English about 1400. *See Stanford Dictionary of Anglicised Words and Phrases* (1892).] [*OED; Three Kings Cologne* (c. 1400), 22; Scott, *The Surgeon's Daughter,* (1827), ch. xiii.]

Khana,[1] **khanna, connah** [18C. H/P. *khāna*.] 'compartment', apartment, department, receptacle etc.' A house. 'Used almost *ad libitum* in India with most incongruous words' as *bobachee* (*bāwarchī*), –*connah* (*khānā*), 'cook-house'; *buggy-connah*, 'coach-house'; *bottle-khana*, 'wine-cellar'; *tosha-khana*, 'repository of presents'; *tyconna*, 'subterranean apartment'; *moorghi-khana*, 'hen-house', or, in Anglo-Indianm, argot, a place set aside specially for women in European clubs in India. [YB; Seton-Karr, *Selections* (1784-1823), i. 41.]

Khana,[2] **conner** [19C. H. *khānā*.] 'food, meal, dinner, repast.' [*OED;* Atkinson, *Curry & Rice* (1857).]

Khanna coolie *See* **Dabawala**.

Khanjar, candjare etc. [17C.] H/P. *khanjar*.] An Eastern dagger. *See* **Kirpan** and **Kuttar**. [*OED* & YB; *Eng. Fact. in India* (1618-69; ed. 1906-27). Also *handjar, hanjar*. (Purchas, *Pilgrimes* (1588; 1625-6), ii. ix.]

Khansama, consumah, consumer [17C. H/P. *khānsamān*, 'a house-steward'.] Lit. 'Master of the household goods'. In Anglo-Indian households, the title of the chief table-servant and purchaser of food. (*See* **Butler**.) 'The Anglo-Indian form *consumer* seems to have been not uncommon in the 18C., probably with a spice of intention.' [YB & *OED*.] Also *Khansamaship*. [*Anglo-Indian Domestic Sketch*, published by Thacker (Calcutta, 1849); Danvers, *Letters* (1609; ed. 1896-1900).]

Khanum [19C. H/P. *khānum* and *khānim*.] The feminine of the title **Khan**. *See* **Begum** [*OED* & YB; J. Morier, *Adventures Hajji Baba* (1824), i. xxiv. 256.] *See* **Khatum** and **Begum**.

Khapra (beetle) [19C. H. *khaprā*, 'destroyer'.] A small brownish-black beetle, *Trogoderma granarium*. A pest, native to India and elsewhere, of stored grain. [*OED;* E. C. Cotes in *Indian Museum Notes* (1896), iii. 19.]

Kharaj, kharatch *See* **Khiraj**.

Kharif, khurreef [19C. H/Ar. *kharīf*, 'autumn'.] In India, the crops or the harvest of the crops, sown at the beginning of the summer rains (April and May), and gathered in Autumn; including rice, the tall millets, maize, cotton; rape, sesamum, etc. [YB & *OED*.] *See* **Rabi (Rubbee)**, the spring crop and harvest. [Broughton, *Letters from a Mahratta Camp* (1809; ed. 1813).] *See* **Tur**.

Kharoshti [19C. S. *kharostī*.] One of the two oldest alphabets in India, used for about seven centuries from *c.* 300 BC in N.W. India; derived from Aramaic. Cf. **Brahmi**. [*OED;* A. Cunningham, *Coins Ancient India* (1891), 36.]

Khas, khass, kauss, coss [18C. H/Ar. *khāss*, 'special, particular, royal'.] (1) Estates in the hands of Government, which are said to be held *khās*. (2) *Khās*-mahal, the women's apartments. [YB.] (2) *Dewan-i-Khās*, the special or Royal Hall of Audience, or **Durbar**, in the palaces of the great Mughal and Muslim princes of India; in contrast to *Dewan-i-Am*, Hall of Public Audience. [YB; Stockdale, *Indian Vocabulary* (1788).]

Khasiya, khasi [18C.] (1) The oldest Indo-Aryan race in the cis-Tibetan Himalaya, between Nepal and the Ganges. 'Khasiyas are Hindus in religion and custom, though there is some suggestion of their Tibetan neighbours in their aspect.' [YB.] (2) Also, a Mongoloid people found in the Khasi and Jaintia Hills in N. E. India. [*OED;* Seton-Karr and Sandeman, *Selections from Calcutta Gaz.* (1865), ii. 218.]

Khaskura, khaskra [20C.] An Indic dialect spoken in Nepal = *Gurkhālī* or *Nepāli. [OED; R. L. Turner in Northey & Morris, Gurkhas* (1928), iv. 70.]

Khassadar, kassidar [19C.] A local militiaman, an irregular soldier performing police duty on caravan routes on the N. W. Frontier. [*OED;* Holdich, *Indian Borderland* (1901), xii. 273.]

Khatak [19C. Tib. *k'a-btāgs.*] In Tibet, a scarf to be presented to or by visitors, as a form of salutation. [*OED;* Schlagintweit, *Buddhism in Tibet* (1863), xiii. 190.]

Khatib, khateb [17C. H/Ar. *katib.*] A Muslim preacher, who recites the **Khutbah** from the **Mimbar** in the mosque on Fridays. [*OED;* Purchas, *Pilgrimes* (1625-6), ii. ix. xix.]

Khatri [17C.] *See* **Kshatriya.**

Khatum, kadum [19C. H/P. *khātūn,* a lady.] A courtesy title placed after a Muslim lady's name. [*OED;* J. Morier, *Ayesha* (1834), i. iv. 80.] *See* **Begum** and **Khanum.**

Khayal, khyal, kheal [19C.] A traditional type of song in N. India, with instrumental accompaniment, usually with two main themes. [*OED;* Willard in *Tagore's Hindu Music* (1882).]

Khedda, kheddah [18C. H. *khedā,* fr. S. *ākheta,* 'hunting'. (H. *khednā,* 'to chase').] An enclosure erected for the capture of wild elephants = **corral** of Sri Lanka. (Pg. *curral,* 'cattle-pen'). [*OED & YB; Lives of the Lindsays* (1780-90; ed. 1849), iii. 191.]

Khel [19C. Pasht./Ar. *khel,* 'a company, a troop, a party'.] Affixed to a man's name to designate his tribe, among the Pathans. [Whitworth, *Anglo-Indian Dict.* (1885).]

Khet [19C. H. *khet.*] A tract of cultivated land in India. Cf. **Khot.**[1] [*OED;* Robinson, *In My Indian Garden* (1878), 176.]

Khichri *See* **Kedgeree.**

Khidmutgar, khedmutgar, khitmutgar, khitmatgar [17C. H/P. *khidmat,* 'service' + *gār,* 'agent'.] Lit. 'one rendering service'. A male servant who waited at table. [*OED & YB; Indian Antiquary* (1632; ed. 1871-1933), IX.]

Khilafat [20C. H/Ar. *kilāfat.*] (1) Spiritual headship of Islam residing in the former Sultans of Turkey. [*OED.*] (2) The Muslim anti-British movement in India after the treaty of Sevres in 1920. Hence *khilafatist,* a supporter of this agitation. [*OED;* 'Moplah Rebellion', 50 in Parl. Papers [Cmd. 1552 (1921), XXVI. 237.]

Khilat, killut, killaut, khelat [17C. H/Ar. *khil'at,* fr. *khala'h,* 'a reward'.] (Gift of) a dress of honour presented by a superior or ruler on ceremonial occasions as a mark of favour or

distinction; any handsome present given by a superior. [YB & *OED; Eng. Fact. in India* (1638); 1618–69; ed. 1906–27).] *See* **Seerpaw.**

Khir [19C. H. *khīr.*] Boiled rice, sugar and milk. [Hawkins, *CIWIE.*]

Khiraj, kharaj, kharatch [18C. H/Ar. *kharāj,* 'tribute'.] Tribute levied by Muslims upon conquered unbelievers (**kafirs**); also land tax. In India it was usually the land-revenue paid to Government. A common expression in India was *lākhirāj,* 'rent-free'. [YB.] *See* **Lackerage.** [Seton-Karr, *Selections* (1784–1823), 1. 49.]

Khis-khis [19C. H/Mar. *khisnā,* 'to drop off'.] Clear the way! Make way! *See* **Pyse** and **Po-Po.** [YB; Hockley, *Pandurang Hari* (1826; ed. 1873), i. 46.]

Khoa [19C. H./Beng. *khoā.*] A kind of concrete, of broken brick, lime etc. used for floors and terrace-roofs. [YB.] *See* **Soorki.**

Khoja, coja [17C. H/P/Turk. *khōjah, khwājah.*] (1) A title of respect; a teacher in a Muslim school or college; a scribe, a clerk. [*OED & YB;* Foster, *Letters* (1615; ed. 1896-1900), IV. 16; Purchas, *Pilgrimes* (1625).] (2) In India, especially applied to eunuchs. [YB; Capt. Jacques in *Articles of Charge* etc. (1786), Burke, vii. 27.] (3) A member of a Muslim sect or converts to Islam from Hinduism, mainly in W. India, retaining some Hindu customs. [*OED.*] Also *attrib. See* **Shaikh** & **Borah.** [*Encycl. Brit.* (1882), XIV. 64/1; C. Eliot (1882), *Hinduism & Buddhism,* (1921), III. LVIII. 455.] *See* **Shia.**

Kho-kho [19C. Mar. *khō-khō.*] A chasing game between teams of 12. [Hawkins, *CIWIE.*]

Khond, Kandh [19C. Tribal name.] A Dravidian people of Orissa and their language. [*OED.*] Also *attrib,* or as *adj.* [S. C. Macpherson in *Jrnl. Royal Asiatic Soc.* (1852), XIII. 217.]

Khot[1] *See* **Khet.**

Khot,[2] **Khoti** [19C. Mar. *khot.*] Person holding or farming villages on a peculiar tenure called *khotī,* differing in different parts of the country where it applied, e.g. similar to a petty **Zemindar** in Bengal and Konkan; in N. Konkan, originally revenue-farmers without ownership or hereditary rights, but they usurped both with time. [YB; Wilson, *Glossary* (1855).]

Khowar [19C. Tribal name.] A Dardic language spoken in Chitral, N. W. Pakistan. [*OED.*] Also *attrib* or as *adj.* [*Encycl. Brit.* (1882), XIV. 9/2.]

Khubber, khabar, kubber [19C. H/P. *khabar,* 'news'.] Information, report, rumour. Espec.

Shikar news, e.g. 'Pucka khubber' of a tiger or other big game animals. [YB & *OED*; Mundy, *Pen and Pencil Sketches* (1828; ed. 1858), 53.]

K(h)ubberdaur [17C. H/P. *khubber-dār*.] *See* prec. 'Take care!' It was the usual cry of **Chowkidars** to show that they were awake. As a noun it meant a 'scout' or 'spy'. [YB; Bernier, *Travels* (E. tr. 1684; ed. Ball, 1889); Broughton, *Letters from a Mahratta Camp* (1809; ed. 1813), 25.

Khud, khudd, kudd [19C. H. *khad* fr. S. *khanda*, 'a gap, a chasm'.] A precipitous hill-side, a deep ravine or ditch; a steep valley or embankment. The word was in constant Anglo-Indian colloquial use at Simla and other Himalayan stations. Also *khud-stick*, a long, straight stick pointed with a metal tip; and *khud-climbing* (1906). [*OED* & YB; Bacon, *First Impressions Hindustan* (1837), ii. 146; Kipling, *Departmental Ditties* (1886).]

Khuda [19C. H/P. *khuda*, 'God'.] *Khuda-Hafiz*, Muslim goodbye. *See* **Hafiz**. [Hawkins, *CIWIE*.]

Khus-khus, cuscus-cuss, khaskas [17C. H/P. *khaskhas*.] The aromatic fibrous roots of a grass, *Vetiveria zizanioides* which abounds in the drier parts of India, where, and elsewhere, it is used during the hot dry winds to make screens or **Tatties**, which are kept constantly wet in window and door openings to allow their fragrant evaporation to cool the house. (*Note*: the Tamil name for these roots, *vettivēru* (lit: 'The root which is dug up'), provides not only the botanical name but also the French word for these roots, *vetyver*. [YB & *OED*; *Eng. Fact. in India* (1618-69; ed. 1906–27).] *See* **Vetiver**.

Khutbah, khitbah, khutba [17C.] The sermon during the Friday service in Muslim mosques. [*OED*; *Eng. Fact. in India* (1618-69; ed. 1906-27).]

Khutput [19C. Mar. *khatpat*, 'wrangling and worry'.] Used as a slang term for intrigue and corruption, especially in the court intrigues of the native princely states. [YB; Frazer, *Records of Sport* (1881), 204.]

Khyal *See* **Khayal**.

Khyber-Pass [18C. Properly *Khaibar*.] (1) The famous pass from Afghanistan to N. Pakistan. [*OED* & YB; Forster, *Travels* (1790; ed. 1808), ii. 65-6.] (2) Rhyming slang = 'arse'. [*OED*; Harrison, *Reported Safe Arrival* (1943), 32.] Also ellipt. the *Khyber*.

Kiblah [18C. H/Ar. *qiblah*, 'that which is opposite'.] The direction towards the great mosque

at Mecca to which Muslims turn at prayer (**Namaz**); a niche in the mosque or other religious buildings on the side towards Mecca. [*OED*; J. Pitts, *Acc. Mahometans* (1704), 40.]

Ki-hi, koi-hai *See* **Qui-hai**.

Kikar [19C. H. *kīkar*.] Indian name for a species of acacia, *Acacia arabica*, yielding gum arabic. *See* **Babool**. [*OED*; *Cassell's Family Mag.*, Oct. 1883.]

Kil, kila [16C. Tam/M. *kīl* fr. Ar. & P. *kīr*, and *kīl*, 'pitch or bitumen'.] [YB; Stanley, tr., *Three Voyages of Vasco da Gama* (1561; Hak. Soc., 1869).]

Killadar [18C. H/Ar. *kal'a*, 'a fort' + *dār*, agent suffix.] The commandant of a fort or castle. [*OED* & YB.] Also *killādari*, the office or tract of land of a *killadar*. [Orme, *Hist. of Milit. Trans.* (1778; ed. 1803), ii. 217.]

Killa-kote [19C. Comb. of Ar. P. & H. words (*kil'a* for *kal'a* and *kōt*, 'a fort'.] 'Used in Western India to imply the whole fortifications of a territory. [YB; Drummond, *Illustrations*, etc. (1808).]

Kilta, kilter [19C. Origin unknown.] Himalayan wicker, or leather-covered basket, strapped on the back of the carriers. Also, attrib. = made of wicker. [*OED*; Cumming, *From Hebrides to Himalayas* (1876), ii. v. 134.]

Kincob, kingcob, kingwab, etc. [18C. H/P. *kimkhāb*.] A rich Indian stuff, damask or brocade, embroidered with gold and silver. [*OED* & YB.] Also attrib. [Malcolm, *Anecdotes*, etc. (1712; ed. 1808).] (*The Voiage & Travaile of Sir John Maunderville* (1400), has 'cammaka'.)

Kindal [20C.] An Indian tree, *Terminalia paniculata*, with hard wood like walnut. [Webster, *3rd New Intern. Dict.* (1976).]

King-cobra [19C.] A venomous elapid snake, (*Ophiophagus hannah*), of India, China, the Philippines etc. = **Hamadryad**. [*OED*; E. H. Aitkin, *Naturalist on the Prowl* (1894), 39.]

King-crow [19C.] The glossy Black Drongo, *Dicrurus adsimilis*, found all over India. Hindi names: *Bujangā, Kōtwāl, Kālkalachi*. [*OED* & YB; Jerdon's *Birds* (1862); E. H. Aitken, *Tribes on My Frontier* (1883), 143.]

Kinnar [19C. S. *kinnara*.] Celestial musician, with a man's body and a horse's head, or vice-versa, who sings the praises of the Gods; sometimes regarded as a kind of **Gandharva**. [H. Wilson, tr., *Visnu Purāna* (1840).]

Kinnari *See* prec. Primitive two-stringed musical instrument fixed on three gourds.

Kipling, 1865-1936 (1) *Kiplingese* (1899). The literary style of Kipling; imitation of that style.

(*Daily News*, Dec. 1899) [*OED*]. (2) *Kiplingesque* (1894). Attitude of superiority over and responsibility for the welfare of native peoples; The White Man's Burden. Also *Kiplingish, Kiplingite, Kiplingize*. [*OED; Sunlight Yr. Bk.* (1894; 1895), 77.]

Kirana [19C. H. *kirāna*.] Grocery. [Wilson, *Gloss*, 1855.]

Kirbee, kurbee [19C. H. *karbī*; S. *kadamba*, 'The stalk of a pot-herb'.] The stalks of **Jowar**, used as cattle food. [YB; Broughton, *Letters from a Mahratta Camp* (ed. 1892), 41.]

Kirpan [18C. Punj. *kirpān*.] Sword worn by orthodox Sikhs. *See* **Five K's.** [*OED; Seir Mutaquerin* (tr. 1789), i. 87; J.D. Cunningham, *History of the Sikhs* (1849); J. J. Gordon, *Sikhs* (1904), IV. 41.]

Kirtan, keertan [19C. S. *kīrtana*.] A devotional song with a moral theme. [*OED*.] *See* **Bhajan.**

Kisan [19C. H. *kisān*; S. *khrsana*, 'one who ploughs'.] Peasant, agricultural worker. [Wilson, *Gloss*. (1855).]

Kishmish, kismas [17C. H/P. *kishmish*.] Small stoneless raisins, alias sultanas, from Iran. [YB; Fryer, *New Acct.* (1673); Watt, *Econ. Dict.* (1889).]

Kismet, kismat [19C. H/Turk. *kismet*, Ar. *qismat*, fr. *qasama*, 'to divide'.] Portion, lot, fate, destiny. [*OED*.] *See* **Karma, Taqdir.** [E. B. Eastwick. *Dry Leaves* (1849), 46.]

Kissmiss [19C. Anglo-Indian.] Corr. of *Christmas*, by native servants. But it was usually called **Burra Din**, 'the great day'. [YB.]

Kist, kist-bundi [18C. H/P/Ar. *kist*, 'portion, instalment + *bundī*, 'closure'.] An instalment of the yearly land revenue or other payment in India. The contract settlement of these instalments is *kist-bundi* [*OED* & YB; *Ann. Reg.* (1764), 192/2; Verelst, *A View etc.* (1772), app. 56.]

Kittul, kitool [17C. Sin. *kitūl*.] The jaggery palm, *Caryota-urens*, the leafy stalks of which yield a strong black fibre for ropes, brushes, etc. [*OED* & YB; R. Knox, *Hist. Ceylon* (1681), 15.]

Kittysol, kitsol, kittisol [16C. Pg. *quita-sol*, fr. *quitar*, 'take away' + *sol*, 'sun'.] A sunshade or Chinese umbrella of oiled paper (1875). Also *Kittysol-Boy* (1813): a servant who carried an umbrella over his master's head. *See* **Roundel, Chatta.** [*OED* & YB; Parke's *Mendoza* (1588); Milburn, *Oriental Commerce* (1813).]

Kling, Kaling(a), Kling [17C. Mal. *keling*.] A somewhat disparaging term for Tamils settled in Malaysia, at first as indentured labour on rubber estates, who came from the Coromandel coast. (An ancient people (Kalingas) mentioned in the edicts of Asoka.) [*OED* & YB; E. Scott, *Exact Discourse* (1606).]

Knol-kohl, nol-kole [19C. Dutch. *knollkool*, 'turnip-cabbage', or *khol-rabi* (1807). [*OED*.] 'cabbage turnip'.] The *Brassica oleracea*, grown a great deal in India. 'The stalk at one point expands into a globular mass resembling a turnip, and this is the edible part.' [YB; Birdwood, *Bombay Products* (1880); Vancouver, *Agric. Devon.* (1807), 191.]

Koel, kokila, coel [18C. H. *koīl* fr. S. *kokila*.] The Indian cuckoo, *Eudynamys scolopacea* or *honorata*. The name imitates its cry during the mating season. Its distribution is throughout the entire Indian Union, Bangladesh, Pakistan, Sri Lanka and Burma. [*OED* & YB; Erskine, tr., *Baber's Mem.* (1826), 323; Jerdon· *Birds* (1862); Sir W. Jones, *Letters* (1821; 1791), 11. 157.]

Koft-gari(-work) [19C. H/P. *kōft; kōftgarī*, 'beaten work'.] Indian damascene work, in which a pattern traced on steel is inlaid with gold. *Koft-work* (1880). [*OED; Birdwood in Cole, Obj. Indian Art* (1874), 60.]

Kofta [19C. H. *kofta*, 'pounded meat'.] A rissole, or spiced meat or fish ball. [*OED; W. H. Dawe, Wife's Help to Indian Cookery* (1888), 71.]

Koh-i-noor, kohinor [19C. H/P. *kōh-i-nūr*, 'Mountain of Light'.] The name of one of the most famous and magnificent diamonds in the world. After a great many vicissitudes and changes of hands from *c.* AD 1300 it passed into the possession of the English on the annexation of the Punjab in 1849, and is now among the British Crown jewels. Fig. something the most superb of its kind. [*OED;* Elphinstone, *Caubul* (1839), i. 68; Thackeray, *Pendennis* (1849), lxvi.]

Kohl [18C. H/Ar. *kuhl*.] A powder, usually sulphide of antimony, used as a cosmetic to darken the eyelids and eyebrows = **Surma.** Also vb. to darken with *kohl; cf. alcohol. See* **Kajal.** [*OED; W. C. Browne, Trav. in Africa, etc.* (1799), xxi. 318; Moore, *Lalla Rookh Veiled Proph* (1817), II.]

Koi-hai *See* **Qui hi.**

Kokam, corcopali [16C. M. *kodukka* + *puli*, 'acid'; Mar. *kokam*, 'mangosteen'.] The Indian tree, *Garcinia indica* or *purpurea* (of the same genus as the **mangosteen**) from whose seeds a fatty oil is drawn, known as *kokam–, kokun–,* or *Goa–butter*. The tree also yields a gum-resin and gamboge, largely used as a pigment, giving a bright yellow colour; also, a drastic purgative. [YB; Watt, *Econ. Dict.* (1889-93); Eden, *Varthema* (1576).]

Kokila [18C.] *See* **Koel.**

Kokoon [19C. Sinh. *kokūn.*] A large Sri Lankan forest tree, *Kokoona zeylanica.* [*OED; Treas. Bot.* (1866), 650/1.]

Kol, Kol Kole, Cole [18C. Disputed origin.] Munda-speaking tribes of Chota Nagpur and Bengal; a member of any of these tribes. [*OED;* J. T. Blunt, *Jrnl.* 2 Feb. in *Asiatick Res.* (1795; 1803), 111. 61.]

Kola [19C. Beng. *Kola.*] A class of Hindus whose main occupation is basket-weaving or mat-making. [*OED;* E. Balfour, *Cycl. India,* 2 edn., (1873), 111. 255/1.]

Kolam [20C.] The **Rangoli** of southern India. [Hawkins, *CIWIE.*]

Kolarian [19C. H. *kolar.*] Non-Aryan linguistic stock of India, the **Munda** group; the name for India in very ancient times. [*OED;* G. Campbell in *Jrnl. Asiatic Soc. Bengal* (1866), xxxv. 11. 28.]

Kolatam [19C. Tam. *kōl,* 'stick' + *āttam,* 'dance'.] A S. Indian folk dance accompanied by the striking of sticks. [Webster, *3rd New Intern. Dict.* (1976).]

Koleroga [19C. Kan. *kolerōga* fr. *kole* 'rat' + S. *roga,* 'disease'.] Areca-palm disease fr. the fungus *Phytophthora areca.* [Webster, *3rd New Intern. Dict.* (1976).]

Koochparwani [19C. H. *kūchch,* 'any' + *parva,* 'care' + *nahin,* 'no'.] Slang: Couldn't care less! or a careless good-for-nothing person. [Hawkins, *CIWIE.*]

Kookri *See* **Kukri.**

Koonbee, kunbee, koolumbee [16C. H. *kunbī* fr. S. *kutumba.*] The cultivating class of Gujarat and the Konkan. 'In the Deccan the title distinguished the cultivator from him who wore arms and preferred to be called a *Mahratta.*' In N. India, the *Kurmī.* [*OED* & YB; Drummond, *Illustrations,* etc. (1808); Linschoten, *Discours of Voyages* (E. tr. 1598).]

Konkee, koonki *See* **Coomkee.**

Koot [16C. H. *kūt* fr. S. *kūshta.*] The costus of the Roman writers. *See* **Putchock.** [YB; Barret in Hakluyt (1584), ii. 413.]

Kooza *See* **Coojah.**

Korakan [19C.] Sinh/Tam. *kurakkan* = **Ragi** [Webster, *3rd New Intern. Dict.* (1976).]

Koran, Currawn, etc. [17C. Ar. *qurān,* 'recitation', fr. *qara'a,* 'to read'.] The sacred book of Muslims; oral revelations by Mohammed collected in writing after his death. Hence: *Koranic* (1811). [*OED;* Purchas, *Pilgrimes*

(1625), II. iii. v. 264.]

Kos, koss *See* **Coss.**

Koshoon [18C. Turki, *koshūn,* 'whatever is composed of several parts'.] A military term used by Tippoo Sultan for 'a brigade, or a regiment in the larger continental use of that word'. [YB; Hanway, *Travels* etc. (1753), I. ii. 252.]

Kotal, kotul [19C. Pushtu, *kōtal.*] A mountain pass; the ridge or summit of a pass. [*OED* & YB; Elphinstone, *Caubul* (1809; 1839), i. 51; *Times* (15 Oct. 1880).]

Kothi [19C. H. *kothi;* S. *koshta.*] Residence, house, mansion, warehouse, business premises. [Whitworth, *Anglo-Indian Dict.* (1885); Wilson, *Gloss.* (1855).]

Kotwal(i), cotwal, cutwaul, etc. [16C. H/P. *kotwāl,* 'castle commandant'.] A chief officer of town- or city-police in India, a native town magistrate. Hence: *kotwali,* police-station, lock-up. 'The office of *kotwāl* in Western and Southern India, technically speaking, ceased about 1862, when the new police system (under Act, India, V of 1861 and corresponding local Acts) was introduced.' [YB & *OED.*] Also *Kotwali,* police-station (1845). [Litchfield, *Castañeda* (1582), 50; Sir T. Roe, *Embassy to the Court of the Great Mogul* (1615-19).]

Krait, karait [19C. H. *karait.*] A venomous snake of India of the genus *Bungarus,* espec. B. *caeruleus,* common in Bengal. [*OED;* Fayber, *Venom. Snakes Ind. Penins.* (2nd ed. 1874), 14.]

Kranti [19C. H. *kranti.*] Revolution. Also *Kranti Vir,* 'Leader of the Revolution'. Special title of V.B. Phadke. *See* **Inqilab.** [Hawkins, *CIWIE;* Platts, *Dict.* (1884).]

Kris, cris, crease, creese [16C. Mal. *krīs.*] Malay dagger of snake-like shape. Also 'creased', 'stabbed with a *Kris*' and vb. trans. [*OED* & YB; Litchfield's *Castañeda* (1582); Drake's Voy. in Hakluyt (1600; 1577-80), III. 742.]

Krishna [19C. S. *Krishna.*] A great Hindu deity, one of **Vishnu's Avatars:** lover of **Radha.** Also *Krishnaism* (1885); *Krishnaist* (1889); and *Krishnaite* (1889). *See* **Hare Krishna.** [*OED;* Monier-Williams, *Indian Wisdom* (1875), XII. 352.]

Krita(-Yuga) [19C. S. *krita yuga.*] The first and best **Yug,** *krta,* the best throw at dice (the 4). [Whitworth, *Anglo-Indian Dict.* (1885).]

Kriti, Krithi [20C.] In S. Indian music, a song composed, not improvised. [*OED;* A.H.F. Strangways, *Mus. Hindostan* (1914), iii. 84.]

Kshatriya, Kshatri, Khatri, Khuttry, Cuttry Shuddery [17C. H. *Khattrī;* S. *kshatriya,* fr. *kshatra,* 'dominion, rule'.] A member of the Hindu **Twice-born** military caste, traditionally rulers and warriors; the second in the hierarchy of the four main castes: **Brahmin, Kshatriya; Vaishya, Sudra.** [*OED* & YB; *Eng. Fact. in India* (1618-19; ed. 1906-27); Lord, *Banians and Persees* (1630), I. 5.]

Kuchipudi [20C. Place-name. *Kuchelapuram,* afterwards *Kuchipudi.*] Classical dance-drama of Andhra Pradesh, performed by boys and men, founded by Sidhyendra Yogi (*c.* AD 500.) [Rina Singha and R Massey, *Indian Dance, Their History and Growth* (1967).]

Kudumbosee [19C.] The ceremony of 'Kissing the Feet' of a person of rank, or of 'touching the feet with the right hand and then kissing the latter, or more generally making "salaam" with it'. [Fanny Parkes, *Wanderings of a Pilgrim* (1850).] *See* **Pranam.**

Kuhar *See* **Kahar.**

Kukang [19C. Mal. *kūkang.*] The Slow Lemur or Loris (*Stenops Javanicus* or *Nycticebus tardigadus*) found from India to Indonesia. [Wood, *Nat. Hist.* (1861), I. 207.]

Kuki [18C.] Any one of several peoples inhabiting the hills of Manipur and Mizoram; a member of one of these; also the language. [*Asiatick Researches* (1799), II. 188.]

Kukri, kookry [18C. H. *kūkrī.*] A curved knife, broadening towards the point, used by the **Gurkhas.** 'A bill, admirably designed and poised for hewing a branch or a foe.' [YB & *OED;* Kirkpatrick, *Nepaul* (1811), v. 118.]

Kulfi [20C. H. *kulfi.*] Milk-rich ice-cream, traditionally cone-shaped. [Hawkins, *CIWIE.*]

Kulin [19C. S. *kulīna,* fr. *kulin;* 'well-born'.] A Bengal Brahmin of the highest class. Also attrib. [*OED; Atlantic Monthly,* Dec. 1866.]

Kulkarani, kulkurnee, coolcurnee [18C. Mar. *kulkarnī,* fr. *kula,* 'a tribe' + *karanī,* 'writer'.] A village accountant and writer (**Cranny**) in central and western parts of India. = the **Patwārī** of N. India. *See* **Curnum** and **Talati.** [YB; Gladwin, *AyeenAkbari*(1783), ii. 338.] *See* **Saswat.**

Kulla, kulah, kullah [20C. H/P. *kulah,* 'cap'.] Cap worn under the turban by Muslims. [*OED; Chambers' Journal,* 29 May 1920.]

Kullah, kula, kla, kalah [18C. Pegu, *Gola;* S. *Gauda.*] Ancient name of N. Bengal; a Burmese name for a native of continental India; an Indian Buddhist immigrant to Burma; also, a Western foreigner. [*OED;* Symes, *Embassy,* (1800), xii. 290.]

Kulli [20C. Place in Baluchistan (Pakistan).] Pertaining to the pre-historic culture of S. Baluchistan, characterized by polychrome vases, small clay objects, female figurines, animals, whistles and carts. [Webster, *3rd New Intern. Dict.* (1976).]

Kullum *See* **Coolung.**

Kumari [H. *Kūmārī.*] Maiden, honorific title. 'Miss' (Fem. of *Kumar,* 'boy'). An epithet of Durga and others. Cape Comorin (Kanya Kumari) received its name from the Durga temple there. [Whitworth, *Anglo-Indian Dict.* (1885).]

Kumbal, kumbli *See* **Cumbly.**

Kumbh Mela [19C. S. *kumbha,* 'pot' (the 'generative pot', representing the womb) + *mela,* 'a fair'.] A festival in the sign of Aquarius, held every 12 years at sacred sites where bathing washes away the sins of Hindu bathers. [A. K. Coomaraswamy, *Yakshas* (1928), ii. 26; Wilson, *Gloss.* (1855).]

Kumbi [20C. H. *kumbi.*] The yellow Silk-Cotton Tree, alias Torchwood Tree, *Cochlospermum gossypium,* whose gum-filled branches are used as torches. *See* **Kuteera.** [Webster, *3rd New Intern. Dict.* (1976).]

Kumbuk *See* **Arjun.**

Kumkum [20C. H. *kunkum,* 'saffron'.] Red powder used by Hindu women for making a mark on the forehead. Also the spot so made. [*OED;* K. Van A. Gates, tr., *Ramabai Ranade's Himself*(1938), VII. 57.] *See* **Namam.**

Kumpass [19C. H. *kampās.*] Corr. of English 'compass'.] Applied additionally to theodolites, sextants and other surveying instruments. [YB; *Confessions of an Orderly* (1866), 175.]

Kumri, Coomry and **Joom** (other names are: dhya, **Taungya** and **Podu**).

Kunbi [16C. H. *Kurmī.*] Member of an Indian farm-labouring caste (**Sudra**). [*OED;* Philip, tr., *Linschoten's Discours Voy.* (1598), i. xxix.]

Kundiah, kundha [19C. H. *kandā.*] Flat cakes of cow-dung mixed with a little straw and water and dried in the sun and used for fuel. *See* **Ooplah** and **Bratty.** [YB; Broughton, *Letters from a Mahratta Camp* (1813).]

Kundalini [20C. S. *kundalinī,* fr. *kundalin,* 'circular, coiled', fr. *kundala,* 'a ring'.] In **Tantra,** the divine power coiled like a snake at the root of the spine (*muladhara chakra*), a manifestation of **Kali.** [Eliade, Cosmical Homology and Yoga, *Journal of the Indian Society of Oriental Art* (1937), 188.]

Kunkur *See* **Kankar.**

Kurakkam, coracan [17C. Sinh. *kurukkan.*] An Indian cereal grass, *Eleusine coracana* (**Ragi**) grown extensively in Sri Lanka. The staple food of poorer Sri Lankans. [*OED;* R. Knox, *Hist. Relation Ceylon* (1681), I. iii. xi.]

Kurta, khurta [20C. H. *kurt(h)a.*] A loose-fitting tunic or shirt, worn by Indian men and women. [*OED;* W. G. Lawrence in T. E. Lawrence, *Home Lett.* (1913; 1954), 485.]

Kurung, kurunj [19C. H. *kurung;* Mar. *kurunj;* S. *kurunja.*] A tree, *Pongamia glabra,* whose seeds yield *kurung*-oil used in India as lamp-oil. *See* **Poonga-Oil** [*OED; Treas. Bot.* (1866), 919/1.]

Kusha [19C. S. *kuso.*] The grass, *Desmostachya bipinnata,* sacred to Hindus, used extensively in Hindu religious ceremonies. [Whitworth, *Anglo-Indian Dict.* (1885).]

Kushti [20C. H. *kūshti.*] Wrestling. [Hawkins, *CIWIE.*]

Kusti [19C. P/Guj. *kustī.*] woollen cord worn round the waist by orthodox **Parsis,** 'consisting of 72 threads to represent the chapters of the *Yashna* of the *Zend-Avesta.* [*OED;* J. Gardner, *Faiths World* (1860), II. 620/1.] *See* **Sudder-Kusti.**

Kusumbha, coosumbah [19C. H/S. *kusumbha.*] (1) Safflower, or 'bastard saffron', *Carthamus tinctorius,* producing a red dye and a medicine in place of saffron. (2) Saffron, *Crocus sativa.* (3) Also the name of a narcotic beverage made of opium or hemp (*Cannabis indica*). [YB; Malcolm, *Mem. of Central India* (1823).]

Kutcha *See* **Cutcha.**

Kuteera, kutera, kutira [19C. H. *katīrā.*] A gum obtained from the shrub *Cochlo-spermum gossypium,* and also from several species of *Sterculia. See* **Kumbi.** [*OED;* T. Thomson, *Chem. Org. Bodies* (1838), 676.]

Kuttar, kuttaur [17C. H. *katār,* fr. S. *kattāra,* 'a dagger'.] 'A kind of dagger peculiar to India, having a solid blade of diamond section, the handle of which consists of two parallel bars with a cross-piece joining them. The hand grips the cross-piece, and the bars pass along each side of the wrist.' [YB & *OED;* Ovington, *Voy. Suratt* (1696), 236; Fryer, *New Account.* (1672-81; 1698), 93.]

Kuzzanna [17C. H. *khizāna;* Ar. *khazīnah* 'a treasure'.] The usual word for the district and general treasuries in British India; *khazānchī* = treasurer. [YB; Hedges, *Diary* (1681-8; Hak. Soc. ed. 1886), i. 103.]

Kuzzilbash [17C. Turk. *kizilbāsh,* 'red-head'.] 'Persianised Turks of the **Shia** persuasion, many of whom took service with the Delhi emperors, and a considerable number with British frontier cavalry regiments in India.' [YB; Fryer, *New Account* (1672-81; ed. 1698), 356.]

Kyah [19C. Beng. *Kyah.*] The Indian Swamp Partridge, *Francolinus gularis,* and found in Nepal, Tibet and Sikkim. [Jerdon, *Birds of Continental India* (1862).]

Kyar *See* **Khair.**

Kythee, Kayati [19C. H. *kaithī.*] A form of cursive **Nagari** character, used by Banyas etc. (fr. H. *Kāyasth;* S. *Kāyastha,* a member of the writer-caste). *See* **Cranny.** [Whitworth, *AngloIndian Dict.* (1885); YB.]

Lac, lacca, laque, etc. [16C. H. *lakh; S. lākshā* Cf. E. *lake;* Fr. *laque;* Pg. *laca.*] 'A transparent red colour.' (a) Dark-red resinous incrustation produced on certain trees (e.g. **Dhawk** and **Peepul**) by the puncture of the *lac* insect, *Tachardia lacca,* or *Coccus lacca;* used to make *shellac, lac-dye, stick-lac, seed-lac, gum-lac,* sealing-wax and varnishes. (b) The crimson colour of *lac; lac-*pigment (1677). (c) Lacquer (1598). (d) *Lac-*coated ware (1662). *See* **Sticklac**. [*OED* & YB; Eden, *Treat. New. Ind.* (1553).]

Lackerage, lackiraz [18C. Ar. *la-khirāj* (treated as one word, *lakhiraj*= 'rent free').] *See* **Khiraj**. [YB; Seton-Karr, *Selections* (1784-1823), i. 49.]

Ladakhi [Place name, *Ladakh* + *ī.*] The language and native of Ladakh; a dialect of Tibetan. [*OED;* Knight, *Where Three Empires Meet* (1893), viii. 123.]

Laddu, luddoo [19C. H. *laddū.*] A ubiquitous Indian sweet confection of balls of sugar, ghee, wheat and gram flour mixed with rasped coconut. By extension, a well-fed, chubby child. [YB; Hockley, *Pandurang Hari* (1826; ed. 1873), i. 197.]

Lady-fish [18C.] Small fish of Indian and many other eastern coastal waters prized for eating, *Sillago sihama,* or *domina.* [*OED;* Cooke, *Voy. S. Sea* (1712), 341.]

Lafanga [19C. H. *lafungga.*] Rascal, boaster, scoundrel. [Platts, *A Dict. of Urdu* etc. (1884).]

Laggar [19C. H. *laggar.*] The common falcon, *Falco biamicus jugger,* generally found at *c.* 2500 ft. in the Himalayas; rare in S. India and Assam. *See* **Jugger**. [Jerdon, *Birds of India* (1862).]

Lahnda, Lahndi [20C. Punj. *lahndā,* 'western'.] An Indo-Aryan language of Western Punjab. Also *attrib.* [*OED;* Risley and Gait, *Rep. Census India,* (1901), 1.211.]

Lakh, lack [16C. H. *lākh; S. laksha.*] In India 100,000 written as 1,00,000, espec. 'one lakh rupees'. In Malaysia 10,000. *See* **Crore**. [*OED* & YB; Hawkins in *Early Travels in India.* (1608-13; 1583-1619; ed. 1921); Litchfield's *Castañeda* (1582), f. 33.]

Laksamana, Laxaman, Laquesimena [17C. Mal./S. *lakshmana,* 'having fortunate tokens'.] (1) Name of Rama's half-brother, who drew the pentacle, the magic figure, to protect Sita against the onslaught of Ravana. (2) A Malay honorific title meaning 'Warden of the Coast' or admiral, originally assumed by Hang Tuah according to the *Sējarah Mēlayu (Malay Annals).* [*OED* & YB; Danvers & Foster, *Letters* etc. (1615; ed. 1900), IV. 6.]

Lakshmi, Laxmi [S. *Lakshmi.*] Hindu goddess of good fortune, identified with *Shri,* wife of **Vishnu;** the benign aspect of **Shakti**, the supreme goddess. Many festivals are celebrated in her honour. [Whitworth, *Anglo-Indian Dict.* (1885).]

Lall-shraub [18C. H. *lāl-sharāb,* 'red wine'.] The universal Anglo-Indian name for claret in India. [YB; Busteed, *Echoes of Old Calcutta* (c. 1780; ed. 1857), 123.]

Lall [17C. H/P. *lālā,* 'domestic tutor' in Persia.] In India a child's bearer. In N. India applied to an Indian clerk writing the vernacular, or to a respectable merchant. [YB; Verelst, *View* etc. (1772), App. 218.]

Lama [17C. Tibet. *bLma* (silent *b*).] A Buddhist monk of Tibet and Mongolia. The Dalai lama (now in exile in India) denominates the chief Lama, formerly ruler of Tibet. *Lamasery,* a *Lama-*monastery. Also *lamaism; -ist.* (1817) [*OED* & YB; tr. Martini, *Conq. China* (1654), 13; Bernier, *Travels* (E. tr. 1684), 135.]

Lamballie, lomballie, lombardie, lambadi, etc. [18C. H. *Lāmbārā;* Mar. *Lamban.*] A wandering tribe of dealers in grain, salt, etc. (*See* **Brinjarry**). The name, now obsolete, may have been derived from their carrying salt (S. *lavana*). [YB; Orme, *Hist. of Milit. Trans.* (1778), ii. 102; Crooke, *Tribes of N.W.F.P.* etc. (1896).]

Lambardar *See* **Lumberdar**.

Lanchara, lantcha [17C. Mal. *lanchār,* 'swift'; Pg. *lanchara.*] A small swift vessel used by the Portuguese in the E. Indies in the 16th & 17th centuries [*OED;* & YB; Pinto, Cogan's trans. (1653), ix. 27.] (Cf. E. *launch*).

Landwind, landtorne [16C. Anglo-Indian trans. of Pg. *terrenho.*] A wind, so termed in S. India, that blows seaward during the night and early morning, sometimes with dangerous effects. The opposite wind was known as the 'Seatorne'. [*OED* & YB; Danvers, *Letters* (1615), 1. 206; Phillips, tr., Linschoten, *Discours* etc. (1598).]

Langar [19C. H/P. *langar.*] Free kitchen, alms-house; army-kitchen. In Marathi any extensive establishment is called *langarkhāna.* [Whitworth, *Anglo-Indian Dict.* (1885).]

Langooty, lungooty, longot [16C. H. *langotī*.] A pocket handkerchief loin-cloth, 'the scantiest modicum of covering worn for decency by some of the lower classes when at work, and tied before and behind by a string round the waist'. [YB.] *See* **Lungi**. [*OED; Indian Antiquary* (1579; ed. 1871-1933), IX.]

Langra [19C. H. *langra*.] Mango of Uttar Pradesh. [Hawkins, *CIWIE*.]

Langur, lungoor [19C. H. *langūr*; S. *lāngūlin*, 'tailed'.] The slim, long-tailed, white-bearded Indian monkey (genus *Presbytes*) identified by Hindus as the monkey-god, *Hanuman*. [OED; & YB; Heber, *Journey* etc. (1826), 11. 85.]

Lanka, Lunka [20C. S. *Laṅka*.] The oldest and the newest name of Ceylon = 'an island'. The full title is *Sri Lanka Janarajaya*. (The Republic of Sri Lanka.) *See* **Lungkah**.

Lantana [18C. Mod. L. *lantana*.] Prolif., ubiquitous and troublesome flowering and prickly shrub in India of the family *Verbenaceae* (*Lantan aculeata*). [*OED*; Bartam, *Carolina* (1791), 103.]

Lantea [17C. Orig. unknown.] A swift kind of rowing boat often mentioned by Portuguese writers. [YB; *Pinto* (Cogan's trans. 1653 by II.Ç. Gent), 69; *c*. 1560, Caspar da Cruz in Purchas (1625-6), 111. 174.]

Larani [19C. H. *laraī*, 'fighting'.] 'The biting and annoyance of fleas and the like'. (Not in Fallon or Platts.) [YB.]

Larin, larine [16C. P. *lāri*.] From Lar, a place on the Persian Gulf. 'A peculiar kind of money used on the W. coast of India, in the Maldive Islands and on the Persian Gulf, in the shape of a small rod of silver bent double unequally.' [YB & *OED; Master Caesar Fredericke* (*c*. 1563) in Hakluyt (ed. 1807), ii. 343; Fitch in *Early Travels in India* (1583-1619; ed. 1921.)

Larkin [17C. Anglo-Indian. Poss. fr. Robert Larkin, chief of the E.I.C. factory at Patani (1616).] A kind of drink. [YB; P. Della Valle, *Journeys* (E. tr. by G. Havers, 1664).]

Lascar, lascari(n) [16C. H/P. *lashkarī*, native soldiers, fr. P. *lashkar*, 'an army', 'a camp'.] (1) An East Indian sailor (1625-73). (2) A 'tent pitcher' (1798). (3) An inferior class of artillery man; a *gun-lascar* (1598). *See* **Classy**. *Lascaree* was a short hunting-spear or javelin for throwing (1712). [*OED* & YB; Linschoten, *Discours of Voyages* (E. tr. 1598); Purchas, *Pilgrimes* (1625-6), I.v.650.] *See* **Serang**.

Lascarine, lascareen [16C. Pg. *lasquarin;* P. *lashkarī*.] *See* prec. An East Indian soldier; also a policeman (1825). [*OED;* Philips, *Linschoten* (1598), 1.XXXIX, 74.]

Lashkar [17C. H/P. *lashkar*, 'army, camp'.] A camp of *sepoys* (1634); a body of armed men, esp. of tribal Afghans. *See* **Lascar**. [*OED;* Sir T. Roe, in Purchas, *Pilgrimes* (1625), 1. 559.]

Lassi [20C. H. *lassī*.] Aerated buttermilk. [Hawkins, *CIWIE*.]

Lasya [20C. S. *lāsya*.] A graceful, soft, rounded, style of female dancing. [*OED*.] *See* **Tandava**. [Sastri and Ayyangar, in *Sankara Acharya Saundarya-Lahari* (1937), 160.]

Lat¹ [19C. H. *lāt*.] Corr. of *lot*, in an auction. [YB; Carnegy, *Kachahri Technicalities* (1877).]

Lat,² lath [19C. H. *lāt(h)*.] (1) Staff, pole. (2) Obelisk or monumental column, e.g. Buddhist columns of eastern India and elsewhere. [*OED* & YB; *Asiatic Ann. Reg. Misc. Tracts*. (1800), 312/2.]

Laterite [19C. L. *later*, 'brick' + *ite*.] 'A reddish, porous, brick-like argillaceous formation impregnated with iron peroxide and hardening on exposure to the atmosphere, which is found in places all over S. India. Laterite was the usual material for road metal in S. India, as **Kunkur** was in the north. In Sri Lanka it is called **Cabook**.' [YB & *OED;* Buchanan, *Mysore* etc. (1807), ii. 440-41.]

Lathi, lattee, lathee [19C. H. *lathī*, fr. S. *yashtī*, 'a stick'.] A long, heavy, iron-tipped stick or bludgeon used as a law enforcement weapon by Indian police. [*OED* & YB.] *See* **Lat(i)**. [Fanny Parkes, *Wanderings of a Pilgrim* (1850), i. 138.]

Lāt Sāhib [19C. Corr. of *Lord Sāhib*.] The title by which the Governor-General of India was generally known in the vernaculars. Also extended to Lieutenant-Governors, who became *Chotā Lāt Sāhibs*. Also written *Lārd Sāhib*. A bishop was known as *Lāt Padre Sāhib* and the Chief Justice as *Lāt Justy Sāhib*. [YB; Heber, *Narrative* etc. (1844), i. 69.]

Latteal [19C. H. *lāthīyāl*, 'a club-man'.] A hired ruffian, or **Goonda**. Also *lāthīwāllāh* [YB]. *See* **Lathi** [*Life in the Mofussil*, Anon. (1878).]

Lavani [19C. H. *lāvani*.] Kind of folk-song. [Hawkins, *CIWIE*.]

Law officer [Anglo-Indian.] A Muslim learned in Muslim law; a functionary of the judges' court in the districts, and of the **Sudder** courts of the Presidency. At first the law-officers were **Cazees** and **Mufties**, with some superintendence from senior servants of the **Company**, but their posts were abolished in 1864. There were also Hindu Law officers (**Pundits**) in cases concerning Hindus, but it would appear that they ceased to function before 1860. [YB; *Regulation passed by the Governor-General and Council* (11 April 1780).]

Laximana *See* **Laksamana**.

Leep [19C. H. *līp.*] To wash or plaster with cow-dung and water. *See* **Lipi**. [*OED;* Kipling, *Second Jungle Book* (1895), 80.]

Left-hand. *See* **Balagai** and **Yedagai**.

'Lemon' = Lime [17C. Pg. *limāo;* Ar. *līmah;* P. *limūn;* Mal. *limau;* H. *nimbū;* S. *nimbū.*] 'the lime'. The fruit of the *Citrus aurantifolia*. [*The Travels of Sir T. Herbert* (1638).] *See* **Nimbu**.

Lemon-grass [19C. H/S *nimbu,* the lime.] A grass, *Andropogon citratus,* cultivated in Sri Lanka and elsewhere for its oil, sometimes called Oil of Verbena, used in perfumery, and as a mosquito deterrent. The name is also applied to another grass, *A. schoenanthus,* which yields Rusa oil, and grows wild in India. [*OED* & YB; Royle, *Ess. Antiq. Hindu* Med. (1837), 82.]

Leopard [14C. L. *leo,* 'lion' + *pard,* 'panther'; S. *prdakus,* 'tiger, panther'.] An Indian carnivore, *Felis panthera* or *pardus*. The name is supposed to indicate a hybrid of a lion and 'pard' (panther). [*OED* & YB.] *See* **Bagh(wagh)** [Jerdon, *The Mammals of India* (1874); Chaucer, *Monk's Tale* (c. 1386), 271; Blanford, *Fauna of British India,* (1888-91), 68.]

Lepcha [19C. Native name.] A member of a Mongoloid people native to Sikkim; their language (Tibeto-Burman); pertaining to the Lepchas and their language, spoken in Eastern Nepal, Sikkim and Darjeeling. [*See* **Rong**. [*OED;* Hamilton, *Acct. Kingd. Nepal* (1819), II. i. 118.]

Lewaya [Sin. *lewaya.*] 'lagoon, saltpan'. [Hawkins, *CIWIE*.]

Leza [19C. Orig. unknown.] A heavy, hard, grey-brown, smooth, lustrous timber of an Indian tree, *Lagerstroemia tomentosa,* used for furniture, floors and panels. [Webster, *3rd New Intern. Dict.*]

Lezim [19C. H.] A kind of bow with chains attached, used in gymnastics. [Hawkins, *CIWIE*.]

Lichi, litchi, leechee, lychee [16C. Ch. *lī-tchī.*] The fruit of the tree, *Lichi chinensis,* introduced into Bengal from China in the 18th C. but mentioned by the Portuguese and others from the 16th C. [*See.* Sonnerat, *Voy. aux Indes Orientales* (1782), III. 255. [*OED* & YB; Parke's *Mendoza* (1588), i. 14; Dampier, Voy (1697; 1729), II. i. 24.]

Lila [19C. S. *līla.*] Hinduism: The playful activity of the Supreme Spirit in the Universe. Play, sport, amusement; amorous sport; wonderful acts; theatrical performance. *Lila-ghar,* 'pleasure-house'. [*OED;* H. H. Wilson in *Asiatick Researches* (1828), XVI. 115.]

Lilac [17C. H. *līl;* S. *nīla,* 'dark blue'.] The shrub, *Syringa vulgaris,* producing fragrant blue or white blossoms. *See* **Anil** and **Indigo**. Also *attrib.* (In Scotland Hobson-Jobsonised as 'Lily-oak'. [YB; Bacon, *Essay on Gardens* (1625).]

Lingam, linga, ling [18C. H/S *lingga(m)* 'mark, token'.] A phallic symbol of **Shiva**-worship. Hence; *lingamism,* worship of *lingams* (1843). [*OED* & YB; T. Phillips, tr. *Thirty-four Conferences* etc. (1719), 326] *See* **Pandaram**.

Lingayat, Lingait, Lingayet, etc. [17C. Mar. *Lingā-īt;* Kan. *Lingāyata.*] A member of a Saivaite sect in W & S. India, whose adherents wear the *linga* in a small gold or silver box suspended round the neck, and who are buried upright in their graves instead of being cremated. This sect was founded in the 12th C. by *Basava*. [YB; Monier-Williams, *Brahmanism* (1891); Fryer, *A New Account* (1672-81), 153.]

Linguist(er) [17C. Anglo-Indian. fr. L. *lingua,* 'tongue'.] An old word for an interpreter, formerly much used in India and the Far East, 'probably adopted from Pg. *lingua* used for an interpreter'. [YB]. *See* **Topass** and **Dubash**. [Danvers, *Letters* (1612; ed. 1896-1900), i. 68. 'Let. to Gov. Fort St George' in Dalrimple, *Orient Report* (1760), 1. 396.]

Lipi [20C. S. *līpī,* 'plastering'.] Writing in general, handwriting, script, alphabet. *See* **Leep**. [Hawkins, *CIWIE*.]

Lip-lap [18C. Dutch slang, poss. from Jav. *laplap,* 'a dish clout' (Klinkert).] A vulgar and disparaging nickname given in the old Dutch East Indies to Eurasians, corresponding to Anglo-Indian **Chi-Chi (Chee-Chee)** applied to Eurasians in India. Also applied to any Dutch child born in the East Indies. *See* **Country-Born, Mustees, Castees, Eurasian, Anglo-Indian**. [*OED* & YB; Wilcocke, tr. Stavorinus, *Voy. E. Indies* (1798), 1. ii. v. 315.]

Lok, log [19C. H. *lok* 'people'.] (The) people, e.g. Kipling's *bandar-log,* 'monkey people'. Hence, *Baba-log,* 'children'; *Bhadra-lok,* 'upperclass people'. [*OED*.] *See* next. [Kipling, *Second Jungle Book* (1895).]

Lok Sabha [20C. H. *lok,* 'people' + *sabhā,* 'assembly'.] The people's assembly. The Lower House of the central Indian parliament, the *Rajya Sabhā* being the Upper House. [*OED.*] *See* next. [Binani and Rama Rao, *India at a Glance* (1954), 178.]

Loknayak [20C. H. *lok,* 'people' + *nayak,* 'hero'.] The People's Hero: Jayaprakash Narayan's popular political nickname. Also *Lok Sangharsh-Samiti,* 'People's Struggle Committee', formed by Jayaprakash Narayan in 1975 to force Indira Gandhi to resign her premiership. [Rajni Kothari, *Politics in India* (1970).]

Long-cloth [16C. Poss. corr. of **Lungi.**] First applied to Indian (white) cotton shirtings exported to England; calico manufactured in long pieces. [*OED* & YB; Rates Custom-House (1545), d. iii. *Notes and Extracts, Fort St. George* (9th Nov. 1670, 1670-81).]

Long-drawers [17C.] Old-fashioned Anglo-Indian equivalent for **Pyjamas.** *See also* **Mogul Breeches, Shalwars, Sirdrars, Pyjamas.** [YB; Pietro Della Valle, *Voyage,* E. tr Havers (1664; ed. Hak. Soc.), i. 43]

Long-shore wind [19C.] The damp unpleasant wind that blows from the south in some seasons in Madras, espec. July to September. [YB; Maitland, *Letters from Madras* (1836-39), 73.]

Loo [19C. H. *lū* fr. S. *ulkā,* 'flame'.] A hot wind laden with dust, in Bihar and the Punjab. [*OED;* Kipling, *Phantom Rickshaw* (1888), 78.]

Loocher [19C. H. *lūchchā.* Anglo-Indian colloquial.] 'a lewd loafer' 'a blackguard', 'a libertine'. Also *loochajee.* [YB; *Or. Sporting Mag.* (1828-33; ed. 1873), i. 121; Hockley, *Pandurang Hari* (1826).]

Loochi [20C. H. *lūchchi.*] Thin puffed **Puree.** [Hawkins, *CIWIE.*]

Loosewallah [20C.] Anglo-Indian hybrid. A loose person, a thief. *See* **Wallah.** [Hawkins, *CIWIE.*]

Loot [18C. H. *lūt,* fr. S. *lōtra.*] 'booty, plunder, pillage; or S. *lunt,* 'to rob'. Also trans. vb. to *loot* (1845). Long a familiar item in Anglo-Indian colloquial, it has now become standard English. Also *looties,* a body of irregulars chiefly concerned with plunder in warfare. [Orme, *Hist. Milit. Trans.* (1757); *OED* & YB; Stockdale, *Indian Vocabulary* (1788). *See* **Wag.**

Looty, lootie-wallah [18C. H. *lūtīwālā.* 'A plunderer'.] *See* **Wallah.** A member of a gang of *looties,* marauders. [*OED* & YB; Orme, *Hist. Milit. Trans.* (1757), 11. vii. 129; Munro *Narrative* (1780-84; ed. 1789), 295.]

Loquot, loquat [19C. Ch. *luh kwat,* 'rush orange'.] A Chinese and Japanese fruit (-tree),

Eriobotrya japonica, naturalized in India and elsewhere. Not unlike a plum. [*OED* & YB; Hoole, *Missions in Madras & Mysore* (1820-28; ed. 1844), 159.]

Loranthus [19C. Bot. L. fr. *lorum,* 'strap' + Gr. *anthos,* 'flower'.] A parasitic plant of the family *Loranthaceae,* found in India. [*OED;* Lindley, *Veg. Kingd.* (1846), 789.]

Lorcha [17C. Pg. *lorcha* (of uncertain origin).] A fast sailing vessel built in China, with European style hull and Chinese rig, usually carrying guns. [Occurring in *Pinto* (1540). *OED* & YB; Cogan, tr. of Pinto's *Travels,* (1653), xv. 47.]

Loris [18C. Poss. fr. Dutch *loeris,* 'booby, clown'.] Kind of lemur; small, slender, tailless, nocturnal, Sinhalese mammal, *Loris gracilis,* the 'slender loris'. [*OED;* Goldsmith, *Nat. Hist.* (1774), 11.373.]

Lory [16C. Mal. *lūrī, nūrī,* 'parrot', family *Loriīnae.*] (Cf. *lorikeet,* dim. of *lory* (1784), genera *Loriculus*). Imported into southern India as early as the 14th century. It is called in the vernacular by a name signifying 'Five-coloured parrot' (Kan. *panchavarna-gini*). [*OED* & YB; Galvano, *Discoveries of the World* (E. tr. Bethune (1555); ed. Hak. Soc., 1863), IV. 424; Linschoten, *Discours of Voyages* (E. tr. 1598; Hak. Soc., 1807), i. 307; Fryer, *New Acct. E. India & Persia* (1672-81), 116.]

Lota(h), lootah [19C. H. *lotā.*] A small round (brass) pot used for drinking-water and sometimes for cooking. Also extended to the spherical pipkins of earthenware used by Indians. *See* **Chatty, Ghurra.** [*OED* & YB; Williamson, *Vade Mecum* (1810), ii. 284; *Chron. in Ann. Reg.* (1809), 310/1.]

Lote [19C. Mod. Hind. *lōt.*] Corr. of English ('bank-) note'. Sometimes *bānklōt.* [YB.]

Love-Bird [18C. H. *latkan,* 'pendent'; because it sleeps upside down hanging by its claws.] The Indian lorikeet, *Loriculus vernalis.* [YB; Salim Ali, *Handbook* etc. (1969); Sparrman, *Voy. to the Cape of Good Hope* (1785).]

Lubbye, lubbee [19C. Tel. *Labbi;* Tam. *Ilappai* (poss. Dravidian corr. of *'Arubī*).] Tamil speaking Muslims in S. India 'supposed to be, like the **Moplahs** of the west coast, the descendants of Arab emigrants by inter-marriage with native women'. [YB.] An energetic and industrious people. *See* **Navayat.** [YB; Wilks, *Hist. Sketches* (1810-17), i. 243.]

Luckerbaug [18C. H. *lakrā, lakarbaghā,* 'hyena', lit. a 'stick'.] Name applied to the leopard or to the hyena, referring to the bar-like stripes on the animal. [YB; Hickey's *Bengal Gazette* (24 June 1781).]

Luddoo *See* **Laddoo.**

Lugow, to [19C. fr. H. *lagā-nā*, 'to apply, attach, join, fix'.] (Example of Anglo-Indian custom of using the imperative form (*lagao*) of a Hindi verb as an infinitive.) 'To lay a boat alongside the shore, or wharf, to moor.' [YB.] (*See* **Bunow, Puckerow, Foozilow.**) [YB; Davidson, *Travels in Upper India* (1843), ii. 20.]

Lumberdar, lambardar [19C. fr. E. number + *dār*, 'agent'. H. *lambardār*,] 'the man who is registered by a number.' Also the registered headman of an Indian village. 'The cultivator who, either on his own account or as the representative of other members of the village pays the government dues and is registered in the **Collector's** Roll according to his number.' [YB & *OED*; H.H. Wilson, *Gloss.* (1855); A. Wilson, *Abode of Snow* (1875), 97.]

Lungi, loonghee, lungyi [17C. H/P. *lungī*.] Also Burmese *lungyi*. Cloth wrapped round the hips, like a Malay *sarong*; loosely tied or tucked in at the waist. Also, the material for this. *See* **Langooty, Dhoti.** [*OED* & YB; *Eng. Fact. in India* (1619); 1618-69; ed. 1906-27).]

Lungkah, lunka(h) [Tel/S.] *Lanka*, name of the islands of the Godavari delta (cf. *Sri Lanka*). A kind of strong Indian cheroot made from Lanka tobacco. *See* **Trichy.** [YB & *OED*; Conan Doyle, *Sign of Four* (1889).]

Lungooty *See* **Langooty** and **Lungi.**

M

Ma [H. *mā.*] Mother. *See* **Mata.** [YB.]

Ma-Bap [19C. H. *ma,* 'mother' + *bap* 'father'.] 'Āp mā-bāp hai khudā-wand!' 'You my Lord, are my mother and father.' 'This was an address from a native seeking assistance, begging release from a penalty, or reluctant to obey an order, which the young *sahib* heard at first with astonishment but soon as a matter of course.' [YB.]

Macaque [18C. Pg. *macaco,* 'monkey, ape'.] Squat, short-tailed monkey of the genus *Macaca.* Some species are trained to pick ripe coconuts. *See* **Rhesus** and **Bandar.** [*OED;* Blythe (1840), tr., *Cuvier's Anim. Kingd.* (1849), 58; E. Balfour, *Cycle. India,* 3rd ed. (1885), ii. 753/2.]

Macareo [16C. Orig. unknown.] 'A term applied by old voyagers to the phenomenon of the *bore* or great tidal wave, as seen espec. in the Gulf of Cambay, and in the Sitang estuary in Pegu.' [YB; Frederick, *Voyage* (1568; Hakl. ed. 1807), ii. 342.]

Mace [16C. Malay *ĕmas,* 'gold', poss. fr. S. *māsha,* 'a weight; *c.* 17 grams'.] (a) In the Malay archipelago, a small gold coin, or a weight. (b) In China, money of account about 1/10 of a silver *liang. See* **Masha.** [*OED* & YB; Linschoten, *Discours of Voyages* (E. tr. 1598), 44.]

Machan, muchan [19C. H. *machān;* S. *mancha.*] A raised observation platform for **Shikar,** or crop protection: 'to watch a tiger, to guard a field, or what not'. [YB & *OED;* Sanderson, *Thirteen Years,* 3rd ed. (1882).] *See* **Pela.**

Machardani [19C. H. *machchar,* 'mosquito' + *dani,* container.] A mosquito-net. [Whitworth, *Anglo-Indian Dict.* (1885).]

Machis [19C. Anglo-Indian.] Kitchen Hindustani for 'matches'. [YB.]

Machwa *See* **Mashwa.**

Madal(a), maddale [20C.] Double-headed drum of Nepal and Eastern India. *See* **Mridangam.** [*OED;* Strangways, *Mus. Hindustan* (1914).]

Madapollam [17C.] Place-name, on the Southern Delta-branch of the Godavari, properly *Madhavapalam* (Tel. *Madhavayyapalam*). A kind of fine white piece-goods, intermediate between calico and muslin, originally made at Madapollam. [*OED* & YB; Danvers, *Letters* (1610; ed. 1896-1900), i. 74.]

Madrafaxao [19C.] A gold coin (185 grs.) of Gujarat, probably referring to one of the many rulers of Gujarat named Muzaffar Shah. [YB; Thomas, *Pathan Kings* (1871), 353.]

Madras [17C.] Place-name: Capital city of Tamil Nadu. Orig. *Madraspatam* (1673). 'Applied to large bright-coloured handkerchiefs of silk warp and cotton woof' (1830, obs.) Also, *Madras*-muslin (1882); *Madras*-lace (1882), and other textiles, e.g. *Bleeding Madras* (1862), a cloth in which the colours run and change after washing. *Madras*-stucco = **Chunam** (1864). [*OED* & YB; Fryer, *A New Acct. of E. India & Persia* (1672-81), 38, 39; M. Scott (1833), *Tom Cringle* (1842), xvi.]

Madrasa(h), medresseh [17C. H/Ar. *madrasa(h)* fr. *darasa,* 'to study'.] A Muslim college. Orig. a seminary of higher Sunni learning to produce scholars (*ulama*) of the *Asha'rī* school, qualified to run the government according to orthodox Sunni ideas. [Davies, tr., *Olearius' Voy. Ambass.* (1662), 214.]

Madrasi [19C. H. *Madrasī.* Adj. pert. to Madras.] Inhabitant of Madras. [*OED;* Chambers' *Journal,* Feb. 1878, 115/1.]

Madura Foot [19C.] Place-name in S. India. A fungoidal disease of the foot, *maduromycosis* or *mycetoma* (at one time thought to be incurable except by amputation of the foot), which occurs in the Madura district and elsewhere, espec. in places where the 'black soil' prevails. [*OED* & YB; Fox, *Skin Dis. Parasitic Orig.* (1863), 16.]

Magar *See* **Mugger.**

Magrib, maghrib [19C. Ar. *magrib.*] 'West', to which Muslims in India and Pakistan, etc. turn in times of prayer (**Namaz**). Also *Maghribi,* language and native of the Maghrib (N. W. Africa). [Lane, tr., *Arabian Nights Entertainments* (1840), ii. xviii. 600.]

Mahabharat(a), The [19th. S. *mahā,* 'great' + *Bharata,* an ancient Hindu dynasty.] One of the **Puranas.** The great Sanskrit epic by Vyasa, concerning the war between Bharata's descendants, in which the five Pandava brothers, with **Krishna's** help, are victorious over their enemies, the **Kauravas.** [*OED.* Hastings *Let.* (4th Oct. 1784); Wilkins, tr., *Bhāgvat Geeta* (1785).]

Mahadeva [19C. S. *mahā,* 'great' + *deva,* 'god'.] The great god **Siva.** [Whitworth, *Anglo-Indian Dict.* (1885).]

Mahajan, mahajun [19C. H. *mahā,* great + *jan,* 'man'; S. *mahājana,* head of a tribe or caste.]

(1) Moneylender, broker, banker. (2) Trade or craft guild, often coterminous with caste. (3) *Mahajani* = a style of writing **Devanagari.** [*OED* & YB; Wilson, *Gloss. of Judicial and Revenue Terms* (1855); *Gloss. to 5th Report* (1813).]

Mahal, mahaul [17C. H/Ar. *mahall,* fr. *halla,* 'to lodge'.] (1) Private apartments or lodgings. [*OED;* Herbert, *Trav.* (1638), 71.] (2) Summerhouse or palace. [*OED;* Purchas, *Pilgrimes* (1625), 1. iv. 428; Finch in *Early Trav.* (1608).] (3) Territorial division in India; ward of a town; tract of land for farming or **Shikar.** (Also *mahalla.*) [*OED* & YB; *Indian Antiq.* (1793).] (4) Coarse, woven carpet made in Iran. [*OED;* Lewis, *Pract. Bk. Orient. Rugs* (1911), xiii. 201.]

Mahaleb [19C. Ar. *mahalab.*] A kind of cherry, *Prunus mahaleb,* whose fragrant kernels are strung as necklaces by the women of Sind and other parts of India. [*OED;* Simmonds, *Dict. Trade* (1858).]

Mahamaya [19C. S. *maha,* 'great' + *maya,* 'illusion'.] Hinduism: The transcendent power of illusion. [Sir Charles Eliot, *Hinduism & Buddhism* (1921), ii. 210.]

Mahannah *See* **Meeana.**

Mahant(a) [19C. H. *mahant,* 'a religious superior'.] Head of a Hindu **Mutt** (monastery) or a **Sikh Gurdwara;** (temple) priest. [*OED; Asiat. Reg. Misc. Tr.* (1800), 247/1.]

Maharaja(h) [17C. S. *mahā,* 'great' + *raja,* 'sovereign'.] Indian prince; *Maharaj* (1826). A title of some Indian princes. So, *Maharani,* a *Maharajah's* wife (*rani,* 'queen', 'princess') (1855). [*OED;* Fryer, *A New Acct. of E. India & Persia* (1672-81; ed. 1698).]

Maharana [19C. S. *mahā* + *rānā* (dial. var. of *rajah*).] As prec., espec. in the title of the *Maharana* of *Udaipur* (Rajputana). [*OED;* Malcolm, *Mem. Cent. India.* (1823), 1. viii. 342.]

Maharashtri, Maharashtra [19C. S. *mahā* + *rāshtrī,* fr. *rāshtrā,* 'kingdom!', great kingdom.] The ancient **Prakrit** language of the Maharashtra region of India, the modern descendant of which is **Marathi (Maharatti).** Also **Maharashtrian,** adj. & sb. [*OED.*] [Colebrooke, in *Asiatick Res.* (1803), vii. 227.]

Maharishi [18C. H. *maharishi* fr. S. *mahā-rishi,* 'great sage'.] *See* **Rishi** and **Guru.** A Hindu sage, or a popular leader of spiritual thought. [*OED;* Wilkins, tr., *Bhāgvāt Geeta* (1785), 144.]

Mahasamadhi [20C. S. *mahā* + *samadhi.*] 'deep contemplation.' In Hinduism and Buddhism, the highest state of **Samadhi:** profound meditation on the supreme being. [Sir Charles Eliot, *Hinduism & Buddhism* (1921), 1.83.]

Mahatma [19C. S. *mahā* + *atman,* 'great souled'.] Hinduism, Buddhism: one possessing preternatural powers; a great spiritual being; a **Brahman** sage. *The Mahatma:* the honorific title given (1931) to the great modern Indian Leader, M. K. Gandhi (1869-1948). Hence *Mahatmaism* (1905). [*OED; Daily News,* 14 Feb. 1855.]

Mahavihara *See* **Vihara.**

Mahavira [19C. S. *Mahāvīra;* 'Great Hero.'] The last of the 24 **Tirthankaras;** also an honorific title among Jains. (The epithet *Mahāvīra* is also applied to Vishnu, Rama, Hanuman and Garuda.) *The Cambridge Hist. of India* (1922), 1.154.]

Mahayana [19C. S. *mahā* + *yāna,* 'vehicle. 'The great Vehicle'.] One of the two great systems of Buddhism, later and more widespread than the little vehicle, **Hinayana.** Also *Mahayanism, -ist, -istic.* [*OED;* Fergusson, *Tree and Serpent Worship* (1868), 65.] *See* **Yogacara** and **Zen.**

Mahomet(an) *See* **Mohammedan.**

Mahout, mohaut, etc. [17C. H. *mahāut, mahāwat,* S. *mahā-mātra,* lit: 'great in measure'.] The driver and attendant of an elephant. [*OED* & YB; Davies, tr., *Mandelslo's Travels* (1662), 81.]

Mahrata, Mahratta [18C.] *See* **Maratha.**

Ma(h)rathi, Mahratti, Moratty, etc. [17C.] Pertaining to the **Marathas** and their language. [*OED;* Fryer, *A New Acct. of E. India and Persia* (1672-81; ed. 1698), 174.]

Mahratta Ditch [18C.] An excavation dug in 1742 on the landward sides of Calcutta to protect it from the attacks of the **Marathas.** 'Hence the term "The Ditch" as a disparaging name for Calcutta, and **Ditchers** for its citizens.' [YB.] There was an excavation of the same name at Madras excavated in 1790. [YB; Orme, *Hist. of the Milit. Trans.* (1763).]

Mahseer, maseer, masal [19C. H. *mahaser.* (Poss. deriv. fr. S. *mahā-siras,* 'big-head').] A large fresh-water cyprinoid fish of the larger species of *Barbus,* resembling the barbel. (*Barbus tor*). [*OED* & YB; Buchanan, *Eastern India* (1809; ed. 1838), iii. 194 and *Fishes of the Ganges* (1822), 304.]

Mahsud, Mahsood [19C.] Tribal name. A member of one of the principal tribes of Waziristan noted for their bellicosity. Also *adj.* [Balfour, *Cycl. India* (1873).]

Mahwa, mahua, moa, mohwa, etc. [17C. H. *mahwa*, fr. S. *madhūka*, fr. *madhu*, 'sweet'.] A large flowering tree, *Madhuca indica*, and *latifolia* (family *Sapotaceae*) from whose orange-pink, fleshy edible flowers an intoxicating drink is brewed. The timber is strong and durable. A related tree is the Indian Butter Tree, *Madhuca butyracea* (1889), whose seeds yield an oily butter-like substance. Also, *mowrah meal*, the dried and powdered residue of the seeds of the *mahwa* tree after the oil has been extracted, used as a pesticide to kill worms in turf (1939). The bark is used to cure leprosy, the flowers to relieve coughs, biliousness and heart trouble, the fruit for tuberculosis and blood diseases. Altogether a most rewarding tree. [*OED & YB*; Boulger, *Uses of Plants* (1889); Finch in *Early Travels in India* (1583-1619).]

Maida [H. *maida*.] Fine wheat flour. [Hawkins, *CIWIE*.]

Maidan, mydan, meidaun [17C. H/P. *maidān*.] An open-space, parade-ground in or adjoining a town; any open plain with grass on it; a *chaugān* (see **Chicane**), ground; a battlefield. [*YB & OED*; Finch in *Early Travels in India* (1583-1619; ed. 1921).]

Mainato [16C. Tam/Mal. *maināttu*.] A washerman or **Dhoby**. [*YB*; Linschoten, *Discours* (E. tr. 1598); Cogan's *Pinto's Voyages* (1653).]

Maistry, mistry, mystery [18C. H. *mistrī* fr. Pg. *mestre*, 'a foreman, a master workman'.] An artisan, mason, bricklayer, mechanic, fitter, blacksmith, etc. In W & S. India *maistry*, as used in the household, generally meant the cook or tailor. See **Caliph** (**Calefa**). [*YB & OED*; Wellington, *Wellesley's Despatches* (1798).]

Maithili [19C.] The Indo-Aryan dialect of Bihari. Also the script. [*OED*; Grierson, *Introd. Maithili Lang. of N. Bihar* (1881).]

Maithuna See **Mithuna.**

Maitreya [19C. S. *maitrī*, 'friendship'.] Buddhism: the name of the future Buddha. Also the artistic representation of this Buddha. [*OED*; Monier-Williams, *Buddhism*, (1889), iv. 135.]

Majlis, medjelis, etc. [19C. H/Ar. *majlis*.] 'Assembly, council.' Also, reception room. [*OED*; Balfour, *Cycl. India* (1885).]

Majoon, majun, majum [18C. H/Ar. *majūn*, lit. 'kneaded'.] Compound of medicines kneaded with syrup into a soft mass', espec. applied to an intoxicating confection prepared from a selection of the leaves of *Cannibis indica* with milk, *ghee*, sugar, poppy-seeds, the flowers of the thorn-apple (**Datura**), the powder of *nux vomica* etc. [*YB & OED*; Lyndsay *Journal of Captivity* (1781; ed. 1840), iv. 222.]

Makai [19C. H. *makā, makai*.] Indian corn, maize, *Zea mais*. [Whitworth, *Anglo-Indian Dict.* (1885).]

Makara [19C. H/S. *makara*.] Mythical Hindu sea-creature, sometimes a crocodile (**Mugger**) with an antelope's head; the equivalent of Capricorn in the signs of the Zodiac. [*OED*; Balfour, *Cycl. India* (1857).]

Malabar [16C. Place name. Etym. uncertain. Poss. fr. Dravidian *malai*, 'hill' + P(?) *bar*, 'region'.] (1) The name of the sea-board country which the Arabs called the 'Pepper Coast'; the ancient *Kerala* of the Hindus; now the modern state of **Kerala**. [Litchfield, *Castañeda* (1582).] (2) The word was applied by the Portuguese to the inhabitants of Malabar (1582) and to the language of the region (1552), though it was also used for **Tamil** as well (see next). See **Malayalam, Malayali.** The word is also used for a kind of handkerchief (1882) and attributively in the names of plants, products, etc., e.g. Malabar bark, genus *Ochna*, (1885); –catmint, *Anisomeles malbarica* (1813); –laurel, *Melastoma malabathrica* (1882); –leaf, *Cinnamomum malabathrum* (1840); –nightshade, the chenapodiaceous genus *Basella* (1787), –nut, *Justicia adhatoda* (1753); –(fish) oil (1883); –plum, the rose-apple, *Eugenia jambos* (*Jambosa vulgaris*) (1855); –rose, *Hibiscus rosa malabarica* (1840); –creeper (*Argyneia malabarica*); –cars, the seed vessels of a tree (*Codaga palli*) (1773); –itch, a kind of ringworm. Hence, *Malabarese, Malabarian, Malabaric, Malabarish.* [*OED & YB*; Watt, *Econ. Dict.* (1889-92).]

Malabar(s) [16C. See prec.] 'A name applied by the Portuguese not only to the language and people of the country thus called, but also to the **Tamil** language and the people speaking Tamil.' [YB]. See **Malayalam.** [Litchfield, *Castañeda* (1582); Lancaster in Purchas (1602; ed. 1625-6), i. 153.]

Malabar Rites [17C. See prec.] Certain Hindu practices which the Jesuit missions in S. India, espec. the mission of Father de Nobili (1606) permitted to their converts despite Papal prohibitions, espec. in 1623. [YB; Pope Gregory XV, Constitution (31 Jan. 1623).]

Malabathrum [17C. L. *malobathrum*; Gr. *malobathron*; S. *tamāla-pattra*, fr. *tamāla*, various trees + *pattra*, 'leaf'. H. *tamāl*.] A classical

export from India. The dried aromatic leaves
of various species of *Cinnamon* valued as a
medicine, perfume and for domestic uses.
See **Tejpat.** [*OED* & YB; Purchas, *Pilgrimes*
(1625), i.i.i. 43; Holland, *Pliny* (1601), 1. 378;
Royle, *Essay on the Antiquity of Hindoo
Medicine* (1837).]

Maladoo [19C.] *Chicken maladoo* was a popular
article in the Anglo-Indian menu; sliced or
pounded re-cooked chicken or mutton. (Pg.
malhado, 'beaten-up', seems a poss. origin
for the Anglo-Indian word.) [YB.] Cf. **Brass-
Knocker.**

Malayalam [19C.] The Dravidian language *Mala-
yā-lam*, related to **Tamil**, **Telugu**, and
Kannada; spoken in **Kerala**. Also attrib. [*OED*
& YB; Logan, *Man. of Malabar* (1887-91);
Harkness, *Anc. and Mod. Alphabets Pop.
Hindu Lang.* (1837).]

Malayali [19C.] A native speaker of **Malayalam**,
fr. *mala* 'mountain' + *-al*, 'possess'. [*OED;*
Caldwell, *Comp. Gram. Dravidian Lang.*
(1856), 491.]

Maler, Male, Moler, Muler, Mal [19C. Fr.
Dravidian *mala*, 'a mountain.'] *See* prec.
Dravidian hill-men living in the **Rajmahal**
hills of N. India and their language. Also
called **Rajmahalai** and **Malto** (1884). [*OED;*
Buchanan, *Jrnl. Survey Bhagalpur* (1811;
ed. 1930), 133.] *See* **Pahari.**

Mali, mallee, molly [18.C. H. *mālī*, fr. S.
mālika, 'garland maker'. Cf. *māla*, garland.] Any Indian gardener, originally one
of the gardener caste. [*OED* & YB; Long,
Sel. Rec. Ft. William (1759; ed. 1869),
182; Williamson, *East Indian Vade Mecum*
(1810).]

Malik [19C. H/Ar. *mālik*, pres. pple. of *malaka*,
'to rule.'] Chief or headman of a village or
other community in India and elsewhere.
Owner, employer, as opposed to **mazdoor**,
worker. [*OED;* Wilson, *Glossary* (1855).]

Malish [19C. H/P. *mālish*, massage.] *See*
Shampoo. Also the 'grooming of a horse, and
the threshing & treading out of corn'. [Whit-
worth, *Anglo-Indian Dict.* (1885).]

Malto [19C. Native name.] A Dravidian language
of the **Maler** people, living in the **Rajmahal**
hills of N. India, also called **Rajmahali**. [*OED;*
Droese, *Introd. Malto Lang.* (1884).]

Malum(sahib) [19C. H/Ar. *mu'allim*, lit. 'the
instructor.'] 'In a ship with English officers
and native crew, the mate is called *malum
sahib.*' [YB; Stanley, tr. *Correa*, Hak. Soc.
(1869); Logan, *Malabar* (1887).]

Mamiran, mamira, momiri [17C. Native name.]
An ancient medicine; a specific for eye-
diseases, from Himalayan and trans-Hima-
layan regions made from certain bitter roots,
e.g. *Thalictrum foliosum.* In the Punjab
known as *mamīra*, and also *pīliarī*. [YB; Watt,
Econ. Dict. (1889-93); Bernier, *Travels* (E. tr.
1684), 136.]

Mamlatdar, mamlutdar [19C. Mar. *māmlatdār;*
Ar. *mu'āmala*, affairs, business + 'owner'.]
The title of a native chief civil officer in
Bombay in charge of a **Taluk**, corresponding
nearly to the **Tahsildar** of a **Pergunna** in
Bengal 'but of a status somewhat more impor-
tant'. [YB; Hockley, *Pandurang Hari* (1826;
ed. 1873), i. 42.] *See* **Tanadar.**

Mamool (sb), **mamooli** (adj) [19C. H/Ar. *māmūl.*
lit: 'practised, established, customary', pre-
cedent, ordinary. [YB; Wilson, *Glossary* (1855).]

Mamoty, mamooty, momatty, etc. [18C. Tam.
manveti, 'earth-cutter'.] A digging tool used
all over India: 'a hoe with the helve set at an
acute angle with the blade'. [YB.] *See* **Fowra.**
[*OED* & YB; Forrest, *Sel. Lett. Govt. India,*
(1782), 111. 855.]

Manchua [17C. M. *manji, manchi;* S. *mancha*,
'cot'.] 'so called apparently from its raised
platform for cargo.' A large cargo-boat with a
single mast and a square sail much used on
the **Malabar** coast. '*Manchua*' is the Portuguese form. [YB; Yule, *Hedge's Diary* (1681–
8; Hak. Soc. ed. 1886), ii. 154; Litchfield,
Castañeda (1582).]

Mand. [19C. H. *manduā.*] An Indian grass,
Eleusine corocana, 'called Natchlee and Nagla
Ragee; also **Murwa.**' [*Chambers Encyclopedia*
(1862), iv. 6/2.]

Mandadore, mandor [17C. Mal. *mandor,* Pg.
mandador. 'One who commands.'] Overseer;
a native superintendent; a hospital assistant.
[YB; Fryer, *A New Acct.* etc. (1672-81; ed.
1698), 67.]

Mandala [19C. S. *māndala,* 'disc, circle'.]
Buddhism: A symbolic painting of a magic
circle used for devotional purposes, e.g. in
meditation. In Jungian Psychol., a dream
circle symbolizing the striving for self-complete-
ness and unity. Also attrib. [*OED;* Max
Mueller, *Hist. Anc. Sanskrit. Lit.* (1859), i. 218.]

Mandapa(m) [19C. S. *mandapam.*] Temple-porch
in S. India. Also temporary wedding erection.
[YB.] *See* **Mantap.** [Buchanan, *Mysore* etc.
(1807), i.ii. 15.]

Mandarin [16C. Pg. *mandarim;* H. *mantri;* S.
mantrin, 'counsellor', fr. *mantra,* 'counsel',

fr. *man* 'mind'.] In India and elsewhere, a counsellor, or sometimes an 'officious official'. In modern usage, a VIP (esp. a reactionary or old-fashioned one). Also, a mandarin orange, a kind of small orange, *Naranja mandarina* (1820). Also attrib. [*OED* & *YB*; Litchfield, tr. *Castañeda* (1581); Linschoten, *Discours* (E. tr. 1598); Boswell, *Johnson* (1791), 1. 5.]

Mandi [19C. H. *mandi*.] Wholesale market; mart. [Wilson, *Glossary* (1855).]

Mandir(a) [19C. H. *mandir;* S. *mandir,* fr. *mand,* 'to be glad'.] Temple; refuge of Hindu ascetics. *Raj-mandir,* royal palace. [Wilson, *Gloss.* (1855); Whitworth, *Anglo-Indian Dict.* (1885).]

Mando(o)r(e), mandur [19C. Malay, *mandor;* Pg. *mandador,* 'he who gives orders'.] Worker, as opposed to **Malik,** employer. A foreman in Malaysia among Tamil workers. Cf. **Kangani.** [*OED;* Hickson, *Naturalist in North Celebes* (1889), 65; Sandhu, *Indians Malaya* (1969), iii. 114.] See **Tindal**.

Mangalsutra [19C. S. *mangalsutra,* 'lucky thread'.] Thread or necklace with a piece of gold etc. worn by a Hindu wife (not by a widow). [Wilson, *Glossary* (1855).]

Mangelin, mangiar, etc. [17C. Tam. *manjadi;* Tel *manjali;* S. *manju,* 'beautiful'.] A small weight corresponding roughly to one or two carats, used in S. India and Ceylon (Sri Lanka) for weighing precious stones; the seed of the *Adenanthura pavonina,* used for this purpose. See **Ruttee.** [*OED* & *YB;* Eden, *Decades,* (1555), 234; Barret (1584) in Hakluyt (1599; ed. 1807).]

Mango [16C. Pg. *manga;* Tam. *mankay* (*mān,* 'mango-tree' + *kay,* 'fruit'.); S. *amra;* Malay *mangga.*] 'The royal fruit of the *Mangifera indica,* when of good quality is one of the richest and best fruits in the world.' [*YB.*] The green, unripe fruit is used for pickles. See **Achar** (1619). The tree is sacred to Buddhists, and is regarded by Hindus as a transformation of the god *Prajapati,* the lord of all living things. vb. 'to mango' = 'to pickle as green mangoes are pickled' (1728). Also attrib. Mango-blossom (1841); –fool (1864), mangoes pulped and mixed with cream; –ginger, *Curcuma amada;* (1840); – tope (1800) a mango orchard; –pickle (1699). [*OED* & *YB;* Varthema, *Travels,* E. T. (1576); Lichfield, tr., *Castañeda.* (1582). 1. XVL. 42.] See **Tope**.

Mango-bird [18C. See Prec.] Anglo-Indian name of the beautiful golden oriole, *Oriolus kundoo.* Its 'loud mellow whistle from the mango-groves [Topes] and other gardens ... is associated in

Upper India with the invasion of the hot-weather'. [YB & *OED;* Albin, *Nat. Hist. Birds* etc. (1738), 111. 45; Robinson, *In My Indian Garden* (1878), 59; Jerdon, in *Madras Journal.* (1839), x.]

Mango-fish [18C.] The golden-coloured **Topsy-Fish,** *Polynemus risua* or *paradiseus* of excellent taste. Perhaps *tapsee* or *topsy* fr. H. *tap(as)si,* 'an ascetic, or penitent', but the connection between this etymology and the fish is baffling. See **Topsy-Fish.** [*OED* & *YB;* Edwards, *Nat. Hist. Birds* (1751); Hickey, *Bengal Gazette,* 3 March, 1781.]

Mango-showers [19C.] Showers falling in March and April when the mangoes begin to ripen. [YB.]

Mangosteen [16C. Mal. *mangustin, manggis.*] The fruit of the E. Indian tree *Garcinia mangustana.* [*OED;* Phillip, tr., *Linschoten* (1598), 1. liv. 96/2.]

Mango-trick [17C.] 'One of the most famous tricks of Indian jugglers, in which they plant a mango-stone, and show at brief intervals the tree shooting above ground, and successively producing leaves, flowers and fruit.' [YB.] But as Bernier (1667) has said, 'as for me I am with all my curiosity none of those happy men, that are present at, and see these great feats'. [YB; Fryer, *A New Acct.* etc. (1672-81; ed. 1681), 192.]

Mani-stone, or **-wall** [19C. Tib. *mani,* fr. S. *mani,* 'precious stone'.] Stone carved with the Tibetan-Buddhist chant, 'Om Mani Padma Hum', 'Hail to the Jewel in the Lotus'. Also a Tibetan prayer-wall covered with piously inscribed stones. [*OED;* Schlagintweit, *Buddhism in Tibet* (1863), xiii. 196.]

Manilla-man [19C. Hybrid.] Tel. *manela vadu,* 'an itinerant dealer in coral and gems'. Perh. fr. S. *mani,* 'a jewel', with reference poss. to Pg. *manilha,* 'a bracelet'. [YB.] Cf. **Cobra Manilla.** [Wilson, *Glossary* etc. (1855).]

Manipuri [20C. Place name.] (1) Pertaining to the state of Manipur in N. E. India. (2) Style of dancing developed in Manipur for men and women, seen in the **Raslila** (folk drama). (3) The people and one of the people of Manipur (1911). (4) The Tibeto-Burman language of Manipur (1918). [*OED;* Pettigrew, *Tāngkhul Nāga Gram. and Dict.* (1918); Gait, *Hist. Assam* (1906), viii. 195.]

Manjee [17C. H. *manjhi;* S. *madhya.*] (1) 'One who stands in the middle.' 'The master or steersman of a boat or any native river-craft.' [Hedges, *Diary* (1683).] (2) Headman among the Paharis or Hill-people of *Rājmahal* Hills in the Santal Parganas District of Bengal. [Wilson, *Gloss.* etc. (1855).] (3) 'An important Dravidian tribe on the borders of the N.W. Province and Chota Nagpur.' [YB, 558.] [*OED;* Campbell, *Wild Tribes of Khondistan* (1864), 120.]

Mannikhjore [19C. H. *mānikjor* (from *mānik*, 'a ruby', according to Platts).] The white- necked stork, *Ciconia leucocephala*, alias 'The Beefsteak Bird' in Bengal [Jerdon's *Birds of India* (1862)], because palatable when cooked in that fashion. Distributed practically throughout India; up to about 3000 ft. in the Himalayas. [YB; Davidson, *Travels in Upper India* (1843), ii. 165.]

Mansabdar, munsubdar [17C. H/P. *mansabdār.* The holder of office of dignity.' (Ar. *mansab*, 'rank').] A Mughal officer granted territory and rank on condition of supplying a certain number of horses to the government. Frequently the term merely indicated that the holder was in the employment of the State without any particular office but bound to yield certain services on call. [YB; Sir T. Roe, *Embassy to the Court of the Great Mogul* (1615–19).]

Mantap(a) [19C. Kan. *mantapa.*] Temporary shrine-like structure, or a temple-porch. *See* **Mandapam**. [Buchanan, *Mysore* etc. (1807), i. ii. 15; Whitworth, *Anglo-Indian Dict.* (1885).] *See* **Vimana** and **Gopura**.

Mantra(m), muntra [18C. S. *mantra*, 'instrument of thought' fr. *man*, 'to think'.] A sacred Vedic text used as a prayer or incantation; a magic formula. Also *mantravadi*, 'a dispenser of magic charms'. [*OED* & YB; Colebrooke, 'Vedas' in *Asiatic Res.* (1808), viii; Halhed, *Code* (1776), 17.] *See* **Om**.

Mantri, muntree [19C. S. *mantri* fr. *mantrin*, 'wise, eloquent', skilled in sacred texts.] A minister or high official of government; the word the Portuguese made into **Mandarin**. *Mantralaya*, ministerial office, building. [*OED* & YB; Maria Graham, *Journal* (1812), 200; Tod, *Annals and Antiquities of Rajasthan* (1829).]

Manvantara [20C. S. *Manu* + *antara*, 'period'.] 'The period or age of a Manu or cosmic deity, held equal to 4,320,000 years. There are 14 such periods which make up a **Kalpa**.' [*OED;* Lyell, *Princ. Geol.* (1830); James Joyce, *Ulysses* (1922).] *See* **Brahma**.

Maramari [20C. H. *maramāri*.] Street fight; rough house; murderous assault. [Hawkins, *CIWIE*.]

Maramut, murrumut [18C. H/Ar. *marammat*, 'repair'.] In a specialized sense the title of 'that branch of the executive which included the conservation of irrigation tanks and the like.' [YB; Ives, *Voyage from England to India* (1754; ed. 1773), 156.]

Maratha, Maratta, Mahratta [17C. H. *Marhatā;* S. *mahā*, 'great' + *rashtra*, 'kingdom'.] A famous Hindu warrior race, whose 17th century hero and leader was Shivaji, much venerated to this day in Maharashtra. *See* **Mahratta Ditch**. [*OED* & YB; Fryer, *New Acct.* etc. (1672-81), 174; Orme, *Hist. Milit. Trans.* (1778).]

Mardana [20C. H. *mardāna*.] Men's quarters in a house. Cf. **Zenana**. [Hawkins, *CIWIE*.]

Marg¹ [19C. H/S. *marg*, 'way, road'.] Also *marga*, the path to salvation; the eightfold path. [Webster, *Third New Intern. Dict.* (1976).]

Marg,² merg [19C. H/P. *merg*.] Mountain meadow in Kashmir. [*CIWIE*.]

Margi [20C.] Follower of **Anand Marg**, sectarian movement started in Bihar in 1955.

Margosa [19C. Pg. *amargosa*, 'bitter.'] The S. Indian name for the **Neem** tree, yielding a bitter oil; the *Azadirachia indica*. [*OED* & YB; Ainslie, *Mat. Med. Hindostan* (1813).]

Markhor, markhore [19C. P. *mār-khōr*, 'Snake-eater'.] A large wild Himalayan goat, *Capra falconeri*, of a slaty grey colour with long spiral horns. [*OED* & YB; Edwardes, *A Year on the Punjab Frontier* (1851), i. 474.]

Marking-nut [18C.] Nut of the tree *Semercarpus anarcadium*, which yields a black dye used by **Dhobies**. [*OED;* Ellis in *Phil. Trans.* (1756), xlix.]

Martaban [16C. Place-name, fr. Talaing, *Mūt-ta-main*.] A large glazed pottery vessel used for storage purposes, once famous all over the East, and known as 'Pegu Jars'. Also applied in the Punjab to 'a small deep jar with an elongated body, used by Hindus and Muhammedans to keep pickles and acid articles'. [Halifax, *Mono. of Punjab Pottery;* Linschoten, *Discours* (E. tr. 1598), 30; Fryer, *New Acct.* etc. (1672-81), 180.]

Martil, martol [19C. H. *mārtol*, Pg. *martello*.] 'A hammer.' Espec. one used in war after the 15th century. Cf. *mār-nā*, 'to strike'. (A purely imaginary connection.) [YB.]

Marwari, Marwaree, Marwarry [19C. S. *maru*, 'desert'.] A man of the *Mārwar*, or Jodhpur country in Rajasthan, otherwise known as a **Banya**; most frequently **Jain** by religion, and moneylender, banker and businessman by vocation. [OED & YB; Carnac, *Trans. Lit. Soc. Bombay* (1819), i. 297.]

Maryacar(s) [17C. M. *Marakkar*, 'doer or follower of the Law' (*marggam*).] Malabar Catholics or Muslims. (The *Madras Gloss.* derives the word from *marakkalam*, 'boat-possessing'; a title of **Moplah** Muslims of Malabar.) [YB; Logan, *Malabar* (1887-91), i. 332; Drummond, *Illustrations*, etc. (1808).]

Masala, mussalla [18C. H/P. *masālih*, pl. of *maslaha*, 'materials, ingredients, things for the good of'.] Spices, curry-stuffs, frequently used to add pungency and 'interest' in Indian cookery. [YB; Munro, *Narrative of Milit. Operations* (1780), 85.]

Mascabar [19C.] Poss. H. *mās-ke-ba'ad*, *māskā-wār*, 'after a month', or fr. H. *maskabar*, the monthly statement of cases decided during the month. [YB; Wilson, *Glossary* (1855); Platts, *Dict.* (1884).]

Mash [19C. II. *māsh*, fr. S. *māsha*, 'a bean'.] A common Indian pulse, *Phaseolus radiatus*. [OED & YB; *Asiat Ann. Reg. Misc. Tracts* (1800), 44/1.]

Masha [19C. H. *māshā*.] A weight = **8 Ratties** = 15 grains Troy, orig. based on the weight of the seed of the bean *Phaseolus mungo*. [OED; Stoqueler, *Oriental Interpreter* (1848), 148/2.] See **Mace**.

Mashalla! [19C. Ar. *māshāllāh*.] God's Will be done! [OED; Ogilvie, *Imperial Dict.*, Suppl., (1855).]

Mashwa, machwa, muchwa [19C. Mar. *mashwā*, fr. *machchh*, 'a fish'.] A small, open, extremely swift, fishing boat, 'very sharp in the bows'. [OED & YB; Whitworth, *AngloIndian Dict.* (1885).]

Masjid, mosque, moschy [17C. H/Ar. *masjīd*, 'a place of Muslim worship'.] Lit. the place of *sujūd*, 'prostration.' See **Mosque**. [OED; Purchas, *Pilgrimage* (1613).]

Mascola(h), musoola, mussoolah, etc. [17C. Unknown etym., but may be from Mar. *māsolī*; Konk. *māsalī*, 'fish'.] A capacious surf-boat used on the Coromandel Coast, 'formed of planks sewn together with coir twine; the open joints being made good with a caulking or wadding of twisted coir'. [YB.] See **Catamaran**. [OED; Fryer, *A New Account* etc. (1672-81), 37.]

Mata [19C. H/S. *mātā*, mother.] *Bharat Mata* = 'Mother India'. *Mata-ji*, term of great respect for a matron. This word is 'applied to various goddesses, most often to Devi or Durga, but also to the mother earth'. [Whitworth, *Anglo-Indian Dict.*]

Mate, maty [19C. Origin obscure, but perh. fr. S. *metha*, 'an elephant keeper', or S. *mitra*, 'associate, friend or M. *metti*, 'a menial servant'.] 'An assistant under a head-servant', espec. in S. India. Also *mate-bearer*, an assistant body-servant; **Jomponi**-mate; and **Cooly**-mate. Also, in the sense of a 'head-man'. See **Mocuddum**. [YB; Williamson, *E. Ind. Vade Mecum* (1810).]

Math, mutta, muth [19C. H/S. *matha*, 'hut, cottage'.] A Hindu monastery for celibate (mendicant) priests and novices. [OED & YB; Prinsep, *The Baboo* etc. (1834); Forbes, *Ras Mala or Hindoo Annals* etc. (1856).]

Mathadi [20C. Mar. *māthadi*.] A porter. [Hawkins, *CIWIE*.]

Matka [19C. H. *matka*.] 'earthenware pot.' Also the 'numbers game' (gambling on numbers), popular in India. [Whitworth, *Anglo-Indian Dict.* (1885).]

Matra [19C. S. *mātra*.] Musical beat or a sub-division of one within a rhythmic phrase; vowel sign in **Devanagri**. [OED; Pringle, *Indian Music* (1898).]

Matrani, matranee [19C. H. Corr. of *mehtarānī*.] Female house-sweeper. A grand title for the lowest menial house-servant in Anglo-Indian (and other) households. See **Mehtar**. [OED & YB; Forbes, *Or. Memoirs* (1813); Sherwood (c. 1804) in *Life Mrs Sherwood* (1854), 294.]

Matross [17C. Origin obscure. (But cf. Dutch *matroos*, and Fr. *matelot*.)] An inferior class of soldier in the Artillery; disused by 1793. See **Classy**. [OED & YB; Fryer, *A New Account* etc. (1672-81).]

Matt [17C. Tam. *māttu*; perh. S. *mātra*, 'measure'] Very pure gold = 9 *ma·tu*, inferior 5 or 6 *māttu*. [YB; Foster, *Letters* (1615), iii. 156.]

Maulana, Mulana [19C. H/Ar. *maulā·ā*, 'our lord; *maula*, 'lord, master'.] Title of a learned Muslim. [OED; Wilson, *Relig. Sects. of Hindus* (1832).]

Maulvi, moolvee, maulwi [17C. H. *mulvī* fr. Ar. *maulawiyy* fr. *maula*, 'lord, master', Mullah.] A Muslim judge; doctor of the Law; teacher of Arabic and Persian; a learned man. See **Mullah** and **Law-Officer**. [Purchas (1611), *Pilgrimes* (1625), ii. ix. xv.]

Maumlet [19C. Kitchen H. *māmlat*.] 'Omelette.' (*Māmlēt* is 'marmalade'.) [YB.]

Maund [16C. H/P. *man*, poss. cogn. with Gr. *mna* and L. *mina*.] Anglo-Indian form of the weight (now about 40 kg.) which has been current in W. Asia 'from time immemorial', and in India since about the 8th century AD and possibly earlier. Also a liquid measure, 9.81 British imperial gallons. [OED & YB; Barret in Hakluyt, Voyages (1584), ii. i. 271.]

Mawa [20C. H. māhwa.] Milk thickened by boiling. [Hawkins, CIWIE.]

Maya [19C. S. māyā.] In Hindu philosophy, illusion, the phenomenal world. [OED; Colebrooke (1823), Trans. Roy. Asiatic Soc. (1827), i. 30.]

Mayla See **Mela.**

Mazar, mazaar [19C. H/Ar. mazar.] Muslim tomb, shrine, mausoleum. Mazar-e-Sharif, 'tomb of the saint'; tomb of the caliph Ali in Afghanistan. [Enc. Brit. Micropedia (1977), vi.]

Mazdaism [19C. fr. Avestic mazda, the name of the good principle (Ahura-mazda, Ormuzd) of ancient Iranian theology.] The ancient Iranian religion as taught in the Avesta; **Zoroastrianism.** Also, Mazdeism, Mazdaist, Mazdean. [OED; Smith, Anc. Hist. East, (1871), III. xviii. 384.]

Mazdoor [19C. H. mazdūr.] 'Porter, labourer'; mazdoori, porterage; wages. Worker as opposed to **Malik,** 'master, owner'. [Wilson, Glossary (1855).]

Mazhabi, Muzbi [19C. H/Ar. mazhab, 'religion'.] Convert to Sikhism from Islam; spec. in the Punjab a converted Chuhra (a sweeper caste). [OED; Cunningham, Hist. Sikhs (1849).]

Mearbar [17C. H/P. mīrbahr, 'master of the bay'.] A harbour-master. Mirabary (mīhrbahrī) are 'ferrydues'. [YB; Fryer, A New Account etc. (1672-81), 98.]

Mecca, Meccan [17C. Dial. var. of Makkāh.] Prophet Mohammed's birthplace.The object of numerous annual Indian Muslim pilgrims aspiring to the holy title of 'Ha(d)ji'. Fig. goal or aspiration; a holy birthplace revered of a faith or policy; a sacred spot or resort. [OED.] Dryden has 'Meccan'. [Hind and Panther (1687), iii. 1098.]

meana, myanna, mohanna [18C. H/P. mīyāna, 'middle-sized'.] 'A small litter suspended under a straight bamboo ... and shaded by a frame covered with cloth, not admitting the passenger to lie at length ...' [YB; Seton-Karr, Selection from Calcutta Gazettes (1784-1823), i. 49.]

Meerass(sb.), **meerassy**(adj.), **meerassidar**(sb.) [19C. H/Ar. mīrās(ī), mīrāsdar, fr. waris, 'to inherit'.] Inheritance, hereditary, a holder of hereditary property. [Fifth Report, etc. (1812).

774.] [YB; Meadows Taylor, Story of My Life (1877), ii. 211.]

Meerch See **Chilli.**

Megpunna(ism) [19C.] The practice of murdering indigent parents for their young children, who are afterwards sold as slaves. [W.H. Sleeman, Report on the System of Megpunnaism (Serampore Press, 1839).]

Mehmandar [17C. H/P. mehmāndār, fr. mihamān, 'stranger', 'guest'.] In India & Persia, a person appointed to be a courier to a distinguished traveller. [OED; 1623, St. Pap. Coll. (1622-24; 1878), 161; Sir T. Herbert, Trav. (1634), 51.]

Mehtar, maitre [19C. Beng/P. mihtar, 'a great personage', 'a prince'.] Ironic honorific for a man of the sweeper or scavenger caste. See **Bheestie, Bungi, Matrani.** [OED & YB; Williamson, The East Indian Vade Mecum (1810), I. 276.] See **Toty** and **Sweeper.**

Mela, mayla [19C. H. melā, fr. S. melā, 'meeting, concourse'.] Hindu fair or festival, almost always connected with some religious celebration. [OED & YB; Mrs Meer Hassan Ali, Observations (1832); Misc. Tracts in Asiat. Ann. Reg. (1800), 245/2.]

Memsahib [19C.] The Anglo-Indian hybrid (maam + sahib) designating respectfully the status of a European married woman, colloquially abbreviated to 'The Mem'. Madam Sahib was used at Bombay and Doresani (See **Doray**) in Madras. (See also **Burra Beebee.**) Transf. one who behaves like a European woman (1873). [OED & YB; Household Words, 19 Dec. 1857.]

Mendang, mendung, mendong [20C. Tib. mendung.] A wall sacred to Tibetan Buddhists, composed of flat stones inscribed with Buddhist texts or with Buddhas. [OED; Hammerton, Countries of the World (1925), VI. 3946/2.]

Mehndi, mendy, mendee [19C. H. mehndī, fr. S. mendhikā.] A henna-yielding plant, Lawsonia inermis; the henna itself, much used among Muslims and Hindus from N. India to give hair and beards a copper tint, and to dye the hands, feet and nails of betrothed girls and Indian dancers everywhere in India. The plant is of ancient lineage under the name of 'Camphire'. 'My beloved is unto me as a cluster of camphire in the Vineyards of Engedi' (Song of Solomon), and mummies have been found with hennaed nails. Extracts from its leaves have been used for leprosy, skin diseases, ulcers, as well as for perfume. [YB; Forbes, *Or. Mem.* (1813); Mrs Sherwood, *Ayah and Lady* (1817).]

Mercall, marcal [18C. Tam. *marakkāl.*] A grain measure used in Madras, varying considerably in different localities. [*OED* & YB; Wellington, *Despatches* (1803); T. Brooks, *Coins E. Indies* etc. (1776), 7.]

Merg See **Marg²**.

Mihrab, Mehrab [19C. Ar. *mihrāb,* 'praying place'.] (1) Niche in mosque wall indicating direction of Mecca. See **Kiblah**. [*OED;* Williams, tr., *Ali Bey's Travels* (1816), II. xvi. 217.] (2) A niche motif on a prayer rug in the shape of a *mihrab* in a mosque. [*OED;* Lewis, *Pract. Book. Orient Rugs* (1911), X. 121.]

Milk-bush, -hedge [18C.] A ubiquitous Indian bush, *Euphorbia tirucallī,* often used for hedges on the Coromandel Coast, in Gujarat and elsewhere in India. 'It abounds in acrid milky juices.' [YB; Ives, *Voy. from England to India* (1773); Munro, *Narr.* (1780), 80.]

Mimansa, mimamsa [18C. S. *mīmānsā,* 'profound thought', 'investigation' fr. *man,* 'to think'.] One of the six systems of Hindu philosophy (*darshanas*). (1) *Nyaya,* logical analysis, through perception, inferences, comparison, testimony. (2) *Sankhya (samkhya),* dualistic (*dvaita*) realism. (3) *Vedanta,* 'end of the Veda', complete knowledge of the **Veda** = *Uttara mimansa.* (4) **Yoga,** union of the individual self with the universal spirit. (5) *Vaiseshika,* the harmony of philosophic theory with moral and spiritual attitudes of life and theistic faith. Advocates an atomic theory of cosmology. (6) *Mimansa,* aims at the solution of the problem of liberation (**moksha**) from the sequence of birth, death, re-birth (*samsara*) by disciplined and critical examination. *Purva Mimansa,* describes priestly duties. *Uttara Mimansa,* usually called *Mimansa.* [*OED; Asiatick Researches* (1788), I. 352.]

Mina See **Myna**.

Minar [17C. H/P. *minar,* Ar. *manārat,* fr. *nar* 'fire'. (Cf. *manar,* 'lighthouse'.] The tall tower, the minaret of a mosque (**Masjid**), from which the **Muezzin** calls the faithful to prayer (**Namaz**) five times a day. [*OED;* Sir T. Herbert (1665), *Trav.* (1677), 142.]

Minbar, mimbar [19C. Ar. *minbar.*] Pulpit in a mosque. Also attrib. [*OED;* Williams, tr., *Travels of Ali Beg* (1816), II. vi. 84.]

Mir See **Amir, Ameer**. [Purchas, *Pilgrimes* (1625), I. iii. xiii. 282.]

Mirchal [18C.] See **Morchal**.

Miras [19C. H. *mirās.*] 'Hereditary land.' *Mirasdar,* holder of such land. [Wilson, *Glossary* (1855).]

Mirza [17C. P. *mīrzā,* fr. *mīr,* 'a prince' + *zād,* 'born'.] See **Ameer, Emir.** (1) A royal prince (placed after the name). (2) A title of honour of an official or learned man. (3) A patronymic among Parsees in India. [*OED;* Purchas (1613), *Pilgrimage* (1614), 422.]

Mirzapur [19C.] A type of carpet manufactured at Mirzapur in Uttar Pradesh. [*OED; Cardinal & Harford's Price List of Oriental Carpets* (1882).]

Misree, miscery [19C. H. *misrī,* 'Egyptian', fr. *misr,* 'Egypt'.] 'The Sugar of Egypt.' Sugar candy. [YB.] See **Sugar**. [Williamson, *The E. Indian Vade Mecum* (1810).]

Missal [19C. H/Ar. *misl,* 'similitude'.] The body of documents in a particular case before a court. (The word was also used in its original sense of 'a clan'.) [YB; Wilson, *Glossary* (1855); Cave Brown, *Punjab and Delhi* (1861).]

Mistry See **Maistry**.

Mithai [19C. H. *mīthai.*] 'Sweetmeats.' [Hawkins, *CIWIE*.]

Mithan, mytton, mythun, etc. [19C. Assamese, *methōn.*] Hybrid of the **Gaur** and domestic cattle, *Bos (Bibos) frontalis*). The **Gayal**. [*OED;* Dalton in *Jrnl. Asiatic Soc. Bengal* 1845, xiv.]

Mithuna [20C. S. *maithuna,* 'twins'.] Sculptured frieze of men and women in erotic embrace; the union of the soul with the divine, of Siva with Parvati, Vishnu with Lakshmi. [O.C. Gangoly, *The Mithunan Indian Art* (1925), 22.]

Mlechcha [19C.] S. *mlechchha.*] Barbarian, foreigner, outsider, a non-Indo-Aryan. [Whitworth, *Anglo-Indian Dict.* (1885).]

Mobed [17C. P. *mūbid,* corr. of Pahlavi, *magopat,* 'Lord Magus.'] A title of **Parsi** family priests. See **Herbed, Dastur, Dokhma, Agiary.** [YB; Malcolm, *Hist. of Persia* (1815); Lord, *The Religion of the Parsees* (1630).]

Moccuddama [H/Ar. *mukaddama.*] 'a piece of business.' Espec. 'a suit at law'. [YB; Wilson, *Glossary* (1855).]

Mochi See **Moochy**.

Mocuddum, mokaddam [16C. H/Ar. *mukaddam,* 'a headman'.] Headman of a village, responsible for revenue (*see* **Lumberdar**); local head of a caste (*see* **Chowdry**); headman of a body of peons, or of a gang of labourers (see **Mate**). [OED & YB; Linschoten in Hakluyt (1598); Sir T. Roe, *Embassy* (1615-19); Wilson, *Gloss.* (1855).]

Modelliar, Mudeliar, Modliar [17C. Tam. *mudaliyar*, an honorific pl. from *mudali*, 'chief'.] A native headman or chief military officer among Jaffna Tamils of Sri Lanka. Also 'a caste title assumed by Tamil people who styled themselves **Sudras** (an honourable assumption in the South)'. [YB & OED; Davis, tr., *Mandelslo's Trav.* (1662), 112.]

Mofussil [18C. H. *mufassil*, fr. Ar. *mufassal*, 'separate', detached, particular.] Rural as opposed to urban; 'up the country'. Outside the **Presidencies:** 'rural localities of a district as contradistinguished from the **Sudder** or chief station which is the residence of the district authorities'. [YB.] Hence: *mofussilite* (1845) and *mofussilize* (1863). Also attrib. [OED & YB; Hickey, *Bengal Gazette*, 31 March 1781; T. B. Macaulay, in *Life* etc. (1836), i. 399.]

Mog(h)ul, Mogol, Mughal [16C. H/P. *Mughal*, a mispronunciation of *Mongol*.] Properly, a person of the great nomad race of Mongols, but in India it came to be applied to all foreign Muslims from the countries W. & N.W. of India except the **Pathans**. The Pg. form is *Mogor*, used by some early English tavellers. (1) A follower of Babur, founder of the Mughal empire in Hindustan in 1526. (2) A follower of Genghis Khan in the 13th century. (3) 'The Great Mogul.' The Emperors of Delhi, of the House of Timur, espec. Akbar (1609). [Birdwood, *First Letter Book* (1609), 305.] (4) Any great personage or autocrat (1678). (5) Best quality playing cards with picture of the Great Mogul on the wrappers (1842). (6) Mogul breeches, **Longdrawers** or **Pyjamas** (1625). (7) A kind of plum, the Magnum Bonum (1718). (8) Mogul engine, a locômotive of a special type hauling heavy trains (1884). Also *Moghlai*, 'Mogul style'. [OED & YB; Foster, *Early Travels in India* (1583).]

Mogra [17C. H. *mogra*.] The Arabian jasmine, *Jasminum sambac*. [OED; Davies, tr., *Mandelslo's Travels* (1662).]

Mohalla [H/Ar. *mohālla*.] A locality in a town. [Hawkins, *CIWIE*.]

Mohammed, Mahomet, Mahommed [17C. Ar. *muhammed*.] Founder of the religion of Islam. [OED; Sir T. Herbert, *Travels* (1634).]

Mohammedan, Muhammedan, Mahometan [17C. See prec. Ar. lit 'laudable'.] (1) *Muslim, Islamic;* (2) A follower of Mohammed; a believer

in *Mohammedanism*. [OED; Wilson, *Brit. India* (1844).]

Moharram, Muharram, Mohurrum [17C. Ar. *Muharram*, 'sacred'.] The first month of the Muslim lunar year. But in India the Shia period of fasting and mourning during the first ten days of that month in memory of the deaths of Hassan and his brother Husain (AD 669 and 680), ending in the ceremonies of the '*Ashūrā-a*, commonly known in India as 'the Mohurrum'. See **Hobson-Jobson**. [OED & YB; Bedwell, *Arabian Trudgman* (1615); J. T. Wheeler, *Madras in Olden Time* (1861), II. 347.]

Mohini Attam [20C. fr. *Mohini*, the supreme seductress of Hindu mythology (fr. S. *much*, confuse, bewilder) + Tam. *attam*, 'dance'.] Graceful solo dance for women, originally from Kerala; showing the influence of the **Kathakali** style, gentle and graceful. [OED; Venkatachalam, *Dance in India*. (1940), xii. 109.]

Mohur (Gold) [17C. H/P. *muhr*, 'a seal' (S. *mudra*.] The chief gold coin of India from the 16th century and from 1776 of British India, worth at that time 14 **sicca Rupees**. In 1835 it was worth 15 silver rupees. This coin was in use from the foundation of the Muslim Empire in Hindustan by the *Ghūri Kings of Ghazni, c.* AD 1200, tending to a standard weight of 100 *ratis* (**Ruttees**) of pure gold. [YB & OED; Finch in *Early Travels in India* (1583-1619).]

Mohurrer, mohrer [18C. fr. Ar. *muharrir*, 'an elegant, correct writer'.] A *writer* in an Indian language. [YB; Verelst, *View of Bengal* (1765).]

Mohwa See **Mahwa**.

Moksha [18C. S. *moksha*, fr. *much;* 'to loose, to release'.] Salvation, spiritual liberation in Hinduism and Jainism. The final liberation of the soul exempted from further transmigration; the bliss attained by this liberation. Also called **Mukti**. [OED.] See **Nirvana**. [Wilkins, tr., *Bhāgvat Geeta* (1785).]

Mole Islam [19C. Poss. Punj. *mūla*, 'unfortunate'.] A class of Hindus in the time of Sultan Mahmud Bigarra, Butler's 'Prince of Cambay'. In W. Punjab (now Pakistan) the descendants of Jats forcibly converted to Islam were known as *Mūla*, or 'unfortunate'. [YB; Ibbetson, *Ethnography* (1883), 142; Drummond, *Illustrations* etc. (1808).]

Moley, molly [19C. Corr. of 'Malay'.] Anglo-Indian expression denoting the 'wet' curry used in Tamil Nadu, a large amount of coconut being one of the ingredients. 'The word is a corruption of "Malay", the dish being simply a bad imitation of the Malay original.' [YB; Wyvern, *Culinary Jottings* (1885).]

Molly *See* **Mali.**

Monal, monaul, moonaul, etc. [18C. H. *munāl, monāl*.] The Himalayan or Impeyan pheasant, *Lophophorus impeyanus*, 'rivalling the brilliance in hue, and the metallic lustre of the humming birds on the scale of the turkey'. [YB & *OED*; Latham, *Synops. Birds* (1769); Kipling, *Second Jungle Book* (1895), 39.]

Monegar, maniakarer [18C. fr. Tam. *maniyak-kāran*, 'an overseer'; *maniyam*, 'superintendence'.] The village headman in Tamil Nadu; equivalent to **Patel** in the Deccan. [Phillips, *Account* etc. (1767), 83.]

Mongoose, mungoose [17C. Mar. *mangūs*.] Popular Anglo-Indian name of the Indian ichneumons, small carnivorous mammals of the genus *Herpestes*, which prey on venomous snakes, and were sometimes kept as pets in Anglo-Indian households for this purpose. In Arabia called 'Daughter of the Bridgeroom' *(bint'arus)*; in Egypt, 'Pharaoh's Cat' (Katt *Faraūn*). [*OED* & YB; Burton, *Arabian Nights* (1886), ii. 369; Fryer, *New Account* etc. 1672–81).] *See* **Mungo, Quirpele**.

Monkey-Bread Tree [18C.] The Anglo-Indian name for the Baobab, *Adansonia digitata*. 'A fantastic-looking tree with immense elephantine stem and small twisted branches, laden in the rains with large white flowers, found all along the coast of W. India.' [Birdwood MS.] [*OED* & YB; W. Aiton, *Hortus Kewensis* (1789), II. 439.]

Monsoon [16C. Pg. *monçao*, fr. Ar. *mawsim*, 'fixed season'.] A seasonal wind prevailing in India and S. Asia, blowing from the S.W. in summer (the rainy season, or 'the Rains') and from the N.E. in winter (the 'dry-monsoon'). Also any wind which has periodic alternations, e.g. Trade-Wind (1691) [*OED* & YB; Barrett in Hakluyt's *Voy.* (1599), II. i. 278.]

Moobarek, mubarak, Bombay rock [(Sailors' Hobson-Jobson) H/Ar. *mubārak*, 'blessed, happy'.] Int. 'Welcome!' 'Congratulations!' uttered by Muslims on *Id* and other festive occasions. *See* **Id**. [YB; Sir T. Roe (1619; Hak. Soc. 1899), ii. 468.]

Moochulka [19C. H. *muchalka*.] A written obligation or bond. [*OED* & YB; Wilson, *Gloss.* (1855); Wellington, *Desp.* (1803), I. 323.]

Moochy, mootshee, mochi [19C. H. *mochī*.] Worker in leather; shoemaker, cobbler, saddler, upholsterer. [*OED* & YB; Tytler, *Considerations* (1815), i. 103; Lady Sale, *The First Afghan War* (1841-2).]

Moodooga [19C. Tel. *moduga*.] A tree, *Butea frondosa*, or *monosperma*, yielding *moodooga-oil*, a clear oil obtained from the seeds, considered by native doctors to possess anthelmintic properties. [*OED*; Lindley and Moore, *Treasury of Botany* (1866).]

Mooghdur [19C.] Dumb-bells. [*Anglo-Indian Domestic Sketch: A Letter from an Artist in England* (Calcutta, 1849).]

Mookam [19C. H. *mūkkam*.] Place of encampment near a village, especially reserved for travellers. [Rousselet, *Travels in Central India* etc. (1865; tr. 1875).]

Mookhtyar, mooktear [19C. H/Ar. *mukhtār*, 'chosen'.] An authorized agent, an attorney. *Mukhtyār-nāma*, 'a power of attorney'. [YB; Trevelyan, *The Dawk Bungalow* (1866), in *Frazer's Mag.*, xxiii. 218; Lewin, *A Fly on the Wheel* (1885), 336.]

Moolvi *See* **Maulvi.**

Moong, moongo, mung [17C. H. *mūng*; S. *mudga*.] A pale-green **Dal**, or 'green gram'. A kind of vetch, *Phaseolus mungo*, in common use in India, recommended by physicians as a diet for fever. Used throughout India for food; the fibre for mats. [*OED* & YB; Danvers, *Letters* (1611), i. 141.]

Moonga, mooga [17C. Beng. *mūga*.] A kind of wild silk, the produce of *Antheraea assama*, collected and manufactured in Assam. [YB; Purchas, *Pilgrimes* (1625), 1005.]

Moonjah, munjah [19C. H. *munj*; S. *munja*.] An Indian name for the plant and the fibre of the *Arunda karka*, used for making ropes. [*OED*; Royle, *Fibre Plants of India* (1855), 32.]

Moonshi, munshi [17C. H/Ar. *munshī*, fr. *ansha'a*, 'to educate [a youth]', 'to compose a written document'.] A secretary, a reader, an interpreter, a teacher, espec. of Indian languages to foreigners. [*OED* & YB; *The Indian Antiquary* (1622), LX; Halhed, *Code Gentoo Laws* (1776), I. 17.]

Moonsif(f), munsif [19C. H/Ar. *munsif*, 'just, honest'.] 'In British India the title of a native civil judge of the lowest grade.' [*OED* & YB; *Gloss. to Fifth Report*, Sel. Comm. E. Ind. Comp. (1812), 31.]

Moor, Moorman, Moorish (adj) [16C. Pg. *Mouro*.] A Muslim in India, particularly through Portuguese habitual use of the term. 'The *Moors* of the Malabar coast were middlemen, who had adopted the profession of Islam for their own convenience and in order to minister for their own profit to the constant traffic of merchants from Ormuz and Arabian Ports.' [YB.] *See* **Moplah, Islam,** and **The Moors.** *Moorish* = Muslim, and the Hindustani language. [*OED* & YB; Hickock, tr., Frederick's *Voy.* (1588), 23; Middleton, *Voyage* (1604).]

Moora [19C. Sea Hind. *mūrā,* fr. Pg. *amura.*] A tack, or tacking, in sailing. [YB; Roebuck, *Naval Dict.* (1811).]

Moorah [17C. Poss. Mar. *mudā, mudī.*] 'Cases of rice straw bound together to contain certain quantities of grain, the former [*mudā*] larger and the latter [*mudī*] smaller.' Also, *moodah,* M. *mūta,* fr. *mūtu,* 'to cover.' 'A fastening package, espec. packages in a circular form.' [YB.] *See* **Culsey.** [Danvers, *Letters* (1611), I. 116.]

Moorat *See* **Muhurat.**

Moorghee, murgghi [19C. H. *mūrghi.*] A fowl, a hen. Also *half-murghee* or *kharcha;* not fully grown but large enough for the table. [Whitworth, *Anglo-Indian Dict.* (1885).]

Moorpunky, -ee [18C. Corr. of *morpankhī.* H. *mor,* 'peacock' + *pankhī,* 'a fan'.] A pleasure-boat, peacock-shaped, formerly used on the Ganges. [*OED* & YB; Long, *Selections* etc. (1748-67).]

Moors, The [18C. fr. *Moor.*] In the 18th century, the Hindustani and Urdu languages. Also termed the *Moorish* or 'black-language'. *See* **Moor.** [*OED* & YB; MS. Letter of James Rennell, 10 March 1767.]

Moorum [19C. Poss. Mar. *murum,* 'a fissile kind of stone' *(murukallu* is the Telugu word for **Laterite**).] A word in W. India for gravel, espec. as used for road-metal. *See* **Cabook.** [YB; Gribble, *Cuddapah* (1875).]

Moorva [18C. S. *mūrva.*] Bow-string hemp. [*OED;* Sir W. Jones, in *Asiatic Res.* (1794), IV. 271.]

Moory, moorees [17C. Poss. fr. Pg. *morim,* 'shirting', or fr. **Moor,** a Muslim.] A kind of Indian calico, or long-cloth, once principally manufactured at Nellore and Chingleput. [*OED* & YB; Pringle, *Diary Fort St. George* (1682-5), iv. 41; Balfour, *Cycl. of India* (1885), ii. 982.]

Mootsuddy [17C. H. *mutasaddī,* fr. Ar. *mutasaddi.*] A native accountant, **Writer** or clerk. [YB; Hedges, *Diary* (6 Jan. 1683).]

Moplah, Mapila [17C. M. *māppila.*] Indigenous Muslim inhabitants of Malabar (Kerala) descended from the Moors and Arab settlers married to Malabar women. Sometimes also applied to the Syrian Christians of Cochin

and Travancore. [*OED* & YB; *The Diaries of Streynsham Master* (1675-80).] *See* **Navayat.**

Mora, morah [18C. H. *morhā.*] A wickerwork stool or footstool in common use in India, and in Anglo-Indian colloquial speech. [*OED* & YB; Capt. Blunt in *Asiatic Res.* (1795), vii. 92; Mrs Sherwood, *Stories Ch. Catech.* (1813),vii. 45.]

Morcha [20C. H. *morcha.*] Procession, protest march. (Generally for political or industrial purposes.) [Hawkins, *CIWIE.*]

Morchal, mirchal [17C. H. *morch'hal.*] A fan or fly-whisk made of peacock's feathers. [YB; Fryer, *New Acct.* etc (1672-81), 95.]

Mordeshin, -een, mordcxim, mort-dc-chien [16C. Pg. *mordexim* fr. Mar. *modchī,* 'cholera', fr. *modnen,* 'to break up, to sink'.] *See* **Cholera Morbus.** Names in India for Cholera, in use up to the end of the 18th century. (*Mort-de-chien,* 'a dog's death', is fanciful folk etymology, based on phonological similarity to *mordesheen*). [Phillip, tr. *Linschoten* (1598), I. xxiv. 67.] Known also to Anglo-Indians as the 'Wandering Jew' because of its ubiquitous spread during (seasonal) epidemics. [Wilkinson, *Two Monsoons* (1976), 172.]

Morning Glory [19C. E. (Mar. *bhauva*).] A convolvulaceous, profusely flowering creeper, with large blue flowers, *Ipomoea purpurea* and other species, flourishing in many parts of India. Also called by Anglo-Indians, *Railway-Creeper* and *Porter's Joy.* [*OED;* Pursh, *Flora Americae Septentrionalis* (1814), I. 146.]

Moslem, Mussulman, Muslim [17C. Ar. *muslim,* 'resigning or submitting oneself to God'.] (1) One who professes Islam. (2) Adj. Of or pertaining to the Muslims. *Mussulmans* = Anglo-Indian expression for the **Urdu** language. *See* **Mohammedan** and **Moors.** [*OED* & YB; Bedwell, *Arab Trudg.* (1615); Sionita in Purchas (1619), ii., 504.]

Mosque [17C. Pg. *mesquita,* fr. Ar. *masjid.*] *See* **Masjid.** 'The Mosque'; those attending mosque services; the congregation of the Faithful; Islam. [*OED* & YB; Sir T. Roe, in Purchas (1616), i. 537; Burke, *Corr.* (1799), II. 270.]

Motiya(s) [19C. Beng. *motiya.*] Porters in Bengal who would carry any parcel on the head, which might be too bulky for the hands of domestic servants in Anglo-Indian households. *See* **Cowra.** [*Anglo-Indian Domestic Sketch: A Letter from an Artist in India to his mother in England* (Thackers, Calcutta 1849), pp 78-88.]

Moturpha [19C. H/Ar. *muhtarifa,* 'an artisan'.] 'A number of miscellaneous taxes in Madras and Bombay such as were called **Sayer** in Bengal.' [YB; *Gloss. 5th Report Sel. Comm. E. Ind. Comp.* (1813).]

Mouse-Deer [19C.] A small deer-like animal of the genus *Tragulus;* the Indian and Malaysian chevrotain, weighing under 6 lbs. [*Penny Cycl.* (1836), VI; Blanford, *Mammalia* (1888-91).]

Mridang(am) [19C. S. *mrdamga.*] Barrel-shaped drum with two heads, beaten by hand, formerly made of clay, now usually of wood. *See* **Madal.** [*OED;* Hipkins, *Mus. Instruments* (1888).] *See* **Tabla, Pakhawaj, Madal.**

Mubarak *See* **Moobarek.**

Muchalka [19C.] See **Moochulka.**

Muchwa *See* **Mashwa.**

Muckin(g), mukkin [late 19/20C. H. *makkhan.*] 'butter'. Regular Army slang. [Partridge, *Dict. of Slang* etc. (1979).]

Muckna [18C. H. *makhnā*, fr. S. *matkuna*, 'a bug, flea, a beardless man, a tuskless elephant.'] A young tuskless male elephant, or one with rudimentary tusks. [*OED & YB; Lives of the Lindsays* (1780), iii. 194.]

Mucoa, mukuva [17C. M. and Tam. *mukkuvan* (sing) and *mukkuvar* (pl) Lit. 'diver(s)'.] Fishermen on the W. coast of India. 'It was among these, and among the corresponding class of *Paravars* on the East coast, that F. Xavier's most noted labours in India occurred.' [YB; Purchas, *Pilgrimes* (1625), 553.]

Mudalali, mutalali [19C. Mar. *mud(d)al*, 'capital, principal, stock'.] Cf. **Modeliar** and M. *mutalali.* A rich trader or proprietor, a businessman. [*OED;* Wilson, *Glossary* (1885).]

Mudeliar *See* **Modeliar.**

Mudder,-ar, madder, mudar etc. [19C. H. *madār;* S. *mandāra.*] Shrubs of the genus *Calotropis*, esp. *C. gigantea*, the root-bark of which yields a diaphoretic medicine, and the inner stem bark, a strong silky fibre known as **Yercum** (1826). *See* **Ak** and **Aal.** 'The plant abounds with an acrid milky juice which the Rajputs are said to employ for infanticide.' [*OED & YB;* Robinson, *Med. Chirurg. Trans.* (1819), X. 32; Stewart, *Punjab Plants* (1869).]

Muddle [19C.] *See* **Budlee** (Doppelganger).

Mudra, moodra [19C. S. *mudrā.*] Significant positions or intertwinings of the fingers in dance and religious worship. 'Also a movement or pose in **Yoga.**' [*OED;* Ward, *Acct. Hindoos* (1812), II. 26.]

Muezzin [16C. fr. Ar. *mu'addin.*] A Muslim mosque official who proclaims the regular hours of prayer from the **Minar.** [*OED;*

Purchas, *Pilgrimes* (1613), 603.]

Mufti, mufty¹ [17C. H/Ar. *muftī.*] An expounder of the Muslim Law; the utterer of the *fatwa* (**Fatwah**). The *Kaži* (**Cadi**) carries out the judgement of the *Muftī.* See **Law-Officer, Moolvi.** [*OED & YB; Notes and Extracts, Fort St. George* (1670-81).]

Mufty² [19C. *See* prec.] Army slang for 'plain clothes', 'civvies', worn by one who has the right to wear uniform. The transition from ¹ to ² was perhaps because the 'civvy' attire affected at that time resembled the oriental dress of the Mufti. [*OED & YB;* 'Quiz' *Grand Master* (1816), II. 50.]

Mug,¹ moog *See* **Moong.**

Mug,² Mugg, Mugh [16C. Beng. *Magh.*] Bengali name for natives of Arakan and Chittagong, formerly considered by Anglo-Indians to be the best cooks in Calcutta. Attrib. *Mug* language (1897). [*OED & YB;* Fitch (1585) in Hakluyt (1807), ii. 389; G. O. Trevelyan, *The Dawk Bungalow* (1866), 389.]

Muga, mooga [17C. Ass. *mūga.*] Raw golden silk of Assam, from the cocoons of the *Antheraea assamensis* moths. [Streynsham Master, *Diaries* (1675-80).]

Mugger, muggar, muggur [17C. H. *magar;* Mar. *makar;* S. *makara,* 'a sea-monster'.] The destructive broad-snouted crocodile of the Ganges and other Indian rivers (*Crocodilus palustris*). [*OED & YB.*] *See* **Makara.** [Hawkins in Purchas (1625), I. 436.]

Muggrabee, maghribi [19C. Ar. *maghrabī*, 'western'.] Obs. in India now, but appears as '*Mograbbin*' in *Quentin Durward.* Formerly used to apply to 'western Arabs, or Moors proper'. [YB & *OED;* Lane, tr., *Arabian Nights Entertainments* (1834), II. xviii. 600.]

Muhajir [20C. H. *muhājirūna.*] Refugee, emigrant. [Webster, *3rd New Intern. Dict.* (1979).]

Muhammedan *See* **Mohammedan.**

Muhurat, moorat [H. *muhūrt.*] Auspicious time for beginning; opening ceremony. [Hawkins, *CIWIE.*]

Muhurtam [19C. S. *muhūrtam.*] Brahmins' sacred thread ceremony. [Abbé Dubois, *Character, Manners etc. of the People of India* (1817).]

Muhurrum *See* **Moharram.**

Mujahid [20C. H/Ar. *mujahid.*] Warrior. [Hawkins, *CIWIE.*]

Mukaddam *See* **Mocuddum.**

Mukiya, mukhi [19C. Guj. *mukha*, 'mouth' + *īya*, 'person'. 'One who speaks for others'.] Village headman, a **Patel.** [Whitworth, *Anglo-Indian Dict.* (1885).]

Mukti [18C. S. *mukti*.] Hinduism & Jainism. Spiritual liberation, freedom. [*OED*.] *See* **Moksha**.[Wilkins, tr., *Bhāgvāt Geeta* (1785), 140.]

Mulki [H/Ar. *mulk*, 'a kingdom'.] Person of the former Hyderabad State.

Mull¹ [19C.] Contr. of **Mulligatawny**. Applied as a distinctive 'title' to members of the Madras Presidency service and to the inhabitants of Madras jocularly. *See* **Qui-hi** and **Ducks**. [*OED* & YB; 'Quiz' *Grand-Master* (1816), vi. 145.]

Mull² [19C. H. *malnā*.] To rub, massage, anoint. *See* **Shampoo**. [*OED*; Mrs Sherwood, *Lady of Manor* (1825-9), V. xxix. 74.]

Mull³ [17C. H. *malmal*.] A thin variety of Indian **muslin**. *See* **Mulmul**. [*OED*; *Hugli Letter Book* (1668); Jane Austen, *Northanger Abbey* (1798), x.] *See* **Qui-hi** and **Ducks**.

Mullah, Moolah [17C. H. *mullā*, fr. Ar. *maulā*.] In India, a learned man, a teacher, a doctor of the Law, a man who reads the **Koran** in a house for 40 days after a death. In India also a schoolmaster. [*OED* & YB; Terry in Purchas (1616), ii. 1467.]

Mulligatawny [18C. Corr. of Tamil *milagu-tannīr*, 'pepper-water'.] A spicy, peppery, curry-flavoured S. Indian soup, frequently on Anglo-Indian domestic menus. *See* **Mull¹** and **Rasam**. [*OED* & YB; Seton-Karr, *Selections from Calcutta Gaz.* (1784-1823); Southey (1829), *Sir T. More* (1831), II. 286.]

Mulmul¹ [17C.] *See* **Mull**.³

Muncheel, manjeel [19C. M. *manjīl*. S. *mancha*.] A kind of hammock-litter slung on long poles, used on the Malabar coast as a substitute for a **Palankin** or **Dooly**; similar to the **Dandy** of the Himalayas, but more elaborate. [YB & *OED*; Buchanan (1808), *Christian Research* (1819), 171.]

Munda [19C. Native word for a Kolarian tribe.] (1) A member of an ancient Indian people of pre-Aryan stock surviving in N.E. India. (2) A group of languages of East Central India, of the Austro-Asian family. Attrib. of or pertaining to the *Mundas* or their language, cf. **Kolarian**. [*OED*; Hodgson, *On Aborigines of India* (1847), iii. 150; Grierson, *Linguistic Survey of India*. (1904), II. 1.]

Mundu [M. *mundu*.] White sarong, extensively worn in Kerala. [Hawkins, *CIWIE*.]

Munga [19C.] The bonnet macaque of S. India, *Macacus sinicus*. [*OED*; J. E. Gray, *List Spec. Mammalia, Brit. Mus.* (1845), 7.]

Mungo¹ [19C.] Variant of **Mongoose**.

Mungo-root² [18C.] Mungo-root: the plant *Ophiorhiza mungos*, a supposed antidote against snake-venom. [*OED*; Mortimer in *Phil. Trans.* (1738), xi. 442.]

Muni, mooni [18C. S. *muni*, 'impulse', fr. *man*, 'to think'.] Hermit, ascetic; one moved by inward impulse; a seer, a saint. [*OED*; Wilkins, tr., *Bhāgvāt-Geeta* (1785), ii. 41.]

Munia [19C. H. *muniā*.] Bird smaller than a sparrow, of sub-family *Estrildinae*. Various species in India, Sri Lanka and Pakistan. Ali & Ripley, *Handbk. Birds Ind. & Pak.* (1974), Vol. 10.]

Munjeet [19C. Beng. *manjīth*; H. *majīth*; S. *manjistha*.] The Bengal Madder, *Rubia cordifolia*, a dye plant. [*OED* & YB; Hastings, 'Letter of Commission to George Boyle', quoted in Woodcock, *Into Tibet* (1971); Bancroft, *Perm. Colours* (1813), II. 278.]

Munshi *See* **Moonshi**.

Munsif *See* **Moonsif**.

Munzil [17C. H/Ar. *manzil*, 'descending or alighting'.] Hence the halting place of a stage or march; a day's stage. [YB; Hedges, *Diary* (30 July 1685).]

Murabba [19C. H. *marabba*.] Jam. [Hawkins, *CIWIE*.]

Murchana, murcchana [19C. S. *mūrchanā*.] Modulation of a musical note. [*OED*; Day, *Music in S. India* (1891), ii. 23.]

Murdabad [20C. H/P. *murdah*, 'a corpse'.] Int. 'Death for ever!' (Political ejaculation: *Apartheid murdabad!* 'Down with Apartheid!') *See* **Zindabad**. [Hawkins, *CIWIE*.]

Murghi *See* **Moorghee**.

Muria, Morea [19C. (Native word).] (1) A member of a hill people of Bastar in India, a tribe of the **Gonds**. (2) Of or pertaining to these people. [*OED*; Hislop (1863), *Aboriginal Tribes of Central Provinces* (1866), i. 22.]

Murid [19C. H/Ar. *murid*.] Disciple of a **Pir**; a disciple; a member of the second order of the *Sufi 'way'*, aspiring to the third order; a schoolchild. [*OED*; Malcolm, *Hist. Persia* (1815), II. xxii. 396.]

Murwa [19C. H. dial. *maruwā*.] A kind of millet, *Eleusine coracana*. Also, a fermented liquor brewed from this. *See* **Mand**. [*OED*; *Nat. Encycl.* (1847), i. 236.]

Musambi [19C. Fr. place-name *Mozambique*.] Sweet, tight-skinned orange, *Citrus sinensis*. [Hawkins, *CIWIE*.]

Musbee(s), Mazhabis [19C. H/Ar. *mazhab*, 'religious belief'.] A class of Sikhs originally said to be of low caste *(Churha)* Hindu converts. Some of the converts seem to have originally been Muslims. Also, a corps of pioneers, the 32nd Bengal N.I. (Pioneers). [*OED* & YB; Cunningham, *Hist. Sikhs* (1849), 379.]

Mushaira [19C. H. *mushaïra.*] Meeting where poets recite their poems. [Hawkins, *CIWIE.*]

Mushrues, mushroos [19C. H/P. *mashrū,* 'lawful'.] Cloth with silk warp and cotton weft. [YB; Mrs Mir Hassan Ali, *Observations* (1832).]

Musk [14C. H. *mushk,* 'scrotum', 'testicle', ult. S. *mushka,* 'scrotum', 'a cod of musk'.] The Musk-rat (1598), *Crocidura murina,* found in the Far East and parts of India. Also the *Musk*-deer, *Moschus moschiferus,* which produces 'Tibet (or *pouchea*) musk'. A scented reddish brown secretion from a gland or sac of the male musk-deer, the basis of many perfumes. [*OED* & YB; Fryer, *New Acct.* etc. (1673); Linschoten, Hak. Soc. (1598); Trevisa, *Barth. De P.R.* (1398), xvii, xix.]

Muslim *See* **Moslem** and **Mussulman.**

Muslin [17C. fr. *Mussolos* (Mosul) Ar. *mausil.*] Fine cotton fabric. [W. Biddulph in T. Lawrence's *Travels* (1609), 43.]

Musnud [18C. H. *masnad,* fr. Ar. *misnad,* fr. *sanada,* 'to lean against'.] A cushioned seat. One used by emperors and princes in place of a throne. *See* **Gaddi.** [*OED* & YB; Orme, *Hist. Milit. Trans.* (1763), I. iv. 254.]

Mussal, massaul [17C. H/Ar. *mash'al,* 'a torch'.] 'Usually made of rags wrapped round a rod and fed at intervals with oil from an earthern pot.' [YB & *OED*; Fryer, *New Acct.* etc. (1672-81), 34.]

Mussalchee, mussaulchee [17C. *See* prec + *chī,* 'torch-bearer'.] In origin a torch-bearer going before his master to light the way. In time degenerated to a cook's assistant, dishwasher, scullion. [*OED* & YB; Finch (1610), in Purchas, *Pilgrimes* (1625), I. 432.]

Mussalla *See* **Masala.**

Mussuck, mussooke [17C. H. *mashak;* S. *masaka.*] A goat skin water-bag carried by a **Beastie** *(bhishtī).* [Hawkins (1610), in Purchas, Pilgrimes (1625), I. 427.]

Mussulman [16C. H/P. *musulmān* (pl-*māns*).] Muslim(s) with incorrect *Mussulmen.* [*OED* & YB; Edward in Hakluyt (1568), i. 442; Foxe, *A. and M.* (1563-83), 759/2.]

Musselmans [18C. *See* prec.] The **Urdu** language (obs.). [Rennel, MS. Let. (1767); Yule, 448/1.]

Must(h), mast [19C. H/P. *mast,* 'drunk'.] Applied in India specially to male animals such as elephants and camels, in a state of periodical excitement. Also *musty,* violent, excited. [*OED* & YB; Forsyth, *Highland India* (1871), 287.]

Mustee(s), mestee(s), mistices, mestiz [16C. Pg. *mestiço.*] A half-caste, part Portuguese part Indian. *See* **Castees, Topaz (Topass), Dobash** and **Chi-chi.** [*OED* & YB; Candish (1699), in Hakluyt (1588), IV. 337; Wheeler, *Madras in Olden Time* (1816), I. 356.]

Muster [17C. Pg. *mostra.*] A pattern or sample. A *muster*-card was a pattern-card. [*OED* & YB; 1601, 'Old trans. of Galvano' in Hakluyt (1807), 83.]

Mutlub [19C. H/Ar. *matlab* fr. *talab,* 'he asked'.] Properly means a question, hence intention, wish, object. 'In Anglo-Indian use it always meant "purpose, gist" and the like.' Also *matbalī* (adj)', 'opinionated'. [YB.]

Mutt, muth *See* **Math, Mahant, Gurdwara.**

Muttee [19C. H. *mutti.*] Earth, soil. [Hawkins, *CIWIE.*]

Mutter [19C. H. *mutter.*] A variety of edible pea, *Pisum sativum.* [Hawkins, *CIWIE.*]

Muttongosht [19C.] Anglo-Indian, Domestic Hind. for 'mutton'. Lit: 'mutton-flesh'. [YB.]

Muttongye [19C.] Sea-Hind. *matangat,* a (nautical) martingale; a corr. of the English word; a rope for guying down the jib-boom to the dolphin-striker. [YB; Roebuck, *Naval Dict.* (1811).]

Myna, mina, miner [17C. H. *maina.*] The Indian 'talking starling', of the genus *Acridotheres* or *Sturnus.* 'They are among the most teachable of imitative birds, articulating words with great distinctness.' [YB & *OED*; *Eng. Fact. in India* (1618-69).]

Myrobalan [16C. L. *myrobalanum,* Pg. *myrabalan.*] Name applied to certain dried fruits and nuts (genus *Terminalia*) of astringent flavour used medicinally and exported from India from an early date, 'with a high reputation in the medieval pharmacopoeia'. [YB.] These and other dried fruits were sold in India by *Kebuli-wallahs,* itinerant Pathan vendors from Afghanistan. Also used for tanning purposes. [*OED* & YB; Elyot (1533), *The Castel of Helth* (1541), 68.]

Mysore Thorn [18C. Anglo-Indian.] A prickly bush, *Caesalpinia sepiaria.* 'Armed with short-sharp, recurved prickles, it was much used as a fence in the Deccan. Hyder Ali planted it round his stronghold in Mysore,

Mysorin

hence it is often called "Hyder's Thorn", *Haidar kā jhār.'* [YB; Lady Falkland, *Chowchow*, 2nd ed. (1857), i. 300.]

Mysorin [19C. fr. *Mysore*.] Anhydrous ortho-carbonate of copper, found in Mysore State (now Karnataka). [*OED*; Ure, *Dict. Arts.* (1839), 236.]

N

Naan, nan [20C. H. *nān*.] Thick oval slabs of N. Indian and Pakistani leavened bread, baked in the *tandūr* (Indian oven). [*OED; Guardian*, 8 Dec. 1967.] *See* **Chupatty, Roti**.

Nabob [17C. Pg. *Nababo* fr. H. *Nawwāb* = Ar. plural of sing. *Nāyab* (**Naib**), 'a deputy'.] (1) Originally, as a **nawāb**, a deputy-governor of a province under the great Mogul. Later an honorary title of rank without office, and occasionally bestowed on Muslims of 'distinction and good service'. [YB; R. Coverte *Voy*. (1612), 36.] (2) In the 18th Century, when the transactions of Clive made the word 'nabob' familiar in England', it was applied to any Anglo-Indian who returned 'home' after 'shaking the Pagoda Tree' with immense success (1760). Otherwise, an ostentatiously wealthy person or, colloquially, a 'nob'. (No etym. connection.) [Horace Walpole (1764), *Letters* (1857), iv. 222.] Derived expressions: (1) Nabob-fortune (1795); (2)-hunting (1771); (3)-maker (1862); (4)-land (1764); (5)-plunderer (1775); (6) Nabobery (1834); (7) Nabobical (1763); (8) Nabobish (1885); (9) Nabobism (1884); (10) Nabobship (1753); (11) Nabobess (1767). [*OED* & YB.]

Nacoda, nacoder, nakhoda, nockado, knockada, etc. [17C. H/P. *nā-khodā*. 'A skipper', fr. *nāw*, 'boat' + *khūda*, 'master'.] Master of native vessel. (Hobson-Jobsonized by Malays into *Anak kuda*, 'son of a horse'.) [*OED* & YB; Saris in Purchas, *Pilgrimes* (1625). I. iv. 385; Wallace, *Fifteen Years in India* (1822), 241.]

Nada, naad [20C. S. *nāda*, 'sound'.] Elemental sound, considered as the source of all sounds and a source of creation; the 'inner' sound of the body. [*OED;* 'A. Avalon', *Tantra of Great Liberation* (1913), xxiii.]

Nadaswaram, nagasara [20C. S. *nāda* + *svaram*, 'sound'.] Conical reed instrument, longer and louder than the **Shehnai**. [Hawkins, *CIWIE*; P. Holroyde, *Indian Music* (1972), 274.]

Naga¹ [18C. S. *nāga*, 'serpent, snake'.] Hindu myth: A serpent demon, half human, half snake; courageous, violent, handsome and symbol of the cycles of time, living in the underworld and still worshipped in S. India. The offspring of Kadru and Kasyapa, supposed to be the guardians of Patala or the subterranean regions. [*OED;* Wilkins, tr. *Bhāgvāt Geeta* (1785).]

Naga² [19C. Tribal name, perh. from S. *naga*, 'mountain' or S. *nagna* 'naked'.] (a) A tribal native of Nagaland, which divides Assam from Burma. [*OED* & YB.] (b) The Tibeto-Burman language of the Naga tribes. [*OED;* McCosh, *Topography of Assam* (1837), xiv. 156.]

Naga³ [19C. H. *nanga*, fr. S. *nagna*, 'naked'. (Cogn. with E. 'naked'.)] A naked ascetic mendicant belonging to any Hindu sect; spec. one belonging to a Dadu Panth sub-sect, whose members were allowed to carry arms and serve as mercenaries. [*OED;* H. H. Wilson, in *Asiatick Researches* (1828), xvi. 80; *Rajputana Gazetteer* (1879), ii. 147.]

Nagara [20C. H/S. *nāgara*.] An Indian drum; *See* **Nobat**. [Holroyde, *Indian Music* (1972).]

Nagari [17C. H/S.] *nāgarī*, 'of the city'. *See* **Devanāgarī**.

Nagasara *See* **Nadaswaram**.

Naib [17C. H. *nāib* fr. Ar. *nāyab*.] Deputy; deputy-governor. *See* **Nawab** and **Nabob**. [*OED* & YB; Hedges, *Diary* (11 Oct. 1682).]

Naik, naique [16C. H. *nāyak*, fr. S. *nāyaka*, 'a leader, chief general'.] (a) Title of honour among Hindus in the Deccan; a governor. [Linschoten in Hakluyt (1598); Hickock, tr. Frederick's *Voy*. (1588), 16.] (b) A native captain or headman (Portuguese usage, 1538). [Cogan, *Pinto* (1653).] (c) A military officer; in later Anglo-Indian use, a corporal or non-commissioned officer of **Sepoys**. [Sir A. Campbell, *Regs. for the Hon. Company's Troops* (1787).] (d) A Telugu caste, whence the general name of the kings of Vijayanagara (1325–1674) and of the Lords of Madura (1559–1741) and other places. [*OED* & YB; Lord Valentia, *Voyages* (1809), i. 398.]

Nainsook(s) [18C. H. *nain*, 'eye' and *sukh* 'pleasure'.] A fine soft white calico or **Jaconet** (1769); one of a large number of Indian **Piece-goods** exported in the 18th century. [*OED* & YB; *Spirit of the Public Journals* (1804), VII, 59.]

Nair, Nayar [16C. M. *nāyar*, fr. the same Sanskrit origin as **Naik**.] Malabar matrilineal military caste; at one time the dominant caste in Malabar (Kerala). [*OED* & YB; Foster, *Early*

Trav. in India (1583-91); Litchfield, tr., *Castañeda* (1582); Logan, *Malabar* (1887-91), i. 131.] *See* **Tambaranee**.

Naja, naia [18C. Mod. L. fr. H. *nāg*, 'snake'.] A genus of highly venomous snakes, eg. *Naja tripudians*, the Indian cobra. [*OED; Chambers Cycl. Supp.* (1753).]

Najeeb, nujeeb, nujeeve [18C. Ar. *najĭb*, 'noble'.] 'A kind of half-disciplined infantry soldier under some of the native governments; also at one time a kind of militia under the British receiving this honorary title as being gentlemen volunteers.' [YB; E.A. Bond, *Trial of Warren Hastings* (1790; 1859–61), ii. 393.]

Naka [19C. Mar. *nākā*.] Road junction or check-post. [Hawkins, *CIWIE*.]

Nakkoo [20C. Kash. *nakkū*. 'The nosey one'.] *See* **Nark**. (Romany: *nāk*, 'nose' fr. S. *nāsa*.) A person with an outsize nose and curiosity; a 'Nosey Parker'. [Rushdie, *Midnight's Children* (1981).]

Nakshatra(s) [20C. S. *nakshatra. nakt*, 'night' + *kshatra*, 'dominion'.] (*See* **Kshatriya**.) Lit. 'dominion over the night'. Hindu mythology: one of the 28 lunar mansions, the *Nakshatra(s)* comprise the Constellations in which dwells the moon (**Soma**), the principle of immortality. [Whitworth, *Anglo-Indian Dict.* (1885).]

Nala *See* **Nullah**.

Nalkee [18C. H. *nālkĭ*, perh. fr. S. *nalika*, 'a tube'.] A kind of litter, formerly used by persons of rank, or a bride's litter in Bihar. *See* **Palki**. [YB; tr. of *Seir Mutaqherin* (1789), iii. 269; Sleeman, *Rambles* (1844).]

Nal(l)a(h) *See* **Nullah**.

Nama(m) [16C. S. *nāmam*.] The mark pasted on the foreheads of **Vaishnavites** with the vertical red line in the middle painted with **Kumkum**. Also *Namadaɩi*, one who wears the *namam*. [Whitworth, *Anglo-Indian Dict.* (1885).]

Namaskar(a) [20C. S. *namaskara; fr. namas*, 'bowing' + *kara*, 'doing'.] A Hindu greeting, with bowed head and palms of the hands put together in the attitude of prayer. *See* next. [*OED;* Parsons, *Mysore City* (1930), 88.]

Namaste [20C. S. *namas*, 'bowing' + *te*, dat. of *tuam*, 'you'. (Alternatively *nam*, (God's) name + *aste*, 'truth'.)] Spoken greeting accompanying **Namaskar**. Also, vb. intr. to *namaste* (1967). [*OED*]. (The distinction between **Namaskar** and **Namaste** is not always distinctly drawn by native speakers.)

Namavali [20C. H. *namāvali*.] A sheet printed with the name of a Hindu deity, revered by devotees, e.g. of Rama or Krishna. [Hawkins *CIWIE*.]

Namaz, namaj [19C. P. *namāz*, 'prayer', akin to S. *namas*, 'obeisance'.] Muslim worship at the five specified times of the day. (1) *Namāz-i-Subh*, from dawn to sunrise; (2) *Salātu 'z-Zuhr*, start of decline of the Sun; (3) *Salātu 'Asr*, midway between (2) & (4); (4) *Salātu' Maghrib*, just after sunset; (5) *Salātu' 'sha*, when night has closed in. And an additional post-midnight prayer, *Namāz-i-Tahjjud*. Also *Namāzgāh*, 'prayer- place' in a mosque. [Mrs Meer Hassan Ali (1832), *Observations Mussulmauns India* (ed. 1978), 82; Wilson, *Glossary* (1855); Whitworth, *Anglo-Indian Dict.* (1885).]

Nambeadarim [16C. M. *nambiyadiri, nambiyattiri*.] A general, a prince of ancient Malabar. (*Nambiyar* = the title of a division of the **Nairs**.) [YB; Litchfield's *Castañeda* (1582), f. 147; Logan, *Malabar* (1887-91), i. 121.]

Nambudari, Namboo(d)ree [18C. M. *nambūdiri* (M. *nambu*, 'the Veda' + *ōthu*, 'to teach' + *tiri*, 'holy'.). A **Brahmin** of Malabar (Kerala)] [YB; Hamilton, *A New Acct. of the E. Indies* (1727),i.312;Logan,*Malabar*(1887-91),i.118.]

Namdharis [19C.] They are also called *Kūkas*, 'the Shriekers'. An austere sect within Sikhism, founded by Balak Singh, 1727-1862; who sought Sikh rule in the Punjab. *See* **Khalsa**.

Nam-ke-waste (adj.) Nominal, not real. [Hawkins, *CIWIE*.]

Nanak Panthi [16C.] A Sikh theocratic movement, founded by Guru Nanak (1538) with primary emphasis on peaceful tenets and objectives. Cf. **Khalsa**. [Webster, *3rd New Intern. Dict.* (1979).]

Nandi[1] [19C. S. *nāndi*, 'the happy one', 'joy, vigour, freshness'.] The Bull, **Shiva's** vehicle, *(vahan)* whose statue or figure is usually found in Shaivaite temples, symbolizing fertility. Also, a benediction or invocation spoken at the beginning of an Indian drama and usually addressed to **Vishnu** or **Shiva**, but sometimes to **Buddha**. [*OED;* Colebrooke in *Asiatick Researches* (1807), IX. 425.]

Nandi[2] [19C. Tel. prob. fr. S. *nandin*.] Any of various plants, e.g. Ben-teak, the wood of an E. Indian tree, *Lagerstromia lanceolata*. [*OED; Treas. Bot.* (1866), 1128.]

Nappy [19C.] A barber. [Hawkins, *CIWIE*.]

Narayan An incarnation of **Vishnu.**

Nard, nardus [14C. L. *nardus;* Gr. *nardos;* Heb. *nērd';* S. *narada, nalada;* Ar/P. *naradin,* 'Indian *spikenard'*.] (1) An aromatic balsam or ointment used by the ancients, derived from the *spikenard* plant. [Wyclif, *John,* (1382), xii. 3]. (2) An aromatic plant (esp. that yielding the ointment) *Nardostachys jatamansi(s).* [Percivall, *Sp. Dict.* (1591); Milton, *Paradise Lost* (1667), v. 293.] (3) Matgrass, *Nardus stricta,* or the common *nard.* [*OED* & YB; Sir W. Jones in *As. Res.* (1790), ii. 410.] Also *nardiferous* and *nardine.*

Narghile, nargeela, nargileh [18C. P. *nārgīl;* S. *nārikera-kela,* 'coconut'. (Of which the receptacle for the tobacco was made.)] Orig. the **Hubble-Bubble** or **Hookah** in its simplest form as made from a coconut shell. [*OED* & YB; Ives, *Voyage from England to India* (1754), 271.]

Nark [19C. Perh. fr. Romany *nāk,* 'nose'; akin to S. *nāsa,* 'nose'.] A 'nosey' person; police spy, informer. Also vb. trans. *to nark,* 'to watch, to spy on'. *See* **Nakoo.** [*OED;* Hotten, *Slang Dict.* (1859).]

Narsimha, Narsingh [19C.] Man-lion incarnation of **Vishnu** in his 4th. **Avatar,** for the destruction of Hiranyakasipu who had been promised by Brahma that he would be slain neither by man or beast. [Whitworth, *Anglo-Indian Dict.* (1885).]

Nasbandi [20C. H.] Vasectomy. Advocated as a means of population control during the Emergency in India (1977). [Hawkins, *CIWIE.*]

Nasik-square (-cube) [19C. Indian place-name + 'square'.] Magic squares and cubes, so named and described by a mathematician, the Rev. A. H. Frost [*Camb. Math. Jour.,* (1857)] from his long residence in Nasik, an ancient Hindu holy city in Maharashtra. [*OED* & YB; P. Frost in *Q. Jrnl. Math.,* 1866, vii. 94.]

Nasrani, Serani, Nastrayne, etc. [16C. Ar. *Nasrāni.*] A Christian, so called by Muslims = *Nazarene.* [*OED;* Newberry (1583), Letter 15 July in Purchas, *Pilgrimes* (1625).]

Nastaliq [18C. H./P. *nashkhī,* 'copy' + *talik,* 'hanging'.] Cursive Persian script with rounded forms and elongated horizontal strokes. Also called *Talik.* [*OED;* Ouseley, *Pers. Miscellanies* (1705), i.i.7.]

Nat¹ [19C. Burm. *nāt;* S. *nātha,* 'lord'.] Myth: A term applied to all spiritual beings, angels, elfs, demons or what not, including the gods of the Hindus. [YB.] Also, *natworshipper* (1833). [*OED* & YB; Hamilton, *Acct. Kingdom Nepaul* (1819), i.i.57.]

Nat,² nut [19C. S. *nata,* 'dancer, actor, tumbler'.] A member of 'an itinerant class of entertainers', esp. in N. India. *Nati,* language of the Nats. [*OED.* Sb. and attrib. Richardson, *Asiatick Res.* (1801), vii. 457.]

Nataraja [20C. Lit. 'prince of dancers', fr. S. *nata,* 'dancer' + *rājan,* 'prince', 'king'.] A name of **Shiva,** the Hindu god of creation and dissolution, in his role as lord of the dance, when he symbolizes cosmic energy. Also, a figure depicting **Shiva** as lord of the dance. [*OED;* Smith, *Hist. Fine Art India and Ceylon* (1911), vii. 249.]

National Calendar *See* **Saka.²**

Natya(-shastri) [20C. S. *nātya,* 'dance' + *shāstri,* 'instruction'.] Indian dancing, and dance-drama, orig. in the temple. *Nātyashāstra,* the earliest book on Indian dancing, believed to have been written by Bharata. *See* **Nritta** and **Nritya.** [Radhakrishnan, *Hist. Phil.* (1952-3), i.383.]

Naubat [19C. H/Ar. *naubat.*] Indian music: a large kettle-drum. Also a drum-band at the palace gateway, playing at fixed intervals. [Whitworth, *Anglo-Indian Dict.* (1885).]

Naubat-khana [19C. *See* prec.] Guardhouse, or chamber at the palace gate where the band played. [Whitworth, *Anglo-Ind. Dict.*]

Naund [19C. H. *nānd.*] A coarse earthen vessel of large size, resembling in shape an inverted beehive, and useful for many economic and domestic purposes. [YB; Fanny Parkes, *Wanderings of Pilgrim* (1850), i. 250.]

Nautch, natch [19C. H. *nāch,* fr. Prak. *nachcha,* fr. S. *nritya, nrit* 'to dance'.] (1) Performance (esp common in 18th century) of professional dancing by *'nautch-girls'* (1809). *See* **Devadasi.** Hence: to *nautch* (vb. intr.) (1851), and *nautched* (1835). [Broughton, *Lett. Mahratta Camp* (1809).] (2) Any kind of Anglo-Indian stage entertainment or ball. (3) Also, a **Poggly**-*nautch,* a wild fantastic dance, by a crazy dancer and a **Pootly**-*nautch,* a puppet-show. *See* **Bayadere, Dancing-Girl** and **Rum-Johnny.** [Mrs Sherwood, *Stories* (1817), 291.] (4) A nautch girl. [Browning, *Fifine* (1872), xxi; *OED* & YB.]

Navayat, Navait, Naitee, etc. [17C.] Perh. fr. P. *naītī,* fr. *Nāit,* name of an Arab clan of Muslims of mixed race in S. Karnataka and the Konkan, corresponding more or less to the **Moplahs** of **Malabar,** and the **Lubbyes** of the **Coromandel** Coast. [YB; Purchas, *Pilgrimes* (1625), 554.]

Nawab, nabob, nahab [18C. H. *nawwāb,* pl. of Ar. *naīb,* 'deputy'.] Muslim Governor or nobleman. *See* **Nabob** = a wealthy retired Anglo-Indian. [*OED;* Tavernier, E. tr. (1684), ii. 99; Mill (1758), *Brit. India* (1817), III. 276.]

Nawar [H. *nawār.*] Webbing. [Hawkins, *CIWIE* (1984).]

Naxalite(s) [20C. fr. *Naxalbari.* (Place-name.)] (One of) a body of violent agrarian revolutionaries, who began a struggle to capture the lands of owners at Naxalbari in West Bengal, near the Sino-Indian border. Hence *Naxalism.* [*OED; Times,* 9 Jan. 9/1, 1969).]

Naya paisa [20C. H. *naya,* 'new' + *paisa,* 'pence'.] 1/100 rupee. *See* **Paisa, Pice, Pie.** [*OED; India: Ref. Ann.* (Ministry of Information Gov't of India, 1956).]

Nayika [20C.] Beautiful woman; heroine; primadonna, (leading) woman dancer, a 'star'. [Hawkins, *CIWIE.*]

Nazar. *See* **Nuzzer.**

Nazir [17C. H./Ar; *nāzir,* inspector, fr. *nazar,* 'sight', 'vision'.] A native official in the Anglo-Indian law courts. Also an inspector. [*OED; English Fact. in India* (1618-69); Grant, *Hist. Ind.* (1878), I. ixxxi. 431/1.]

Neelam [16C. H. *nīlām,* fr. Pg. *leilão.* Ar. *i'lām,* 'proclamation, advertisement'.] An auction or public **Outcry.** [YB; Linschoten, *Discours of Voyages* etc. (1598).]

Neelgye, nilghau *See* **Nilgai.**

Neem [19C. H. *nīm;* Mar. *nimb,* S. *nimba.*] The tree, the **Margosa,** *Azadirachia indica,* grows ubiquitously in India, the leaves and bark being used medicinally, while the tree in itself is sacred to Hindus. The young leaves are eaten on the Hindu New Year's Day [**Ugadi** fr. S. **Yuga** + **Adi** 'beginning'] to ward off sickness during the ensuing year. Hindus festooned their houses during smallpox epidemics, or to keep evil spirits away when there was a birth or death in the house. Dried leaves keep out moths and cockroaches etc. and are used as poultices for festering wounds and boils, and the bitter bark reduces fevers. The fruit is a purgative and anthelmintic, and gives **Margosa**-oil for leprosy, skin-diseases and rheumatism. The stalks are used as

toothbrushes, and the timber for boats and furniture. Practically every part of this 'all-purpose' tree is of value. [*OED* & YB.] *See* **Buckyne.** [Cowen, *Flowering Trees and Shrubs in India* (Bombay, 1965); Forbes, *Or. Mem.* (1813).]

Neera, neri, nira [17C. H. *neri, nīr,* 'sap'.] Fresh juice drawn from certain palm-trees 'in an earthen vessel is as sweet and pleasant [to drink] as Milk' [Ovington]. *Neri* is Gujarati for some form of **Toddy.** [YB; Ovington, *A Voyage to Surat in the Year* (1689), 237.]

Nefa [20C. Acronym.] North-East Frontier Agency (1947-65) or Administration (1965-72).

Nelly, nele [19C. M. *nel,* 'rice in the husk', Tel/Tam. *nelli* 'rice-like'.] The Dravidian equivalent of **Paddy.** [YB; Logan, *Malabar* (1887-91), III. 265.]

Nelumbium, nelumbo [18C. Sinh. *nelumbu.*] Genus of water-beans, family *Nymphaeceae,* including the E. Indian or sacred lotus, *N. nucifera,* with white or pink flowers. [*OED;* A.L. de Jussien, *Genera Plantarum* (1789); M. Adamson, *Familles des Plantes* (1763); E. Darwin, *Botanic Garden* (1794), II. 169; Curtis's *Bot. Mag.* (1806), XXIII. 903.]

Nenuphar [15C. Ar. and P. *nīnūfar, nilufar;* S. *nīlōtpala* (*nīla,* 'blue' + *utpala,* 'lotus') = 'Blue Lotus'.] Water lily (*Nymphaeaceae*), esp. the white or yellow species. In early use, freq. in *oil,* syrup and water of *nenuphar.* [*OED; COD;* Elyot (1533), *Cast Helth* (1534), 76.]

Nercha [17C. M. *nerchcha,* 'a vow'.] Offerings to saints, or to temples; or particular forms of devotion. Among Hindus, the use of **Ghee** instead of oil to feed the lamp before an idol of a Hindu god. [YB.]

Nerrick, nerruck, nirk [18C. H/P. *nirkh.*] A tariff, rate or price-list, esp. one published by government. [YB; Wellington, *Despatches* (1799), i. 56.]

Ness [19C. Guj. *nes.*] A group of herdsmen's huts. [Whitworth, *Anglo Indian Dict* (1885).]

Neta [20C. Beng. *neta.*] Leader. *See* next.

Netaji [20C. *See* prec. + *jī* (honorific title).] Respected great leader, espec. applied to Subhas Chandra Bose (1897-1945); president Indian National Congress, 1918 and 1939; founder and leader of the Indian National Army (Azad Hind Fauj) and of a 'Provisional Government of Free India' in Singapore, 1943.

Ngapi [19C. Burm. *ngapi,* 'pressed fish'.] 'The odorous delicacy described under **Balachong.**' [YB; Yule, *Mission to Ava* (1855).]

Nibbana *See* **Nirvana.**

Nidhi [20C. S. *nīdhi.*] Fund. [Hawkins, *CIWIE* (1984).]

Nigger [16C.] Anglo-Indian derogation of the 'native'. 'The use originated, however, doubtless in following the old Portuguese use of *negros* for "the blacks" with no malice prepense, without any intended confusion between Africans and Asiatics.' [YB & *OED;* Litchfield's *Castañeda* (1582), f. 19; Danvers (1608), *Letters* (1896-1900); I. 10; Trevelyan, *Cawnpore* (1865), 47.]

Nigger-blarney [20C. H. *nigar bani,* lit. 'looking at'.] Fig. 'favouritism'. [Flora Annie Steel, *Voices in the Night* (1900).]

Nikka(h) [19C. H/Ar. *nikah.*] Marriage; permanent Muslim marriage as opposed to *muta,* a temporary alliance understood to be so by both parties, with appropriate compensation for the 'wife' at the end of the 'arrangement'. *See* **Shadi.** [Whitworth, *Anglo-Indian Dict.* (1885).]

Nilgai, nylghau, neelgye [17C. H. *nīl,* 'blue' + *gaī,* 'cow' fr. P. *nīlgaw.*] Large, short-horned Indian antelope; the 'blue bull' *(Boselaphus tragocamelus,* allied to the *addax* and *gnu* of Africa.) [*OED* & YB; Bernier, E. tr., *Travels* (1684).]

Nilla, nillaes [17C. Etym. obscure, but perh. H. *nīlā,* 'blue'.] A kind of (blue) cloth, one of many Indian **Piece-goods,** exported to Europe from India in the 18th century. [*OED* & YB; J. F. Merch, *Warehouses Laid Open* (1696), 30.]

Nilu [20C.] Thick undergrowth.

Nimbu, limbu [20C. H/S. *nimbū;* Pg. *lima;* Ar. *līma,* 'lime' (1673).] Fruit of the tree, *Citrus aurantifloria. See* **Lemon.**

Nimbu-pani [20C. Indo-Pg. *See* prec. + *pāni,* 'water'.] Anglo-Indian lime-juice + (sugar) + water + (ice), popular everywhere in India, espec. in the 'hot season'. [*OED;* Mrs B. Singh, *Indian Cookery* (1961), 184.]

Nimukwallah [19C. H. *nimak* 'salt' + *wallah* 'man', 'keeper'.] A loyal and faithful servant or follower; one 'true to his salt'. [Hawkins, *CIWIE.*]

Nipah [16C. Mal. *nīpah.*] The stemless palm *Nipa fruticans* abounding in the Ganges delta and eastward to Malaysia, the Philippines and N. Australia. The leaves are used for thatch and the sap for vinegar and the distillation of spirits or **Arrack.** [*OED* & YB; Hickock, tr., Federick, *Voy.* (1588), 236; Royle, *Bot. Himalayan Mount.* (1839), 408.]

Nirah *See* **Neera.**

Nirankari(s) [19C.] Peaceful reform movement of Sikhism founded by Dayal Das (d. 1855). Opposed to **Khalsa** or militant Sikhs. *Nirankār =* (God is) formless. [*Encycl. Brit.,* 15th ed., (1974), Microp. VII. 355.]

Niragrantha, Nirgantha [19C. S. *nir,* 'out' + *grantha,* 'tying'.] Jainism; 'Free from ties'. Early Jaina religious community headed orig. by *Mahāvīra.* Term now out of use. [Sir Charles Eliot, *Hinduism & Buddhism* (1921), i. III.]

Nirmanakaya [19C. S. *nirmānakaya,* 'body of magic transformation', fr. *nirmāna,* 'measuring, creating, magical creation', *nir,* 'out' + *māti,* 'he measures' + *kāya,* 'body'.] The historically manifested body of Buddha in the doctrine of *trikāya,* the three bodies or aspects of the Buddha: *dharma-, sambhoga-,* and *nirmāna-kāya.* [Sir Charles Eliot, *Hinduism and Buddhism* (1921), ii. 33.]

Nirvana, Nibbana, Niba [17C. S. *nirvāna,* 'extinction', fr. *nirva,* 'be extinguished', fr. *nis,* 'out' + *va',* blow'.] Hinduism and Buddhism: The highest *sukha* or bliss *(arhat);* the extinction of individual existence, of all desire and passion, the attainment of perfect beautitude and absorption into the Supreme Spirit. Psychology: 'The Nirvana Principle.' In psychoanalytic theory, the attraction felt by the psyche for a state of non-existence, which Freud connected with the death-wish, countering the tensions set up by the pleasure-principle (1920). *See* **Moksha.** Colloquial: 'Nirvana suggests rather a Mohammedan Paradise or blissful Elysian fields to the minds of the masses.' [Max Mueller, *Lect. on Buddhistic Nihilism* (1869).] Also, *Nirvanic,* relating to, or resembling *Nirvana.* [*OED* & YB; Purchas, *Pilgrimes* (1625), 506.]

Nishada [19C. H/S. *nisada.*] Name of a wild Non-Aryan tribe; member of a low caste. Also the offspring of a **Brahmin** and a **Sudra.** Cf. **Mlechcha.** [Whitworth, *Anglo-Indian Dict.* (1885).]

Nishin *See* **Purdah.**

Nizam, The [17C. Turk. *Nizām.* Ar. *nidām,* 'order, arrangement'.] The hereditary title of the rulers of the former Deccan State of Hyderabad; in full, *Nizām-ul-Mulk* (Pg. *Nizamaluco),* governor of the empire founded by Asaf Jah, **Subahdar** of the Deccan (1713-48). Hence: *Nizamate* (1887), the Nizam's territory; *Nizamut* (1764), the office or authority of the Nizam. [*OED* & YB; Johnson (1601), *Kingdom and Commonwealth* (1603), 45; Macaulay (1840), *Ess. Clive* (1897), 509.]

Nokar [19C. H/P. *naukar*.] 'A servant, domestic, (military or civil.)' Also: *Naukar-logue* [fr. *log*, 'people', and *Naukar-chākar*, 'the servants'.] 'One of those jingling double-barrelled phrases in which Orientals delight even more than Englishmen.' [YB.] Cf. **Rumble-tumble**. *See* **Chakur**. [YB; Burnes, *Travels into Bokhara* (1835), i. 238.] *See* **Oolta-poolta**.

Nol-kole *See* **Knol-Kohl**.

Non-Regulation (adj) [19C. Anglo-Indian.] 'The style of certain Provinces of British India, ... in which the ordinary Laws (or **Regulations** as they were formerly called) are not in force, or are in force only so far as they are specially declared by the Government of India to be applicable. [YB & *OED*; *The Travels of Sir John Mandeville in the E. Indies* (1860); Stoqueler (1846), *Handbk. Brit. India* (1854), 122.]

Norwester [19C. Anglo-Indian.] A sudden and violent storm during the hot weather (April-June), preceded by a 'dust-storm' and followed by hail and torrents of rain in N. India. *See* **Typhoon**. [YB; Williamson, *Vade Mecum* (1810), ii. 355.]

Nowroze [17C.] P. *nau-rōz*.] 'New [Year's] Day'. The first day of the Solar year, observed in India by the **Parsis**. [YB; Foster, *Letters* (1614), iii. 65.]

Nowshadder, nouchadur [19C. H. *naushādar* (S. *narasāra*.)] Salammoniac, *ammonium chloride*. [YB; Burnes, *Travels into Bokhara* (1834), ii. 366.]

Nritta [19C. S. *nritta*.] One of three main components of Indian classical dancing, the other two being, **Natya** and **Nritya**. *Nritta* is loosely termed *pure* dance, being entirely concerned with rhythmic movement, and **Natya** depicts ideas and themes, and the dramatic elements of the dance, while **Nritya** reflects the moods sentiments and feelings inherent in it. *See* **Bharatanatyam**. [*OED*; Coomaraswamy & Duggirala, tr., *Mirror of Gesture*, (1917), 14; Monier-Williams, *Indian Wisdom* (1875), XX. 463.] *See* **Tillana**.

Nritya [19C. S. *nritya*.] See prec. See **Natya-shastri**.

Nujeeb *See* **Najeeb**.

Nullah, nala [17C. H. *nālā*, 'brook, rivulet, ravine'.] A watercourse. In Anglo-Indian use, more often a dry ravine or river-bed. [*OED* & YB; Foster (1636), *English Fact. in India* (1618-69).]

Numda(h), numna [19C. H. *namdā*; P. *namad*, 'carpet, rug'. (S. *namata*).] Felt, or coarse woollen cloth, often embroidered and used as a rug or carpet; a saddle-cloth or pad made of felt. [YB; Hanway, *Hist. Acct. of British Trade* (1774), i.226.]

Nuncaties [19C. H. *nankhatāi*, poss. fr. P. *nān*, 'bread', + Mar. *khat*, 'six'.] A kind of rich cake (spec. to Bombay) composed of six ingredients: wheat-flour, eggs, sugar, butter or **Ghee**, yeast and almonds. [YB.]

Nut¹ [19C. H. *nath*, fr. S. *nāsa*, 'the nose'.] The nose-ring used traditionally as an adornment by Indian women. [*Trans. Lit. Soc. Bom.* (1819), i. 284.]

Nut² *See* **Nat.²**

Nut-cut (sb. and adj) [19C. H. *natkhat*.] Rascal(ly), rogue, roguish. [*OED*; Stoqueler, *Oriental Interpreter* (1848), 175/2.]

Nut Promotion [16C.] 'From its supposed indigestible character, the kernel of the *cashew-nut* is so called in S. India, where roasted and hot, it is a favourite dessert dish.' [YB; Linschoten (1598; Hak. Soc., 1807), ii. 28.]

Nuzzer, nazar, nuzzerana [18C. Ar. *nazr*, 'gift, vow or votive offering'.] A ceremonial present; a douceur or gift from an inferior to a superior, the converse of **Inam**. [*OED* & YB; Verelst, *View of Bengal* (1765), 127; *Trial Joseph Fowke* (1776), 3/I.]

Nyaya [19C. S. *nyāya*, 'rule, model, maxim, logic', fr. *ni*, 'down, back' + *eti*, 'he goes'.] One of the six Brahmanical systems of orthodox Hindu philosophy dealing with logic and epistemological analysis, the others being **Vaiseshika, Sankhya, Yoga, Mimansa** and **Vedanta**. *Nyaya* involves a critical examination of the objects of knowledge by means of the canons of logical proof; a system by means of which the mind is led to a logical conclusion, uninfluenced by other philosophical considerations. [Sir Charles Eliot, *Hinduism & Buddhism* (1921), ii. 39.]

O

Oart [17C. Pg. *(h)orta*, 'a garden'.] A coconut grove (espec. in Western India). [YB; Fryer, *A New Acc. E. India and Persia* (1672-81).]

Odissi *See* **Orissi.**

Odhni [H. *odhni*.] *See* **Dupatta.**

Ollah [17C. Tam. *olai*; M. *ōla*, 'a palm-leaf'.] Especially the leaf of the **Palmyra**, *Borassus flabellifer*, prepared and used (in S. India) for writing on; a letter or document so written. [OED & YB; Linschoten, Hak. Soc. (1598), ii. 45; Tennent (1859), *Ceylon* (1860), I. x. 512.]

Om, aum [18C. S. *ōm*.] Hinduism and Buddhism: a sacred utterance of assent, or **Mantra**, recited in prayer and meditation; used at the beginning of all prayers, hymns and religious texts; the Greatest Mantra, or Word of Power. 'Om is the world of heaven and the sun, and where it is resolved into three letters, *a, u,* and *m.*' [*Aitareya Brāhmana*.] [OED; Sir W. Jones in *Asiatick Researches* (1788), 1.262; Keith in *Encycl. Relig. & Ethics* (1917), ix. 490/2.]

Om mani padme hum [18C.] *See* prec. Lit: 'Hail! Jewel in the Lotus!' In Tibetan Buddhism, a **Mantra** or mystic formula intoned in prayer and meditation. *See* **Padma**. [OED; Bogle, *Narr. Mission Tibet* (1774), iii. 29.]

Omander [19C. Etym. obscure.] Ebony obtained from the E. Indian tree, *Diospyros ebenaster*. Akin to **Calamander**. [OED; Holtzapffel. *Turning & Mech. Manip.* (1843).]

Omeduar, omedwaur [19C. H. *ummedwār* (*ummed*, 'hope').] Lit. 'a hopeful one'. 'An expectant, a candidate for employment, one who awaits a favourable answer to some representation or request.' [Wilson.] [YB; Colebrooke, *Elphinstone: Life* (1816), i. 344.]

Omlah [18C. Ar. '*amalā(t)*, pl. of *amil*.] (*See* **Aumil.**) Indian officials, clerks and other staff of a civil court or **Cutcherry** collectively. [OED & YB; *Lives of the Lindsays* (1778), iii. 166.]

Omrah, ombra [17C. Ar. *umara*, pl. of *amir* (*see* **Ameer**), 'commander, lord'.] Applied collectively to the higher officials or dignitaries of a Muslim Court, espec. that of the Great Mughal. 'In old European narratives it is used as a singular for a lord or grandee of [the Mughal] Court.' [YB & OED; Finch, in *Early Travels in India* (1583-1619).]

Omum-water [19C. Tam. *omam*, fr. S. *yamāni* (H. *ajwān*).] A well-known herbal medicine in S. India, 'made from the strong-smelling carminative seeds of an umbelliferous plant, *Carum copticum*'. [YB; Hanbury and Flückiger, *Pharmacographia* (1874).]

Oolta-poolta [19C. H. *ūlta-pūlta*.] Topsy-turvy, upside-down. 'Another of those jingling double barrelled phrases in which orientals delight even more than Englishmen.' [CIWIE; YB.] Cf. **Nokar, Chakar.**

Oont [19C. H. *ūnt*.] A camel. Also *oont-wallah*, a camel keeper or driver. [OED; Speid, *Our Last Years in India* (1862).]

Ooplah [17C. H. *ūpla*.] 'Cow-dung patted into cakes and stacked for fuel. In S. India called **Bratty.**' [YB.] Also called **Kundah**. [*Ords. at Fort St. George, Notes and Exts.* (1672), i. 56.]

Oord, oorud [18C. H. *urad*.] A variety of *dāl* (*see* **Dhall**) or pulse, the produce of *Vigna mungo* (black gram), highly esteemed and cultivated in all parts of India. *See* **Popper**. [YB; *Asiatic Res.* (1792), vi. 47.]

Oorial *See* **Urial.**

Ooriya, Oriya, Uriya [18C. Re: Orissa State, language and people, H. *uriya*.] 'The Ooriyah bearers were an old institution in Calcutta, as in former days palankeens were chiefly used.' [YB; Carey, *Good Old Days of Honble. John Company* (1882), ii. 148.]

Opal [14C. Prob. ult. S. *upala*, 'precious stone'.] Irridescent, milk-white or bluish stone; a kind of hydrous silica, first brought from India. [OED & YB; Trevisa, *Barth. De Prop. Rerum* (1398), xvi. lxxii.]

Opium [14C. H. *afim*; L. *opium*; Gr. *opion*; Ar. *afyun*; (Indo-Iranian *āp-*, water).] The inspissated narcotic drug of the *Papaver somiferum*. 'The Indians use much to eat Amfion.' [OED & YB; Linschoten in *Hakluyt* (1598), ii. 127.] *See* **Posta.**

Organ [18C.] Anglo-Indian (perh. fr. P. *arghan*, 'an organ').] An oriental form of *mitrailleuse*. [YB; Compton, *A part. Acct. of the European Milit. Adventures of Hindustan* (1784-1803), 61.]

Orissa [17C. S. *Odrashtra*, 'land of the Odras'.] *See* next. [Sir T. Roe, *Embassy to the Court of the Great Mogul* (1615-19).]

Orissi, Odissi [20C. fr. *Orissa*, a state in the Indian union.] (S. *Odrashtra*, 'the land of the Odras'.) A very ancient Indian dance-form from Orissa, based on several old texts (e.g. *Natya-Shastra, Abhinaya Darpanam* and

Abhinaya Chandrika) and on Hindustani music. It was performed by dancing girls, *Maharis*, dedicated for service in the temples of Orissa, together with their male counterparts, the *Gotipuas*. *See* **Devadasi**. [*OED;* Fabri in *Marg* (Bombay, 1960), xiii. ii. 5.]

Ormessine, armozeen, ormuzine [16C. Etym. doubtful.] A kind of stout silk, 'almost invariably black, used for hat-bands and scarfs at funerals by those not family mourners. Sometimes sold for making clergymen's gowns.' [YB; The *Stanf. Dict.* (1892), gives Ormuzine, 'a fabric exported from Ormuz'. [*OED* & YB; Caes. Frederick in *Hakluyt*, (1566), ii. 334.]

Orombarros [18C. Anglo-Indian; fr. Malay *Orang baharu*, 'new man'.] 'An expression imported from the Malay factories to Continental India.' A beginner, novice, **Griffin**. [YB; Lockyer, *An Acct. of the Trade in India* (1711).]

Ortolan [19C. Anglo-Indian.] Name applied to two Indian birds by Anglo-Indians: (1) a small lark, *Calandrella brachydactyla*: H. *bargel*; (S. *varga*, 'a troop'); (2) sometimes in S. India to the finch lark (*Pyrrhalauda grisea*). [YB.]

Ottam thullal, Ottantullal. A popular form of entertainment in Kerala; song and dance with topical allusions. Lit. 'running and jumping'; in Malayalam, known as 'the poor man's **Kathakali'.** [Singha & Massey, *Indian Dances* (1967), 90.]

Otto, otter *See* **Attar.**

Outcaste (sb. & vb.) [19C. Anglo-Indian.] One who has lost caste or is casteless. *See* **Harijan, Pariah, Scheduled-caste** and **Tribe,** and **Untouchables.** [*OED;* Kipling, *Jungle-Book* (1894), 37.]

Outcry [17C. Anglo-Indian.] Auction by public announcement. *See* **Neelam.** [YB; Minsheu, *The Guide into the Tongues* etc. (1627).]

Overland [17C.] Anglo-Indian expression applied specifically to the Mediterranean route to India from Antioch or thereabouts to the Persian Gulf, before the construction of the Suez Canal. [YB; Fryer, *A New Acc. of E. India & Persia* (1672-81), 89.]

Owl [18C. H. *aul*.] 'Any great calamity or epidemic, such as a plague, cholera', etc. [YB; *Asiatic Res.* (1787), ii. 307; Sleeman, *Journey in Oudh* (1849-50; ed. 1858), ii. 103.]

P

Pachisi [19C. H. *pachisi*, lit. 'of *pachchis*' = 25.] A four-handed game played in India on a board with **cowries**; so named from the highest throw, 25. A simpler European form of the game is *Ludo*. [*OED*; *Asiatic Ann. Reg. Misc. Tracts* (1800), 314/2.]

Pada, padam [19C. S. *pādaĺ*, 'a foot'.] (1) An Indian lyrical poem set to music. [*OED*; Growse, *Mathura* (1880), 212.] (2) A group of words forming a section of Sanskrit verse. [*OED*; Monier-Williams, *Brahmanism & Hinduism* (1887), xv. 409.] (3) A mode of reciting this. *See* **Samhita.**

Paddy, padi [19C. Mal. *pādī*.] Rice in the husk or in the straw. (Cf. Kan. *bhatta*. *See* **Batty,** unhusked rice.) Also *Paddy-bird* (1727), the pond-heron, *Ardeola gravii*, found throughout the Indian Union, Bangladesh, Pakistan, Sri Lanka and Burma. (H. *bōgli* and *andhā bagla*, 'blind heron'. *Paddy-field* (1759) = rice-field, generally in its flooded state. *Paddy-crop*, the rice harvest. [*OED* & *YB*; Sir Francis Drake's *Voyage*, in *Hakluyt* (1580), iv. 246.] *See* **Nelly.**

Padishah, padsha(w), podshaw [17C. H/P. *pādishāh*, fr. *pad*, 'throne' + *shāh*, 'prince'. (ult. fr. P. *pati* (S. *pati*, 'master, lord, ruler').] Emperor; espec. in India the Great Mughal, and later the Sovereign ruler of Great Britain as the Emperor/Empress of India. [*OED* & *YB*.] *See* **Kaiser-i-Hind.** [Danvers, *Letters*, (1612), i. 175; Sir T. Herbert, *Some Yeares Travels* etc. (1638), 169.] *See* **Shah.**

Padma [18C. S. *padma*.] The lotus, or water-lily of Asia. In India a religious (Hindu) symbol. (*See* **Om mani padme hum**) and a civil decoration of honour (20C.) *Padma Vibhushan, Padma Bhushan, Padma Shri*. Also a large number, 100 **Crores.** [Bogle, *Narr. Mission Tibet* (1774), iii. 29.]

Padouk, padauk [19C. Burm. native name.] The tree, *Pterocarpus dalbergioides; or macrocarpus;* its rose-wood-like timber. [*OED*; H. Malcom, *Trav. S. E. Asia* (1839), I. ii. 189.]

Padre [16C. Pg. *padre*, 'Father'.] First applied to Catholic (Portuguese) priests (later embraced all Christian ministers) in India. The general meaning nowadays is equivalent to 'chaplain'. The Padre's Godown' = British soldiers' slang for the graveyard. [*OED* & *YB*; Fitch in *Hakluyt* (1584), ii. 381.]

Padyatra [20C. H/S. *pada*, 'foot' + *yatra*, 'procession'.] A walk undertaken for a social or political purpose in India, to influence Government or other authorities to take action on the objective(s) of the *padyatra*.

Pagar, paggar [19C. Mar. *pagār*, fr. Pg. *pagar*, 'to pay' (used as a noun.)] In general use in the Bombay dialect for wages. [*YB*; Wilson, *Abode of Snow* (1875).]

Pagoda, pagod [16C. Pg. *pagode;* poss. fr. P. *butkada*, 'idol-temple', fr. *but*, 'idol' + *kada*, 'habitation'. (Cf. Prak. *bhagodi*, 'divine, holy', and S. *bhagavati*, 'god-endowed, divine'.] This word is used in different senses. (1) An idol temple (India and China); especially a sacred tower or pyramid (*see* **Gopura**), often built over the relics of Buddha or saints. *See* **Dagoba, Tope, Stupa, Chedi.** [*OED* & *YB*; Litchfield's *Castañeda* (1582), i. xiv. 34.] (2) An idol. [*OED* & *YB*; Litchfield (1582), lxviii. 140.] (3) A gold or silver coin, formerly current in S. India, with a representation of a pagoda-temple thereon. *See* **Pagoda-Tree.**[2] [*OED* & *YB*; Phillips, *Linschoten* (1598), i. xxxv. 60/1.] (4) A small structure built in imitation of the real thing. [*OED*; Morse, *Amer. Geog.* (1796), ii. 492.] (5) A person superstitiously worshipped and likened to an idol; a '*God-man*' (1719). Also *Pagod(a)- worship* (1719); *-gods* (1719); *-sleeve* (18th C.); *Pagodite*, a soft mineral, *agalmatolite*, carved into the shapes of *pagodas*, statuettes etc. (1837). [*OED*; D' Urfey, *Pills* (1719), ii. 315.]

Pagoda-tree [19C.] *See* prec. (1) The Indian **Banyan**-tree, *Ficus indica*. *See* **Bo-Tree.** [*OED* & *YB*; *Treas. Bot.* (1876), 836/1.] (2) Phrase: 'to shake the Pagoda Tree', to make a quick fortune in India, often unscrupulously, thereby becoming a **Nabob** (1836). 'A mythical tree, feigned' to produce Pagodas, sense 3 in prec. [*OED*.] Cf. Malay *Pokok ěmas*, 'the Tree of Gold', a miniature of a tree with leaves of gold, sent in former times from Malay chiefs to the King of Siam as a tributary gift. [*Blackwood's Magazine* (1877), 575; T. Hook, *Gilbert Gurney* (1836).]

Pagri *See* **Puggri.**

Pahari [19C. H. *Pahārī*, (language) of the mountains, fr. *pahār*, 'mountain'.] An Indo-Iranian group to which belong the languages spoken in the lower ranges of the Himalayas from Nepal to Chamba. Also *Pahari painting.* *See* **Maler.** [*OED;* F. Buchanan, *Jrnl. Survey Bhagalpur* (1811; 1930), 133.]

Pahlavi, Pehlevi [18C. P. *Pahlavi,* Parthian.] (1) The ancient Persian language of the **Zoroastrians,** akin to the dialects of **Zend-Avesta,** characterized by a number of inflections agreeing with those of **Sanskrit.** (2) Name, by followers of **Zoroaster (Parsis),** of the characters in which are written the ancient translations of their sacred books. (3) Now generally designates a mode of writing the language used in Persia under the Sassanian Kings. *See* **Parsi.** 'Where the language is transcribed either in Avesta characters, or in those of the modern Persian alphabet, it is called *Pazand* [**Pazend**]; a term supposed to be derived from the language of the *Avesta, paitizanti* with the meaning 're-explanation'. [*OED* & YB; W. Jones, tr., *Astarabadi's Hist. Nadir Shah* (1773); Haug, *Essays on the Sacred Lang., Writings & Relig. of the Parsis* (1878).] *See* **Pulwaun.**

Pahlwan, pulwaun [18C. H/P. *pahlwān,* lit: 'a native of ancient Persia'.] (*See* prec.) A champion; a professional wrestler; a man of extraordinary strength; a prize-fighter. [YB; Hanway, *Hist. Acct. of the British Trade over the Caspian Sea,* (1753), iii. 104.]

Paigambar [H. *paigambar.*] Prophet. [*CIWIE.*]

Paijama *See* **Pyjama.**

Pairi [20C. Pg.] A variety of mango, in India, with a pointed tip. [*CIWIE.*]

Paisa, (pl.) paise, -a, paisas [19C. H. *paisa.* 1/100 of a **Rupee.**] In India, *paise* (1957); in Pakistan *paisa* (1966), and Nepal (1969), and 1/100 *taka* in Bangladesh. *See* **Pice, Poisha, Pie** and **Naya Paisa.** [*OED;* *Enc. Brit.* (1884), xviii. 343/1.]

Pak [20C.] Abbr. of **Pakistan.** Also *Paki(s)* (1964), abbr. of *Pakistani(s).* Also *Paki-bashing* (1970), violent attacks on *Pakistani* immigrants in Britain. [*OED;* C. Rahmat Ali, *Pakistan* (1935); *Guardian,* 15 April 1964.]

Pakhal *See* **Puckauly.**

Pakhawaj [19C. H. *pakhawaj.*] A double-headed drum, made of clay, used in Indian music, espec. in N. India. [*OED;* Taylor, *Proc. R. Irish Acad.* (1867), ix. 116.] *See* **Tabla, Mridangam.**

Pakhora *See* **Pakora.**

Pakhtun, Pakhtoon, Pushtun, Pashtun [19C.] The **Paktu/Pashto**-speaking tribes of **Afghanistan;** also called **Pathans** and **Afghans.** *See* next. [*OED;* Elphinstone, *Acct. Kingdom of Caubul* (1815), ii. i. 151.]

Pakhtoonistan, Pakhtunistan [20C. 'Land of the Pathans.'] A variable 20C. political theory and aspiration of the **Pathans** for an independent or semi-autonomous state, absorbing parts of Pakistan and Afghanistan.

Pakhtoonwali, Pashtunwali [19C. Pakht./Pusht. *pakhtūnwalī, pashtūnwalī.*] The unwritten code of Pathan ethics, marked by three obligations: *badal* (revenge), *nanawatai* (the right to seek asylum), *maelmastya* (the entitlement of a stranger/enemy to hospitality and protection of life). [Holdich, *The Indian Borderland* (1880-1908).]

Pakistan [20C.] Earlier 'Pakistan', from initials of Punjab, Afghan Frontier, Kashmir, Sind, and the last three letters of Baluchi*stan.* These were predominantly Muslim parts of undivided India. A separate independent Muslim state was created on 15 August 1947, consisting of West and East Pakistan (the latter now Bangladesh, formerly East Bengal). Otherwise explained as 'The Land of the Pure'. *Pakistani,* a citizen of Pakistan and pertaining to Pakistan. *See* **Pak.** [*OED;* C. Rahmat Ali, *Pakistan* (1935); L.S. Amery (1941), Letter 25 Jan. *in* J. Glendevon *Viceroy at Bay* (1971), xvi. 198.]

Pakora, pakhora [20C. H. *pakora.*] A dish of diced or chopped vegetables coated with batter or stuffed into pastry and deep-fried. [*OED;* Masters, *Bhowani Junction* (1954), xxiii. 192.]

Pal [17C. Romany, *pal,* 'brother, mate'. (S. *bhratar,* 'brother').] In modern English, colloquially, a friend, mate, chum. [*OED;* *Hereford Diocesan Register* (1681-2).]

Palagilas [Anglo-Indian.] A Domestic Hindustani word for 'asparagus'. [YB; *Punjab Notes and Queries,* ii. 189.]

Palampore, palempore [17C. Poss. fr. *Palampur,* a town in Gujarat, once famous for its production of **Chintz,** perh. with contamination from Urdu and Persian *palang posh,* an ornamental bed-cover (English slang **Posh**?)] A kind of beautifully patterned Indian chintz bed-cover, formerly exported to Europe. Both the word and the material are now obsolete. [*OED* & YB; Fryer, *A New Acct.* (1672–81).] *See* **Salempore.**

Palanquin, palankeen, palkee, palankee, etc. [16C. Pg. *palanquim;* H. *palki;* Pali, *palanki;* S. *palayanka,* 'bed, couch'.] A covered box-litter, used in India and elswhere, by travellers, borne by 4 or 6 men by means of a pole projecting fore and aft. Now obsolete. *See*

Palkee-gharry. [*OED* & YB; Hickock, tr., C. Frederick's *Voy.* (1588), 10 (ll).]

Palas, pulas(h) [18C. H. *palās*, fr. S. *palāsa*.] The **Dhak**-tree, or Flame of the Forest, *Butea fron-dosa* and *superba*. See **Dhak**¹. [*OED*; Cole-brooke in *Life* (1873; 1799), 407.] *See* **Teesoo**.

Palay, pala [19C. Tam. *palay*.] Name of two Indian shrubs with milky juice. (a) *Crypto-stegia grandiflora*, which yields a flax and rubber latex. (b) *Wrightia tinctoria*, which produces an inferior indigo. [*OED*; Lindley, *Treasury of Botany* (1866).]

Pale Ale (Indian) [18C. Anglo-Indian.] The name of a sort of beer formerly brewed for consumption in India. [YB; Advt. in Seton-Karr, *Selections from Calcutta Gazettes* (1784-1823).]

Pali [17C. S. *palibhasha* (*pali*, line, row, series, + 'bhasha', language').] The **Prakrit** langu-age of the sacred canonical texts of **Bud-dhists**, called elliptically *Pali*. The *lingua franca* of N. India from the 5th or 6th to the 2nd century BC. Also, the *Pali Plague*, which raged from 1815 to 1822 in Kutch and Gujarat. [*OED* & YB; De la Lourbere, *Siam* (E. tr. 1693).] *See* **Sanskrit**.

Palkee [17C.] *See* **Palanquin**. [*OED* & YB; J. Phillips, tr., *Tavernier's Voy.* (1678), ii. ii. 175.]

Palki-bearer [19C.] *See* **Bearer**. [*OED*; Lang, *Wand. India* (1859), 121.]

Palki-dak (dawk) [19C.] *See* **Dak (Dawk)**. [*OED*; Mrs Cuffles, *Mem. Mrs. Valentine* (1882), ii. 24.]

Palkee-gharry [19C. *See* prec. H. *gāri*, 'a carriage or vehicle'.] A carriage shaped some-what like a palanquin on wheels. Sometimes termed a '*palankin-coach*'. [*OED* & YB; Brad-don, *Life in India* (1872).] *See* **Palanquin**.

Palla, pallav [H. *pallav*.] The border on the width of the **Sari** that hangs over the shoulder—generally the left one.

Pallavi [19C. Orig. uncertain.] In the music of S. India, the first section of a song. [*OED*; Day, *Music and Musical Instruments in S. India* (1891), v. 60.]

Palmyra [17C. Pg. *palmeira*.] The Fan-Palm, *Borassus flabellifer*, grown in India and Sri Lanka with many uses. 'It produces **Jaggery** (palm-sugar); the wood makes rafters and laths, and the fronds give material for thatch, mats, umbrellas, fans and a substitute for paper.' A Tamil proverb ascribes to it 801 uses, but its chief product is **Toddy** and **Arrack**, from the sap of the flowering branches; fermented (**toddy**) and distilled (**arrack**). Hindus and Buddhists venerate it, as their sacred texts were inscribed on its leaves, and its leaves and fruits are used on ceremonial occasions, hanging from door-ways, and on marriage **Shamianas**. Also called the **Brab**-*tree* and the **Toddy**-*palm*. Some vernacular names are: H. *tal*; Tel. *tadu*; Mar. *tadi*; Sinh. *tal*. [*OED* & YB; Fryer (1673), *New Acct. of E. India & Persia* (1672-81), 199.] *See* **Ollah**.

Pambre [17C. Mar. *pāmarī*.] 'A sort of silk cloth'. Used as a scarf, turban, head-cloth, mantle etc. of 'pure silk, or cotton and silk, with an ornamental border'. [YB; Foster (1616), *Letters* (ed. 1896-1900), iv. 344; Fryer, *New Acct. of E. India & Persia* (1672-81), 79.]

Pan, pawn [17C. H. *pān*, fr. S. *parna*, 'a leaf'.] The **Betel**-leaf. *Pan*, or *pan-supari* in full (*see* **Supari**), an astringent combination of chopped **Areca**-nut, lime and other ingredients accor-ding to taste, wrapped in a *betel-leaf*, and offered to departing guests, or otherwise used as a form of ceremonial hospitality. *Pan* is also bought from stalls and shops to be found in every town in India. [*OED* & YB.] *See* **Pandan**. Also, *pan-wallah* (1955); -box (1922); -chewing (1892); -garden (1923); -juice (1901). [Sir T. Roe (1616), in Purchas (1625), i. iv. xvi.]

Panchama [19C. S. *pachama*, 'fifth'.] A member of the fifth division of early Indian society, outside the four main castes (**Brah-min, Kshatriya, Vaishya, Sudra**). Also called *Pancham Bandam*. A *Panchama* was a former **Pariah** or **Outcaste**. (*See* **Harijan, Untouchable, Scheduled Caste** and **Sche-duled Tribes**.) [*OED*; Buchanan, 'Journal', 30 Apr. in *Journey from Madras* (1800), 1. i. 19.]

Panchang(am) [19C. S. *pānchāngī, panch*, 'five' + *angi*, 'body'.] An Indian almanac containing information on five subjects: Solar and Lunar Days, Asterisms, *Yogas*, and *Karanas* (certain astrological divisions of the days of a month). Also used for the Brahmin who keeps and interprets the almanacs. [YB; Buchanan, *Journey through Mysore*, etc. (1800), i. 234.]

Panchayat, punchayet [18C. H. *panchāyat*, fr. *pānch*, 'five' + *ayat*.] 'A council of five persons; a village-council in India, to oversee and decide on village matters.' Also *panchayat samiti* (1969), a committee of five; *panchayat raj* (1963), the rule of the *panchayat*. Other terms related to 'panch' are: (1) *Panchayat*, an assembly of five witnesses, as a 'Court of Arbiters or Jury'. (2) *Pancha(h)*, one of its members; (3) *Panchshil*, the five Buddhist principles forbidding, (a) the taking of life, (b) theft, (c) fornication and adultery, (d) lying, (e) use of intoxicants, (4) *Panchshila*, the five principles of 'peaceful co-existence' formulated between India and China in 1954. Alias: *Punch-Sheel* (*Times*, 18 July 1955). [*OED* & YB; Dosambha Framji (1778), *H. of the Parsis* (1884), ii. 219.] *See* **Punch¹**, **Sarpanch**.

Panchen, Banchen, Pantchan [18C. Tibet. abbr. of *pandita-chen-po* (S. *pandit*), 'The Great Learned One'.] A Tibetan Buddhist title of respect (esp. applied to the *Panchen Lama*, next in importance to the *Dalai Lama*.) [*OED*; Bell, *Travels from St. Petersburg.* (1763), 1. 284.]

Panchway, paunchway [18C. Beng. *pansi*; M. *pensoia*, 'boat'.] A light kind of boat or **Ding(h)y** used on the rivers of Bengal, similar to a **Budgerow**. [*OED* & YB; Grant, *Acct. of the Loss of Calcutta* (1757); Grose, *Voy. E. Ind.* (1757), 20.]

Panda¹ [19C. Nep. *panda*.] (a) The Himalayan cat-bear, *Aelurus fulgens*, a racoon-like animal. [Swainson, *Nat. Hist. Quadrupeds* (1835); (b) A large black and white bear-like animal, *Ailuropoda melanoleuca*, native of China. (1901). [*OED*; Lancaster, *Trans. Linn. Soc.* (1901), viii. 165.]

Panda² [H. *panda*.] A Hindu temple-priest, senior to a **Pujari**. [*CIWIE*.]

Pandal, pendaul [18C. Tam. *pendal* (S. *bandh*, 'to bind'), 'a shed'.] A booth (for marriages), an arbour; a marquee for great occasions, but for temporary use only. [*OED* & YB; J. T. Phillips, *Acct. of the Relig, Manners and Learning of the People of Malabar* (1717), 19.]

Pandan [19C. H. *pandan*, fr. *pan* + *dan*, 'box'.] A small receptacle for holding the various ingredients of **Pan**. [*Catal. Colon. and Ind. Exhib.* (1886), 51.]

Pandaram [18C. Tam. *pandaram*.] A low caste Hindu ascetic mendicant or a priest in Sri Lanka and S. India, often serving in **Siva** temples, decorating the **Ling(h)am** with flowers and blowing the trumpets when offerings are made. [Wheeler (1711), *Madras*, (1861), 11. 163; *OED* & YB.]

Pandava *See* **Mahabharata**.

Pandit *See* **Pundit**.

Pandy [19C. Surname *Pande*: high-caste, Bengal personal name (fr. S. *Pandita*).] Common name among the Brahmin sepoys of the Bengal army. 'The most current colloquial name for the sepoy mutineer during 1857-58.' [YB & *OED*; Greathed, *Letters During the Siege of Delhi* (1857), 99.]

Pangara, pangaia, pangala [16C. Pg. *pangaio*.] 'A two-masted barge with lateen sails' [Rivara], or 'a barge with one mat sail of coconut leaves'. (Lancaster, *Voyages*) [YB; Barker (1519), *Hakluyt*, 11. 588.]

Pani, Pawnee, pahni, parnee [19C. H. *pānī*, water.] The word was extensively used in Anglo-Indian compounds, such as *bilayutee pawnee*, 'soda-water' (fr. *bilāyatī*, 'foreign') (1885). (*See* **Blighty**); *brandy-pawnee*; *khushbo pawnee* (European scents); etc. [YB.] Cf. Romany *pani, paani, pauni*. Also in Anglo-Indian usage = *Rain* (1859) and *pawni-game* = teetotalism (1893). *Guzzle-pawnee* (20C.), Indian Army punning nickname for men named Drinkwater. [Partridge, *Dict. of Slang* (1979).]

Pani, kalla [19C. H. *kālā pānī*, 'Black Water'.] The sea, a voyage over which a caste Hindu dreaded to make because of the pollution suffered in the process. (This taboo has disappeared even among orthodox Brahmins of the present day.) The Black Water was feared also by lower castes and casteless Indians because it often involved their transportation to penal settlements. [YB; Malcolm, *Central India* (1823), i. 446.]

Pani-wallah [20C. H. *pānī* + *wala*, 'water-man'.] A water-carrier. *See* **Bhistie (Beastie)**. [YB; Orwell, *Burmese Days* (1934), xxv. 368.]

Panicale [18C. Indo-Portuguese, poss. fr. H. *pānī*, 'water' + Tam. *kāl*, 'leg'.] An Indian disease; a swelling of the feet. (Blutean, 1727-8). *See* **Cochin Leg** (Tam. *ānaikāl*). [YB.]

Panikar, panyca [16C. M. *panikan*, 'a fencing master, a teacher', fr. *pani*, 'work + *karan*, 'doer'.] More recently, an astrologer. [YB; Litchfield, *Castaneda*, (1582), f. 36 v.]

Paninean, paninian [19C. S. *Pāniniyā*, fr. name *Pānini*.] Of or pert. to the Sanskrit grammar of *Pānini* (6th or 5C. BC); adhering to the rules formulated by *Pānini*. [*OED*; Colebrooke, *Asiatic Res.* (1801), vii. 204.]

Panir [H. *panīr*.] Indian cottage cheese made from milk curdled with lime-juice, strained and pressed solid.

Pansala [19C. Sinh. *pānsala* (fr. *pān*, 'leaf' + *sala*, 'dwelling'). S. *parnasālā* (Pali. *pannasālā*).] A Buddhist temple or monastery; orig. a forest hut constructed of leaves. [OED; Hardy, *Eastern Monachism* (1850), xiii. 129.]

Pant [19C.] E. *pants*, 'trousers'. Also: *pantpiece*, 'trouser-length', and *half-pant*, trousers reaching to above or about the knee, English 'shorts'. Back formation from *pants*, which is regarded as the plural of 'pant' (poss. fr. USA). [Shands, *Some Peculiarities of Speech in Mississippi* (1893), 40.]

Panth [19C. H. *panth*. S. *patha*, 'way, path'.] A religious order espec. Sikh *Panth*(s). *See* **Dalit Panther**, [Whitworth, *Anglo-Indian Dict.* (1885).]

Panthak(y) [P. panthak(i).] A chief priest of the **Parsis**.

Panthee, panthi [19C.] *See* prec. The follower of any particular sect or teacher, or a European who 'goes native' or *Panti*. [Kipling, *The Man Who Would be King* (1888).]

Panther [10C. Gr. *panther;* perh. S. *pundarikas*, 'tiger'. Leopard (*Felis pardus*) (but applied vaguely in early use). *See* **Leopard**.

Pap(adj) [19C. S. *pāp* (H. *pāp*).] Sinful, evil, wicked, vicious, accursed. [Sir Charles Eliot, *Hinduism & Buddhism* (1921), I. 107.]

Pap(am)(sb) [S. *pāpam* (H. *pāp*).] Sin, evil, vice, guilt. [Sir Charles Eliot, *Hinduism & Buddhism* (1921), i. 107.]

Papad(d)am, pop(p)adam, popper-cake [19C. Tam. *pappadam* (abbr. of *paruppu-adam*, 'lentil cake'.] Thin lentil cakes (seasoned with asafoetida, **Jeera** etc.) and fried or toasted till brittle. *See* **Hopper**. [OED & YB; Forbes, *Oriental Memoirs* (1813), ii. 50.] *See* **Oord**.

Papaya, pawpaw [16C. Pg. *papayo*.] A giant herbaceous plant, *Carica papaya*, indigenous in tropical America, but now ubiquitous in India, producing large, succulent salmon-pink fleshed fruit, rather like an elongated melon, considered by YB to be an 'insipid not to say nasty fruit!' (*Chacun à son gout*). A milky latex from the green, unripe fruit is a vermifuge, and papain from the latex is used for making chewing gum, and tenderizing meat (1890). [OED & YB; Phillips (1598), tr., Linschoten (1855), ii. 35.]

Papiya [19C. H. *papiya*.] The Brain-fever Bird, or Common Hawk Cuckoo, *Cuculus varius varius*, distributed in the Indian Union from about 2500 ft., in the Himalayas south to Sri Lanka. In the hot weather its call becomes insistent, even obstreperous. In Hindi it is rendered as *Pee-kāhān?* ('Where is my love?') and in Marathi, *Paos-ala* ('Rain's coming'),

repeated *ad nauseam*. (The pied Crested Cuckoo *Clamator jacobinus* is also called *Papiyā* in Hindi). [W. E. Brooks, *Ornith Observations* etc. (1879).]

Para [18C.] The hog-deer or *Babiroussa. Cervus (Axis) porcinus*, related to the **Chital**. Lives in the alluvial grass plains of N. India, Pakistan and Sri Lanka. [Hawkins, *Ind. Nat. Hist* (1986).] *See* **Spotted-deer**.

Parabyke [17C. Bur. *pārabeik*.] A kind of exercise-book common in Burma and parts of India at one time = Kan. *kadatam*, consists of paper made from the Daphne shrub, blackened with charcoal and written on with a steatite pencil. [YB; De la Loubere, *Historical Relation of Siam* (E. tr., 1693), 12.]

Parangi, paranghee [19C. Sinh. *parangi*, fr. S. *phiranga*, 'Frankish', European.] The old name given to the disease in Sri Lanka now identified as yaws. Orig. the disease of the foreigners, i.e., the Portuguese. [OED.] *See* **Feringhee**. [Marshal, *Notes Medical Topogr. Interior Ceylon* (1821), iii. 43.]

Parao [19C. H. *parao*.] Camp or halting place. [Kipling, *Kim* (1901).]

Parbutty [19C. Corr. of Tel. + Kan. *pārapatti, pārupatti*, Mar. + Konkani. *pārpatya* fr. S. *pravritti*, 'employment'.] 'A subordinate village officer, a **Writer** under a **Patel**, sometimes the village crier etc. in the Madras Presidency.' [YB; Buchanan, *Mysore* (1807), ii. 151-2.]

Paratha [20C. H. *parātha*.] Pancake of unleavened bread, fried on a griddle. [OED; Morphy, *Recipes of all Nations* (1935).]

Pardao [16C. Ind. Pg. *pardao*, poss. corr. of S. *prātapa*, 'splendour, majesty'.] 'A gold coin from the native mints of Western India, which entered largely into the early currency of Goa, and the name of which afterwards attached to a silver money, of constantly degenerating value.' [YB & OED; Litchfield, *Castañeda* (1582), i.iv.117.]

Pargana *See* **Pergunnah**.

Pariah, Parriar [17C. Tam. *paraiyar*, pl. of *paraiyan*, lit. 'hereditary drummer', fr. *parai*, the large drum beaten at certain S. Indian festivals.] (1) One of a low (but not the lowest) caste in S. India, whose members once supplied most of the domestics in Anglo-Indian households in S. India. 'They are also low in habits, frequently eating carrion and other objectionable food, and addicted to drink.' [YB & OED; Purchas (1613), *Pilgrimage* (1614), 494.] (2) Hence (erroneously) any person of low caste, or no caste at all. [OED; Wheeler (1711), Madras in Old. Time (1861), ii. 550.] (3) Also erroneously, and now most frequently in English, a social outcaste of any kind or race anywhere. [OED; Shelley (1819), Lett. Pr. Wks. (1888), ii. 286.] Hence: **Pariah-dog** (1626) (See **Pi-dog**); **Pariah-arrack** (1671); **Pariah-kite** (1880); and Pariah-dom (1878); pariah-ship; pariah-brig, (1929), a sea vessel built in India.

Pariah-arrack [17C.] See **Pariah** and **Arrack**. In the 17th and 18th centuries this was the name commonly given to the poisonous native spirit commonly sold to European soldiers and sailors. [YB & OED] See **Fool's Rack**. [Langhorne (1671-2) in Wheeler (1861), iii. 422.]

Pariah dog [18C.] The stray mongrel dog that scavenges the refuse of the streets of India. 'So-called from being a low-bred, casteless animal'. [YB & OED; Munro, Narrative of Milit. Ops. (1780-84), 36.]

Pariah-kite [19C. H. chīl.] The common Indian forked-tail hawk, the cheel (Milvus migrans), excessively bold and impudent, a voracious scavenger of 'offal and garbage, earthworms, winged termites, lizards, mice, disabled or young birds and almost anything that can be procured.' [OED & YB; Jerdon, Birds of India (1862); Salim Ali, The Book of Indian Birds, 23.] Cf. **Brahminy kite**.

Parishad [20C. Beng./H. fr. S. parishad (pari, 'about' + sad, sidati, 'sit down'), 'assembly', 'council'.] In India and Bangladesh, an assembly group or local council (cf. English parish council). Also, **Zilla parishad**, 'district council'. [OED; Mookerji, Local Govt. Anc. India (1919), i. 29.]

Parmahansa(s) [19C. S. parama, 'best' + hansa, 'a supreme spirit'.] A caste reputed to eat human flesh; Siva devotee(s). Otherwise, an ascetic of the highest order; one who has controlled and subdued all his senses by abstract meditation. See **Aghori**. [Edward Moor, Hindu Pantheon (1810).]

Parsi, Parsee [17C. Fr. Farsi fr. Fars, Persia (now Iran).] A guebre. A descendant of Persians who fled from Muslim religious persecution from Persia to India in the 7th and 8th centuries AD in order to preserve their freedom to adhere to their religion, **Zoroastrianism**. [OED & YB; Terry (1615) in Purchas, Pilgrimes (1625), ii. 1479.] See **Pahlavi**.

Parvati [19C. S. fr. parwata, 'a mountain'.] Siva's wife in his character of a jovial mountain god. [Whitworth, Anglo-Indian Dict. (1885).]

Parvoe, purvo [17C.] See **Prabhu**.

Pasador [19C. Sea-Hind/Pg. passador.] A marlin spike [YB; Roebuck (1811).]

Pashmin(a) [19C. fr. P. pashm, 'wool'.] Underfur of hairy quadruped. Fine cloth made from goat's wool, used for cashmere shawls. See **Toos** [OED; Mrs A.G. F.E. James, Ind. Indust. (1880), xxi. 36.]

Pashto, Pushtoo, Pustu, Pakhtu, Paktoo [18C. Pashtō.] The name of the language of the tribes in S.W. Afghanistan, and Pakhtu, of those in N.E. Afghanistan. Their language is intermediate between the Iranian and Sanskrit families of the Indo-European languages. Also called **Afghani** in the time of Babur. [OED; Elphinstone, Acc. Caubul (1815), ii. ii. 168.]

Pashtun See **Pakthun**.

Pat [19C. Sea-Hindi pāt.] A can or pot (fr. English). [YB.]

Pata [20C. H/S. pata, 'cloth, canvas'.] (Religious) picture painted on a canvas scroll. [OED; Bhattacharyya, Study on Vastuvidya (1948), 261.]

Pataca, patacoon [16C. M/Pg. pataca.] (1) A term, formerly current in India, used for a dollar or piece of eight. In 17C. worth about 4s. 8d. English. [OED & YB; Logan (1528), Malabar (1887-91), i. 329.] (2) The monetary unit of Macao and Timor. [OED; 1584 in Hak., Voy. (1811), 11. 411.]

Pat(t)amar, patimar [16C. Pg. patamar; Mar. pattamāri, fr. patta, 'tidings' + māri, 'carrier'.] (1) A courier or **Dak**-runner. [OED & YB; Phillips, Linschoten (1598), 73/2.] (2) An Indian dispatch boat, spec. a lateen-rigged sailing vessel, with one, two or three masts, used on the west coast of India. [OED & YB; Churchill, in Collect. Voy. (1704), iii. 740/2.]

Patana [19C. Sin. patana, fr. S. pat, 'to fall'.] A glade usually with sloping sides, in the jungle-covered mountains of Sri Lanka. [OED; Barker, Rifle and Hound in Ceylon (1854), viii. 218.]

Patch [17C. abbr. of Tel. pach' chadamu.] A particular kind of cotton cloth; two cloths joined together. [YB; Foster, Engl. Fact. in India (1651-4; ed. 1915).]

Patcharee, patcherry, parcherry [18C. poss. H. pich'hārī, 'the rear', or Tam. parash + sheri', a pariah village', or the quarters on the outskirts of a village.] 'The name applied in European corps to the cottages which used to form the quarters of married soldiers.' [YB; Accts. Fort St. David, 21 Feb. 1747 (MS. in IOL).]

Patchouli, patch-leaf, putcha-leaf [17C. H. *pacholi,* or Tam. *pachchilai* (*pachchai*, 'green' + *ilai*, 'leaf'.] Also known as *patchleaf* (1673). A sweet-smelling plant, *Pogestemon patchouli,* grown throughout India and the Malay peninsula. Perfume distilled from its dried flowering spikes and leaves. Also, *patchoulied,* perfumed with *patchouli* (1925). [*OED* & YB; Fryer, *New Acct.* (1698), 209.]

Pateca [16C. Indo-Pg. *pateca; Ar. battikh.*] Watermelon, *Citrullus vulgaris.* [YB; Phillips, *Linschoten* (1598), 97; Fryer, *New Acct.,* (1672-81), 76.]

Patel, patil, potail [17C. H. *patel;* Mar. *patil,* 'roll or register'.] The hereditary headman of a village, having control of village affairs, and forming the medium of communication with officers of Government in central and southern India. *See* **Monegar** and **Adigar**. [*OED* & YB; Foster (1614), *Letters* (1602-17), ii. 281.] Also **Mukiya, Saswat**.

Pathan, Puttan [17C. H. *Pathan;* Pashto, *Pukhtanah,* pl. of **Pakhtun**.] *Pathan* and **Afghan** are terms often loosely employed as synonymous, esp. to people in India of Afghan descent. A member of an Afghan tribe, esp. one inhabiting the Afghanistan-Pakistan border areas, whose language is **Pashto**; noted for courage and fierceness in battle. In India, Pathans are often watchmen. Also called **Pakhtun**. [*OED* & YB; Hawkins in Purchas (1614), i. 220.]

Paths(h)ala [S. *path,* 'school' + *sala,* 'room'.] Traditional Hindu (Sanskrit) school. [Hawkins, *CIWIE*.]

Patit [20C. H. *patit,* 'fallen', 'apostate'.] Term applied to Sikhs in Britain who cut their hair and beards, and cease wearing turbans.

Patka [19C. H. *patka*.] Girdle, sash.

Patna [16C. City name fr. H. *pattana,* 'the city'.] Name of a district and chief city in Bihar (the *Pataliputra* of the Greeks), famed, *inter alia* for its *Patna* rice, a small-grained variety principally used in curries and other savoury dishes. [*OED* & YB; Fitch (1586), *Hakluyt* (1807), ii. 388.]

Patola [17C. Kan./M. *pattuda,* 'silk-cloth'.] Intricately woven silk fabric of Patan in Gujarat.

[YB; Birdwood (1605), *Letter Book* (1600-19), 74.]

Patta, pottah [18C. H. *patta;* Tam. *pattiam* (perh. S. *patta,* 'a tablet'.)] Title deed. A deed of lease defining and certifying land tenure. *See* **Patwari**. [*OED* & YB; Burke, Articles of Charge against Hastings (1778), vi. 591.]

Pattar(s) [M. *pattar,* 'foreign'.] Brahmins settled in Malabar, and permitted to form alliances with **Nayars (Nairs)**.]

Pattawala, puttywalla [19C. H. *patta,* 'belt' + *wala,* 'person'.] A belted, uniformed servant or messenger attached to an office or business, the belt being his badge of office. *See* **Chuprassi** and **Peon**. [*OED* & YB; Monier-Williams, *Modern India* (1878), 34.]

Patello, patellee [17C. H. *patelā.*] A large flat-bottomed boat on the Ganges. [YB; Yule (1680), Hedges, *Diary,* Hak. Soc. ii. 15.] *See* **Woolock**.

Pattidar [19C. H. *patti,* 'a share', 'a division of a village' + *dar,* 'holder'.] Hereditary shareholder in village land. [H. H. Wilson, *Glossary* (1855).]

Patwari, putwari, potwari [19C. H. *patwārī,* fr. *patta* + *wari*.] Village registrar, or accountant under a **Zemindar**. *See* **Kayasth** and **Prabhu**. [*OED;* Patton, *Asiatic Monarchies* (1801), 118.]

Paunchway *See* **Panchway**.

Paut, pat [19C. H. *pāt,* 'leaf', 'indigo plant', 'juice'.] The jute fibre, also the leaves of the indigo plant made into bundles for delivery. [*OED; Trans. Soc. Arts.* (1801), xix. 235.]

Pawl [19C. H. *pāl;* S. *patala,* 'a roof'.] 'A small tent with two light poles, a ridge-bar and steep sloping sides. [*OED* & YB.] *See* **Shooldarry, Rowtee**. [Kirkpatrick, tr., *Tippoo's Lett.* (1811), 49.]

Pawn *See* **Pan**.

Pawnee *See* **Pani**.

Payen-Ghaut [18C. fr./P. *pāin,* 'below' + H. & Mar. **Ghat**.] 'The country on the coast below the **Ghats** or passes leading up to the tableland of the Deccan.' [YB; Munro, *Narrative* (1789), 252.]

Pazend *See* **Pahlavi** and **Zend**.

Peda, pedha [H. *pedha.*] Indian sweetmeat of milk boiled till thick, with sugar, cardamon, pistachio and a variety of flavourings.

Peeada, Piyada *See* **Peon**.

Peechy [late 19C. Military slang fr. H. *pīchhe.*] Soon, without delay, presently. [Frazer & Gibbons, *Soldier & Sailor Words & Phrases* (1925).]

Peenus [17C. H. *pīnas,* corr. of *pinnace.*] (1) A class of **Budgerow** rigged like a brig or brigantine on Bengal rivers. [YB; Cocks (1615), *Diary,* Hak. Soc. i. 22.] (2) Also, in N. India, sort of palankin used by a bride. [YB.]

Peepul, pipal, peepal [18C. H. *pīpal,* fr. S. *pippala.*] The Indian tree, *Ficus religiosa,* or **Bo-tree** sacred to Hindus and Buddhists; to the latter because Siddhartha meditated beneath it, found enlightenment and became known as the Buddha; to the former because Brahma, Vishnu and Shiva were reputed to have been born beneath its branches. Consider the possible connection of the word *Pīpal* with poplar. [*OED* & YB; *Asiatick Res.* (1788), i. 390; Kipling, *Life's Handicap* (1891).]

Peer *See* **Pir.**

Peg [18C.] E. *peg.* One of a set of pins fixed at intervals in a drinking vessel. Anglo-Indian: Measure for spirits about 56 millilitres, or one fluid ounce; beverage of spirits esp. brandy and (soda) water. *See* **Blighty-Pani.** Also, *Peg-table,* a small, low occasional table. *See* **Teapoy.** [*OED;* Strutt, *Compleat View* (1775), I. 48.]

Pegu ponies [19C. Place-name.] Ponies at one time imported from Burma to India, until the annexation of Pegu, after which the local demand absorbed them. [YB; *Madras Mail,* 19 Feb. 1880.]

Pehranu [19C. Sind. *perhanu.*] A shirt with full-length sleeves. [R. Burton, *Hist. of Sindh* (1851).]

Pela [Sin.] A watch-hut on stilts. Cf. **Machan.** [Hawkins, *CIWIE.*]

Pelong [17C. Deriv. uncertain; perh. fr. Malay *pēlang,* 'striped'.] A kind of material used for gowns in S. India. [*OED;* Charter to Fort St. George (E.I.C.) (1687), f. 5.]

Peon [17C. Indo-Portuguese. In many Indian languages. Pg. *peao* (fr. *pe,* 'foot'), 'footman' (also, a pawn in chess). It is not a corr. of H. *piyada,* meaning the same as peon, 'though the words are ultimately akin in root.' YB.] Orig. a foot-soldier, thence an 'orderly' or messenger. Now in India, Pakistan, Bangladesh, Sri Lanka and Malaysia, an 'office-boy'. *See* **Chuprassy** [*OED* & YB; Finch (1609) in Purchas, *Pilgrimes* (1625), i. 421.]

Pepper [11C. Ult. S. *pippalī,* 'berry, pepper-corn'.] The Sanskrit word 'means not the ordinary pepper of commerce', black-pepper, *Piper nigrum,* but 'long pepper', *Piper longum,* indigenous in Kerala, Sri Lanka and

Bangladesh [*OED* & YB; Aelfric (*c.* AD 1000), *Gram.* ix. (Z). 44; Trevisa (1398), Barth. De P. R., *xvii.* cxxxi. (Bodl. MS.)

Perahera [17C. Sin. *perahera,* 'protection, safety'.] A religious Hindu or Buddhist procession in Sri Lanka, of praise, thanksgiving or of intercession. [*OED;* Knox, *Hist. Relation Ceylon* (1681), iii. iv. 78.]

Pergunnah, paraganza [17C. H/P. *paragana,* S. *pragan,* 'to reckon up'.] A sub-division of a 'district' comprising a number of villages. *See* **Zilla.** [*OED* & YB; Foster (1614), *Letters* (1602-17; ed. 1896-1902), ii. 106.]

Perpet, perpetuano, perpetuana [16C. Trade-name. (L./Sp. *perpetuo.*)] A light glossy twilled stuff of wool made in England from the 16th century which took its name from its durability. Exported to India and elsewhere in the East in the 17th and first part of the 18th centuries. [*OED* & YB; B. Jonson, *Cynthia's Revels* (1599), III. ii.]

Peshcubz [18C. P. *pesh-kabz,* 'fore-grip'.] 'A form of dagger, the blade of which has a straight thick back, while the edge curves inwardly from a broad base to a very sharp point.' [YB; Long, *Sel. from Records Ft. St. George* (1748-67), 497.]

Peshcush, piscush [17C. P. *pesh-kash (pēsh,* 'fore, 'in front' + *kash,* 'drawing').] First fruits; tribute; quit rent; present; offering; a fine. 'In the old English records most generally used in the sense of a present to a great man.' [YB & *OED;* Foster, *Eng. Fact. in India;* Herbert, *Trav.* (1634), 156.]

Peshkar [19C. H./P. *peshkar.*] Court aide, front man, deputy. *See* **Saristadar** (Sheristadar.) Whitworth, *Anglo-Indian Dict.* (1885); Kuldip Nayar, *The Judgement* (1977).]

Peshkhana, pesh-khidmat, peshkhaima [17C. H/P.] All three mean 'fore-service'. *Peshkhāna,* 'house(s) in front'; *Pesh-khidmat,* lit. 'fore-service'; *Pesh-khaima,* 'advance tents'. These expressions refer to the practice of sending tents, retinue, food, accoutrements and paraphernalia of the march or expedition every night in advance, to be ready for the main party the next day. [YB; Bernier, *Travels Mogul Empire* (1658-64; E. tr. 1684), 115.]

Peshwa, peishwa [17C. H/P. *pēshwa,* 'leader, chief, guide'.] The chief minister of the Maratha power. From 1749 the Peshwas became the hereditary rulers of the Maratha confederacy, after supplanting the descendants of Shivaji, until the surrender of the last Peshwa, Baji Rao, in 1817. [OED & YB; Fryer (1673), *New Account* (1672-81), 79.]

Petersilly [Dutch, *petersilie*, 'parsley'.] 'The name by which 'parsley' is generally called in N. India. [YB.]

Peth [18C. H/Mar. *peth*.] Market, division of a city, bazaar, suburb. *See* next. [Whitworth, *Anglo-Indian Dict.* (1885).]

Petta(h) [18C. Tam. *pettai;* Mar. *peth;* S. *petaka*.] 'The extramural suburb of a fortress or the town attached and adjacent to a fortress.' In S. India, sometimes' itself fortified. [YB; *Orme* (1763), *Hist. Milit. Trans.* (ed. 1803), 1. 147.]

Phansigarh [19C. H. *phānsi*, 'a noose' + *garh.* 'place'.] The place of execution by hanging. [Maud Diver (1843), *Honoria Lawrence* (1936), 255.]

Phansigar, phanseegar [18C. H. *phānsi*, 'a noose' + *gār* (agent suffix).] One of a band of criminal stranglers and assassins. *See* **Thug**. [OED & YB; Forbes, *Or. Mem.* (1813), iv. 13.]

Pheriwala [H. *pheri*, 'around' + *wala*, 'agent'.] A hawker. [Hawkins, *CIWIE*.]

Pheran [19C. Kash/P. *pairahan*.] A long full-sleeved woollen, or silk gown worn by men and women in Kashmir, eminently suitable for the **Kangri**, fire-pot. [OED; *Encyl. Brit.* (1882), 12/1; W.R. Lawrence, *Valley of Kashmir* (1895), xix 464/2.]

Phoorza [18C. Guj. *phurjā*, fr. Ar. *furzat*.] 'a notch', 'a bight', 'river-mouth', 'harbour', 'custom-duty'. Custom-house. [YB; Alexander Hamilton (1727), *New Acct. E. Indies* (ed. 1744), ii. 19.]

Phulkari, phoolkaree [19C. H. *phūlkārī*, 'flowered embroidery'.] Flower-embroidered cloth; cotton sheets, embroidered in silk, once part of a Hindu and Sikh bridal trousseau in N. India. Each girl was supposed to embroider one of these for her marriage. [OED & YB; Lady Dufferin, *Viceregal Life* (1887), 336.]

Phut (adv.) [19C. Slang fr. H. *phatna*, 'to burst'.] Slang, to be a failure, to collapse, to fizzle out. Phrase: 'to go *phut*'. [OED; Kipling, *The Naulakha* (1892); Partridge, *Dict. of Slang* (1979); Steevens, *With Kitchener to Khartum* (1898), 143.]

Phut-phut [19C. *See* prec.] Reduplication of *phut*, echoic of the sound of an engine, motor-cycle, scooter, etc. Hence, *Phut-phuti*, a motor-cycle. [Hawkins, *CIWIE*.]

Pi-(dog) [19C. Contraction of **Pariah**.] Any

(stray) mongrel dog. (Also: *pie-* & *pye-*.) [Hawkins, *CIWIE*.]

Pial *See* **Pyal**.

Picar [17C. H. *paikār* (corr. of P. *pa'e-kar, pa'e* 'foot'.] A retail-dealer; an intermediate dealer or broker. (English slang, a *piker*.) [YB; Hedges (1683), *Diary*, Hak. Soc., i. 133.]

Piccalilli [18C. Etym. unknown.] A pickle; formerly called 'Indian Pickle.' [Mrs Raffold (1769), *Eng. Housekeeper* (1778), 357.]

Pice [17C. H. *paisā*, perh. fr. *pa'ī* (*see* **Pie**), and S. *Pad(i)*, 'a quarter'.] A copper coin, $\frac{1}{4}$ **Anna**. Also, slang, *picey* (1927), 'mean, niggardly, miserly'. [OED & YB; Peyton in Purchas, *Pilgrimage* (1614), i. 530.]

Picota [19C. Origin unknown of Indo-Portuguese use in 16C.] An additional allowance or percentage added as a handicap to the weight of goods.' [YB; A. Nunes, *Livro dos Pesos da Yindia* (1554), 18.]

Picot(t)a(h) [19C. Pg. *picota*. A.S.] Indian term for a device for raising water, consisting of a long lever pivoted on an upright post, weighted on the short arm, and bearing a line and a bucket on the long arm. 'It is the *dhenkli* **(Denkli)** of N. India, the *shadaf* of the Nile, and the old English *sweep, swape*, or *sway-pole*.' [YB & OED; Buchanan, *Journ. Mysore* (1807), i. 15.]

Pie, pai, pi [19C. H/Mar. etc. *pa'ī*.] *See* **Paisa**. The smallest copper coin of the Anglo-Indian currency; 1/12th of an anna, 1/192 of a rupee. [Lang, *Wand. India.* (1859), 69.]

Piece-goods [17C.] A technical term originally used for Indian cotton goods exported to England and, after the imposition of crippling duties in the 18th and 19th centuries on this trade, for the Manchester goods exported from England to India, which ultimately killed off Indian exports, and inflicted grave damage on the Indian economy of the time. Over a hundred different kinds of Indian piece-goods were exported in the heyday of the trade, with such exotic names as: *Allieballies, Aunneketchies, Bejutapauts, Callipatties, Cattaketchies, Chunderbannies, Dosooties, Habassies, Humhums, Jamadannies, Muggadooties, Sastracundees, Tarnattannes* and *Ventepollams*, as well as the now better-known varieties such as *Bandannas, Chintzes, Calicoes, Dungarees, Ginghams, Muslins, Seersuckers* and *Taffetas*. [OED & YB; *London Gazette*,1665, No. 12/1; James Mill, *Brit. Ind.* (1817), I. I. iii. 45.]

Piffer [19C. Acronym.] Member of the Punjab Irregular Frontier Force, raised in 1849 to police the NWFP of India. (Also, any of the regiments which succeeded it. [*OED; Pall Mall Gazette*, 24 Oct. 1892.]

Pigdanny, pigdaun [17C. H. *pīkdān*, fr. *pīk*, the expectorated juice of chewed **Pan** + *dān*, 'a receptacle'.] A spittoon. [YB; Fryer (1673), *New Account* (1672-81).]

Pig-sticking [19C.] This mounted Anglo-Indian sport of 'hog-hunting' with spears was popular from the 17th century, though the term seems to have been introduced much later. [*OED* & YB; Thackeray, *Vanity Fair* (1848), ix.]

Pilau, pilaw, pilow, pilaf(f), etc. [17C. H/P. *pilāw, pulāo*, and S. *pulāka*, 'a ball of boiled rice'.] A dish of rice boiled with meat, fish or fowl, with spices, raisins, etc. Especially popular among Muslims and Anglo-Indians (1612). [*OED* & YB; Coryat (1612), *Journal* in Purchas, *Pilgrimes* (1625), x. xii; Aliph Cheem, *Lays of Ind* (7 ed. 1883), 2.]

Pin [20C.] Acronym of Postal Index Number, of six digits.

Pinda, peenda, pindee [18C. S. *pīnda*, 'lump'.] a ball of boiled rice offered to the souls of their ancestors by Hindus at funerals and **Shraddhas**, as far back as the third generation, to succour the departed spirits, until they become **Pitris**. The *shraddha pindas* are offered to the *pitris* [GCW]. Phrase: 'to perform pindee'. [*OED*; Wilkins, tr., *Bhāgvat Geeta* (1785), 139; Sir William Jones, tr., *Inst. Hindu Law* (1796), iii. 67; Ward, *Acct. Writings & Manners Hindoos* (1811), II. v. 550.]

Pindar, pindarry [18C. Etym. obscure but poss. fr. place-name *Pandhar*. (H. *Pindārī, Pindārā;* Mar. *Pendhārī*.)] One of a band of mounted marauders and plunderers in Central India (1720-1820). Also, their dialect. Cf. **Dacoit**. [*OED* & YB; see *Indian Antiquary* (May 1900), xxix. 140, Stockdale, *Indian Vocabulary* (1788).]

Pin-drop silence [20C.] The Anglo-Indian version of the silence in which one can hear a pin drop. [Paul Bruton, *A Search in Secret India* (1914).]

Pinjrapole, panjrapol [19C. Guj. *pānjrāpol, pinjrapor*, fr. *pānjra*, a cage, S. *panjara* + *pol*, 'enclosed space'.] In India an enclosure for old and sick animals (often kept up by the Jains and Parsis of Gujarat and by the early Buddhists). A *pinjrapol* has been described as a 'Cheshire Home' for cows. [*OED* & YB.] *See* **Goshala**. [Drummond, *Illustrations Grammatical Parts Guzarattee* etc. (1808).]

Pintado [16C. Pg. *pintado*, a 'painted' cloth.] *See* **Chintz**. 'Some of the finer Indian chintzes were at least in part, finished by handpainting.' [YB; Drake (1579), *World Encompassed*, Hak. Soc., 143; Birdwood (1602), First Lett. Bk. E.I.C. (1893), 34.]

Pipal *See* **Peepul**.

Pir, peer, peor [17C. H/P. *pīr*.] A Muslim saint or holy man; used elliptically for the tombs or shrines of such persons.] Finch (1609), in Purchas [1625], i. 438.] *See* **Sheikh**.

Pisachee, pishachee [19C. S. *pisāchī*, 'a she-demon; Masc. *pisāchā*.)] (1) Spirits of the dead, espec. those who have met with violent deaths. (In Tamil *pey*.) [YB & *OED*; Buchanan, *Journey from Madras* (1807), III. xiv. 17.] (2) 'A Dravidian dialect. still to be recognized in the speech of the *Paraiya* [**Pariah**] who cannot pronounce distinctly some of the pure Tamil letters.' [YB.] (3) *Pisāchā bhāshā;* In Hindu drama, a gibberish, or corruption of Sanskrit. (Sometimes applied to English.) (4) A mode of Hindu marriage, *Pisachavivaha*, 'when the lover without sanction of the girl's parents, takes her home by means of talismans, incantations and such-like magical practices, and then marries her'. [Shea & Troyer, *The Dabistan* (1843).] (5) The word was applied also to the small circular storms called by Europeans 'Devils'. [*OED* & YB; *Asiatic Journal* (1816), II. 367/1.]

Pishcash *See* **Peshcush**.

Pishpash [19C. Prob. H/P. *pash-pash*, 'shivered or broken in pieces', fr. P. *pashīdan*.] An Anglo-Indian (nursery) word for a slop or rice-soup with bits of meat in it. [*OED* & YB; A. Prinsep, *Baboo* (1834), II. 85.]

Pita [H. *pitā*.] Father. *See* **Pitri**. [Hawkins, *CIWIE*.]

Pitaka [19C. S. *pitaka*, 'basket'.] A division of the sacred books of the Buddhists; there are 3 pitakas: *Sutra* (rules), *Vinaya* (discipline) and *Abhidharma* (metaphysics), compiled after the Buddha's death. [Whitworth, *Anglo-Indian Dict.* (1885).]

Pitarrah, batarara, petarah [19C. H. *pitārāh;* fr. S. *pitaka*, 'a basket'.] A box, originally of basket-work, used in travelling by palanquin, to carry the travellers' clothes, 'two such being slung to a **Banghy'**. [*OED* & YB; *Asiatic Costumes* (1828), 61; W. D. Arnold, *Oakfield*. (1853), 1. 223.]

Pitri [19C. H/S. *pitri* 'Father'.] The deified ancestor; the venerated spirit of a deceased ancestor and of mankind's ancestors. Generally worshipped among Hindus. *Pitriloka*, 'heaven'. See **Pinda, Pita** and **Shraddha**. [Dubois, *Indian Manners* etc. (1817); Whitworth, *Anglo-Indian Dict.* (1885).]

Pitta [19C. Tel. *pitta*, 'anything small'.] A small bright-plumaged passerine Indian bird, *Pitta brachyura* (Hindi name *naorang*) found in well-wooded areas of India from the foothills of the Himalayan south. [*Penny Cycl.* (1840), xviii. 194/2; Ali & Ripley, *Handbook Birds India & Pakistan* (1968), 4/250.]

Play-back, -singer, -musician [20C.] In Indian movies, a substitute voice or musician for the actor or actress when song or music are required. [*OED*; Barnouw and Krishnaswamy, *Indian Film* (1963), 164.]

Po-po [17C. M. *po*, 'get out of the way!', cf. **Khis-khis** & **Pyse**.] [YB; *Linschoten* (1598), Hak. Soc. (1807), i. 280.]

Podar [17C. H. *poddār*, corr. of P. *fotadār*, fr. *fota*, 'a bag of money'.] A treasury official, employed 'to weigh money and bullion and appraise the value of coins.' [YB; Fort St. Geo. Cons., 2 Dec. 1680; Verelst, *View of Bengal* (1772).]

Podshaw See **Padshah**.

Podu [19C. Tel. *podu*.] Cultivation practices in West India, equivalent to **Kumri** in S. India. See also **Jhoom**. [Wilson, *Glossary* (1855).]

Poggle See **Puggle**.

Poisha [Beng. *poisha*.] 1/100th of a **Taka** (in Bangladesh). Cf. **Paisa**.

Poligar, pallegar [17C. Tel. *palegādu*; Mar. *palegar*; Tam. *palaiakkaran*.] Holder of a **pollam**, or feudal estate in S. India; a feudal chief or predatory follower of such chief. By the 19th century he had become much the same as a **Zemindar**. [*OED* & YB; Wheeler (1681), *Madras* (1861), 1. 118.]

Poligar-dog [19C. See prec.] A large breed of hairless dog found in S. India. [YB; Col. W. Campbell, *The Old Forest Ranger* (1853), 12.]

Pollam [18C. Tam. *palaiyam*, Tel. *pālemu*.] See **Poligar**. [*OED* & YB; Burke's (1783), Speech on Fox's E. I. Bill (*Wks.* iii. 488).]

Pollock-saug, -sag [19C. H. *pālak*, 'spinach' + *sāg*, 'leaf (vegetable)'.] A poor vegetable, alias 'Country spinach', *Beta vulgaris*, or

bengalensis. Also called 'Bengal Beet'. [YB; Riddell, *Indian Domestic Economy* (7th edn. 1871), 579.]

Polo [19C. *Baltī, polo*, 'ball'; Tibetan, *pulu*.] 'The game of hockey on horseback.' [YB.] Of *Balti* (Indus Valley) origin; first introduced at Sibsagar and, later, Calcutta from native Indian practice, esp. Manipur. See **Chukka**, and **Chicane**. [Vigne, *Trav. Kashmir* (1842), ii. 289.]

Polonga, tic-polonga [17C. Sinh. *tic*, 'spot(ted)' + *polongarā*, 'viper'.] A very poisonous Sri Lankan snake, *Vipera russelli*, variously called 'chain viper', 'necklace-snake', 'Russell's viper', and 'Cobra manila'. [YB; Knox, *Hist. Rel. Island Ceylon* (1681), 29.]

Pom(m)elo, pampelmoose, pummel-nose, pompel moose, etc. [17C. Anglo-Indian, but etym. unknown.] The fruit of *Citrus grandis*, 'the largest of the orange tribe'. [YB.] Also called the **shaddock**, fr. the name of Capt. Shaddock who reputedly took the seed from India to Barbados early in the 18th century. It is grown in many parts of India and the Far East, especially in Malaysia and Indonesia, where it reaches perfection, and is known in Bengal as *Batavi nimbu*, the 'Batavian lime'. [*OED* & YB.] Ives calls the fruit 'pimple-noses'. [Ives, *Voy. to India* (1773), 468.]

Pomfret, paumphlet [16C. Prob. fr. Pg. *pampo*.] Embraces many species of the family *Stromatoides*, found on all the Indian coasts. Also: *White pomfret*, the general name; *Silver pomfret*, when immature; *Black or Grey pomfret*, when mature. [*OED* & YB; *Linschoten* (E. tr. 1598; Hak. Soc., ii. II.); Hamilton, *New Acc. E. Ind.* (1727), I. 393.]

Pongal, Pongol [18C. Tam. *ponkal*, 'boiling' (of rice).] The Tamil New Year Festival observed early in January, the first ritual act of which is the boiling of the new rice; a kind of harvest festival; hence a dish of cooked rice. [*OED* & YB; F. Magnus, tr. (1788), Sonnerat's *Voy. East-Indies*, I. v. 142.]

Poodle-faker [20C. Anglo-Indian slang.] A man, espec. orig. a naval or military officer, who lays himself out (for the time being) to cultivate and ingratiate himself with female society. In ref. to *lap*-dogs. Its use in India may have had some ref. to **Fakir**(?). [*OED*; 'I. Hay', *Knight on Wheels* (2nd edn., 1914), iii. xxiii. 228; Engel, *Music Ancient Nations* (1864), 59.]

Pooja, See **Puja**.

Poojari See **Pujari**.

Poolbundy [18C. H/P. *pulbandī*, fr. *pul'a* 'bridge' + *bandi*, 'embankment', 'securing of bridges and embankments'.] Former name, in Bengal, of a civil department in charge of embankments. Also sometimes used improperly for the embankment itself. [YB; Verelst, *View of Bengal* (1772), App. 213.]

Poon, peon, pohoon [17C. Kan. *ponne;* M. *punna;* Tam. *punnai;* Sinh. *pūna;* S. *punnāge.*] A timber tree, *Calophyllum inophyllum*, furnishing ships' masts and spars, and wood for building purposes. Also 'poon-oil' from its seeds, used medicinally and as lamp-oil. [OED & YB; Dampier, *Voy.* (1699), II. 1.64.]

Poonac [19C. Tam. *punnaku;* Sinh. *punakku.*] Coconut-oil cake, used as fodder and manure. [OED; Whitworth (1885).]

Poonah[1] (adj) [19C.] The former summer capital of Maharashtra. *Poonah*-painting on rice- (or other thin) paper; imitating oriental work by application of thick body-colour, with little or no shading, and without background. Also: *Poonah*-paper. *Poonah*-brush. (Modern spelling Pune.) [OED; *Examiner* (1821), 272/2.]

Poona(h)[2] (adj) [20C.] Alluding to the **Pukka** lifestyle supposedly characteristic of British officers stationed there during the **Raj**. [OED; G. Treast, *Best One-Act Plays, 1938* (1939), 63.]

Poonga-oil [19C. Tam. *punga;* M. *pūngam.*] A dark-yellow oil expressed from the seeds of the *Pongamia glabra* or *Pongam-tree*, used in India as a lamp-oil, and for treatment of skin diseases. *See* **Kurung**. [OED; *Treas. Bot.* (1866), 919/1.]

Poo(n)gye [19C. H. *pūngī.*] A snake-charmer's pipe. A nose-flute. [Engel, *Music Ancient Nations* (1864), 59.]

Poorub, poorbea [17C. H. *pūrab, pūrb,* 'the East, fr. S. *pūrba, pūrva,* 'in front of'.] 'In upper India the term meant Oudh, the Benaras division and Bihar. Hence *Poorbea* (*Pūrbiya*), a man of those countries who was, in the days of the old Bengal army, often used for a sepoy, the majority being recruited in those provinces.' [YB; Sir T. Roe, *Embassy to the Court of the Great Mogul* (1615-19).]

Pootly nautch [19C. H. *putlī-nach.*] A puppet dance (show). In full: *kāth-putlī-nāch,* 'wooden- puppet-show'. [YB.] Also *Pootleepuppet,* a mere nothing; a man of no standing or consequence. *See* **Nautch**. [1856 in Maud Diver's *Honoria Lawrence* (1936), 464; Mrs. Sherwood's Stories (1817), 221.]

Pop(p)adam, popper-cake *See* **Pap(p)adam**.

Porgo, purgoo [17C. Anglo-Indian corr. of an Indian corr. of Pg. *barco, barca.*] 'Any kind of sailing-boat [used] by early Portuguese visitors to the East.' [YB; Hedges (1683), *Diary,* Hak. Soc., i. 65.]

Portia [19C. Corr. of Tam. *Purvarassu,* 'flower-king'.] The Umbrella-tree, *Thespesia populraea* alias **Bhendi** or The Indian Tulip Tree, of the family *Malvaceae*. It is a tropical evergreen tree bearing large crinkled yellow flowers from which, and from the fruit, a yellow dye is obtained. Its fruit juice is used as a cure for scabies and other skin diseases, a tonic is concocted from the roots and the inner bark provides a tough fibre for cordage, while the bark and wood contain tannin and yield a red dye. [OED & YB; Cleghorn, *Forests and Gardens in S. India* (1861), 197.]

Posh [20C. Etym. obscure.] Slang: smart, splendid, first-class, elegant.] Anglo-Indian usage considered this word (erroneously) to be an acronym based on the expression 'Port Out Starboard Home', referring to the most comfortable, expensive way of travelling by ship to and from India. *See* **Palampore**. [OED; Wodehouse, *Tales of St. Austin's* (1903), 37.]

Posta [17C.] A spiced infusion of **Opium**, fr. H/P. *pōst,* 'skin', 'rind', 'poppy-head'. [OED; Fryer, *Acc. E. India & P.* (1698), 32.]

Post(h)een, postin [19C. Pash. /P. *postīn,* fr. *post,* 'a hide or pelt'.] An Afghan leathern (sheepskin) pelisse with the fleece on. [OED & YB; Elphinstone (1815), *Acc. Caubul* (1842), ii. 59.]

Poti, pothi [H. *pothi.*] A palm-leaf book. [Hawkins, *CIWIE*.]

Potwari *See* **Patwari**.

Pottah *See* **Patta** and **Patwari**.

Poya [Sin. *poya.*] Buddhist rest-days, at new moon, first quarter, and full and last quarter of the moon. [Hawkins, *CIWIE*.]

Praag [16C. S. *Prayāga,* 'the place of sacrifice'.] The old Hindu name of Allahabad, espec., of the river confluence of the Jumuna, Ganges, and the mythical Saraswati, sacred to Hindus. *See* **Tirtha**. [YB; Fitch (1585), in *Hakluyt*, ii. 386.]

Prabhat-pheri [20C. H. *prabhāt,* 'morning' + *phēri.*] 'morning-procession or walk.' Esp. of Indian politicians singing political songs. [Hawkins, *CIWIE*.]

Prabhu, parbha, parvoe, purvo, parbhu [17C. S. *prabhu,* 'lord or chief'.] The popular name of the 'writer caste' in Western India, 'an honorific title assumed by the caste of **Kayasth(a)**, one of the mixed castes which commonly furnished *writers.*' [YB.] A Bombay term only. *See* **Cranny**. [Forrest, *Bombay Letters, Home Series* (1676-7), I. 125.]

Pradakshina [19C. S. *pradaksinā*, fr. *pra*, 'in front' + *daksinā*, 'right'.] Devotional clockwise circumambulation, in the *sanctum sanctorum* of Hindu and Buddhist temples, as a form of worship. [*OED;* E. Moor, *Hindu Pantheon* (1810), 327.]

Prakrit, Pracrit [18C. S. *prākrta*, 'natural, unrefined, vulgar', opp. of **Sanskrta**, 'refined, polished, prepared'.] A general name for the vernaculars that existed alongside, or evolved from, **Sanskrit,** bearing the same relation for example, as the Romance languages bear to Latin. The most completely preserved of the old Prakrits is **Pali,** the language of the sacred Buddhist scriptures, in Sri Lanka, Burma and elsewhere. The Prakrits are used by ladies, and by inferior characters, in the Sanskrit dramas. Also *Prakritic* (1875) and *Prakritize* (1881) [*OED* & YB; J. Cleland, *Way to Things by Words* (1766), 88.]

Prakriti [19C. S. *pra*, 'higher' + *kriti*, 'action'.] Hinduism: Nature; Cosmic Nature and Man's Nature; that which acts constantly to maintain a balance of the three **Gunas (Sattva, Rajas,** and **Tamas)** in contrast to **Purusha** (spirit). (**Sankhya** philosophy.) [Sir Charles Eliot, *Hinduism & Buddhism* (1921), II. 217.]

Pralaya [20C. S. *pralaya*.] Dissolution, destruction, espec. of the whole world at the end of a **Kalpa**. [*OED;* Joyce, *Ulysses* (1922).]

Prana [19C. S. *prana*, 'the breath of life'.] The life principal; life-giving force or inspiration. Hence, *pranic* (adj), and *pranayama*, the Hindu (**yoga**) system of breath control, which became an important part of a *Sufism* in Iran and Ghazni as early as the 10th century. [*OED;* Colebrooke in *Trans. R. Asiatic Soc.* (1830), II. ii.]

Pranam [19C. S. *pranām.*] Respectful bow or salutation. *See* **Namaste, Kudumbosee, Namaskara**. [Hawkins, *CIWIE.*]

Prasad(am) [19C. H. *prasād*, fr. S. *prasāda*, 'clearness, kindness, grace'.] Offerings (coconut etc.) to the temple god, afterwards shared among devotees. Also divine grace or favour. (Sb. attrib.) [*OED;* H. H. Wilson, in *Asiatic Res.* (1828), xvi. 83; Hopkins, *Relig. India* (1895), xv. 429.]

Pratyahara [19C. S. *pratyāhāra*.] Yoga phil. Self-mastery, restraint, withdrawal of the senses from external objects. [*OED;* Cowell, tr., *Acharya's Sarvana-Darshana Samgraha* (1882), xv. 267.]

Presidency, President [17C.] An area in India administered by a *President,* was called a *Presidency,* and such a *President* was the head of the East India Company's **Factory** in that area. *Presidency-towns* were Madras (1683); Bombay (1687); Calcutta (1699). [*OED* & YB; Fryer, *Acct. E. India & P.* (1698), iv.]

Prickly-Heat [18C.] 'A troublesome cutaneous rash, *Lichen tropicus,* in the form of small red pimples which itch intolerably.' [YB.] It affects many Europeans and some Indians in the hot-weather season. *See* **Red Dog**. [*OED* & YB; Wesley (1736), *Wks.* (1830). I. 36; 1807 in *Lord Minto in India* (1807-14; ed. 1880).]

Prickly pear [18C.] Various cactaceous plans of the genus *Opuntia,* and some *Euphorbias;* at one time called *Cactus Indica,* now spread throughout India, with pear-shaped, fleshy, edible fruit. Also the fruit itself. [*OED* & YB; Grainger, *The Sugar-Cane Bkl.* (1764).]

Prow, parao, prahu, prawl [16C. Pg. *proa,* the fore part of a sailing vessel, transferred by synecdoche to the whole vessel, e.g. in Malay *prahu;* M. *paru,* 'a boat'.] A general term for any vessel, but usually for small, swift craft. [*OED* & YB; Litchfield's *Castañeda* (1582), f. 62 C.]

Pucka *See* **Pukka**.

Puckauly, puckaul pakhal(i) [18C. H. *pakhāli*, fr. *pakhāl*, 'a water-skin'.] A water-carrier. *See* **Bheestie**. [*OED* & YB; Munro, *Narrative* (1789), xiii 183.]

Puckerow, puckerow [19C. H. *pakrana*.] 'to cause to be seized.' (Imp. *pakro,* cause (him) to be seized, or, perhaps more correctly the imp. of a compound verb *pakarāo,* 'seize and come', or in our (English) idiom, 'go and seize'. 'But *puckerow* belongs essentially to the dialect of the European soldier and in that becomes of itself a verb 'to puckerow', i.e. 'to lay hold of' (generally a recalcitrant native). The conversion of the Hind. imperative into an Anglo-Indian verb infinitive, is not uncommon; compare **Bunow, Dumbcow, Gubbrow, Lugow**. [YB & *OED;* Trevelyan, *The Dawk Bungalow* (1866), 390.]

Pug, pug-mark [19C. H. *pug;* S. *padaka,* 'a foot'.] In Anglo-Indian usage, the paw-marks of a wild animal. Also: *puggy, puggi* (1824) (H.

pagī) 'a professional tracker; the name of a caste, or rather an occupation, whose business is to track thieves by footmarks and the like.' (1824). [YB & *OED;* 1831 in *Orient. Sport. Mag.* (rpt. 1873), ii. 178.]

Puggle, puggled, puggly, poggle [19C. H. *pāgal,* 'a madman, an idiot'.] An Anglo-Indian colloquialism for a fool, foolish; idiot, idiotic. Hence. a *poggle-nautch,* a frenzied dance; *poggle-khana,* lit. 'a fool's meal', a picnic; *poggle-gymkhana,* 'light-hearted club (equestrian) competitions; *poggle-pahni,* 'idiot-water', rum; and *puggled, poggled,* 'mad-drunk', or Anglo-Indian equivalent of 'round the bend', 'off one's rocker', 'a screw loose', etc. [*OED* & YB; Shipp, *Memoirs* (1829), II. viii. 233.]

Pug(g)ree, pug(g)ri, puggerie [17C. H. *pagrī,* 'a turban'.] An Indian light turban; a scarf or veil wound round a **Topi** (1859); 'Key-money': in India, the under-the-counter additional pre-payment by the buyer made to the seller of a house or other property to 'wrap up' the sale. *Puggree dālna,* 'to put a turban on someone's head' = to cheat (slang). Also *Puggree-wallah* (1808), 'a native'. [*OED* & YB; Sir T. Herbert (1665), *Travels* (ed. 1677), 140; E. Jenkins, *The Cooli* (1871).]

Puhur, pore, pyre [17C. H. *pahar,* fr. S. *prahara.*] A fourth part of the day and of the night; a watch, or space of eight *gharis* (*see* **Ghurry**). [YB; Bruton (1633) in *Hakl.* (1807), v. 51; Fryer (1673), *New Acct.* (1672-81), 186.]

Puja, pooja [18C. H/S. *pūjā.*] Hinduism: any religious rite, but above all that performed by a **Pujari** in a Hindu temple in worship of the idol or god of that temple. '*Jhandā Ji pūjā*', or 'pooja of the Flag', was the Sepoy term, for what in St. James's Park is called 'Trooping of the Colours'. Used in the plural, *poojas* are the festivals of **Durga Puja**, or **Dusserah** in October-November. [*OED* & YB; Halhed (1776), *Code of Gentoo Laws,* Pref. (1863), xcix; Trevelyan, *Competition Wallah* (1866), 295.]

Pujari poojari [19C. H/S. *pujārī.*] An officiating Hindu priest of a Hindu temple, who also performs religious ceremonies of a private and public nature outside his temple. [*OED* & YB; F. Hamilton (1813), *Jrnl. Shahabad Survey* (1926), 129; Monier–Williams, *Brahmanism & Hinduism* (1891).] See **Panda²**.

Pukka, pucka [17C. H. *pakkā,* 'ripe, mature, cooked'.] A term of abundant uses: e.g.

'genuine', of a coin or contract; 'thorough', of an undertaking or investigation; 'ripe', of fruit; 'metalled', of roads; 'permanent', of appointments; 'brick and stone built', of buildings. A *pukka sahib* is, or should be, 'a real gentleman', 'the genuine article'. The antithesis of this term is **Cutcha**. '*Semi-pukka*' = 'half and half', e.g. a stone and mud building. [*OED* & YB; Fryer, *Acct. E. India & P.* (1698), 205.]

Pula [16C. Tam. *pillai; M. pilla,* 'child'.] The title of a superior class of (so-called) **Sudras** (espec. **Curnums**). 'In Cochin and Travancore it corresponds with Nayar. [*See* **Nair**.] It was granted by the sovereign, and carried exemption from customary manual labour.' [YB; Litchfield's *Castañeda* (1582), iv. 2.]

Pulicat, pullicate [17C. Place-name on the Madras coast. Tam. *pala Velkādu,* 'old Velkadu'.] A kind of cotton piece-goods used for handkerchiefs similar to **Bandanna**(s), first made at Pulicat. [YB; Danvers (1611), *Letters* (ed. 1896-1900), i. 133.]

Pulao *See* **Pilau**.

Pulla [19C.] A fish that comes to salute a saint's tomb and then returns to the sea without turning round, lest it should dishonour the saint by turning its back. [Honoria Lawrence, *Journal.*]

Pultan, pultan [19C. H. *paltan,* corr. of *battalion,* poss. with some confusion of *platoon.*] 'It was the usual native word for a regiment of native infantry: it was never applied to one of Europeans.' [YB; (1800) *Arbuthnot's Mem. of Munro* (1881), lxix.]

Pulwaun [18C. H. *pahlwan;* P. **Pahlavi**. 'A native of ancient Persia.'] A champion, a professional wrestler or strong-man, cf. Malay *pahlawan,* 'a champion'. (Influenced by *awan,* 'to fight'.) [YB; Hanway, *Hist. Acct. Brit. Trade* (1759) iii. 104.]

Pulwar, pulwah [18C. H. Beng. *palwār.*] A light, keelless boat used on the rivers of Bengal, 'carrying some 12 to 15 tons'. [YB & *OED;* Holwell, *Hist. Events* etc. (1765), 1. 69.]

Pummelo *See* **Pomelo**.

Pun [17C. H. *pana.*] A certain number of cowries; generally, eighty. (S. *pana* = 'a stake played for a price, a sum', hence both a coin (whence **Fanam**) and a certain amount of cowries. [YB; Hedges, *Diary,* 2 Oct. 1683.]

Punch¹ [19C.] Short form of **Panchayat**.

Punch² [17C. Attributed (doubtfully) to H. *pānch,* 'five' (P. *panj,* S. *pancham*).] An intoxicating concoction traditionally made of five ingredients: viz., *arrack*, sugar, lime-juice, spice, and water, with variations. A beverage now usually made with wine, spirits, hot- water, or hot-milk, with sugar, lemons, spice, cordial, or some of these. Also: *punch-bowl* (1658); *-house* (1652), the Portuguese and Anglo-Indian drinking tavern in India; and *punchery* (1825), etc. [*OED* & YB; R. Addams 28 Sept. 1632, Let. to T. Colley Merchant at Pattapoli (IOL).]

Pundit, pandit [17C. H/S. *pandita*, 'learned [man]'; *panda*, 'learning, understanding'.] Cf. Pg. *pandito*, 'a learned Hindu', one well-versed in **Sanskrit**, philosophy, religion and Hindu law. The pundit of the Supreme Court was a Hindu law-officer who advised the British judges on questions of Hindu Law. This office became extinct in 1862. Also, any learned expert or teacher, often applied jocularly. Also *punditry* (1926) and *pundita* a female *pundit*. [*OED* & YB; Bernier (1684), *Travels*. E. tr., 85 (ed. Constable), 264; J.I.M. Stewart, *Madonna of Astrolabe* (1977), iii. 51.]

Punjab(i) [17C. H. *punjāb(i)* fr. P. *panj*, 'five' + *ab*, 'water'.] An extensive region of the Indian subcontinent, so called because of its five rivers: **Indus**, Jelum, Chenab, Ravi, Beas. (If the Sutlej is included the Indus is excluded.) Now divided between India and Pakistan. Also *punjabi*, loose shirt; *punjabis*, shirt and trousers in Punjabi style; *Punjabi head*, forgetfulness (1949); *Punjabi-bat* (1984), a new concept, representing the life-style and ethos that binds together Punjabis of different religious persuasions. [*OED* & YB; *Today*, 30 April 1984; Sir T. Herbert) (*c*. 1630), *Travels* (ed. 1677), 63.]

Punji, panji(e), panja, punge [19C. Prob. fr. a Tibeto-Burman language.] A sharpened (poisonous) bamboo stake set in a hidden hole in the ground as a trap for enemy attackers (or occas. animals). Also: *punji-stake* and *punji-stick*, and vb. intrans. 'to punji'. [*OED*; E. Dalton, *Descriptive Ethnol. Bengal* (1872), ii,]

Punkah [17C. H. *pankhā*; S. *pakshaka*, fr. *paksha*, 'a wing'.] (1) Formerly a fan made from the **Palmyra** leaf, *Borassus flabellifer*, or 'fan-shaped'.] [Finch in Purchas, *Pilgrimes* (1625), iv. iv. vi. 439.] (2) A large swinging fan made of cloth suspended on a frame from the ceiling or rafters, and worked by a rope pulled by a *punka*-wallah (1807). Anglo-Indian phrase: 'under the punkah' = 'sub-rosa,' '*entre nous*'. [Ld. Minto (15 Sept. 1807), in

Life & Letters (1880), 27.] (3) Any mechanical or electric fan. [*OED* & YB.] Also: *punkah-coolie* (1859); *-wallah* (1857); *-ropes* (1870); and a verb, *punkawing* (1625).

Punsaree [19C. H. *pansārī*, fr. S. *panyasāla*, 'a market, warehouse'.] A native drug-seller. [YB; Fraser, *The Persian Adventures* (1830), iii. 23.]

Punya [S. *pūnya*.] Virtues; (adj.) sacred. [Sir Charles Eliot, *Hinduism & Buddhism* (1921), I. 107.]

Purana(s), Poorana(s) [17C. S. *purāna*, 'old, legendary'.] A class of sacred poetical works in Sanskrit, 18 in all, containing the myths and legends of the Brahmins. Hence: *Puranic* (1809) [*OED* & YB; Toland, *Christianity not Myst.* (1696), 31; Tavernier, *Travels* (E. tr. ed. Constable, 1684), 335.] See **Smriti**.

Purdah [17C. H/P. *pardah*, 'curtain, veil'.] (1) A curtain, espec. to screen women from the sight of men and strangers. See **Harem**, **Zenana**. [*Misc. Tracts in Asiatic Ann. Reg.* (1800), 64/1; Lord Valentia, *Travels* (1809), I. 100.] (2) Seclusion of women. Phrase: 'In Purdah' = *purdah nashin* [*Daily Tel.* (1865), 28. Nov. 8/6.] (3) Striped cotton cloth, or other curtain material. [Simmonds, *Dict. Trade* (1858).] Transferred uses: (medical) isolation or quarantine; secrecy. (Galsworthy, *Swan Song* (1928), II. v. 143.] Also: *purdah*-lady (1902); *-wallah* (1847); *-system* (1894); *-women* (1900); *-girl* (1971); *-costume* (1905); *-curtain* (1955); *-glass* (1973); *-party* (1975). And, *purdah nashin*, a woman who observes the rules of seclusion, 'behind the curtain'. Hence: *purdahed* (1832). See **Gosha** and **Burka** [*OED* & YB.].

Purdesee, pardesi [19C. H. *par(a)desi*, 'one from a foreign country'.] 'In the Bombay army the term was universally applied to a sepoy from North India, and in the N.W.F.P., to a wandering tribe of swindlers and coiners.' [YB; Kipling, *Kim* (1901).]

Puree, puri [20C. H. *puri*.] A small disc of wheaten cake, fried in **Ghee** and oil. [Hawkins, *CIWIE*.]

Purnima [19C. S. *purni*, 'full' + *ma(na)* 'moon'.] Full moon, the 15th day of the Hindu synodical month. [Whitworth, *Anglo-Indian Dict.* (1885).]

Purohit [S. *purōhita*, fr. *puras*, 'before' + *hita*, 'placed'.] Hindu family priest, generally hereditary. [Whitworth, *Anglo-Indian Dict.* (1885); Sleeman, *Rambles & Recollections* (1844), 140.]

Purree [19C. H. *peori.*] A yellow colouring matter, from which 'Indian-yellow' is prepared; the magnesium salt of purreic acid, $C_{19}H_{16}O_{12}$. [*OED;* Fownes, *Chem* (4 ed. 1852), 582.]

Purum [20C. Anthrop.] Name of a tribe of mongoloid people living near the Indo-Burmese border whose kinship system is characterized by matrilineal, cross-cousin marriage. [*OED;* J. Shakespear, *Lushei Kuki Clans* (1912), II. ii. 150.]

Purusha [19C. S. *purusha,* 'man'.] Hinduism: In **Sankya** philosophy, spirit (male) as opposed to **Prakriti,** matter (female), the union of which creates individual souls and the phenomenal world. [Whitworth, *Anglo-Indian Dict.* (1885).]

Purwana, perwanna, perwauna [17C. H/P. *parwāna,* 'an order'.] A grant or letter under royal seal; a letter of authority from an official to his subordinate; a licence or pass. [YB.] *See* **Hosbolhookum.** [Hedges, *Diary,* 10 Oct. 1682 (Hak. Soc. 1886), i. 34.]

Pushto *See* **Pashto.**

Putchuk, putchook, putchock [16C. Etym. uncertain.] A trade name for a Himalayan fragrant root, *Aplotaxis auriculata,* alias *Aucklandia costus,* used in making incense and *joss-sticks. See* **Costus** and **Agarbatties.** [YB; Caesar Frederick (1588), in Hak. (1807), ii. 343.]

Putney, putnee [18C. H/Beng. *pattañi, patnī,* fr. *patnā,* 'to be agreed'.] (1) Goods commissioned or manufactured to order. [YB; Long (1755), *Selections Records Ft. William* (1748-67).] (2) A kind of sub-tenure in Bengal, held by a *patidar. See* **Pottah (Patta).** [YB; Wilson, *Glossary* (1855); Grant, *Rural Life in Bengal* (1860), 64.]

Puttee, putty[1] [19C. H. *pattī,* 'band, bandage'.] A long strip of cloth wound spirally round the leg from ankle to knee (by soldiers and others) for protection. 'A special kind of cloth appears in the old trade-lists under the name of *puteahs.*' [YB.] Also: *Putty-wallah* (one with a belt', a messenger (1878), adj. putteed. *See* **Chaprassi (Chuprassi).** [*OED;* Drew, *Jummoo* (1875), 175.]

Puttee, putty[2] [19C. *See* prec.] 'In the N.W.P. an original share in a joint or coparcenary village or estate comprising many villages.' Hence: *putteedaree* (H. *pattidārī*), 'tenure of this kind'. [YB; Raikes, *Notes on the N.W.P. of India* (1852), 94.]

Puttee, putty[3] [19C. Kan. *patti.*] A written statement of any kind. In S. India, soldiers' pay. [YB; Wilks, *Hist. Sketches* (1810-27; 2nd ed. 1869), I. 415.]

Puttoo [19C. H/Punj. *pattu,* fr. old Kash. *patu,* allied to S. *pata,* 'woven stuff', 'cloth'.] Fabric made of the coarse hair of the Cashmere goat; tweed. [*OED;* Keith Young (1857), *Siege of Delhi* (1902), 110; *Maud Diver* (1844), *Honoria Lawrence* (1936), 292.]

Putwa [19C. H. *patwā.*] 'The *Hibiscus sabdariffa,* from the succulent flowers of which very fair jelly was made in Anglo-Indian households. It is also known as the Rozelle or Red Sorrel.' [YB; Riddell, *Indian Domestic Economy* (1871), 337; Watt, *Dict. Econ. Prod. India* (1889-93), iv. 243.]

P.W.D. [Anglo-Indian.] From initials of Public Works Departments; a government department in charge of public buildings, roads, bridges, canals, etc. etc.

Putwari *See* **Patwari.**

Pyal, pial [16C. S. Indian langs. *poyal,* 'seat or bench'.] A raised platform for sitting-out purposes; a verandah in S. India. [*OED* & *YB.*] *See* **Chabootra.** Also attrib. *pyal-school* [Litchfield's *Castañeda* (1582), vi. 3; Gover in *Ind. Antiq.* (1873), II. 52.]

Pyjama(s), pajama(s) [19C. H. *pae,* 'foot' + *jāmah,* 'clothing'.] Loose drawers or trousers tied round the waist, worn by women and men in India, espec. Sikhs (men) and Muslims (both sexes). Adapted by Anglo-Indians and afterwards others, as a sleeping-suit, with jacket. Also, *beach-pyjamas* (1928); *pyjama-party* (1928); and jocularly *pyjams* (1926) and *pyjies* (1962). *See* **Mogul Breeches, Shalwars, Long-Drawers.** [*OED* & YB; *Misc. Tracts in Asiat. Ann. Reg.* (1800), 342/2; J. Betjeman, *Summoned by Bells* (1960), vii. 66.]

Pyke, paik [17C. H. *paik;* M. *payak;* P. *paik,* 'a foot-runner'. (S. *padātika*).] A footman, an armed attendant, an inferior police and revenue officer, a messenger, a courier, a village watchman, a foot-soldier. *See* **Peon.** [YB; Sir Paul Rycaut, *Present State of the Ottoman* Empire (1687), 19; Hunter, *Orissa* (1872), ii. 269.]

Pyse, pice [19C. H. *po'is.*] 'look out!' 'make way!' (S. *pasya,* 'look!' 'see!'). Cf. **Khis-Khis** & **Po-Po.** [YB; Elphinstone's *Report on Murder of G. Shastry,* in *Papers Relating to E.I. Affairs,* 14.]

Q

Qabr [19C. H/Ar. *qabr.*] Grave, tomb of a Muslim. *Quabristan*, Muslim cemetery. [Whitworth, *Anglo-Indian Dict.* (1885); Hawkins, *CIWIE.*]

Qaid-i-Azam or **Quaid-i-Azam** [20C. H/Ar. *qaid-i-azam*, 'Great leader'.] (Applied to Mohammed Ali Jinnah, who became the Qaid-i-Azam of the new Muslim state of Pakistan in 1947.) [Allan Moorhead, *The Rage of the Vulture* (1948).]

Qawal [H/P. *qawāl.*] Professional singer. *Qawali*, programme of music and song. [Hawkins, *CIWIE.*]

Quamoclit [19C. YB gives the fanciful and very unlikely etym. (taken from Fanny Parkes) as a corr. of S. *kāma-lata*, 'the creeper of *Kama*', Hindu god of love. The *OED* & Webster associate the word with a Mexican origin.] Anglo-Indian; the name given to the Red Jasmine (*Ipomea lobata*). [*OED* & YB; Fanny Parkes, *Wanderings of a Pilgrim* (1850), I. 310. 11.]

Quedda See **Keddah**.

Queen of the Night The shrub *Cestrum nocturnum*, whose jasmine-like flowers emit a powerful scent at night.

Queen's Flower [19C.] A deciduous tree *Lagerstroemia flos-reginae*, bearing purple or mauve or pink blossoms. 'Second only in importance to the **Teak**, the timber of the Queen's Flower is of great value for posts, boats, casks and furniture.' [*OED*; Cowen, *Flowering Trees and Shrubs in India* (1965); *Cent. Dict.* (1891).]

Qui-hi, Koi-hai, Ki-hi, etc. [19C. H. *koi-hai?* 'Is anyone there?'] The popular distinctive nickname of the (Bengal) Anglo-Indians (*koi-hais*), from the usual manner of their calling servants in clubs and homes. Cf. **Mull** (in Madras) and **Duck** (in Bombay). [*OED* & YB; 'Quiz', *The Grand Master, or Adventures of Qui-Hi in Hindostan, a Hudibrastic Poem* (1816).]

Quilla See **Killa**.

Quirpele [Tam. *kirippillai*, 'little squeaker'.] The mongoose, *Herpestes griseus.* [YB.] See **Mongoose**.

Qul [Ar. *qul.*] Prayers for the dead. [Hawkins, *CIWIE.*]

R

Rabi, rubbee [18C. H/Ar. *rabi*, 'the Spring'.] In India the crops, or the harvest of the crops, sown after the rains and reaped in the following spring or early summer. Such crops are wheat, barley, **Gram**, linseed, tobacco, onions, carrots, turnips. [*OED* & *YB*.] *See* **Kharif.** [Verelst, *View of Bengal* (1772), App. 167.] *See* **Tur.**

Rabri [H. *rabri*.] Milk boiled with sugar till thick, and afterwards flavoured and enriched with almonds, saffron, cardamoms, etc. [Hawkins, *CIWIE*.]

Rack *See* **Arrack.**

Radaree, rahdari, rawdarrie [17C. H/P. *rāhdari*, fr. **Rahdar**, 'road-keeper'.] A transit duty; sometimes blackmail. Also the sending of prisoners by escort from one police post to another. [*OED* & *YB*; Forrest, *Bombay Letters*. Home Series (1667), i. 213.]

Raddi, ruddee [H. *raddi*.] Rubbish, refuse, trash. [Hawkins, *CIWIE*.]

Radha *See* **Krishna.**

Raga, rag [18C. H/S. *rāga*, 'colour, tone'.] The melodic base of Indian classical music. Any one of about 60 melodic formulae of such music, with rules for improvisation, but having the shape, rhythm and ornamentation prescribed by tradition. Each *raga* has definite melodic qualities that distinguish it from all other *ragas*. Also fig. [*OED*; Sir William Jones in *Asiatick Res.* (1788), I. 264.] *See* **Tal(a)** and **Vadi.**

Raga-rock [20C.] Rock music in the style of a *raga*, with improvisation. [*Journal Mus. Acad. Madras* (1968), XXXIX. 7.]

Ragi, raggy [18C. H. *rāgī*.] A cereal grass, *Eleusine coracana*, cultivated for its grain; the grain itself. (This word is derived from S. *rāga* 'red' on account of the colour of the grain). Largely cultivated as staple food in S. India. Sown from the end of June to the end of August. [*OED* & *YB*; Gleig, *Life of T. Munro* (1792), iii. 92.]

Ragmala [20C. S. *ragmala*, 'garland of ragas'.] 'Musical' painting. Transposition into painting of the values contained in melodic themes and poetry. [V.A. Smith, *Hist. of Fine Art in India & Ceylon*.]

Rahdar [17C. H/P. *rāhdār*, fr. *rāh*, 'road' + *dar*, 'agent'.] A road-keeper, or toll-gatherer. Hence: *rahdarage* (1698), the toll. *See* **Radaree**. [*OED* & *YB*; Sainsbury (1623) in *Calendar State Papers, E. Indies* (1622-4), III. 163.]

Rahu [19C. S. *rahu*, 'the seizer'.] A demon; inauspicious time; the spirit who causes eclipses by attempting to devour the sun and the moon. [Whitworth, *Anglo-Indian Dict.* (1885).]

Railway Institute [20C. Anglo-Indian.] In India a club for railway employees; sometimes one for Europeans and Eurasians and another for Indians. [*OED*; J. Masters, *Bhowani Junction* (1954), I. V. 42.]

Rains, The [17C. Anglo-Indian.] 'The common Anglo-Indian colloquial for the Indian rainy season.' [*YB*.] *See* **Winter** and **Monsoon.** [Bernier, *Travels* (E. tr., 1684), 138.]

Rain-tree [19C. Anglo-Indian. Hindi name, *Belaiti siris*.] A large, handsome tree *Enterolobium saman*, recognized by its canopy of evergreen, feathery foliage and puffs of pink flowers; brought originally to India from central America 'In India ... the name (Rain-Tree) was given because of a curious habit possessed by the tree of intermittently spraying the ground beneath with moisture.' [Cowen, *Flowering Trees in India* (1965), 42.]

Rais, reis [16C. H/Ar. *ra'īs*, fr. *rās*, 'head' chief. Also Pg. *arraes, arrais*.] (1) In Ar. meaning the captain or master of ship, not the owner. [*OED* & *YB*; Washington, E. tr., *Nicholay's Voy.* (1585), I. vii.] (2) In India 'a native gentleman of respectable position'. [*YB*; *Pioneer Mail*, 13 April 1900.] (3) A chief or governor. [*OED*; Taverner, E. tr., *Travels* (1678), I. V. 228.]

Raita [19C. H. *raita*.] Vegetables in curd. [Hawkins, *CIWIE*.]

Raj [19C. H. *rāj*, 'sovereignty'.] Anglo-Indian, The Raj; British dominion or rule in India, 1858-1947. In full, *The British Raj* (1859). Also transf. *See* **Gram-Raj, Swaraj** and **Ram-Raj.** [*Asiatic Ann. Reg. Misc.* (1800), tr., 261/2; M. Thompson, *Story of Cawnpore* (1859), XVI. 229.] *See* **Raja-Yoga.**

Raja(h), Roger [16C. H/S. *rājā*, 'king', 'one whose duty is to please'.] An Indian king or prince; an honorific title for petty chiefs or important **Zemindars.** 'Among the English vulgarisms of the 18th century (also, 17th) we find the word barbarized into *Roger*.' [*YB*.] Also, *rajaship*. [*OED* & *YB*; Eden, *Decades* (1555), 22.4.]

Raja Yoga [19C. S. *rajan* 'king' + *yoga*.] (*See* **Yoga**.) A form of **Yoga** by which the devotee attains control over his mind and emotions. Also *raja-yogin*, a devotee of *raja-yoga*. [*OED*; Dvivedi, *Raja Yoga* (1885), I. 44.]

Rajas [19C. S. *rajas*.] Hinduism : One of the three **Gunas** (qualities); 'Activity, aggression, passion'. *See* **Tamas** and **Sattva**. [Sir Charles Eliot, *Hinduism & Buddhism* (1921), II. 298.]

Rajasthani [20C.] The Indo-European language of *Rajasthan* (erstwhile Rajputana). *See* **Rajput**. Also, adj. pertaining to this language and the Rajasthan people; spec. used for a style of Indian dancing. *See* **Kathak**. [*OED*; *Jrnl. R. Asiat. Soc.* (1889; 1901), 787.]

Rajmahal(i) [19C. (fr. the name of the Rajmahal Hills of N. India).] An aboriginal language of Central India = **Maler**. [*Jrnl. Asiat. Soc. Bengal* (1848), XVII. II. 553.]

Rajpramukh [20C. H. *rājya*, 'state' + *pramukh*, 'chief or head'.] Governor of certain princely states, between 1948 and 1956, or of the unification of a number of such states, before their absorption into the Indian Union. Also, *Uparajpramukh*, a deputy governor of such a State or States. [*OED*; *Britannica Bk. of Year* (1949), 339/1.]

Rajput, Rajpoot, Rashboote, etc. [16C. H. *Rajpūt*, S. *rāja*, 'king' + *putra*, 'son'.] A member of the Hindu warrior caste of Rajputana, claiming descent from the original **Kshatriyas**. A typical British *Hobson-Jobsonism* is the form *Rashboots*, 'a name shaped by a certain sense of aptness' as the old English travellers considered them to be 'mainly a pack of banditti'. [YB & *OED*; 1598, tr. Linschoten's Voy. xxvii. 48; Also attrib. 'a *Rashboote Gentile* in Sir. T. Roe, *Jrnl.*, 9 Oct. 1616.] *See* **Thakur**.

Rajya Sabha [20C. H/S. *rajyah sabha*, lit. 'State Assembly'.] The Upper House or Council of States of the national parliament of the Indian Union; of not more than 250 members, of whom (in 1980) 232 were elected by State Legislative Assemblies and 12 were nominated by the President of India. *See* **Lok Sabha**. [*OED*; *Whitaker's Almanack* (1948), 772/1.]

Rake [20C. Anglo-Indian.] The coupled bogies forming a railway train. [*OED*; *Sunday Standard* (Bombay), 6 July 1969.]

Rakhi [19C. H. *rakhī*, 'defence'.] Thread bracelet, esp. that given on **Coconut Day** to one considered as a brother. [Hawkins, *CIWIE*.]

Rakshas(a) [19C. S. *rakshasa*.] Hindu mythology: Demon, malignant, hideous, repellent and bloodthirsty. Something to be guarded against or warded off, esp. one of a band of demons at war with **Rama** and **Hanuman**. Also, an artistic representation of such a demon. [*OED*; Chambers's Encycl. (1866); Singha & Massey, *Indian Dances,* (1967), x. 106.]

Rakshi, raksi [19C. Nep. *raksi*, Tib. *rag-si*.] A liquor distilled from rice or grain in Nepal and Tibet.[*OED*;Wright,*Hist.Nepal* (1877),ii. 30.]

Rama [17C. S. *Rama*, lit. 'pleasing', fr. *ram*, 'to rejoice'.] The hero of the **Ramayana,** and the 7th **Avatar** of **Vishnu**. *See* **Sita**. *Rām-Rām* is a common Hindu greeting, and *Ramna-raj* in Gujarati is a proverbial expression for a time of peace and prosperity. [Whitworth, *Anglo-Indian Dict.* (1885).] *See* **Rakshas(a), Vairagi**.

Ramadan, Ramdam, Ramazan [16C. H/Ar. *ramadhan* (P. *ramazān*), fr. *ramada*, 'to be hot'.] The ninth Muslim lunar month observed as a 30 days fast during daylight hours by all Muslims. Transf. 'A lent or Ramadan of abstinence from opium.' [*OED*; De Quincey, *Confess.* (1822), II. 126; Hak., *Voy.* (1599), II. 203.]

Raman-Effect, The [20C.] The discovery by Sir C.V. Raman (1880-1970), Indian Nobel prize-winner, of the change in the frequency of light after passage through gas etc. Also, *Raman-line; -band; -shift; -active; -spectrum*. [*OED*; *Nature*, 29 Sept. 1928, 477/2.]

Ramapithecus [20C. fr. *Rama* + Gr. *pithikos*.] A fossil anthropoid ape, known from remains found in N. India and E. Africa. Hence, *ramapithecine*, a closely-related fossil anthropoid, or pertaining to it. [*OED*; *Discovery*, July 1934, 197/2.]

Ramasammy [19C. Corr. of *Ramaswami*, 'Lord Rama'.] A common Hindu personal name in S. India. Used as a generic name for Hindus. Espec. applied to Indian coolies in Ceylon (Sri Lanka). Also a twist of cotton in a tube used for a cigar-lighter. *See* **Fuleeta**. Slang; *Ramasammy* (1891), a family quarrel, a noisy gathering, a rumpus; a scrap (fight). [YB; Thackeray, *Book of Snobs* (1848), Ch. 1; *Cornhill Mag.*, Nov. 1880, 582–3.] *See* **Swami**.

Ramayana, The [18C. S. *Rāmā*, 'the Hindu god' + *ayana*, 'a going'.] A Sanskrit epic, ascribed to the poet Valmiki, concerning the exploits of Rama, the 7th **Avatar** of **Vishnu**. Also attrib., e.g., the *Ramayana epic, -influence*. [*OED*; *Asiat. Res.* (1788), I. 351.] *See* **Ramlila**.

Ramazan *See* **Ramadan**.

Ramchukor [19C.] The Himalayan snow-cock, genus *Tetrao gallus*. *See* **Chikhor** (1815). [YB; Jerdon, *Birds of India* (1862).]

Ramlila, Ram Lila [19C. H. *Rām(a)* + *līlā*, 'sport, deeds'.] A dramatic representation of episodes from the **Ramayana**, commemorating the victory of Rama over *Ravana*, performed during the festival of **Dusserah**. See **Ras Lila**. [*OED*; Oman, *Great Indian Epics* (1894), I. iii. 71.]

Ramoosy [19C. Mahr. *Ramosī*.] Name of a tribe or caste in W. India (said to be from Mahr. *ranavāsī*, 'jungle-dweller'.) Orig. a community of thieves; afterwards employed as watchmen, **Chokidar(s)**, by Anglo-Indian families, on the principle of setting a 'thief to catch a thief'. The *Ramosī* dialect was used as a secret argot among *Ramoosies*. [YB; Alexander Mackintosh, *Acct. Tribe Ramoosies* (1833), 19; E. H. Aitken, *Tribes on my Frontier* (1881).]

Ramphul [H. *ramphal*.] The tree, *Anona reticulata*, whose fruit is like a large red custard-apple. [Hawkins, *CIWIE*.]

Rampuri [H. *rāmpuri*.] Flick-knife. [Hawkins, *CIWIE*.]

Ram Rajya [20C.] The object of the Indian freedom struggle = Utopia, the Kingdom of Ram, used by Gandhi to mean a society free from oppression, inequality and injustice.

Ram-Ram! [17C.] 'The commonest salutation between Hindus meeting on the road; and invocation of the deity.' [YB.] See **Po-Po, Khis-khis** and **Pyse**. [*Tavernier* (E.tr. 1684, ed. Ball), 1. 263.]

Rana [17C. Nep & H. *rānā*, 'prince', fr. S. *rājana*, 'royal'.] A title equivalent to **Raja**. (1) The title used by the Nepal ruling family from 1846-1951. [*OED* & YB.] (2) Masc. of **Rani**. [Fryer (1673), *New Acct.* (1672-81), 162.]

Ramraj [20C. H. *Rama* + *raj*, 'government'.] The kingdom of God (in India). Cf. **Raj, Gram- raj** and **Swaraj**.

Randy [18C. poss. fr. E. *rant*, to use violent language.] *Rand* in Marston's *Malcontent*, IV. 4. Also prov. E. *randy*, 'wild', 'mad'; 'to toss about', 'to copulate' (as animals). Perh. influenced by H. *randi-baz*, 'a lecher'. 'Sexually excited, lecherous, lustful.' Cf. Mahr. *randiya*, 'libertine, lecher', 'addicted to women'. [Partridge, *Dict. of Slang* (1961), Vol. ii; J. Halliwell, *Dict. of Archaic & Provincial Words* (1847); Grose, *Prov. Gloss.* (1787).]

Rangoli [20C. H. *rangolī*.] Traditional floor decoration of sprinkled rice flour. [Hawkins *CIWIE*.]

Rangri, -ee [19C.] A form of the Malvi dialect of Rajasthan. [*OED*; J. Malcolm, *Mem. Central India* (1823), II. xiv. 166.]

Rani, Ranee, Rannie [17C. H. *rānī*, fr. S. *rājnī* (= *regina*), fem. of *rajan*, **Rajah**.] A Hindu queen; a Rajah's wife. Also, an honorific title. See **Rana**. [*OED* & YB; Fryer (1673), *Acct. E. India* (1672-81, P. IV. iii. 162.]

Rao, Raw, Row [18C. H. *rao*, 'chief prince', fr. S. *rajan*, 'king'.] (1) In W. & N.W. India a title given to a chief or prince, and affixed to the names of other distinguished men. [*OED*; 1799 in *Asiat. Res.* vi. 67; (2) a common personal or family name in S. India.

Ras(a)¹ [18C. S. *rasa*, 'juice'] Hinduism; essence, character, feeling, sentiment. [*OED*; F. Wilford in *Asiat Res.* (1799), vi. 503.]

Rasa² [19C. S. *rāsa*, 'dance, sport'.] A rustic Manipuri Indian dance (commemorating that) performed by **Krishna** and the **Gopis**; a festival celebrating this. [*OED*; H. H. Wilson in *Asiat. Res.* (1828), XVI. 92.]

Rasam, resam [Tam. *rasam*.] Spiced pepper-water. See **Mulligatawny**. [Hawkins, *CIWIE*.]

Rasamala [19C. M. *rasamala*, fr. S. *surasa*, 'sweet' + *mala*, 'garland'.] A tall E. Indian tree, *Altingia excelsa*, or *Liquidambar altingia* yielding a sweet-smelling resin. [*OED*.] See **Rose-Mallows**. Also attrib. [Raffles, *Java* (1817), I. 43.]

Raseed [19C. Anglo-Indian fr. H. *rasīd*, 'corr. of the English 'receipt', shaped probably by the Persian *rasīda*, 'arrived'.] Viz. an acknowledgement that a thing has 'come to hand'. [YB; Burton, *Sind Revisited* (1877), I. 282.]

Rasgulla [20C. H. fr. *ras*, juice + *gol*, ball.] A spongy Indian sweetmeat, made from milk, sugar, various flavours and soaked in syrup. [Veeraswamy, *Indian Cookery* (1936), 207.]

Rasika, [S. *rasika*.] Connoisseur; one who appreciates with interest and feeling. [Hawkins, *CIWIE*.]

Raslila, Ras Lila [S. *ras līla*.] A folk dance-drama on the **Radha-Krishna** theme, commemorating the *ras* which Krishna danced with the **Gopis** of Vrindavan. It is found in many parts of India, but is a special feature in the *Ras Mandals* during the festivals of *Vasanth, Holi* and *Janamashtami* at Vrindavan and Mathura. This folk-dance has traditionally three parts: *Nrtya ras*, prologue; *Sangeet*, didactic piece; and *Lila*, the dance proper, which is danced in a circle. See **Ram Lila**. [Singha & Massey, *Indian Dances* (1967), 134.] See **Manipuri**.

Rasta-roko [20C. H. *rasta*, 'road' + *roko*, 'shut, stop', imp. of *rokana*.] Road-closure. A 20th century political device of protest in India against authority, or propaganda for a social or religious cause, by blocking all traffic on the road. *See* **Bandh, Gherao, Dharna.**

Ratemahatmaya [19C. Sinh. fr. *rate*, 'of the district' + *mahatmaya*, 'great [souled] man'.] The chief headman of a Kandyan district in Sri Lanka. [*OED; J. Davy, Acct. Interior Ceylon* (1821), V. 147.]

Rat-bird [19C. Anglo-Indian.] The striated bush-babbler, *Chatterhoea caudata* (Dumeril). [*OED* & YB; *See* E. H. Aitken, *Tribes on my Frontier* (1883).]

Rath, ruth, rut [19C. H. *rath*, 'a chariot'.] (1) 'A native carriage drawn by a pony, or oxen, and used by women on a journey'. [YB & *OED;* Mrs Sherwood (1813) in *Life* XXV (1847).] (2) A temple chariot on which the temple idol is carried on festival days. [YB; Wilks, *Sketches* (1810-17).] (3) The name of the chess-piece. 'rook', in India. [YB.]

Rat-snake *See* **Dhaman.**

Rattan, rotan, rota [16C. Malay, *rōtan*, prob. fr. *rāut* (*rawat*) 'to pare, to trim, to strip'.] Species of *Calamus;* stem of this, or sticks made therefrom, 'when split, are used to form the seats of cane-bottomed chairs'. Hence; *Rattan*-chair; -furniture; -mat; -rocker; -rope; -screen; -ware. [*OED* & YB; Linschoten, *Voyages* (E. tr. 1598); Pepys, *Diary,* 13 Sept. 1660.]

Ratti, ruttee, rettie [17C. H. *rattī,* fr. S. *raktikā,* fr. *rakta,* 'red'.] The seed, a pretty scarlet pea with a black spot, of a leguminous creeper, *Abrus pecatorius,* used as a goldsmith's weight; known in England as 'Crab's Eyes'. [*OED* & YB; Purchas, *Pilgrimes* (1625), I. iii. 223; *Tavernier* (1684), E. tr., ii. 140; ed. Ball. ii. 89.] *See* **Mangelin.**

Rauza *See* **Roza.**

Rava [Mar/H. *rawa.*] Semolina. [Hawkins, *CIWIE.*]

Ravanastron [19C. Orig. unknown.] A stringed instrument played with a bow. Freq. associated with the lengendary king, Ravana; cf. S. *rāvanahasra.* 'a stringed instrument'. [*OED;* C. Engel, *Music of Most Ancient Nations* (1864), II. 81.]

Ravine Deer [19C. Anglo-Indian.] The Indian gazelle, *Gazella Benettii.* [YB; Blanford, *Mammalia* (1888–91), 526.]

Rawas [Mar. *rawas.*] The Indian Salmon, *Eleutheronema tetradactylus.* [Hawkins, *CIWIE.*]

Rayat *See* **Ryot.**

Razakar [20C. H. *Razākar.*] A Muslim volunteer, who pledges to fight in defence of his religion; a member of a fanatical body dedicated to this end. Immediately after Independence the Razakars fomented tensions in some parts of the country, espec. in Hyderabad. [*OED;* Keesing, *Contemp. Archives,* 31 July – 7 Aug. 1948, 9421.]

Reas, rees [17C. Pg. *real,* pl. *reis.*] 1/25th of an anna; 1/400th of a rupee. Small money of account formerly in use in Bombay. [YB; Fryer (1673), *New Acct.* (1672-81), 207.]

Rebab, rabab [18C. Ar. *rebāb, rabāb.*] A stringed musical instrument among the Muslims of India; plucked or bowed, of Arabian origin. [*OED;* T. Shaw, *Trav. Barbary* and *Levant* (1738), 270.]

Red Dog [18C.] *See* **Prickly-Heat.**

Reeper, reaper [18C. Mar. *rīp.*] In Anglo-Indian house – building, small laths laid across the rafters of a sloping roof to support the tiles. [*OED;* & YB; Wheeler (1734-5), *Madras in the Olden Time* (1861), III. 148.]

Regur, regar [19C. H. *regar,* 'black soil'; Tel. *rēgada,* 'clay'.] The peculiar black loamy calcareous soil rich in clay, called by Anglo-Indians 'black cotton soil', particularly located on the Deccan Plateau, and formed mainly by the weathering of basaltic rock. [*OED* & YB; *Edin. New Philosoph. Jrnl.* (1828), VI. 119; *Ma. Geol. India.* (1879), i. 434.]

Reh [19C. H. *reh;* S. *rej,* 'to shine, shake, quiver'.] 'A saline efflorescence which comes to the surface in extensive tracts of upper India, rendering the soil sterile.' [YB; Watt, *Econ. Dict.* (1889-93), VI. pt. i. 400; W. Crooke, *The North-Western Provinces of India* (1897), 32.] *See* **Usar.**

Reinol, Reynold [16C. Pg. *reino,* 'the Kingdom (of Portugal)'.] Used by Portuguese at Goa for a 'Johnny Newcomer', and sometimes 'to distinguish the European Portuguese from the country-born'. [YB.] *See* **Castees, Griffin, Creeper.** Linschoten, *Voyages,* E. tr. (1598), ch. xxxi; A. Hamilton, *New Acct.* (1744), i. 251.]

Residency [18C. Anglo-Indian.] The official residence of a representative of the Governor-General or of the East India Company at an Indian native Court. Also attrib. 'Residency ground.' [*OED; Asiat. Ann. Reg.* (1800), II. 19/1.]

Resident [18C. Anglo-Indian.] (1) The chief of the East India Company commercial establishments in the provinces up to the organization of the Civil Service in Warren Hastings' time, and for a short time the European chief of districts. [YB & *OED; Long, Selections Ft. William* (1748-67), 3.] (2) Later, the representative of the Governor-General at an important native Court, e.g. at Lucknow, Delhi, Hyderabad and Baroda. [YB & *OED; Wellesley* (1798), *Despatches* (1837), i. 99.]

Respondentia [17C. Anglo-Indian fr. Mod. L.] An old trade technicality. 'Money which is borrowed, not upon the vessel as in bottomry, but upon the goods and merchandise contained in it, which must necessarily be sold or exchanged in the course of the voyage, in which case the borrower personally is bound to answer [respond to] the contract.' [YB & *OED.*] *See* **Jawab.** [Pringle, *Diary Ft. St. George* (1682-85), IV. 123.]

Ressaidar [19C. H/P. *Rasaīdār,* fr. *rasaī,* 'quickness of apprehension; fitness, perfection' + *dar,* 'agent'.] An Indian subaltern of irregular cavalry under the **Rissaldar.** [YB.]

Rest-House [19C. Anglo-Indian.] Government staging bungalows for officials and others 'on tour', erected at intervals of 12 or 15 miles along the roads. Much the same as **Dak-Bungalows.** Superior Rest-houses for Senior government officials are *Circuit Houses.* [*OED* & YB; Cordiner, *Desc. Ceylon* (1807), I. 205.]

Resum [19C.] Lascar's Hind. for *ration.* [YB; Roebuck, *Naval Dict.* (1811).]

Rezai, rosye [18C. H. *rāzāī,* poss. through P. *razā'ī* fr. *razidan,* 'to dye'.] Quilted coverlet or counterpane. [*OED* & YB; Busteed (1784), *Echoes of Old Calcutta* (3 ed., 1857), 195.]

Rhesus [19C. (Arbitrary use of Gk. *Rhēsus,* mythical king of Thrace).] Small catarrhine monkey common in N. India, of the genus *Macaca.* In full, *Rhesus monkey* (*Macacus rhesus*). *See* **Macaqe, Bandar** and **Rillow.** [*Penny Cycl.* (1839), xiv. 236/1.]

Rice [13C.] The food plant *Oryza sativa,* the staple food of S. India. 'it is quite poss. that Southern India was the original seat of rice cultivation. (Tam. *arisi,* 'rice deprived of husk'). Numerous combinations, e.g. *wild rice, Indian rice, rice-arrack, rice-field, rice-eater, rice-bird,* etc. etc. [*OED* & YB; *Close Roll* (c. 1234), 18 Hen. III. (1905), 381.]

Rice-Christian [19C. Anglo-Indian.] An Anglo-Indian (sarcastic) term for an Indian convert to Christianity, who sought conversion for a 'meal-ticket'. [*OED; Q. Rev.* (1816), XV. 352.]

Ricksha(w) [19C.] Abbr. of **Jinricksha.** *See* **Jennyrickshaw.** Also, auto-; scooter-; cycle-. [*OED;* Kipling, *Phantom Rickshaw* (1889), 17.] *See* **Trishaw.**

Rig Veda [18C. S. *Rigveda,* fr. *ric,* 'praise' + *veda,* 'knowledge'.] The oldest and chief **Veda,** prob. dating from *c.* 1200 or 1300 BC. [*OED;* Halhed, *Gentoo Laws* (1776), Pref. xxxii; *Trans Philol. Soc.* (1886–7), 658.] *See* **Yama.**

Rilawa [19C. Sinh. *rilawā.*] Cf. **Rillow.** The toque or red monkey, *Macaca Sinica* (or *Macacus pileatus*) of Sri Lanka. [*OED;* Tennant, *Ceylon* (1859), I. 229.]

Rillow [17C. Sinh. *rilawā.*] Bonneted Rillow, the Bonnet Macaque of S. India. [*OED;* R. Knox, *Ceylon* (1681), vi. 26.]

Ringal [19C. H. *ringal.*] Himalayan bamboo, growing at altitudes between 1000 and 2000 metres, *Arundinaria.* [Hawkins, *CIWIE.*]

Rishi, -ee [18C. S. *rishi* (uncertain etym).] A sage an ascetic, a saint, inspired poet. *See* **Maharishi,** 'great sage'. [*OED;* J. Cleland, *Way to Things by Words* (1766), 91.]

Rissala(h), ressala(h) [18C. H/P/Ar. *risāla.* Lit: The charge or commission of a *rasūl* (a civil officer employed to make arrests).] A troop of cavalrymen of regiments of native irregular cavalry or native corps of horse in India. [*OED* & YB; W. Hastings (1758), Let. in Gleig, *Mem* (ed. 1843), I. 147.]

Rissaldar, ressaldar [19C. H/P/Ar. *risāldār* (*risāla,* see prec.) + *dār,* 'agent'.] Orig. in upper India the commander of a corps of Hindustani horse, though in S. India it was applied to officers of infantry. Later applied to the native officer commanding a *Rissala* in a regiment of 'Irregular Horse'. [YB & *OED.*] *See* **Ressaidar.** [*Asiat. Ann. Reg.* (1800), 34/1; Kipling, *Barrack Room Ballads, East & West* (1892), 76.]

Rita, rta [S. *rta,* 'fit, right, true'.] The **Vedic** concept of cosmic order, that establishes regularity and righteousness in the world. [Radhakrishnan, *Ind. Phil* (1923), i. 78]

Rock-pigeon [19C. Anglo-Indian.] The common sand-grouse, *Pterocles exustus h̃industani,* found in dry areas throughout the Indian Union, except Assam. [*OED* & YB.] Hindi name: *Bhat teetar.* [Newton in *Encycl. Brit.* (1885), XIX. 84/2.]

Rock-snake [19C.] Anglo-Indian for the *python molurus,* in thick jungle near water. It kills its prey by smothering it with its thick coils; it is often upto 20 ft. long. [Whitworth, *Anglo-Indian Dict.* (1885).]

Rogue-(elephant) [19C. Sinh. *hora, sora* = S. *chora*, 'thief'.] Term used by Europens in Sri Lanka and India for an elephant, now generally (if not always) a male, living alone and usually a bold marauder and a danger to travellers. Also sometimes termed **Goonda** which means a rogue. [*OED* & YB; Tennant, *Ceylon* (1859), II. viii. iii. 327.]

Rohilla [18C. Pasht. *rōhīlah*.] (1) Inhabitant of *rōh* 'mountain' which came to represent a large part of E. Afghanistan. [*OED* & YB; Scott (1745), E. tr., *Hist. of the Dekkan*, 218.] (2) 'A name by which Afghans settled in the Bareilly district of N. India came to be known, and which gave a title to the erstwhile province *Rohilkand*, made independent in 1744, but ceased to exist in 1774. [*OED* & YB; Hastings, *Diary*, 21 Aug. 1773.]

Rohu [H. rohu.] Large freshwater fish, *Labeo rohita*, valued for food and sport. [Hawkins, *CIWIE*.]

Rohun, rohunna [19C. H. *rohun(na)*.] The febrifugal bark of the *Soymida febrifuga*. (The bark of *Strychnos nux-vomica* is also known as Rohun in Bengal.) [Simmonds, *Dict. Trade* (1858).]

Rolong [19C. Pg. *rolāo*.] Semolina. Used in S. India, and formerly in W. India for fine flour. *See* **Soojee**. [Forbes, *Or. Mem.* (1813), i. 47.]

Romal, Roomaul [17C. H/P. *rūmāl*, (*rū*, 'face' + *māl*, 'rubber').] 'A pocket handkerchief in Anglo-Indian usage. Otherwise a towel or muffler, or an ornamental handkerchief carried by a high born *parda* (**Purdah**) lady, attached to her *batwa* or tiny silk handbag.' [YB.] 'The handkerchief or bandage used by **Thugs** to strangle their victims.' [*OED*; 1615 in Cocks' *Diary*, Hak. Soc. i. 179; Sleeman, *Ramaseana* (1834), 145.]

Romany sb. + adj.[19C. Gypsy *dom*, man; S. *doma*, 'low-caste person, earning a living as a singer and dancer.'] The word *Romany* is related to N. Western Indian languages of the Indo-European family, e.g. *Rajasthani, Punjabi, Gujarati, Hindi*, etc. Also *Romany chal*, malc gypsy (1843). *Romany chi*, female gypsy (1857), *Romany rye*, nongypsy associate of gypsies (1851). [Vaux, *Flash Dict.* (1812); Borrow (1841), *Zincali* (1846), Introd. 5.]

Roocka, rocca, rooka¹ [17C. Fr. H/Ar. *ruk'a*.] A letter, a written document; a note of hand. [YB; Ft. St. Geo. Consns, 25 May 1680.]

Roocka, rocca, rooka² [17C. Tel. *rokkamu*; S. *roka*, 'buying with ready money', from *ruch* 'to shine'.] An ancient coin in S. India. [Grable, *Manual of Cuddapah* (1875), 296.]

Roorkee-chair [20C. Anglo-Indian fr. *Roorki*, place name in Uttar Pradesh.] A collapsible chair, with wooden frame and canvas back and seat. Also *Roorkee*-work, a kind of canvas-work made in Roorkee. [*OED*; 1905 in *Army & Navy Coop. Soc. Rules & Price List*, 15 March, 261/2.]

Roosa, rusa [19C. Anglo-Indian/H. *rūsa*.] *Roosa*-grass; an Indian grass, *Andropogon schoenanthus* or *Cymbopogon martini*, yielding *roosa*-oil by distillation. [*OED*; *Pop. Econ. Bot.* (1853), 279.]

Rooty [19C. Corr. of H. *rōtī*, 'bread'.] Anglo-Indian slang; *Rooty-gong*, long-service medal. [*OED*; Sala in *Illustr. Lond. News*, 7 July 1883, 3/3; Fraser & Gibbons, *Soldier & Sailor Words & Phrases* (1925).]

Rose-Apple *See* **Jamboo**.

Roselle, rosella [19C. Anglo-Indian.] The Indian Hibiscus, *Hib. sabdariffa*, from the fleshy calyx of whose flowers an 'excellent sub-acid jelly' is made. Also called red or Indian sorrel, fr. French *oseille (de Guinée)*. 'Roselle is probably a corruption of oseille.' *See* **Putwah**. [*OED* & YB; *Tait's Mag.* (1857), xxiv. 164.]

Rose-mallows [16C. Anglo-Burmese Hobson-Jobsonism. S. *rasa-māla*, 'perfume garland'.] The resin also known as Liquid Storax, of the *Liquidambar altingia*, native to Tenasserim, and used for medicinal purposes. The gum is used as incense. *See* **Rasamala**. [*OED* & YB; Linschoten, *Voyages* (Hak. Soc., E. tr. 1598), I. 150.]

Rosy Pastor [19C. H. name, *tilyar*.] Alias the Rose-coloured starling, *Sturnus roseus*. A migrant starling found all over India in Winter. [Ali and Ripley, *Birds of Ind. & Pak* (1972), 5. 163.]

Roti [20C. H. *rotī*, 'bread'.] A cake of unleavened Indian bread. (Now also current in the W. Indies. *See* **Rooty, Naan, Chapati, Paratha**. [*OED*; Chambers, Jrnl. 29 May 1920, 407/1.]

Rottle-rattle [17C. Pg. *arratel*; Ar. *ratl*. The 'Arabian pound'.] A weight used in India from the 14C. [YB; Danvers (1612), *Letters* (1896-1900), i. 193.]

Round [17C. Anglo-Indian.] Used in the sense of patrolling, going the round(s). Hence 'Rounder', 'gentleman of the Round', 'whose duty it was to visit the sentries'. [YB & *OED*; Pringle

(1683), *Diary Ft. St. George* (1683-85), 1st Ser. ii. 33.]

Roundel [17C.] An old Anglo-Indian word for an umbrella. [*OED* & YB; Fryer (1673), *New Acct.* (1672-81), 30.]

Rowannah [18C. H/P. *rawānah,* fr. *rawā,* 'going'.] A pass or permit. [YB; Verelst, *View of Bengal* (1772), App. 127.] *See* **Dustak**.

Rowce [19C. H. *raus.*] A Himalayan tree, *Cotoneaster bacillaris,* 'from which alpenstocks and walking sticks are made'. [YB; Fanny Parkes, *Wanderings of a Pilgrim* (1850), ii. 241.]

Rownee, renny [H. *raonī* (origin obscure).] 'A fausse-braye, i.e. a subsidiary enceinte, surrounding a fortified place on the outside of the proper wall and on the edge of the ditch.' [YB; J. Skinner (1799), *Mil. Mem.* (ed. 1851), i. 172.]

Rowtee [19C. H. *rāotī.*] A kind of small tent with pyramidal roof, and no projection of fly, or eaves. [YB; Broughton, *Letters,* ed. Constable (1813), 20.] *See* **Pawl, Shooldarry**.

Roy [H. *raja.*] A common (Bengali) variation of the title *rāī,* **Raja.** Also as a family name, e.g. Ram Mohun *Roy.* [Whitworth, *Anglo-Indian Dict.* (1885).]

Roza, rauza [19C. H. *rauza,* fr. Ar. *rauda.*] A garden, espec. the *rauda* of the great mosque at Medina. In India applied to the **Taj-Mahal,** 'called by the natives the *Taj-rauza'.* [YB; Forbes, *Or. Mem.* (1813), iv. 41.]

Rozya *See* **Rezai**.

Rubbee *See* **Rabi**.

Rudraksha [19C. S. *rudra,* 'Shiva', fr. *rud,* 'to weep'. (Hindu myth says Rudra wept when he was born) + *vaksha,* 'eye'; Shiva's eye.] The rosary worn by **Shaivite** devotees, strung with berries, from the shrub *Elaeocarpus ganitrus,* said to be Rudra's tears. [Stutley, *Dict. of Hinduism* (1977).]

Ruffugur [18C. H. *rafūgar,* fr. P. *rafū,* 'darning'.] A craftsman who repairs Kashmir shawls and other woollen fabrics. 'Such a man was employed by the East India Company to examine the manufactured cloths and remove petty defects in the weaving.' [YB; 1750 in 'Bengal Letter to E. I. Co.' Feb. 25. I.O.L. MSS.]

Rukh, ruk [19C. H. *rūkh,* fr. Prak. *rukka,* 'tree'.] In India, a forest (reserve) or scrub-land. [*OED;* Kipling, *Many Inventions* (1893), 191.]

Rumal *See* **Romal**.

Rumble-tumble [Anglo-Indian.] Scrambled eggs (Guj. *burghi*). *See* **Ackoori**. [A. E. James, *Ind.*

Household Management (1879), 88.]

Rum-Johnny[1] [19C. Hobson-Jobsonism, perh. from *Ramazānī,* allegedly a common Muslim name.] 'A low class of native servant who plied on the wharves of Calcutta in order to obtain employment from newcomers.' [YB; Williamson, *Vade Mecum* (1810), i. 191.]

Rum-Johnny[2] [18C. Anglo-Indian. Sl. fr. H. *rāmjanī,* S. *ramā-janī.*] 'a pleasing woman', 'a dancing-girl'. Among soldiers and sailors, 'a prostitute'. [1799 in *Life of Colebrook,* (1873), 153.]

Rumna [18C. H. *ramnā,* fr. S. *ramana,* 'causing pleasure'.] A 'chase' or reserved hunting ground. [YB; Vansittart, *Narrative Bengal* (1760-64), i. 63.]

Rupee [17C. H. *rūpiyah,* fr. S. *rūpya,* 'wrought silver'.] The standard monetary unit of the Anglo-Indian currency system, and of the Mughal Empire. It is now the unit in India, Pakistan and Sri Lanka. *See* **Anna, Pice, Paisa.** (Cf. *Rouble.*) [*OED* & YB; Withington (1612), *Trav.* (1735), 289.] *See* **Sicca**.

Rusa [19C. Malay, *rūsa.*] The East-Indian red-deer, a sub-genus of *Cervus.* [Beveridge, *Hist. India* (1862), I. Introd. II.]

Russud [19C. H/P. *rasad.*] 'Provisions of grain, forage, and other necessaries got ready by the local officers at the camping ground of a military force or official cortege.' [YB; H. H. Wilson, *Glossary* (1855).]

Rut *See* **Rath**.

Ruttee *See* **Ratti**.

Rye [19C. Romany, *rāi*] Gentleman. (cf. S. *rāja,* ruler.) *See* **Romany.** [*OED.* Borrow, *Lavengro* (1851), II. xxvi. 242.]

Ryot, rayat [17C. Fr./H. *raiyat,* fr. Ar. *ra'iyah,* 'flock herd', 'fr. *ra'a,* 'to pasture feed'.] 'It is by natives used for a subject in India, but its specific Anglo-Indian application is to 'a tenant of the soil, an individual occupying land as a farmer or cultivator.' [*OED* & YB; Purchas, *Pilgrimes* (1625), I. iii. 223.] *See* **Taccavi**.

Ryotti [18C.] *See* prec. Beng *raiyati* (of land in Bengal) held on a permanent tenure in return for payment of a certain rent. [*OED;* Verelst, *View of Bengal* (1772), 69.]

Ryotwar(i), ryotwarry [19C. *See* prec. *ryot* + *wār(i),* 'pertaining to'.] Direct settlement of land tenure between government and the **Ryot** without the intervention of a **Zemindar** or landlord. Hence: The *Ryotwary System.* [*OED* & YB; Sir T. Munro (1827), in Gleig, *Life* (1830), III. 353.]

S

Sabha [20C. H/S. *sabhā*.] Conclave, assembly parliament. *See* **Lok Sabha,** and **Rajya Sabha.** [*OED*; Keith in *Camb. Hist. of India* (1922), I. iv. 96.]

Sable-Fish [19C.] *See* **Hilsa** [YB; Bp. Heber, *Narr. of Journey* etc. (1844), I. 81.]

Sabzi, Subjee [H. *sabzī*,] Greens, vegetables. *See* **Subjee.** [Hawkins, *CIWIE*.]

Sachiv [H. *sachiv*.] Secretary; *sachivālaya*, secretariat. [Hawkins, *CIWIE*.]

Sacred cow [19C. Anglo-Indian.] (1) The cow as an object of veneration among Hindus. [*OED*; J.L. Kipling, *Beast and Man in India* (1891), vi. 116.] (2) Fig. someone or something who must not be criticized; literary copy that must not be cut or altered. [*OED*; *Atlantic Monthly*, March (1910), 308/1.] (3) Fig. an idea, institution, legal decision, political theory etc., etc. held to be immune from questioning or criticism. [*OED*; M. Mitchell, *Gone With the Wind* (1936), xiii. 240.]

Sadhana [19C. S. *sādhanā*, 'means to the goal', fr. *sadh*, 'to succeed, attain'.] Dedication: to an aim; discipline, religious training. *See* **Sadhu.** [*OED*; Sarkar, *Hindu Syst. of Relig. Sci. & Art* (1898), vii. 137.]

Sadhu [19C. S. *sādhu*, 'good, pious'.] A Hindu holy sage, ascetic, holy man, saint. Hence *sadhuism* (1803). Also 'In his sadhuship', a humorous title for a *sadhu* (1954), and *sadhri* (fem. of *sadhu*), a female sage, a chaste woman (1942). [*OED*; *Encycl. Metrop.* (1845), XXI. 672/2.]

Sadr *See* **Sudder.**

Safa [H. *safa*.] Turban. A variable length of cloth wound around the head in various caste and community ways in different parts of India. [Hawkins, *CIWIE*.]

Safflower [16C. Etym. dub. Influenced by assoc. with **Saffron** and flower, sometimes termed 'bastard saffron'.] (The dried petals of) the plant *Carthamus tinctorius*. The Hind. name is **kusumba**, or *kusum*. Exported from India for the manufacture of a red dye, used espec. in rouge; also the name of the dye. The oil from the seeds is used in cooking and making margarine. [*OED* & YB; L. Mascall, tr., *Bk. Dyeing* (1583), 20; Capt. Saris (1612) in *Purchas* (1625-6), i. 347.]

Saffron [13C. Ult. Ar. *za'farān*.] (1) Orange-coloured stigmas of the Autumn *Crocus sativus* grown in Kashmir, and used for colouring and flavouring confectionery and liquors. Also, *Safranin*, the colouring of saffron. [*OED* & YB; *Trin. Coll. Hom.* (c. 1200), 163.] (2) In S. India, the name for **Turmeric**, which the Portuguese called *açafrao da terra* ('country saffron'). (Hind, *haldi*). [*OED* & YB; *Chambers Cycl.* (1727-41).] Also attrib. saffron-coloured, -crocus, -wood, -flower, -pear, -plum, etc.

Sag¹ [19C. H. *sāg*.] Greens, spinach, pot-herbs. [Wilson, *Glossary* (1855).]

Sag² [19C. Mar. *sāg*.] The teak tree, *Tectona grandis*, native of India and Burma, and extensively cultivated elsewhere; valuable for its hard, white-ant resistant timber, extensively used for furniture, ships and buildings. The wood, bark and flowers can be used medicinally to relieve headaches, dyspepsia, bronchitis and stomach complaints. [Cowen.] *See* **Teak.** [Whitworth, *Anglo-Indian Dict.* (1885).]

Sagar-pesha [18C. H/P. *shagird-pesha*, lit. *shāgird*, 'a disciple, a servant' + *pesha*, 'business'.] Camp-followers, or a body of servants in a private establishment. [YB; Long, *Selection Records Ft. William* (1748-67), 513.]

Sago, sagow, sagoe [16C. Mal. *sagu*, via Pg. *sagu*.] The farinaceous pith of the palm *Metroxylon laevis* etc. used as food and starch. [YB; Eden, *Decades* (1555), 229; Litchfield's *Castañeda* (1582), E. tr. vi. 24; Drake (1628), *The World Encompassed* (Hak. Soc. 142).]

Sagwire [17C. Pg. *sagueira*, fr. **Sagu.**] The **Gomuti** (Malay) palm, *Arenga sacharifera*, which yields *sago* of an inferior sort. Its most important product, however, is the sap which produces **Toddy,** and which in former days also afforded almost all the sugar used by natives in the islands (of the Indian Archipelago) as well as poisonous juice for the darts of the blow-pipe, *sumpitan* (Mal.) [*OED* & YB; Grew, *Musaeum* (1681), iv. iii. 377; Forrest, *Voy. Calcutta to Mergui* (1791), 73.]

Sahib [17C. H/Ar. *sāhib* (companion).] Title given to, or assumed by, former Anglo-Indians and other Europeans in India, meaning 'lord' or 'master'. (*See* **Dorai.**) Often affixed to the name of an office: Inspector *Sahib*; Colonel *Sahib*; Collector *Sahib*; even Sergeant *Sahib*; *Lat* (Lord) *Sahib* (Governor or Governor-General); *Lat Padre Sahib* (Bishop), or to the

proper name of an important, or self-important, person, e.g. Tippu *Sahib*, Nana *Sahib*,
Robertson *Sahib*, or to the rank of Indian
potentates, e.g., Khan *Sahib*, *Nawab Sahib*,
Raja and *Maharaja Sahib*, and *Mem-Sahib*,
a European wife of a *sahib*, etc., etc. *Shahzada Sahib*, applied to the Prince of Wales
(Nov. 1921). Also *Sahib-log* (1848), European
officer-class, or gentlefolk, in India; *Sahib-dom*
(1901) (obs.), the quality or condition of being
a *sahib; Sahib-hood* (1946), same as prec;
Sahiba(h), 'mistress', 'lady' (1849). The word
is also used as a general vocative *Sahib!* 'Sir!'
Oont-Wallah-Sahib, 'camel-keeping gentleman'. [*OED & YB; Deccan Herald*, 6 March
1984; Ovington, *Voy. Suratt* (1696), 326;
Fryer (1673), *New Account* (1672-81), 417.]

Sahitya [20C. S. *sahitya*.] 'Association, agreement, composition, literature, lyrical verse'.
The lyrical verse that forms part of an Indian
dance-song. [*OED;* F. Bowers, *Dance in India*
(1953), 46.]

Sahiwal, sanhiwal [20C.] Name of a Punjab
town, now in Pakistan. A cow or bull belonging to the breed so called, originally native to
the Punjab, but now used in tropical regions
elsewhere to denote cattle distinguished by
small horns, and a hump on the back of the
neck. [*OED; Rep. Agric. Research Inst. &
Coll.* (1914-15), 10.]

Sahukar *See* **Sowcar, Soucar.**

Sailab [20C. H/Punj *sailāb(ā)*, 'flood, torrent', fr.
P. *sail*, 'flowing' + *āb*, 'water'.] Cultivation by
using flood-water from rivers in N. India and
Pakistan, as opposed to *barani* (rain)
cultivation. [*OED;* J. Douie, *Punjab, NWFP &
Kashmir* (1916), xiv. 142.]

Sainik [19C. H. *sainik*.] A soldier. *See* **Jawan,**
and **Sena.** Also *sainika-sabha*, a court-martial.
[Wilson, *Glossary* (1855).]

Sais, saïs *See* **Syce.**

Saiva [19C. S. *saiva*.] A devotee of **S(h)iva.**
Hence, *Shaivism (Sivaism)* (1877), and
Shaivite (Sivaite) (1867). [*OED & YB;* E.
Moor, *Hindu Pantheon* (1810), 15; F. M.
Milman (1867), *Bishop Milman, Mem. of,*
(1879), 48.] *See* **Tambaranee.**

Saj [19C. H. *saj*.] The Indian laurel, *Terminalia
alata*, or *tomentosa*. Yields an excellent hard
timber. [R. W. Lane, tr., *Arabian Nights*
(1839), ii. xiii, 384.]

Sajjan [H. *sajjan*.] Gentleman. [Hawkins, *CIWIE.*]

Saka¹ [17C. S. *saka*.] (1) A member of an ancient
Indo-Scythian people originating in Central
Asia. [P. Holland, tr., *Pliny's Nat. Hist.* (1601),

vi. xvii. 123.] (2) The language of these
people = *Khotanese*. [Lane *in* Birnbaum
and Puhvel, *Anc. Indo-European Dial*
(1961), 223.]

Saka² [19C. S. *sāka*.] In Indian chronology
designating or pertaining to an era from AD
78. The National Calendar established by the
Indian government from 1957 is reckoned by
this era. [*OED; Encycl. Brit. Macropaedia*
(1974); Wilson, *Glossary* (1855).] *See* **Shaka.**

Sakta, shakta [19C. S. *sakta*, 'relating to power,
or to the **Sakti**'.] 'One who worships Sakti',
divine energy, especially as identified with
Durga. [*OED;* E. Moor, *Hindu Pantheon*
(1810), 116.]

Sakti, Shakti [19C. S. *shakti*, 'power, energy', fr.
sak, 'to be able'.] All-pervading divine energy,
the female principle, espec. when personified
as the wife of a god, as **Durga**, the Mother Goddess of the Hindus, is the *Sakti* of **Siva.** [*OED;* E.
Moor, *Hindu Pantheon* (1810), 10.] *See* **Tantra.**

Sal, saul [18C. H. *sāl*, fr. S. *sāla*.] The timber
tree, *Shorea robusta*, yielding **Dammar.** Its
valuable timber is strong, durable and heavy
[*OED & YB;* Holwell, *Hist. Events* etc. (1766),
i. 200.]

Sala¹ [19C. H. *sālā*, 'brother-in-law', fr. S. *syala*.]
'used elliptically as a low term of abuse.' [YB.]
Also *sussoor*, 'father-in-law', used in the same
way, cf. French, 'et ta soeur'. [YB; Wilson,
Glossary (1855); A.K. Forbes (1856), *Ras
Mala* (ed. 1878), 616.]

Sala² [19C. H/S. *sālā*, 'house'.] Rest-house, inn.
See **Dharmsala.** [*OED;* Alabaster, *Wheel of
Law* (1871), 265.]

Salaam(s) [16C. H/Ar. *salām*, 'peace'.] A Muslim
salutation; compliments. In full *'alaikum
salaam*, 'peace be unto you'. (English coll.
corr. 'So long' = 'good-bye'.) Used as a vb.
trans. and intrans. (1693). Hence, *Salaaming*
(1816). [*OED & YB;* Litchfield's *Castañeda*
(1582), E. tr. iii. 445; Fryer (1673), *New Acct.*
(1672-81), 18.]

Salabad, sallabad [17C. Mar. *salabād*, 'peren-
nial'.] Apparently a factitious word fr. P. *sāl*,
'year', and Ar. *abad*, 'ages'. 'An obsolete term
for 'the customary or prescriptive exactions of
the native governments and for native and
prescriptive claims in general.' [YB; *Fort St.
Geo. Consns.*, 27 Sept. (1680), 35; Stockdale,
Indian Vocab. (1788).]

Salagram, saligram [18C.] S. *salagrāma. See*
Shalgram.

Saleb, salep, saloop [18C. H/Ar. *tha'lab*, shortening of Khasyu*'th-thalab* (lit. 'fox's testicles'.)]

Tubers of various species of *orchis*, reputed to have restorative powers, once commonly known as *Sa'lab misri*, or *Salep-misry* (the Salep of Egypt) in India. [*OED* & YB; A. Hamilton, *New Acct. of E. Indies* (1727), i. 125; Bailey, *Household Dict.* (1736), 519.]

Salempore, salempoory [16C. fr. *Salempur*, a town in Tamil Nadu. (Tel. *sale*, 'weaver' + S. *pura*, 'town'.)] Blue cotton cloth (occas. white) made at Nellore, S. India. *See* **Palampore**. [*OED* & YB; Phillip, tr., Linschoten (1598), i. 28/1.]

Sallekhana [19C.] Jain rite of euthanasia; death by voluntary starvation; first on rice and water, then only water, finally nothing. Mahavira, the founder of Jainism, died in this way at the age of 72. [Max Mueller, *Sacred Books of the East* (1884-95), xxii & xlv.]

Salootree, salustree [19C. H. *sālotar, sālotrī*, 'a farrier or horse-doctor fr. S. *sālihotri*, 'a horse' (fr. *sali* 'rice, corn' + *hotri*, 'sacrificing'.)] The *salotari* of a cavalry regiment ranked as a **Duffardar (Dafadar)**. [YB; 1831 in *Or. Sport. Mag.* (reprint (1873), ii. 223; Whitworth, *Anglo-Indian Dict.* (1885).]

Salwar *See* **Shalwar**.

Samadh [19C. *See* next.] The tomb of a holy Hindu or **Yogi**, assumed to have achieved **Samadhi** rather than to have died. [*OED*; *Asiat. Res.* (1828), xvi. 39.]

Samadhi [18C. S. *sāmādhi*, 'a placing together', fr. *sam*, 'together' + *a*, prefix + *dha*, 'to place'.] (1) The state of union with creation into which a perfected **Yogi** or holy man is said to pass at his apparent death; the voluntary burial of such a person before death in anticipation of this state; the site of the burial of a holy man. (*See* prec.) [*OED*; *Asiat. Res.* (1795), iv. 218.] (2) The highest state of meditation, in which the distinctions between subject and object disappear and unity with creation is achieved; the last stage of **Yoga** (1806). [*OED*; *Trans. Roy. Asiat. Soc.* (1827), i. 25; A. Huxley, *After Many a Summer* (1939), II. I. 189.] *See* **Samyama**.

Samaj, somaj [19C. S. *samaja*, 'a meeting', fr. *sam*, 'together' + *aj*, 'to drive'. H/Beng. *samāj*, 'society'.] An assembly or congregation in India; a church or religious body, as in **Brahmo Samaj** (1828), **Arya Samaj** (1875), and *Prarthana Samaj* (1867). *See* **Brahmoism**. [*OED*; C.M. Davies, *Unorthodox London* (1875), 2nd Ser. (2 ed.), 193.]

Saman [18C. S. *sāman*, 'chant'.] A sacred text or verse forming the third of the four kinds of Vedas; the name of the Veda thus formed. So *Sāmaveda*, the name of the third. Also, *Samaveda-samhita*, a collection of texts used for composing *saman*-hymns. [*OED*; *Asiat. Res.* (1798), v. 364.]

Sambal, semball [19C. Malay, *sambal*.] A highly seasoned Malayan condiment, consisting of raw vegetables, fruit, spices and vinegars and used as a relish. *See* next [*OED* & YB; Raffles, *Hist. Java* (1830), i. 98.]

Sambar, sambhar [20C. Tam. *sambhar*.] A highly seasoned sauce of **Dal**, vegetables, spices, tamarind juice, etc. in South Indian cuisine, eaten with **Idli(s)** and **Dosa(s)**. Also attrib. [*OED*; S. Rangarao, *Good Food from India* (1957), vii. 68.]

Sambook, sambuq, sambuk [16C. Ar. *sanbūk*.] A kind of small one-masted vessel formerly used in Western India, smaller than the *bagalā*. (*See* **Buggalow**.) 'chiefly used to communicate between a roadstead and the shore or to go inside the reefs.' [YB & *OED*; Litchfield, *Castañeda* (1582), i.x. Burton, *Pilgr. El-Medinah and Meccah* (1855), i. 263.]

Sambur, sambre, samba [17C. H. *sa(m)bar*; S. *sambara*.] Either of two large deer, *Cervus unicolor* or *C. equinus*, native to India and S. Asia. 'It grows to a height of 14 hands, is dark brown in colour, has a massy neck clothed with bristling hair and long antlers.' [GCW.] Known as the Indian elk, or the *Rusa Aristoteles* [Jerdon, *Mammals of India* (1874); *OED* & YB; Fryer (1673), *New Acct.* (1672-81), 175.]

Samhita, sanhita [19C. S. *samhita*, fr. *sam* 'together' + *dha*, 'to place'.] Linguistics: A text treated according to **Sandhi**; a verse of the **Veda(s)** which is the continuous text formed from the **pada** or separate words by the appropriate phonetic sound changes. *See* **Saman**. [*OED*.] Also attrib. [Colebrooke in *Asiat. Res.* (1805), viii. 476.]

Samiti, samity [20C. H. *samiti*, 'meeting, committee.'] In India and Bangladesh, an assembly or a committee. *Mahila Samitis*, Women's Institutes, founded in Bengal (1930). *Panchayat Samitis*, District Council Committees. [*OED*; M.L. Darling, *Rusticus Loquiter* (1930), v. 124.]

Samjow, sumjao, samjao [19C. H. imp. of *samjhānā*, 'to cause to know, warn, correct, usually with the implication of physical coercion'. [YB.] *See* **Puckerow, Bunow, Gubbrow, Lugow**. [YB; Hockley (1826), *Pandurang Hari* (ed. 1873), ii. 170.]

Samosa, samusa, samoosa [20C. H. *samōsā.*]
In India, a triangular envelope of pastry, fried
crisp in **Ghee** or oil, stuffed with spiced meat
or vegetables. [*OED;* R.P. Jhabvala, *To Whom
She Will* (1955), ix. 67.]

Samprasarana [19C. S. *samprasārana,* lit. 'a
stretching out, extending', fr. *sam* 'together'
+ *pra,* 'forth' + *sārana,* 'extension'.]
Linguistics: In Sanskrit, the interchange
between the vowels *i, u, ri, lri* and their
corresponding semi-vowels *y, v, r, l;* hence a
similar process in other Indo-European
languages. [*OED;* Goldsticker, *Panini: His
Place in Sanskrit Lit.* (1861), 169.]

Samsara, sangsara [19C. S. *samsāra,* 'a
wandering through', fr. *sam,* 'together,
completeness' + *sar,* 'to run, glide, move'.]
Hindu Philosophy: The endless cycle of birth,
death, re-birth to which life in the material
world is bound. Metempsychosis. Also, *sam-
sarin,* state of being (Jainism). [*OED; Encycl.
Brit.* (1886), xxi. 289/1.]

Samskara [19C. S. *samskāra,* 'a making
perfect, preparation', fr. *sam,* 'together' + *kr*
'to make, perform'.] Hindu philosophy: 1. A
purification ceremony or sanctifying rite,
which purifies from the taint of sin contracted
in .the womb, leading to regeneration and
marking a stage or an event in life; one of the
12 rites enjoined on the first three classes of
the **Brahmin** caste. [*OED; Asiat. Res.* (1807),
ix. 288.] 2. A mental impression, instinct or
memory. [*OED; Trans. Roy. Asiatic Soc.*
(1827), i. 562.]

Sama-veda *See* **Veda.**

Samvat, samwat, samwatsara [19C. S. *samvat.*]
A year; espec. the luni-solar year of the era of
Vikramaditya, King of Malwa, who began his
reign in 57 BC. In India, the luni-solar year
was the interval between the new moon in
one sign of the Zodiac and the new moon in
the same sign again. [Whitworth, *Anglo-
Indian Dict.* (1885).]

Samyama, sanyama [19C. S. *samyama,*
'restraint, control of the sense', fr. *sam,*
together' + *yam,* 'sustain, hold up' (*yama,*
'rein, bridle, self-control).] Hindu Philosophy:
Name of the three final stages of meditation
which lead on to **Samadhi,** or the state of
union. [*OED; Trans. Roy. Asiatic Soc.* (1828),
iii. 164.]

Sanad *See* **Sunnud.**

Sanatan [19C. S. *sanatan,* 'eternal'.] *Sanātana
Dharma,* orthodox Hinduism; and *Sanātana
Dharma Mahāmandal,* a Hindu reform and
revivalist movement of the last third of the
19C. Cf. **Arya Samaj.** [Hawkins, *CIWIE.*]

Sandal(wood), sanders, saunders, sandlewood
[15C. H. *chandan;* S. *chandana.*] (1) The
scented wood of the *Santalum* trees from
which a strongly aromatic oil is distilled.
[*OED* & *YB;* Lydgate and Burgh, *Secreta
Secretorum* (tr. *c.* 1450).] (2) An unscented
dye-wood, *Pterocarpus Santalinus* = Red
Sanders. [YB; Milburn, *Orient Commerce*
(1825), 249.] (3) The name is also applied to
substitutes for the true sandalwood. [*OED;*
Lindley, *Veg. Kingd.* (1846), 553.] (4) A
perfume derived from sandalwood oil, used in
soap and cosmetics. [*OED;* E. Rimmel, *Bk.
Perfumes* (1865), viii. 143.] (5) The oil is used
as a genito-urinary antiseptic. [*OED;* W.H.
White, *Textbk. Pharmacol. & Therapeutics*
(1901), 586.] (6) Sandal (wood)-colour, a light
yellowish brown, a once fashionable shade
(for dress materials). [*Daily Express* (Advt.),
Sept. 1926.] (7) Sandal-wood English =
Beach-la-Mar (*Beche-de-Mer,* also *Biche-*),
Pg. *bicho do mar (Pidgin-English).* [Jesper-
sen, *Language* (1922), 216.] (8) An ointment
is made of powdered sandalwood. [Lydgate
and Burgh, *Secreta Secretorum* (tr. *c.* 1450).]

Sandarac [14C. Poss. fr. H. *sandaros.* Pg.
sandaraca.] Red arsenic sulphide = realgar.
[*OED;* Trevisa (1398), *Barth. De PR.* (1495),
xix, xxix, 878.]

Sanders [14C.] *See* **Sandalwood.**

Sandesh [20C. Beng. *sandesh.*] A Bengali
sweetmeat of curdled milk, sugar, and
pistachio nuts, resembling cheese fudge.
[*OED;* D.R. Gupta, *Best Stories Mod. Bengal*
(1944), I. 72.]

Sandhi, sundhi [19C. S. *samdhi,* 'a placing
together', fr. *sam,* 'together' + *dha,* 'to
place'.] Linguistics: Assimilative phonetic
changes, or morphemic alternation, espec. as
determined by phonemic environment (e.g.
samdhi, becoming *sandhi*), occurring in
Sanskrit (and extended by modern linguistics
to analogous changes in other languages) in
the final and initial sounds of words in a
sentence (*internal sandhi*) and in the final
stems in word formation (*external sandhi*).
'The permutation of letters occasioned by the
junction of syllables.' Also attrib. & comb., e.g.
sandhi-form, *sandhi*-system, *sandhi*-alter-
nants, etc. [*OED;* Carey, *Gram. Sungskrit
Lang.* (1806), i. iii. 15.]

Sandhya [19C. S. *samdhyā,* 'a holding
together', 'junction'.] Cf. **Sandhi.** (a) Twilight

(personified as the daughter of **Brahma**.) [*OED*; Whitworth, *Anglo-Indian Dict.* (1885).] (b) The period preceding a **Yuga** or age of the world. [*OED*; *Chambers Encycl.* (1868), X. 327/1.] (c) Morning or evening prayers. [*OED*; *Encycl. Brit. Macropaedia* (1974), viii. 850/1; Monier-Williams, *Brahmanism & Hinduism* (1891), 401.]

Sunga, sanga [19C. Kulu, *sanga*.] A bridge made of beams used in the Himalayas, projecting from each bank, slightly pointing upwards, each set of beams laid to project beyond the lower ones, till the space left in the middle can be crossed by single timbers. [*OED*; G.E. Mundy, *Pen & Pencil Sk. Ind.* (1832), I. iv. 241.]

Sangam(a) [19C. S. *samgam*, fr. *sam*, 'together' + *gam*, 'go'.] The confluence of rivers, esp. of Ganga, Jumuna (Yamuna), and the invisible (myth.) Saraswati. Also called *Triveni* or *Tribeni* at Allahabad. *See* **Saraswati**. [Lady Falkland, *Chow-Chow: being Selections of a Journal kept in India* (1857); Fanny Parkes, *Wanderings* etc. (1850), I. 213.]

Sangar, sungar, sanga [19C. Pusht. *sangar*; Punj. *sanghar*.] A breast-work of stone, 'such as is commonly erected for defence by the Afridis and other tribes on the Indian N.W. Frontier' (now Pakistan). [YB & *OED*; Sir T. Seaton (1841), *Cadet to Colonel* (1866), I. viii. 215; W. S. Churchill in *Morning Post*, 25 July 1909, 5/7.]

Sangh(a), Samgha [19C. H. *sangha*, fr. S. *sangha*, fr. *sam*, 'together' + *han*, 'to come in contact'.] (1) Buddhism: The community or order of monks. (2) Association, assembly, e.g., *Jan Sangh*, the People's Party, a modern Indian political party. [*OED*; P. Bigandet, *Life or Legend of Gaudama* (1858), 234.]

Sangit, sangeet [S. *sangit*.] Music. Devotional songs and poems sung by the chorus in Indian dance-dramas. [Singha and Massey, *Indian Dances* (1967), 166.]

Sanguicel [16C. Prob. fr. *Sanguicer*, a Pg. name for *Sangameshwar*, an ancient port in Karnataka.] A kind of small vessel used in naval warfare by the Portuguese. [YB; Linschoten, *Voyages* (1598), ch. 92.]

Sankaracharya [20C. S. fr. *sam*, 'prosperity' + *kara*, 'causing' + *acharya*, teacher, guide'.] The name of the '*acharya*', a S. Indian *Saivite* Brahman who founded the sect of the *Smartas*; a follower of Sankaracharya, famous teacher of **Vedanta** philosophy (prob. 8th century AD); used as the title of one of the

various Indian religious teachers and leaders that came after him. He taught the identity of soul (**Atma**) with **Brahman**, achieved by spiritual discipline and meditation. The system is sometimes referred to as **Jnana Marga**, 'The Way of Knowledge'. [*OED*; K.M. Pannikar, *Survey of Indian Hist.* (1947), xii. 133.]

Sankhya, sanchya, samkhya [18C. S. *sāmkhya*, lit. 'relating to number', prob. referring to the 25 principles of the *Sankhyan* philosophy; founded prob. by Kapila.] One of the 6 orthodox philosophical schools or *darshans* of Hinduism, the other 5 being *Yoga*, *Nyāya*, *Vaiseshika*, *Mīmansa*, and *Vedānta* or *Uttara-Mīmansa*, all being based on the dualism of matter and soul (**Prakriti** and **Atma**.) [*OED*; C. Caul in *Asiat. Res.* (1788), i. 344.] *See* **Purusha**.

Sannah, sannow, sannoes [17C. (Obscure origin.)] One of the very numerous cotton 'piece-goods' at one time exported to England from India. [*OED* & YB; J.F. Merchant *Warehouse* (1696), 36.]

Sannyas, Sunnyas, Sannyasi, Sunnyasi, Sunyasee [17C. H. *sannyāsī* fr. S. *sannyāsin*, 'laying aside, abandoning, ascetic', fr. *sam*, 'together' + *ni*, 'down' + *as*, 'to throw'.] A **Brahman** (Brahmin) in the fourth stage (*ashrama*) of his life, the four *āshramas* being: (1) **Brahmachari**, the stage of the celibate (Vedic) student. (2) **Grihastha**, the married state of the householder, (3) **Vanaprastha**, the state of retirement to life in the forest. (4) *Sannyas*, the final renunciation of all wordly interests and responsibility. Also, a religious **Fakir** or ascetic mendicant (not always the genuine article) and, 'A body of banditti in Bengal [c. 1760-75] claiming to belong to a religious fraternity'. [Long, 526-767.] [*OED* & YB; Purchas, *Pilgrimage* (1613), v. ix. 417; Monier- Williams, *Brahmanism & Hinduism* (1891), 55; Somerset Maugham (1938), *Writer's Notebook* (1949), 280.]

Sansar(i) [19C. S. *sansara*, 'the world', fr. *sansri*, 'to revolve'.] Worldly, mundane; engaged in secular life as opposed to **Tyagi**; a **Sadhu** whose order permits him to marry. Cf. **Sanyogi** and **Viyogi**. [Whitworth, *Anglo-Indian Dict.* (1885).]

Sansi, Sansiya, Sansya [19C. Origin uncertain.] A person of a degraded and outcaste tribe of the Punjab, who 'was required to live outside towns, to eat his food in broken vessels, to wear the clothes of the dead, and to be excluded from all intercourse with other people'. The women of this tribe were reputed to practice prostitution. [OED; Gunthorpe, *Notes on Criminal Tribes* (1882), xiii 78; Crooke, *Tribes and Castes N.W. Provinces & Oudh* (1896), iv. 277.]

Sanskrit, Sanscrit, Samskrit, Samskrt, etc. [17C. S. *Samskrta,* 'put together, highly-wrought, well-formed, perfected', fr. *sam,* 'together' + *kr,* 'to make, to do, to perform' + p.p. ending *-to.*] The ancient and sacred language of India; the oldest known member of the Indo-European group, in which Hindu literature from the **Vedas** onwards is composed. In the narrower sense the word refers to 'classical Sanskrit' (opp. to the 'Epic' and 'Vedic'), whose grammar was formulated and fixed by Panini, about the 4th century BC. 'The term *Sanskrit* came into familiar use after the investigations into this language, by the English in Bengal (viz. by Wilkins and Jones, etc.), in the last quarter of the 18th century.' [YB.] Hence: *Sanskritic,* pertaining to *Sanskrit* (1848). Also *Sanskritization,* the adoption by a lower caste of the symbols of a higher caste, or translation into *Sanskrit* (fr. *Sanskritize.*) And: *Sanskritist* (1889), a person well-versed in *Sanskrit,* or who bases a mythological theory upon *Sanskrit* (1864). [OED & YB; Purchas, *Pilgrimage* (1617), v. xi. 636.]

Sant [19C. H/Punj. *Sant,* 'saint'.] Title of **Sikh** religious leader; ascetic devotee of the Sikh religion. [Macauliffe, *The Sikh Religion;* Khushwant Singh, *The Sikhs* (1953).]

Santal [18C.] **Sandal-wood.** Also, Chem. a substance ($C_8H_6O_3$) obtained fr. sandal-wood (1894). [OED; 1727-41 Chambers *Cycl.;* Muir & Morley, *Watts Dict. Chem.* (1894), iv. 427.]

Sant(h)al, Sonthal(s) [19C. Native name.] A Kolarian people of N.E. India; a member of these people; their language, **Santali.** They worship Sing Bonga and Marang Buru and burn their dead. [OED & YB; *Asiat. Res.* (1798), iv. 359.]

Santali, Santalee [19C. See. prec.] The Munda language, an Austro-Asiatic language (Grierson) of the Santals, without literature or written characters. [Whitworth, *Anglo-Indian Dict.; OED;* L.O. Skrefsud, *On Non-Aryan Lang. Ind.* (1873), iii.]

Santalol [19C.] Fragrant liquids, $C_{15}H_{24}O$, found in **Sandal-Wood** oil. [OED; *Pharm. Jrnl.* 1, 118./1. 1895.]

Santara, Sungtara [19C. H/P. *sangtara.*] The name of a loose-skinned mandarin orange, *Citrus reticulata* (perh. fr. Cintra). [YB; Kirkpatrick, *Nepaul* (1811), 129.]

Santoor, santir [19C. Ar. *santir;* P. *sāntūr.*] The dulcimer. A multi-stringed musical instrument in India, mounted on legs, played by plucking with two plectrums or striking with two hammers. *See* **S(h)atantri.** [OED; Layard, *Discov. Nineveh & Babylon* (1853), xx. 454.] *See* **Suvaramandala.**

Sanyogi [19C. S. *sanyogi,* fr. *sam,* 'together' + *yoga,* 'junction' (fr. *yuj.* 'to join').] A married man, a householder of a religious nature, as opp. to **Viyogi.** *See* **Sansari(i)** and **Tyagi.** [Whitworth, *Anglo-Indian Dict.* (1885).]

Saphir d'eau [19C. Fr. *saphir d'eau,* 'sapphire of water'.] A translucent blue variety of cordierite found in Sri Lanka. [OED; R. Jameson, *Syst. Mineral* (ed. 1820), 1.174.]

Sap(p)an [16C. Tam. *shappangam;* M. *chapannam;* Mal. *sapang.*] The wood and red dye of the Indian and Far-Eastern tree, *Caesalpinia sappan* and related species. *See* **Brazil-Wood.** [OED; Linschoten, *Voyages* (E. tr. 1598), 36.]

Sarangi, sarungi [19C. S. *sarangī.*] An Indian stringed musical instrument resembling a violin. *See* **Sarinda.** [OED; *Illustrated Catalogue Great Exhibition* (1851), IV. 913/2.]

Saraswata [19C. S. *Saraswata.*] Relating to **Saraswati;** the name of the second subdivision of the Gauda Brahmans. [Whitworth, *Anglo-Indian Dict.* (1885).]

Saraswati [19C. S. *Saraswati.*] (1) The name of a holy subterranean mythical river said to reappear to join the confluence of the Ganges and Jumuna. *See* **Sangam.** [Fanny Parks, *Wanderings of a Pilgrim* (1850), I. 213. (2) The Hindu goddess of eloquence and learning, considered to be the **Sakti,** the active power or wife of **Brahma,** the creator. [Whitworth, *Anglo-Indian Dict.* (1885).]

Sardar *See* **Sirdar** and **Sirdar-Bearer.**

Sari, saree [16C. H. *sārī.*] A long wrapping garment (generally colourful), of cotton, silk or other materials, worn by Hindu women. One end is wrapped several times around the waist, the other end being thrown over the left shoulder, and often, for protection and purposes of modesty, over the head. [OED & YB; Linschoten, *Voyages* (E. tr. 1598), 28.]

Sarinda [19C.] Dial. var. of **Sarangi.**

Saristadar *See* **Sheristadar.**

Sarkar *See* **Sirkar.**

Sarod, saroda, sarode, etc. [19C. H. *sarōd.*] An Indian stringed musical instrument of

Persian origin. Cf. **Sitar** and **Veena**. [*OED; Proc. R. Irish Acad.* (1865), ix. i. 115.]

Sarowar [H. *sarowar.*] A lake; **Tank**. [Hawkins, *CIWIE.*]

Sarpanch, Sir Punch [19C. H. *sarpanch.*] Head arbitrator, foreman of a jury or council; a village headman in Northern India; the head of a **Panchayat** village council. [*OED;* Wilson, *Glossary* (1855); F.G. Bailey, *Politics and Social Change* (1963), i.i. 55.]

Sarpech *See* **Surpeach.**

Sarptoli [19C. Mahr. *sarptoli.*] The harmless green whipsnake, *Passerita mycterizans*. Large specimens grow to 6 ft. in length. [Whitworth, *Anglo-Indian Dict.* (1885).]

Sarson [H. *sarson.*] The herb *Brassica campestris*, yielding mustard. [Hawkins, *CIWIE.*]

Sarus, Cyrus, Syras, serious (soldiers' slang) etc. [17C. H. *saras;* S. *sarasa*, the 'lake-bird'.] The Indian red-headed grey crane, *Grus antigone*, generally found in pairs, held almost sacred in some parts of India and whose 'fine trumpet-like call, uttered when alarmed or on the wing, can be heard a couple of miles off. [Jerdon, *Birds of India* (1862).] 'The British soldier Hobson-Jobsonized this word to "serious" and was "fond of shooting him for the pot".' [YB & *OED;* Fryer (1672), *New Account* (1672-81), 117.]

Sarvadharma, samabhavana [20C. S. *sarva*, 'all' + *dharma*, 'duty'.] Religious toleration.

Sarvashri [H. *Sarva Shrī*, fr. *sarva*, 'all' + *shri*, 'title'.] Esquire, Everyman, Messrs. [Hawkins, *CIWIE.*]

Sarvajanik [H/Mar. *sarvajanik*, fr. *sarva*, 'all' + *jana*, 'people'.] Relating to all people; public. [Hawkins, *CIWIE.*]

Sarvodaya [20C. H/S. *sarva*, 'all' + *udaiya*, 'uplift, prosperity'.] The welfare of all; social service; the name given to the new social order advocated by Mahatma Gandhi (1869-1948) and his followers. [*OED;* M.K. Gandhi, *Sarvodaya* (1908).]

Sarwan, surwan [19C. H/P. *sārbān*, fr. *sār*, 'camel' + *bān*, 'keeper'.] A camel-driver. [*OED* & YB; M. Sherer, *Sk. India* (1821), 242; Mundy (1828), *Pen & Pencil Sketches* (1832), II i.i.]

Sasin [19C. Nep. *Sasin.*] The Blackbuck or Indian antelope, *Antilope cervicapra*. *See* **Blackbuck**. [*OED; Penny Cycl.* (1834), II. 72.]

Sastra *See* **Shastra.**

Sastri *See* **Shastri.**

Sastrigal [S. *sastrigal.*] Honorific title affixed to a Smarta Brahmin's name. [Hawkins, *CIWIE.*]

Saswat [17C. Mar./S. *saswata*, 'perpetual'.] A name given to certain offices, such as **Patel**, (1614); **Kulkarni** (1783); **Deshmukh** (1801); and **Deshpande** (1855) which are hereditary, and therefore highly prized. [Whitworth, *Anglo-Indian Dict.* (1885).]

Satara [19C.] A town in Maharashtra. A ribbed, heavy, broadcloth, with a horizontal weave to it, named after the town in which it was first made. [*OED;* Barlow, *Hist & Princ. Weaving* (1878), 442.]

Sat-bhai, Saht-bai [19C. H. *sātbhāi*, 'seven brothers (or sisters)'.] An Indian jungle babbler, *Turdoides striatus;* a large brown bird with a long tail and a slightly curved bill; generally found in groups, hence the name **Seven Sisters**. [*OED* & YB; Jerdon, *Birds of India* (1863); II. 65; P. Robinson, *In My Indian Garden* (1879), 30. 31.]

Satchitananda [19C. S. *sat*, 'pure being' + *chit*, 'pure consciousness' + *ananda*, 'pure bliss'.] The Supreme Existance; Bliss. [Alain Danielou, *Hindu Polytheism* (1964), 258; Das Gupta, *Hist. Ind. Phil.* (1955), v. 67.]

Satrangi, sitringi, sittringy, sittringee, etc. [17C. H. *shatrangi*, fr. P. *shatranj*.] 'chequers', with ref. to the orig. chequered pattern on a carpet or rug of coloured cotton, now usually of striped pattern. [*OED* & YB; Foster (1606), *Eng. Fact. Ind.* (1921), I. 354; Peachey (1688) in *Hedges Diary* (1888), II. cclxv.]

Satrap [14C. P. *kshatrapha*, S. *kshatra*, 'country + *pa*, 'to protect'.] A subordinate ruler. There were two India satrapates, in Saurashtra and Gujarat fr. AD 150 to AD 388. [YB & *OED;* Wyclif (*c.* 1380), *Wks.* (1880), 7; *Jrnl. Roy. Asiat. Soc.* (New Series) (1890), 639.]

Satsang [20C. S. *satsanga*, 'association with good men', fr. *sat*, 'good man' + *sanga*, 'association'.] Hinduism: A spiritual discourse; a sacred gathering; an otherworldly community. *Satsangi*, a member of such a gathering, association or community. [J.N. Farquar, *Mod. Relig. Movements in India* (1929), iii. 17.]

Satta [20C. H. *satta.*] Commercial speculation; gambling on numbers; the Numbers Game. [Hawkins, *CIWIE.*]

Sattva [19C. S. *sattva*, 'lightness, truth, virtue, harmony'.] Hinduism: One of the three 'qualities' or **Gunas**. *See* **Rajas** and **Tamas**. [Sir Charles Eliot, *Hinduism & Buddhism*

(1921), ii, 298; V. Bhikshu, *Sankhya-Sara* (1862).]

Satu [19C. H. *sattu*.] Coarse gram flour, parched and made into a paste with water. [Whitworth, *Anglo-Indian Dict.* (1885).]

Satya [19C. S. *satya*, 'truth', speaking the truth.] Hinduism & Jainism: truthfulness. *Satya meve jayatam*, 'Let Truth Prevail', the national motto of modern India. [*OED*; Whitworth, *Anglo-Indian Dict.* (1885); C.S. Lewis, *Abolition of Man* (1943), i.]

Satyagraha [20C. S. *satya*, 'truth' + *āgraha*, 'pertinacity'.] Lit. insistence on truth. Friendly passive resistance. Used by Gandhi as the means of solving social and political conflict in India, esp. in conjunction with **Ahimsa** (non-violence). *Satyagrahi*, one who practises *satyagraha* (1928). [*OED*; M.K. Gandhi, *Non-Cooperation* (1920), 46.]

Saudagar, soudagur [19C. H/Mal./P. *saudāgar*, (*saudā* = 'goods for sale').] A merchant. In India often applied to those who sell European goods in civil stations and **Cantonments.** [YB; Buchanan, *Eastern India* (1807), i. 375.]

Sayar, sayer syre [18C. H/Ar. *sā'ir* (pres. pple. of *sāra*, 'to go', or *sa'ara*, 'to remain'.] A term applied to revenues from miscellaneous sources other than the land tax, e.g. customs, excise, transit duties, licences, house-tax, etc. levied by the **Zemindars** within their own estates and by the government under the East India Company's rule. In Bombay it was applied only to such **Abkari** revenue collected by village officers, and it came to an end in 1858, when the E.I.C. relinquished control. Hence, *sayerdar*, an officer who collected transit duties. [*OED* & YB; Long (1731), *Selections Rec. Ft. William* (1748-67), 25; W. Hamilton, *East India Gazetteer* (1815), Gloss.]

Sayyid, sayed, sayud, said [18C. H/Ar. *Saiyid*, lit. 'lord prince'.] In India and Muslim countries a title, given espec. to males claiming descent from Husain the elder grandson of the Prophet. A dynasty of Sayyids ruled at Delhi from AD 1414 to 1451. [*OED* & YB; Burke (1788), 'Sp. Agst. W. Hastings', *Wks.* (1821), VII. 91.]

scavenger, scavager [18C. E. (Cf. Anglo-Saxon, *Sceawian*, 'to look at'.)] The title of an official under the East India Company, originally charged with the inspection of goods and the collection of the tax upon those liable to duty.

[*OED* & YB; Feb. 1702, 'List of Persons in the Service of the Honble E. I. Co.'.]

Scheduled Caste(s) & Scheduled Tribe(s) [20C. Anglo-Indian.] Under the Government of India Act, 1935, these castes and tribes, formerly known as the depressed classes or **Untouchables** were designated as Scheduled Castes and Tribes, who were given preference for certain posts. The 8th Schedule of the Indian Constitution provides for the administration of certain scheduled areas and tribes. *See* **Harijan, Pariah** and **Outcaste.** [*OED*; Govt. of India Act 25 & 26. Geo. V. C. 42. 1st sched.' (1935).]

Scimitar-babbler [19C. Anglo-Indian.] A. N. Indian bird, genus *Pomatorhinus*, or *Pomatostomus*, distinguished by a long curved bill. [*OED*; Jerdon, *Birds of India* (1863), II. 31.]

Scrivan [17C. I. Pg. *escrivao*.] An old word in India for a clerk or **Writer;** scrivener. [*OED*; Fryer, *New Acct.* (1673), 112.]

Seacunny, seaconny, secunnie, saucan. [19C.] App. a perversion (after *sea* + *con* (vb) 'to know how'.) of P. *sukkānī*; Ar. *sukkān*, 'rudder'.] A steersman or quartermaster in a ship manned by **Lascars.** [*OED* & YB; *Asiat. Ann. Reg.* (1800), III. 21/1; M. Graham (1840), *Jrnl. Residence India* (1812), 85.]

Seat [20C. Anglo-Indian.] In India, a place for a student in a school or college, and by transference, the actual admission to such an institution. [Hawkins, *CIWIE*.]

Sebundy [18C. H/P. *sibandī* (Etym. obscure).] Irregular native soldiers in the Indian army, maintained for town garrisons, revenue and police duties; charges in the revenue accounts for the upkeep of such troops; also a member of this militia. [*OED* & YB; Burke, 'Nabob of Arcot's Debts', *Wks.* (1792), App. iv, II. 536.]

Seedi, seedy *See* **Sidi** and **Sayyid.**

Seemul *See* **Simul.**

Seer [17C. H. *ser*, fr. S. *setak*.] A measure of weight and capacity, formerly varying in different parts of India, now about 1 kilogram, and 1 litre (or 2.2 lb., and 1.76 pints). Also **Pucka** and **Kutcha**-seer. [*OED* & YB; Foster (1618), *Eng. Indian Gazetteer* (1815), Gloss.]

Seerfish, seirfish [18C. Corr. of Pg. *serra*, lit. 'saw' + *fish*.] An east-Indian combroid fish, *Cybium guttatum*, or *Scomberom orus commerson*, 'reckoned among the most delicate of Indian sea-fish'. [YB.] 'As savory as any Salmon or Trout in Europe.' *See* **Surmai.**

[OED & YB; Hamilton, *New Acct.* (1727); Linschoten, *Voyages* (1598), E. tr., 88; Hamilton, *New Acct.* (1727), I. xxix. 379.]

Seerpaw [17C. H. *saropā*, fr. P. *sar-ā-pā*, 'head to foot', *'cap-a pie'*.] 'A complete suit, presented as a **Khilat** or dress of honour by the sovereign or his representative.' [YB.] *See* **Tashreef**. [OED; Bernier (1671), *Partic. Events Gt. Mogul*, 11. 4; Fryer (1673), *New Acct.* (1672-81), 87.]

Seersucker [18C. Corr. of P. *shīr-o-shakkar*, lit. 'milk and sugar'.] Transf. 'a striped linen garment.' (Or perh. *sir*, 'head' + *sukh*, 'pleasure'. [YB.] A crumpled or puckered linen or cotton dress fabric, orig. made in India, now chiefly applied to imitations made in the USA and elsewhere. [OED & YB; Guyon, *New Hist. E. Indies* (1757), II. 14. 5.]

Seesi, sisi [19C. Echoic. = *seesi*–partridge.] A small sand partridge, *Ammoperdix griseogularis*, found in India and parts of western Asia. [OED; Gould, *Birds of Asia* (1815), VII. Pl. I; Jerdon, *Birds of India* (1863), III. 567.]

Seetulputty, seekulputty [19C. H. *sītalpattī*. Lit. 'cold-slip'.] 'A fine kind of mat made espec. in Eastern Bengal, and used to sleep on in the cold weather ... made from the *mukta pata*, *Phrynium dichotomum.*' [YB; Williamson, *Vade Mecum.* (1810); ii. 41.]

Semul *See* **Sccmul**.

Sena [20C. H. *sena*.] 'army.' Hence *senapati*, *senaputtee*, commander-in-chief, and **Sainik** soldier. *Shiv Sena*, an *extreme* Hindu nationalist political party. [Hawkins, *CIWIE*.]

Sendhee [19C. H. *sendhī*.] 'The sap of the palm fermented in a peculiar manner and very exciting.' [Meadows Taylor, *Story of My Life* (1877).]

Sepoy, seapoy, sipahi [17C. H/P. *sipāhī* (prob. through Pg. *sipae*), 'horseman', 'soldier', fr. *sipāh*, 'army'.] Orig. a horseman, later (1717) an Indian native private soldier in the British-Indian army. Occas. a policeman, and office messenger. *See* **Spahi**. Also *sepoy-crab* (1857), a species of crab found in the Indian and Pacific Oceans. And *Sepoy-Mutiny* or *Rebellion*, a revolt against British rule in India in 1857. *See* **Pandy**. [OED & YB; Sir T. Herbert (1638), *Travels* (ed.1677).] *See* **Naik**.

Serai¹ [17C. H/Ar. *surāhī*.] 'A long-necked earthenware (or metal) flagon for water.' [YB.] *See* **Goglet** and **Surahi**. [OED & YB; Bernier (tr.) (1672), *Hist. Rev. Emp. Gt. Mogol*, IV. 10; Elphinstone (1808) in Colebrooke, *Life* (1884), I. 192.]

Serai,² Serye [17C. H/P. *serāī*.] 'In India ... a building for the accommodation of travellers with their pack-animals, consisting of an enclosed yard with chambers round it.' [YB.] Cf. *caravanserai*. Also, a warehouse (1619). [OED & YB; Foster (1619), *Eng. Fact. in India* (1906), 103; W. Finch (1609) in Purchas, *Pilgrimes* (1625), I. 434; W. Hamilton, *East India Gazetteer* (1815), Gloss.]

Serang, Syrang, Sarang [17C. H/P. *sarhang*.] 'A commander or overseer.' A native boatswain or skipper of a **Lascar** crew of a small native vessel. [Hyde, *Syntagma* (1676), II. 264.] [OED & YB; Wallace (1817), *Fifteen Years in India* (1822), 256.]

Seraphin *See* **Xerafin**.

Serendip, serendib. 'The Arabic form of the name of Ceylon in the earlier Middle Ages.' [YB.] (For example in *Al Birūni* and *Ibn Batuta*.) *See* next.

Serendipity [18C. fr. *serendip* + *ity*.] A word coined by Horace Walpole from the title of a fairy-tale, *The Three Princes of Serendip*, the heroes of which were always making discoveries by accident. The faculty of making happy and unexpected discoveries by accident. Also *serendipitous* (1958). [OED & YB; H. Walpole, *Let. to Mann*, 28 Jan. 1754; E. Meynell, *Life of Francis Thompson* (1926), xiii. 221.]

Serow, surrow [19C. Lepcha, *serow*.] The Himalayan goat-antelope, *Capricornis sumatraensis* or *Nemorhoedus bubalinus*. *See* **Tahr**. [OED & YB; Hodgson (1847) in *Jrnl. Asiatic Soc. Bengal* XVI. II. 697.] *See* **Goral**.

Seth, sett, seat [18C. H. *sēt*, fr. S. *sētha*. said to be a corruption of S. *sreshtha*, 'best or chief'.] A leading Hindu merchant or banker. *See* **Chetty**. [OED & YB; Long (1740), *Select Unpubl. Rec. Govt.* (F. William) (1869), 9; Dow, *Hist. Hindostan* (1772), iii. Diss. i. 109.]

Seven Sisters (or brothers) [19C. Anglo-Indian.] The popular name of a bird (H. *sāt-bhāi*) common throughout most parts of India, (*Turdoides striatus*), so named because it is 'constantly seen in little companies of about that number'. [YB; Robinson, *In My Indian Garden* (1878), 31.] *See* **Sat-bhai**.

Sevika, sevak [H. *sevak*.] A servant. [Hawkins, *CIWIE*.]

Sha,¹ sah [19C. H. *sah* and *sāhu*, fr. S. *sādhu*, 'perfect, virtuous, respectable'.] A merchant or banker (often attached as a surname.) *See* **Sowcar**. [YB; Buchanan Hamilton (c. 1809), *Eastern India* (1838), ii. 573.]

Sha² [19C. Tib. *sha-pho*, 'wild sheep'.] (*See* **shapoo.**) The **Oorial (Urial)**, *Ovis orientalis*. Also applied to the *Ovis vignei*. A species of wild sheep, found in Kashmir, Tibet, etc. [*OED*; Vigne, *Trav. Kashmir* (1842), ii. 280.]

Sha(h)bash [19C. H. *shāh-bāsh*, fr. P. *shād-bash*.] 'Be joyful.' Interj. Well done! Bravo! [YB; Davidson, *Travels in Upper India*. (1843), i. 209; Kipling, *Kim* (1901), iv. 105.]

Sha(h)bunder, Shahbandar, Shawbunder, etc. [16C. H/P. *Shāh-bandar*, and Pg. *Zabandar*, 'King of the Haven'.] Harbour-master 'at native ports all over the Indian seas ... the chief authority with whom foreign traders had to transact ... often also the head of the Customs.' [YB & *OED*; J. Davis (1599) *in* Purchas, *Pilgrimes* (1625), I. iii. 120.]

Shaddock, chadocks [17C. Anglo-Indian.] The fruit, *Citrus decumana*, named after Capt. Shaddock, an **Interloper**, who reputedly first brought it from the East Indies to Barbados at the end of the 17C. (also called **Pompelmoose**). [*OED* & YB; Sloane, *Voy. Jamaica* (1696), 1. 41; Ives, *Voy.* (1754), 19.]

Shade, table-shade, wall-shade [18C. Anglo Indian.] 'A glass guard to protect a candle or simple oil-lamp from the wind, standing on the table or affixed to the wall. [YB & *OED*; Hicky, *Bengal Gazette*, 8 April 1780.]

Shadi [19C. H. *shadī*.] Wedding. [Hawkins, *CIWIE*.] *See* **Nikka.**

Shagreen, shagrin, etc. [17C. var. of E. *chagrin*, fr. P. *saghri*.] A species of rough, granular, untanned leather prepared from the skin of the ass, horse, shark, seal, etc., often dyed green. [*OED* & YB; Frver, *New Acct.* (1672-81), 264.]

Shah [16C. P. *shah*.] 'King, ruler.' Allied to S. *kshatra*, 'dominion'.] Also *shahzada* heir-apparant. *See* **Padisha.** [*OED*; A. Edwards (1566) in Hakluyt, *Voy.* (1589), 378.]

Shahid, shaheed [19C. H/Ar. *shahīd*.] 'a witness', 'a martyr'. This term was espec. used to denote those Pakistanis who died fighting in the Indo-Pakistan wars. Also the name of a Sikh *misl* (confederacy). [Whitworth, *Anglo-Indian Dict.* (1885); *Calcutta Review* (1881), LXXVI, 74.]

Shahin, shaheen [19C. H/P. *shāhīn*, lit. 'royal (bird)'.] An Indian falcon, *Falco peregrinator*, and other species, e.g. the red-naped falcon, *Falco babylonicus*. [Jerdon in *Madras Jrnl. Lit. & Sci.* (1839), X. 81.]

Shahnai *See* **Shehnai.**

Shaitan [17C. H/Ar. *Shaitān* (corr. of Heb. *Sātān*).] The Devil, *Satan*, an evil spirit. 'Shaitan ka-bhai, 'Brother of the Arch-Enemy', a title given to Sir C. Napier by the Amirs of Sind and their followers.' [YB & *OED*; Sir T. Herbert (1638), *Trav*, 2 ed., 241.]

S(h)aka [19C. H/S. *saka*.] Hinduism: an era, espec. that of the birth of *Saliwahana*, a S. Indian King born in AD 78 (e.g. *Saka* era 1807 began on 17 March 1885). *See* **Saka².** [Whitworth, *Anglo-Indian Dict.* (1885).]

Shakespearian Bridge [19C. Anglo-Indian, fr. pers. name, C. Shakespeare.] Foot-bridge of coir rope and bamboo strips. [Hawkins, *CIWIE*.]

Shakha [H. Shakha.] Branch. [Hawkins, *CIWIE*.]

Shakti *See* **Sakti.**

S(h)al(a)gram, salgram, saligram, etc. [18C. H. *salgrām*, fr. S. *sālagrāma*.] An ammonite or other fossil sacred to **Vishnu**. So named from the real or imaginary village, *Village of the Sal tree*, where this stone was orig. found. [YB & *OED*; Gladwyn, tr., *Ayeen Akbery* (1784), II. 29.]

Shalee, shaloo, shella, salloo, etc., etc. [17C. H. *sāloo*. (Cf. Tel. *sālū*, 'cloth').] A soft twilled cotton stuff, of a Turkey-red colour, originally one of the numerous Indian **Piece-goods**. (But Skeat and others think that this word is a corr. of *Chalons*, which French town gave its name to certain stuffs used for bed coverlets.) [YB; Danvers (1610), *Letters* (1896-1900), I. 72.]

Shalwar, shulwar, shulwaurs, sherwal, sherri-vallies, etc. [19C. H/P. *shalwār*.] 'Trousers, or drawers rather of the oriental kind, the same as **Pyjammas, Long-Drawers** or **Mogul-Breeches**.' [YB.] Also *ShalwarKameez*, the long shirt and baggy trousers worn espec. by Punjabis and Muslims of both sexes in India, Pakistan, Bangladesh and elsewhere. [*OED* & YB; Morier, *Adventures Hajji Baba* (1824), II. ix. 144.]

Shama¹ [19C. H. *shāmā*.] A cereal cultivated in India, *Panicum frumentacium (coconum)*, yielding a millet-like grain, used as food. Also: *shamalo(o)*, *shamoola*, and *shàmalo-grass* in the Deccan. [*OED*; Roxburgh (1815), *Flora Indica* (1820), I. 307.]

Shama,² Shamah [19C. H. *shāmā*, fr. S. *syāma*, 'black, dark-coloured'.] An Indian dark-coloured forest song-bird, *Cittocincla tricolor* (or *Copysychus malabaricus*), which 'in confinement imitates the notes of other birds, and of various animals, with ease and accuracy'. [YB; Jerdon (1839), in *Madras Journal Lit. & Sci.*, X. 252.]

Shambogue, shanbague, shanaboga, etc. [18C. Kan. *s(h)āna-bhoga, shanāya.*] 'allowance of grain paid to the village accountant.' (S. *bhōga*, 'enjoyment'.) A village clerk or accountant; paid by a grant of land and portions of the crop. [YB; Buchanan, *Mysore, Canara & Malabar* (1807), I. 268.]

Shamiana, shameeana, semiana, etc. [17C. H/P. *shamiyāna.*] An awning or flat tent-roof, with or without sides (**Kanauts**), stretched from top to top of poles and with no centre pole, formerly used by officials on tour for court or office proceedings, now for ceremonial occasions such as weddings. Also, the striped (calico) material used for such awnings. [OED & YB; Danvers (1609), *Letters* (1896–1900), I. 29.] See **Palmyra**.

Shampoo, champoo [18C. Prob. H. *shampo*, imper. of *shāmpnā*, 'to press'.] (Cf. *Champing* (obs.) 1698 = *shampooing*). In Anglo-India, but now obsolete in English, 'to knead and press the muscles with the view of relieving fatigue, etc.' = *massage*. Nowadays the word designates the washing of the scalp and hair with a shampoo preparation and water. Also, *dry shampoo*, a preparation of powdered starch, etc. used for cleansing the hair. [OED & YB; [Noble?], *Voy. E. Indies*, etc. (1762), 226; Mrs Sherwood, *Autobiog.* (1857), 410.]

Shanbaff, sinabaff [16C. H/P. *shanbāft.*] A cotton stuff often mentioned in the early narrative as an export from Bengal and other parts of India. The word is sometimes derived from *sīna-bafta*, 'China-woven' cloths. [Birdwood, *Report on the Old Records of the India Office*, 1891; YB; Varthema, *Travels* (1576), E. tr. 269.] See **Mull²**.

Shandy [Tam. *shandi.*] A market. [Hawkins, *CIWIE.*]

Shantih [20C. S. *shantih* Peace.] 'The peace that passeth understanding' is our equivalent of this word. [T.S. Eliot, *Collected Poems, 1907-35* (London, 1936).]

Shapu, shapoo [19C. Tib. sha-pho. 'wild sheep'.] The **Urial** *ovis orientalis*. See **Sha²**. [OED; A.L. Adams in *Proc. Zool. Soc.* (1858), 526.] See **Urial**.

Sharab, sherab See **Shrub, Sherbet** and **Syrup**.

Sharaddha See **Shraddha**.

Shariat, shariah, sheriat [19C. H./Ar. *sharīa*, 'law, justice', fr. *shara*, 'law'.] The canon law of Islam, consisting of the teaching of the Koran and the traditional sayings of Prophet Mohammed. [OED; R.F. Burton, *Personal Narr. Pilgrimage to El-Medinah* (1855), II. xxi. 281; *Encycl. Brit.* (1877), VII. 113/2.]

Sharif, shereef, sherifi, etc. [16C. H./Ar. *sharīf*, 'noble, glorious, a person of rank', fr. *sharafa*, 'to be exalted'.] A descendant of Prophet Mohammed through his daughter Fatima. Also, the title of certain Muslims of rank. Also *shereefa, shareefa*, wife of a *shereef, shareef.* [OED; Hak, *Voy.* (1599), II. II. 104.]

Sharpa See **Sherpa**.

Shastra, shaster, sastra [17C. H. *shastr*, fr. S. *shastra*, 'a rule, a precept, a sacred code'.] Any one of the sacred writings of the Hindus. [OED & YB; Lord *Banians* (1630), 40; Koestler, *Lotus & Robot* (1960), I. 59.]

Shastri, shastree [17C. H. *shāstrī*, fr. S. *shāstrin.*] One who is learned in, or teaches the *Shastras*, or any branch of Hindu learning. [Howell (*c.* 1645), *Litt. Suppl.*, xiv. (1892), 662.]

S(h)atatantri-Veena See **Santoor**. [Hawkins, *CIWIE.*]

Shatrungi See **Satrangi**.

Shawk [19C. Anglo-Indian. A blend of shit + hawk.] the shit-hawk, an Indian vulture, *Neophron percnopterus*. See **Shite-Hawk**. [Partridge (1870), *Dict. of Slang* (1937), 2nd vol.]

Shawl [17C. H/P. *shāl.*] A rectangular piece of wearing apparel, woven orig. in Kashmir from the hair of the Tibetan shawl-goat, and worn over the shoulders. The word has been adopted in Hindustani and other Indian languages and thence into many European languages. Also: *Shawl-dance* (1813); *shawl-goat* (1793); *shawl-wool (pashm)* (1879); and *shawlie* (1914), one who wears a shawl. [OED & YB; J. Davies (1662), *Ambassador's Trav.*, Bk. vi. 235; *Stanf Dict.* (1882); Sterne, *Letters to Eliza* (1767). x.] See **Toos**.

Sheeah See **Shia**.

Sheermaul [19C. H/P. *shīrmāl.*] 'a cake made with flour, milk and leaven; a sort of brioche' (P. *shir*, 'milk' + *mal*, 'crushing'. [Mrs Meer Hassan Ali, *Observations* (1832), i. 101.]

Sheesham, shisham See **Sissoo**.

Shehnai, Shahnai [20C. H. *shahnāī*, P. *shāhnāy.*] An Indian oboe-like musical instrument. [OED; Fox Strangways, *Music of Hindostan* (1914), i. 46; Ld. Harewood, *Tongs & Bones* (1981), xii. 195.]

Sheikh [16C. H/Ar. *shaikh*, 'old man'.] In India, one of a dissenting sect of Muslims; a general term for a Hindu convert to Islam; a Muslim saint. See **Pir**. [YB; Linschoten, *Voyages* (E. tr. 1598); *Eden's Hist. Trav.* (1577), 331 b.]

Shendi [19C. H. *shendi.*] Tuft of hair left on crown of head (of Brahmins), otherwise the *chuda* or *chonti.* [Whitworth, *Anglo-Indian Dict.* (1885).]

Sherbacha [19C. H. *Sherbaccha,* 'little lion'.] A small cannon; blunderbuss. [Whitworth, *Anglo-Indian Dict.* (1885).]

Sherbaff, serebaffe, etc. [17C. Prob. P. *shir,* 'lion' (used to denote excellence of quality) + *baf,* stem of *baftan,* 'to weave'.] A kind of rich silk. [*OED;* Foster (1619), *Eng. Fact. in India,* 63.]

Sherbet [17C.] *See* **Shrub.**

Sheristadar, sherishtadar, sarishtadar [18C. H/P. *sarishta-dar,* 'office-holder'.] Lit. *sar,* 'head' + *rishta,* 'thread' + *dar,* 'holder'. One who is able to pull strings. The head clerk or registrar of an Indian Court of Justice. *See* **Chitnis.** [*OED* & YB; *Min. Evid. Trial W. Hastings* (1775; 1788), I. 1033; *Bengal Rev. Regulation* (1786), 19 July, xix.]

Sherryvallies *See* **Shalwar.**

Sherpa [19C. Tib. *sharpa.*] One of the Himalayan people living near Mount Everest; a mountain guide. [*OED;* B. H. Hodgson in *Jrnl. Asiatic Soc. Bengal* (1847), XVI. 1237.]

Sherwani [20C.] H. *sherwāni.* A man's coat buttoning up to the neck. [*OED.*] *See* **Achkan, Angarkha.** [Encycl. Brit. (1911), XIV. 419/1.]

Shia(h), sheeah, etc. [17C. Ar./P. *Shi'a,* 'sect'.] One of the two great Muslim sects, which differs from the other, the **Sunni** in venerating Hazrat Ali (Prophet Mohammed's cousin and son-in-law) and in regarding the **Imams,** his descendants, as the true successors to the Caliphate, the three first caliphs of the **Sunni** being regarded as usurpers. A great many Indian Muslims are Shias. Hence *Shiite,* belonging to the Shia. *See* **Bo(h)ra,** and **Khoja.** Also *attrib* & *adj.* [OED & YB; Purchas, *Pilgrimes* (1625), 995; Fryer, *New Acct.* (1672-81), I. IV. 29; *Pioneer* (Lucknow) 13 Aug. 1969, 4/8.]

Shibar, shibbar [17C. Mar. *shibar.*] Poss. fr. P. *shahi-bar,* 'royal carrier'. A kind of large, coastal vessel. *See* **Pattamar.** [YB; Hedge's *Diary* (1684).]

Shigram, shigrampo [19C. H/Mar. *shīgr.* fr. S. *shīgra,* 'quick'.] 'A Bombay and Madras name for a kind of hack palanquin carriage.' [YB.] A clumsy vehicle drawn by horse, bullock or camel. *See* **Jutka** and **Cranchee** [OED & YB; A. Wilson, *Abode of Snow* (1875), 18; H. Miller (1841), *in* W. W. Peyton, *Life* (1883), iv. 57.]

Shikakai [T. *shikkakai.*] The soap-pod wattle, *Acacia concinna* [Hawkins, *CIWIE.*]

Shikar [17C. H/P. *shikār.*] Sport (in the sense of hunting, shooting, fishing); the game or prey. Also vb. 'to hunt animals for sport'. (1872.) [*OED* & YB; Finch (1613) in *Purchas* (1625), 1. 428.]

Shikara [19C. Kash./H. *shikarā.*] Long narrow Kashmiri boat. [*OED;* Drew, *Jummoo and Kashmir* (1875), viii. 181.]

Shikargah [19C. P. *shikār,* 'hunting' + *gāh,* 'enclosed-preserve'.] (1) A hunting preserve. [YB; J. Burnes, *Visit to the Court of Sinde* (1831), 103.] (2) Patterns of figures and groups of animals woven into Banaras brocade and Kashmir shawls. [YB; *see* Marco Polo (Tr. Yule, 1871), Bk., Ch. 17.]

Shikari, shikaree, shekary etc. [19C.] *See* Prec. A hunter, sportsman. (1) 'A native expert, who either brings in game on his own account, or accompanies (European) sportsmen as guide and aid. [*OED* & YB; Johnson, *Sketches of Field Sports* (1822), 25.] (2) The (European) sportsman himself. [H.A. Leveson, *The Old Shekarry* (1860-75).] (3) A shooting boat, used on the Kashmir lakes. *See* **Shikara.** [*OED* & YB; Drew, *Jummoo and Kashmir* (1875), viii. 181.]

Shikast(a) [18C. P. shikast, 'broken.] Cursive Persian writing. [*OED;* Sir W. Jones, *Gram. Pers. Lang.* (1771), 15; Kipling, *Kim* (1901), xiv. 364.]

Shikhara, shikara [19C. S. shikhara, 'point, peak, spire'.] A pyramidal tower on a Hindu temple, sometimes with convex sides. [*OED;* Tod, *Annals & Antiquities of Rajasthan* (1829), I. 670; Fergusson, *Hist. Indian & Eastern Architect.* (1891), II. ii. 221.]

Shikra(h) [19C. H/P. *shikra.*] A small Indian hawk, *Accipiter badius.* Sometimes used in falconry. [*OED;* Jerdon in *Madras Jrnl. Lit & Sci.* (1839), X. 83.]

Shin [19C. Native name, *Shīn.*] A (member of a) Dardic people of the Gilgit Agency of Kashmir. [*OED;* Drew, *Jummoo and Kashmir* (1875), xviii. 428.]

Shina [19C.] The Indo-Aryan language of the *Shins.* [*OED;* Cunningham, *Ladakh* (1854), ii. 37.]

Shinbin, shinbeam [18C. Bur. *shin,* 'to put together', 'side by side' + *byin,* 'plank'.] A thick teak plank split from a green tree and used in constructing the side of a ship. Also, (obs.) *shin-log* (1842). [YB; *Madras Courier,* 10 Nov. 1791.]

Shinwari [19C. Native name, *Shinwāri*.] A (member of) a nomadic Afghan. tribe of the Khyber Pass area. [*OED; Encycl. Brit.* (1875), I. 232/I Kipling, *Phantom Rickshaw* (1888), 85.]

Shiraz [17C. P. *Shirāz*.] Name of former capital of Persia (Iran). 'The wine of Shiraz, much imported and used by Europeans in India in the 17th century and even later.' [YB & *OED*; Sir T. Herbert, *Trav.* (1634), 65.]

Shireenbaf [17C. P. *shirinbaf*, 'sweet woof'.] 'A kind of fine cotton-stuff, but we cannot say more precisely what.' [YB; Danvers (1609), *Letters* (ed. 1896-1900), i. 29; Fryer (1673), *New Acct.* (1672-81), 88.]

S(h)iromani. [S. *shiromani*.] Title of scholarly distinction. [Hawkins, *CIWIE*.]

Shisham [19C. H. *shisham*, cogn. with S. *shinshapā* = Sissoo.] [*OED* & YB; Eastwick, *Dry Leaves from Young Egypt* (1849), 96; Kipling, *Soldiers Three* (1890), 31.]

Shishmahal, shishmuhull [19C. H/P. *shisha-mahal*, lit. 'glass apartment' or 'palace'.] 'A hall or suite of rooms lined with mirrors and other glittering surfaces, usually of a gim-crack aspect' in Indian Palaces. [YB; Fanny Parkes, *Wanderings of a Pilgrim* (1835), i. 365.]

S(h)ishya [S. *shishya*.] Disciple, pupil. [Hawkins, *CIWIE*.]

Shite-hawk [19C. Anglo-Indian.] An Indian scavenger vulture, *Neophron percnopterus*. Transf. an outsider, an unpleasant person. Also the badge of the 4th Indian Division (1940). *See* Shawk. [Partridge (1870), *Dict. of Slang* (1937), vol. 2.]

S(h)iva, Siwa, Shiv, etc. [18C. S. *siva*, 'the Auspicious One'.] One of the three deities of the Hindu trinity, Trimurti, the other two being Brahma and Vishnu. This god appears in many forms, e.g. as: (1) *Maheshvara*, 'the great god', the creator of music, dance and drama. (2) *Nataraja*, 'the Divine Dancer', who dances the *tāndava* to destroy the universe and create a new one by yet another dance. (3) *Sadashiv or Shanker*, 'Ever Blessed', or 'the Creator'; symbolized in the Lingam and Yoni. (4) *Rudra or Mahakala*, 'the Destroyer, the 'Great Dissolver', whose Sakti or consort is Kali, the Mother Goddess. (5) The wild, jovial Himalayan god, whose wife is Parvati.

Shiva is usually represented with three eyes, perhaps indicating the present, the past and the future, and with a crescent moon on his forehead which may indicate the measurement of time. His neck is blue from the stain of the poison he drank at the 'churning of the ocean'. *See* Amrita.

The holiest of Hindu rivers, the Ganges (*ganga*) flows from his hair; as *Bhairava* he wears a necklace of skulls and garlands of serpents. His *vahan* or vehicle is the bull, Nandi. He dwells on Mt. Kailasa in the Himalayas, with Parvati, his wife, and his two sons Ganesa, the elephant-headed deity, and Karttikeya with six heads.

Also: *Shaivism, Saivism, Shivaism* (1901), devotion to *Shiva* as the greatest of the Hindu gods. *S(h)aivite, shivite* (1880), a devotee of *Shiva*. *S(h)ivaistic* (1891), relating to the worship of *Shiva*. *Sivalaya, Siwalaya* (1885), fr. *Siva* + *alaya*, 'an abode'. A *Shaivite* shrine or temple, espec. one containing only the Lingam, *Sivaratri, Siwaratri* (1885), fr. *siva* + *ratri*, 'night'. The 14th of the Krishna-paksh, fr. S. *Krishna*, 'black + *paksha*', 'a side, a part', the dark half of the month, the fortnight from the full moon to the new moon. [*OED*; Major John Corneille (1760), *Jrnl. Service in India* (ed. 1960); *Asiat. Res.* (1788), I. 248; Monier-Williams, *Brahminism & Hinduism* (1891).] *See* Tantra, Durga.

Shivir, shibir [H. *shibir*.] A camp. [Hawkins, *CIWIE*.]

Shoe-flower [18C. Lit. trans. of Tamil *shapāttupu*.] Name given in Madras to the flower of the *Hibiscus rosa-sinensis*; so-called because it was used to blacken shoes. [*OED* & YB; Ives, *Voyage* (1754; ed. 1773), 475.]

Shoe-goose, syagush [18C. Corr. H/P. of *siyāh-gosh*.] Lit. 'black-ear', i.e. lynx (*Felis caracal*), once used for (antelope) hunting. [YB; A. Hamilton, *New Account* (1727), i. 124.]

Shoebite [Anglo-Indian.] Blister caused by un-suitable footwear. [Hawkins, *CIWIE*.]

S(h)loka, sloca [19C. S. *shloka*, 'sound, noise, call, hymn, stanza, etc'.] 'A couplet or distich of Sanskrit verse, each line containing 16 syllables.'[*OED; Asiat. Ann. Reg.* (1800), I. 80/1.]

Shoke [18C. H/Ar. *shauk*.] A hobby, a favourite pursuit or whim. [YB; Lt. Col. J. Skinner (1796), *Milit. Mem.* (1851), I. 109.]

Shola¹ [19C.] *See* Sola.

Shola² [19C. Tam. *sholāi*.] A thicket or jungle, a wooded ravine in S. India. [YB; Markham, *Peru & India* (1862), 356.]

Shoocka, shukha [18C. H/Ar. *shukka*, lit. 'an oblong strip'.] A letter from a king to a sub-ject. [Letter of Lord Cornwallis in *Corresp.* (1787; ed. 1859), i. 307.]

Shooldarry, shoaldarree, sholdarry [19C. H. *chholdārī* (of obscure origin).] 'A small tent with steep sloping roof, two poles and a ridge-piece, and with very low walls.' [YB.] *See* **Pawl**. [Elphinstone (1808), *Life* (ed. 1884), I. 183.]

Shooter-sowar *See* **Shutur-sowar**.

Shrab *See* **Sherbet, Shrub**.

S(h)radd(h)a [18C. H. *shrāddh*, S. *shrāddha*, 'faith, trust'.] Ceremonial periodic obsequies in which food and water are offered in honour and for the benefit of a deceased relative. These ceremonies occur on occasions of rejoicing as well as of mourning. The first *shrāddha* is performed on the day after the 10 days of mourning are over, and thereafter usually repeated once a month for the first year, afterwards once a year. *Shrāddha* also refers to the offerings themselves. *See* **Pinda** and **Pitri**. [*OED;* Seton-Karr (1787), *Select. Calcutta Gaz.* (1864), I. 209.]

S(h)ramdan [20C. H. *shram*, 'hard work' + *dan*, 'gift'.] 'A gift of labour' for public purposes. [Hawkins, *CIWIE*.]

Shri, sri, shree [18C. S. *shri*.] (1) Prosperity; or the goddess of prosperity, *Lakshmi*, wife of *Vishnu*. (2) Prefix of reverence to the names of dieties, holy places, sacred books, spiritual teachers, etc. Elliptically for *Sri Ganesha*. (3) Also written at the commencement of books, letters, and writings generally. (4) A title of respect, = Mr or Esquire. Also: *Shrimati* = Mrs, Madame, lady. (5) And, *Shrijut*, an honorific title. [*OED; Asiat. Res.* (1799), VI. 475; Molesworth, *Dict. Marathi & English* (1857); Whitworth, *Anglo-Indian Dict.* (1885); Wilson, *Glossary* (1855).] *See* **Thiru**.

Shroff [16C. H/Ar.*sharaff(a)*, 'exchange, expenditure'.] A money-changer. Also, an expert employed in banks to examine money to test its genuineness. Also, *shroffage* (1629), the commission charged for *shroffing* money and, *shrooferage* (1675-80). [*OED* & YB; Linschoten, *Voy.* (E. tr. 1598), 66; Foster (1629), *Eng. Fact. in India* (1909), iii. 35.]

Shrub, shrab [17C. H/Ar. *sharāb*, 'drink'.] Wine, spirits, or any intoxicating beverage. Hence: Port-*shrub;* sherry-; *lal-* (red-wine); brandy-; beer-. Also, **Sherbet** (1603), fr. P. *sherbet*. (1) A cooling drink of the East, made with fruit-juice and water, often cooled with snow. (2) European imitation of this made with effervescing *sherbet*-powder. [*OED* & YB; Sir T. Herbert, *Travels* (1638), 241; Sir W. Scott, *The Surgeon's Daughter* (1827); Dickens, *Sk. Boz. and Miss Evans* (1835).]

Shruti [S. *shru* 'to hear'.] Basic tonic scale in Indian music. Lit. 'heard'. Also, a *shruti-box*, a drone instrument often used with or instead of a **Tamboura (Tanpura)**.

S(h)ud(d)h [19C. H/S. *suddha*, 'pure, bright'.] A term used after the name of a month to denote the *Suklapaksh*, or bright half of the month. [Whitworth, *Anglo-Indian Dict.* (1885).]

Shudra *See* **Sudra**.

Shukriya [H. *shūkriya*.] Int: Thanks! Thank you! [Hawkins, *CIWIE*.]

Shulwar *See* **Shalwar**.

Shums(h)eer, shamsheer [17C. H/P *shamshīr*, scimitar.] The Asian sabre. [YB; Sir T. Herbert, *Travels* (1638), 228.]

S(h)unyata [20C. S. *shūnya*, 'zero'. All & none'.] The ever-changing state of the phenomenal world. [Sir Charles Eliot, *Hinduism & Buddhism* (1938), II. 38.]

Shutur-sowar, shooter-sowar [19C. H/P. *shutur*, 'camel ' + *sowar*, 'rider'.] A camel-rider. Such riders were attached to the establishment of the Viceroy on the march. *See* **Sowar**. [*OED* & YB; Marquess of Hastings, *Journal* (1815), I. 337; Col. Mountain, *Mem.* (1834; 1857), 135.]

Sicca [17C. H/Ar/P. *sikkah*.] 'die for coining', 'coined money', used as an adj. with *rupee*. (1) Orig. a newly coined rupee, accepted at a higher value than that worn by use. [*OED* & YB; Foster (1619), *Eng. Fact. in India* (1906), I. 113. (2) Latterly, a Bengal government rupee current from 1793 to 1836 of a greater weight than the Company's rupee. As last coined, it weighed 192 grains of which 176.13 were of pure silver. [GCW.] [*OED* & YB.] Also *sicca*-weight (1833). *See* **Chick** and **Rupee**. [India Regulation vii of 1833.]

Sicleegur, chickludar, sikalgar [19C. H. *saikalgar*, fr. Ar. *saikal*, 'polish'.] A furbisher of arms, a sword-armourer; a sword-or-knife-grinder. (This in Madras, is turned into *chickledar*. Tel. *chikili-daradu*.) [YB; Hockley (1826), *Pandurang Hari* (ed. 1873), i. 216.]

Sickman [17C.] 'Hindustani sepoy patois meaning 'one who has to go to hospital', and generally *sikmān ho jānā* means to be disabled. [YB; Yule (1665), *Hedges Diary*, (Hak. Soc., 1886), II. cclxxx; C.J. Davidson, *Travels* (1843), i. 251.]

Siddhartha [19C. S. *siddha*, 'accomplished' + *artha*, 'object'.] One who has accomplised his object; the name of the Buddha; a perfected bodyless being, freed from the cycle of re-births. [*OED;* H. H. Wilson, *Sk. Relig. Sects Hindus* (1846), ii. 17; M. Miller (1856), *Chips* (1867), II. xvi. 102.]

Siddhi [19C. S. lit. 'fulfilment' (see prec.).] Supernatural, magical powers acquired by meditation or other practices in Hindu or Tibetan Buddhistic religions. [OED; Schlagintweit, *Buddhism in Tibet* (1863), vi. 56; A. Huxley, *Grey Eminence* (1941), ix. 218.]

Sidi, Seedy [17C. H. *sīdī*; Mar. *siddhi*; Ar. *saiyid*, 'lord' (whence 'Le Cid').] (1) A Muslim title of honour, in India given to African **Sunni** Muslims, some of whom 'furnished the Moghul empire with the chief naval officers on the western coast'. [GCW.] [Orme (1679). *Fragments* (1805), 78; Fryer (1673), *New Acct.* (1672-81), 147.] (2) An Abyssinian Sea-raider on the western coast of India. [Grose, *Voyage* (1757), i. 58.] (3) In later use, an African negro, '*Seedy boy*' was the Anglo-Indian term for a Zanzibar man. Cf. **Sayyid, Syed.** [OED & YB; Burton, *Arabian Nights*; Forbes, *Orient. Mem.* (1813), III. 167.]

Sigri [Guj. *sagdī*.] A charcoal brazier used for cooking. [OED; J.R. Lawrence, *Indian Embers* (1949), 56; Masters, *Bhowani Junction* (1954), 127.]

Sika [20C. Beng. *Sika*; S. *sikya*, 'sling'.] A rope-hanger for suspending baskets. [OED; *Observer*, 15 Sept. 1974, 40.]

Sikh, Seikh, Seek, etc. [18C. H/Punj. *Sikh*, from S. *sishya*, 'disciple'. The Anglo-Indian spelling *Seek* perh. by association from H. *sikh*, 'learning', from *sickna*, 'to learn'.)] A member of a military community of the Punjab, whose monotheistic, eclectic religion (*Sikhism*) was founded by Guru Nanak Shah, a Hindu reformer of the **Kshatriya** caste, early in the 16th century, whose aim was to unite Muslim and Hindu religions and people. In the two centuries following the foundation of *Sikhism*, there were ten *gurus*, the ninth being executed by Aurangzeb, after which event there was never again peace between the Mughals (Muslims) and the Sikhs. The tenth *guru* denominated every *Sikh* male, '*Singh*', 'a lion' and the whole community **Khalsa.** (Ar. *khalsa*, 'pure, genuine'.) Originally the bulk of the Sikhs were of the **Jat** community who had long settled in the Punjab. The holy book of the Sikhs is the **Granth (Sahib)**, in which the sayings of the first four *gurus*, collected by Arjun the fifth *guru*, with compositions added by later *gurus*, various saints (**Sants**) and others, are known as **Adi-Granth** (First Book). The language is metrical, in Hindi, in **Gurumuki** characters. [OED & YB; Wilkins (1781), *Asiatic Rev.* (1799), I. 288; Orme,

Hist. Milit. Transactions (1781), II. 22; Cunningham, *Hist. Sikhs* (1849), iii. 96/1.]

Sikkim [19C. Name of kingdom, now a state of India.] Used attrib. to designate certain indigenous trees, etc., e.g. the Sikkim stag, the Sikkim oak. [OED; *Treas, Bot.* (1866).]

Sikra, See **Shikhara.**

Silajit, Shilajatu, Silajeet [19C. H. *shila-jit*; S. *silājit, silājatu*, 'bitumen', fr. S. *silā*, 'rock' + *jit*, 'conquering', or *jatu*, 'essence'.] The name of various solid or viscous substances found on rock in India and Nepal used in Indian medicine, espec. a substance probably consisting mainly of dried animal urine. [OED; F. Buchanan (1811-12), *Acct. Bihar & Patna* (1936), II. iii. iii. 467.]

Silappadikaram, Silapadigaram [Tam. *Silappadigāram*. 'Tale of the Anklet'.] Tamil epic composed between the 2nd and 5th (or 9th) centuries AD. [Basham, *A Cultural Hist. of India* (1975), 304.]

Silboot, silpet, slippet [19C. Domestic Hindustani.] A slipper (*Silboot* is an example of 'striving after meaning'.) (The Railway *sleeper* was in the same way corrupted into *silīpat*.) [YB.]

Silk-cotton [17C.] The silky, elastic down obtained from certain bombaceous and other tropical trees (*see* next) and chiefly used for packing, stuffing cushions and pillows, making paper etc. See **Kapok, Simmul.** [OED; Dampier (1697), *Voy.* (1698), I. vii. 164.]

Silk-cotton Tree [18C.] One or other of various species of tropical trees producing silk-cotton (**Kapok**), e.g., *Ceiba petandra* (white flowers) and *Bombax ceiba* (red flowers). [OED.] See **Sim(m)ul.** [E. Cooke, *Voy. S. Sea* (1722), 117.]

Silladar, silledar, silahdar [19C. P. *silāhdār*, 'armour-bearer, squire'. fr. *silāh*, 'arms, armour' + *dār*, 'one who has, owner'.] Its Anglo-Indian application is to a soldier, in a regiment of irregular cavalry, who provides his own arms and horse (as distinguished from a *bargir*. Sometimes referred to as a corps or regiment of such men. [OED & YB.] [Wellington (1802) *Gurw. Disp.* (1841), I. 322; P. Mason, *Matter of Honour* (1974), i. 26.]

Sillaposh [18C. H/P. *silāh*, 'armour' + *posh*, fr. *poshīdan*, 'to wear'.] An armour-clad warrior or a bodyguard. [YB; W. Franklin (1799), *Mil. Mem. of George Thomas* (ed. 1805), 165.]

Silmagoor [19C.] Ship H. for 'sail-maker'. [YB; Roebuck, *Naval Dict.* (1811).]

Silpa, silpin [H/S. *silpa.*] Hindu Arts: The guiding canons of ancient Hindu sculpture. (Lit. any manual of mechanical art.) [Wilson, *Glossary* (1855).]

Simkin, simpkin, samkin [19C.] Domestic H. corr. of *champagne.* [YB; W. D. Arnold, *Oakfield* (1854), ii. 127.]

Sim(m)ul, simool, semul, seemul, and sometimes **symbol** & **cymbal.** [H. *semal;* S. shalmali.] The **Silk-Cotton Tree** (Red), *Bombax ceiba,* or Indian **Kapok.** Found all over India, except in the driest areas. Also in Sri Lanka, Burma and Malaysia. Its *Kapok* is used for stuffing pillows and cushions, and its wood for matches, coffins, packing cases and the lining of wells. It produces also *mocharas,* a brown astringent gum used as a tonic. [*OED* & YB; Buchanan-Hamilton, *E. India* (1807), ii. 789; *Penny Cycl.* (1835), IV. 2/2.]

Sind(h), Scinde, Sindy, etc [16C.] Local name fr. *Sindhu* and *Indus* (river). Territory on the Indus below the Punjab, east of Rajputana (Rajasthan) and now in Pakistan. Also *Sindhi:* (1) The largely Sanskritic language of Sind. [Fitch (1583), *Hakluyt* (ed. 1807), 885.] (2) *Sindhi,* an indigenous inhabitant of Sind, **Sunni** by religion. [Elphinstone, *Acct. Kingdom of Caubul* (1815), IV. V. 500.] [*OED* & YB; Hughes, *Dict. of Islam* (1885); Whitworth, *Anglo-Indian Dict.* (1885).]

Sindhia Name of one of the four Maratha leaders who rose to independent power; the family name of the former rulers of Gwalior State. [Whitworth, *Anglo-Indian Dict.* (1885).]

Sindur [H. *sindur.*] 'red lead', vermillion, the red stripe in the parting of a Hindu wife's hair. [Hawkins, *CIWIE.*]

Sinduriyar See prec. The name of a caste, which deals in red lead and grain. [Whitworth, *Anglo-Indian Dict.* (1885).]

Singalese, Singhalese, Cingalese, Sinhalese, etc. [16C. S. *Sinhala,* 'Ceylon', or 'Dwelling of Lions'.] Pertaining to Ceylon (now Sri Lanka), its inhabitants and its Indo-European language, *Sinhala.* The *Sinhalese* are Buddhists and their sacred books are in **Pali.** [*OED* & YB; Fitch (1583), *Hakluyt* (ed. 1807), ii. 397; Pinkerton, *Mod. Geogr.* (1802), II. 313.]

Sing(h)ara [18C. H. *singhārā;* S. *sringar* 'a horn'.] The **water-chestnut** plant of India, *Trapa bispinosa,* and its edible fruit. Usual. *attrib.* with *nut.* [*OED* & YB; Forster, *Journey from Bengal to England* (1790), ii. 29; *Penny Cycl.* (1834), II. 478/2.]

Singh, Sing [17C. H. *singh,* fr. S. *sinha,* 'the powerful one, lion'.] A great warrior, a title borne by several of the warrior castes of North India, such as **Rajputs** and **Sikhs,** a name given to the latter by Gobind, the tenth *Guru,* who assumed it himself to signify that thenceforth they should be soldiers. [*OED;* Foster (1623), *Eng. Fact. in India* (1908), 218.]

Sinhala [20C.] = **Sinhalese.**

Sipahselar [19C. H/P. *sipāhsālār,* 'army-leader'.] A commander-in-chief, a generalissimo. [YB; *N. India Notes and Queries.* (1803), iv. 17; M.H. Ali Khan Kirmani, *Hist. Hydur Naik* (E. Tr. Miles, 1842), 61.]

Sircar, sirkar, sarkar, circar [17C. H/P. *sarkār,* fr. *sar,* 'head' + *kār,* 'agent, doer'. (1) The court or palace of an Indian King or Prince. [*OED;* Foster (1619), *Eng. Fact. in India* (1906), I. 160.] (2) A province, a revenue division. [YB & *OED;* Foster (1627), *Eng. Fact. in India* (1909), III. 176.] (3) The state or Government. [*OED* & YB (1798); *Wellesley's Desp.* (1877), 61.] (4) Bengali house steward. [*OED* & YB; Verelst, *View Eng. Govt. Bengal* (1772), v.] (5) Indian 'Writer' or accountant. [*OED* & YB; Williamson, *Vade Mecum* (1810), I. 200.] (6) Purchasing clerk employed in a merchant's office. [*OED* & YB; Fanny Parkes, *Wanderings of a Pilgrim* (1850), I. 21.] (7) A Bengali broker. [YB & *OED; Asiatic Costumes* (1828), 41.]

Sirca baksheesh. See **Higher Standard.**

Sirdar, sardar [17C. H/P. *sardār,* fr. *sar,* 'head' + *dār,* 'possession'.] (1) In India, a military chief, leader or general. [*OED* & YB; Sandys, *Trav.* (1615), 211.] (2) *Sirdar-bearer,* an Indian valet or body-servant. See **Bearer.** [*OED* & YB; *India Gaz.,* 2 Sept. 1782; W. Hamilton, *East India Gazetteer* (1815), (Gloss). (3) A recruiter of plantation labour. [Hawkins, *CIWIE.*] (4) A title of respect. [Hawkins, *CIWIE.*] (5) *Sirdar-ji,* a common form of address to a Sikh. [Hawkins, *CIWIE.*] Hence *Sirdarship,* the office of *Sirdar.* [*Daily Chronicle.* 10 Oct. 1898, 6/3.]

Sirdar-melon [19C. Pusht. *sarda.*] The melon *Cucumis melo* is *Sirdar melon.* [*OED; Encycl. Brit.* (1880), XIII. 836/2.]

Sirdrars [19C. Domestic Hindi, *sīrdrāj,* 'short drawers', underclothing.] **Long-Drawers.** (A chest of drawers was also called '*Drāj kā almaira*'.) [YB.]

Sirgang [19C. Beng. *sirgang.*] An East Indian corvine bird, *Cissa chinensis,* alias Green Magpie. [*Century Dict.* (1891).]

Siris, Sirris [19C. H. *siris.*] (1) One or other of the leguminous trees of the genus, *Abizzia*, native to India and other tropical areas in Asia and Africa. [*OED* & YB.] (2) A similar tree belonging to the genus *Acacia*, esp. *Acacia sirissia*. Also its timber. 'A closely kindred tree, *Acacia julibrissin* (Boivin), affords a specimen of scientific 'Hobson-Jobson'. The specific name is a corruption of *Gulābreshm* 'silk-flower'. [YB.] *Attrib.* 'Siris boughs' [Kipling, *Dep. Ditties* (1886), 114; Stewart & Brandis, *Flora N. West India* (1874).]

Sirki, sirky [19C. H. *sirkī.*] The upper part of the culm of a species of a tall Indian reed-grass, *Saccharum munjia* or *sara*. 'A kind of unplatted matting formed by laying the fine cylindrical culms side by side, and binding them in single or double layers ... to lay under the thatch of a house, to cover carts and palankins, to make chicks and table-mats.' [YB.] *See* **Surkunda**. [*OED* & YB; *Asiat. Res.* (1801), vii. 463; Williamson, *Vade Mecum* (1810), I. 489.]

Sisodia Family name. Name of the rulers of the former **Rajput** state of *Udaipur* from the 13C. [Whitworth, *Anglo-Indian Dict.* (1885).]

Sissoo, shisham, sessu etc. [19C H. *sīsū.*] A valuable Indian timber-tree, *Dalbergia sissoo*, used for construction of buildings, joinery, boat-and-carriage-building and furniture. *See* **Shisham**. [*OED* & YB; Williamson, *Vade Mecum* (1810), II. 71.]

Sita, Seeta [20C. S. *sīta*, lit. 'furrow'.] Hinduism: The daughter of King Janaka and wife of **Rama**. (*See* **Ramayana**.) Sita was an incarnation of **Lakshmi** and received her name because she was born in a furrow in a ploughed field of her own desire and free will. Hence her epithet *ayonija*, 'not womb-born'. [Sir Charles Eliot, *Hinduism & Buddhism* (1921), I. 72.]

Sitaphul [19C. H. *sītaphal*, 'the fruit of Sita'.] *Anona squamosa*. *See* **Custard Apple**.

Sitar, sitarre [19C. H. *sītar.*] An Indian guitar; a long-necked fretted musical instrument, usually with three to seven metal strings played with a plectrum. Also *sitarist* (1966). [*OED*; Stocqueler (1845), *Handbk. Brit. India* (1854), 26.] *See* **Surbahar, Veena**.

Sitringee *See* **Satrangi**.

Sitting-up. [18C.] A curious old-time Anglo-Indian custom. Newly-arrived ladies 'sat-up' in the evening, often in the homes of some ladies of rank or fortune, to receive male and female visitors of the **Station**, in order to become acquainted with them and their functions in the social and official hierarchy. [YB; Busteed (1777), *Echoes of Old Calcutta* (1857), 124; Munro, *Narrative of Milit. Ops.* (1780-84), 56.]

Siva, Siwa *See* **Shiva**.

Sivatherium [19C. Mod. L. fr. **Siva** & Gr. *therion*, 'wild beast'.] An enormous fossil ruminant with four horns discovered in the sub-Himalayan hills. [*OED*; Falconer & Cautley, *Asiatic Res.* (1835), XIX. I. 2.]

Skeen, Skyn [19C. Tibet. *skyin.*] The Himalayan ibex, *Capra sibirica*. [*OED*; D. Herbert in *Asiat. Res.* (1825), XV. 397.]

Sky-clad *See* **Digambar**.

Sky-races [19C. Orig. obscure.] The suggested connection with Westminster School slang, *sky*, meaning 'an outsider', seems remote. Sky Races in India and Burma in the 19th century were confined to amateur riders on untrained mounts over a roughly marked-out course in the early mornings under the sky of the uncertain weather of the monsoon season, with stakes limited to Rs 50 or so. [*OED*; Atkinson, *Curry and Rice* (2nd. ed. 1858), xviii; Lady Dufferin (1885), Jrnl., 11 June, in Our *Viceregal Life in India* (1889), I. iv. 157.]

Sling, Seling [18C.] Himalayan place-name *Sining* in Kan-su. 'A stuff made of goat's wool at the place so-called.' [YB; Bogle's Narrative (*c.* 1774) in *Markham's Tibet* (1876), 124.]

Smriti [19C. S. *smrī*, 'remember'.] Hinduism: Tradition; that which is remembered. This term includes the Sanskrit texts which, though not directly revealed (*sruti*), have been founded on revelation and delivered by human authors. *Smriti* may be said to denote almost the whole of post-vedic literature; a class of religious texts consisting of law-books, epics and **Puranas**. [Monier-Williams, *Religious Thought & Life in India* (1883).]

Snake-bird [19C.] A bird, *Anhinga rufa melanogaster*, the Darter, quite common in Bengal (Beng. *goyār*). 'A black water-bird like the cormorant with longer, slenderer snake-like neck. [*OED*; Ali & Ripley, *Birds of India & Pakistan* (1968), 1. 43; *Fish. Exhib. Catal.* (4th ed. 1883), 152.]

Snake-flower [A.I./H. *Sarpa kumbha*.] 'Snake-Pot', the *Arisaema wallachium*.

Snake-gourd [19C. Anglo-Indian.] An edible Indian gourd, *Trichosanthes anguina*. [*OED*; Henfrey, *Bot.* (1857), 479.]

Snake-juice [19C.] Illicit 'country' liquor. [Hawkins *CIWIE*.]

221

Snake-stone [17C. Anglo-Indian.] A porous or absorbent substance considered to be a cure for snake-bite, or a remedy against poison. [*OED* & *YB*; Fryer (1673), *New Acct.* (1672-81), 53.]

Snake-wood [16C. Anglo-Indian.] (a) A tree or shrub of the genus *Strychnos*, esp. *S. colubrina*, the wood of which was used as a remedy for snake-bite. [*OED*; Phillip's *Linschoten* (1598), I. LXXV. 121/1.] (b) Also the plant *Ophioxylon serpentinum*, used as an antidote for snake-bites. Both found in India, Sri Lanka and the Far East. [*OED*; Burnett, *Outlines Bot.* (1835), 4614.]

Sneaker [18C. Anglo-Indian.] 'A large cup, (or small basin) with a saucer and cover', for punch, brandy, etc. [*YB*; Letter (1772) in Forbes, *Or. Mem.* (1810), IV. 217.]

Snooker(s) [19C.] A game played on a billiards table, combining 'pyramids' and 'pool'. Said to have been invented at the Jabalpur Officers mess by Sir Neville Chamberlain about 1875, and perfected at the Ooty Club about six years later. The name appears to have come from the Royal Military Academy, where a fresh-man was known as a 'Snooker', prob. fr. the slang expression *Snook*, 'sneak about'. [Partridge, *Dict. of Slang.* (1979); *OED*; Drayson, *Pract. Billiards* (1889), 110; Glasfurd, *Rifle in Indian Jungle* (1905), 70.]

Snow rupee [19C. Corr. of Tel. *tsanauvu*.] 'authority, currency'. 'An excellent example of the Hobson-Jobson type.' A genuine rupee.

Sola, Solar, Solah [19C. H. *sholā*; Beng. *solā*.] A tall leguminous swamp-plant, *Aeschynomene paludosa* or *aspera*, of India, the pith of which is used to make light-weight hats, 'Sola Topis', corrupted by Anglo-Indians to *Solar Topis*, 'led astray by the usual striving after meaning'. [*YB* & *OED*; Fanny Parkes (1836), *Wandr. Pilgr.* (1850), II. 100.] See **Terai**.

Soma [19C. S. *sōma* = Zend. *haōma* = P. *hōm(a)*.] Hinduism: (1) Supposedly the 'moon-plant' *Asclepias acida* or *Sarcostemma viminale* (or *accidum*) deified in Vedic ritual and religion; the *Sama Veda* incantations now fallen into disuse, may have been arranged to this end. (2) Its fermented juice, a kind of **Amrita**, was believed to confer eternal life and vigour on gods and men. Mixed with **Ghee** and flour this fermented liquor was offered to the gods in sacrificial ritual (*Somayajna* preceded by the *Somakaryam*), and finally drunk by the officiating Brahmin **Pujaris**, who partook of divinity in this way.

(3) The plant and its juice are also venerated by Parsis and dubiously identified with one or other species of *Asclepias* or *Sarco-stemma*. (4) *Soma* was said to be the plant by means of which Indra conquered Vritra. [*OED*; Cole-brook in *Trans. Royal Asiatic Soc.* (1827), I. 455; Trottler, *Hist. India* (1874), 1. i. 4.] See **Yajna**.

Somba, sombay [17C. Mal. *sembah-an*.] A present. [*YB*; Foster (1614), *Letters* (ed. 1896-1900), ii. 112.]

Sonar [19C. H/S. *suwarna*, 'gold' + *āra*, 'wor-ker'.] The bazaar goldsmith. One of the *Pan-chāls* (Marathi), a collective name for five castes of artificers – the *Sonār*, *Sutār*, *Lohār*, *Kānsār* and *Pātharwat* (gold-smith, carpenter, blacksmith, metal-worker and stone-mason.) [Whitworth, *Anglo-Indian Dict.* (1885).]

Sonf. [H. *sonf*.] Aniseed seeds. Comes with the bill after a restaurant meal, to be chewed as a digestive.

Sonthal *See* **Santal**.

Soodra *See* **Sudra**.

Sooji, suji, soojee, soojy [19C. H. *sūjī*.] A coarsely-ground flour obtained by grinding Indian wheat; a nutritious food prepared from this resembling semolina; porridge. Also *sooji* **Halwa** (1955), a kind of sweet pudding. [*OED* & *YB*; Williamson, *E. Ind. Vade Mecum* (1810), II. 136.] See **Rolong**.

Sooranji [19C. Guj. *sorangi*, fr. S. *surangi*.] The root of the plant *Morinda citrifolia*; a dye, *morindin*, obtained from this with which **sadhus** colour their cloth. *See* **Morinda**. [Anderson (1848), *Trans. Roy. Soc. Edin* (1849), XVI. 438.]

Soorki [18C. H/P. *surkhī*, 'redness', 'brick-dust'.] A mortar made with pulverized brick mixed with lime. *See* **Khoa**. [*OED* & *YB*; Stephen (1777), *Nundcomar & Impey* (ed. 1885), ii. 201; Stavorinus, *Voyage to the E. Indies* (E. tr., 1798), I. 514.]

Soorma *See* **Surma**.

Soosy, soosie, sussy [17C. H/P. *sūsī*.] A mixed striped fabric of silk and cotton once manu-factured in India, used especially for making trousers for Muslims. [*OED* & *YB*; Foster (1621), *Eng. Fact. in India* (1906), 338.]

Soubash(dar) *See* **Subah(dar)**.

Soucar, Sah(o)ukar, Sowcar [18C. H. *sāhūkār*, perh. fr. S. *sādhu*, 'right' + *kar*, 'agent'.] Guj./Mar. *sāvakār*. A Hindu banker, money-lender or broker, corresponding to the **Chetty** of S. India. Hence, *Soucaring* (1785), 'money-lending'. [*OED* & *YB*; Burke, *Sp. on Nabob of Arcot's Debts, Wks.* (1785), VI. 289.] *See* **Sha**[1].

Sow, abbr. for *Sowbhagyavati.* Sanskrit title prefixed in S. India to the name of a woman whose husband is alive. [Hawkins, *CIWIE.*]

Sowar, sawar [19C. H/P. *sawār,* 'horseman'.] A native cavalryman; a mounted orderly, policeman, etc; a native trooper, espec. one belonging to the irregular cavalry. Also, *shooter-sowar,* (H/P. **Shutur-Sawar**), and *oont-sowar,* the rider of a dromedary or swift camel. [*OED* & *YB*; James, *Milit. Dict.* (1802); Scott, *Surgeon's Daughter* (1827), xiii.]

Sowarry, sawari, sewarry, suwarree, etc. [18C. H/P. *sawārī* (fr. prec.)] A cavalcade of mounted riders attending a person of high rank or state officials. Hence, a *sawari* horse, camel or elephant is one used for riding (1835). [*OED* & *YB*; *Trial Maharaja Nund-coomar* (1776),43/2.]

Spahi, sipahi [16C. Turk/P. *sipāhī.*] Orig. a member of the Turkish irregular cavalry and later of native Algerian cavalry in the French army. 'The *spahī* is totally different from the *sepoy* and is in fact an irregular horseman.' [YB.] *See* **Sepoy.** [*OED* & *YB*; Shute, tr. *Cambini's Turkish Wars* (1562), 53; Hedges' *Diary* (Hak. Soc., 1886), I. 299.]

Spatchcock [18C. Orig. Irish, but later Anglo-Indian.] A fowl dispatched, split open, plucked, dressed and grilled in summary fashion. *See* **Sudden-Death.** Also vb. trans. & intrans. [*OED*; F. Grose, *Dict. Vulgar Tongue* (1785); Mrs James, *Ind. Household Manual* (1865), 34.]

Spin [19C. Anglo-Indian. Abbr. fr. 'spinster'.] An unmarried woman; used in playful or derogatory sense. [*OED* & *YB*; G.F. Atkinson, *Curry and Rice* (1860); 'Aliph Cheem' (Yeldham) (1872), *Lays of Ind* (1876), 93.]

Spotted-deer [17C. Anglo-Indian.] The Indian **Chital.** (S. *chitra,* 'spotted'.) [YB; Fryer (1673), *New Acct.* (1672-81), 71.]

Squeeze [19C. Anglo-Chinese slang. (sb.)] A forced or illegal exaction or import made by Asian servants or officials. (vb) To extort or exact, to obtain by force or pressure, an illegal 'gratification'. [*OED* & *YB*; *Fankwae, or Canton before Treaty Days, by an old Resident* (1881), 36.]

Station]19C. Anglo-Indian.] In India, a place where the British officials of a district, or the officers of a garrison (not in fortress) resided and conducted their allotted duties and led their social lives. Also, the aggregate society of such a place. *See* Hill-Station. [*OED* & YB;

Mrs Meer Hassan Ali, *Observations* (1832), I. 196.] *See* **Sitting-up**.

S.T. (1) Sales Tax; (2) State Transport (bus); (3) Member of **Scheduled Tribe.** [Hawkins, *CIWIE.*]

Stepney [20C.] (1) A motor-car spare-wheel with inflated tyre (but orig. no spokes), perh. from Stepney Street, Llanelly, in Glamorganshire the orig. place of manufacture. Now any spare-wheel wherever manufactured. [*OED*; *West. Gaz.,* 3 Dec. 1907, 4/3.]

Stick-insect or **animated stalk** [18C.] The name, in India and elsewhere, applied to insects of the family *Phasmidae,* 'which have the strongest possible resemblance to dry twigs or pieces of a stick, sometimes 6 or 7 inches in length'. [YB & *OED*; Ives (1754), *Voy. from England to India* (1773), 20.]

Sticklac(k) [18C. E. *stick* + H. *lac.*] **Lac** in its natural state, encrusted on sticks found and collected in the jungles of Central India. [*OED* & YB; *Lond. Gaz.,* 1704, No. 4059/4.]

Stridhan(a), stredhan(a) [18C. S. *stri-dhana.*] 'Woman's property'. Hindu law: Property belonging to a woman which follows a law of succession different from that which regulates other property. The term is to be found in the works of Colebrooke and Sir William Jones, 1790-1800, afterwards introduced into European legal treatises. [YB; Sir Henry S. Maine, *Early History of Institutions* (1875), 321.] Manu defines it as: 'What was given before the nuptial fire, what was given at the bridal procession, what was given in token of love and what was received from a mother or brother, or father, are considered as the six-fold separate property of a married woman.' [Whitworth, *Anglo-Indian Dict.* (1885); Manu, *Institutes,* ix. 194; Wilson, *Glossary* (1855).]

Stupa [19C. S. *stūpa* fr. *stūp,* 'to pile up'. Pali, *thūpa.*] Buddhism: A solid dome or tumulus-like structure built to contain relics of the *Buddha* or others revered by Buddhists. Famous *stupas* in India are at Sanchi, Bharut and Amaravati, and other spots consecrated as the scenes of his acts. *See* **Tope.** [*OED* & YB; Fergusson, *Ind. & East. Archit.*(1876),I.]

Subah, soubha, soobah [18C. H/P. *sūba.*] A province of the Mughal empire (e.g. the *subah* of the Deccan or of Bengal). Also frequently used as short for Subahdar, 'the viceroy of a *subah'. See* next. [*OED*; Hanway (1753), *Trav.* (1762). II. xiv. v. 362; Orme (1753), *Hist. Fragments* (1805), 400.]

Subahdar, subadar, soubadar, soobadar [17C. Prec. + *dar*, 'possessor, master'.] (1) The viceroy of a **Subah** or province. [*OED* & YB; Orme, *Hist. Milit. Trans.* (1763), i. 35.] (2) A local commandant or chief officer. [*OED* & YB; Fryer (1673), *New Acct. E. India & Persia* (1672)-81; ed. 1698), 77.] (3) The chief native officer of a company of **Sepoys** [*OED* & YB; MS in India Office Lib. (1747), Cons. Fort St. David.] Also, (a) *subahdar-major*, the local commandant of a regiment of sepoys. [*OED; Eng. Hist. Rev.* (1819; 1913), April, 269.] (b) *subahdary* (1764) and *subahship* (1753), the office of status of a *subah* or province; also the territory governed = **Subah**. [*OED; State Papers* in *Ann. Reg.* (1764), 190; Orme (1753), *Hist. Frag.* (1805), 399.] (c) *subhedar*, chief administrative officer in the former Baroda State. [GCW, 1885.]

Sub-cheese or **subcheese** [19C. H/P. *sub*, 'whole' + *chīz*, 'thing'.] Everything; all there is; the 'whole shoot' (Indian Army colloq.) See **Cheese**. [*OED*; Partridge, *Dict. of Slang* (1961), vol. 2; Hotten, *Slang Dict.* (1864), 98; E. Lear, *Jrnl.*, 4 May 1874.]

Subji, sabji, subjee [19C. H. *subzī*, 'greenness, verdure, fr. *sabz* (P. *sebz*) 'green'.] The leaves and seed capsules of Indian hemp, *Cannabis indica*, used for making *bhang*; also a drink made from an infusion of *bhang*. See **Hashish, Charas, Ganja** and **Bhang**. [*OED; Penny Cycl.* (1836), vi. 239/2.]

Subud [20C. Contraction of Sanskrit *sushīla*, 'right living' + *budh*, 'to awake' + *dharma*, 'custom.] Taken together they mean 'Right living according to the highest that is possible for man in submission to God's Will.' [E. Van Hien, *What is Subud?* (1968), ii. 25.] *Subud* is a system of exercises, founded in 1947 by the Javanese mystic, Pak Muhammad Subuh, to enable one to approach a perfect state by means of the divine power. [*OED*; J.G. Bennett, *Concerning Subud* (1958), vi. iii; A. Huxley (1959), Let. 12 Aug. 1969, 874.]

Suclat, suklat, sackcloth [17C. P. *sakallāt*.] 'To the north of India the name given to a stuff imported from the borders of China.' [YB.] Certain woollen stuffs and European broadcloth. [YB; Fryer (1673), *New Acct.* (1672–81, ed. 1689), 224.]

Sudden death [19C. Anglo-Indian.] Slang for a fowl served as a spatch-cock. 'The bird was caught in the yard, as the traveller entered, and was on the table by the time he had bathed and dressed.' [YB; & *OED*.] See **Spatchcock**. [Berncastle, *Voy. to China* (1850), i. 193.]

Sudder, sadr, sooder [18C.] H/Ar. *sadr*.] 'Chief', foremost or highest part of anything; chief place or street, etc; used in combination as exemplified below. Applied espec. to high government departments or officials. (1) The chief seat of government, the presidency as opposed to the provinces or **Mofussil**. (2) Mostly applied to establishments or individuals employed in the judicial and revenue administration of the state. See **Adalat**. For example, (a) *Sudder-adawlat (sadr adālat):* The Supreme Court and Court of Final Appeal in India (of the East India Company). By Act viii, 1842, the court of highest civil and administrative jurisdiction in all the Presidencies. (b) *Sudder Board:* The 'Board of Revenue' (historically at Calcutta and in the Bengal Presidency). (c) *Sudder-diwani-adalat:* The Chief Civil Court. (d) *Sudder-faujdari-adalat:* The Criminal Court. (e) *Sudder-Ameen:* A chief Commissioner or Arbitrator: a class of civil judges under the British Government; a rank of native judges, one above **Munsif (Moonshif)**. (f) *Sudder-Jumma:* The total of revenue payable directly to government, exclusive of collection charges. (g) *Sudder-Cutcherry:* The principal revenue office of a district or estate; that of the Collector or *Zamindar*. (h) *Sudder-Talukdar:* Commissioner = **Subha**. (i) *Sudder-Station:* The chief station of a district, where the collector, judge and other chief civil officials resided and where their courts were. [*OED* & YB; Wilson, *Glossary* (1855); *Gent. Mag.*, 1787, 1281/2; Prinsep, *The Baboo & Other Tales* (1834), I. iii. 50; *Stanf. Dict.* (ed. 1892).]

Sudra,[1] **Soodra, Sooder,** etc. [17C. H. *shūdra*, fr. S. *sūdra*. Etym. doubtful.] A member of the lowest of the four great Hindu castes; except in S. India where members of this caste claim to be next after the *Brahmins*, there being no indigenous South Indian **Kshatriyas** or **Vaisyas**. Manu describes the Sudras as the feet of the creator, born to serve the other three castes. Henry Lord called them *Shudderies* in his *Discoverie of the Sect of the Banians* (1630), xii. [*OED* & YB; Phillips, *Acct. Relig. Manners and Learning Malabar* (1717). ii. 6.]

Sudra[2] [P. *sudra*.] Loose **mulmull** shirt worn by orthodox Parsis. Also, *sudra-kusti*, the shirt and the woollen sacred thread to be worn for two years by men and women after initiation. *See* **Kusti**. [Hawkins, *CIWIE*.]

Sufedposh [H. *sufedpōsh*.] White-collared. [Hawkins, *CIWIE*.]

Sufi [17C. Ar. *Sūfī*, lit. 'man of wool'.] One of a sect of Muslim ascetic mystics who in later times embraced pantheistic views, and borrowed ideas and practices from Christian and Buddhist monasticism, and philosophy from Neo-platonism and Upanishadic concepts, making them an integral part of Muslim life. The Sufi theory of the unit of Being or Oneness of Existence (*Wahdatu'i-Wujūd*) is similar to the yogic definition of ultimate Reality. In India, the Sufis were influenced by *Hatha-Yoga*, which taught them their meditative practices and gave them knowledge of herbs and chemistry. The emergence of the Punjabi **Sants** (Kabir and Nanak) was the result of two centuries of interaction between the Muslim Sufis and the Hindus, while Hindu mysticism gave new vitality to *sufism*. Sufis practised *pās-i-anfās* (breath control); *Chilla* (40 days of hard ascetic exercises in a cell or lonely place; *Chilla'-i-ma'kūs* (40 days ascetic exercise with head on ground and legs tied to the roof or branch of a tree); and *Samā* (song recital) to arouse ecstasy in their audiences. [Basham, *Cultural History of India* (1975).] (*Sufi* has often erroneously been connected with *Sophy*.) Also, *Sufian* (1585), adj. belonging to the *Sufis*; sb. a *Sufi*. *Sufic* (1884), pertaining to the *Sufis* or their mystical system. *Sufism* (1836) and *Sufiism* (1817). The Sufi mystical system. *Sufist* (1913) = **Sufi**. *Sufistic* (1836), pertaining to Sufism. [*OED*; Greaves, *Seraglio* (1653), 178.]

Sugar [13C.] English, cogn. with S. *sharkara*, 'grit or gravel', Prakrit. *sakkara*, 'ground or candied sugar'. P. *shakar*, and Ar. *sukkar*. *See* **Jaggery**. [*OED* & *YB*.] In English at least as early as the 13th Century. [*Househ. Exp. R. de Swinfield* (Camden) (1289-90), 116; Forrest, *Bombay Letters* (1630), i. 5.]

Sumbul, sumbal, sambul [18C. H/Ar. *sunbul*.] A term applied to the roots of certain plants (and to the plants themselves) which are grown in India as a tonic and antispasmodic; esp. (a) the spikenard, *Nardostachys jatamansis*; (b) the Musk Root, *Ferula (Euryangium) sumbul*; (c) Valerian; (d) also, the *Erytherina suberosa*. Attrib. *sumbul-balsam, -oil, -root*. [*OED*; Sir William Jones, 'Spikenard Ancients' in *Asiat. Res.* (1790), II. 408.]

Sumjao [19C.] *See* **Samjao**.

Summerhead [16C. A Hobson-Jobson form of Pg. *sumbriero*, E. *sombrero*.] A sun-umbrella or parasol. 'It was a name in the Bombay Arsenal [according to Maj. Gen. Keating] for a great umbrella.' [*YB* & *OED*; Hakluyt, *Voy.* (1598), II. 258; Douglas, *Glimpses of Old Bombay* (1845), 86.]

Sundri, Soondry [19C. Beng. *sundarī*, fr. S. *sundara*, 'beautiful, handsome'.] A tree, *Heritiera minor*, which grows in clusters abundantly in the Ganges–Brahmaputra delta, providing a tough and durable timber. [*OED*; *Encycl. Brit.* (7 ed., 1831), IV. 241/1; *Blackwood's Mag.*, Aug. 1907, 252/1.]

Sundook-wallah [19C.] A **Box-wallah**. [Mrs Sherwood, *Lady of the Manor* (1847).]

Sunga *See* **Sanga**.

Sungar *See* **Sangar**.

Sunn [18C. Beng/H. *san*, fr. S. *sāna*, 'hempen'.] A leguminous shrub, *Crotolaria juncea*, or Indian hemp, with long narrow leaves and bright yellow flowers, widely cultivated in India and S. Asia generally for its fibre; used for rope, cordage, sacking, etc., often called Bengal-, or Country-hemp. *See* **Janapa**. [*OED* & *YB*; *Phil. Trans.* (1774), LXIV. 99.] Transf. applied to the *Hibiscus cannabinus*. *See* **Dhang**. [Lindley, *Vegetable Kingdom* (1846), 369.]

Sunna(h), Sunnah, Soona, etc. [17C. H/Ar. *sunnah (sunnat)*, 'form, way, course, rule'.] The body of traditional sayings, law and customs attributed to Prophet Mohammed and supplementing the Koran, compiled about 100 years after his death, and containing subsequent changes. *See* next. [*OED*; Lovell tr., *Thevenot's Trav.* (1687), I. 48.]

Sunni, Sunnee, Soonnee [17C. H/Ar. *Sunni*, 'lawful', fr. prec.] An orthodox Muslim follower of the **Sunna**; Ar. *Ahlu's Sunnah*, 'the people of the path, traditionist'. *Sunnis* hold the *Sunnah* as transmitted in their **Hadis** to be of equal authority to the Koran. *Sunnis* acknowledge the first four *Khalifahs* as the rightful descendants of the Prophet, and are thus opposed to the **Shiahs**. [*OED* & *YB*; Sir. T. Herbert, *Trav.* (1634), 159; (Ft. William).] *See* **Bohra, Khoja**.

Sunnism, Suniism [19C.] Doctrines of the Sunnites. [*OED*; *Chamber's Encycl.* (1892), ix. 398/2.]

Sunnud, sanad [18C. H/Ar. *sanad*, 'signature, deed, diploma, seal of magistrate etc'.] 'A document conveying to an individual emoluments, titles, privileges, offices, or the government rights to revenues from land etc. under the seal of the ruling authority.' [HHW; OED & YB; J. Long (1759), *Sel. Unpub. Rec. Govt.* (1869), 184.]

Sunnyas, Sunnyasi *See* **Sannyas, Sannyasi.**

Sunya [19C. S. *sunya* 'zero, nought, naught, void.] Maths: 'The first epigraphic evidence for zero occurs in India in the Bhojadeva inscriptions at Gwalior around A.D. 870.' [Basham (ed.), *Cult. Hist. Ind.* (1975), 57.] Relig.: 'Kabir (1440-1518) called God by many names including *Sūnya* (the Void).' [Ibid., 274; Whitworth, *Anglo-Indian Dict.* (1885).] *See* next.

Sunyata [20C.] S. *sūnyata,* emptiness, non-existence, *fr.* **Sunya.** Buddhism: 'The concept of the essential emptiness of all things and of ultimate reality as a void beyond wordly phenomena.' [*OED;* Suzuki, *Outl. Mahāyāna Buddhism* (1907), vii. 173.]

S(h)uryawadi [19C. S. *sunya* + *wādi,* 'assertion'.] One who asserts that nothing exists. [Whitworth, *Anglo-Indian Dictionary* (1885).]

Supari [17C. H. *supāri,* 'betel-nut'.] The areca-palm, and its nut chewed with **Betel** leaves etc. The whole combination is properly termed **Pan-supari** 'which is politely offered to visitors and which intimates the termination of the visit'. [YB & OED; Sir T. Herbert, *Trav.* (1638), (2 ed.), 28.]

Sura[1] [18C. H. *sur,* fr. S. *sura,* 'god, deity'.] A good angel or genie in Hindu mythology. [*OED;* T. Maurice (1795), *Hindostan* (1820), I. i. xii. 417.]

Sura(h)[2] [17C. Ar. *surah.*] A chapter of the Koran, in which there are 114 chapters each divided into verses. [*OED;* W. Bedwell, *Moham. Impost.* (1615), 11.45.]

Sura[3] [16C. H/S. *surā,* 'spirituous liquor, wine'. (S. *surakara,* 'coconut-tree'.)] **Toddy;** the fermented sap of various species of palm such as the wild date, coconut and palmyra. [*OED* & YB; Phillip, tr. *Linschoten* (1598), I. lvi. 101/2.]

Sura(h)[4] [19C.] Perh. a pronunciation of **Surat?** *See* **Surat(s).** A soft twilled silk fabric. [*OED; Young Englishwoman,* May 1873, 234/1; *Truth,* 19 May 1881, 686/2.]

Surahi [19C. H/P. *surāhī.*] A long-necked metal or earthenware water pot. *See* **Serai.**[1] [YB; Elphinstone (1808), *Life* (1884), i. 183.]

Surat(s) [17C.] Port city Gujarat. A kind of coarse, inferior cotton piece-goods once manufactured in *Surat.* Also the cotton itself,

Surat-cotton. 'Surat in English slang is equivalent to the French *Raftot,* in the sense of "no great shakes", an adulterated article of inferior quality.' [YB & *OED;* Sainsbury (1643), *Cal. Crt. Min. E. Ind. Co.* (1909), 329.]

Surbahar [19C. Beng. *surbāhār.*] An enlarged **Sitar,** popular in Bengal. [*OED;* S.M. Tagore, *Universal Hist. Music* (1896), 88; Basham, *A Cultural History of India* (1975), 233.] *See* **Veena.**

Surkunda [19C. H. *sarkanda; S. sara,* 'reed-grass' + *kanda,* 'joint, section'.] A very tall reed-grass, *Saccharum sara,* or *munjia.* From the upper part of the flower-bearing stalk the **Sirky** is derived. [YB; Grant Duff, *Notes on an Indian Journey* (1876), 105.]

Surma, soorma [17C. H/P. *surma(h).*] A black powder consisting of sulphide of antimony of lead, used by Indian women for darkening the eyebrows and eyelids; **Kohl.** [*OED* & YB; Lovell, tr., *Thevenot's Trav.* (1687), I. 56; Grose, *Voy. East Indies* (1757; 1772), 2nd ed. ii. 142.]

Surmai Bombay name of the **Seer-fish.** [Hawkins, *CIWIE.*]

Surpeach, serpeych [17C. H. *sarpēch,* fr. P. *serpēsh.*] An ornament of gold, silver or jewels worn in front of the turban. Also a band of silk and embroidery worn round the turban. *See* **Culgee.** [*OED* & YB; Hanway, *Trav.* (1753), IV. 191.]

Surpoose [17C. H. *sarpōsh,* fr. P. *serpush,* 'veil', fr. *ser,* 'head' + *pūsh,* 'covering' = 'head-cover'.] A cover of a basin, dish, **hookah**-bowl etc., 'corrupted into our *Tarboosh (tarbūsh),* and '*Tarbrush*' of the wandering Briton.' [YB.] *See* **Tarbrush.** [*OED* & YB; Fryer, *New Acct. E. Indies* (1698), 130; Shipp, *Mem. Milit. Career* (1829), II. vi. 159.]

Surra [19C. Mahr. *sura,* 'air breathed through the nostrils'.] A disease of horses and other domestic animals in India and elsewhere, supposed to be caused by a microbe, *Trypanosoma evansi.* [*OED;* Billings, *Nat. Med. Dict.* (1890).]

Surrapurdah [19C. H/P. *sarāparda.*] 'A canvas screen surrounding royal tents or the like.' *See* **Canaut.** [YB; Elphinstone, *Acct. Kingd. Caubul* (1815; 1839), 2nd. ed., I. 101.]

Surrinjaum [19C. H/P. *saranjām,* lit. 'beginning- ending'.] 'Used in India for "apparatus", "goods and chattels", and the like. But in the Maratta province it had a special application to grants of land or rather assignments of revenue, for special objects, such as keeping up a contingent of troops for service, to civil officers for the maintenance of their state, or for charitable purpose.' [YB.] [Malcolm, *Hist. Central India* (1823; 1824), 2nd ed., i. 103.]

Surrinjaumee, Gram- [S. *grāma*, 'a village', and prec.] 'Gram-serenjammee, or peons and pykes stationed in every village of the province to assist the farmers in collections and to watch the villages and crops on the ground....' [YB; 'Revenue Accts. of Burdwaun', *in* Long (1767), *Selections from unpublished records of Government (Fort William)* (1748-67), 507.]

Surrow *See* **Serow.**

Surwa(u)n, Sarwan [19C. H/P. *sārbān*, fr. *sār*, 'camel' + *bān*, 'keeper'.] A camel-driver. [*OED* & YB; J.M. Sherer, *Sketches of India* (1821), 242.]

Suryanamaskar [S. *surya*, 'sun' + *namaskar*, 'salutation'.] Early morning **Yoga** exercises. [Hawkins, *CIWIE*.]

Susi *See* **Soosy.**

Susu, Soosu, Sousou [19C. Beng. *sūsū*.] The gangetic dolphin, *Platanista gangetica*, which also inhabits the Brahmaputra. [*OED*; Roxburgh, *Asiat. Res.* (1801), VII. 171.]

Sutra [19C. S. *sūtra*, 'string', (hence) rule, fr. *siv*, 'sew'.] In Sanskrit literature, a short mnemonic rule in grammar, law or philosophy, requiring expansion by means of a commentary. Also applied to Buddhist text-books; the name of one of the three Buddhist **Pitakas,** that which prescribes rules for Buddhists. [*OED*; Colebrooke (1801), *Ess. Sanscrit and Pracrit Lang.* (1837), 1]. 5.]

Suttee [18C. H/S. *satī*, 'faithful or virtuous wife'. (*sat*, 'good'; *satya*, 'truth').] (1) A Hindu widow immolated on the funeral pyre with her husband's body, a former Brahminical rite. [*Parl. E. Indian Aff. Hindoo Widows* (1786; 1821), 3.] (2) The act of immolation; the supreme act of wifely fidelity (1813). This application of the word was of Anglo-Indian origination. The proper Sanskrit terms for the act are: *Sahagamana* (departing together) and *Sahamarana* (dying together). The custom was abolished by law in British India in 1829, though instances have occurred since then. Phr. 'to do or perform *suttee*'. Fig: *Sutteeism.* [*OED* & YB; *Parl. E. Indian Aff. Hindoo Widows* (1821), 33.] *See* **Johar.**

Suttoo, sutto [19C. H. *suttū(a)*] (1) Grain (e.g. barley) parched and ground into coarse flour. (2) A gruel made by stirring finely ground

Gram in water (1908). [*OED*; A.H. Church, *Food Grains Ind.* (1885), 100.]

Suvarnabanik [20C. Beng. *suvarna*, 'gold' + *banik*, 'maker'.] Goldsmith.

Sva, Swa [19C. S. *sva*.] One's self, the ego. Adj. one's own. *See* **Swadesh(i)** and **Swaraj.** [Wilson, *Glossary* (1855).]

Svara, suara [18C. Musical note.] (Cf. Malay *suara*, 'voice'.) *Suara kalpana* (*OED:* a musical passage.) [*OED*; Sir W. Jones, *Asiat. Res.* (1792), III. 68; Basham, *A Cultural History of India* (1975), 214.]

Svarabhakti [19C. S. *svara*, + *bhakti*, lit. 'sound or vowel separation'.] Linguistics: The process of insertion of a glide or 'parasitic' vowel between two consonants. This term was taken from the Hindu grammarians by the German philologist Johannes Schmidt. [*OED*; Sayce, *Sci. Lang.* (1880), I. 317.]

Suvaramandala = **Santoor.**

Svarga, swarga [19C. S. *svarga*.] Hinduism: The heaven of Indra, of the inferior gods. [Whitworth, *Anglo-Indian Dict.* (1885).]

Svarita [20C. S. *svarita*] A falling glide used in the recitation of Vedic texts. Also in extended use. [*OED*; Macdonell, *Vedic Gram. for Students;* Sommerstein, *Sound Pattern Anc. Greek* (1916), 448; (1973), v. 122]

Swadeshi [20C. Beng. *swa*, 'one's own' + *desh(i)*, 'country (things)', i.e. home industries. The name of a political and national movement, originating in Bengal, advocating the boycotting of foreign goods, and the using of Indian-made goods only. Hence: *Swadeshism* (1907). [*OED*; *Times*, 26 Oct. 1905, 3/6; O' Malley, *Mod. India & West* (1941), xvi. 762.]

Swami, Swammy, Sammy, etc. [18C. H. *Swāmī*, fr. S. *Svāmin*, 'master, prince'.] (1) A Hindu idol. The 'Sammy' of the British soldiers' argot. *See* **Ramasammy.** [*OED*; & YB; Ives, *Voy. Ind.* (1773), 70; Partridge, *Dict. of Slang* (1960).] (2) A Hindu religious teacher (1901). [*OED*; *Daily News*, 2 Dec. 1901, 5/1.] (3) A term of respectful address to Brahmins. [YB; Stanley's tr. of Barbosa's *Desc. Coasts E. Africa & Malabar* (1866), 99.] (4) Also attrib. (a) *Sammy-house*, a Hindu pagoda or shrine. [*OED* & YB; Orme, *Hist. Milit. Trans. Indostan* (1778), x. II. 443.] (b) *Sammypagoda*, an old Indian coin, with **Krishna's** effigy on one side and Lakshmi's on the other, formerly current at Madràs. [*OED* & YB; Milburn (1813), *Orient. Comm.* (1825), xix. 233.] (c) *Sammy-work*, or Jewellery, gold and silver ornaments made originally and chiefly in Trichinopoly, 'in European shapes covered with grotesque mythological figures'. [YB & OED; Birdwood, *Industr. Arts. Ind.* (1880), I. 152.] (5) An Indian pedlar of fruit (1913). [YB; Partridge, *Dict. of Slang* (1960).]

Swamp-deer *See* **Barasingha**.

Swaraj [19C. S. *svaraj*, 'self-ruling', fr. *sva*, 'one's own' + *raj*, 'to reign or rule'.] Self-rule (for India); the political and nationalist agitation demanding this from Britain. Also: *Swarajist* (1908), *Swarajism* (1923) and *Purna Swaraj*, perfect or complete national independence (c. 1930). [OED; *Encycl. Metrop.* (1845), xxi. 679/2; *Westn. Gaz.*, 24, June 1908, 5/1.] *See* **Raj**.

Swastika [19C. S. *svastika*, fr. *svasti*, 'well-being, luck'.] A primitive symbol, a cross of equal arms each with a limb of the same length at right angles to its end, all in the same direction, usually clockwise. Used backwards as the emblem of the Nazis from 1933. [OED; Alabaster, *Wheel of Law* (1871), 249.]

Swatantra [19C. S. *swa* + *tantra*, lit. 'One's own thread'.] One who is independent or free to act for himself. The name of a modern Indian right-wing political party (1959). [OED; Wilson, *Glossary* (1855).]

Swati, Swautee, Swatee [19C.] An inhabitant of Swat. (Of or pertaining to) a member of an Indo-European tribe originating in the former North West Frontier Province; also called *Kohistanis.* [OED; Elphinstone (1815), *Acct. Caubul* (1842), I. 417.]

Swayamsevak [20C. Voluntary service, fr. *swayam*, 'one's self' + *sevak*.] [Hawkins, *CIWIE*.]

Swayamwara [19C. S. fr. *swayam*, 'one's self' +

wara, 'choice'.] A Hindu ceremony in which a maiden chooses her husband by putting a garland round his neck in public assembly, a practice common in the heroic ages of the Hindus. [OED; Milman in *Q. Review*, 1831, XLV-17; Wilson, *Glossary* (1855).]

Sweeper [19C.] In India, a person of the lowest caste or no caste, traditionally employed to perform the most menial of household tasks, e.g. the cleaning of privies and drains. *See* **Toty** and **Mehta**. [OED; Lang, *Wand. India* (1859), 259.]

Sweet-Apple [18C.] Anglo-Indian corruption (Hobson-Jobsonism) of **Sitaphal?** *See* **Custard-Apple**. [OED & YB; Lee, *Introd. Bot.*, (1760), App., 305.]

Syce, sais, saice [17C. H/Ar. *sāis*, fr. *sūs*, 'to tend a horse'.] Orig. in India, a groom, a follower on foot of a mounted horseman or of a carriage. Later, a motor-car driver, a chauffeur. *See* **Gora-wallah** and **Horse-keeper**. [OED & YB; Greaves, *Seraglio* (1653), 141; Busteed (1779), *Echoes Old Calcutta.* (1882), 230; Thackeray, *Newcomes* (1854), lxvi.]

Sycee, sisee [18C. Ch. *si, sai, sei*, 'fine silk'.] Fine uncoined silver in lumps of various sizes, used by the Chinese as a medium of exchange in Indo-Chinese trade, so called because, if pure, it may be drawn out into fine threads. [OED & YB; Lockyer, *Acct. Trade in India.* (1711), 135; Jrnl. *Asiat. Soc. Bengal.* (1834), App. 291.]

Syed, Syud *See* **Sayyid** and **Sidi**.

Syras, Cyrus *See* **Sarus**.

Syrup *See* **Sherbet** and **Shrub**.

T

Tabasheer, tabashir, tabaxir [16C. H/Ar/P. *tabāshīr*, 'chalk, mortar', Pg. *tābaxīr*.] A silicious substance, white or translucent, formed in the joints of bamboos. Also called 'Bamboo Salt' and 'Sugar of Bamboo'. Used medicinally. [*OED* & *YB*; Phillip tr., *Linschoten's Voyages* (1598), 104/2.]

Tabela [20C. Anglo-Indian. E. *stable*.] A (buffalo) stable. [Hawkins, *CIWIE*.]

Tabla, tubla [19C. H./fr./Ar. *tābl*.] Indian music: A pair of small kettle-drums played with the fingers, the larger, the left-hand one, bass, the right-hand one, tenor. *See* **Mridangam** and **Pakhawaj**. [*OED*; *Proc. R. Irish Acad.* (1865), IX. I. 117; Strangways, *Mus. Hindostan* (1914), IX. 227.] *See* **Madal**.

Taboot, tabut [17C. H/Ar. *tabūt*, 'a wooden box or coffin'.] A flimsy model of a Muslim tomb, esp. that of Hussain, the third *imam*, at Kerbala, carried in the *Muharram* processions. *See* **Tazia**. *Taboot* is also the name of the ark of the covenant presented, according to Muslims, by God to Adam. [GCW; *OED* & *YB*; (1622); Foster, *Eng. Fact. in India* (1908), II. 94.]

Taccada [19C. Sinh. *takkada*.] The Malayan rice-paper plant, *Scaevola lobelia*, found in India, Sri Lanka and elsewhere in tropical Asia, Australia and Polynesia. Used for making artificial flowers etc. [*OED*; *Treas. Bot.* (1866), 1027/2.]

Taccavi, tuckavee [19C. H. *takāvī*, fr. Ar. *kavī*, 'strength, reinforcement'.] Money advanced to a **Ryot** by his superior to enable him to carry on his cultivation, and recoverable with his quota of revenue. [YB; Buchanan, *Mysore* (1807), ii. 188; Wilson, *Glossary* (1855).]

Tack-ravan [18C. H./P. *takht*, 'throne' + *ravān*, 'travelling'.] A royal litter carried on men's shoulders, signifying a moving throne. [YB.] (Wilson disputes this and gives 'A plank or platform on which public performers, singers, and dancers are carried on men's heads in festival and religious processions'. Whitworth agrees with Wilson.) [Hanway, *Acc. British Trade Caspian Sea.* (1753), IV. 169.]

Tahr, Tehr, Tair [19C. Himalayan name.] A wild goat of the genus *Hemitragus*, found in the Himalayas. Sometimes confused with the *thar*, the Nepali name of the **Goral** (goorul), a goat-antelope of Nepal. *See* **Serow (Surrow)**.

[*OED* & *YB*; Hodgson, in *Proc. Zool. Soc. Lond.* (1835), 492; Jerdon (1867), *Mammals India* (1874), 286.]

Tahsil, tahseel [18C. H./Ar./P. *tahsīl*, 'collection'.] A subdivision of a district in India for revenue collection. (*See* **Zillah**.) Hence, *tahsīldar*, the chief revenue-officer of a subdivision of a district under Mughal rule, and retained by the British. Also, formerly, sometimes applied to the cashier in a Calcutta business house. (Possibly from a confusion with *tahvīldar*, 'a cashier'.) [YB & *OED*; Verelst, *View of Bengal* (1772); Williamson, *Vade Mecum* (1810), I. 209.] *See* **Tanadar**.

Tailor-bird [16C.] One of a number of species of Asian passerine singing birds, of the genera *Orthotomos, Prinia, Sutoria*, etc. which stitch together leaves to form a cavity for their nests. Orig. a particular species, *Orthotomos sutorius*, or *longicauda*, or *Sutoria sutoria* of India and Sri Lanka. [*OED* & *YB*; Pennant, *Ind. Zool.* (1769); Aitken, *Tribes on my Frontier* (1881), 145.]

Taj, tuj [17C. P./Ar. *tāj*, 'crown'.] A crown or headdress of distinction (as worn by the king of Oudh, for example). Also short for the *Taj Mahal* at Agra, erected in 1632-50 by the 5th Mughal emperor *Shah Jehan* to commemorate his favourite wife, *Mumtāz-i-Mahal*, 'Ornament of the palace' (d. 1631). (*Tāj* is a vernacular·form of the second syllable of Mumtaz.) Slang: *taj* = 'ripping, spiffing, first rate', c.1900-12 (Partridge). [*OED* & *YB*; Bernier (1684), E. tr. *Voyages* (ed. Constable 293), 94-6; *Illustr. Catal. Gt. Exhib.* (1851), iv. i. 918/2.]

Taka, tucka [19C. H. *takā*; Beng. *tākā*; S. *tantaka*, 'stamped silver money'.] (1) Formerly in Bengal = one rupee. Elsewhere in India valued variously. *See* **Tanga**. [Broughton (1800), *Letters from a Mahr. Camp.* (ed. 1892), 84; YB.] (2) Now it is a monetary unit in Bangladesh. [*OED*; *Guardian*, 22 Aug 1972, 10/4.] *See* **Tical**.

Takaza, tagada, tagade, etc. [19C. H./Ar. *takāza*.] Extra-legal dunning methods to obtain settlement of a claim or debt; enforcing payment by various kinds of annoyance, as by stationing persons at the house of debtor from morning to night; obstructing the entry of water or food into the debtor's house, or by the claimant threatening to fast unto death. *See* **Dharna, Traga** and **Gherao.** [Wilson, *Glossary* (1855).]

Takerary [19C. H./Ar. *takrar* 'dispute'.] Quarrelsome, contentious, litigious. [Wilson, *Glossary* (1855); Hawkins, *CIWIE.*]

Takht [18C. H./P. 'throne', 'Chair of state', 'symbol of royalty'.] Hence *takht-nishin*, 'the reigning monarch', and *takht-rawan* (**Tack-Ravan**), 'a royal litter', or 'a moveable platform for public performances'. [*OED* & YB; Hanway, *Acct. Brit. Trade* (1753), iv. 169; Wilson, *Glossary* (1855); Whitworth, *Anglo-Indian Dict.* (1885).]

Takin [19C. (Native name in Mishmi).] A horned ruminant, *Budorcus taxicolor*, of Assam and Tibet. [Hodgkin, in *Jrnl. Asiat. Soc. Bengal* (1850), xix. 65.]

Takla [19C. Mahr. *tāklā*.] A small bush, *Cassia tora*, with yellow flowers and pods; the young leaves are edible, and the seeds yield a blue dye. [Whitworth, *Anglo-Indian Dict.* (1885).]

Takli [20C. H. *takli*.] A small spindle. Gandhian ideology was symbolized by the spindle and the spinning-wheel, **Charkha.** [Hawkins, *CIWIE.*]

Taklif [19C. H./Ar. *taqlif*.] Trouble, inconvenience. [M. Diver (1844), *Honoria Lawrence* (1936).]

Taksha [19C. Punj. *tākshā*.] A small plant, bearing a rose-coloured pea-shaped flower, the leaves of which are used for the elimination of maggots in sheep. [Whitworth, *Anglo-Indian Dict.* (1885).]

Taksir [19C. Ar. *taksir*, fr. *tasr*, 'to break'.] A magic square, a set of numbers so arranged that the sum of each row or column or diagonal line is the same. Such squares are worn as charms. [Whitworth, *Anglo-Indian Dict.* (1885).]

Tal, talao [19C. H. *tāl*.] A pond, lake or reservoir. As in place-name *Nainital*. *See* **Tank.** [Wilson, *Glossary* (1855); Whitworth, *Anglo-Indian Dict.* (1885).]

Tal(a) [19C. S. *tāla*, 'hand-clapping'.] The rhythmic improvisation or pattern in Indian music, which prescribes the length of the time cycle in terms of the units as well as the distribution of stresses within the cycle. **Raga** and *tala* are the two main elements of Indian classical music. *See* **Jati.** [*OED*; Wilson, *Glossary* (1855); Basham, *Cultural Hist. India* (1975), 213; Menuhin (1977), xii. 258.]

Talagoya [Sinh. *talagoya*.] The monitor, *Varanus bengalensis*. [Hawkins, *CIWIE.*]

Talak [18C. Ar. *talāq*.] Divorce or dissolution of marriage according to Muslim law, whether reversible or not, in a set form of words. [*OED*; Wilson, *Glossary* (1855); C. Hamilton, tr., *Hedaya* (1791), I. iv. 200.]

Talapoin [16C. Pg. *talapāo*, fr. *Talaing* (Old Peguan) *talapoi*, 'my lord'.] Title of Buddhist monks, corresponding to Burmese *pongyi*. This term was used by the Portuguese, and afterwards by French and other continental travellers, including British of the 17th century, to indicate Sri Lankan (Ceylonese) and other Buddhist monks. [*OED* & YB; Fitch (1586), in *Hak. Voy.* (1599), II. 261; Purchas (1613), *Pilgrimage* (1614), 461.]

Talati,¹ talatty [19C. Guj. *talātī*.] The village accountant, usually a government servant, but not hereditary like the **Kulkarni.** [Wilson, *Glossary* (1855).] *See* **Patwari, Curnum.**

Talati,² talathi [19C. Mar. *talāthī*.] Collection of revenue from the cultivators; the officer collecting it = *talatdar*. [Wilson, *Glossary* (1855).]

Tali, talee, tally [19C. Tam. *tāli*, fr. S. *tāla*, 'the palmyra' (**Talipot**).] A trinket of gold tied on the neck of the bride by the bridegroom at the time of marriage; the term and practice are common to all the people throughout India. [*OED* & YB; Forbes (1813), *Orient. Mem.* (2nd. ed. 1834), ii, 312.]

Taliyamar [19C.] Sea-Hind. for 'cut-water'. Pg. *talhamar.*] [YB; Roebuck, *Naval Dict.* (1811).]

Taliera [19C. Beng. *tālier*, fr. S. *tāl*, fr. *tāla*, fan-palm. H. *tar(r)a*.] An Indian and E. Indian palm *Corypha taliera*, allied to and resembling the **Talipot,** but not nearly so high. [*OED*; Roxburgh, *Hortus Bengal* (1814).]

Talipot [17C. Sinh. *talapata*; M. *tālipat*; H. *tālpāt*; S. *tālpattra*.] Leaf of the palmyra or fan-palm, *Borassus flabelliformis*; transferred in Sri Lanka and S. India to the leaf of *Corypha umbraculifera*, noted for its great height and its enormous fan-shaped leaves, which were much used as material to write on. *See* **Tali.** [*OED* & YB; Knox, *Hist. Ceylon* (1681), 15.

Talliar, tarryar, talari [17C. Tam. *talaiyārī*, fr. *talai*, 'head'.] The vilage watchman; one of the subordinate officers in the villages of S. India. [*OED* & YB; *Fort St. George Consns.* (10 Feb. 1680); 1693 in Wheeler, *Madras in the Olden Time* (1861), I. 267.]

Tallica [17C. Ar. *ta'likah*.] An invoice or schedule. [YB; Hedges' *Diary*, 26 Dec. 1682.]

Taluk, talook [18C. H./Ar. *ta'alluk*, 'estate, proprietary land', fr./Ar. *alaqa*, 'adhere', 'to be affixed', 'to suspend from or depend on'.] A hereditary estate belonging to an Indian proprietor; a subdivision of a **Zillah** or district, comprising a number of villages, place for revenue purposes under a **Collector;** a collectorate or 'department of administration; an estate resembling the holding of a **Zemindar'.** [1793, *Bengal Permanent Settlement Reg.* in *Bengal Code* (1913); *OED* & *YB;* 1799 in Wellington, *Suppl. Desp.* (1858), I. 370; Wilson, *Glossary*, 1855.]

Talukdar, talookdar [18C. H. *ta'aluk + dār*, 'possessor, holder'.] The hereditary holder of a **Taluk**, or the officer in charge of a *taluk* or the division of a *Zillah;* a collector of revenue from the cultivators, either on behalf of the state or of the farmer of the revenue whose undue exactions it was his duty to prevent. Also: *talukdāri*, the tenure, office, or estate of a *talukdār.* [*OED* & *YB;* Verelst, *View of Bengal.* (1772), App., 233; *The Times*, 5 Oct. 1904.]

Talwar, tulwar, tulwaur [18C. H. *talwār* (also, *tarwar*), fr. *S. tarwart*, 'a sabre', 'a sword'.] 'A Rajput bridegroom sometimes sends his *tulwar* as his proxy at his wedding. [GCW; *OED* & *YB;* Jackson, *Journey from India* (1799), 49; (A. Prinsep), *Baboo* (1834), I. viii. 125.]

Tamarind [16C. Sp./Pg./It. *tamarindo;* Med.L. *tamarindus;* ult. fr. Ar. *tamr-hindī*, 'the date of India'.] (1) The fruit of the tree, *Tamarindus indica*, a brown pod containing one to twelve soft brown seeds covered in a soft acid pulp, valued as a medicine and in cookery as a relish. [*OED* & *YB;* Elyot (1533), *Cast. Helthe* (1539), 60. Litchfield, tr., *Castañeda, Cong. E. Ind.* (1582), i. x. 94.] (2) The tree itself, supposed to be a native of the E. Indies. Also, the *tamarind-fish* (pomfret) preserved in the acid pulp of the tamarind fruits (1858). *OED* & *YB;* Purchas (1614), *Pilgrimage*, 2 ed., 483; *Mem. of Col. Mountain* (1857), 98.]

Tamas [19C. S. *tamas.*] One of the three **Gunas;** inertia, heaviness, darkness. The other two are: **Rajas** and **Sattva.** [Sir Charles Eliot, *Hinduism & Buddhism* (1921), II. 298.]

Tamasha, tumasha, tomashaw, tomasia, etc. [17C. H/Ar/P. *tamāshā*, 'walking about for amusement, or entertainment', fr. *masha(y)*, 'walk'.] A public function, an entertainment, display, show, spectacle, anything that at-tracts and amuses spectators. Transf. fuss, commotion (1882). British army in India colloq. Late 19-20C. [Partridge.] [*OED* & *YB;* Finch in *Purchas* (1625-6), i. 436; Crawford, *Mr. Isaacs* (1882), x. 213.]

Tambac [18C.] A native Indian name of **agal-loch** or **aloes**-wood. [*OED; Chambers Cycl.* (1727-51).]

Tambaranee [16C. M. *tamburan*, 'Lord, God or King', fr. *tam*, 'one's own' + *puran* 'lord'.] Title of honour among the **Nairs,** and is also assumed by the **Salva** monks in the Tamil regions. The junior male members of the Malyali Raja's family, until they come of age, are called *Tambān* and after that *Tamburān.* The female members are similarly styled *Tambatti* and *Tamburatti.* [YB; Varthema, *Travels*, E. tr. Eden (1576); Logan, *Malabar*, (1887-91), Gloss, iii.]

Tamboo [20C. H./P. *tambū*, tent.] A temporary rough shelter in a trench. (Milit. slang, 1914-18.) [*Sphere*, 19 Feb. 1916, 188.]

Tamboura See **Tanpura.**

Tamil, Tamul [18C. Native name, *Tamir, Tamil.* (Dutch and Pg. *Tamul.*) Known in the 8th century. Pali and Prakrit *Damila, Davila. Davida;* S. *Dramila, Dramida, Dravida.*] A member of a S. Indian and Sri Lankan non-Aryan race, belonging to the **Dravidian** stock; the language spoken by this people; the leading member of this *Dravidian* family of languages. Also *Tamilian, Tamulic, Tamulian.* [*OED* & *YB;* Wepery, *Grammar Malabar Lang.* (1778); *Asiatic Researches* (1788), I. 246.]

Tamra-pat [19C. H./S. *tāmrā*, 'copper' + *patta*, 'a tablet'.] An engraved copper plate (on which a grant of land or of privileges is engraved). [Wilson, *Glossary* (1855).]

Tana, thana [19C. H. *thāna, thānā*, 'a place of standing, a post', fr. S. *sthāna*, 'a place'.] A police station. Orig. a military station or fortified post, used to preserve peace and collect the revenue. [*OED* & *YB;* Wellington (1803), in *Gurw. Desp.* (1837), II. 251; Mrs B.M. Croker, *Village Tales* (1896), 212.]

Tanadar, thanadar [19C. Prec. + *dār*, 'agent, holder'.] The head officer of a police station. 'In a native state a revenue and magisterial officer corresponding generally with the **Mamlatdar** and **Tahsildar** of British India.' [GCW.] 'This word was adopted in a more military sense by the Portuguese.' [YB.] Also, *t(h)ānadāri*, 'A system by which lands, belonging to petty native states under chiefs incapable of effective control, were formed into circles and placed under the magisterial jurisdiction of special *thānādārs'*. [Whitworth, *Anglo-Indian Dict.* (1885); *OED* & YB; C. James (1802), *Milit Dict.* (1816); Forbes (1813), *Or. Mem.*, 2nd ed. (1834), ii. 5.]

Tandava [S. *tāndava.*] Shiva's fierce and wild dance of destruction and re-creation of the universe; a traditional style of dancing in India of a vigorous and masculine character. See **Lasya**. [*OED;* Ld. Ronaldshay, *India: Bird's-Eye View* (1924), xxi. 272.]

Tandoor, tandur, tandour [17C. H. tandur, P./Ar. *tannūr;* Turk. *tandūr,* 'an oven'.] In India, a large earthen oven. Also: *tandoori,* food baked in a *tandoor,* or this style of cooking. [*OED;* J. Davis, tr., *Olearius Voy. Ambass.* (1662), 294; Fraser, *Trav. Koordistan* (1840), I. vi. 160.]

Tanga, tunga, tanka [16C. H. *tanka;* Pg. *tanga;* S. *tanka,* 'weight'.] A name (orig. of a weight) of various coins (or moneys of account) in India and elsewhere, whose value varied greatly at different times and places. See **Taka (Tucka)**. [*OED* & YB; Phillip, *Linschoten* (1596), xxxv. 69/I; Markham (1876), *Narr. Mission George Bogle to Tibet,* xiii. 129.]

Tangham. See **Tangun**.

Tangi [19C. Pasht. *tangai,* pl. *tangī;* P. *tang,* 'narrow'.] A gorge or defile on the N.W. Frontier of India (now Pakistan). [*OED; Q. Jrnl. Geol. Soc.* (1854), x. 467.]

Tangun, tanyan [18C. H. *tāng(h)an,* app. Fr. Tibet *tanān.*] The vernacular name of the strong little pony of Bhutan and Tibet. [*OED* & YB; Hodges, *Travels in India, 1780-83,* (ed. 1793), 31; Aitchison (1774), *Treaties* (1876), I. 153.]

Tanjore-Pill [19C.] From *Tanjore,* a city in S. India. A specific said to have been used 'with great success against the bite of mad dogs, and that of the most venomous serpents'. [YB; *Asiatic Journal* (1816), ii. 381.]

Tank [16C. Guj. *tānkh;* Mar. *tānken;* Pg. *tanque;* perh. S. *tadāga.*] In India, an Anglo-Indian term designating a pond, pool, lake, or reservoir. 'This is one of those perplexing words which seem to have a double origin, in this case one Indian, the other European.' [YB & *OED;* Parkes' *Mendoza* (1588; Hak Soc., 1853), ii. 46; Terry (c. 1616), *Voy. E. Ind.* (1655), 105.] See **Tal**.

Tanka¹ See **Taka, Tanga**.

Tanka,² thanka [20C. Tib. *t'an-ka, t'an-ka.*] Tibetan religious scroll-painting on woven

material, hung in temples and carried in processions. [G. Roerich, *Paintings* (1925), 17; A.K. Gordon, *Tibetan Relig. Art.* (1952), 15.]

Tanpura, tanpoora [16C. H/P. tanbūr; Ar. *tunbūr.*] A droning musical instrument, with four metal strings, plucked by the fingers and played as an accompaniment to the main instrument, such as the **Sitar** and **Veena** in Indian classical music. [*OED;* Washington's tr. *Nicholay's Voy.* (1585), iii. i. 69; Engel *Mus. Anc. Nat.* (1864), 51.] See **Shruti, Vina**.

Tantra [18C. H./S. *tantra,* 'loom', 'warp', hence groundwork, doctrine, principle, system, fr. *tan,* 'stretch, extend'.] One of a class of Sanskrit religious works, of comparatively recent date, (c. 6th Century AD.), relating to **Shakti**-worship, chiefly of a magical and mystical nature, inculcating esoteric rites in honour of different forms of **Siva** and **Durga**. Also in Tibetan Buddhism, with sexual and occult overtones. Hence, *tantric* (1891), *tantrika* (1855) = *tantrist, tantrism* (1877), and *tantrist* (1905). [*OED; Asiatic Researches* (1799), v. 53.]

Tany pundal [19C. Tam. *tanni pandal,* 'water shed'.] 'Small buildings where weary travellers may enjoy temporary repose in the shade and obtain a draught of water or milk.' See **Chuttrum, Choultry, Dharmasala**. [YB; F. Buchanan, *Mysore,* etc. (1807), i. ii. 15.]

Tapas(ya) [19C. S. *tapas(yā).*] Austere or ascetic devotion; self-inflicted suffering; invoked by Gandhi as one of the methods of civil disobedience and passive resistance against the British. [*OED;* Malcolm in *Asiat. Res.* (1810), xi. 267; A. Huxley, *Island* (1962), ix. 137.

Tappal, tappaul [18C. Tam., Tel., Mahr., Kan., Guj: *tappa, tappalu, tappe, tapo,* etc.] A stage, a halting place, where relays were posted; also the relay itself; the post; the carriage, relay and delivery of letters (in S. India), and one who carries the mail. See **Dawk (Dhak)** [*OED* & YB; Jas. Anderson, *Corr.* (1791), 64; Ld. Valentia, *Voy* (1809), I. vii. 385.]

Tar¹ [19C. H. *tar,* 'a wire', a thread, 'a string of a musical instrument'.] Transf. 'a wire', 'a telegram'. [*OED;* Kipling in *Harper's Weekly,* 30 Dec. 1893, 1246/3.]

Tar² [19C. H. *tār,* S. *tāla.* 'A palm tree'.] The palmyra or fan-palm, *Borassus flabelliformis,* from which **Toddy** is extracted. The name is sometimes applied to the *Corrypha* and other palms which do not yield *toddy*. [Wilson, *Glossary* (1855).] *See* **Targola**.

Tara, tare [16C. Pg./M. *taram*, a coin.] 'A small silver coin current in S. India at the time of the arrival of the Portuguese'. [YB; Eden's *Varthema* (1576); Fryer, *New Acct.* (1673), 55.]

Tarbrush¹ [18C. E.] Fig. in such phrases as 'a dash, or touch of the tar-brush', signifying a person of dark complexion; a half caste. *OED. See* **Chee-cheeh, Mustees, Eurasian.** [Grose *Dict. Vulg. Tongue.* (1796); Lang, *Wand. India* (1859), 50.]

Tarbrush,² tarboosh [18C. H./Ar. *tarbūsh*.] A cap of cloth, of felt, head-cover. *See* **Surpoose.** [*OED* & YB; W.J., tr., Bruyn, *Voy. Levant.* (1702), xx. 91.]

Tare and Tret [E./Pg. *tara*; Ar. *tarhah*, 'that which is thrown away' + *tret* (orig. and hist. obscure, but poss. fr. Fr. *traite*, 'a draught'), 'an allowance on goods sold by weight after the deduction of *tare*'.] The two ordinary deductions in calculating the net weight of goods to be sold by retail. Used in Indian trade records. [*OED* & YB; Jon Bee, *Dict.* (1823).]

Tarega, tareghe [16C. Tel. *taraga*; Tam. *taraga*; M. *taragu*.] Broker and brokerage; commission, a small deduction from the price of articles purchased claimed by the agent of the purchaser. [H.H.W.]. *See* **Dastur(i)**. [Fitch in Hakluyt, *Principal Navigations* (1599).]

Targola [H. *tār*, 'toddy-palm, + *golah*, 'ball'.] The jelly-like fruit of the **Toddy** palm. [Hawkins.]

Tarkashi [19C. H. *tār-kasī*.] Lit. wire-drawing.] Wire inlaid in wood by Indian craftsmen; also the articles so produced. [*OED*; Birdwood, *Handbk. Brit. Indian Section* (Paris Universal Exhibition (1878), 79.]

Taro Sacred bull's urine said to subdue the forces of evil when applied to the face and lips.

Tarwad [19C. M. *tarawāa, tarawāta*.] A matrilineal joint family (of *Nayars*) in Kerala, whose property belongs to the females of the *tarwad* and the males have no power of alienating it. [Wilson, *Glossary* (1855).]

Tashreef, tashrif, tasheriff [17C. Mar. *tasrīf*; Ar. *tashrīf*, 'honouring'.] 'Conferring honour upon anyone, as by paying him a visit, presenting a dress of honour, or any complimentary donation'; the presents or honorarium so paid. In south India, complimentary presents made by the cultivators to the native revenue officer at the time of fixing the annual assessment. [1674 in Wheeler *Madras in the Olden Time* (1861), i. 84; Wilson, *Glossary* (1855).] *See* **Seerpaw, Khilat**.

Taslim, tasleem [17C. H. *taslīm*.] Ceremonial salutation. [Bernier, *Travels in the Mogul Empire* (1656-68, tr. 1684).]

Tat,¹ taut [19C. H. *tāt*.] Coarse canvas made from various fibres, esp. jute, and used as sacking; sackcloth. [*OED; Trans. Lit. Soc. Bombay* (1820), III. 244.]

Tat,² tatt [19C. Short for **Tatty**. [*OED;* Maria Graham, *Jrnl. Resid. India* (1812), 125.]

Tat,³ tatt [19C.] Short for **Tattoo**, a native pony of India. [c.1840 in Parker, *Bole Ponjis* (1851), II. 215; *OED* & YB.]

Tatpurusha [19C. S. *tatpurus(h)a*. lit. 'his servant'.] 'A compound in which the first element qualifies or determines the second while the second retains its grammatical independence as noun, adjective or participle.' [*OED;* M.-Williams, *Elem. Gram. Sanscrit* (1846), IX. 157.]

Tattoo, tattu [18C. H. *tatū*.] An Indian native pony. *See* **Tat.³** [*OED* & YB; Seton Karr (1784), *Select. fr. Calcutta Gaz.* (1864), I. 15.]

Tatty [18C. H. *tattī*.] A screen or mat made of the roots of the fragrant **Cuscus** grass, which is placed in a doorway or window opening during the hot weather and kept wet constantly to cool and freshen the air in the room. *See* **Tat,²** & **Thermantidote**. [*OED* & YB; Williams in *Phil. Trans.* (1792), LXXXIII. 131.]

Taungya, toungya [19C. Burm. fr. *taung*, 'hill' + *ya*, 'plot, garden'.] A Burmese system of agriculture, known in India as **Jhoom** and **Coomry**. [*OED* & YB; *Encyl. Brit.* (1876), iv. 560/2.]

Tawa, tava(h) [19C. H./Punj. *tavā*, frying-pan, griddle'.] A circular griddle for cooking **Chupatties** & other items of Indian cuisine. [*OED;* H. Lawrence (c. 1843), *Jrnls* (1980), viii. 134.]

Taweez [19C. H/Ar. *ta'wīz*.] Lit. 'praying for protection by invoking god or by uttering a charm. Also, an amulet or phylactery, and a structure of masonry over a tomb. [YD, Lt.-Col. Fitzclarence, *Journal of a Route across India* (1819), 144; Hockley (1826), *Pandurang Hari.* (1873), i. 148.]

Tazee [19C. H/P. *tāzī*, 'invading, invader', fr. *tāz*, 'running.'] 'A favourite variety of horse, usually of Indian breed.' Also a kind of greyhound. *See* **Yaboo.** [1815 in Elphinstone *Caubul.* (ed. 1842), i. 189; YB.]

Tazia, Tazea [19C. H./Ar. *ta'zīyat*, 'consolation, condolence'.] 'In India the word is applied to the **Taboot,** or model in flimsy material of the tombs of Husain and Hassan carried in the Muharram festival procession, and afterwards thrown into water or buried.' [YB & *OED;* Broughton (1809), *Let.,* 26 Feb. 1813, 72; Kipling, *In Black and White* (1889), 94.]

Tea, tay, cha, chai, etc. [16C. Sb. and attrib. Ch. (Amoy dial.) *t'e, (Mand. dial.), ch'a;* P/H. *chā;* Mal. *teh.* (The earliest mention of tea (*chaw*) in the old Records of the India Office seems to be in 1615).] (Leaves of) a plant, *Thea chinensis or Camilla thetfera,* from which a beverage is made; the beverage itself. In Anglo-Indian parlance, early morning bedside tea was known as *bed-tea* (in **Butler-English** *beg-tea,* or **Begti**). [*OED* & YB; Phillip, tr., *Linschoten* (1598), I. xxvi. 46/1; Pepys, *Diary,* 25 Sept. 1660.]

Teak [17C. Pg. *teca;* M. *tēkka;* Tam. *tēkku;* Tel. *tēku;* Tulu, *tekki;* Kan. *tēgu,* etc.] A large E. Indian tree (*Tectona grandis*) with a dark, heavy, oily wood of great strength and durability, widely used for furniture, house construction, ship-building, etc., etc. Medicines concocted from the wood are native remedies for headaches, dyspepsia, stomach complaints. Its ashes are reputed to improve eye-sight, and from its bark and flowers, a preparation is extracted to relieve bronchitis; the sap of its leaves is used as a red dye. [*OED* & YB; Cowen, *Flowering Trees* etc. (1965); Fryer *Acct. E. India & P.* (1698), 142.] See **Sag²**.

Tea-planter [19C. One who cultivates tea on a plantation. [*OED;* Kipling *Plain Tales* (1887), 112.]

Teapoy, tepoy [19C. H. *tīn,* 'three' + *pāe,* 'foot'.] Small, (usually) three-legged occasional table. (By erroneous association with *tea,* a table with three or more legs, that is a tea-, or tea-time table, often with a receptacle, a 'tea-caddy', to hold tea.) The word appears to be constructed on analogy with **Charpoy.** [*OED* & YB; Mrs Sherwood, *Lady of Manor* (1828), VI. xxix. 246.] [Sir John Kaye, *Peregrine Pulteney* (1844), I. v. 112.]

Teek, thick [19C. H. *thīk,* 'exact, precise, punctual'.] *Teek-hai,* 'O.K.', 'all right' (orig. Indian Army colloq.). And *tiggerty-bo,* or *ticketty-*boo (R.A.F. slang, fr. *c.* 1922, for 'All correct, in good order'.) [YB; G. W. Johnson, *Stranger in India* (1843), I. 290.]

Teela [Beng. *tīla.*] An isolated conical hillock.

Teerut See **Tirtha.**

Teesoo, tesu, tesso, etc. [19C. H. *tēsū.*] The brilliant orange-red flowers of the Indian tree, **Dhak** or **Palas,** *Butea frondosa,* and *B. superba;* the yellow dye obtained from these. [*OED;* Playfair, tr., *Tale of Shereef* (1823), 333; Royle, *Bot. of Himalayas* (1835).]

Tehr See **Tahr.**

Tejpat, tezpat [19C. H. *tajpāt;* S. *taja-puttra,* 'pungent leaf'.] The Indian name for *Malabathrum* or the leaf of the cinnamon tree. [YB; Fanny Parkes, *Wanderings of a Pilgrim* etc. (1850), i. 278.]

Telinga [17C. H. *tilangā,* S. *tailanga* (of uncertain origin, but 17th century English writers used this word to denote the **Telugu** language, and in Hindustani a *Telugu* is called *Telinga,* and the *Telugu* country **Tilangana.**] (1) The **Telugu** language. [*OED;* Fryer, *Acct. E. India & P.* (1698), 33.] (2) One of the *Telugu* people. [*OED* & YB; *Asiat. Ann. Reg.* (1800), 186/2.] (3) A native Indian soldier dressed in quasi-European fashion; a **sepoy.** [*OED* & YB; Long (1700), *Select. Unpubl. Records* (1869), 235.] (4) A **Dhoney** or Indian coastal vessel on the Coromandel coast. [*OED;* Simmonds, *Dict. Trade* (1858).] Also, the *Telinga potato,* the edible tuber, *Amorphophallus campanulatus.* [*OED.*]

Tellicherry-bark [19C. fr. *Tellicherry,* a town in Kerala, north of *Calicut.*] The medicinal bark of the *Wrightia dysenterica;* also called *Conessine-bark.* [*OED;* Good, *Study of Med.* (4 ed., 1824-34), I. 626.]

Tellicherry-chair [19C.] A sort of sedan or carrying chair once used in Malabar. Cf. **Tonjon, Tomjohn.** [YB; Col. James Welsh, *Milit. Reminiscences* (1830), ii. 40.]

Telugu, Teloogoo [18C. Native name. Orig. and deriv. uncertain.] (1) The Dravidian language spoken in *Tilangāna,* now Andhra Pradesh. 'It is this language that used to be called Gentoo.' [*OED* & YB; Fryer, *Acct. E. India & P.* (1698), 33.] (2) One of the Dravidian people who speak this language. [*OED;* Seir Mutaqherin (1789), II. 93; Comb. *Telugu*-speaking person (1903).] See **Telinga.**

Tembool [16C. S. *tāmbūla.*] **Betel**-leaf. 'It gives its name to the *Tambolis* or *Tamolis,* sellers of betel in the N. Indian bazaars.' [YB; Eden, *Varthema's Travels* (1576).]

Temple-tree = **Champak.**

Tempo [20C.] An Indian three-wheeler haulage vehicle. [Hawkins, *CIWIE*.]

Tendu [20C. H. *tendū*.] The ebony tree, *Diospyros melanoxylon*, with date-like fruit. [Hawkins, *CIWIE*.]

Terai,[1] terye [18C. H. *tarāī*, moist (land).] Name of a belt of marshy jungle between the lower foothills of the Himalayas and the plains, where the *terai-hat*, which was a wide-brimmed felt hat with a double crown, was first worn by travellers, hunters and Europeans, (generally in former times) when the sun was not so hot as to require the use of a **Sola-topi**. [*OED* & YB; Kirkpatrick, *Acct. of Nepaul* (1811), 40.]

Terai[2] (fever) [19C.] *See* prec. **Bengal fever**, a severe form of malaria. [YB; Moore, *Family Med. for India* (1879), 211.]

Thakali [20C. Nepal *takālī*.] (A member of) one of the tribes of Nepal of Mongol origin; the language of this tribe. Also attrib. [*OED*; Northey & Morris, *Gurkhas* (1928), xii, 202.]

Thakur, thakoor [18C. H. *thākur*; S. *thākkura*, 'a deity'.] A term of respect, Lord, master, etc. espec. applied to **Rajput** nobles; to men of the Bhils and other wild races; to Bengali Brahmins or men of 'good family'; and as an ironic honorific to barbers. (Cf. **Caleefa, Beastie, Mehtar**.) In Bengal, anglicized in one outstanding family to *Tagore*. Also: *Thakurai*, the rank or office of a *thakur*; *Thakurani*, a goddess, a lady, a Rajput chief's wife; *Thakurgarh*, a place of worship. [*OED* & YB; 1798 in *Life of Colebrooke* (ed. 1873), 462; *Misc. Trav. in Asiat. Ann. Reg.* (1800), 312/1.]

Thali[1] [20C. H. *thālī*.] A metal dish or plate on which Indian food is served. [*OED*; *Times*, 13 Oct. 1969).]

Thali[2] *See* Tali.

Thana(dar) *See* Tana(dar).

Thanga obs. var. **Sangha**.

Thanka var. **Tanka**.

Theka *See* Thika, Teek, Thik.

Thermantidote [19C.] An antidote to heat. A rotating fan fixed in a window opening, encased in wet **Tatties** and used in India to drive into a room a current of cool air. 'It is in fact a winnowing machine fitted to a window aperture.' Introduced in 1830. [*OED* & YB; W.G. Osborne, *Court & Camp Runjeet Sing* (1860), 132; Fanny Parkes (1830), *Wanderings of a Pilgrim* (1850), i. 208.]

Thik *See* Teck.

Thika, ticca, ticker, theka, etc. [19C. H. *thīka(h)*, 'hire, fare, fixed price, contract'.]

Anybody engaged by the job or on contract. Hence: *ticca-garry*, 'hired carriage'; -*doctor*, 'a surgeon temporarily employed by government on contract'; -*cook*, 'hired for the occasion'; -*palanquins*; -*bearers*, etc. Also, *thikadar, teekadar, tuckadar, thekadar*, etc. Farmer, householder on lease, middleman, contractor. [*OED* & YB; *Gloss. Fifth Report* (1813); Kipling, *Soldiers Three* (1889), 10.]

Thiru [19C. Tam. *tiru*.] Honorific title prefixed to a man's name in *Tamilnadu*; also to the names of many places in S. India, often anglicized to *Tri*, as in *Tripetty* for *Tiru-pati*, and used chiefly in the sense of the Sanskrit **Shri**, implying auspicious, venerable, sacred, honourable, etc. [Wilson, *Gloss.* (1855).]

Thread (Sacred-) *See* Juneo and Kusti.

Thug, Thag, Theg, T'hug [19C. H. *thag*; Mahr. *thag, thak*, 'a cheat, swindler'.] A member of a class of murderers and robbers in India of different tribes and castes, whose 'calling' was hereditary and who murdered travellers and pilgrims by strangulation with handkerchiefs (**Romals**) after gaining their confidence, and then burying them; associated with the worship of **Kali**; suppressed by law in 1836. Also applied to child-abduction. *See* **Phansigar** and **Dacoit**. Transf. any cutthroat, ruffian, bully-boy, etc. Also *thugdom* (1839), the domain of *thugs*; *thuggess* (1859), a female *thug*; *thuggism* (1856) = *thuggee* (1837), the system of murder and robbery by *thugs*; *thuggish* (1953), resembling a *thug*; *thuggery* (1839), ruffianism; *thugocracy* (1984), government by thugs or by unbridled ruffians or murderers. [*OED* & YB; *Observer*, 4 March 1984; 1810 in *Hist. & Pract. Thugs* (1837), 329; Sleeman, *Ramaseeana* (1836), 145.]

Thumri [19C. H. *thumrī*.] A popular form of N. Indian vocal or instrumental music based on the romantic-religious literature inspired by the **Bhakti** movement. [*OED*; Willard, *Treat. on Mus. Hindoostan* (1834), 89; Ld. Harewood, *Tongs & Bones* (1981), xvii. 257.]

Thunder-box [19C.] A commode; a box with a seat with a hole over a removable receptacle for faeces and urine, which was taken out, cleaned and replaced by a **Sweeper** in N. India or a **Toty** in S. India. (Cf. 'thunder-mug', an 18th century chamber-pot.) [*OED*; Auden & Isherwood *Journey to War* (1939), vii. 182; Partridge (c. 1870), *Dict. of Slang* (1937), II.]

Tibet, Thibet, Tibat [19C.] The name of a central Asian country, used attrib. for (1) Tibetan goat's wool or imitation; (2) a heavy material made from this wool; (3) fine stuff for women's dress material. Also, *Tibetan*, a native and the language of Tibet (member of the Tibeto-Burmese sub-family of the Sino-Tibetan language group). [*OED* & YB; Scott, *Surgeon's Daughter* (1827); Parkhill, *Hist. Paisley* (1857), xiii. 97; Malte-Brun, tr., *Universal Geogr.* (1822), I. 571.]

Tibetian [18C.] = Tibetan. [*OED*; Astley, *New Gen. Coll. Voyages* (1747), iv. ii. iv. 451/2; G. Borrow, *Zincali* (1841), ii. iii. 108.]

Tical [17C. Burm. *tik'l*, representing Pg. *tical*; H. *tankā, takā*.] An E. Indian trade-term used by the Portuguese and others fr. the 16th century, especially in Siam (Thailand) and Burma, applied to a silver coin roughly equivalent in value to the Indian rupee (orig. the **Taka** or **Tanga**). [*OED* & YB; Foster, *Letters*, (1615), iv. 107; Malcolm, *Trav.* (1849), 41/1.]

Ticca See **Thika**.

Ticka See **Tika, Tilak, Tilka**.

Ticket [20C.] A postage stamp. [Hawkins, *CIWIE*.]

Ticky-Tock [18C.] A rhythmic refrain used by Indian musicians accompanying the dance movements of **Nautch**-girls. [YB; Ives, *Voy. from England to India* (1754), 75.]

Tic-polonga [17C. Sinh. *tit-polongā*, fr. *tita* (in comb. *tit*.) 'speck, freckle, spot' + *polongā*, 'viper'.] An extremely venomous snake of India and Sri Lanka; the chain-viper, necklace-snake, or Russell's viper, *Daboi or Vipera Russelli*, or **Cobra Manilla**. [*OED*; Knox, *An Hist. Relation of the Island of Ceylon* (1681), 29; Mrs Heber (1825) in *Heber's Narr. Journey* (1828), II. xxvii. 258.]

Tier-cutty [18C. Mal. *tiyar-katti*.] The knife used by a Kerala toddy-drawer (a member of the **Tiyan** caste) for scarifying the toddy-palms. [Logan, *Malabar* (1792), iii. 169; YB.]

Tiffin [18C.] Prob. fr. *tiffing* (English slang), 'eating out of meal-times', connected with *to tiff*, 'to take a little drink or sip', which was specialized in Anglo-Indian usage. [*See* Grose, *Lexicon Balatronicum* (1785).] A light mid-day meal or snack. Also, *Tiffin-carrier*, several metal containers superimposed one on another to carry various items of a meal, taken at work or away from home, as at a picnic or while travelling. [*OED* & YB; Grose, *Dict. Vulg. Tongue* (1785); *Ward* (1800) in *Carey's Life* (1885), vi. 137.]

Tiger [16C. Gr./Lat. *tigris*; Pg. *tigre*. Cf. H/S.

tir, 'an arrow', and S. *vyāghrā* (in the *Arthaveda*).] The *Felis tigris*. Mentioned by Arrian (*Indica* XV) *c*. 325 BC. The Bengal-or Royal-tiger: the tiger of Bengal where it attains its typical development. [*OED* & YB; *De Rebus in Oriente* in Cockayne's *Narrat.* 38; *c*. 1386, *Squire's Tale*, 411; Fitch (1586) in Purchas (1625-6), ii.]

Tika, teeka, ticka, tilak, tilka [19C. H. *tikā*, tilak; S. *tilaka*, fr. *tila*, 'a sesamum seed'.] A mark on the forehead made with coloured earth or unguents, as an ornament; to mark sectarial distinction; accession to the throne; at betrothals, espec. among *Kayasths* and **Rajputs**; a so-called 'caste-mark'. Also: *tīka-wālā sāhib*, the vaccination official. Cf., (1) Kan. *nama*, a sectarian mark on the forehead by followers of Vishnu in the form of a trident, the middle line red or yellow, the outer ones white. [*OED* & YB; Mir Husain Ali, *Life of Tipu* (1796), 25; Wilson, *Glossary* (1855); *Tod. Annals & Antiquities* (1829), i. 262; Fanny Parkes, *Wanderings of a Pilgrim* (1850), i. 259.] (2) *Tripundra* (S. 'three lines), the *Saivaite* mark on the forehead, consisting of three horizontal lines, made with **Sandal**-paste or burnt cowdung ashes. [Wilson *Glossary* (1855).] (3) *Urdh(w)apundra* (S. *urdhwa*, 'straight' + *pundra*, 'line'. The forehead mark made by *Vaishnavas*, consisting of two perpendicular lines joined above the nose by a curved line to represent the footprint of *Vishnu*. [Whitworth, *Anglo-Indian Glossary* (1885); Wilson, *Dict.* (1855).]

Tikka [20C. H. *tikka*.] Small pieces of meat or vegetable marinaded in spices and cooked on a skewer. Attrib. as in *tikka* **kebab**. Also with qualifying word, e.g., chicken *tikka*. [*The Times*, 28 May 1955, 5/1; L. Cody, *Bad Company* (1982), xxx. 200.]

Til, teel, teal [19C. H. *til*; S. *tilā*.] The Indian name of the plant, *Sesamum indicum*, whose seeds yield edible oil. A **Kharif** crop. *See* **Gingili**. [*OED* & YB; *Penny Cycl.* (1840), xvi. 417/1; Stoqueler (1845), *Handbk. Brit. India.* (1854), 514.]

Tilangana [18C.] *See* **Telinga**. The tract of land east of Bijapur between the rivers Godavari and Krishna, the homeland of the *Telinga* or *Telugu* people. [Rennell's *Memoir* (3rd ed. 1703), cxi; YB.]

Tilka See **Tika** etc.

Tillana [19C. S. *tillāna*.] An item of **Nritta** (pure dance) in **Bharatanatyam** between the **Padas**, with a number of alluring sculpturesque poses and variegated patterns of movement executed with grace and elegance. *See* **Nritya**. [Coomarasamy & Duggirala, tr., *Mirror of Gesture* (1917), 14; Monier-Williams, *Indian Wisdom* (1875), xx.]

Tincal, tincar [17C. Malay, *tingkal;* H. *tankār, tinkār;* S. *tankana.*] Crude borax, found in India and a number of Asian countries in lake deposits. [*OED* & YB; 1635 in Foster, *Crt. Min. E. Ind. Co.* (1907), 99.]

Tindal [17C. H. *tandel;* Mal. *tandal;* Tel. *tandelu.*] (1) The chief or headman of a body of men, espec. of a ship's crew of **Lascars,** or of a gang of **Coolies;** a boatswain; a foreman. [*OED* & YB; Fryer, *Acc. E. India & P.* (1698), 107.] (2) A personal attendant. [*OED;* Lang, *Wand. India* (1859), 36.] *See* **Mandor**.

Tiparry, tipari [19C. Beng./H. *tipārī, tepārī.*] The Cape Gooseberry, *Physalis pubescens.* [Robinson, *In My Indian Garden* (1878), 49-50; *OED* & YB.]

Tirtha, teertha, teerut [19C. H. *tirth, tīrtha,* 'a passage', fr. S. *tri,* 'to cross over'.] Among Hindus a place of pilgrimage and bathing, generally on the banks of holy rivers, espec. at the confluence of two (or more) such rivers, as at Hardwar, where the Ganges (**Ganga**) is said to take its rise, and at **Prayag** (Allahabad) at the confluence of the Jumuna, Ganges and the legendary subterranean river Saraswati. [YB; Sleeman, *Journey through Oude* (1844), ii. 4.]

Tirtht(a)nkar(a) [19C. S. *tirthankura,* fr. **Tirth** + *kura,* 'maker'. 'passage- or pilgrimage-maker'.] One who makes a passage through life; head of a sect. Among Buddhists, an ascetic; among Jains any of the 24 prophets or early teachers revered as deities, as having crossed the river of time and made a path for others to follow. *See* **Arhat, Vairagi**. [*OED;* Smith (1835), *Life of John Wilson* (1878), vi. 205.]

Titar, teetar [19C. H. *tītar, tītur.*] The Grey Francolin or Grey Partridge of India, *Francolinus ponticerinus,* otherwise known as *Ram-titar* and *Gora-titar.* [Jerdon, *Birds of India* (1862).]

Tiyan, Tiva, Tir [19C. M. *Tīyan* or *Tīvan.*] The third, or toddy-tapper caste of Malabar (Kerala). The word signifies 'islander', fr. M. *Tīvu* (S. *dvipa*), 'an island', and this caste is supposed to have come from Sri Lanka. *See* **Tier Cutty**. [YB; Logan, *Malabar* (1800), i. 110.]

Toady bacha [*today* + *baccha,* 'youngster'.] An obsequious person, sycophant, bootlicker, otherwise a 'toad-eater'. *See* **Chamcha**. [Hawkins, *CIWIE* (1984).]

Tobra [19C. H. *tobrā.*] The leather nose-bag containing a horse's feed, tied over the mouth by a thong which is passed over the horse's head. [YB; Drummond, *Illustrations* etc. (1808).]

Toco, toko [19C. Perh. the imp. of H. *toknā,* 'to censure, to blame'. (Cf. **Bunnow, Dumbcow, Lugow**.) But poss. public school slang, fr. Gr. *tokos,* 'interest'. [Partridge.] Slang (obs): A thrashing, chastisement, corporal punishment. [*OED* & YB; John Bee, *Slang Dict.* (1823).]

Toddy, taddy, tarrie, etc. [17C. H. *tārī* (with H. cerebral 'r' approaching English 'd'), fr. H. *tār,* 'palm-tree; S. *tala,* 'the palmyra'.] (1) The (fermented) sap of the palmyra or *tar* palm, *Borassus flabellifer,* and other species of palm, esp. the *Caryota urens,* the wild date *Phoenix sylvestris,* and the coconut *Cocos nucifera.* Used as a beverage in India and other tropical countries. [*OED* & YB; Finch (1609-10) in Purchas, *Pilgrimes* (1625), I. 436.] (2) A beverage composed of whisky or other spirituous liquors with hot water and sugar. [*OED* & YB; Burns, *Holy Fair* (1786), xv.] (3) Used in India as yeast to leaven bread. [YB.] Also: toddy-cat, the palm-civet, *Paradoxurus hermaphroditus* (1867); toddybird, the *Plocens baya,* which feeds on palm-sap (1698); toddy-shrike, the palmyra-swallow, *Artemus fuscus;* toddy-tapper, one who climbs palm trees to collect toddy sap (1937); *toddy-shop* (1842); *toddy-fly* (1681); and *toddyize* (1836), to cause to drink *toddy.* [*OED.*] *See* **Sagwire** and **Tar²**.

Tola, tole, toll [17C. H. *tolā;* S. *tulā,* 'a balance', fr. *tul,* 'to weigh'.] An Indian weight, about 12 grams (180 grains), the weight of a silver rupee, but varying at different times and places. [*OED* & YB; Hawkins (1610) in Purchas (1625-6), I. 217.]

Tombac(k) tambac, tombaga [17C. Malay *tēmbaga;* Pg. *tāmbaca,* 'copper'.] (1) An alloy of E. Indian origin of copper and zinc, in various proportions. Used in the manufacture of bells and gongs. [*OED* & YB; Lancaster (1602), Voy. India in Purchas (1625-6), 153.] (2) A musical instrument made of this alloy (rare). [*OED;* J. Davis (1602), tr. *Mandelslo's Travels* (1669), I. 30.]

Tom-tom, tum-tum, tong-tong [17C. H. tamtam. Cf. Sinh. *tammatana;* Malay, *tongtong.*] An onomatopoeic expression. An Indian or other E. Indian drum; 'extended also to the drums of barbarous people generally'. [*OED.*] Usually beaten with the hands. When badminton was introduced at *Satāra,* natives called it *Tamtam phūl khel, tam-tam* meaning 'battledore', and the shuttlecock looked like a flower (*phūl*). Tommy Atkins promptly turned this into '*Tom Fool*' [*Calcutta Rev.* xcvi. 346, YB.] [*OED & YB;* Wheeler (1693), *Madras* (1861), I. 268; Dickens, *Sketches by Boz.,* 'The Steam Excursion'.]

Tonga, tanga [19C. H. *tāngā.*] A light and small two-wheeled horse-drawn carriage and cart used in India. Also *tonga-wallah,* 'tongadriver' (1945). [*OED & YB; Settlement Report Nasik* (1874); Crawford, *Mr. Isaacs* (1882), ix.]

Tomicatchy, tunnyketch [18C. Tam. *tannirkāssi,* abbr. of *tannir-kāsatti,* 'water-woman'.] The name of the domestic water-carrier in Madras, who is generally a woman, and acts as a kind of under housemaid. [YB.] *See* **Beastie (Bhisti).** [*Madras Courier,* 26 April 1792).]

Tonjon, tomjohn [19C. (Origin uncertain).] A sort of sedan chair, slung on a single pole and carried by four bearers, like a palanquin; alias **'Tellicherry-chair'.** [Welsh, *Milit. Reminiscences* (1840), ii. 40; *OED & YB;* Mrs Sherwood (*c.* 1804), *Autobiog.* (1854), xvi. 300.]

Tony *See* **Dhony, Doney.**

Toolsy *See* **Tulsi.**

Toon, toon-wood, tun [19C. H. *tūn; S. tunna.*] The tree *Cedrela toona,* and its timber, resembling mahogany, but softer and lighter in colour. Used for furniture and cabinetmaking. Also called Indian mahogany. [Maria Graham (1810), *Jrnl. Resid. India* (1812), 101; *OED & YB.*]

Toos [19C. Tib. *tūs.*] Tibetan **Shawl**-goat; its wool (**pashmina**), and the material woven from it. [YB; Kirkpatrick, *Acct. of Nepaul* (1811), 134.]

Tootnague *See* **Tutenag.**

Topaz, topas(s) [17C. Pg. *topaz,* said to be fr. M. *tōpāsh* and H. *dōbāshī,* 'a man of two languages'. *See* **Dubash.** (A fancied derivation from H. *tōpī,* 'hat', the term forming *topi-wallah,* 'hat-man', European, has been current since the middle of the 18th century).] A dark-skinned half-caste of Portuguese descent, whose occupation might be soldier, ship's scavenger, bath-attendant or interpreter, depending on circumstances. [*OED & YB;* Fryer (1673), *New Acct. E. India & Persia* (1672–81).] *See* **Linguist(er)**.

Topchee, topchi [17C. H. *top,* 'cannot', and *chī,* agent'; P. and Turk. *tōp.*] A term formerly employed in the Ottoman Empire and India for a gunner or artilleryman. Also *topkhanawalla.* [*OED;* 1623 in Foster, *Eng. Factories India* (1908) 234.]

Tope¹ [17C. Tel. *tōpu,* Tam. *tōppu.*] A grove, orchard, clump of plantation trees, espec. **Mango.** [*OED & YB;* Fryer (1678), *New Acct. E. India & P.* (1672-81), 40.]

Tope² [19C. H./Punj. *tōp;* Prak./Pali *thūpo; S. stūpa.*] A dome or tumulus of masonry to hold saintly relics or to commemorate some religious occasion, usually of **Buddhist** or **Jain** origin, numerous examples of which may still be seen in Indian and other eastern and far-eastern countries. *See* **Stupa.** [*OED & YB;* Elphinstone, *Caubul* (1815), I. 80.]

Tope,³ top [17C. H. *top,* 'a cannon', P./Turk. *tōp.*] *See* **Topchi.** Also, *Tope-Khana* (1656), the Artillery Park or Ordance Department. [YB; Rycaut, *Present State of the Ottoman Empire* (1687), 94; Holwell, *Hist. Events Bengal & Indostan,* (1765), I. 96.]

Topi, topee [19C. H. *topī,* 'a hat'. Poss. an adaptation of Pg. *topo,* 'top'.] In India a pithhat, esp. the **Sola-topi** (erroneously 'Solar' by sound association). Orig. applied by Indians to the European hat, then specialized in Anglo-India as a name for the pith-hat or sunhelmet. *See* **Sola.** [*OED & YB; Court Mag.* (1835), 207/2.]

Topi-wallah, topee-wallah [19C. H. *topīwālā,* 'one who wears a hat'.] A European or, disparagingly, 'one claiming to be so'. [YB.] In Bengal, a hat-maker, a milliner. [*OED & YB;* Drummond, *Illustrations of Grammatical Parts of Guzaratee and Mahrattee* (1808); Hockley, *Pandurang Hari* (1826), vi. I. 88.]

Topsy-, tipsy-, tupsi-fish [18C. Hobson-Jobsonism fr. H. *tapsi* (*machh*); S. *tapasya matyas;* 'fish generated by heat' in the Spring season, *Phalguna* (Feb. March), when the mango blossoms. (*See* **Mango**-Fish.) The *Polynemus paradiseus* or *risua,* inhabiting the Hughly and Irrawaddy estuaries, and considered a great delicacy locally. Also called the Penitent-Fish, conjecturally because they have long hairs like some Hindu religious ascetics 'who never shave, but who like the Topsy-fish disappear during the rainy season'. [*OED* & YB; Buchanan, *Fishes of the Ganges* (1822); Hickey's *Bengal Gazette*, 3 March 1781; Hamilton, *Desc. of Hindostan* (1820), I. 58; Cantor in *Proc. Zool. Soc.* (July 1839), 116.]

Toran(a) [19C. H. *tōran*; S. *torana*, 'arched portal'.] A sacred Buddhist gateway, of wood or stone, consisting of a pair of uprights with one or more (often three) cross-pieces; sometimes elaborately carved, e.g. the gateways to the Great Tope at Sanchi. [*OED*; Robins, *Temple of Solomon* (1887), 27.]

Torma [19C. Tib. *tōrma*.] Sacrificial burnt offering in Tibetan Buddhist ceremonies. [*OED*; Waddell, *Buddhism of Tibet* (1895), xii. 297.]

Tosha-khana, toshaconna [17C. P/H. *tosha-khāna*.] The repository of articles received as presents attached to a government office, or great man's establishment; formerly a special department attached to the Foreign Secretariat of the Government of India. [YB; Sir Thomas Roe, *Embassy Court Great Mogul* (1615-19) (Hak. Soc., ii. 300; Lady Dufferin, *Viceregal Life* (1885), 75.]

Tostdaun [18C.]. Milit. H. *tosdān*; P. *toshadān*, 'provision-holder'.] A cartouche-box. [YB; *Society in India* by an Indian Officer (1841), ii. 223.]

Toty [19C. Tam. *totti*; Kan. *totīga*.] In S. India a low-caste man employed as labourer, messenger, scavenger, etc. [YB; Wilson, *Glossary* (1855); Le Fanu, *Man of Salem* (1883), ii. 221.] *See* **Sweeper, Mehta**.

Tourmaline [18C. Sinh. *toramalli*.] A general name for the cornelian, orig. found in Sri Lanka. [*OED*; R. Wilson in *Phil. Trans.* (1759), LL. I. 308.]

Tower-of-silence [19C.] A tower or **Dokhma**, on the summit of which the Parsees place their dead to be eaten by birds. [*OED*; *Chamber's Encycl.* (1865), vii. 300.]

Towleea [19C. Pg. *toalha*; H. *tauliya*. (Cf. Malay *toala*).] A towel. [YB; *Panjab, Notes & Queries* (1885), ii. 117.]

Traga [19C. Poss. fr. Guj. *trāgu*.] The self-infliction of a wound designed to force a debtor to pay his debt, or redress an injury; espec. by a **Bhat** in order to enforce the fulfilment of an engagement for which he had pledged his personal surety. A commonly used form of *traga* was made by penetrating both cheeks with a sword or other sharp implement, and in this state to dance before the person against whom *traga* was made. This had to be performed without the slightest show of pain which, if displayed, would have destroyed its efficacy. An extreme form of **Dharna** and punishable by law. [*Bombay Reg.*, xiv. 1827 (Wilson); YB; 1803 in Wellington's *Despatches* (ed. 1837), ii. 387; Forbes, *Oriental Memoirs* (1813), ii. 91.]

Trichy, trichi (trichies, tritchies) [19C. (Coll. abbrev. of place-name Trichinopoly).] The familiar name of the **Cheroots** made at Trichinopoly (or Tiruchirappalli) in Tamil Nadu; 'long and rudely made, with a straw inserted at the end for the mouth'. [*OED* & YB; Burton, *Sind Revisited* (1877), I. i. 7.]

Trimurti [19C. S. *tri*, 'three' + *mūrti*, 'form'.] (1) Hinduism: The Hindu Trinity, or Triad: **Brahma, Vishnu** and **Shiva**. Typified by the three mystic letters A,U,M, combined as OM, and sometimes interpreted respectively as Creator, Preserver and Destroyer, though otherwise these functions are considered as being interchangeable, and conceived as aspects of one ultimate reality. [*OED*; J. F. Davies, *Chinese* (1836), II. xiii. 107; Monier-Williams, *Hinduism* (1877), vii. 87.] (2) A three-faced statue of Brahma, Vishnu and Shiva [*OED*; E.B. Havell, *Handbk. Indian Art* (1920), III. i. 203.]

Tripitaka [19C. S. *tri*, 'three' + *pitaka*, 'basket'.] The 'three baskets' of the Hinayana Buddhist writing, which are named the Sutra, Vinaya and *Abhidharma*, compiled many years after the death of the Buddha. [Whitworth, *Anglo-Indian Dict.* (1885).]

Trishaw [20C. Adaptation of Japanese **Jinricksha**. fr. *tri*, 'three' + *ricksha*, strength-cart.] A tricycle *rickshaw* pedalled by a man or driven by an engine; used ubiquitously in India as a taxi. *See* **Ricksha(w)** & **Jenny-Rickshaw**.

Tristubh [19C. S. *tristubha*.] A vedic metre of ten to thirteen syllabus. *See* **Jagati** and **Gayatri**. [*OED*; *Penny Cycl.* (1843), xxvi. 177/1.]

Trisul(a), trishul [19C. S. *trisūla*, fr. *tri*, 'three' + *sūla*, 'spear-head'.] A three-pointed figure or ornament, used as an emblem of **Siva**; also as a Buddhist symbol. [*OED*; Albaster, *Wheel of Life* (1871), 249.]

Truchman tarjuman [17C. *See* **Dragoman**. H/Ar. *tarjaman*.] An interpreter [Purchas, *Pilgrimage* (1613). *See* **Dubhash, Topass**.]

Tsongdu [20C. Tib. *t'sogs du*, 'an assembly meets'.] The Tibetan National Council or Assembly. [*OED; Spectator*, 18 Feb., 243/2.]

Tucka [19C. H. *takā;* Beng. *tākā*.] In Bengal it was used for a rupee, elsewhere in India it had different values. *See* **Tanga**. [YB; Broughton, *Letters from a Mahr. Camp.* (1809; ed. 1892), 84.]

Tuckavi *See* **Taccavi**.

Tuckeed, takid [19C. Ar/H. *takīd*, 'emphasis, injunction'.] *'Tākīd karnā'* = 'to enjoin stringently, to insist'. *Tuckeed-chitty*, 'a letter of injunction, a written mandate or directions'. [YB; Wilson, *Glossary* (1855).]

Tuckiah [19C. P/H. *takya*, 'a pillow or cushion'.] The hut or hermitage of a **Fakir**. [YB; Wellington (1800), *Despatches* (ed. 1837), I. 78; Mr Mackenzie, *Life in the Mission* etc. (1847), ii. 47.]

Tulip-tree = **Bhendi** (*Thespesia populnea*) in India.

Tulsi, toolsy [17C. H. *tūlsī; tūlasī*.] The holy basil-plant of the Hindus, *Ocimum sanctum;* sacred to *Vishnu* and frequently planted in a vase on a pedestal in the vicinity of a Hindu temple, or a domestic shrine, in which sometimes the ashes of a deceased relative are preserved. Also used medicinally by **Ayurvedic** doctors. [*OED* & YB; Fryer (1673), *Acct. E. Indies & P.* (ed. 1698), 199.]

Tulwar *See* **Talwar**.

Tumasha *See* **Tamasha**.

Tumlet [Dom. H. *tāmlet*.] Corr. of *tumbler*. [YB.]

Tumtum [19C. Derivation uncertain. Poss. a corr. of *tandem*.] A dog-cart or two-wheeled country carriage. [Trevelyan, *Competition Wallah* (1864), vi. 139; 1807 in *Stanford Dict.* (ed. 1892).]

Tunca, tuncaw, tankha [18C. P/H. *tankhwāh* (pronounced *tankhā*).] (1) An order or draft of money, a bill of exchange, an assignment by the ruling authority upon the revenue of any particular locality in payment of wages, pay, gratuity, or pension, or in repayment of advances or any specified head of charge. [Wilson, *Gloss.* (1855); Orme, *Hist. Milit. Trans.* (1778), ii. 361.] (2) In its most ordinary more modern sense it was a word for the wages of a monthly servant. [YB.]

Tundice [20C. A.I. hybrid H./E.] An ice-cooled container. [Hawkins, *CIWIE*.]

Tupsee *See* **Topsy-Fish**.

Tur [19C. H. *tūr;* S. *tuwari*.] The pulse, *Cajanus indicus*, a **Kharif** and a **Rabi** crop, the green pods of which are used as vegetables, the beans are made into **Dhal**, and the dried stalks were reduced to charcoal to make gunpowder. *See* **Arhar, Moong, Oord**. [Whitworth, *Anglo-Indian Dict.* (1885).]

Turmeric [16C. E. fr. Fr. *terre mérite*. Mod. L. *terra merita* (16th century).] Powder made from the root-stock of the East Indian plant *Curcuma longa*, used in curry powder; as a yellow dye, a chemical test, a condiment and a medicine. [*OED*.] *See* **Haldi**. [*Rates of Custome* (1545), c vj b.]

Tus *See* **Toos**.

Tussore, tussah, tusser, tasar [17C. H. *tasar;* S. *tasara*, 'a shuttle'. (perh. fr. the form of the cocoon. (YB).] A coarse brown silk, made in and exported from India, produced by *Antherea mylitta* or *paphia* and other species of silkworm. [*OED* & YB; 1619 in Foster, *Eng. Fact. in India* (1906), 112.]

Tutenag, tootnague [17C. Mar. *tuttināg*, said to be fr. S. *tuttha*, 'copper sulphate' + *nāga*, 'tin, lead'; cf. Pg. *tutenaga*, an alloy of copper, zinc and nickel, sometimes called 'white copper', and resembling 'German-silver'.] Also used at one time for zinc in the Indian trade. The word was Hobson-Jobsonised into 'tooth an egg' metal. [Foster, *Eng. Fact. in India* (1908), II. 135; *OED* & YB.]

Tuxall, takasau, taksal [18C. H. *taksāl*, fr. S. *tankasālā*, 'coin-hall'.] The Mint and *takasālī*, an officer or master of the Mint; a person whose occupation is coining. [YB; 1757 in Wheeler, *Early Records*, 248.]

Twice-born [18C. trans. of S. *dvija*.] An epithet of the three higher castes of Hindus: **Brahmin, Kshatriya, Vaishya;** the investiture with the sacred cord (**Janeo**) being deemed to constitute a second birth. [*OED*; Sir W. Jones, *Inst. Hindu Law* (1794), II. 169; Elphinstone, *Hist. India* (1841), I. i. iv. 79.]

Tyagi [19C. Fr. S. *tyāj*, 'to leave, to give up'.] One who has abandoned terrestrial objects and thoughts. The opposite of **Sansari**. *See* **Viyogi**. [Whitworth, *Anglo-Indian Dict.* (1885).]

Tyan [18C. M. *tīyyan*, fr. *tīvu* (S. *dvīpa*), 'an island'.] A Kerala caste of **Toddy**-tappers, supposedly from the island of Sri Lanka. [YB.] *See* **Tier-cutty**. [Logan, *Malabar* (1792), iii. 169.]

Ty(e)khana, tyconna [18C. H. *tah-khana*.] 'Nether-house', in which it was the subterranean custom to pass the hottest part of the day during the hot season in some parts of India. [*OED* & YB; *Seir Mutaqherin* (E. tr. 1789), iii. 19; Lang, *Wand. India* (1859), 196.]

Typhoon, tuffon, touffon, etc. [16C.] (1) [P./Ar./H. *tūfān;* Gr. *tūphon.*] A violent storm of wind and rain; tempest; hurricane; tornado. A violent storm or tempest occurring in India. (2) [Ch. *tai-fung,* 'big-wind' (1699).] A violent cyclonic storm or hurricane occurring in the China seas and adjacent regions, chiefly during the typhoon season, July-October. *See*

Nor-Wester. [*OED* & YB; Hickcock's tr., *Frederick's Voy.* (1588), 34.6; Purchas, *Pilgrimage* (1613), iv. xix. 448.]

Tyre, tyer The common name in S. India for curdled milk, or cream beginning to sour. *See* **Dahi.** [*OED* & YB; Purchas, *Pilgrimage* (1613), v. xi. 428; Halhed, *Code Gentoo Laws* (1776), Pref. 41.]

U

Uddiyana [20C. S. *uddīyana,* 'rising up'.] One of the physical exercises (**Asanas**) in **Yoga**. [S. Kuvalayananda, *Popular Yoga* (1949), I. iii. 51; Koestler, *Lotus and Robot* (1960), iii. 117.]

Ulema, ulama [19C. Ar/P/Tur. *'sulema,* pl. of *alim,* 'knowing, learned, wise', fr. *'alama,* 'to know'.] Body of Muslim doctors of the law under the authority of Sheikh-ul-Islam; Muslim doctor or divine. [*OED;* Whitworth, *Anglo-Indian Dict.* (1885); Tennyson, 'Akbar's Dream' (1892), 45.]

Ulus [19C. Turk. *ūlūs.*] The name applied in Afghanistan either to a whole tribe or to independent branches of a tribe. 'The word seems to mean a clannish commonwealth.' [*OED;* Elphinstone, *Caubul* (1815), II. ii. 159.]

Umedwar [19C. H/Ar. *umed,* 'hope'.] An expectant; a candidate for employment; an unpaid probationer; one who awaits a favourable answer to some representation or request. [Whitworth, *Anglo-Indian Dict.* (1885).]

Unani, yunani [19C. H. *Yunan.*] A system of Indian medicine said to be of Greek (Ionian) origin. [Whitworth, *Anglo-Indian Dict.* (1885).]

Untouchable [20C.] A casteless Hindu or aboriginal whose touch or proximity pollutes a caste Hindu; e.g. a **Sweeper, Mehtar, Toti, Chuckler,** etc. Now called **Scheduled Castes, Harijans, Dravidas, Dalits,** etc. Also, Untouchability (1924). In 1949 in India and 1953 in Pakistan 'the term and the social restrictions which accompany it were declared illegal'. [*OED; Indian Spectator,* 23 Oct. 1909, 843/2; Priestland, *Priestland's Progress* (1981), vi. 93.]

Upanayana(m) [20C. S. *upa,* 'below' + *ni,* 'to leave'.] The ceremony of investiture of a Hindu into the order of a twice-born man with the sacred thread or *Janeo.* This rite is enjoined for a Brahmin in his eighth year, for a Kshatriya in his eleventh and for a Vaishya in his twelfth, but the time may be extended in each case. [Whitworth, *Anglo-Indian Dict.* (1885).]

Upanishad [19C. S. *upa,* 'near to' + *ni-shad,* 'to sit or lie down'.] Sitting at the feet of a teacher. Mystical or secret doctrine. The Third division of the **Veda;** its speculative metaphysical interpretation concerning the deity, creation and existence. [*OED;* Colebrooke in *Asiatic Res.* (1805), viii. 446; Max Mueller, *Lect. Sci. Lang.* (1861), 145.] *See* **Vedanta**.

Up-country, up-the-country [18C.] In India, sb. an inland district or part of the country, as distinct from the cities and main centres of government; also adv. & adj. uses. [*OED;* J. Corneille, *Journal of My Service in India,* (c. 1760), Ms printed by Folio Society (1966), ed. Michael Edwardes; Trevelyan, *Competition Wallah* (1864), 31.]

Upma [20C. Tamil *ūpma.*] A salted confection of flour. [Hawkins, *CIWIE.*]

Upper Roger [18C. A Hobson-Jobsonism of the Sanskrit **Yuva Raja,** 'Young King'.] Heir-apparent, Crown Prince. [YB; 1755 in Dalrymple's *Oriental Repertory* (1808), i. 92.]

Urdu, Oordoo [18C. P/H. *Urdū;* Turki *ordū,* 'camp'. Ellip. for *Zabān-i-urdū,* 'language of the camp'. Cf. 'horde'.] The **Hindustani** langauge, allied to **Hindi,** but with copious Persian, Arabic and Turki vocabulary, and written in a Perso-Arabic script. Orig. spoken at the Mughal courts of Delhi and Lucknow and by Indian Muslims generally; now the national language of Pakistan. [*OED* & YB; Hanway, *Hist. Acct.* (1753), I. 247; Gilchrist, *Gram. Hindustanee Lang.* (1796), 261.]

Urial, oorial [19C. Punj. *Urial.*] The wild Himalayan Sheep, a sub-species of *Ovis orientalis,* also called the **Sha²** or **Shapoo**. [YB; *Athenaeum,* 31 Dec. 1887, 897/3.]

Urs [19C. H/Ar. *ūrs.*] Offerings of food, incense, or lamps, made by Muslims on various occasions at the shrines of Muslim saints, and espec. on the 12th of *Babi-ul-awal,* the anniversary of the death of Prophet Mohammed; also nuptials, marriage, a marriage feast. [*OED;* Newbold, *Straits of Malacca* (1839), I. V. 252.]

Usar, ushar(a) [19C. H/S. *ūshar.*] Saline (soil); land alkaline and unfit for cultivation; barren, fallow (land), commonly called **reh**. [Wilson, *Glossary* (1855).]

Usharafi *See* **Ashrafi**.

Uspuk, hanspeck [19C. A.I./H. *aspack,* corr. of E. handspike.] Also Sea-Hindi *hanspeek.* [Roebuck, *Naval Dict.* (1811).]

Ustad [19C. H/P. *ūstad.*] A master, a teacher, one skilled in art, music, science, etc. (Cf. sp. *usted.*) [*OED;* Wilson, *Glossary* (1855); Ved Mehta, *Portrait of India* (1967), 40.]

Uthamna [H. *uthāmana.*] Hindu mourning ceremony held on third day after death. [Hawkins, *CIWIE.*]

V

Vacca, Vakea-nevis [17C. Ar. *wākia'h*, 'an event, new'; *waki'ah-navis*, 'news-writer'.] Among the Mughals, 'a sort of registrars or remembrancers. Later they became spies who were sent into the provinces to supply information to the central government.' [YB; Fryer (1673), *New Acct. E. India & P.* (1672-81; ed. 1698), 80.]

Vadi [S. *vādī*.] The *jīva-svara* or the most prominent note of a **Raga**.Also *vadyam*, instrumental music. [Fox Strangways, *The Music of Hindostan* (1914).]

Vadiyar [19C. Tam. *vadiyar*.] Family Brahmin priest. [Hawkins, *CIWIE*.]

Vahan(a) [19C. S. *vāhana*.] Vehicle, esp. bird or beast traditionally ridden by a Hindu god. [*OED*; Moore, *Hindu Pantheon* (1810), 16; J.L. Kipling, *Beast & Man in India* (1891), vi. 122.]

Vahini, bahini [Beng. *vāhini*.] Army. [Hawkins, *CIWIE*.]

Vaid, baid, vaidya [H/S. *vaidya*.] An **Ayurvedic** (Hindu) physician. Cf. **Hakim²**. [Wilson *Glossary* (1855); Sleeman, *Rambles and Recollections* (1844), 107.]

Vaidika [19C. fr. S. *Veda*, equivalent to English **Vedic**.] Relating to the **Vedas**. A Brahmin learned in the vedic texts. [Wilson, *Glossary* (1855).]

Vairagi, byragi, viragee, etc. [H./S. *vairāgi*. Lit. 'one devoid of passion,' fr. *vi*, without' + *rag*, 'passion'.] Religious mendicant; applied to different classes of vagrants, but particularly to those devoted to the worship of **Vishnu**, espec. in the form of **Rama**; generally an ascetic professing to have subdued all worldly emotions, and depending on alms. Also *vairagan*, a female *vairagi*. [W. Hamilton, *East India Gazetteer* (Gloss), (1815).]

Vaisakha, *See* **Vesak.**

Vais(h)eshika [19C. S. *visish*, 'to distinguish'.] One of the six systems (**darsans**) of orthodox Hindu philosophy analysing the cosmos by distinguishing nine elements, each without cause and eternally distinct, namely five atoms (earth, air, fire, water and mind) and four other entities (ether, time, space and soul.) [Whitworth *Anglo-Indian Dict.* (1885).]

Vaishnava [19C. S. *vaishnava*.] A worshipper of *Vishnu* in one or other of his incarnations. In Bengali the term becomes *Boishnab*. [YB.] It also designates a body of bankers and merchants who are followers of Vishnu. *See* **Vishnu**. [Ward, *Hist. Hindoos* (1811; 2nd ed. 1815); ii. 13; Wilson, *Glossary* (1855); YB.]

Vaisya, Vaishya [17C. S. *vaishya*, 'peasant, labourer, fr. *vis*, 'to enter into, to settle down on'.] The third of the four Hindu castes according to Manu's code, and the last of those ranking as 'twice-born *(dvija)*. *Vaisyas* are traditionally landowners and merchants and are represented by the great mercantile class of **Banyas**. [*OED*; Sir T. Herbert, *Trav.* (1634), 34; Sir W. Jones, *Inst of Manu* (1794), i. 34.]

Vajra [18C. S. *vajra*.] Hinduism and Buddhism: a thunderbolt or mythical weapon, espec. one wielded by Indra. [*Asiatick Res.* (1788), I. 241; Beauchamp's tr., *Dubois, Hindu Manners* (1897), II. iii. v. 638.]

Vakil, vakeel, wakil [17C. H/Ar. *wakil*.] (1) A person invested with authority to act for another, an agent, an ambassador, a representative. [*OED* & YB; Foster (1622), *Eng. Fact. in Ind.* (1908).] (2) In India, also, an attorney, an authorized public pleader in a court of justice, a barrister. [*OED* & YB; Sir. T. Herbert, *Trav.* (1634; ed. 1677), 316; 1689 in Ovington, *Voy. Surat* (1969), 415.] (3) Among the Marathas the hereditary assistant of the **Deshmukh**. [Wilson, *Glossary* (1855).]

Vaklatnama, wakalatnama(h) [19C. *See* prec. + *namah*, 'a document'.] Power of attorney, letter of authority, credentials. [Wilson, *Glossary* (1855).]

Valima [H. *valima*.] A banquet. [Hawkins, *CIWIE*.]

Vanaprastha, Wanaprastha [19C. S. *vana*, 'forest' + *prastha*, 'proceeding'.] A man of one of the first three Hindu castes who has entered the third *asrama* or stage of life and has proceeded to a life in the forest, in preparation for the final **Sannyasi** stage. *See* **Brahmacharya, Grihasta**. [Wilson, *Glossary* (1855).]

Vanaspati [20C. H/S. *vanaspati*, 'lord of the wood, forest tree'.] Hydrogenated vegetable oil, often used instead of **Ghee** in cooking in India. [*OED*; *Food Manufacture* (1949), XXIV. 500/2.]

Vanda [19C. S. *vanda*.] A genus of epiphytal orchids found in India and tropical Asia, bearing large, showy flowers; a plant of this genus. [*OED*; *Encycl. Brit.* Suppl. (1801), II.]

Varna, varan, barna, baran [19C. H/S. *varna*, lit. 'colour'.] Class, **caste**. The names of the four *varnas* of Hindus according to *Manu* are **Brahmin, Kshatriya, Vaishya** and **Sudra**; the system or basis of this division. [*OED; Penny Cycl.* (1838), XII. 230/I.]

Varsha [19C. H/S. *varsha*, lit. 'rain, the rainy season', 'annual, celebrated annually'.] Rites performed on anniversaries. Also, related to the rainy season. [Wilson, *Glossary* (1855).]

Varsi, barsi *See* prec. Rites performed on the first anniversary of a death. [Hawkins, *CIWIE.*]

Varuna, Waruna [19C. S. *varuna*, fr. *vri*, 'to envelop'.] The Hindu God of the sky; the all enveloper; one of the oldest **Vedic** Gods. 'Corresponds in name and partly in character with the Greek Uranus'. Also *varuni*, a Hindu festival in honour of Varuna. [Wilson, *Glossary* (1855); Whitworth, *Anglo-Indian Dict.* (1885).]

Veda, Bead, Beda, etc. [17C. H. *ved, bed;* S. *vēda*, 'knowledge, sacred knowledge, sacred book', *vid*, 'to know'. (Cf. E. *wit*.)] Any one of the four *Vedas*, the ancient sacred books of the Hindus, entitled *Rig-, Yajur-, Sama-*, and *Atharva-Veda;* the body of sacred literature contained in these books. Hence *Vedic* (1839) fr. **Vaidika**, relating to the *Vedas*, or to the language of the *Vedas*, an early form of Sanskrit (2000-500 BC); *Vedism* (1882); *Vedist* (1896); *Vedaic* (1865); *Vedaism* (1887). Also applied to other works or systems of supposedly inspired origin, e.g. *Ayur-Veda*, the science of life or longevity, medicine; *Dhanur-Veda*, the science of the bow or military science; *Gandharbar-Veda*, the science of music. [*OED* & *YB*; Bernier, E. tr., *Voyages* (1684), 104; Scrafton, *Hindostan* (1763), 4; Colebrooke, *Asiat. Res.* (1808), VIII. 387.] *See* **Upanishad**.

Vedanta [19C. S. *Veda + anta*, 'end'.] One of the six **darshans**, or systems of orthodox Hindu philosophy, founded on the **Upanishads**, which are the end of the **veda**; the non-dualistic pantheistic 'final truth', which teaches that all souls are but part of the eternal soul and that all matter is illusion'. [GCW.] Also *Vedantic, -ism, -ist. [Asiat Res.* (1788), I. 223; *OED*; Colebrooke (1828), 'Philos. Hindus' in *Trans. Roy. Asiat. Soc.* (1827), I. 19; Max Mueller, *India* (1882), vii. 270.]

Vederala [Sinh. *vederala*.] A village doctor in Sri Lanka. [Hawkins, *CIWIE.*]

Vedda, Wedda [17C. Sinh. *veddā*, 'archer, hunter'.] A member of an aboriginal forest tribe of Sri Lanka. [Tam. *vedu*, 'hunting'.] [*OED* & *YB*; Knox, *Hist. Ceylon* (1681), 61; Tylor (1881), *Anthropology* (1904), vi. 164.]

Veddoid [20C.] *See* prec. Pertaining to (a member of) a racial group typified by the **Veddas**, with dark skin, short stature and wavy hair, and occurring generally in parts of S. Asia. [*OED;* Kroeber (1923), *Anthropology* (2nd ed., 1948), iv. 139.]

Veena, Vina [18C. H/S. *vīna*.] An Indian musical instrument with fretted finger-board to which seven strings fitted with pegs attached, and a gourd at each end, played by plucking; the Indian Lyre. *See* **Sitar, Tamboura** and **Surbahar.** [*OED;* Eliza Hamilton (1796), *Lett. Hindoo Raja* (1811), I. 211; Sir W. Jones in *Asiatick Res.* (1788), I. 265.]

Vellard [18C. Pg. *vallado*, 'a mound or embankment'. Cf. Mar. *walhad*, 'to cross over'.] The term is applied to the causeways built between Bombay and the neighbouring islands to serve both as moles to exclude water and as dry passages over the marshy land. [GCW; YB; Douglas, *Bombay and Western India* (1893); Maria Graham, *Journal Resid. India.* (1812), 8.]

Vendu-Master [18C. fr. vendue (dial.), 'sale, auction'. Poss. of Pg. origin in India.] An Agent (of government) with functions similar to that of a **Chowdry**, or an auctioneer. [*OED* & *YB; India Gazette*, 17 May 1781; SetonKarr *Selections from Calcutta Gazettes* (1793), ii. 99.]

Venetian [17C. *venetian*.] A coin (the *sequin* of Venice) current in India and adjacent countries in 17th and 18th centuries. [*OED* & *YB*; Fryer (1675), *Acct. E. Indies* (1698), 406; Burnes, *Trav. Bokhara* (1835), I. 90.]

Veni [Mar. *venī*.] String of flowers used to decorate women's hair. *See* **Gajra**. [Hawkins, *CIWIE.*]

Veranda(h) [17C. Orig. fr. India. (*See* H. *varandā;* Beng. *bārandā;* mod. S. *baranda*); but appears to be an adoption of Pg. and older Sp. *varanda, baranda*, 'railing, balustrade, balcony'.] An open portico or roofed gallery along the side(s) of a building as a protection or shelter from the sun and rain. [*OED* & *YB*; Cogan's *Pinto's Voyages and Adventures* (1653), 102; Lockyer, *Acct. Trade India* (1711), 20; Ld. Valentia, *Voyages & Travels to India* (1809), I. 424.]

Verdure [18C. fr. Pg. *verduras*.] This word appears to have been used [in India] in the 18th century for vegetables, adapted from the

Portuguese.' [YB; Long, *Selections Fort William* (1748-67; ed. 1869), 35.]

Verge, varem [18C. fr. Pg. *varsea, varzia, vargem,* 'a plain field, or a piece of level ground, that is sowed and cultivated'. [YB.] A term used in S. India for rice lands. [Logan, *Malabar* (1749), iii. 48.]

Vesak, Visakha [19C. S. *vaisākhā,* fr. *vi-sākhā,* 'branched'.] The 1st month of the Hindu solar year (April-May), & the second of the luni-solar. Also the name of a constellation, 'An important Buddhist festival commemorating the birth, enlightenment, and death of the Buddha, observed on the day of the full moon Visakha'. [*OED;* Wilson, *Glossary* (1855); E. J. Thomas, *Life of Buddha* (1927), iii. 34.]

Vettyver, vetiver, vitivert, wattie, waeroo, etc. [19C. Tam. *vettivēru,* fr. *ver,* 'root'.] The fragrant **Cuscus** grass and the perfumed oil distilled from it. [Heyne, *Tracts on India* (1814), II; *OED* & YB; Thornhill, *Haunts Indian Official* (1899), 18.]

Veva, wewa [S. *veva.*] A reservoir. [Hawkins, *CIWIE.*]

Vibhuti [S. *vibhuti.*] 'Sacred ash, often produced miraculously by Indian saints or god-men.' [Hawkins, *CIWIE.*]

Vidana [17C. Sinh. *vidana;* S. *vadana,* 'the act of speaking'.] In Sri Lanka, the title of the village headman, who conveys the orders of Government to the people. A *Vidhana Sabha* is the Legislative Assembly of an Indian State. [YB; Knox, *Historical Relation Ceylon* (1681), 51.]

Vidyapith [S. *vidya,* 'knowledge, learning, science, art'.] Traditional Hindu school. [Hawkins, *CIWIE.*]

Vihara, wihare [17C. S. *vihārā, vihri,* 'to walk about'.] A place where Buddhist teachers met and walked about; a hall surrounded by cells of monks; a Buddhist monastery or temple. 'The wide diffusion of such establishment, has left its trace in the names of many noted places, e.g. *Bihar, Kuch Behar,* and the *Vihar* water-works at Bombay.' [YB.] See **Chaitya.** [*OED* & YB; Knox, *Ceylon* (1681), III. iii. 74; L. Woolf, *Village in Jungle* (1913), I. 12.]

Vikram(a) era [19C. S. *vikrama.*] The era commences with the year 57 BC so that to find the *Vikram Samvat* (year), 57 is to be added to any year AD, eg. AD1927 + 57 = 1984. [Tod *Annals & Antiquities of Rajasthan* (1829), i. 104.]

Vilayati See **Blighty.**

Villu [Sinh. *villu.*] Lake, swamp. [Hawkins, *CIWIE.*]

Vimana [19C. S. *vimāna.*] (1) In an Indian temple the central tower enclosing the shrine. See **Gopura, Mantapa.** [*Chamber's Cycl.* (1863), V. 552/1.] (2) Hindu Mythol: A heavenly chariot of the gods. [*OED;* Whitworth, *Anglo-Indian Dict.* (1885); Kramrisch, *Hindu Temple* (1946), II. 344.]

Vina See **Veena.**

Vinaya [19C. S. *vinayā,* lit. 'leading (away)'.] Buddhist monastic rules of conduct for the order of **Bhikshus.** [*OED;* A. Cunningham, *Ladakh* (1854), xiii. 383.]

Vindaloo [19C. Prob. fr. Pg. *vin d'alho,* 'wine + garlic (sauce)'.] An Indian dish of curry with meat, fish or poultry, in a sauce of garlic, vinegar, spices, etc. [*OED;* W.H. Dave, *Wife's Help to Indian Cookery* (1888); Barr & York, *Official Sloane Ranger Handbk.* (1982), 27/1.]

Vir(a) [19C. S. *vira,* lit. 'bold, brave'.] The name of the last **Arhat** of the Jains. Also in modern Indian decorations for bravery, e.g. Param Vir, Maha Vir. See **Tirth(a)nkar(a).** [Whitworth, *Anglo-Indian Dict.* (1885).]

Visarga [19C. S. *visārga.* Lit. 'emission'.] A sign in the Sanskrit alphabet representing a hard (voiceless) aspiration; also the sound itself. [*OED;* H.H. Wilson *et al., Dict. Sanscrit & Eng.* (1819), XLII; W.S. Allen, *Phonetics in Anc. India.* (1953), II. 50.]

Vishnu, Vistney, Wistchnu, Vishnou [17C. S. *Vishnu,* prob. fr. *vish,* 'all-pervader, worker'.] The second of the great Hindu Triad (**Trimurti**), but by his worshippers (Vishnuites) identified with the Supreme deity and regarded as the preserver of the world. The husband of *Lakshmi.* Also: Vishnuism – **Vaishnavism** (1871); Vishnuite – Vaishnavite (1883). [*OED;* Sir T. Herbert, *Trav.* (2nd ed. 1638), 42; Sir W. Jones (*c.* 1790), 'Hymn to Nārāyena', *Wks.* (1790), VI. 368.] See **Narayan.**

Viss, vyase [16C. Tam. *visai,* 'division', S. *vihita,* 'distributed'.] A weight used in S. India and Burma about 1.5 kilos (3½ lbs.). [*OED* & YB; Hickock, tr., *Federici's Voy. & Trav.* (1588), 32; Yule, *Mission to Ava* (1858), 256.]

Viyogi [19C. S. fr. *vi,* 'apart' + *yoga,* 'junction'.] One who is separated from society, as opposed to the **Sanyogi.** See **Sansari, Tyagi.** [Whitworth, *Anglo-Indian Dict.* (1885).]

Vizier, wuzeer, wazir [17C. H/Ar. *wazīr,* lit. 'porter'.] Hence one who bears the onus of responsibility. A high state official, governor, viceroy of a province, prime-minister under a Muslim ruler. In India sometimes an honorific title of a great noble, e.g. The Nawab Wazir of Oudh. *See* **Wazir.** [*OED* & YB; Danvers (1612), *Letters* (1896-1900), i. 173.]

Vriddhi [19C. S. *vrddhi*, lit. 'increase'.] Sanskrit grammar: (1) The strongest grade of an ablaut series of vowels. (2) The process of phonetic change in which vowels of the middle grade are strenthened to achieve this grade. Cf. **Guna** [*OED;* H.H. Wilson, *Skr. Gram.* (1841).]

W

Wada,[1] Vada [H. *wada.*] A ball of fried pulse stuffed with potato, etc. [Hawkins, *CIWIE.*]

Wada,[2] wadi [19C. Mar. *wādā,* fr. *wād,* 'a hedge', fr. S. *wāta,* 'enclosed', fr. *wat,* 'to surround'.] An enclosure, the courtyard of a house; a large joint-family house with all its precincts and inhabitants. Also, *wadi,* a country residence of which the garden is the main feature. See **Bagh.[1]** [Whitworth, *Anglo-Indian Dict.* (1885).]

Wada,[3] Wayda [19C. Mar/H. fr. Ar. *wayada.*] A promise, an agreement, engagement, a contract, especially with a fixed term. Also: *wadadar,* a contractor, a government officer responsible for the collections of a **Zamindari**; *wadadari,* making a contract or engagement. [Wilson, *Glossary* (1855).]

Wagh [Mar. *wagh.*] Tiger, leopard. See **Bagh.[2]** Also *waghdewa,* 'tiger-god'. The tiger as a god, worshipped by some wild Indian tribes. [Whitworth, *Anglo-Indian Dict.* (1885).]

Wah! [H. *Wāh!*] Excl. Excellent! Bravo! [Hawkins, *CIWIE.*]

Wahabi(s) [19C. Ar. *Wahhabi.*] Follower(s) of Mohd. ibn Abd al-Wahhab (1691-1787), an Arabian Muslim puritan reformer, who attempted by force to eliminate the beliefs and practices (espec. of the Shias), which had grown up after the 3rd century of Islam. In India, *Wahabism* was introduced by Sayyid Ahmed Brelwi after his return from Mecca in 1823. He instigated a holy war (**Jihad**) against the Sikhs and was killed in 1831. The Indian Wahabis have made Patna their main centre. The term *Wahabi,* in India, became an abusive expression equivalent to 'infidel' (**Kafir**). [*OED;* Waring, *Tour to Shiraz* (1807), 119; Wilson, *Glossary* (1855); Whitworth, *Anglo-Indian Dict.* (1885).]

Wakf, waqf [19C. H/Ar. *waqf.*] A bequest or endowment for religious or charitable purposes among Muslims; also the property given in this way. And *wakf-nama,* 'a written deed of endowment. [*OED;* Lane, *Acct. Manners & Customs of Mod. Egyptians* (1836), I. 159; Whitworth, *Anglo-Indian Dict.* (1885).]

Wakil See **Vakeel.**

Waler [16C.] A horse imported into India from Australia, espec. from New South Wales. [*OED; New South Wales* (1849), vii. 65; Trevelyan, *Dawk Bungalow* (1866), 223;

Kipling, *Plain Tales; Rout of White Hussars* (3rd ed., 1888), 215.]

Walla(h) [18C. H. *wāla.*] A suffixed morpheme expressing relation, denoting a person who does any act, performs any function, or is charged with any duty or belongs to any trade or profession, place, etc. Europeans commonly used it as a noun equivalent to 'man', 'agent', 'chap', 'fellow', etc. Used by Anglo-Indians in such hybrids of English-Hindustani or Hindustani-Hindustani as *Competition wallah* (1856), an East India Company official selected by examination; *box wallah* (1834), an itinerant pedlar, (and by extension, a European commercial traveller or businessman); *punkah-wallah* (1864), a menial who kept the old cloth *punkah* going; *lootie wallah* (1782), a member of a gang of thieves; *howdahwallah* (1863), an elephant used for passengers; *amen-wallah* (19th-20th C.), an army chaplain, and by extension any reverend gentleman; *base-wallah* (1915), a soldier employed behind the lines, not in the front line; *jungle-wallah* (1826), a man of the jungle, uncivilized; *Empire-Day wallahs,* flag-wagging jingoists.[Edmund Candler, *Siri Ram Revolutionist* (1912).] *oont-wallah-sahib,* 'a camel-keeping gentleman'. [*Deccan Herald,* 6 March 1984]. *poultice-wallah* (1870), a doctor's assistant, a para-medical; *loose-wallah* (1850), a rascal, thief; *lemonade-wallah* (1890), a teetotaller; *janker-wallah* (1920), a soldier under punishment; *jake-wallah* (1900), a 'meths' addict; *bilti-wallah sahib* (1907), one who acts quickly; *ground-wallah* (1915), an R.A.F. non-flying man; *goo-wallah* (1900), a man of the sanitary squad; *gen-wallah* (1936), an information officer; *jerrypurana-wallah* (19C.-20C.), a dealer in old newspapers and bottles = *Kabaddi-Wallah, Daddi-Wallah;* *barrow-wallah, burra wallah* (1914), the Big Man, the chief, No.1; *char-wallah,* one who supplies the tea or a teetotaller (1933); *crab-wallah* (1900), an evil person (fr. H. *kharab,* 'bad'); *admi-khane-wallah* (1875), a man-eating-tiger. *Agra-wallah* (1776), a resident of Agra; *bhangy-wallah* (1810), a **Sweeper, Pariah, Untouchable.** *Sani-wallah* (1875), a riding-camel-keeper. *Pant-Wallah* = **Beastie;** *Topi-wallah, Ready-made- Clothes-Wallah* (1894), an itinerant pedlar of ready-made clothes; *Daddi-wallah* (H. *dari*, cotton stuff, carpet), old clothes & junk man. *See* **Jerry Purana-wallah; Kabaddi-wallah.** *Gao-wallah* (1855), a cowherd; *Ghar-wallah* (1855), a master of the house; *Putty-wallah* (1850), an office messenger who wears a belt (H. *patti*). And three related special compounds, each one representing a particular form of **Dharna:** (1) *Tasmiwallah*, one who twists a strap around his neck and throws himself on the ground, 'a strap-rigger'. (2) *Doriwallah*, who threatens to hang himself, unless he gets satisfaction; (3) *Dandi-wallah*, who rattles sticks and stands cursing until he gets what he wants. [*OED* & YB; *Indian Antiquary* (1872), i. 162.]

Wallandez = **Feringhee.** Hollander. [Whitworth, *Anglo-Indian Dict.* (1885).]

Wallum [M. *wollam*.] A wide-beamed boat used in the backwaters of Kerala. [Hawkins, *CIWIE*.]

Wanderoo [17C. Sinh. *wanderu, vandura*; H. *bandar*; S. *vanara*, 'monkey' fr. *vanar*, 'forest'. Perh. orig. 'forest dweller'. (Cf. Malay *orang hutan*, 'orang outang', lit. 'forest-being'.)] The Sri Lankan grey langur, *Presbytis entellus thersites*, but sometimes misapplied to the lion-tailed macaque of Malabar (Kerala), *Macacus silenus* (after Buffon). [*OED* & YB; Knox, *Hist. Rel. Ceylon & E. Ind.* (1681), I. vi. 26; Hornaday, *Two Years in Jungle* (1885), xxiii. 274.]

Watan, wutun, wuttun [19C. H/Ar. *watan*, 'country, native country'.] Among the Marathas it came to mean a hereditary estate, office, privilege, property, or means of subsistence, a patrimony. Also: *watandar*, the holder of a hereditary right, and *watanwari*, 'a patrimonial estate'. [Wilson, *Glossary* (1855).]

Water-chestnut [19C.] The *Trapa bispinosa*, the *Saligot. See* **Singhara** (H. *singhārā*). [*OED* & YB; Adams etc., *Man. Nat. Hist.* (1854), 402.]

Water-hyacinth [19C.] Fast-spreading water-plant with pale blue flowers, *Eichornia crassipes*, extensively established and proliferating in many parts of India. [*OED*; Webber in *Bull. U.S. Dept. Agric.* (1897), XVIII. 13; Thompson, *Indian Day* (1927), xiv. 111.]

Wazir(i) [19C.] (Member of) a Pathan tribe of N.W. Pakistan. Also *Vaziri, Vizeeri, Wuzeera.* [*OED*; Elphinstone, *Caubul* (1815), III. iii. 385.]

Weather, cold In India, November-March. [Hawkins, *CIWIE*.]

Weather, hot [19C.] In India, the months before and after the monsoon rains.

Weaver-bird *See* **Baya** *(Ploceus philippinus).*

Wewa, veva [S. *vevā*.] Reservoir. [Hawkins, *CIWIE*.]

Whistling Teal [19C.] (1) Lesser Whistling Teal, *Dendrocygna javanica* (1821, Salim Ali.) H.*silhi.* (2) Large Whistling Teal, *Dendrocygna bicolor* (1816, Salim Ali). Beng. *Bada sharal.* [YB; Jerdon, *Birds of India* (1862).]

White-ant(s) [17C.] A very destructive social insect of the *Neuropterus* order, which proliferates throughout India doing immense damage; also called *termite* and *emmet.* Cf. Pg. *formigas biancas.* [Bluteau's *Dict.,* 1713.] [*OED* & YB; Locke, *Jrnl.* (17 Nov. 1684); Hamilton, *New Acct. E. Indies* (1729), II. xlvii.,

White jacket [19C.] 'The old custom in the hot weather, in the family or at bachelor parties, was to wear this at dinner. It became a regular item in an Anglo-Indian outfit.' [YB; Ld. Valentia, *Voyages & Travels* (1802-6; ed.

Widow [S. *vidh*, 'to lack, to be destitute', and S. *vidhavā*, 'widow'. H. *avira. obeera.*] *See* **Grass Widow**, first used in India in the 19th century. [Wilson, *Glossary* (1855).]

Wilayati(i) *See* **Vilayat** and **Blighty.**

Winter [16C.] The rainy season on the West coast of India. [YB; Barker (1592), in *Hakluyt* (ed. 1807), ii. 589-90; Finch (1610) in *Purchas* (1625-6), i. 423.] *See* **Monsoon, Rains**.

Woffadar [19C.] 'Faithful fellow.' [Barter, *The Seige of Delhi* (1869; ed. 1984, Folio Society).]

Wood-apple [19C.] The fruit of the *Feronia elephantum*, an E. Indian gum-yielding tree allied to the orange; or the tree itself; also called *Elephant-apple.* [*OED* & YB; Simmonds, *Dict. Trade* (1858); Yule in *Geog. Mag.* (1875), 49-50.]

Wood-oil [18C. = *Gurjun-balsam* or-*oil* (Beng/H. *garjan.*).] A name for several oils or oily substances from various trees: (a) *Dipterocarpus alatus.* (b) The E. Indian satinwood, *Chloroxylon swietenia*, (c) *Aleurites cordata* = *Tung-oil.* [*OED* & YB; 1759 in Dalrymple *Oriental Repertory* (1793), I. 109.]

Woolock, oolock [17C. Beng/Turk. *ula.*] A kind of boat once used in Bengal, 'round, smooth-sided, (with the planks) laid edge to edge and fastened with iron clamps, having the appearance of being stitched'. [YB.] *See* **Pattello.** [YB; Hedges (1683), *Diary* (Hak. Soc. ed. 1807), i. 76; Symes, *Embassy Kingd. Ava* (1795; ed. 1800), 233.]

Woordy-major, Wordie-major [18C.] Perh a corr. of Kan. *varadi*, 'news, an order, message, information'.] A native adjutant in the regiments of Indian Irregular Cavalry. [YB; Forest, *Bombay Letters* (1784), ii. 323; Cave-Browne, *Punjab & Delhi* (1861), i. 120.]

Wootz, Woots, Wutz [18C. Poss. a misprint for *wook*, representing Kan. *ukku*, 'steel' (pron. with initial 'w'.] A crucible steel made in S. India by fusing magnetic iron ore with carbonaceous matter. [*OED* & YB; *Phil. Trans.* (1795), LXXV. 322; Baldwin (1869), *Preh. Nations* (1877), vi. 229.]

Writer [17C.] (1) A clerk in the service of the East India Company; the junior grade of covenanted civil servants. (2) A copying clerk in an officer, native or European (1764). *See* **Cranny.** [*OED* & YB.] Hence *writership* (1763). [Wheeler (1678), *Madras* (1861), 64; Kipling, *Life's Handicap* (1891), 345.]

Wug [19C. Sind. *wag* or *wagu*, 'a herd of camels'.] Mistakenly taken by Europeans to mean **Loot**, perh. because camels were the commonest form of plunder among *Baluchis* and *Sindhis*. [YB; Letter of Sir C. Napier, in *Life* (1851), iii. 298.]

X

Xerafine, Xeraphin, Xerafin, Seraphin [16C. Pg. *xerafin*, 'a silver coin'.] Formerly current in India, where it was worth about a rupee. (Cf. Ar. *sharife*, orig. the name of a gold coin.) *See* **Ashrafi**. [*OED* & YB; Lichefield's *Castañeda* (1528), 56; A. Hamilton, *New Acct. E. Indies* (1727), i. 249.]

Y

Yaboo, yabu, yabou [18C. H/P. *yābū.*] One of a breed of large ponies or small horses in Afghanistan, Iran and adjacent countries. *See* **Tazee.** [*OED* & YB; Hanway (1753), *Travels* (1762), II. xiv. vii. 367; 1880 in Ld. Roberts, *41 Years in India* (1897), lxi. II. 353.]

Yab-yum [Tib.] In **Tantric** Buddhism, ritual sexual union. [Hawkins, *CIWIE.*]

Yagna [S. *yagna.*] Hinduism: Religious self-mortification, e.g. *snake-yagna,* sitting in a cage with poisonous sakes.

Yagya, Yaga [19C. S. *yāg(ya).*] A sacrifice, an offering, an oblation. [Wilson, *Glossary* (1855).]

Yajana [19C. S. *yajana.*] Sacrificing, offering sacrifices, the duty of the first three castes. [Wilson, *Glossary* (1855).]

Yajna [19C. S. *yajna.*] A sacrifice, performance of a sacrifice, offering libations of **Soma,** or oblations of butter. [Wilson, *Glossary* (1855).]

Yak [18C. Tib. *yak.*] The Tibetan ox, *Bos grunniens,* found wild and domesticated in Tibet, where it is the ordinary beast of burden. Its hair is woven into tents and spun into ropes; its milk a staple of diet, and its dung used as fuel and the tails for decoration, and as fly flappers. *See* **Chowry.** *Yakdan* = a yak's burden; *Yak-corps; Yak-hair; Yak-tail; Yak-lace* = a heavy kind of lace made from its hair. [*OED* & YB; *Asiatick Res.* (1795), iv. 351; Turner (1700), *Embassy Tibet* (1800), 186; Candler, *Unveiling of Lhasa* (1905), xiv. 268.] *See* **Zho.**

Yakdan [19C. P. *yakdān,* 'ice-container'.] Portmanteau, trunk. [Morier, *Adv. Hajji Baba* (1824), II. vii. 112; Masters, *Bhowani Junction* (1954), xxxvii. 320; Kaye, *Far Pavilions* (1972), I. 13.]

Yaksha [18C. S. *yaksha.*] A supernatural being, demigod or spirit; tutelary guardian of a place. A statue or carving of one of these. [*OED;* Wilkins, tr., *Bhagvat Geeta* (1788), xi. 92; Barth, *Religions of India* (1882), v. 164.]

Yama [19C. S. yama, lit. 'a rein or curb'.] Hinduism: The God who presides over the spirits of the dead. In the **Rigveda** he is the first man that died and acts as the guide to the home of later departed spirits. In post-vedic times he was the judge of the dead, sending each soul after trial to Heaven *(swarga)* or Hell *(naraka).* Also: *Yamdut (yama duta,* 'a messenger'.) A messenger of death, and more prosaically a nickname for a policeman, as *yamduts* are supposed to seize and maltreat sinners at the time of death. [Southey, *The Curse of Kehama* (1809); Wilson, *Glossary* (1855).]

Yantra, jantra [19C. H./S. *yantra.*] A machine, an instrument, an engine; a mystical diagram used as an aid to meditation in **Tantric** worship. [*OED;* Wilson, *Glossary* (1855); M.-Williams, *Hinduism* (1877), ix. 129.]

yar [19C. H./Ar. *yar.*] A friend, chum, mate. A term of familiarity. [Wilson, *Glossary* (1855).]

Yatra, jatra [19C. S. *yatra,* fr. *ya,* 'to travel'.] Going about, travelling, espec. to holy places; pilgrimage and pilgrims. In Bengal a dramatic representation. Also, *yatri, jatri,* a pilgrim. [Wilson, *Glossary* (1855).]

Yavana, yavan, jaban [19C. S. *yavana,* 'foreigner'.] Applied orig. to the Greeks (Ionians) but in later times to Arabs and Europeans. In Tamil, *yavanar* (plural) = artificers and low-class Muslims. [Wilson, *Glossary* (1855).]

Yercum [19C. Tam. *yerkum.*] An East-Indian shrub, *Calotropis gigantica,* or the fibre obtained from its bark; also the species, *C. procera,* both used medicinally. *See* **Mudder (Mudar).** [*OED;* Ainslie, *Mat. Ind.* (1826), I. 486; Lindley, *Flora Med.* (1838).]

Yeti [20C. Tib. *yeh-teh.*] A Sherpa (Tibetan) name for the Abominable snowman, a hypothetical sub-human animal, supposed to leave giant tracks in the snow in the higher Himalayas. [*OED; Times,* 13 Nov. 1937, 13/5; Hillary, *Nothing Venture Nothing Win* (1975), xv. 238.]

Yoga [19C. H./S. *yoga.* lit. 'union'. (Cf. E. *yoke;* Lat. *jugum.*).] Hinduism: Union with the Supreme Spirit; a system of ascetic practice, meditation, mental concentration, by means of which superhuman faculties are claimed to be acquired; one of the six *darsans* or systems of orthodox Hindu philosophy. Also *Bhakti-yoga,* devotion to Krishna; *Hatha-yoga,* physical exercises, **asanas;** *Karma-yoga,* salvation through action; *Kundalini-yoga,* Tantric discipline. Now a widespread cult outside India. [*OED;* W. Ward, *View Hindoos* (3rd ed. 1820), iv. 125; Orwell, *Road to Wigan Pier* (1937), xiii. 254.] *See* **Raja Yoga, Suryanamaskar.**

Yogacara [19C. S. *yogācāra,* fr. *yoga* + *ā-cāra,* 'conduct, practice'.] (a) A school of **Mahāyāna** Buddhism, which teaches that only consciousness is real. [Monier-Williams, *Buddhism* (1889), x. 225; Conze, *Buddhism* (1951), vii. 165.] (b) An adherent of this school, which disappeared from India about AD 1100. [R.W. Frazer, *Indian Thought* (1915), ix. 181.]

Yogi, jogee, jogi, etc. [17C. H. *yogī*, fr. S. *yogīn*, fr. *yoga*.] (1) A devotee of *yoga* philosophy, but applied also to any ascetic or religious mendicant, and sometimes, ironically, to a 'conjuror' or 'magician'. Also: *yogini*, a female *yogī*; one of a class of malicious female demons, espec. an attendant on **Durga** or **Siva**. [*OED* & YB; Purchas, *Microcosmus* (1619), lvii. 543.] (2) = **Yoga**. [*OED*; 1925 in A. Huxley, *Let.* (25 Feb. 1969), 242.] *See* **Samadhi**.

Yogi-bogeybox [20C. nonce-word. fr. **Yogi** + bog(e)y + box.] The paraphernalia of a spiritualist. [*OED*; Joyce, *Ulysses* (1922), 180; *Spectator*, 15 Jan. 1965, 73/1.]

Yogic [20C.] Of or pertaining to **Yoga**. [*OED*; Streeter and Appasamy, *Sadhu* (1921), v. 136; A. Huxley (1946), *Let.* (26 Oct. 1969), 551.]

Yojan(a) [18C. H. *yojan*, fr. S. *yojana*, 'yoking'.] The distance travelled at any time, varying from one locality to another in India from about 4 to 10 miles (lit. distance travelled without unyoking). [*OED* & YB; W. Chambers (1784) in *Asiat. Res.* (1788), I. 155; E. Arnold,

Ind. Idylls (1883), 171.]

Yoni [S. *yonī*.] Hinduism: A figure or symbol of the female organ of generation as an object of veneration among Hindus and others. Hence *yonic*. [*OED*.] *See* **Linga(m)**. [*Asiat. Res.* (1799), III. 363; Whatham in *Amer. Jrnl. Relig & Psychol.* (1906), II. 44.]

Yuga(a), yoog, yoogu [18C. H. *yug*, fr. S. *yuga*, 'yoke'.] In Hindu cosmology, any of the four ages in the duration of the world, (or the aggregate of these) which are, (1) the *Krita*, or *Satya-yuga* (1,728,000) years; (2) The *Dwarpura-yuga* (1,296,000 years); (3) the *Treta-yuga* (864,000 years); (4) the *Kali-yuga* (432,000 years); making a *Maha-yuga* of 4,320,000 years. The world in 1985 was in the year of the *Kali* age. [*OED*; W. Hastings (1784) in *Asiat. Res.* (1788), I. 237; W. Ward, *View Hindoos* (3rd ed. 1820), iv. 315.] *See* **Sandhya**.

Yunani *See* **Unani**.

Yusufzai [19C. P. *yūsuf*, Joseph + *zāī*, 'bringing forth'.] (1) (A member of) a Pathan tribe in the NWFP of India. (2) Of or pertaining to this tribe. [Elphinstone, *Caubul* (1815), III. i. 38; M.M. Kaye, *Far Pavilions* (1978), xi. 170.]

Yuvaraja, jubaraj [19C. H. fr. S. yuva 'young' & *rājā*.] The male heir to an Indian rajah or maharaja; the crown prince. *See* **Upper Roger**. [Lethbridge, *Golden Bk. India* (1893), xv; E.M. Forster, *Hill of Devi* (1953), 161.]

Z

Zabardasti [19C. H./P.*Zabardasti*.] Violence, force, oppression, tyranny. [Wilson, *Glossary* (1855).]

Zabita, Zabeta, Jabita, Jabata [18C. H./Ar. *zābitā*.] A rule, canon, statute, law; established practice, usage; a list, a roll in Telugu. [YB; Wellington (1799), *Despatches*. (ed. 1837), i. 49; Wilson, *Glossary* (1855).]

Zakat, jakat [19C. H./Ar. 'purification'.] Alms, contributions of a portion of property (obligatory on every Muslim possessed of capital), for the poor and needy. Properly a tenth but it may be increased according to the piety of the individual. [Wilson, *Glossary* (1855).]

Zamindar *See* **Zemindar**.

Zamorin, Samorin, etc. [16C. Pg., *samorin, sāmurī* (of disputed origin.)] 'The title for many centuries of the Hindu sovereign of Calicut and the country round.' [OED & YB; Lichefield, *Castañeda*, (1582), I. xiv; R. Johnson (1601), *Kingd. and Commonw.* (1603), 204, *Pioneer Mail*, 13 April 1900.]

Zarathustrian [19C. Fr. *Zarathustra*.] The old Iranian form of the founder of the ancient Persian religion. *See* **Zoroastrian** and **Parsi**. [OED; Tylor, *Prim. Cult.* (1871), I. ii. 49.]

Zar(i) [19C. H./P. *zar*, 'gold' + *i* = gold-stuff or gold-brocade.] Also *zar-baft*, 'cloth of gold'; *zar-doz* (sewing), 'an embroidery'; '*zar-gar*', 'a goldsmith'. *See* **Zerbaft**. [Wilson, *Glossary*, (1855).]

Zebu [18C. A.I./Fr *zébu*. (Buffon states this name was used at a fair in Paris in 1752.)] The humped species of ox, *Bos indicus* (the **Brahminy Bull**) domesticated in India and elsewhere from ancient times. (Cf. Zobo?) [OED & YB; Goldsmith (1744), *Nat. Hist.* (1776), III. 23; W. C. Martin, *Ox* (1847), 19/1.]

Zedoary, zeduarye, etc. [16C. Ar. *zedwār*.] The aromatic tuberous root of some species of *Curcuma* of India and neighbouring countries used as a drug, having properties similar to those of ginger. *See* **Zerumbet** and **Cassumunar** (yellow zedoary). [OED & YB; *Treas. Health* (c. 1550), I. vi; Royle, *Antiquity of Hindoo Medicine* (1837), 77.]

Zemindar, zamindar, jem(m)adar [17C. H./P. *zamīn*, 'land', + *dār*, 'agent, holder'.] (1) Orig. under Muslim rule in India, a *Zemīn- dār* was ordinarily a landholder responsible for collecting land revenues on behalf of the rulers, generally on a non-hereditary basis, from land held by a number of cultivators, while retaining a percentage (usu. 10%) for himself. (2) Gradually many *zemīndārs* became hereditary landowners and under British rule they paid the land revenues direct to the British government. Now any land-owner. [OED & YB; Hedges (1683), *Diary* (Hakl. Soc., ed. 1886), I. 77; Sir H. Maine,*Village Communities* (3rd ed. 1876) 163.] *See* **Taluk, Zillah**.

Zemindary, Zamindary, jamindary, etc. [18C (*See* Prec.)] The system of holding lands and farming revenues by means of **Zemindars**; the office or jurisdiction of a *zemindar*; the territory administered by a *zemindar*. Also *zemindarship* (1698). [OED; Scrafton (1757), *Indostan* (1770), 81; *Ann. Reg., St. Papers* (1764), 191/2.] *See* **Wada³**.

Zen [18C. Jap. *zen chin chan*, 'quietude', fr. S. *dhyāna*, 'meditation.'] A sect of **Mahayana** Buddhism, emphasizing meditation and self-awareness, introduced into Japan from China in the 13th century. [Scheuchzer, tr., *Kaempher's Hist. Jap.* (1727), I. ii. v. 199; *Spectator*, 15 July 1960, 101.] Also attrib. and comb., esp in *Zen-Buddhism*; *-Buddhist* (1881). And *Zendo*, 'a Zen meditation hall'. (1959). [OED; *Trans. Asiatic Soc. Japan* (1881), IX. 179.]

Zenana, zananah, jenana, etc. [18C H./P. *zenāna, zanāna*, fr. *zan*, 'woman'. (Rel. to Gr. *gunē*.)] (1) In India and Iran, the secluded women's quarters of a household; a **harem**; also used for the secluded women themselves. [OED & YB; Long (1760), *Sel. Records Ft. William* (1748-1767), 236; *Trial of Maharajah Nundacomar* (1776), 66/2.] (2) *Zenana-cloth*. A light, thin material used for womens' dresses (1900). [OED; *Westminster Gaz.*, 6 Dec. 1900, 2/2.] (3) The *Zenana* Missions, which carried out Christian missionary educational work for and among Indian women. [OED & YB.] *See* **Purdah**.

Zend, zand [17C. P. *zand(a)*, 'interpretation, commentary'.] This word has come to be the name of the language of the sacred writings of the **Parsis** = **Zend Avesta**. Also called *Old Bactrian*, a member of the Indo-European family of languages. (Anqetil du Perron used *Zend* (1771), abstracted from *Avesta-va-*

Zend, as the name of the language. *See* next.)
[*OED* & YB; Lord, *The Religion of the Parsees, the Proeme* (1630).]

Zend Avesta [17C. P. *Zand(a)wasta*, and *Avesta-va-Zend*, 'Avesta with interpretation'.] The sacred writings of the *Parsis*, usually attributed to *Zoroaster*. *See* **Zoroastrian** and **Zarathustrian.** [*OED* & YB; Lord, *The Religion of the Parsees, the Proeme* (1630); Sir. T. Herbert, *Travels* (1677), 54.]

Zerbaft, Sherbaff [17C. H/P. *zar*, 'gold' + *baft*, 'woven'.] Gold brocade. *See* **Bafta** and **Zari.** (For alternative etymology *see* **Sherbaff.**) [*OED* & YB; Lovell, tr., *Thevenot's Travels* (1687), II. 92; Yusuf Ali, *Mon. on Silk Fabrics* (1900), 86.]

Zerumbet [16C. H/P. *zerunbād*.] An E. Indian plant of the genus *Curcuma*, and its aromatic root used, like the allied **Cassumunar** and **Zedoary,** as a tonic drug. [*OED* & YB; Eden, *Decades* (1555), 296; J. Davies, tr., *Mandelso's Travels* (1662), II. 151.]

Zho, Zo, dzo, zobo, dsomo, etc. [19C. A.I./Tib. *mdso*.] A hybrid bred from a male **Yak** and the domestic cow in N. India. (-*bo* = masc. suffix, and -*mo* = fem. suffix. *zhomo* = a female *zho*.) Cf. **Zebu.** [*OED* & YB; Moorcroft, *Travels* (1841), I. 272; Sir J. Hooker, *Himalayan Journals* (1805), I. 203.]

Ziarat [18C. H./Ar. *ziyārat*.] Pilgrimage; going on pilgrimage to a Muslim shrine; in India, also, visiting the grave of a deceased person on the third day after the burial, when the Koran is read and prayers are recited, and offerings made to expiate the sins of the deceased. [*OED*; Halhed, tr., *Code Gentoo Laws* (1776), xiii. 187; M. Diver, *Desmond's Daughter* (1916), II. IX. 121.] *See* **Haj**.

Zid [20C. H. *zid*.] Strong dislike (against someone or something.) Also *ziddi*, 'obstinate'. [Hawkins, *CIWIE*.]

Zillah [18C. H/Ar. *zila*, lit. 'a rib, a side', thence, a district, division.] An administrative district in India; a *collectorate*. Also: *ziladar*, *zillahdar*, the **Collector** of a *zillah*; *zilladari*, the office or jurisdiction of a *ziladar*; *zillah*

parishad, *see* **Parishad.** [Warren Hastings in Hunter, *Annals of Bengal* (4th ed., 1772), 388; Stocqueler (1845), *Handbk. Brit. India* (1854), 340.] *See* **Pergunnah, Tahsil**.

Zindabad [20C.] P. *zinda(gi)*, 'life' + *bad.*, 'Long live …)! as in *'Nehru zindabad'*, or *'Inquilab zindabad'*, 'long live [the] revolution'. Opp. of **murdabad**, 'death to …!' [Wilson, *Glossary* (1855); Subba Rao, *Indian Words in English* (1954).]

Zirbad [P. *zīr-bad*, 'below the wind'.] Leeward; applied by seamen to countries east of India. Prob. adopted from the Malay 'di-bawa angin'. [YB.]

Zoolum, zulum, zulm [19C. H./Ar. *zūlm.*] Tyranny, extortion, oppression, a heavier assessment than people can bear. Also, *zalim*, an oppressor, an extortioner. [Wilson, *Glossary* (1855); Whitworth, *Anglo-Indian Dict.* (1885).]

Zopadputti, zopti [20C. Mar. *zodapatti*.] A hutment, colony, slum. [Hawkins, *CIWIE*.]

Zoroastrian [18C. Zend. *Zarathustra;* P. *Zardusht.*] The name given to (an adherent of) the religion of the **Parsis,** called after the founder Zoroaster (Zarathustra) who is said to have lived in the 6th century BC. The Parsis brought this monotheistic religion with them to India in the 7th century AD. There are three orders of priests, namely *dastar*, *mobed* and *andhyaru*. *See* **Zend** (Avesta). [*OED*; Warburton, *Pope's Essay on Man* (1743), II; T. Maurice (1795), *Hindostan* (1820), II. iv. iii. 249; Byron, 'Let. to F. Hodge', 3 Sept. 1811.]

Zumbooruk, Zamburka [18C. H. *zambūrak*, fr. P. *zambūr*, 'hornet'. Cf. P. *zemberek*, 'crossbow'.] A small swivel-gun, espec. one carried on the back of a camel; resembling a *Jinjal* but shorter and of larger calibre; a falconet. Hence *zumboorukchi*, a gunner. [*OED* & YB; tr., *Seir Mutaqherin* (1789), iii. 250; J.B. Fraser, *Journ. Khorasan* (1825), 198; R.F. Burton, *Abeokuta* (1863), I. 75.]

Zyadah [19C. H./P. *zyādah.*] 'Too much, more than enough.' [Maud Diver (1856), *Honoria Lawrence* (1936), 461.]

SUGGESTED REFERENCE AND READING

Unless otherwise stated, the place of publication is London

Dictionaries and Glossaries

The Oxford English Dictionary and Supplements, Oxford, 1928, 1972, 1976, 1982, 1986.

Webster's Third New International Dictionary of the English Language. New York, 1971.

Bliss, A.J., *A Dictionary of Foreign Words and Phrases in Current English*, 1966.

Fenell, C.A.M., *Stanford Dictionary of Anglicised Words and Phrases in Current English*, 1954.

Fryer, John, *A New Account of East India and Persia*, 1698.

Hasan Ali, Mrs Meer, *Observations on the Mussulmans of India*, 1852; reprint OUP, Karachi, 1978.

Hawkins, R.E., *Common Indian Words in English*, OUP, New Delhi, 1984.

Heber, Bishop Reginald, *Narrative of a Journey Through the Upper Provinces of India*, 1884.

Onions, C.T., ed., *The Oxford Dictionary of Etymology*, Oxford, 1966.

Parkes, Fanny, *Wanderings of a Pilgrim in Search of the Picturesque*, 1950; reprint, OUP, Karachi, 1975.

Partridge, E., *A Dictionary of Forces Slang*, 1848.

Partridge, E. *A Dictionary of Slang and Unconventional Language*, 1961.

Rao, G. Subba. *Indian Words in English*, Oxford, 1954.

Roebuck, T., *An English-Hindoostani Naval Dictionary*.

Scott, C.P.G. 'The Malayan Words in English', *Journal of the American Oriental Society*, New Haven, 1897.

Skeat, W.W., *An Etymological Dictionary of the English Language*, Oxford, 1882.

Sleeman, Sir William, *Ramasseeana, and the Vocabulary of the Peculiar Language of the Thugs*, Calcutta, 1836.

Small, Rev. G.A., *A Laskari Dictionary*, 1882.

Stephen, Leslie and Sidney Lee, eds., *A Dictionary of National Biography*, 1908.

Watt, Sir G., *A Dictionary of the Economic Products of India*, Calcutta, 1889-93.

Whitworth, G.C., *An Anglo-Indian Dictionary*, 1885.

Wilkins, Sir Charles, *Glossary Prepared for the Fifth Report of the Select Committee of the House of Commons on the Affairs of the East India Company*, 1813.

Wilson, H.H., *Glossary of Judicial and Revenue Terms*, 1855.

Yule, H. and A.C. Burnell, *Hobson-Jobson : A Glossary of Anglo-Indian Words and Phrases*, 1886.

Literature, Memoirs, Diaries, Letters, etc.

Aberigh Mackay, G., *Twenty One Days in India, Being the Tour of Sir Ali Baba, K.C.B.*, 1880.

Aitken, E.H., *Behind the Bungalow*, Calcutta, 1889.

Allen, Charles, *Plain Tales from the Raj*, 1975.

'Aliph Cheem' (W. Yeldham), *Lays of Ind.*, Calcutta, 1889.

Anon., *Hartley House*, Calcutta, 1789.

Arnold, Edwin, *The Book of Good Counsels*, 1861.

255

—— *The Indian Song of Songs*, 1875.

—— *The Light of Asia*, 1879.

—— *Mahabharata : Indian Lyrics*, 1883.

—— *The Light of the World*, 1891.

Arnold, W.D. ('Punjabi'), *Oakfield, or Fellowship in the East*, 1853.

Atkinson, G.F., *Curry and Rice, or the Ingredients of Social Life at 'Our Station' in India*, 1859.

Bhupal Singh, *A Survey of Anglo-Indian Fiction*, Oxford, 1934.

Butler, Iris, *The Viceroy's Wife : Letters of Alice, Countess of Reading, 1921-5*; Boston, 1969.

Byron, Lord George Gordon, *The Bride of Abydos*, Boston, 1814.

—— *The Giaour*, Boston, 1813.

—— *The Corsair*, New York, 1814.

—— *Don Juan*, 1818-24.

Candler, E., *Sri Ram Revolutionist*, 1912.

—— *Abdication*, 1912.

—— *Youth and the East*, 1924.

Chaucer, G., *The House of Fame*, c. 1384.

—— *Troilus and Criseyde*, c. 1374.

Colebrooke, Sir T.E., *Life of the Hon. Mountstuart Elphinstone*, 1884.

Coleridge, Revd. H.I. (SJ), *Life and Letters of St. Francis Xavier*, 1872.

Cowasjee, Saros, *Stories from the Raj*, 1983.

Crawford, F. Marion, *Mr Isaacs : A Tale of Modern India*, 1882.

Croker, Mrs B.M., *The Company Servant : A Romance of Southern India*, 1907.

Cunningham, H.S., *Chronicles of Dustypore*, 1875.

Dalhousie, Marquess of, *Private Letters*, ed. J.G.A. Baird, 1910.

Derozio, H.L.V., *The Fakir of Jungheera and Other Poems*, 1871.

Diver, Maud, *Capt. Desmond, V.C.*, 1907.

—— *Lilamani*, 1910.

—— *The Englishwoman in India*, 1909.

—— *The Great Amulet*, 1908.

—— *Desmond's Daughter*, 1907.

—— *The Hero of Herat*, 1909.

—— *The Judgement of the Sword*, 1913.

—— *Honoria Lawrence*, 1936.

Dryden, John, *The Indian Emperour*, 1663.

—— *The Indian Queen*, 1664.

—— *Aurengzebe*, 1675.

Dyson, K.K., *A Various Universe*, OUP, New Delhi, 1978.

Eden, Hon. Emily, *Up the Country*, 1866.

—— *Letters from India*, 1872.

Eliot, T.S., *A Choice of Kipling's Verse*, 1941.

Emerson, R.W., 'Brahma', 1857, in *May Day and Other Poems*, Boston, 1867.

Falkland, Viscountess (Amelia Cary), *Chow Chow, Being Selections from a Journal Kept in India*, 1857.

Faye, Eliza, *Original Letters from Calcutta*, 1779-1815; edn. 1817 (with introduction and notes by E.M. Forster, 1925).

Fenton, Mrs E.S., *The Journal of Mrs. Fenton*, 1826-30; ed. Sir Henry Lawrence, 1901.

Forbes, J., *Oriental Memoirs*, 1813.

SUGGESTED REFERENCE AND READING

Forster, E.M., 'Reflections on India', *The Nation/Athenaeum, xxx*, 21 Jan. 1922.

—— *Passage to India*, 1924.

—— 'Indian Entries', *Encounter 18* (May–June 1962).

—— *The Hill of Devi*, 1967.

Frazer, R.W., *A Literary History of India*, 1898.

Graham, Maria (afterwards Lady Calcott), *Journal of a Residence in India*, Edinburgh, 1812.

—— *Letters on India*, 1814.

Greenberger, A.J., *The British Image of India: A Study in the Literature of Imperialism*, 1880-1960; edn. 1960.

Greig, Miss Hilda ('Sydney C. Grier'), *In Furthest Ind: the Narrative of Edward Carlyon of the Honourable East India Company's Service*, 1894.

Grierson, H.J., 'Edmund Burke', *Cambridge History of English Literature*, vol. 1, 1922.

Guthrie, T.A., ('F. Anstey'), *Baboo Hurry Bungsho Jabberjee, B.A.*, 1897.

—— *A Bayard from Bengal*, 1902.

—— *Hajji Baba of Ispahan*, 1824.

—— *Hajji Baba in England*, 1828.

Henty, G.A., *With Clive in India*, 1884.

—— *Through the Sikh War*, 1884.

Hickey, W., *Memoirs*, 1749-1809; ed. Alfred Spencer, 1913-25.

Hockley, W.B., *Pandurang Hari, or Memoirs of a Hindoo*, published pseudonomously, 1826.

—— *Tales of the Zenana, or a Nawab's Leisure Hours*, 1827.

Howe, Suzanne, *Novels of Empire*, New York, 1949.

Hunter, Sir William, *The Old Missionary*, 1895.

—— *The Thackerays in India*, 1895.

—— *India of the Queen and other Essays*, 1903.

Husain, Sajjad, *Kipling and India*, 1965.

Iyengar, Srinivasa, *Indian Writing in English*, 1962.

Jones, Sir William, *Letters*, ed. G. Cannon, 1970.

—— *Collected Works*, ed. Baron Teignmouth, 1807.

—— *Dissertation on the Orthography of Asiatick Words in Roman Letters*, Asiatick Researches, vol. 1, Calcutta, 1784, pp. ix-xvi.

Kincaid, D., *Cactus Land*, 1933.

—— *Durbar*, 1933.

Kipling, John Lockwood, *Beast and Man in India*, 1891.

Kipling, Rudyard, *Departmental Ditties*, Lahore, 1886.

—— *Plain Tales from the Hills*, Calcutta, 1888.

—— *Soldiers Three*, Allahabad, 1888.

—— *The Story of the Gadsbys*, Allahabad, 1888.

—— *In Black and White*, Allahabad, 1888.

—— *Under the Deodars*, Allahabad, 1888.

—— *Wee Willie Winkie*, Allahabad, 1888.

—— *The Phantom Rickshaw*, Allahabad, 1888.

—— *City of Dreadful Night*, Allahabad, 1890.

—— *The Light that Failed*, New York, 1890.

—— *The Smith Administration*, Allahabad, 1891.

—— *The Naulahka* (with W. Balestier), New York, 1892.

—— *Barrack-Room Ballads*, New York, 1892.

—— *Many Inventions*, New York, 1893.

—— *Jungle Books*, New York, 1894-5.

—— *The Day's Work*, New York, 1898.

—— *Kim*, New York, 1901.

—— *Just So Stories*, New York, 1902.

Knighton, W., *Tropical Sketches: Reminiscences of an Indian Journalist*, 1885.

Lear, Edward, *Indian Journal*, 1873, ed. Ray Murphy, 1953.

Leslie, C., *Goat to Kali*, 1948.

Macaulay, Rose, *The Writings of E.M. Forster*, 1938.

Macmillan, Margaret, *Women of the Raj*, 1988.

Marlowe, Christopher, *Tamburlaine the Great*, 1590.

—— *Dr Faustus*, 1604.

Marshman, J., *Samachar Durpun, or Mirror on News*, 1818, seqq.

Mason, P. ('P. Woodruff'), *Call the Next Witness*, 1945.

—— *The Island of Chamba*, 1950.

—— *The Wild Sweet Witch*, 1947.

Master, Streynsham, *Diaries*, 1675-80; ed. R.C. Temple, 1916.

Masters, John, *The Nightrunners of Bengal*, 1951.

—— *Bhowani Junction*, 1954.

—— *Coromandel*, 1955.

Maugham, Somerset, *The Razor's Edge*, 1944.

Milton, John, *Paradise Lost*, pt. ii, 1667.

Moore, Thomas, *Lallah Rooke, an Oriental Romance*, 1817.

Mundy, T., *Rung Ho!* 1914.

—— *King of the Khyber Rifles*, 1917.

—— *Hira Singh's Tale*, 1918.

—— *Told in the East*, 1920.

Myers, L.H., *The Root and the Flower*, 1935.

—— *The Pool and Visnu*, 1940.

Norway, Nevil Shute ('Nevil Shute'), *The Chequer Board*, 1947.

Oaten, E.F., 'Anglo-Indian Literature', *Cambridge History of English Literature*, vol. xiv, 1967.

Parry, Benita, *Delusions and Discussions : Studies on India in the Indian Imagination*, 1830-1930; ed. 1972.

Payne, P.S.R., *The Great Mogul*, 1950.

—— *Blood Royal*, 1952.

Perrin, Alice, *Idolatry*, 1909.

—— *The Anglo-Indians*, 1912.

Prichard, Iltidus, *The Chronicles of Budgepore*, 1870.

Prinsep, A., *Baboo, and Other Tales Descriptive of Society in India*, 1834.

Prinsep, Val. C., *Imperial India, an Artist's Journal*, 1879.

'Quiz', *The Grand Master or Adventures of 'Qui Hi' in Hindostan : a Hudibrastic Poem in Eight Cantos* (illustrated by Rowlandson), 1816.

Richards, Private Frank, *Old Soldier Sahib*, 1936.

Rivett-Carnac, J.H., *Many Memories*, 1910.

Robinson, P.S., *In My Indian Garden*, 1878.

Rutherford, A., ed., *Kipling's Mind and Art*, 1964.

Savi, Ethil, *By Torchlight*, 1931.

Scott. H.S. ('Henry Seton Merriman'), *Flotsam : the Study of a Life*, 1896.

Scott, Sir Walter, *Guy Mannering*, 1815.

—— *The Surgeon's Daughter*, 1827.

Sencourt, R., *India in English Literature*, 1923.

Shelley, P.B., *Adonais*, 1821.

Sherwood, Mary Martha, *Little Henry and His Bearer*, 1814.

Sita Rama, *From Sepoy to Subadar*, E.tr. Lt. Col. Norgate, 1873; ed. James Lunt, 1970.

Skinner, Lt. Col. J., *Military Memoirs*, ed. J.B. Fraser, 1851.

Sleeman, Maj. Gen. Sir W.H., *Rambles and Recollections of an Indian Official*, ed. V.A. Smith, 1893.

Southney, R., *The Curse of Kehama*, 1810.

Stanford, J.K., ed., *Ladies in the Sun: the Memsahibs' India*, 1709-1860; edn. 1962.

Steel, Flora Annie, *From the Five Rivers*, 1893.

—— *The Flower of Forgiveness*, etc. 1894.

—— *The Potter's Thumb*, 1894.

—— *Tales from the Punjab*, 1894.

—— *On the Face of the Water*, 1897

—— *The Hosts of the Lord*, 1900.

—— *In the Guardianship of God*, 1900.

—— *A Prince of Dreamers*, 1908.

—— *King Errant*, 1912.

—— *Mistress of Men*, 1917.

—— *The Builder*, 1928.

—— *The Garden of Fidelity*, 1930.

—— *Indian Scene*, 1933.

—— *The Complete Indian Housekeeper and Cook* (with Mrs Grace Gardiner), 1888.

Sterne, L., Journal to Eliza, Brit. Mus. Addit. MS. 34527, c. 1773.

Stokes, M., *Indian Fairy Tales*, 1879.

Stoqueler, J.H., *The Oriental Interpreter and Treasury of East Indian Knowledge*, 1840.

Taylor, Philip Meadows, *The Confessions of a Thug*, 1839.

—— *Tippoo Sultan*, 1840.

—— *Tara, a Mahratta Tale*, 1863, 1874.

—— *Ralph Darnell*, 1865, 1879.

—— *Seeta*, 1872, 1880.

—— *A Noble Queen*, 1878, 1880.

—— *Story of My Life*, 1877.

—— *Major Gahagan*, 1838-9.

Thackeray, W.M., *Book of Snobs*, 1848.

—— *Vanity Fair*, 1848.

—— *Henry Esmond*, 1852.

—— *Pendennis*, 1849 50.

—— *The Newcomes*, 1854-5.

Thompson, E., *Krishna Kumari*, 1924.

—— *The Other Side of the Medal*, 1925.

—— *An Indian Day*, 1927.

—— *Night Falls on Siva's Hill*, 1929.

—— *A Farewell to India*, 1930.

—— *At the End of the Hours*, 1938.

Tompkins, J.M.H., *The Art of Rudyard Kipling*, 1959.

SUGGESTED REFERENCE AND READING

Trevelyan, G.O., *Letters of a Competition Wallah*, 1864.
—— *The Dawk-Bungalow, or is his appointment pucka ?* 1866.
Waterfield, W., *Indian Ballads and Other Poems*, 1868.
Western Literature, The Indian Theme In, eds. J.T. Reid, J.G. Mills, B. Parlier, and Heimo Rau (Department of Modern Indian Languages, University of Delhi), 1963.
Weston, Christine, *Indigo*, New York, 1943.
Williamson, V.M., *The East India Vade Mecum*, 1810.
—— *Oriental Field Sports*, 1808.
Wilson, A., *The Abode of Snow*, 1875.
Woolf, Leonard, *The Village in the Jungle*, 1913.
—— *Stories from the East*, 1921.

History and Politics

Ali, A. Yusuf, *A Cultural History of India During the British Period*, Bombay, 1940.
Bearce, G.D., *British Attitudes Towards India*, 1784-1858; edn, 1961.
Brown, Hilton, *The Sahibs: The Life and Ways of the British in India as Recorded by Themselves*, 1948.
Bidwell, S., *Swords for Hire: European Mercenaries in Eighteenth Century India*, 1971.
Burke, Edmund, *Works*, 1852.
Carey, W.H., *The Good Old Days of the Honble. John Company*, 1882.
Caroe, Sir Olaf, *The Pathans*, 1958; OUP, Karachi, 1983.
Chamberlain, M.E., *Britain and India: The Interaction of Two People*, 1974.
Churchill, Winston, *India : Speeches and Introduction*, 1931.
Danvers, F.C., *The Portuguese in India*, 1894.
Datta, K.K., *The Advanced History of India*, 1950.
Dodwell, H.H., ed., *The Cambridge History of India*, 1922-53.
Dow, Alexander, *History of Hindostan*, 1768-72.
Duff, James Grant, *History of the Mahrattas*, 1826.
Edwards, M., *A History of India*, 1961.
—— *The Last Years of British India*, 1963.
—— *The High Noon of Empire*, 1965.
—— *British India*, 1772-1947; edn. 1967.
—— *Glorious Sahibs, the Romantic as Empire Builder*, 1799-1838; edn. 1968.
Elliot, Sir Henry Miers, *History of India as told by its own Historians*, ed. J. Dowson, 1866-77.
Elphinstone, Mountstuart, *History of India*, 1841.
—— *Account of the Kingdom of Caubool*, 1815.
Garratt, G.T., ed., The Legacy of India, 1967.
Golant, W., *The Long Afternoon : British India (1601-1947)*, 1975.
Greenberger, A.J., *The British Image of India*, 1969.
Griffiths, Sir Percival, *The British in India*, 1946.
Heimsath, C.H., *Indian Nationalism and Hindu Social Reform*, 1964.
Hicky, J.A., *Hicky's Bengal Gazette*, 1780.
Hockley, W.B., *The English in India*, 1828.
Holwell, J., *Zephaniah, Narrative of the Deplorable Deaths of the English Gentlemen who were suffocated in the Black Hole*, 1758.
Hutchins, F.G., *The Illusion of Permanence, British Imperialism in India*, 1967.

SUGGESTED REFERENCE AND READING

Hunter, Sir William, *The Indian Empire*, 1882.

—— *History of British India*, 1899.

The Imperial Gazetteer of India, vols I-IV, Oxford, 1909.

Kaye, Sir John, *The History of the Sepoy War in India*, 1857-8; edn. 1864-76.

Khushwant Singh, *History of the Sikhs*, 1469-1964; edn. 1964-7.

Kincaid, D., *British Social Life in India*, 1608-1937; edn. 1938.

Letters of Simpkin the Second on the Trial of Warren Hastings, 1791.

Lewin, Lt.-Col. T., *A Fly on the Wheel, or How I Helped to Govern India*, 1885.

Litchfield, Nicola, *Lopez de Castaeda's First Booke of the Historie of the Discoverie and Conquest of the East Indies*, E. tr. 1582.

Lyall, Sir Alfred, *The Rise and Expansion of the British Dominion in India*, 1893.

Macaulay, T.B., 'Indian Education', Minute of Feb. 1835.

Maclagan, Sir E.D., *The Jesuits and the Great Mogul*, 1932.

Malcolm, Sir John, *Life of Robert, Lord Clive*, 1836.

—— *History of Central India*, 1823.

—— *A Sketch of the Political History of India*, 1811.

Mason, P., *A Matter of Honour*, 1974.

Mc Crindle, J.W., *Ancient India as described by Ktesias the Knidian*, 1882.

—— *Ancient India as described by Megasthenes and Arrian*, 1877.

—— *Ancient India as Described by Ptolemy*, 1885.

Mill, James, *The History of British India*, 1817 (completed by H.H. Wilson, 1858).

Mudford, P., *Birds of a Different Plumage : A Study of British-Indian Relations from Akbar to Curzon*, 1974.

Munro, Capt., Innes, *Narrative of Military Operations against the French, Dutch and Hyder Ally Cawn*, 1780-84; edn. 1789.

Munro, Sir T., *Life of by the Rev. G.R. Gleig*, 1830.

Orme, Robert, *History of the Military Transactions of the British*

—— *Nation in Indostan from the year 1745;* edn. 1763-78.

—— *A General Idea of the Government and the People of Hindostan*, 1752.

—— *Historical Fragments of the Mogul Empire, of the Morattoes, and of the English Concerns in Indostan from the year 1659,* edn. 1782.

Plumb, J.H., *England in the Eighteenth Century*, 1963.

Prinsep, H.T., *History of Political and Military Transactions in India during the Administration of the Marquess of Hastings*, 1825.

Sainsbury, W. Noel, *Calendar of State Papers, East Indies*, 1513-1629; edn. 1862.

Sale, Lady, *A Journal of the Disasters in Afghanistan*, 1841-2; edn. 1843.

Smith, V.A., *The Oxford Student's History of India*, Oxford, 1951.

—— *The Oxford History of India*, ed. T.G.P. Spear, Oxford, 1958.

Spear, T.G.P., *The Nabobs: A Study of the Social Life of the English in Eighteenth Century India*, 1932.

Tytler, A.F., *Considerations on the Present Political State of India*, 1815.

Tench, Charles Chevenix, *The Frontier Scouts*, 1985.

Tod, James, *Annals and Antiquities of Rajasthan*, 1829.

Wales, Quaritch, *The Making of Greater India*, 1951.

Wellington, The Duke of, *Despatches*, edn. 1837.

Welsh, Col. J., *Military Reminiscences*, 1830.

Wilson, C.R., and W.H. Carey, *Glimpses of Olden Times : India Under the East India Company*, 1968 (reprint).

Woodruff, P. (P. Mason), *The Men Who Ruled India*, 1965.

SUGGESTED REFERENCE AND READING

The Arts

Ambrose, K. and Ram Gopal, *Classical Dances and Costumes of India*, 1937.

Archer. M. and W.G., *Indian Painting for the British*, 1770-1880, edn. 1955.

Archer, M., *British Drawings in the India Office Library*, 1969.

—— *'Company' Drawings in the India Office Library*, 1972.

Archer, W.G., *Central Indian Painting*, 1958.

Ashton, Sir Leigh, ed., *The Art of India and Pakistan*, 1910.

Barett, D.E. and B. Gray, *Painting in India*, 1963.

Bence-Jones, M., *Palaces of the Raj : Magnificence and Misery of the Lord Sahib*, 1973.

Birdwood, G.C.M., *The Arts of India*, 1880.

Blake, A.A., *The Music of India* (New Oxford History of Music, vol. I, 1957).

Brown, P., *Indian Painting under the Mughals*, 1924.

Fergusson, J., *A History of Indian and Eastern Architecture*, 1910.

Gover, C.E., *The Folk-Songs of Southern India*, 1871.

Goetz, H., *Five Thousand Years of Indian Art*, 1959.

Havell, E.B., *The Building of New Delhi*, c. 1912.

—— *Indian Architecture*, 1913.

—— *A Handbook of Indian Art*, 1920.

Irving, R.G., *Indian Summer, Lutyens, Baker and Imperial Delhi*, 1981.

Mundy, Gen. G.C., *Pen and Pencil Sketches in India*, 1858.

Popley, H.A., *The Music of India*, 1950.

Prinsep, Val C., *Imperial India: An Artist's Journal*, 1879.

Natural History

Aitken, E.H., *Common Birds of India*, ed. Salim Ali, *1946*.

Ball, V., *Jungle Life in India*, 1880.

Blanford, W.T., *The Fauna of British India : Mammalia*, 1888-91.

Cleghorn, H., *Forests and Gardens of S. India*, 1861.

Cowen, D.V., *Flowering Trees and Shrubs in India*, 1965.

Day, F., *The Fishes of India*, 1876-8.

Forbes, H.O., *A Naturalist's Wanderings in the Indian Archipelago*, 1885.

Hamilton, Buchanan Francis, *The Fishes of the Ganges River*, Edinburgh, 1822.

Hanbury and Fluckiger, *Pharmacographia : A History of the Principal Drugs of Vegetable Origin*, 1874.

Hawkins, R.E., ed, *Encyclopedia of Indian Natural History*, Delhi, 1987.

Hooker, Jos., Notes of a Naturalist, *Himalayan Journals*, 1855.

Jerdon, T.C., *The Birds of India*, Calcutta, 1862.

—— *The Mammals of India*, Calcutta, 1874.

Roxburgh, W., *Flora Indica*, ed William Carey, 1832.

Robinson. P., *In My Indian Garden*, 1878.

Russell, P., *An Account of Indian Snakes*, 1803.

Salim Ali and S.D. Ripley, *Handbook of the Birds of India and Pakistan, together with those of Nepal, Sikkim, Bhutan and Ceylon*, 1968-74.

Sanderson, G.P., *Thirteen Years Among the Wild Beasts of India*, 1882.

Voigt, *Hortus Suburbanus Calcuttensis*, Calcutta, 1845.

SUGGESTED REFERENCE AND READING

Religion, Philosophy, Indology, etc.

Aclan, T., *A Popular Account of the Manners and Customs of India*, 1908.

Antiquary, The Indian: A Journal of Oriental Research, Bombay, 1872, et seqq.

Barnett, L.D., *The Heart of India*, 1908.

Basham, A.L., *The Wonder That Was India*, reprint 1969.

—— *A Cultural History of India*, 1975.

Beames, J., *Comparative Grammar of the Modern Languages of India*, 1872-9.

Cannon, G., *Oriental Jones*, 1964.

Colebrooke, H.T., *A Digest of Hindu Law*, 1782.

Crooke, W., *The Popular Religion and Folk-lore of Northern India*, 1896.

Danielou, A., *Hindu Polytheism*, 1964.

Dubois, Abbé J.A., *Hindu Manners, Customs and Ceremonies*, 1817 (tr. fr. MS.), H.K. Beauchamp's tr. 1897).

Eliot, Sir Charles, *Hinduism and Buddhism*, 1921.

Farquhar, J.N., *An Outline of the Religious Literature of India*, 1920.

Forster, C., *Sketches of the Mythology and Customs of the Hindoos*, 1785.

Garratt, G.T., ed., *The Legacy of India*, Oxford, 1937.

Grierson, Sir G.A., *The Linguistic Survey of India*, 1898-1928.

Griffiths, Sir P., *The British in India*, 1946.

Halhed, N.B., *Code of Gentoo Laws*, 1776.

Hassan Ali, Mrs Meer, *Observations on the Mussulmans of India*, 1832; OUP Karachi, 1973.

Isherwood, C., *Vedanta for the Western World*, 1945.

Jones, Sir W., *On the Orthography of Asiatick Words in Roman Letters*, 1784.

—— *Code of Manu*, tr. 1789.

Lannoy, R., *The Speaking Tree, A Study of Indian Culture and Society*, Oxford, 1971.

Lord, H., *Display of Two Forraigne Sects in the East: A Discoverie of the Banians: The Religion of the Persees*, 1630.

Mayo, K., *Mother India*, 1927.

—— *Slaves of the Gods*, 1929.

Monier-Williams, Sir Monier, *Religious Thought and Life in India*, 1883.

—— *Brahmanism and Hinduism*, 1891, 4th edn.

Mueller, Max, *Lectures on the Science of Language*, 1861, 1864.

—— *Chips From a German Workshop*, 1875.

—— *The Six Systems of Indian Philosophy*, reprint 1919.

Mukerji, S.N., *Sir William Jones. A Study in 18th Century Attitudes to India*, Bombay, 1987.

Perron, Anquetil du, *Le Zendavesta*, 1771.

Radhakrishnan, S., *Eastern Religions and Western Thought*, Oxford, 1940.

Serjeantson, Dr M.S., *History of Foreign Words in English*, 1937.

Sherring, Revd., *Hindu Tribes and Castes*, 1872-81.

Thomas, E.J., *History of Buddhist Thought*, 1933.

Ward, W., *A View of the History, Literature and Religion of the Hindoos*, 1811.

Warder, A.K., *Indian Buddhism*, 1970.

Williams, R., *Jaina Yoga*, 1963.

Wilson, J., *Indian Caste*, 1877.

SUGGESTED REFERENCE AND READING

Trade and Travel

Abul Fazl Allami, *Ain-i-Akbari*, E.tr. H. Blochmann, 1873; and H.S. Jarrett, 1891-4.

Bernier, Francois, *Travels in the Mogul Empire*, 1656-68; E.tr. Archibald Constable, 1891.

Birdwood, Sir George, *The Industrial Arts of India*, 1880.

—— *The First Letter Book of the East India Company*, 1600-19, edn. 1893.

Bruce, J., ed., *Annals of the Honourable the E. India Company*, 1600-1708; edn. 1819.

Bruton, William, *Newes from East Indies*, 1638.

Burnes, A., *Travels into Bokhara*, 1835.

Burton, Richard, *Goa and the Blue Mountains*, 1851.

—— *Scinde, or the Unhappy Valley*, 1851.

—— *Sindh and the Races that Inhabit the Valley of the Indus*, 1851; OUP Karachi reprint, 1973.

Chardin, Sir John, *Travels into Persia and the East Indies*, 1686.

Cocks, R., *Diary*, ed. E.M. Thompson, Hak. Soc., 1885.

Coryat(e), Thomas, *Traveller for the English Wits : Greeting-Letters from Asmere, the Court of the Great Mogul to Severall Persons of Quality in England*, 1616 (included in the 1776 edition of his *Crudities* [3 vols]).

Danvers, F.C. and W. Foster, eds., *Letters Received by the East India Company from its Servants in the East*, 1602-17; edn. 1896-1900.

Della Valle, Pietro, *Viaggi*, 1614-26; E.tr. G. Havers, 1664; Hak. Soc. 1891.

Douglas, J., *Bombay and Western India*, 1893.

Forbes, J., *Oriental Memoirs*, 1813.

Fryer, Dr John, *A New Account of East India*, 1672-81; edn. 1698.

Foster, W., ed., Early Travels in India, 1583-1619; Oxford edn. 1921.

—— *Letters Received by the East India Company from its Sevants in the East*, 1602-17, edn. 1896-1902.

—— and C. Fawcett, eds., *The English Factories in India (containing, inter alia, accounts, letters and memoirs of Ralph Fitch, John Mildenhall, William Hawkins, William Finch, Nicholas Withington, Thomas Coryate and Peter Mundy)*, 1618-1684; edn. 1906-55.

Gardner, B., *The East India Company*, 1971.

Hakluyt, Richard, *The Principall Navigations, Voiages and Discoveries of the English Nation*, 1589.

Hakluyt Society Publications :

(1) *The Voyages of Sir James Lancaster, Kt., to the East Indies*, 1877.

(2) *India in the Fifteenth Century*, 1857.

(3) *The Travels of Ludovico Varthema*, 1863.

(4) *Cathay and the Way Thither*, 1866.

(5) *A Description of the Coasts of East Africa and Malabar*, 1866.

(6) *Sir William Hedge's Diary*, 1866.

(7) *The Hawkins' Voyages*, 1878.

(8) *The Voyage of John Huyghen van Linschoten*, 1885.

(9) *The Voyage of Pyrard of Laval*, 1888.

(10) *The Travels of Pietro Della Valle in India*, 1892.

(11) *The Embassy of Sir Thomas Roe*, 1899.

(12) *The Journal of John Jourdain*, 1905.

(13) *Fryer's A New Account of East India and Persia*, 1912.

(14) *The Travels of Peter Mundy*, 1914.

(15) *The Suma Oriental of Tome Pires*, 1944.

Hamilton, Alexander, *A New Account of the East Indies*, 1727.

Hamilton, Walter, *Hindustan: Geographical, Statistical and Historical Description of Hindustan and Adjacent Countries*, 1820.

Havers, G., E.tr., *The Travels of Pietro della Valle into East India and Arabia Deserts, whereto is added a relation of Sir Thos. Roe's voyage into the East Indies*, 1664.

Heber, Bishop Reginald, *Narrative of a Journey through the Upper Provinces of India from Calcutta to Bombay*, 1824-5; edn. 1844.

Hedges, Sir William, *Diary*, 1681-8; Hak. Soc., 1866.

Herbert, Sir Thomas, *Some Yeares Travels into Divers Parts of Asia and Afrique*, 1638.

Hodges, William, *Travels in India During the Years 1780-83*; edn. 1793.

Hull, E.H., *The European in India, or the Anglo-Indian's Vade Mecum*, 1878.

Ibn Batuta, *Travels*, E.tr. Sir Hamilton Gibb, 1958-71.

Ives, Edward, *A Voyage from England to India in the Year 1754*; edn. 1773.

Jones, T.W., tr. (also E.tr. by R.A. Eden, 1576), *Lodovico di Varthema's Travels*, Hak. Soc., 1863.

Kaye, Sir John, *Peregrine Pulteney, or Life in India*, 1844.

Linschoten, J.H. vån, *Itinerairie Voyage after Schipvaert van J.H. van L.*, Amsterdam, 1596.

Lockyer, C., *An Account of Trade in India*, 1711.

Lushington, Mrs Charles, *Narrative of a Journey from Calcutta to Europe*, 1728-9; edn. 1829.

Mackay, G., Aberigh (alias 'Sir Ali Baba'), *Twenty One Days in India, being the Tour of Sir Ali Baba*, 1880.

Mandelslo, J.A. de, *Voyages and Travels into the Indies*, 1638; E.tr. 1669.

Manucci, Niccolao, *Storia do Mogor*, 1658-1708; E.tr. W. Irvine, 1907-8.

Markham, C.R., *Mission of G. Bogle to Tibet, and Journey of Thomas Manning to Lhasa*, 1876.

Marshall, John, *Notes and Observations on East India*, 1668.

Master, Streynsham, *Diaries*, 1675-80; ed. R.C. Temple, 1911.

Methold, W., *Relations of the Kingdome of Golchonda and other neighbour Nations within the Gulfe of Bengala*, 1626 (in *Purchas: His Pilgrimes*).

Milburn, W., *Oriental Commerce*, 1813.

Mundy, P., *Travels in Europe and Asia*, 1608-67, ed. Sir R.C. Temple, 1914.

Oaten, R., *European Travellers in India in the 15th, 16th, 17th Centuries*, 1909.

Ovington, Rev. T., *A Voyage to Suratt in the Year 1689*, edn. 1696; reprint by OUP, 1929.

Parks, Fanny, *Wanderings of a Pilgrim in Search of the Picturesque*, 1850.

Phillips. J., *The Six Voyages of J.B. Tavernier through Turkey, into Persia and East Indies*, 1677-8; E.tr. 1684.

Prasad, R.C., *English Travellers in India*, 1980.

Purchas, Samuel, *Purchas: His Pilgrimage*, 1613.

—— *Hakluytus Posthumus, or Purchas his Pilgrimes*, 1625-6.

Roe, Sir Thomas, *Embassy to the Court of the Great Mogoar, King of the Oriental Indies, of Condahy, of Chismer and of Corazon*, 1615. (First published in *Purchas Pilgrimes*, 1625-6.)

Rousselet, Louis, *Travels in Central India and in the Presidencies of Bombay and*

SUGGESTED REFERENCE AND READING

Bengal, 1865, E.tr. Lt. Col. Buckie, 1875.

Shaw, Dr T., *Travels*, 1738.

Sleeman, Sir W.H., *Remaseana, and Vocabulary of the Peculiar*
—— *Languages of the Thugs*, 1836.

—— *Rambles and Recollections of an Indian Official*, 1844.

—— *A Journey through the Kingdom of Oudh*, 1849-50; edn. 1858.

Stephens (Stevens), Thomas, (Jesuit) *Letter from Goa*. (First published in *Hakluyt's Navigations*, 1589.)

Tavernier, Jean-Baptiste, *Les Six Voyages en Turquie, en Perse, et aux Indes*, Paris, 1676. (*See* John Phillips.)

Terry, Edward, *A Voyage to East India*, 1655.

Tod, James, *Annals and Antiquities of Rajasthan*, 1829.

Valentia, Lord George Annersley, *Voyages and Travels to India, Ceylon, the Red Sea, Abyssinia, and Egypt, in the Years 1802-1806*, edn. 1809.

Varthema, Lodovico di, *Itinerario de Ludovico di Varthema Bolognese*, Venice, 1510. (*See* T.W. Jones.)

Watson, J.F.W., *The Textile Manufactures and the Costumes of the People of India*, 1866.

—— *A List of Indian Products*, 1872.

Wilson, A., *The Abode of Snow : Observations on a Journey from Chinese Tibet to the Indian Caucasus*, 1875.